Without a Trace ...

Historical Materialism Book Series

VOLUME 363

The titles published in this series are listed at *brill.com/hm*

Family photo, photographer unknown, public domain. Noah and Miril London

Without a Trace ...

Pogrom, Sweatshop, Gulag: The Jewish Radical Odyssey of Noah and Miril London

By

John D. Holmes

BRILL

LEIDEN | BOSTON

The Library of Congress Cataloging-in-Publication Data is available online at https://catalog.loc.gov

Typeface for the Latin, Greek, and Cyrillic scripts: "Brill". See and download: brill.com/brill-typeface.

ISSN 1570-1522
ISBN 978-90-04-73062-5 (hardback)
ISBN 978-90-04-74538-4 (e-book)
DOI 10.1163/9789004745384

This book is printed on acid-free paper and produced in a sustainable manner.

Contents

PART 3
The Soviet Union

Acknowledgements

Writing acknowledgements for a book one has worked on for a third of a century, receiving enormous assistance from a remarkable number of scholars and others, is a difficult task.

First, let me say some words in gratitude to my dissertation committee, who could not have been better. To its chairman, Soviet historian Yuri Slezkine, whose support down the years has been invaluable. To Russian labor historian Reginald Zelnik, who told me he felt honored to help supervise my dissertation. To Russian historian Victoria Frede, who stepped in at the last moment when Reggie passed, read over the entire dissertation and made a string of valuable suggestions. To sociologist Michael Burawoy, who liked my sociological analyses of Soviet bureaucracy. And to one of America's best-known labor historians, David Brody. I was his last student – in fact, he came out of retirement to participate in my dissertation committee. Having him read over what I wrote on American labor history and find it worthwhile was reassuring and good for my morale.

Other scholars who read over parts of my manuscript and gave useful suggestions were Paul Buhle, Tony Michels, Bryan Palmer, Steven Harris and Stephen Wheatcroft, as did socialist veteran Andrew Busby, who taught me 'The Cloakmakers Union'. He also provided first-rate stylistic advice, as did David Brody. And Alex Colston, master of how to turn a dissertation into a book people want to read, and Steven Hiatt, who finalized the job. Their assistance has been invaluable.

My extended Jewish family provided many of the photographic materials, especially my sister Dolly Holmes, artist, graphic artist, and family repository for old family photos. Her scanning, photo research and touchups were invaluable. As also was scanning and digital repair work by Martin Goodman of the Riazanov Archive.

Others who have assisted the project over the years include Michal Goldman, producer of the documentary film *At Home in Utopia*, and her assistant Andrew Hazelton; Dmitri Reider, who enabled me to arrange a telephone interview with Miril London's old friend Esther Markish in Israel; Dick Lewis's daughter Lucy Lewis, who found and gave me access to the file of his correspondence with my great aunt Rose Risikoff during her visits to the Soviet Union; and NYU Jewish historian Gennady Estraich, formerly managing editor of *Sovetish Heymland* before the collapse of the Soviet Union.

I also thank my hosts overseas, especially my hosts in war-torn Ukraine, whose names I do not list due to the current situation, and whom I discuss in more detail at the end of the Introduction below.

In addition, I need to say that my late parents, Joseph Everett Holmes and Beatrice Hort Holmes, read over and gave detailed and useful comments on every chapter in the dissertation. This work is something of a family project.

Rabbi Gershon Caudill-Steinberg of the Eco-Kosher Cleaning Service, now retired, a former Mormon elder from a Harlan County coal mining family, a relative of the Hatfields, gave solid counsel on Jewish-Mormon relations. Given the central role of coal mining and miners in this book, having a son of a coal miner's family provide spiritual counsel as well as interest and support for the book project down the years was highly useful. His encyclopedic knowledge as a scholar of 'flexodox Judaism', of Jewish theology and traditions, was also helpful. Insofar as any traces of Jewish spiritual values are to be found in this book, that is entirely to his credit – as was first-rate cleaning service.[1]

Many archives and archivists aided me in my research. Of particular note are Leo Greenbaum, first of the Jewish Bund Archive and later of YIVO, and also the late Marek Web of YIVO; Peter Filardo of Tamiment; Tim Davenport of the Early American Marxism website; David Walters of the Marxist Internet Archive; and Emily Turnbull of the Prometheus Research Library. In Moscow, Soviet historian Oleg Khlevniuk, Jewish historian Oleg Budnitsky and oil historian Alexander Igolkin were very helpful, as was Robert Cherny of San Francisco State University, my mentor in my master's program there. His research visits to Moscow preceded mine, and he introduced me to my invaluable Moscow research assistant, Daria Lotareva. In Kiev I was assisted by Ukrainian Soviet historian Yuri Shapoval, and by Soviet Donbass historian Zoia Likholobova in Donetsk. Civil engineers Leonid Prishchepa and Gennady Trikash of Ukrpromvodchermet, the contemporary descendant of Noah London's Donbassvodtrest, deserve special mention for the help they gave me with complex technical Donbass water issues. Their telling me that as late as the early 1950s, when one of them began work there, Noah London was still remembered and respected at his trust was good to hear.

Many ex-Soviet archivists were very helpful in finding me materials about Noah London and his work in the Soviet Union. Especially I wish to thank Boris Lebedev at RGAE, the Russian State Archive of the Economy in Moscow, for finding for me some particularly valuable materials on Noah London's work as an industrial administrator in the mid-1930s that had managed to survive a Khrushchev-era purge of the archive by Noah London's direct superior in those days, Semion Ginzburg. Who, unlike Noah London, survived the Great Terror.

Last not least, my *compañera* Marge Turngren has helped maintain my sanity throughout this whole decades-long project.

1 See https://www.facebook.com/RabbiGershon/.

Figures

Introduction

This book tells the story of Noah and Miril London, who lived and died under the Chinese curse 'May you live in interesting times'. It is a family story, as he was my great uncle and she my great aunt. As Noah London put it in the last letter he managed to send American relatives from the Soviet Union: 'What an interesting life we lived through, what an interesting world we went through, and alas how all of that is passing into the darkness … without a trace as the ripples on the surface of the sea'.[1]

Noah London was the most prominent American radical to be shot at Stalin's orders.[2] As a teenager in Tsarist Russia, he had been an underground Jewish revolutionary. He fled to the US in 1910, where he learned English, attended Cooper Union, and graduated with a degree in civil engineering. He built roads, bridges, subways and tunnels, organized Jewish garment workers into the American Communist Party, and helped found and lead its Jewish section. In 1926, he returned to his transformed homeland, the Soviet Union, participating in the industrial revolution that remade a quarter of the planet. In 1937, he was arrested, shot, and buried in an unmarked grave. Then he was forgotten. Miril, my blood relative, spent seven long years in a *gulag* afterwards. She committed suicide after her release, after she learned her husband's fate.

How is it then that this story of a man who disappeared from the pages of history, seemingly without a trace, is now reaching the light of day? Because Noah London left behind a legacy. In the woods outside the London dacha in the Moscow countryside, he dictated a 43-page English-language manuscript entitled 'Notes on the USSR' – to Miril's younger sister Rose in the summer of 1934.

I did not know Aunt Rose very well. I was not her favorite nephew. I was a brash young Sixties radical who had been an activist in Students for a Democratic Society in my freshman year at Columbia. When I joined SDS in the fall of 1970, the Columbia chapter had a hundred members. At the height of nationwide student strikes against the invasion of Cambodia and the massacre of four antiwar students at Kent State in the spring of that year, the chapter had been

1 Letter to Rose Risikoff, Cora (vacation resort in the Caucasus), Oct. 29, 1935. See Appendix C, page 419. This appendix consists of letters sent from the Soviet Union found among Rose Risikoff's effects after she died.

2 Photographs of a copy of the arrest list page on which his name appears, and of the page with Stalin's signature, are reproduced on page 364.

 | DOI:10.1163/9789004745384_002

400 strong; it seemed pretty big to me at the time. But everyone soon complained about how many people had quit since the spring semester.

It was a 'Worker-Student Alliance' chapter. As a high school student in the political outback of the DC suburbs, I was skeptical of the New Left. It seemed obvious to me that the idea of a revolution led by students was never going to fly. This SDS chapter was run by the Progressive Labor Party, whose slogan was 'Less Talk, More Action, Fight for Socialism!'[3] As the only new recruit at Columbia that year, I was chosen as the Columbia representative on the New York SDS Regional Interim Committee, the RIC. I spent a lot of my time on the phone badgering increasingly burnt-out members to show up at our dramatic weekly confrontations with campus rent-a-cops. But I found the enthusiasm for Stalin of my fellow campus radicals a bit troublesome – the couple across the hall in my dorm who recruited me to SDS had even named their dog Stalin. When I went home for Christmas vacation, my mother was angry at me for getting involved with these people. 'Don't you know that they killed your great uncle?' she asked me. I did not.

When I returned to Columbia, the chapter was engaged in fierce factional warfare between Progressive Labor and more orthodox Maoists. Naturally, both sides wanted to court me as the chapter rep on the RIC – but recoiled when I told them about my uncle Noah. I was not re-elected at the next meeting – but neither was anyone else. The position became a moot point as the organization collapsed. By the end of the school year the Columbia chapter was down to four people. Most of my old SDS friends became orthodox Maoists. One former comrade warned me that all Trotskyites would get an icepick in the head after the Revolution. I pointed out to him that all the good Stalinists like him got a bullet in the neck. He blanched. Many years later, I found out that this was just how Noah London died – though he was never the best of Stalinists.

When I was at Columbia, Rose Risikoff, like so many Jewish radicals of her generation, had moved up in the world and away from her radical past. She was then the Executive Assistant to the Deputy Superintendent of Educational Services of the New York City Board of Education and a former principal.[4] She did not think much of the current radical generation – myself included. Aunt

3 *You Say You Want a Revolution*, ed. by John Levin and Earl Silbar, is the best source for the understudied role of the Progressive Labor Party and the Worker-Student Alliance Caucus of SDS in the Sixties.

4 If she is remembered at all now outside my extended Jewish family, it would be for her article on the effects of the controversial 1968 New York teacher's strike on schoolchildren.

See https://www.tandfonline.com/doi/abs/10.1080/00094056.1969.10729484?journalCode=uced20.

Rose finally revealed the existence of the London manuscript to the rest of the family when she developed heart trouble. She gave it to my father at a family gathering, and she underwent a triple bypass operation shortly thereafter. The operation was a success, but the patient did not survive long.

Jay Everett Holmes, my father, originally planned to write an introduction to the manuscript and publish it. But it was clear to both of us that matters were not so simple. 'Notes on the USSR' is an analysis and critique of the Stalinist regime in the Soviet Union and the Communist International, written from the standpoint of a dissident 'member of the Communist International' who was also a Soviet official. It cannot really be understood without a thorough grasp of its context. I took over the project, and I have been working on it ever since. It was finally published in a partial version in the year 2007, more than seventy years after it was dictated.[5] Now it is reproduced in full as Appendix B to this book.

When I first received the manuscript, I knew very little about Noah London. My family on my mother's side were Jews who emigrated from Tsarist Russia in the aftermath of the 1905 Revolution. They had almost all once been sympathisers of Communism and the Russian Revolution. After Miril and Noah were arrested, family members went off in an array of different political directions as they moved up in the world. One of my aunts told me many years later that family gatherings degenerated into screaming political arguments in the 1940s and 50s. But as everyone got older, the women of the family quietly got together and insisted that the London story not be discussed to avoid strokes and heart attacks.

Rose told my father that Noah had been a prominent Soviet industrial manager and a founding editor of the *Freiheit*, the American Communist Party's Yiddish daily newspaper. Its circulation usually exceeded that of the English-language *Daily Worker*. From my own experiences, I was already well aware of the central role of Jews in American radicalism. Most of the members and all the leaders of my Columbia SDS chapter were Jewish. But Noah London had become an 'unperson', someone disappeared without a trace like so many other victims of Stalinist repression.

In 1988, a year after receiving the manuscript, I interviewed the last editor of the *Freiheit* shortly before it folded. He confirmed what I had heard and told me a bit more. Paul Novick edited the paper for 60 years, and had known Noah and Miril London personally. For this 96-year-old left-wing veteran, the

5 Noah London's 'Notes on the USSR', reproduced in Appendix B. Edited version, *Labour/Le Travail* 60 (Fall 2007): 181–215. A photocopy of the original manuscript is available in the Noah London Collection at the Tamiment Institute at New York University.

Londons were a cherished memory – and their fate a bitter tragedy.[6] That interview inspired me to learn Yiddish and begin researching the forgotten world of American Jewish Socialism and Communism.[7]

I began my research in 1987, before the collapse of the USSR, when Stalinist rule in the Soviet Union was still a contemporary phenomenon. I finished the project in the twenty-first century, by which time the Soviet Union was only a memory. I quickly discovered that Noah London played a prominent role in the earliest days of American Jewish Communism – he was far from an obscure figure in the 1920s. But even by the 1930s, memories had dimmed. When reports reached America of London's execution, an American Trotskyist newspaper asked the question 'Who was Noah London?' and answered:

> He was a founder of the Communist Party of the United States and a leader of its Jewish Federation for years. A true proletarian, raised in the misery and poverty of New York's East Side, he devoted his whole life to the revolutionary movement. Speaker, organizer and writer, he was known to thousands of Jewish workers in New York and elsewhere.[8]

My research on his career and the world of Jewish socialism and garment industry unionism in America continued for more than two decades.[9] I discovered that the picture historians have painted of the irrelevancy of the American Communist Party in the 1920s had a big exception – Jewish New York and the garment industry. I also discovered that Noah London's often insightful early writings shed a lot of light on *the* question for American radical historians and radical trade unionists: what happened to the promising socialist and radical labor movements in America after World War I? The left's lack of influence during the Roaring Twenties was not something foreordained. Noah London was present on stage – and often objecting – when key mistakes were made by what was America's only viable radical organization, the Communist Party.

---

6 Paul Novick, interview by John Holmes, New York, May 26, 1988, Noah London Collection, Tamiment Institute.

7 Irving Howe, *World of Our Fathers* (New York: Simon & Schuster, 1976). The annotated bibliography lists Noah London's many publications. It describes their provenance, as finding them can be difficult. They appear in the *Freiheit* and in various rarer Yiddish left-wing journals findable at New York institutions such as the Public Library, YIVO and Tamiment.

8 'Noah London Reported Executed in Moscow!', *Socialist Appeal*, June 18, 1938.

9 See 'The Life and Times of Noah London: American Jewish Communist; Soviet Engineer; and Victim of Stalinist Terror', Ph.D. dissertation, UC Berkeley, May 2008. An additional product of this research was the article 'American Jewish Communism and Garment Unionism in the 1920s', *American Communist History* 6, no. 2, (December 2007): 171–95.

His role in the early years of the Communist Party has largely been forgotten. Former Communist Melech Epstein's books are a central source for all historians of the American Jewish labor movement, and especially of American Jewish Communism. A political rival of Noah London when they were both leaders of its Jewish section, he consistently downplays Noah London's role in the movement. This significantly contributed to Noah London's near disappearance from the historical record. Epstein even claims in his autobiography that he, not London, was the first *Freiheit* labor editor.[10]

To find solid information about Noah London's career in the Soviet Union, and about the Londons' fate in the Great Terror, I learned Russian, traveled to Moscow and then Ukraine, and researched state, party, economic and security archives. Much of my research focused on the centerpiece of Noah London's career as an industrial manager, in the eastern Ukrainian-Russian borderlands usually referred to as the Donbass, lately sometimes as the 'Donbas' instead. Either way, literally translated, the Don River basin is now a forgotten corner of the world that stepped back into history in the year 2014, when it went into rebellion.

The Donbass was, however, once crucial to the Soviet Union. And the Londons were participants in molding the industrial, economic and social matrix of what became the main energy source and a central industrial heartland of the Soviet Union – but one that rusted into obscurity when the Soviet Union collapsed. During his career in the Soviet coal industry, Noah London found himself entangled in a peculiar triangular relationship among party officials, Soviet engineers and Soviet workers. A Stalinist 'cultural revolution' was underway, and one of its central features was upward social mobility. Upward social mobility can be translated into a single word in Soviet Russian, coined shortly after the Revolution, *vydvizhenie*. Its literal meaning is 'movement outwards', but in Soviet usage it meant 'promotion' out of the working class into officialdom. Soviet historian Sheila Fitzpatrick's writings on the phenomenon of '*vydvizhenie*' have influenced my thought, and we will be talking about *vydvizhenie* quite a bit.[11] Soviet workers, like Jewish immigrants to America, were experiencing a sweeping transformation of their lives.

10 Melech Epstein, *The Jew and Communism: The Story of Early Communist Victories and Ultimate Defeats in the Jewish Community, USA, 1919–1941* (New York: H. Wolff, 1959); Epstein, *Jewish Labor in USA, 1914–1952: An Industrial, Political and Cultural History of the Jewish Labor Movement* (New York: H. Wolff, 1953); *Pages from a Colorful Life: An Autobiographical Sketch* (Miami Beach, FL: I. Block, 1971).

11 Fitzpatrick, *Education and Social Mobility in the Soviet Union 1921–1934*, 1979.

The key moment of this cultural revolution, the 'Shakhty Affair' of 1928, took place in the Donbass coal fields. Mining engineers in the Donbass coal industry were arrested, tried and convicted after confessing their alleged guilt of dubious charges of sabotage of the mines that resulted in the death of miners. This was supposedly at the behest of foreign powers and emigré former owners of the Donbass coal mines. Due to a lengthy and bitter history of brutal conflict between workers and engineers in the mines, this trial was popular among Donbass coal miners, tremendously publicized and given wide credence even in unexpected places. The Shakhty trial was the original model for the more well-known Moscow trials of the 1930s, in which scores of veteran Bolsheviks confessed to sabotage and assassinations on the behalf of Hitler and the Mikado.

The Londons were eyewitnesses and, to some degree, participants in this affair, which has echoes that reverberate in the Donbass to this day. Stalin used the historic hostility between miners and engineers in the Donbass to consolidate his power, while Noah London used the atmosphere of Shakhty to push through the project that became the main focus of his career as a Soviet economic manager. He had come to the Soviet Union to 'build socialism' – to help create a better life for all the peoples of the former Tsarist Empire, constructing a model for the rest of the world. His particular contribution was to provide clean, safe drinking water for the Donbass. Under the Tsarist regime, the scourge of typhus and cholera made life expectancy shorter than anywhere else in the Empire. Clean water for the Donbass was a key priority – for industry, the uppermost factor for Stalin and his entourage, and for the miners themselves, the primary consideration for Noah London. But by 1933, even as his water projects were blessed with success, workers in Ukraine were worrying about food, not water. Every ruble spent on the tremendous accomplishments of the Stalinist industrial revolution, including for waterworks, was one less ruble devoted to feeding the starving. The Ukrainian 'hunger plague', with its death toll in the millions, turned the Londons into secret dissenters from the party line.

However, to the day he died Noah did not want to leave the official Communist movement. As he put it in that secret manuscript he dictated to great aunt Rose: 'While the author considers the present tactics and organizational forms of the [Communist International] and its sections to be fundamentally wrong … he knows that the revolutionary impetus is concentrated within the bounds of the organizations within and around the Communist Party of the World'.[12]

12 'Notes on the USSR', Appendix B, page 382.

Nor was he eager to leave his 'interesting life' in that 'interesting world' as a prominent Soviet official until it became clear that his life and freedom were in danger.

1 Jewish Radicalism: 'Non-Jewish Jews' and the Jewish Labor Movement

According to Rose Risikoff, Bella Kaufman based her book *Up the Down Staircase* on her experiences at the high school where Rose was the principal. Bella Kaufman was a granddaughter of Yiddish novelist Sholem Aleichem, on whose stories the Broadway spectacular *Fiddler on the Roof* was based. According to her *New York Times* obituary, the novel was 'shot through with despair and hopefulness, violence and levity, bureaucratic inanity and a blizzard of official memorandums so mind-bendingly illogical as to seem almost Kafkaesque'.[13] You will read more about despair, hopefulness, violence, bureaucracy and bureaucracies in this book, and perhaps encounter even a few moments of levity, though not as many as I would like. The movie version of *Up the Down Staircase* became a smash success.

I discovered in the course of my research that the London story was emblematic of the sad tale of twentieth-century Jewish radicalism. The 1905 Russian Revolution began a worldwide cycle of war, revolution, destruction and transformation. It was Noah's teenage political baptism of fire, and Miril's as well. It set the mold for the twentieth century paradigm of Jews as representatives of revolution, progress and modernity; and anti-Semitism as the ideology of counter-revolution and reaction. In *The Jewish Century*, Yuri Slezkine writes that 'modernization is about everyone becoming urban, mobile, literate, articulate ... Modernization, in other words, is about everyone becoming Jewish'.[14] Twentieth-century fascists saw Jews as representatives of modernity: the carriers of political, cultural, and social subversion; and advocates of communism, liberalism, democracy and everything else that they lusted to extirpate. The German-Jewish figure of Karl Marx represented evil in Hitler's eyes. Jews embodied a world in which, as Marx described capitalism in the *Communist Manifesto*, 'All that is solid melts into air, all that is holy is profaned ...'

But the Londons were not just victims. Both were respected activists, and Noah was a leader and a thinker. He played a central role in the birth of an

---

13 Margalit Fox, 'Bel Kaufman, Who Told What School Was Really Like, Dies at 103', *New York Times*, July 25, 2014.

14 Yuri Slezkine, *The Jewish Century* (Princeton, NJ: Princeton University Press, 2004), 1.

American Jewish Communist subculture in the 1920s that survived long after the demise of radical Jewish garment unionism. He was the first camp director of Camp Nitgedeiget on the Hudson in upstate New York, the Communist summer camp where this subculture took shape.[15] He was the organizer of the Bronx 'coops' cooperative housing project, which he saw as a vehicle for utopian visions of social transformation unfolding in the early Soviet Union.[16] By then a senior designer for the New York subway system, he was attempting to combine communal Soviet social experimentation with American practicality – and American construction quality. He did his best to continue this mission as an industrial manager on Soviet soil.

The central role Jewish intellectuals played in shaping the modern era is one of the major reasons why Jews became targets of fascist wrath. Jewish socialist intellectual Isaac Deutscher argued in *The Non-Jewish Jew* that Jewish revolutionaries of modern thought like Spinoza, Marx, Freud, Einstein and Deutscher's personal hero, Trotsky, belonged to a tradition of heretics and dissenters who transcend Jewish tradition to herald a message of universal human emancipation. What they had in common was that, as Jews, they dwelt on the borderlines of various civilizations, religions and national cultures. As he put it, 'they were born and brought up on the borderlines of various epochs. Their minds matured where the most diverse cultural influences crossed and fertilized each other … It was this that enabled them to rise in thought above their societies, above their nations, above their times and generations, and to strike out mentally into wide new horizons and far into the future'.[17]

Noah London was not a Spinoza or a Trotsky, or even a Deutscher. By family background, he was not an intellectual at all. He was a very 'Jewish Jew', the son of a blacksmith and store owner from one of the most dirt poor and isolated corners of the Tsarist Jewish Pale to which they were confined, which included contemporary Belarus, much of Poland and the Baltic Republics, and western and central Ukraine. His ideas were molded by the Jewish labor movement that the Trotskys and Rosa Luxemburgs dismissed as parochial. From early adolescence, he sought a broad education. For ages, Jews had been the 'people of

15 Yiddish spelling, like the Yiddish language in general, is varied and mutable. 'Nitgedeiget', the spelling campers themselves usually employed in the English language, is the most well-known transliteration. The technically correct transliteration would be 'kemp nitgedayget'. The spellings employed in this book for this and other Yiddish words may vary with context.

16 Michal Goldman's PBS documentary film, *At Home in Utopia*, powerfully depicts this exciting radical experiment. See Appendix A for Noah London's manifesto for the project.

17 Isaac Deutscher, 'The Non-Jewish Jew', in *The Non-Jewish Jew and Other Essays*, ed. Tamara Deutscher (London: Merlin Press, 1981), 27.

the book', a literate group in preliterate societies. In Western Europe, capitalist modernity enabled Jews to break out of social isolation and become central figures in economic, social, intellectual and cultural life. Yuri Slezkine describes Jews as a 'Mercurian' people. Mercury was the Greek god of mobility, the 'patron of rule-breakers, border crossers and go-betweens; the protector of people who lived by their wit, craft and art'.[18] But in Noah and Miril London's *shtetl*, Jewish upward social mobility hit the brick wall of Tsarist anti-Semitism – unlike in America, or the Soviet Union.

The twentieth century can also be described as the century of the Russian Revolution. Some historians begin a 'short twentieth century' with the start of World War I in 1914 and the Russian Revolution in 1917 and end it with the collapse of the Soviet Union in 1991.[19] The London story unfolds where the Russian Revolution and the 'Jewish Century' intersect. Their lives followed the classic rules of Greek tragedy. Commitment to their radical principles embroiled them in a deradicalizing, corrupted Soviet bureaucracy. They slowly became disillusioned with the cause to which they had dedicated their lives. Disillusionment complete, doom struck. It was not flaws in their characters that decided their fate, but a terrible mistake – pledging allegiance to the Stalinist version of the Soviet project.

The London odyssey sheds light on the nature of that thing called Stalinism, which well-informed biographer Dmitri Volkogonov defined as a 'specific social phenomenon ... synonymous with alienation of the working people from power', which resulted in 'a weakening of the real meaning of socialist values'.[20] Its theoretical essence, the concept of 'socialism in one country', was a revision of Karl Marx's worldview that the original leaders of the Russian Revolution, Lenin and Trotsky, consistently opposed. The horrors of Stalinism stemmed from the determination of Stalin and his entourage to follow this idea to its logical conclusion, whatever the consequences. The Stalinist terror that engulfed the Londons had a devastating impact on twentieth century movements for social transformation, swallowing up and destroying countless of their best activists – both morally and physically, in the Soviet Union and elsewhere. The London story reveals a great deal about what happened to humanity in that century. It may also help us to understand our present day world, and our future as well.

---

18 Slezkine, *Jewish Century*, 8.

19 Eric Hobsbawn, *The Age of Extremes: The Short Twentieth Century, 1914–1991* (London: Little Brown & Co., 1994).

20 Dmitri Volkogonov, *Stalin: Triumph and Tragedy*, trans. and ed. H. Shukman (New York: Grove Weidenfeld, 1991), xxvii.

2 The London Story and Socialism in 'the West'

What will the London story have to tell you about what went on in 'the West', after Noah London died in that ugly year 1937? Exactly half a century later, in 1987, when research began for this book, the final flare-up of the Cold War was just beginning to dissipate. Nearly half the population of planet earth was still living under regimes that proclaimed themselves to be Communist, Marxist and Leninist. Labor, socialist and radical movements of one sort or another still tended to dominate the political scene in much of the rest of the world. The United States of America was still unique in the 'Western world' as that eccentric, peculiar country which lacked a strong Socialist, Communist or Labor Party based in a powerful labor movement. German sociologist Werner Sombart asked the classic question 'Why is there no socialism in America?' as long ago as 1904.[21]

Sociologists and historians debated it for generations. The debate ended after the collapse of the Soviet Union in 1991, as the rest of the world conformed to American hegemony. In the immediate aftermath, philosopher and economist Francis Fukuyama was describing American victory in the Cold War as 'the end of history'. The stock market was booming. Most of the human race seemed to have drawn the conclusion that the free market was the wave of the future. The Soviet collapse seemed to be dragging socialism, radicalism and even the labor movement itself into the dustbin of history. Socialist parties were repudiating socialism, Communist parties were repudiating themselves, and a Democratic president in America was abolishing 'welfare as we know it'.

One of America's most prominent sociologists, Hoover Institute fellow Seymour Martin Lipset, published extensively on Werner Sombart's theme for decades. Like many New York intellectuals, he was a Jewish former Trotskyist, and he stated frankly that he derived a number of his ideas from comments on the question by Marx and Lenin. Among the reasons cited were higher wages, social mobility, racial and ethnic divisions, and especially, in his final works, the role of the 'American ideology' as an alternative to Marxism and class consciousness.[22] In the aftermath of the Soviet collapse, the general intellectual climate

21 Werner Sombart, *Why Is There No Socialism in the United States?* (White Plains, NY: International Arts & Sciences Press, 1976).

22 Seymour Martin Lipset and Reinhard Bendix, *Social Mobility in Industrial Society* (Berkeley: University of California Press, 1959); John H.M. Laslett and Seymour Martin Laslett, eds., *Failure of a Dream?: Essays in the History of American Socialism* (Berkeley: University

has been moving to the right. In the historical profession, sociology and political economy have given way to ideology and culture. As Sombart put it, long ago when more attention was paid in the professorate to sociology and basic economics, socialism in America 'foundered on the reefs of roast beef and the shoals of apple pie'.[23] Of the reasons for the weakness of socialism in America, I believe higher wages and upward social mobility are the key ones. Until the 1980s, when I began my research into the London story, the USA had the highest standard of living in the world, and the 'American dream' had not yet become the American nightmare.

I derived my thoughts about the causes of socialist weakness in America partially from book learning, but even more so from the history of the dominant Jewish side of my family, and my quarter of a century of experience in the old, once well-paid printing trade, out of which I was finally automated during my researches in the former Soviet Union. Like many student radicals of the Sixties, when I got my undergraduate degree I sought to join the working class. As it happens, printing is the family tradition on both sides of the family, including my non-Jewish father's side as well. I had a romantic dream of becoming a radical activist in the oldest and craftiest of all American unions, craft or otherwise, the International Typographical Union, of which Walter Holmes, my grandfather, was a member in Brooklyn. After some alarums and excursions, including working in a nonunion shop busted for counterfeiting, I managed to do so.

In January 1986 I attended the family gathering where old Aunt Rose climbed a ladder to get the London manuscript out of her attic. That year I had something else occupying my time. I was working full-time as a union printer at the *Hayward Daily Review* newspaper, in what was then Oakland's white suburb in the Bay Area. The paper was bought by a union-busting chain. I was suddenly propelled into the job of chapel chairman after the previous chairman quit. I found myself the leader of a rather socially unenlightened composing room with very strong union consciousness, and participating in a multi-union attempt to organize the whole paper. After the company gave up on trying to bust us and offered a concessionary contract, the old chairman was narrowly re-elected. A year or two later I left for a more enlightened, black-owned newspaper, the *Oakland Tribune*, humming 'take this job and shove it' as I walked out the door, and researching the London story became my main hobby. But

of California Press, 1974); Seymour Martin Lipset and Gary Wolfs Marks, *It Didn't Happen Here: Why Socialism Failed in the United States* (New York: W.W. Norton, 2000).

23 Sombart, *Why Is There No Socialism*, 106.

then the *Tribune* went bankrupt. After I and a fellow printer failed in an effort to organize a sitdown strike, I was unsure what to do with the rest of my life. My parents suggested that I go back to school and research the London story. So, with their support and a number of scholarships and fellowships, including a union scholarship, I did so.

At the same time, somewhat to my surprise, I was still able to work part-time on the night shift as a printer at the *San Francisco Chronicle* while taking graduate history classes at San Francisco State and UC Berkeley in the daytime. As it happens, this was more or less how Noah London got his engineering degree at Cooper Union in his first years in America. In 1994, I got to participate in one of the most dramatic strikes in America since World War II, the 1994 *San Francisco Chronicle* strike. This strike resembled the kind of strikes you read about in labor history more than the kind of strikes we get these days.[24] Seeing the power of the working class in action is, perhaps, the reason why I have not followed the classic pattern of the young radical who becomes conservative in old age.

There is also, of course, the question of racial divisions as an obstacle to socialism. In the aftermath of the *Chronicle* strike, with strikers having fought and beaten strike-breaker goons, and with a deaf Hayward printer suing the police after he was beaten for not hearing a police order, I was able to pass a motion, in my mostly white union local of militant labor aristocrats, for freeing America's most famous political prisoner, former Black Panther Mumia Abu Jamal. My skeptical moderate socialist union officers arranged, for once, to have the union meeting take place in the whitest and most socially conservative corner of the local, Hayward, to see if my former shopmates would object. Despite this, the motion passed. For years thereafter, I pushed through regular donations to Mumia's defense fund. Perhaps under the influence of class struggle, racial divisions can break down: economics and class struggle are the key to everything, just as Marx said.

Hourly wages for American workers began a steady decline after American defeat in Vietnam. They have continued to decline ever since, with a brief interruption in the Nineties in the aftermath of Bush Sr.'s victories in the Cold War and the Persian Gulf. In Western Europe, however, the student radicalism of the Sixties spilled over into the working class, with semi-revolutionary con-

24 For more on this dramatic strike, and the history of the *Chronicle*, here is a video of an anniversary presentation as part of San Francisco's Laborfest in 2015. The first speakers deal with the history of the paper, and then the representatives of the different unions to talk about the strike come on. I speak at about the hour mark: www.youtube.com/watch?v=wI_uUAnvW8o.

sequences – inspiring the 'Worker-Student Alliance' wing of SDS which I joined as a freshman at Columbia University in 1970. The resultant political transformations seem superficial in retrospect, but economic gains for workers were dramatic. Popular living standards rose to the US level – and in some countries surpassed it. The 'social market' model became powerfully attractive to German workers, whether in the Western or Eastern halves of the country. In the Soviet Union and Eastern Europe, the rapid economic growth of the Stalin and Khrushchev eras stagnated to a geriatric halt under Brezhnev. This was the material basis for the decline of socialism in Western Europe, and the collapse of Communism in Eastern Europe.

The much-discussed 'decline of the American middle class' has not yet led to a real rebirth of socialism, despite the Sanders phenomenon. The 'American dream' of upward social mobility has yet to fully dissipate. Deindustrialization has crippled the labor movement, but the still dominant position of the USA in the world economy continues to enable some Americans to move upwards into the professions. The children, grandchildren and great-grandchildren of Jewish immigrants toiling in garment sweatshops became the wealthiest American religious group. Their main vehicle for the American brand of '*vydvizhenie*' has been education, just as it would be for Noah London here, and for Soviet workers there. Jews have the highest level of scholastic achievement of any religious group worldwide. In America they have declined a bit lately, notably with respect to Unitarianism, the 'faith', if you want to call it that, that my parents tried to raise me in. Yuri Slezkine's 'Mercurians', the entrepreneurial 'service nomads' of the modern era, provided the model for other once downtrodden ethnic groups to move up in the world in the brave new deindustrialized American 'service economy'.

The story of American Jewish Socialism, Communism and trade unionism, narrated in this book through the eyes of the Londons, sheds light on the short-term causes and day-to-day workings of the failure of American left movements to root themselves in labor, European style. But the main long-term cause for the failure of American socialism, more important even than wage levels, seems to be the same, as this book will talk about, in the Soviet Union – upward working-class social mobility. Noah London would seek to harness this phenomenon for the socialist cause through his Bronx housing project. He enthusiastically supported '*vydvizhenie*' in the Soviet Union, the promotion of rank-and-file workers into the bureaucracy by way of working-class 'affirmative action' for college education, especially in the engineering schools where blue-collar workers like former steelworker Brezhnev began their rise to the top. But he did understand that upward social mobility could be an obstacle to socialist dreams. In one of his letters to Rose from Russia, he described the Soviet Union as 'a society of inequality, but equal opportunity'. Just like America, where 'not brains or culture, but title to money [is] what counts'.[25]

What are the prospects for socialism in the future in America? In September 2001, as I began research in former Soviet archives, I saw on Russian television the woes of the twentieth century finally catching up to the country that won that century's struggles. Since then, Fukuyama's formula about the 'end of history' has taken on an ominous ring. Science fiction writers have turned to apocalypse or fantasy, thinking perhaps that ideas of a positive future are too implausible nowadays to sell paperbacks. Just how will history end – with a nuclear bang or an ecological whimper? The question might receive an unpleasant earlier answer, as the world spirals ever deeper into war, crisis and convulsions. Or perhaps, as socialist thinkers have speculated, a triumph of socialism could represent the beginning of human history, not its end.

3 A Note on Methodology

By the time I began serious research, everyone who knew much about the Londons had died. I did gain some insights from interviewing a handful of aged relatives on his side of the family, who were children when he was alive. I relied heavily on Noah's own writings. Fortunately, they reveal a great deal about him – rarely are they arid treatises. He wrote in Yiddish as a vehicle for self-expression. To convey his thoughts and beliefs as accurately as I can, I have quoted directly from his writings wherever possible. I decided to translate his Yiddish literally and in a practical idiom. If sometimes his language seems a bit clumsy, well, it sounds better in the original. Besides a single brief parenthetical note to one of Noah's letters, I found only one equivalent for Miril. She sent an autobiographical declaration to NKVD head Lavrenti Beria from her *gulag*, in the not quite unfounded hope that he might intervene in her case. Surely this statement is a clouded window into her soul. Nonetheless, it is reproduced as Appendix D.

In the American period of his life, Noah was a far more prolific writer than in his Soviet days. The best guide for understanding his Soviet career was that manuscript smuggled out of the USSR in 1934, and subsequent letters to American relatives.[26] They are invaluable keys for the interpretation of otherwise dry and unilluminating Soviet records.

25 Letter to Rose, Fall 1934. See Appendix C, 415.

26 See Appendices B and C.

A new school of Soviet cultural history arose in the aftermath of the collapse of the USSR in 1991. It seeks to analyze Stalinism through the lens of 'Soviet subjectivity'. One of its most influential practitioners, Jochen Hellbeck, has asked, 'What kind of source material can be expected to make visible individuals' "real" beliefs, if the repressive political environment continuously forced them to censor themselves?' He chose surviving Stalin-era diaries, using them to probe the internal worlds of bureaucrats and intellectuals, whether of Soviet or pre-Soviet molding.[27] They used these diaries as tools for 'self-fashioning', personal transformation into exemplars of 'the new Soviet man'. Hellbeck's findings reveal how similar were the internal worlds of the new Stalinist elite, whatever their original social background – ironical evidence for Karl Marx's proposition that being determines consciousness. Did Hellbeck illuminate how that actually works? Marxists have rarely sought to delve into individual psychology.

The London manuscript was intended to serve a different project. It is certainly a counterexample to Hellbeck's proposition that 'an individual living in the Stalinist system could not conceivably formulate a notion of himself independently of the program promulgated by the Bolshevik state'.[28] But it verifies his argument that the concept that Soviet citizens told the truth in private and lied in public is at the very least an oversimplification. Noah London traveled through many geographical and political worlds, but there was always a fundamental consistency to his worldview. He expressed his basic ideas in many different ways in varying circumstances, publicly and privately.

By revealing his actual thoughts as he took part in Soviet political rituals, the manuscript may give clues to what other protagonists were really thinking. Might it be a sort of 'Rosetta stone' to translate Stalinist discourse – what historian Stephen Kotkin calls 'speaking Bolshevik' – into plain English?[29] I have tried to use it in that fashion in this book.

John Holmes,
October 2020

---

27 Jochen Hellbeck, 'Fashioning the Stalinist Soul: The Diary of Stepan Polubnyi, 1931–39,' in *Stalinism: New Directions*, ed. Sheila Fitzpatrick (London: Routledge, 2000), 77; Hellbeck, *Revolution on My Mind: Writing a Diary under Stalin* (Cambridge, MA: Harvard University Press, 2006).

28 Hellbeck, *Fashioning the Stalinist Soul*, 111.

29 Stephen Kotkin, *Magnetic Mountain: Stalinism as a Civilization* (Berkeley: University of California Press, 1995), 198–237. Internal evidence indicates that the London manuscript was originally dictated in Yiddish.

4 On the Present Conflagration in Ukraine

As I write, we are in the middle of a wave of anti-Russian hysteria in the West. Many US restaurants have taken Russian dressing off the menu. The local pastry shop I go to in my upwardly mobile Rockridge neighborhood in Oakland, California, where my *compañera* and I have been grimly hanging on to our problematic rent-controlled apartment for a third of a century, is now selling *hamantaschen* to benefit Ukraine! Given the history of Jewish–Ukrainian relations I talk about in this book, that is strange.

What I wrote in this book was strongly influenced by my personal experiences researching in Kiev, Kharkov and Donetsk. I will never forget my encounter with a nasty Ukrainian anti-Semite while at the Kharkov Party archive, eagerly explaining how Jews have always been bad for Ukraine. The woman at the desk told me afterwards that she was Ukrainian herself, but that people like that sometimes made her embarrassed to be Ukrainian. The apartment of the woman I stayed with in Donetsk was in the western fringe of the city, into the suburbs, so probably right on the battle front. I suspect her home has been demolished, and would not be surprised if she is among the over 10,000 Donbass citizens who died in the brutal Ukrainian civil war even before Putin invaded the rest of Ukraine. But now I also have to worry about the wonderful couple I stayed with in Kharkov. The retired former missile base commander, with whom I watched some really great Soviet World War II movies, like the story of the 'night witches', was reduced to being a janitor at the Kharkov national theater. Last I heard from him he had been laid off and was dead broke. His Caucasian wife provided the best home cooking I ever encountered in the former Soviet Union. They were my favorite hosts ever. And then there was the woman I stayed with in Kiev, with her gorgeous snow white cat, the princess Alba. Who told me that her own love of gardening and vegetable growing in the countryside showed that I had a point in thinking of Ukrainians as an agricultural people.

Now that we have full-scale war between Russia and Ukraine, I am against both sides; and I certainly don't support Putin's invasion.

December 5, 2023

PART 1

Russia and the Jewish Pale

CHAPTER 1

Origins: Jewish Socialism and Noah and Miril London

> Praise be to the Creator, Who guides His heavenly orbs in their paths and His earthly creatures in their ways! Surely, if our holy books relate that not even the tiniest blade of grass can stick its head above ground unless an angel taps it and says, 'Grow, little grass, get thee up and about', surely, I say, a man must have his angel too, tapping and crying, 'Up and about with thee!' ... Or it may be: 'Go, ye wealthy Jews who lack for nothing, cease twiddling your thumbs and get ye to the bathhouse and start to sweat! ...'
>
> MENDELE MOCHER-SFORIM, in 'The Brief Travels of Benjamin the Third', 1878

Noah London was born on May 17, 1888, in the tiny Belarusian hamlet of Upirovo, a squalid pocket of poverty overrun by pigs who befouled everything. Upirovo in turn festered on the western outskirts of a *shtetl* called Motele, in the Kobrinsk district of Grodno Province, one of the 'northwest provinces' of the Tsarist Empire – contemporary Lithuania and Belarus, roughly speaking. The Jews who lived there, the *litvaks*, called those provinces *lite*, the Yiddish word for Lithuania. They coincided loosely with the heartland of the ancient medieval kingdom of Lithuania – and the heartland of the Jewish Pale of Settlement. The Pale was the only area where Jews were allowed to live in Tsarist Russia – unless of course they were wealthy and 'lacked for nothing'. As Noah drew his first breath, the Pale imprisoned the largest Jewish community in the world.

In 1888 it was a divided community, in transition and under pressure. For ages, Lithuanian Jews had been a commercial 'middleman minority' in a preindustrial world, but by the late nineteenth century, capitalist modernity was squeezing them out of traditional roles and some were finding new ones.[1] In old

1 Slezkine, *Jewish Century*; Abram Leon, *The Jewish Question: A Marxist interpretation* (New York: Pathfinder Press, 1970).

 | DOI:10.1163/9789004745384_003

Lithuania they had been pillars of society, people whose clothes glittered with gold and who wore swords just like the nobility.[2] Its successor state, early modern Poland, became a refuge for Jews escaping Christian anti-Semitism. Polish Jews were a prosperous social élite – and thus a target for peasant wrath – until the Romanov conquest.

Russian anti-Semitism goes back before reliable historical records. In ancient Russian folktales, the giant Zhidovin (the Jew) was the mythic enemy of the hero Il'ya Muromets. Varangian Norsemen constructed the first Russian state in struggle with the commercial, Turkish-speaking Khazar empire, the only significant Jewish polity known to history between the fall of the Temple and the birth of the state of Israel. Their capital Kiev itself likely began as a Khazar river fort – its very name seems to be of Khazar derivation.

After the Varangians destroyed the Khazar empire in the tenth century, a Jewish commercial community developed in Kiev. It attracted Christian converts, whether due to a Khazar heritage of proselytization or simply Jewish educational and cultural superiority. Real or alleged 'Judaizing sects' played a marked role in the history of Russian Orthodoxy, exacerbating its anti-Semitism. When, for example, Ivan the Terrible conquered Polotsk from the Poles in the sixteenth century, all Jews who refused to convert were drowned in the Dvina. His Romanov successors seized the throne with the help of anti-Semitic agitation against the 'false Dimitri'. a Polish-backed pretender who allegedly was a Jew. Romanov Tsars repeatedly expelled all Jews from their empire, until the conquest of most of Poland by Empress Catherine.[3] Which is how the Tsarist Empire, by then the most anti-Semitic country on earth, became the home of the great majority of the world's Jewish population.

Nineteenth-century economic development displaced Jews from traditional roles all over Eastern Europe. In Tsarist Russia, authorities supplemented this trend with deliberate social engineering and anti-Semitic legislation. A tiny Jewish élite managed to penetrate Russian industry and banking. The great majority of the Jewish population was, however, subjected to downward social mobility and became paupers. Noah London's birthplace exemplified the social crisis the Jewish Pale was undergoing during his youth and childhood.

---

2 Leon, *Jewish Question*, 189.

3 David Christian, 'The Kaghanate of the Rus': Non-Slavic Sources of Russian Statehood', in *Challenging Traditional Views of Russian History*, ed. S. Wheatcroft (Basingstoke: Palgrave Macmillan, 2002); Salo Baron, *The Russian Jew under Tsars and Soviets*, 2nd ed. (London: Macmillan, 1976), 3–14.

1 Motele

Motele (Motol' in Slavic languages), was an old *shtetl* whose story is told in its Yizkor Memorial Book. Yizkor books commemorate Jewish *shtetls* annihilated in the Holocaust. They were created by former residents or their children to preserve their stories, lives and ways of life. According to Motele's Memorial Book,

> The name Motol' can be traced back to the legend of the Swedish conquest of the entire area in 5408 (1608 CE) ... the Swedish army encircled the town and set fire to all its sides and with it its people and property. Only one Jew escaped from the inferno – Mordechai 'Motol' the grave digger ... Mordechai the gravedigger labored diligently to build a small house ... after a short time the house became an inn for the many merchants making their way from Pinsk to Minsk ... Jews and non-Jews began to concentrate around the house and slowly the city returned and reformed itself ... But the name Motol' was on everyone's lips and stuck to the city until the Nazi beast turned it to a city without Jews.[4]

When Noah London was born in Motele, its Jewish population was a bit less than a third of its total of some 700 families. Motele was about 25 miles northwest of Pinsk, a small provincial city with the second-highest percentage Jewish population in the whole empire – the only city in the world whose factories worked on Sunday and closed on the Jewish Sabbath. Pinsk was the market center for Polesie, the Pripet marshes region, and Polish ethnographers considered it to be the most economically and culturally backward region of the entire Slavic world.[5]

Timber was the mainstay of the Polesian economy, such as it was. Motele is best known as the birthplace of timber merchant Chaim Weitzmann, the first president of Israel, and one of his relatives was Noah's future wife, Miril. Her father, Chaim Unterman, was also a timber merchant. Motele lay on the banks of the river Iasel'da, in 'one of the darkest and most forlorn corners of the Pale of Settlement, that prison house created by czarist Russia', as Weitzmann put it in his memoirs.[6] A tributary of the river Pripet, it gurgled slowly through marshes and forests, occasionally carrying a raftload of logs off to distant markets.

4 A.L. Poliak, ed., *Hurban Motele* ('Destruction of Motele'), jewishgen.org.

5 Oksana Grabowicz, 'About Polesie', in *The Changing Peasantry of Eastern Europe* by J. Obrebski, ed. B. Halpern and J. Halpern (London: Routledge, 1976), vii–ix.

6 Chaim Weizmann, *Trial and Error: The Autobiography of Chaim Weizmann* (Westport, CT: Greenwood, 1949), 4.

Motele was a typical Polesian *shtetl*. It had no paved roads, nor a post office, a railway station or any other way to communicate with the outside world. It was divided into three sections along its only real street. The marketplace section, Der Mark, was mostly Polish and Belarusian, and that was where the upper classes lived. The middle section was what the Jews called the 'Street of the *Goyim*', where relatively well-off Belarusian artisans resided. On the wrong side of the river lay the 'Street of the Jews' or the *Neistadt*, where Jewish shops were located and Jewish life was centered. This was where the poor lived. According to the Motele Yizkor Book:

> The residents of '*Marak*' were the veterans that according to historical records originally settled it during the seventeenth century. While the residents of '*Nishtut*' were the more recent residents who settled in the city over the years. The distinguishing mark that could differentiate between these two groups was imprinted on the eyelashes of the veterans that helped form their thin mocking looks towards the newer residents. The veterans who had managed to become urbanized and who had grabbed all the best professions looked 'down their noses' at the laborers, the ordinary people of '*Nishtut*'.[7]

Prominent among the tiny sprinkling of prosperous Jews in Der Mark were the timber merchants. Their prosperity was relative. The Weitzmann family, who employed about 60 local peasants in their business, ate meat only once a week. The Jews who lived on the 'Street of the Jews' were dirt-poor peddlers and artisans ... and *luftmenshn* – i.e. people who 'lived on air'.[8] In the words of American Jewish labor historian Steve Fraser:

> No great distance separated the hand-to-mouth existence of the peddler from the twilight world of the *luftmensh* – a figure whose enforced idleness and anomalous place in the cramped universe of the *shtetl* has sometimes been camouflaged by a romantic image of contemplative men pondering the mysteries of life and dreaming of what might be ... With no visible means of support, they lived on hope and hustle, dreaming always of that miraculous stroke of luck, or *mazl*.[9]

---

7 Jehuda Reinharz, *Chaim Weizmann* (New York: Oxford University Press, 1985), 4–5; Poliak, *Hurban Motele*.

8 Weizmann, *Trial and Error*, 6–7; Reinharz, *Weizmann*, 3–5.

9 Steve Fraser, *Labor Will Rule: Sidney Hillman and the Rise of American Labor* (New York: Macmillan, 1991), 3–4.

The abject poverty of the 'Street of the Jews' was a symptom of the extreme economic backwardness of Polesie. In the 1860s, the daily diet of a Jewish family in Grodno province had usually been a pound of bread, a herring and a few onions. Grodno was far from unique. All over the Pale economic modernization and Tsarist anti-Semitism were pauperizing the Jewish population. During Noah's childhood up to 40 percent of the *shtetl* population consisted of *luftmenshn*, though few *shtetls* were as poor as Motele.

The Londons were a fairly numerous family in the *shtetl* of Antopol, in the swamps about 35 miles to the west. According to the Antopol *Yizkor Book*, it was a particularly pious *shtetl*. But Noah's father Moishe was an atheist, according to his American descendants.[10] Perhaps he left the hometown because he found its atmosphere stifling. The pious Jews of Antopol were more prosperous than those of Motele. The land was owned by the noble lady Sofia Dimitrievna Voitosh, whose business manager, Mordecai Sheinboim, got her to do many favors for her Jews. Many were lease-holding farmers – some growing onions, potatoes and cucumbers themselves, others employing Belarusian hired laborers. This unusual situation was a last remnant of the traditional role of Polish-Lithuanian Jewry in pre-modern Eastern Europe.

Noah's grandfather Joseph is the first name on the family tree drawn up by American descendants many years later. In 1841, when he was born, younger Jewish sons all over the Pale were adopting last names, a thing they usually had not had before. Only one son per family was exempt from the military draft under Tsar Nicholas I, so male youth all adopted different last names.

The name 'London' was surely not chosen accidentally. In the stifling medieval confines of Polesie, it must have symbolized Western modernity, prosperity and freedom. Joseph London died in 1891, a few years after his grandson was born. Noah himself would be interested in England all his life. In his secret 1934 critique of Stalinism he would describe England as 'the classical land of the labor movement, a land where world politics and world imperialism are being shaped ...' And when confessing his sins to the NKVD in 1937, he would blame them on a 1932 visit to England, where he lost his faith in world revolution.

10 The primary source for material about Noah London's youth is two short autobiographies written for Moscow party records: *Avtobiografiia Noia Moisseevicha Londona*, 1926, RGASPI, fond 17, opis 98, delo 8957, listy 1–4; and *Biograficheskii ocherk*, 1933, f. 17, op. 100, d. 126451, l. 5–8. I also interviewed Noah London's American nephews Jonas Weitzman (late 1980s), Morris London (late 1980s, April 7, 2005 and June 19, 2005), Abraham Weitzman (Aug. 20, 2004), and Paul Malamud (Aug. 20, 2004). There are brief biographical entries on London in several lexicons of Yiddish writers.

Noah's mother Pia's maiden name was Walensky, though one of her American nephews told me her actual name was Volinetz. A half-dozen Londons, more than a score Volinetzes and four Walinskys would emigrate from Antopol to America in the aftermath of the 1905 Revolution.[11] Moishe London was a fairly prosperous jack-of-all-trades, by low local standards. He was primarily a blacksmith, and the family kept a store selling milk and bread, as well as a smithy. This is how anthropologist Hirsz Abramowicz described the life of a Jewish blacksmith in the Pale: 'Every blacksmith had his own hut, with a forge close by. He would shoe horses, repair wagons, forge plows, sharpen scythes, and make axes, knives and other household utensils … The peasants lived very amicably with the blacksmith, realizing that he was essential to their own primitive existence'.[12]

The Tsarist regime was meanwhile applying steady pressure to drive Jewish artisans out of peasant communities. Under the anti-Semitic 'May Laws', enacted in the aftermath of the wave of pogroms after the assassination of Tsar Alexander II, expulsion of Jews from the countryside turned great numbers of them into *luftmenshn*. The Londons managed to avoid this fate.

In Tabulok, another tiny hamlet on the opposite side of Motele, 'Moshe the Tabuloker' was the blacksmith. His son was David Chez. Moshe and David almost certainly were relatives of the Chess brothers from Motele, who founded America's greatest blues label, Chess Records. According to David Chez: 'Near his shop the *goyim* would come with their horses to put on horseshoes. They would bring corn or potatoes or something else and I would show them where to put it down. I would go with them back and forth and so I got to like them (the horses). The *goyim* had no money so they would bring a treat for the worker and I was the receiver of the goods'.[13]

Noah, David Chez's counterpart on the other side of town, would adopt the pseudonym 'Smith' as an activist in the American Communist underground. In its legal newspapers he would write as 'the engineer N. Paiezon'. According to Jonas Weitzman, a nephew of Noah's, the pseudonym signified 'Pia's son'.[14]

---

11 Malamud interview. The founding chairman of the Antopol *landsleit* society in Harlem was a Max London. There were five Londons and fourteen Volinetzes listed on the Antopol Yizkor Book street map. Bereza & Antopol, https://stevemorse.org/yizkor/index.html.

12 Hirsz Abramowicz, 'Rural Jewish Occupations in Lithuania', in *Profiles of a Lost World*, trans. Eva Zeitlin, ed. Dina Abramowicz and Jeffrey Shandler (Detroit: Wayne State University Press, 1999), 43–4.

13 David Chez, *From Motol to Chicago: An Autobiography by David Chez, 1902–1976*, trans. Rutie Gold, https://www.shtetlinks.jewishgen.org/motol/chez%20memoir.pdf. The Chess brothers also got their start in Chicago.

14 Jonas Weitzman interview, late 1980s. Regrettably, I only interviewed him once, by telephone, before I commenced serious research.

'Pious son' might be another reading. Noah was not averse to puns or Americanisms. Perhaps it was at pious Pia London's urging that young Noah sought education.

Noah wrote in his Soviet party autobiography that he helped his father at the smithy in the summertime, from the age of 12. Until Noah was 15 his family could afford to hire a *yeshiva-bocher* (Yeshiva student) to give home instruction to Noah and his younger brother Harry. Besides the Talmud they studied Russian, Yiddish grammar and arithmetic. Harry wasn't very interested, but Noah was an excellent student, with a particular facility for language. His older sister Chana would sneak in to listen. Later in America she would tell her own son that her brother was one of the two best Jewish students in the region, the other being Chaim Weitzmann. Before Noah was born, the oldest of the five children, Rochlea, emigrated to America with her husband, Nachm Eisenstein, a successful pushcart peddler.[15]

Noah grew up to become a prolific Yiddish journalist. He liked to ground what he wrote in personal experience, but almost never touched on the poverty of his childhood years. One exception is a 1925 piece about backwoods Middle America, the land of the Ku Klux Klan. He had just passed through the area on a trade mission for Soviet industry. He commented that:

> When you are poor and cut off from the world, you live a separate life ... We have here good old-fashioned Americans, and we, the foreigners, feel right at home. I, the outlander, feel more at home in the all-American *shtetls* of Indiana. I see a population of workers and the poor, who all speak the same language and understand each others' troubles. Squalor is everyone's friend ... I detect a home made element here, the element of quiet discontent, of half-hungry, seeking eyes.[16]

Motele was also where Miril London-Unterman grew up, though she did not meet him there. She was a child of the local Jewish elite, far above him on the social scale. Her mother, Bessie, was a first cousin of Chaim Weitzmann. According to the Unterman family tree:

> In 1890 a dashing moustached army sergeant (the first Jew to attain such rank in the Russian Army) returned after six years of military service. He had been drafted because he was the youngest unmarried son of a Pinsk

15 Morris London, Abraham Weitzman, and Paul Malamud interviews; London, *Avtobiografiia; Biograficheskii ocherk*.

16 Noah London, 'In mitl-Amerike', *Freiheit*, May 3, 1925.

> innkeeper … Chaim Unterman hastened to Motele, to meet the girl with whom he had been corresponding in Hebrew from faraway Tula, a military outpost and lumber center. There Chaim met a prosperous merchant, the uncle of Bessie Shapiro … Bessie's mother, widow of a rabbi, objected to the horseback-riding, concertina-playing moustached soldier as a suitor for her oldest daughter, but Bessie insisted that she'd marry Chaim or stay an old maid … Bessie Shapiro and Chaim Unterman were married in 1891.[17]

Chaim Unterman's role in the business was to select trees for export to Prussia. The Untermans raised seven children in Motele; Miril, the oldest, was born in 1891. According to her sisters Sue and Eva, Chaim 'loved music and puzzles and games and sports, and mathematical problems. He was self taught. His wife and children worshipped him … Father was a Russian patriot. He willingly served in the army. He easily distinguished himself by his intelligence, good humor, his musical feats on the accordion, [and by] out-riding, out-dancing, out-singing most of his companions in uniform'.[18] Miril, a merchant's daughter, was admitted to a prestigious *gymnasium*, while Noah had to leave home to continue his studies. His parents could no longer afford his tutor, and he turned up in Vilna as an *orem-bocher* (starving student) in 1904, at the age of sixteen. It was very difficult for Jews to be admitted to higher education, due to Tsarist discrimination. Meanwhile Miril got herself transferred to a trade school in Pinsk, where she studied to be a bookbinder and a dressmaker. Thus while Noah was seeking upward social mobility into the intelligentsia, Miril was voluntarily accepting downward mobility into the ranks of artisanry.

So much education for so many Jewish children was an expensive proposition at the Pinsk *gymnasium*. Under its quota system, Jewish parents had to pay tuition for an equal number of gentile students. A traveling Jewish merchant described this practice in Sholem Aleichem's *Railroad Stories*:

> It was an act of sheer mercy on God's part to find me a commercial high school in Poland where they took a Jew for every Christian – that is, where the quota was fifty percent. There was just one little catch: the Jew had to bring his own Christian with him – and only if your Christian passed the

17 'The Unterman Family Tree', by William Hort, Chaim Unterman's grandson and the author's uncle.

18 Letter, 'Aunt Sue and Eva', to Olivia Holmes (the author's sister), May 23, 1973.

> exams and you were ready to treat him to tuition did you stand a fighting chance ... instead of one millstone around my neck I had two.[19]

Miril's Pinsk trade school turned out to be a hotbed of student radicals – just like the one in Aleichem's *Railroad Stories*. She joined the revolutionary movement there.[20]

2 Vilna and 'Socialist Zionism'

Noah joined the movement in Vilna, now called Vilnius. It was the first metropolis he ever saw – a polyglot city, in which Jews were the dominant nationality. According to the census of 1897, 40.0 percent of its inhabitants spoke Yiddish, 30.9 percent Polish, 20.0 percent Russian, 4.2 percent Belarusian and 2.1 percent Lithuanian. But many of those Russian-speakers were Jews.

Vilna was essentially the capital of the 'northwest provinces' of the Empire and had considerable administrative and military importance. It was as well a historic crucible of Eastern European Jewish civilization. The famed Vilna *gaon* had spread the orthodox message of the anti-Hasidic *misnagdim* from Vilna. Talmudic Vilna rationalism helped lay the basis for the Jewish Enlightenment, the *haskalah*. (Chaim Unterman considered himself a follower of this movement.) It was also a significant Polish cultural center, and had been the capital of the medieval Lithuanian state, though the peasantry in immediately surrounding area were at this point mostly Belarusian. Even though five different nationalities thus had claims on Vilna, it had a reputation for an unusually high level of mutual tolerance.[21]

Noah London tried to enroll in the Vilna Teachers Institute. Admission to this prestigious government-sponsored institution was notoriously difficult, as it was one of only two of its kind for Jews in the entire Empire. As he put it, he *'gotovilsia, daval uroki, golodal, v Institut ne popal'* (prepared for the entrance exam, tutored, starved, wasn't admitted).[22] He was an *ekstern*, an 'external stu-

19 Sholem Aleichem, *Tevye the Dairyman and The Railroad Stories*, trans. and ed. H. Halkin (New York: Schocken, 1996), 226.

20 *Registratsionnyi blank chlena VKP(b)* Maria London, *partbilet* No. 1193080, RGASPI; letter, Beatrice to John Holmes (June 30, 1996); B. Holmes interview (Nov. 30, 1998); B. Holmes, 'Young Girl as Heroine'. She was the author's mother.

21 Theodore Weeks, 'The 1905 Revolution in Vilnius'; Henri Minczeles, *Vilna, Wilno, Vilnius: La Jérusalem de Lituanie?* (Paris: La Découverte, 1993); Abramowicz, 'Vilne di natsionaliteten-shtot', *Vilne: A zamlbukh*, 267–72.

22 London, *Biograficheskii ocherk*.

dent', part of a great wave of *eksternikes* among the Jewish youth in this period. According to Jewish Bund leader Raphael Abramovitch: 'Children of poor parents who didn't have the means to pay a teacher; *yeshiva-bochers*, who once upon a time would have been fed as house guests; young girls who didn't want to wait for marriage – all tried out self-education. Since getting into a Russian school had become almost impossible ... the solution found was to prepare at home for the entrance exams'.[23]

Noah London exemplified an entire category of *poluintelligenty* (half-intellectuals), who played a major role in the Jewish socialist underground. Their background was lower on the social scale than that of the Russian socialist intelligentsia, and many of them had to make their living by working with their hands. As Russian labor historian Allan Wildman puts it:

> Because of the peculiarities of the Jewish social milieu, the categories 'worker', '*poluintelligent*', and '*intelligent*' were quite fluid. The son of an impoverished Jewish middle class family was typically a *poluintelligent*, but, given the tremendous drive such youngsters often had for a Russian education, he might eventually qualify as an *intelligent*. However, to support himself, he might be obliged to learn a craft or trade which qualified him as a 'worker'.[24]

This new Jewish social category came into existence because of Tsarist discrimination. In an intermediate space between the working class and the intelligentsia, these *poluintelligenty* could perhaps be considered examples of Antonio Gramsci's conception of the 'organic intellectual' playing a vital role in the workers movement. In Gramsci's vision 'organic intellectuals' would be carefully trained by revolutionary parties. These 'half intellectuals' were autodidacts, who Bund leader Abramovitch described as 'a new layer of people who could handle the tool we were not able to handle – to write and speak Yiddish to the Jewish worker ...'[25]

---

23 Raphael Abramovitch, *In tsvey revolutsies: Di geshikhte fun a dor* (New York: Farlag Arbeiter Ring, 1944), vol. 1, 30.

24 Allan K. Wildman, *Making of a Workers' Revolution: Russian Social Democracy, 1891–1903* (Chicago: University of Chicago Press, 1967), 174.

25 Susanne Marten-Finnis, 'The Bundist Press', in *Jewish Politics in Eastern Europe: The Bund at 100*, ed. Jack Jacobs (Basingstoke: Palgrave Macmillan, 2001), 14; *Selections from the Prison Notebooks of Antonio Gramsci*, ed. Q. Hoare, G. Smith (New York: International Publishers, 1971), 15–16; Jonathan Frankel, *Crisis, Revolution, and Russian Jews* (Cambridge: Cambridge University Press, 2009), 103–4.

Noah London arrived in Vilna as thousands of young Jews just like him were flocking into a budding new movement, in the aftermath of the infamous 1903 Kishinev pogroms universally blamed on the Tsarist regime. These massacres in Kishinev (nowadays Chișinău in Moldova), in which 49 Jews were killed; a number of Jewish women were raped; over 600 Jews were injured and some 1,500 homes were damaged.[26] The Kishinev pogroms inspired Jewish youth to reject traditional Jewish acquiescence to authority and the 'orthodox' Zionist movement founded by Austrian journalist Theodor Herzl a few years earlier as well. Herzl and his Russian followers were advocating cooperation with the authorities for the sake of Jewish resettlement in Palestine. Rival Jewish-nationalistic socialist parties arose in response, and in the fall of 1904 London joined the largest and most important, the Socialist-Zionist Party (SZP). Vilna was one of its main centers. Yiddish writer Daniel Charney was also living in Vilna in 1904, in an SZP commune that served as party headquarters. According to Charney, the SZP was made up mostly of 'more or less petty-bourgeois elements. These were office workers; *eksternikes* who used to dream of Russian *gymnasia*; teachers; former *yeshiva-bochers*; students; bookbinders and watchmakers, who used to belong to the ideal professions; stockingmakers; milliners; and driftless middle-class daughters, who aspired to a new world. The true Yiddish proletariat … were all with the Bund'.[27] The Jewish Labor Bund, as Charney wrote, was the main Jewish labor and socialist organization in the Jewish Pale, a true mass party. It became the focus of Noah London's life for a decade, after he left the SZP for the Bund. Noah's teenage years as a 'professional revolutionary' in the Bund would shape his entire later life.

The SZP's program made excellent sense to Charney's 'petty-bourgeois elements'. Its leading thinker was sociologist Jacob Lestchinsky, who developed a 'theory of non-industrialization'. Lestchinsky asserted in his 1906 work, *Der yidisher arbeter in Rusland*, that the Jewish situation in the Pale was hopeless. Advancing capitalism was destroying traditional Jewish occupations. Jewish workers were excluded from industrial jobs and confined to increasingly marginal sectors of socio-economic life. Therefore, they could not play a significant role in either the class struggle or the struggle for Jewish rights in Russia. Jews

---

26 Recent research questions whether the Kishinev pogrom was stage-managed by the authorities. Judge, *Easter in Kishinev*; Löwe, *Tsars and the Jews*, 147–56. Dubbed by Löwe as a 'preliminary skirmish of the revolution', it had a transitional character between the probably spontaneous pogroms after the assassination of Tsar Alexander, which sparked Jewish emigration in the 1880s, and the quite different pogroms of later years.

27 Daniel Charney, *Vilne: Memuarn* (Buenos Aires: Tsentral-Farband Fun Poylishe Yidn, 1951), 99. Charney was well positioned to make such judgments. He had one older brother in the central leadership of the SZP and another among the top leaders of the Bund.

would automatically be driven to emigrate to a homeland of their very own – somewhere or other, probably not in Palestine. Russian Zionism, socialist or otherwise, was essentially a movement of despair – not unlike black nationalism in America.[28]

Noah London was the son of a hammer-wielding blacksmith – the future central image of Soviet proletarian iconography. He would pride himself all his life on his ability to work with his hands. But he was also a child of the 'people of the book' in a land where upward social mobility for Jews was blocked. Participating in the Jewish labor movement shaped the ideas of 'half-intellectuals' like young Noah. Jewish socialism evolved together with a militant and assertive Jewish working class in Tsarist Russia – and in New York City as well.

By 1905, the downward social mobility inflicted by economic evolution and Tsarist anti-Semitism revolutionized a community once noted for its political passivity. The Jewish socialism of Noah London was born in the Jewish Pale of Tsarist Russia. The golden age of a worldwide Jewish labor movement would be brief. Its impact on the history of the twentieth century would be considerable.

28 Yoav Peled, *Class and Ethnicity in the Pale: The Political Economy of Jewish Workers' Nationalism in Late Imperial Russia* (New York: St. Martin's Press, 1989), 80–7; John Bunzl, 'Klassenkampf in der Diaspora: Aur Geschichte der jüdischen Arbeitersbewegung', in *Schriftenreihe des Ludwig-Botzmann-Instituts für Geschichte der Arbeiterbewegung*, no. 5 (Vienna: Europaverlag, 1975), 107–8.

CHAPTER 2

The Revolution of 1905

While Noah was trying to concentrate on his entrance exams and Miril was pondering her future, the Russian Empire went to war and Russia's defeat touched off political crisis. Its revolutionizing effects were compounded in the Jewish Pale, where war aggravated an organic economic crisis. On Sunday, January 9, 1905, Father Gapon led Christian factory workers in a march on the Winter Palace in St. Petersburg to petition Tsar Nicholas for reform. Bullets met the marchers. Hundreds died and thousands were wounded on 'Bloody Sunday'. The Russian Revolution of 1905 began, and Jewish workers in the Tsarist Pale mobilized – more quickly and on a larger scale than elsewhere in Russia. Mass strikes rippled through sixty large and small centers of Jewish population, sparking revolutionary developments across the country.[1]

1 A Jewish Revolution in a Jewish Pale

The 1905 Revolution was a milestone in Jewish history. Jews all over Russia and around the world enthusiastically identified with it. The Pale went through a 'Jewish Revolution': decades later, poet David Einhorn wrote that 'I do not know how others number the years. But I count them from 1905'. Jewish socialism of every possible coloration grew explosively in Noah London's Vilna. As one observer put it, 'Any group of *intelligenty*, speaking out publicly, draping itself in any sort of red flag, advancing any kind of theory, even the most intricate, could rally together a considerable number of people, wanting to join the revolution somehow or other'.[2]

After Bloody Sunday the pessimistic Socialist-Zionist program appealed to Noah no longer. He now believed you could change Russia, since there now

1 Ezra Mendelsohn, *Class Struggle in the Pale: The Formative Years of the Jewish Workers' Movement in Tsarist Russia* (Cambridge: Cambridge University Press, 2010), 113–15; S. Dimanshtein, in *1905: Istoriia revoliutsionnogo dvizheniia*, ed. M.N. Pokrovskii (Moscow-Leningrad, 1927).

2 Jonathan Frankel, *Jewish Politics and the Russian Revolution of 1905* (Tel Aviv: Tel Aviv Univeristy Press, 1982); Frankel, *Prophecy and Politics: Socialism, Nationalism, and the Russian Jews, 1862–1917* (Cambridge: Cambridge University Press, 1981), 134; and Frankel, *Crisis, Revolution, and Russian Jewry*, 57–9; Dimanshtein, *1905*, 124–5. Former rabbi Dimanshtein, a Vilna Bolshevik in 1905, was selected by Lenin after the 1917 Revolution to head the *Evsektsiia*, the Jewish section of the Soviet Communist Party.

 | DOI:10.1163/9789004745384_004

were Orthodox Christian Russians in revolt, not only Jews. Fleeing Russia no longer felt necessary. He joined the Jewish Bund, the dominant force 'on the Jewish street'. Bund street meetings became community institutions. In the words of Aleksandr Chemerinsky, a Bund leader in 1905: 'People used to come for every different reason: questions of divorce; a dowry; business partners who had fallen out; a speculator who himself had been outwitted; a young woman who had been deceived; a quarrel in the family; maids with complaints against the ladies of the house – all used to come and one could hardly escape them by telling them that they should rather go to the rabbi'.[3] The Bund was the largest, strongest and best-organized section of Russian Social Democracy. In 1896 Georgii Plekhanov, the founder of Russian Marxism, reported to the Congress of the Socialist International that 'the Jewish workers may be considered the vanguard of the labor army in Russia'. Russia's northwest provinces, Jewish Lithuania, were its bastion, and the Bund's deep roots in the area gave it a mass character. In Vilna, it is estimated that a quarter of the city's Jewish workers were dues-paying members of the Bund in 1905.[4]

The Bund's broad popular support attracted Noah. Throughout his political career he would advocate an orientation 'to the masses' in one form or another. As revolution swept over the Empire, the Bund program fit the moment better than socialistic Zionism. Bundists maintained that the socio-economic peculiarities of the Russian Jewish community were mere symptoms of Tsarist oppression. Overthrowing the autocracy would put an end to pogroms, emigration and the exclusion of Jews from industry. Jewish workers ought to fight side by side with their non-Jewish brothers and sisters, but would need a separate organization to defend their particular interests.

Vilna responded to Bloody Sunday with a powerful general strike. Jewish workers, especially leather workers, played the dominant role. Noah was arrested but released for lack of evidence – and being arrested was serious business in Vilna. According to former rabbi, future historian and Bolshevik Jewish leader Semen Dimanshtein, 'I remember from my own experience how unbelievably brutally they beat the arrestees. They flung arrestees on the floor … and blows with sabers, clubs and boots rained down thick and fast; they beat with special rubber whips, they beat women on the naked skin until their bod-

3 Frankel, *Prophecy and Politics*, 148. Chemerinsky would later follow Dimanshtein as the head of the Evsektsie.

4 Mendelsohn, *Class Struggle in the Pale*, 156; Moshe Mishkinsky, 'Regional Factors in the Formation of the Jewish Labor Movement in Czarist Russia', *YIVO Annual* 14 (1969); Weeks, '1905 Revolution in Vilnius'.

ies were covered by continuous swellings. Afterwards they poured water over them, so as to be able to continue the punishment'.[5]

The arrest was a 17-year-old's initiation into his new trade as a professional revolutionary. In the early summer the Bund called one-day strikes all over the Pale, in support of barricade fighters in Odessa and Lodz. Noah was arrested again shortly thereafter in the *shtetl* of Oshmiany, the capital of the Smorgon district, a Bund stronghold with a militant tradition. In Oshmiany, many Jews were tannery workers, and the Smorgon district was the center of the leather industry in the Pale – the main Lithuanian export industry. In 1905 there also was a huge domestic demand for leather boots and jackets for the army, the navy, the Cossacks and the police – and for leather whips and clubs to use on troublemakers.[6]

Noah's younger brother Harry became a leatherworkers' apprentice at about this time. The method he learned for tanning was simple: you took the hide of an animal and hung it over a tree branch. Leather was one of the best organized labor sectors in the Pale.[7] Both Jewish and non-Jewish workers were employed in the trade, which had a semi-industrial character despite its primitivity, so leather workers fell victim to all the worst features of both modern industry and traditional artisanry. They had no chance to become independent craftsmen, but working conditions and techniques were medievally backward. Wages were decent, but conditions were so bad that leather workers had an average life expectancy of only 40 years.

The Smorgon-based *garber-bund* was an extremely militant industrial union, whose Jewish members enthusiastically supported blows against the Empire. The Bund's Achilles heel in the trade was the non-Jewish workers, who were difficult to organize at first.[8] Things changed after Bloody Sunday, and in Oshmiany, where Noah London worked, Jewish protest strikes rapidly transformed into community-wide battles for higher wages. In the nearby Smorgon *shtetl* itself, non-Jewish leatherworkers struck and marched side by side with their Jewish co-workers the very next week. According to a socialist newspaper account, 'Smorgon was in the hands of the proletariat'.[9]

---

5 Weeks, '1905 Revolution in Vilnius', 7–10; London, *Avtobiografiia*; Dimanshtein, *1905*, 145. Accounts of prisoner treatment from Bundist sources are similar.

6 *Biograficheskii ocherk*; M. Peled, 'A Small Jewish Village, of Blessed Memory', *Oshmana Memorial Book* 1969, jewishgen.org; Mendelsohn, *Class Struggle in the Pale*, 24; Katzenelenbogen, 'Pionir fun der leder-industrie', *Lite*; Mendel, *Memoirs of a Jewish Revolutionary*.

7 Morris London interview; Morris was Harry London's son.

8 Sofia Dubnova-Erlikh, *Garber-bund un bershter-bund* (Warsaw, 1937).

9 A.D. Kirzhnits, 1905: Evreiskoe rabochee dvizhenie, ed. M. Rafes (Moscow: Gosudarstvennoe izdatelstvo 1928).

Noah was released after a couple months in prison at the end of summer and returned to Vilna at the peak of revolutionary ferment in the fall. A national rail strike paralyzed the whole country and turned into a general strike against Tsarist absolutism. According to a Vilna Jewish socialist, the day before Tsar Nicholas capitulated to the strikers and accepted the idea of a constitution,

> the streets are turned into weird black streams of humanity, which all poured in one direction – to the railworkers' club. They marched free as a bird, openly and boldly reading fresh proclamations from all parties in all local languages, calling for a general strike and grandiose demonstrations. The young people marched cheerfully, with bright eyes and shining faces, here and there humming the first notes of revolutionary songs, without the words.[10]

We can be sure that one of these young people was Noah. The Tsarist army was compelled to negotiate its troop deployments that November with the Vilna Bund leader, Aron Devenishskii (Vayter). People were calling him the police chief of Vilna: 'dual power' had arrived.[11]

But an anti-Semitic counterrevolution answered Jewish revolution. Massive pogroms accompanied the days of freedom, beginning simultaneously all across the Empire on October 18, one day after Nicholas issued his constitutional October Manifesto.[12] These pogroms had a historical resonance extending far beyond their immediate victims: Jews became associated with revolution, and anti-Semitism with reaction. In consequence, as pogrom historian John Klier put it: 'pogroms arose out of collisions between revolution and

---

10 A.I. Goldshmit, 'Khaver aron', in *Vayter bukh: tsum andenk fun a. vayter*, ed. Sh. Niger and Z. Rayzen (Vilna: Br. Rozaental, 1920), 82–9.

11 Vladimir Medem, *Life and Soul of a Legendary Jewish Socialist: The Memoirs of Vladimir Medem*, tran. Samuel A. Portnoy (New York: Ktav, 1979), 364–5; Abramovitch, *Tsvey revolutsies*, vol. 1, 227.

12 In recent years, a number of historians have challenged the traditional belief that the regime was directly responsible, arguing that there is no proof in government records. Rogger, *Jewish Policies*; Klier and Lambroza, *Pogroms: Anti-Jewish Violence*; Löwe, *Tsars and the Jews*. Official documents illicitly published in the aftermath indicate otherwise. *Pogromy po offitsialnym dokumentam: Materialy k istorii russkoi kontr-revoliutsii*, vol. 1 (St. Petersburg: Obshchestvennaia Polza, 1908). The consensus at the time was that the pogroms were stage-managed by Deputy Minister of the Interior Trepov, the dominant figure at that moment in the Tsarist regime. He was in secret communication with police officials all over the empire through newly installed telephone lines.

counterrevolution, because Jews were the symbol of the first of these'.[13] The Bolshevik Revolution would reinforce this association.

In some areas of the Tsarist empire, the pogroms had at least a partially spontaneous character. This was particularly true in a corner of the empire now attracting world attention, the eastern Ukrainian borderlands of the Donbass. Jews were not supposed to live in the Donbass, since it was outside the Pale. The Donbass was a traditional site for miners' riots against Jews, doctors and other outsiders, notorious for its social backwardness. Elsewhere in the Pale itself, even in the rest of Ukraine, local authorities had to act more directly if they wanted to spark pogroms – sometimes not too successfully.[14]

'Jewish Lithuania', the Bund stronghold where London was active, was largely exempt from the October wave of pogroms. But anti-Jewish bloodshed elsewhere in the Empire had a demoralizing impact. People were already fatigued by three-quarters of a year of continual strikes, demonstrations and barricade battles. Jewish revolutionaries increasingly understood that it was simply not possible for Jews to overthrow the regime all by themselves, and that Jews would be the worst sufferers from the backlash to a failed insurrection. Jewish workers increasingly became willing to risk armed uprising only if they felt they would be joined by the rest of the population.[15]

In December, Jewish radicals greeted news of a Moscow insurrection of non-Jewish workers with relief and enthusiasm. The Bund, previously unfavorable to its Bolshevik leaders, became their allies. This revolt, which according to some reports almost succeeded, seemed to prove both that the Tsar could be overthrown and that Jews had powerful allies. Simultaneously local radical revolts briefly seized power here and there in the Empire, even in the Donbass. A solid general strike shut down all Lithuania, led by joint committees of the Bund and Russian and Polish Social Democrats. While the Vilna committee debated whether to follow Moscow's example, rebellions chased the police out of a series of Lithuanian *shtetls*. Leatherworkers were the backbone of these village uprisings. Future American labor leader Sidney Hillman led

---

13 John D. Klier, 'Kazaki i pogromy: Chem otlichalis' 'voennye' pogromy?' in *Mirovoi krizis 1914–1920*, ed. O.V. Budnitskii (Moscow: Rosspen, 2005), 57.

14 Charters Wynn, *Workers, Strikes and Pogroms: The Donbass-Dnepr Bend in Late Imperial Russia, 1870–1905* (Princeton, NJ: Princeton University Press, 1992); Weinberg, *Revolution of 1905 in Odessa*; Viktoriya Khiterer, 'The October 1905 Pogrom in Kiev', *East European Jewish Affairs* 22, no. 2 (1992); Michael F. Hamm, 'Jews and Revolution in Kharkiv', in *The Russian Revolution of 1905*, ed. Anthony J. Heywood and Jonathan D. Smele (London: Taylor & Francis, 2005), 156–76; Kirzhnits, *1905*, 214–15; Nathan Weinstock, *Pain de misère: Histoire du mouvement ouvrier juif en Europe* (Paris: La Décourverte, 1984), 210–11.

15 Abramovitch, *In tsvey revolutsies*, vol. 1, 242–3; Dimanshtein, *1905*, 177–9.

the revolt in the *shtetl* of Zagare, near the contemporary Latvian/Lithuanian border. He then organized a Committee of Public Safety to arrest the police superintendent and execute the occasional provocateur.[16] Noah London would cut his teeth in the American labor movement in Hillman's union, just a few years later.

2 A Revolution in Decline

But in Vilna itself, where Noah London was working, the Bund was ceasing to be the decisive factor. The leading role in the October national general strike, in Vilna as elsewhere, had been played by the railworkers. They clearly would need to play the same role in a Vilna revolt. These overwhelmingly Russian railworkers were the only classic 'industrial proletarians' in Vilna, and were much more vital to the economy than the artisans and workshop employees who formed the Bund's social base. 'Tomas', their leader, was a Russian Social Democrat. But the Black Hundreds, the Russian version of fascism in those days, were agitating among them against what they called Jewish domination. And disaffected Russian soldiers in Vilna were not about to mutiny under Jewish leadership. When news of the defeat of the Moscow insurrection reached Vilna, the general strike collapsed. The political atmosphere changed abruptly. Bund leader Vladimir Medem described how: 'the place was unrecognizable ... True, the streets and houses were still the same. But two weeks before it was "our" Vilna, now it had suddenly become an unfamiliar city ... The attitude of the city as a whole ... had changed ... This was the summation of the ill-fated struggle of December. The honeymoon period of the revolution was liquidated'.[17] A punitive expedition was dispatched to the Baltic provinces. Count Witte, the new and supposedly liberal prime minister of Russia, urged Tsar Nicholas to employ 'the most merciless measures', complaining that 'we have too few troops in the Baltic'. A somewhat reluctant Nicholas complained that Witte wanted 'to hang and shoot everybody'.[18] This was not precisely a pogrom, but it was difficult for victims to see the difference.

16 I. Iurenev, 'Rabota RSDRP v Sever-Zapadnom krae (Vil'no) 1903–1913'. *Proletarskaia Revolitsia* 31–32 (1924): 163–82, Kirzhnits, *1905*, 249, 260–8; Fraser, *Labor Will Rule*, 14.

17 Weeks, 'The 1905 Revolution in Vilnius', 12–13; Kirzhnits, *1905*, 259–61; Iurenev, 'Rabota RSDRP v Sever-Zapadnom krae', 171–8; Frankel *Prophecy and Politics*, 154–5; Medem, *Life and Soul*, 370–1.

18 Howard D. Mehlinger, *Count Witte and the Tsarist Government in the 1905 Revolution* (Bloomington: Indiana University Press, 1972), 106–9, 157–60.

The Bund attempted to rally by calling protest strikes for January 9, 1906, the anniversary of Bloody Sunday. In response, a full-blown military pogrom was inflicted on Gomel, a main Bundist center. Led by Cossacks and dragoons, mobs burned down most of the city.[19] Young Noah was arrested in Vilna on the ninth of January, exiled from Vilna Province and sent home. Russia was acquiring a 'constitutional' regime. Stolypin became the Russian prime minister in June 1906, and revolutionaries began donning 'Stolypin neckties' all over Russia (i.e., being hanged). Noah could not safely return home to Motele, so he hid out for a year with one of his many cousins in Antopol.[20]

3 Aftermath of a Jewish Revolution: Noah London, Lithuanians and Leather

In 1907 the Bund sent London to Kovno Province as an underground 'professional'. Mostly agrarian, Kovno's geographical boundaries were similar to those of interwar Lithuania. About 80 percent of the total population was ethnically Lithuanian. The overwhelming majority were peasants, but there was also a small urban Lithuanian labor sector. During the 1905 Revolution, the Bund managed to mobilize these artisans, who had no previous experience of political or trade union activity.[21]

In the aftermath of the revolution, Noah's Bund was starting to face competition from local Lithuanian revolutionaries. The Lithuanian Social Democratic Party (LSDP) was an offshoot of patriotic Polish socialism. It took up an interest in the culture and traditions of the Lithuanian countryside, organized a powerful peasant movement and gradually turned into an ethnically Lithuanian party after its original founders were arrested. Prosperous Lithuanian peasants supported strikes by farm laborers on noble estates, hoping to bankrupt the Polish, Russian or Baltic German landlords so that they could buy up their lands. Nationalist-inclined smallholders often led the movement. LSDP control largely prevented the violence and property destruction that characterized spontaneous rural rebellions elsewhere in the Empire. This movement

19 Heinz-Dietrich Löwe, a 'revisionist' on the question of Tsarist pogrom responsibility, concedes that the local authorities were heavily involved in the Gomel pogrom. Even the official report to Minister of the Interior Durnovo confirms this. Löwe, *The Tsars and the Jews: Reform, Reaction, and Anti-Semitism in Imperial Russia, 1772–1917* (Amsterdam: Harwood, 1993), 221; *Pogromy po offitsialnym dokumentam*, 375–95; Kirzhnits, *1905*, 273–5.

20 London, *Biograficheskii ocherk*; Morris London interviews.

21 London, *Biograficheskii ocherk*; *Avtobiografiia*; Kirzhnits, *1905*, 78; Frankel, *Prophecy and Politics*, 145.

had little contact with the Jewish-dominated labor movement of the cities and *shtetls*. Relations between the Bund and the LSDP were distant but friendly.[22] But by 1907 this was changing. London wrote a decade later that a Yiddish orator from the LSDP

> gave a lecture in Shavel in Kovno province in 1907 about his program … he criticized the program of the Bund and maintained that there should be no Bund in ethnic Lithuania and that it is 'chauvinism' to demand any kind of autonomy for Jews in the future independent Lithuania, and so forth. It was pointed out to the orator that it is laughable to think that the highly developed Jewish intelligentsia, whether from the progressive or conservative elements of Lithuanian Jewry, should assimilate themselves with the Lithuanian peasants, who have the greatest percentage of illiteracy among any nation of European Russia; and that the only socialist movement which can successfully function in Lithuania is among the workers in Lithuania, which are mostly Jewish. He answered that it is not the fault of the Lithuanian peasant that he is backward. But he has a right to demand that the 'foreign' elements should adapt to him in 'his' country.[23]

Shavel's LSDP for its part accused the Bund of allying with Jewish liberals and even conservatives instead of the LSDP during the 1907 Duma elections.[24] Shavel (now Siauliai) would become interwar Lithuania's second-largest city. Two-thirds of its population was Jewish, and Jewish businessmen dominated the Shavel leather trade, which became a world center for leather manufacture in the aftermath of 1905. Local leathermen were transforming and modernizing the industry. The largest, Chaim Frenkl, modeled himself on Henry Ford, and his factory had a thousand employees. Unlike his American model, he had a cooperative relationship with his coreligionists of the Bund.[25] London's previous experience in the Smorgon leather district was surely the reason why the Bund sent him to Shavel.

---

22 Leonas Sabaliunas, *Lithuanian Social Democracy in Perspective, 1893–1914* (Durham, NC: Duke University Press, 1990), 43–65; Vincas Mickevičius-Kapsukas, '1905 god v Litve', *Proletarskaia Revoliutsia* 11, 1922: 57–72.; James D. White, 'The 1905 Revolution in Russia's Baltic Provinces', in *Russian Revolution of 1905*, 55–78.

23 Noah London, 'An internatsionale idish-sotsialistishe konferents', *Naye Velt*, Nov. 1, 1918.

24 Leaflet, Shavel regional LSDP committee, Jan. 1907, 'Proletarier aller lender fareynigt aykh! tsu ale idishe arbeyter fun shavel!', YIVO, RG 117 (US Terr. Coll.), box 58, folder 1.

25 Katzenelenbogen, 'Chaim Frenkl', *Lite*, 1951.

The formerly illegal Bundist leather workers union, the Garber-Bund, was refounded on a legal basis in the immediate aftermath of the Revolution. Its bulwark was the Smorgon region, where according to its leader, Avram der Tate, 'people frequently would turn to the union with complaints, not wanting to have anything to do with the rabbi or the courts'. At one leather factory in Grodno province, the factory owner threatened to close it down after an anarchist attempt to assassinate him – unless his employees agreed to repudiate the anarchists and join the Garber-Bund. The Bund never tried to unionize Shavel, where London was assigned – postrevolutionary Bundist strategy in the industry was conciliatory to cooperative employers like Chaim Frenkl.[26]

Noah London seems to have opposed the Bund's conciliatory labor policies. He wrote more than a decade later that he had argued for more militant union tactics in Bundist internal discussions in Shavel, tactics which he referred to as 'Bolshevik'.[27] In 1908, London returned to Vilna and once again took up the life of an 'external student'. For three years he had traveled the 'northwest provinces' on party assignment, supporting himself through office work, tutoring and writing letters for illiterates.[28] At the age of twenty, Noah London, a blacksmith's son from the backwoods marshes, had gained some serious experience as an underground professional revolutionary. But the movement was collapsing around him.

3.1 *The Aftermath of Defeat: A Cultural Turn*

The Bund had been organizing for a workers' revolution. It had come – and gone. Many Jews were bitterly disappointed with the revolutionary movement's failure to stop the pogroms. The Bund's Socialist-Zionist competitors urged Jews to put faith in themselves, not unreliable *goyishe* allies. They gained influence, with London's old SZP briefly rivalling the Bund in size. But the economic decline of the *shtetl* accelerated after the defeat of the 1905 Revolution. Employers launched increasingly successful attacks on Jewish unions, and their economic gains were abruptly wiped out. What happened to the Garber-Bund was typical: all-Jewish labor and socialist organizations collapsed. Political reaction accompanied economic depression, as nonsocialist elements re-emerged in Jewish politics. Jews, many of them disappointed revolutionaries, emigrated to

---

26 Avram der Tate (Leyb Blekhman), *Bleter fun mayn yugnt*; Sofia Dubnow-Erlich, *Garber-bund un bershter-bund bletlekh fun der Yidisher arbeyter-bavegung* (Varshe: Kultur-lige, 1937). Blekhman was the union's leader. Neither work even mentions the Shavel leather industry.

27 London, *Biograficheskii ocherk*; London, 'A perzenlikhe erklerung', *Proletaryer*, July 20, 1921.

28 London, *Biograficheskii ocherk*.

America in unprecedented numbers. Increasingly the Bund became dependent for survival on American financial support.[29] The battle-hardened Bund underground collapsed as well. Its various Socialist-Zionist competitors disintegrated completely and disappeared from the scene. The demoralization overtaking the Jewish underground affected Vilna Bund leader 'Aron' Devenishskii early. One of his comrades asked him why he fell silent during the 'days of freedom'. He answered:

> Because they are desecrated! ... With thousands of raped Jewish daughters, with murdered Jewish infants, with oceans of Jewish blood and tears ... Guilty for all this is the vile regime ... also the intelligentsia, and perhaps also, the people ... [But] Aron felt that he could not depart at such a moment ... and he returned to his work ... By word and pen, he proved that the revolution was liberal-bourgeois, and that the proletariat, which is actually barely at all organized and absolutely undisciplined, physically and spiritually simply does not have it in its power to carry the revolution alone on its back, and that in itself compels it not to try to anticipate the course of history, which punishes tactical mistakes bitterly ...[30]

The parallels are obvious with the conclusions the Menshevik wing of Russian Social Democracy would draw from the defeat of the 1905 Revolution, that the revolution needed to be restricted to a 'bourgeois' revolution, and that an alliance with the liberal bourgeoisie was necessary. The Bund originally called for the creation of an autonomous Jewish workers' movement struggling to overthrow Tsarism, in alliance with Russian Social Democracy but independent. As Bund and Menshevik leader Abramovich put it many years later, the Bund's founders 'aimed at the creation of an organization of the Jewish proletariat which would form both an organic part of the general revolutionary movement in Russia and also ... represent the specific interests and demands of the Jewish workers and population'.[31] This strategy was put to the test of history in 1905 – and failed.

---

29 Dubnow-Erlich, 'Barg arop', in *Geshikhte fun bund*, vol. 2; *Otchet TsK Bunda* (to 1907 RSDAP congress), RGASPI, f. 271, op. 1, d. 293, l. 2, 7; Frankel, *Crisis, Revolution, and Russian Jews*, 63–9.

30 Goldshmit, 'Khaver aron', 90.

31 Raphael Abramovitch, 'Jewish Socialist Movement in Russia and Poland (1879–1919)', in *The Jewish People: Past and Present* (New York: Jewish Encyclopedic Handbooks, 1946), vol. 2, 369.

In the aftermath the Bund's remnants turned to legal activity, especially Yiddish cultural activity. This new orientation was authentic, not just a 'front' for the Bundist underground. Many veterans left the movement to become Yiddish writers and artists: 'Comrade Aron' became playwright 'A. Vayter', and cultural semi-nationalism became a refuge from the collapse of revolutionary dreams.

4 Noah London, Bundism, Bolshevism and Menshevism

Noah London would later maintain that he had been a 'Bund Bolshevik'. In 1902 the Bund supported the Mensheviks during the famous London Congress at which Russian Social Democracy split between Mensheviks and Bolsheviks. Its delegates walked out when its claim to be the 'sole representative of the Jewish proletariat' was rejected by both sides. Bundists as a result disdained both wings of Russian Social Democracy until 1905. The Bund was a mass organization and saw Menshevik and Bolshevik demands that it should subordinate itself to a feeble Russian Social Democracy as ridiculous and unreasonable. According to Abramovich, the Mensheviks, unlike the Bolsheviks, came to their senses after 1905 and granted the Bund the rightful place in the movement it deserved. But there was nothing unusual about 'Bund Bolshevism'.

In the immediate aftermath of 1905, the Bund still had a larger membership than either the Bolshevik or the Menshevik organizations. Prior to the 1905 Revolution, the Bund's original sympathy for Menshevik advocacy of a looser organizational structure was temporary and hypocritical. Although the Bund began as a 'general Jewish workers union', it soon adopted a thoroughly 'Leninist' mode of organization. Underground union leaders like Avram der Tate (real name Leyb Blekhman) used Lenin's *What Is to Be Done?* as their organization manual.[32] Menshevism for its part became identified with a strategy of alliance with a liberal bourgeoisie by the end of the 1905 Revolution. This strategy was difficult to apply in the Pale, where a 'Jewish revolution' temporarily isolated all nonsocialist political forces on the Jewish street. Ex-rabbi Dimanshtein later asserted, 'It must be said that Jewish liberalism didn't receive any support from Jewish workers in this period. Not because Jewish revolutionary parties were so left, but because Jewish liberals were such flabby, colorless loyal citizens that even the most inveterate Menshevik couldn't put any stake on them. By comparison with Jewish liberalism Russian liberalism looked revolutionary'.[33]

32 Frankel, *Prophecy and Politics*, 236.

33 Dimanshtein, *1905*, 119.

During the 1905 Revolution, the Bund fell into an alliance with the Bolsheviks against the Mensheviks. The Bolshevik tactical orientation was similar to the Bund's. Bundists advocated armed insurrection and enthusiastically hailed that Bolshevik-led Moscow uprising which the Mensheviks labeled a blunder. When Russian Social-Democracy invited the Bund to rejoin its ranks in the spring of 1906 it was at Lenin's prompting, over Menshevik objections.[34]

The Bund actually 'out-Bolshevized' Lenin in organizational terms. The Bolsheviks supported the formation of elected *sovety* (councils, Soviets) of workers' deputies, even though they were originally initiated by the Mensheviks. Lenin overcame resistance against this policy from narrow-minded committeemen, such as a young Georgian Bolshevik who adopted the pseudonym of Stalin, the 'man of steel'. But the Bund, like Stalin but more insistently, opposed such workers councils, believing that they would dilute Bund control over the movement. The Bund wanted complete control over Jewish unions, with no impudent rank-and-filers defying orders from the Bund Central Committee. No workers councils were even allowed to exist in the Bund heartland. All Jewish labor organizations were required to accept Bund leadership and pay the Bund a quarter of their membership dues.

Jewish unions usually accepted these conditions, despite opposition from Bolsheviks, Mensheviks, anarchists and Socialist-Zionists alike. When the Garber-Bund was refounded as a legal organization, Leyb Blekhman kept it firmly under Bundist control, quelling anarchist rebellions. Fistfights frequently broke out at preliminary meetings. A resolution pledging subordination to the Bund was rammed through over fierce opposition at the founding conference.[35] The legal Garber-Bund combined an intolerant attitude to dissidence with a conciliatory attitude toward employers, neither of which were Bolshevik characteristics at the time, least of all the latter. Though one imagines the young Stalin might have approved of intolerance toward dissidents. The attitudes of the leadership of the Garber-Bund, the Bund's strongest bulwark in 1905, would become the hallmarks of Jewish garment unionism on American shores as well.

There was a critical long-term strategic difference between Bundism and Bolshevism. For Lenin, armed insurrection and the 'dictatorship of the proletariat and the peasantry' in Russia were an antechamber to socialist revolution in Western Europe. Lenin initially rejected Trotsky's 'permanent revolution'

34 Kirzhnits, *1905*, 327–30; Frankel, *Prophecy and Politics*, 247–9.

35 Bukhbinder, *Geshikhte fun der Yidisher arbeter-bavegung*, 373–9; Avram der Tate, *Bleter fun mayn yugnt*, 257–82; Dubnow-Erlich, *Garber-bund un bershter-bund*, 94.

formula, which made a direct, immediate connection between revolution in Russia and world socialism. He advocated a revolution in two stages: first democratic in Russia; and then socialist in Western Europe – which then could be followed by a socialist revolution in Russia. But this second stage was not seen as a matter for a distant future.

For the Bund by contrast, the fundamental goal was a 'bourgeois revolution' to overthrow Tsarism, democratize Russia, and solve the Russian Jewish dilemma that Socialist-Zionists saw as unsurmountable. In Noah London's judgment, as expressed in his secret manuscript,

> in 1905 … Lenin did not put as a slogan for the vanguard of the workers 'Overthrow Czarism, Establish a Dictatorship of the Proletariat!' He was against the leftist slogans of Trotsky and other prominent revolutionists 'Down with Czarism – For Workers' Government' … Lenin did not call for the immediate establishment of a workers' government because faith in capitalism was not yet shattered in 1905 …

Whether or not the position he ascribed to Lenin was good Bolshevik orthodoxy, it was excellent Bundist orthodoxy. In 1906 Vladimir Medem, then in the process of becoming the Bund's central leader, criticised the St. Petersburg Soviet led by Trotsky for a 'policy of isolation of the proletariat, leading to proletarian dictatorship'.[36]

For their part, Russian Social Democrats, whether Bolshevik or Menshevik, denied that Russian Jews were a 'nation' and foresaw a future of Jewish assimilation in a democratic Russia, after the overthrow of the Tsar. The Bundist program for Russian Jews, 'national-cultural autonomy', was officially adopted in October 1905 – right in the middle of the general strike that forced the Tsar to accept a constitution. The Bund's leaders were divided. Some saw the Bund as the leadership of the Jewish people in Russia. Others still thought of themselves as simply the leaders of the Jewish section of the proletariat. But the new program signified that the Bund was no longer merely the Jewish detachment of Russian Social Democracy.

At the height of the Jewish Revolution in the Pale there was 'a period of revolutionary dictatorship that was identical with the "dictatorship of the Bund"', as Abramovitch put it.[37] But by then, the significance of Bundist rebellions in backwoods *shtetls* was limited. With the Empire as a whole in turmoil,

36 Kirzhnits, *1905*, 282–3.

37 Abramovitch, 'Jewish Socialist Movement in Russia and Poland', 379.

events in the Pale were peripheral. The revolutionary feats of Jewish leather workers drew diminishing attention. Rejoining the ranks of Russian Social Democracy became a practical necessity. Abramovitch admitted in his memoirs that

> we no longer believed ... that the Jewish worker is the vanguard ... the Russian worker, whom we for so long had considered backward, had become the leader ... the instinctive feeling that not in our cities, but only in the main cities of Russia would the fate of the movement be decided is why nowhere in our region did it go over to armed insurrection. Besides this instinctive feeling, it should be understood that the spiritual oppression which lingered in the Jewish Pale after the terrible October pogrom-wave worked strongly.[38]

Times had changed. The Bund's 1905 'Bolshevik' tactical orientation – armed workers' insurrection organized by an underground professional revolutionary cadre – had not worked. The flirtation with Bolshevism was over. The Menshevik strategy of an alliance with Russian liberalism became attractive. A close and long-lasting kinship developed between the Bund and the Mensheviks, by now clearly the more moderate wing of Russian Social Democracy.[39] The Jewish Revolution had been defeated.

Noah London, a Bund Bolshevik in Shavel in 1907, followed the example of Comrade Aron in Vilna in 1908. He left the underground and in 1909 he went home to Motele, where he was drafted into the army in September. His older sister Rochlea had been buying steamship tickets to America for her younger sisters and brothers and sending them home to Motele. When the army gave Noah leave in May of 1910 to visit his family, younger brother Harry lent Noah his passport and ticket. With Harry's passport, Noah, who closely resembled Harry, was able to cross the border and emigrate to America. He arrived on Ellis Island in July of 1910 – and mailed Harry's passport back. All the London children emigrated in this fashion, following the classic American immigrant pattern of 'chain migration'. Rose, the youngest, had to travel by herself at the age of fourteen, and narrowly avoided rape along the way. Their parents stayed in the old country and died during the Russian Civil War,

38 Abramovitch, *In tsvey revolutsies*, vol. 1, 241–2.

39 Leonard Shapiro, 'The Role of the Jews in the Russian Revolutionary Movement', *Slavonic and Eastern European Review* 40 (1961/62): 148–67.

when the Polesian swamplands were conquered by Polish legionaries, who shot thirty-five Jews in the 1919 Pinsk pogrom.[40]

The Unterman family was leaving Russia, too. According to the traditional family narrative, Miril was sent to America in 1909 because the police were starting to arrest students at her trade school and send them to Siberia. Her father and brother followed her in 1910. Her mother and sisters waited two more years so that Rebecca at least could actually graduate from the *gymnasium*. According to Moscow party records the reality was more complex. Miril successfully graduated from the Pinsk trade school in 1907, and then got a job in a workshop in Brest-Litovsk. She worked there for two years, emigrating in 1909. Fear of police repression in Pinsk is a plausible explanation for her move to Brest-Litovsk, but her parents and siblings followed her there as well.[41]

The family story is that Morris, unlike his sisters, was a poor student. Father Chaim finally admitted that his son would never make a scholar or a rabbi. So he took him along on a business trip to northern Russian forests, outside the Pale, where one of the lumbermen accidentally hit him with a charge of buckshot. Since the Untermans were Jews, the local hospital refused to give him emergency aid. This was the last straw. Chaim announced to his family that it was time to follow Miril to America.[42]

The Londons and Untermans had run into a brick wall in the Pale, and so had Jewish socialism. The Jewish Revolution in the Tsarist Pale was over, and the next Russian Revolution would not be Jewish. It was time to move on.

40 London, *Biograficheskii ocherk*; A. Weitzmann interview; Morris London interviews; Paul Malamud (son of Rose London) interview; Minczeles, *Vilna, Wilno, Vilnius*, 152.

41 'Aunt Sue and Eva' letter, 1973; Unterman Family Tree; B. Holmes letter, 1996; *Registratsionnyi blank chlena VKP(b)* Maria London, *partbilet* No. 1193080, RGASPI.

42 Unterman Family Tree; 'Aunt Sue and Eva' letter; B. Holmes, 'Young Girl as Heroine', 3.

FIGURE 1 Family photo 1896–7, photographer unknown, public domain. Miril at right Anna in center. Morris with toy rifle

FIGURE 2 Family photo, photographer unknown, public domain. Rose as baby, Miril at right. Later than 1900 but in Russia

FIGURE 3
Artist unknown. https://speakoutsocialists.org/bloody-sunday-1905-the-spark-of-revolution-in-russia/

FIGURE 4 From YIVO archives. Bundist demonstration in Dvinsk in Latvia, during 1905 Revolution

אויסגאבע פון דער צייטונג

דאס לעבען

פעטערבורג 1905

פרייז 7 קאפ.

די בלוטיגע טעג.

אקטאבער 1905.

די מצבה.

קרבנות הייליגע און ריינע
פאר אונזער פרייהייט, גליק און פרייד!
דער בייזער שונא האט דעם חלף
נאך ניט אריינגעלעגט אין שייד;

דאס בלוט איז נאך ניט אבגעוואשען
פון זיינע מערדערישע הענד;
עס הענגען נאך די אלטע שלעסער,
עס שטעהען נאך די אלטע ווענד;

ניטא קיין צייט אייך צו בעוויינען, —
מיט דאס איז אנגעזאפט די לופט,
דאס הארץ מיט יאמער און מיט צארען;
דער שטורם נעהט, דער שטורם רופט!

ניטא, ניטא קיין צייט צו קלאגען
אויף אייער בלוט, אויף אייער לייד,
קרבנות הייליגע און ריינע
פאר אונזער פרייהייט, גליק און פרייד!

עס קלאפט דער פויק, די שופרות שאלען,
עס וועהט און פלאטערט אונזער פאהן;
דער קאמפף דער שרעקליכער, דער גרויסער,
ער געהט נאך ערשט, ער הויבט זיך אן. —

און מיט די קולות פונ'ם שטורם
רופט-אויס דעם שונא פלוך און שאנד
און דינגט נאך אייך „אל מלא רחמים"
דאס גאנצע פאלק, דאס גאנצע לאנד!

ש. פרוג.

FIGURE 5 The Bloody Days. Simon Frug. From special issue of Dos Leben dedicated to 1905 pogrom victims. Also from YIVO archives

PART 2

America (1910–1926)

CHAPTER 3

Jewish Socialism and Garment Unionism in the Promised Land

> Imagine a great ship, taking passengers from Europe to America. Deep down in the ship, buried under the third deck, ten feet under the waterline, bad air, no sunshine, a rabble of thousands of immigrant men from many lands speaking many languages lie around in rags. They don't understand each other, they don't understand the swearing of the sailors. They eat bad food, they're treated roughly, but they don't care about any of this, because they're travelling to *di goldene medine* [the Golden Country].
>
> NOAH LONDON, *Der Kamf*, August 1919

America, the Jewish Promised Land. The land of equal opportunity, where pogroms never happen. And the land of the garment sweatshop. The second part of Noah London's story is embedded in the history of Jewish radicalism, rebellion, socialism and garment unionism in the US, up until the day the Londons left America for the Soviet Union. Unfortunately, I was able to find out much less about Miril's socialist and union activism, which was usually behind the scenes. This chapter covers their time as socialists and garment unionists in the Progressive Era, from 1910 or so until 1917, the year of the Russian Revolution, which transformed their lives and the entire world, including America.

For the Londons, emigrating to America was itself a transformational experience. They became Americans – an identity they did not lose when they gave up their citizenship. This is how Noah described their immigrant days in his last letter from the Soviet Union:

> Nobody has yet told the story of our East side of 1910–14, our immigrant years, the years of struggle and adaptation in a new life, of a multitude of Miril's & Noah's which taken together made up a social group, with its social thriving giving to its individual doings a social color & meaning.

 | DOI:10.1163/9789004745384_005

> That period I would define like this: Realization that life is not play in Revolution or romantics. That life is individual steady work & struggle for ends that have a collective significance.
>
> The immigration of the preceding five years was of people who traveled with the drum of the 1905 Revolution still ringing, with the Romanticism and inexperience in life inherent to the Russian intelligentsia of that period.
>
> And so we, your sisters & myself among the cohorts of others like us, have thrown ourselves into the fight to become a good draper, a sleeve-maker ... and then to live a love in the parks, go to theater, have a good time in an East Broadway restaurant and enjoy all of that, without suspecting that for Central Park there are villas on the Hudson, for Coney Island there is Newport ... that there are the wide spaces.
>
> I call these our childhood years in America.[1]

As Noah said, he and Miril represented a whole layer of radicalized Jewish emigrants escaping Tsarist Russia in the aftermath of the 1905 Revolution. The explosion of garment unionism in the Progressive Era continued that revolution on American soil,[2] and garment unionism would come to be known as the 'European' sector of the American labor movement, replicating the European pattern of unionism under socialist influence. The garment industry would be fruitful soil for the growth of moderate and radical socialism and trade unionism – and for conflict between them, just as in Europe. This conflict would lay the basis for the birth of American Jewish Communism, and for the 'civil war' that wracked the garment unions in the 1920s – one of the frameworks for the lives of Noah and Miril. Another framework was the upward social mobility of Russian Jewish emigres on American soil, already well underway as the Londons arrived in America.

1 The American Dream: The Contradictions of Upward Mobility

> Some of the gang have become famous. Al Levy was known to us simply as 'Stinker': now he writes wealthy musical comedies. Abe Sugarman is a proud movie director. He also has become a Spanish nobleman. His Hollywood name is Arturo De Sagaar, no less. Lew Moses shoots craps with high stakes, with skyscrapers; he is a big real estate speculator. Others of

1 Letter, Noah London to Rose Risikoff, Oct. 29, 1935.

2 Melech Epstein, *Jewish Labor in USA*, vol. 1, 348–50, 387–8.

> the boys are humbler comedians. Jake Gottlieb is a taxi driver, and feeds his three kids every day. Harry Weintraub is a clothing cutter. Some of the boys are dead.
>
> MICHAEL GOLD, *Jews Without Money*

Mike Gold would become American Jewish Communism's most successful literary spokesman. As in Gold's *Jews Without Money*, Noah and his siblings came from a lower class background, but their experiences also remind one of those of the hero of Abraham Cahan's *The Rise of David Levinsky*. This book, by the leader of the Jewish Socialist 'old guard' in America, the leader of Jewish socialism in America *before* refugees from 1905 flocked to America's shores, was the first great American Jewish novel. It is the best literary depiction of Jewish upward mobility in the years preceding World War I. The fictional Levinsky emigrated from Russia to America in the 1890s. Despite failure as a pushcart peddler, he climbed the slippery ladder of success in the garment industry, becoming a rich manufacturer, though he discovered that money does not buy happiness – the moral of Cahan's secular parable.

Noah's oldest sister Rochlea, who came to America long before he did, married a Jewish pushcart peddler more successful than Levinsky. Several of their sons became factory owners, and Noah would end up working for one for several years. Another, Harry Eisenstein, also employed London relatives from time to time and had a family reputation as a real-life Levinsky in miniature. Noah may have been thinking about this branch of the family when he wrote in a Soviet Yiddish literary journal that before the 1905 Revolution, 'riffraff used to arrive from Eastern Europe ... who at first sought out the taste of capitalism, and at first impression that taste wasn't bad, compared to the squalor of Lithuania and Poland'.[3]

Tired of that taste, the Londons would return to their transformed homeland in 1926. While cruising the Atlantic in his first class cabin in 1926, on board the ocean liner taking them back home, this is how Noah described his first few months in the Golden Country: 'I have sewed jackets with operators 58 hours a week on Eldridge Street with half a day Sunday for dessert. The second half of the day we went with our boss to play in a casino, and felt that this was our America'.[4]

Noah arrived in America in 1910 with a job already lined up for him, a legal necessity for poor Jewish immigrants. His older sister Chana had married Philip

3 Morris London interviews, 2005; Paul Malamud interview, Aug. 20, 2004; London, *Royte Velt*, Nov. 1928, 86.

4 London, 'Fun "Woolworth" tsum "lvisn"', *Freiheit*, April 28, 1926.

Weitzmann, who owned a factory that manufactured sailor suits for boys. It was one of the main providers of employment verification on the Lower East Side. Philip and Chana's son Abe described many years later how 'they worked for a day or a week or a month or years, but they worked there, which they had to, according to the law. And years and years later, I met people who worked for my father'. All the London children who came to America started out by working at a family factory.[5] It was a real-life model for the fictional sweatshop depicted in *The Rise of David Levinsky*. At Levinsky's shop: 'If one of my operatives happened to have a relative … who wished to emigrate to America, I would advance him the passage money, with the understanding that he was to work off the loan in my employ. That the "green one" was to work for low wages was a matter of course'.[6]

Noah London chose the college route to upward Jewish mobility, and his career would become a classic example of the American Jewish success story.[7] After World War I, American Jews increasingly rose in the world not as a commercial class, as in medieval Eastern Europe, but as the 'people of the book'. This is how he described those days himself, in his 1935 letter to Miril's younger sister:

> Then came the years when the start in life was made. All the initial difficulties were overcome, we acquired a trade or a profession, the language, acquired *citizenship*, in its direct and implied meaning.
>
> We started as full-fledged members of the Community to fight for a better America. When I think of these two periods, I don't know which raises more tender memories. Whether those initial years of childhood when we learned how to take our first steps in life, or the 2nd period when we started to walk on our own feet. Whether I love the old-fashioned Madison St. where I used to come only for supper with pumpernickle and lots of soup and boiled meat and pickled tomatoes, with the Sunday morning spending in the barber shop waiting for the next to be shorn, and hear all the neighborhood gossip for the week, including the gossip in and about the *Forward* … or the City Island swimmings with the Unterman family, baking ourselves in the hot mud in bundles of bodies and legs and young laughing faces, or whether I have better memories of the struggles at the meetings for leadership, fight for our ideas, the struggle for a better America.[8]

5 Abraham Weitzmann interview, Aug. 20, 2004.
6 Abraham Cahan, *The Rise of David Levinsky* (New York: Harper Brothers, 1917), 378.
7 Abe Weitzmann interview; Cahan, *Levinsky*, 526, 529.
8 Letter, Noah to Rose, Oct. 29, 1935.

He applied for admission to Cooper Union's Day School of Technical Science less than a year after his arrival in America. He was admitted for the fall semester in September 1911. In his memoirs, American Communist leader Alexander Bittelman would describe the Cooper Union engineering program he also participated in as a hotbed of Russian-Jewish socialism.[9] But to pay the bills Noah worked at the Weitzmann shop.

Eastern European Jewish immigrants discovered the garment industry when they discovered America, regardless of previous backgrounds – thousands of Jewish immigrants who had never held a needle in their hands became 'Columbus tailors'. Their impact on the garment industry and the American labor movement would be even deeper than its impact on them. And that impact was not necessarily one of radicalization. As Noah put it in the Communist press, 'Disappointment dominated the workers in Russia in the period of reaction. The immigrants which were streaming into America did not bring with them the earlier revolutionary spirit'.[10] But neither were their experiences on American shores always conservatizing. One of the first things he saw when he arrived on American shores was a spectacular New York cloakmakers' strike that began on July 7, 1910, and won after a two month's struggle. Fifteen years later, while reporting on a Toronto strike for the *Freiheit*, he would reminisce that: 'Watching the boys, how they hold the line with such order and self-discipline, how they stand up bravely for their rights ... the feelings I experience I have undergone before as a greenhorn, when I watched the great mass strike that the cloakmakers carried out in 1910 which created the [ILGWU-International Ladies' Garment Workers Union], where the masses struggled and led and knew what they wanted – and later the tailors' strike in 1913 ...'[11]

Noah London would participate in that tailors' strike. And when he himself became a radical labor spokesman, he would identify with those militant New York cloakmakers. His American career would embody all the complexities of the Jewish immigrant experience. His choice of the leftwing camp was far from inevitable, and he became known there as an advocate of realism, practicality and Americanism.

---

9 College transcript, Noah London, Cooper Union, 1911–15; 'Things I Have Learned', Bittelman Collection, Tamiment Library.

10 London, 'Der Arbeyter Ring – vos er iz un vos er darf zeyn', *Emes*, Sept. 23, 1921.

11 London, 'Der politisher strayk in kenede', *Freiheit*, July 2, 1924.

2 Noah London and the Men's Clothing Industry

Noah, a classic Columbus tailor, worked in his brother-in-law's sweatshop until 1914. According to his Moscow Party autobiography he 'organized a union which immediately collapsed, on account of the extreme backwardness of the elements there and on account of the uncomplicated and unskilled work there, which allowed the boss to fire without hindrance'.[12] The exact dates are unclear, but this was probably the 1913 mass New York mens' clothing strike, which helped lay the basis for the creation of Sidney Hillman's Amalgamated Clothing Workers of America (ACWA). Noah's personal ties with his employer helped him keep his job, but were no asset for the task of unionization, though family bonds seamlessly survived Noah's failed attempt to unionize his brother-in-law's enterprise.

The Brotherhood of Tailors sponsored the strike, electing a 'Red Tailors Council' to organize and lead it. This was a militant, socialist-influenced, male and mostly Jewish craft union with a rocky relationship with the AFL-affiliated United Garment Workers (UGW). It was the last of the massive pre-World War I labor revolts that gave birth to powerful garment unions. It was also the most thoroughly organized. According to Jewish labor historian Melech Epstein, 'The Brotherhood of Tailors, and the locals of the other crafts worked a full year to complete preparations. Hundreds of shop meetings were held … Hundreds of strikers were jailed … Many demonstrations, several scores of thousands participating in each, were held throughout the clothing district'.[13]

In the aftermath of the strike the Brotherhood of Tailors elected Joseph Schlossberg of Daniel De Leon's Socialist Labor Party (SLP) as its secretary-treasurer. De Leon was a Sephardic Jew originally from the West Indies island of Curaçao. Under his leadership the SLP, the original US socialist party, became identified with a particularly unbending species of orthodox Marxism. The enormous expansion and radicalization of its New York locals panicked the UGW, a union most of whose members were white Protestant American women in small-town America producing union label overalls for union workmen. Its 1914 convention in Tennessee refused to seat the New York delegation. One member of the UGW Executive Board, Margaret Daley, told the overall delegates that 'the clothing worker delegates were Jews … as decent American women, they must stand solidly against [them]'. She previously had been a leader of the Women's Trade Union League, which had mobilized support for mostly Jewish

12 London, *Biograficheskii ocherk*, l. 5.

13 Epstein, *Jewish Labor in USA*, vol. 1, 415–18.

women's garment strikes. The ousted New York delegates held a rump convention of their own, and soon the new union was launched.[14]

The birth pangs of the ACWA were Noah London's introduction to the American Jewish labor movement. Unionizing men's clothing workers was a challenging experience. A decade later he wrote, 'The general mass of the workforce was unorganized and backward … Undeveloped, unconscious, slaving long hours for miserable wages in unsanitary shops, little understanding that they should or could get something better. For such a working rabble a strong leadership was necessary …'[15] Their leader was former Lithuanian-Jewish revolutionary Sidney Hillman. Hillman had actually been a Menshevik rather than a Bundist in the old country. Accordingly, his style of leadership was less marked by Jewish particularism than that of the former Bundists, and his union would incorporate non-Jews more successfully than other garment unions. It was independent of the AFL of Samuel Gompers, and his ACWA acquired a reputation as America's model progressive union, attracting national attention as the standard-bearer of a 'new unionism' compatible with the progressive spirit of the age.

3 The Untermans in the Promised Land: 'New Womanhood' in the Garment Industry

Miril's experiences in the same time period differed from Noah's due to her previous trade school training. When she came to America she got a job immediately, without needing to resort to family connections, and quickly ascended the occupational ladder to the enviable position of draper. When the rest of the family arrived, the generous Miril presented each of the younger children with a complete wardrobe that she had sewn herself.[16] The Unterman sisters' early years in America have an odd resemblance-in-reverse to those of the fictional Smolinsky sisters depicted in Anya Yezierska's semi-autobiographical 1920s best-seller *Bread Givers*. According to feminist labor historian Alice Kessler-Harris:

> Because [Sara Smolinsky] so effectively captured the tension between an America that longed to maintain the community of a traditional old world and yet sought the material goods and individual satisfactions of

14 Epstein, *Jewish Labor in USA*, vol. 2, 40–5.

15 London, 'Di firer un mase in der Amalgameyted', *Freiheit*, Oct. 5, 1922.

16 B. Holmes, 'Young Girl as Heroine'.

> the new, Smolinsky reached beyond the specifically Jewish situation into the heart of the shared immigrant experience … In the American tradition of self-reliance, she takes her life in her hands and shapes herself after the models provided by her family.[17]

The Untermans did not arrive broke. Miril came first in 1909, and by 1912 the reunited family lived in an attractive, steam-heated five-room apartment in then-prosperous Harlem, not the Lower East Side. Like the Smolinskys, the Unterman children all went to work. Unlike them, they eagerly accepted the role of family breadwinners. Anna, the author's maternal grandmother, preferred work to school in America despite old-country academic achievements, since work gave her increased status in the family. Like Miril, she quickly became a draper, earning more money than the author's grandfather, a journeyman printer, when they married. All the Unterman children were proud to join the working class, mostly in the garment industry. They all supported the American Socialist Party and subsequently the Bolshevik Revolution, except for Rebecca, but even she married a Socialist-Zionist.[18]

Miril was the first of the sisters to join the International Ladies' Garment Workers Union. According to her Moscow party autobiography, she 'took active part in a strike' a year after her arrival, the same year Noah came to America. This was in the aftermath of the famous 1908 shirtwaist 'Uprising of the 20,000'. This first mass strike of women workers in American history put the previously tiny ILGWU on the map of the American labor movement. It paved the way for the 'Great Revolt' of 50,000 mostly male New York cloakmakers in 1910, which impressed her future husband so deeply and established it as the third-largest union in America by 1914.[19] Miril and Anna Unterman's high skill and income levels were not unusual for union militants in the trade. In *Daughters of the Shtetl*, Susan Glenn describes their combination of ambition and militancy:

> It was no accident that many radical women were also highly skilled workers; some of them had perfected their craft in eastern Europe … Their role in the organizational drive illuminates one of the paradoxical qualit-

17 Alice Kessler-Harris, foreword to *Bread Givers* (New York: Persea Books, 2003), xi–xvi.

18 B. Holmes, 'Young Girl as Heroine', 4–5; letter, B. Holmes to John Holmes, 1996.

19 Greenwald, The Triangle Fire, The Protocols of Peace, and Industrial Democracy, Epstein *Jewish Labor in USA*, vol. 1, 387–410.

> ies of Jewish immigrants at this time: their ability to combine individual ambition with a spirit of collective consciousness and labor radicalism … A well-paid draper who could have her pick of jobs told a newspaper reporter that 'she had no personal grievances' but 'struck because all the others should get enough'.[20]

That draper could well have been Miril Unterman. In any case, that was her attitude. This was the period in which the concept of 'New Womanhood' entered the American vocabulary, and its Jewish version took shape in the context of revolt in the garment industry. According to Glenn, 'Long confined to economic and domestic roles, women saw in the labor movement a vehicle for expanding their social and cultural horizons and for joining with men in the civic life of their communities'. But their attitude to marriage and family was not the same as that of the typical 'suffragette'. Glenn: 'If the prototypical middle-class American reformer before World War I was a single woman who eschewed marriage for a public-spirited career … the typical Jewish union member was a teenager with marriage on her mind'.[21]

Chaim Unterman believed in the Jewish Enlightenment movement, the *Haskalah*, not socialism. According to his grand-daughter Beatrice, 'My mother [Anna] once said that he was a Kadet'.[22] The Kadet party, the Constitutional Democrats, were the party of middle-class liberalism in Russia and had developed a powerful aversion to socialism in the course of Russia's revolutionary turmoil. Like the fictional father in *Bread Givers*, Chaim regarded work for wages as beneath him. Like many *Haskalah* devotees, he became a Zionist. When his wife Bessie died, he retired and went to live in Palestine on his life savings and remittances from his children. His hopes for Russia had been disappointed, and in America, he was a Republican and an opponent of unions. But unlike Reb Smolinsky, he did not believe that he had the right to interfere with his daughters' interests in socialism and trade unionism. After all, they were the breadgivers.[23]

---

20 Glenn, *Daughters of the Shtetl*, 185.

21 Ibid., 210, 214.

22 B. Holmes interview.

23 B. Holmes, 'Young Girl as Heroine', 6–7; B. Holmes letter, 1996.

4 Garment Unionism and Jewish Socialism

In 1912, Miril joined the American Socialist Party (SP) and its new-fledged Jewish Socialist Federation (JSF), preceding Noah by two years. Mass strikes of Jewish garment workers were creating the need for an American counterpart to the Bund. The Socialist Party never before had a formal Jewish section: Abraham Cahan's Jewish 'old guard', who dominated the party's New York branch, were assimilators, opponents of any sort of Jewish particularism, Zionist, Bundist or otherwise. The JSF's main leader was J.B. Salutsky (aka Hardman). The former Bundist Salutsky was another veteran of the 1905 Revolution, like Hillman and the Londons. He passed briefly through the ranks of De Leon's SLP when he came to America. Post-1905 émigrés at first were quite dissatisfied with the SP. According to the JSF's historian, Eugene Orenstein:

> These émigré activists and writers tended to sympathise with Daniel DeLeon's Socialist Labor Party ... they often wrote for its Yiddish organ, *Der arbeyter*. Edited by the prominent union leader Joseph Schlossberg ... their newspaper also attracted more intellectual contributors due to its higher standard of Yiddish labor journalism in contradiction to the tendency to pander to the popular taste which was encouraged by Abe Cahan in the pro-Socialist Party *Forward*.[24]

The *Forward* was the highest-circulation Yiddish newspaper in the world and then played the role in the Socialist Party that Tammany Hall played in the Democratic Party. It consciously imitated the yellow journalism of rivals like Hearst and Pulitzer. Murders, serialized romance novels, and gossip about the rich and famous were its staples. As Noah London put it in a mock obituary for Cahan:

> He praised *success* [in English], he wrote about the immense opportunities in America, he preached love for the revolutionary homeland. In fact he meant the cozy middle-class milieu where they dreamed about equal rights, the generation of gymnasium students who strived for education, for heroic deeds, and then got married and went into business and went to the theater and dreamed about true love.[25]

---

24 Eugene Orenstein, 'The Jewish Socialist Federation of the US (1912–1921)', Ph.D. diss., Columbia University, 1978, 28–9.

25 London, 'Itskhok Eyzik un Ab. Kahan', *Freiheit*, July 16, 1924.

People like the hero of Cahan's novel. The most successful human interest feature in the *Forward* was the *Bintel Brief*, a collection of letters to the editor about everyday problems of immigrant life. When not enough letters arrived, Cahan had staff writers invent them.[26] Cahan sought to assimilate Eastern European Jewish immigrants into American society, the American Federation of Labor, and the American Socialist Party, despite the anti-immigrant chauvinism of all three. He therefore opposed the creation of any autonomous Jewish body within the SP with as much vigor as he resisted criticism of his *Forward* or outside interference in its administration. Salutsky's Jewish Socialist Federation came into existence only after a lengthy struggle against opposition from Cahan's 'Old Guard'.

From its inception the Jewish labor movement had an international character, since Jews did not have a homeland of their own. The founding figures of American Jewish socialism were all Russian-speaking Tsarist émigrés – including Cahan. The Socialist Party's opposition to immigration often repelled immigrant socialists, especially refugees from revolutionary Russia. The musty atmosphere of what they called 'gas and water socialism', with its small town mayors, lawyers, professors, ministers and AFL officials, offended veterans of 1905. Decades later, Jewish SP leader Morris Hillquit coined the epithet 'sewer socialism'. He was describing the Socialist administration of Milwaukee, where beer was brewed and socialist Germans were numerous. Socialist election campaigns there focused perennially around the construction of public utilities, especially sewers, and American municipal socialism was difficult to distinguish from other species of progressive urban reform.[27] Noah London as it happened would become a 'water Communist' when he returned to his birthland.

In the immediate aftermath of 1905 American Bundists flocked into the nonpartisan cooperative Arbeyter Ring (Workmen's Circle, WC) instead of either of America's rival socialist parties, the SP and the SLP. The organization, quite small in its early years, grew spectacularly after the Bund dissolved its own American cooperative society. London joined the WC not the SP, shortly after he arrived in New York. A decade later he would write that when he landed at Ellis Island, the Arbeyter Ring was

> The only leader and spokesman for the Jewish workforce … the fresh revolutionary forces of the Jewish workers from Russia streamed into

26 Arthur Liebman, *Jews and the Left* (New York: Wiley, 1979), 337; Howe, *World of Our Fathers*, 533–7, 529n.

27 Bruce M. Stave, ed., *Socialism and the Cities: Essays by Walter Lippman and Others* (London: Kenikat Press, 1975).

> the Arbeyter Ring … They brought in their revolutionary traditions, their seething activity, and struggled to build … a physical and spiritual center of social-cultural life for the Jewish workforce … The worker had in the Arbeyter Ring the bridge which united him with the international socialist movement in general and with the Russian revolution in particular.[28]

After re-emigration to the Soviet Union, he nostalgically recounted how

> the yearly ball and concert of the Berdichev branch for example became the daily preoccupation of Berdichev landsmen in and around New York or Chicago all winter … The Arbayter Ring enriched the impoverished spiritual life of the hard-working, preoccupied immigrant. It founded its own journal, its own publishing house, its own childrens' schools, its own tuberculosis sanitarium. And hundreds of tubercular Jewish workers regained their health there.[29]

Such as Noah London. Members were required to join the union of their trade and to vote only for socialist political parties. By 1915 the Workmen's Circle had 50,000 members, and its initial assimilationist leaders were being replaced by enthusiasts for Yiddish culture, usually Bundists.[30] The Workmen's Circle in time gained a reputation as the Red Cross of the Jewish labor movement.

5 The Dark Side of the American Dream

> New York is a devil's dream, the most urbanized city in the world. It is all geometry angles and stone … No grass is found in this petrified city, no big living trees, no flowers, no bird but the drab little lecherous sparrow, no soil, loam, earth; fresh earth to smell, earth to walk on, to roll on, and love like a woman. Just stone.
>
> MICHAEL GOLD, *Jews Without Money*

While working in the Weitzmann factory, Noah London was living at 306 Madison Street on Manhattan's Lower East Side, which then had the highest

28 London, *Der Emes*, Sept. 23, 1921.

29 London, 'Der Arbeter-Ring fun di fareynikte shtatn un kanade', *Royte Velt* 11 (Nov. 1928): 85.

30 By the 1920s former Bundists would dominate the organization at every level. Isaiah Trunk, 'The Cultural Dimension of the American Jewish Labor Movement', *YIVO Annual* 16 (1976): 358–61.

population density in the world. It was the heart of the New York Jewish immigrant community – and of America's clothing industry. He was studying intensively by day, working long hours in the factory by night, and perhaps already trying to unionize the place besides. His health did not withstand the stress. He developed tuberculosis in the spring of 1912 and spent the summer convalescing, free of charge, in the Catskills, at the Liberty tuberculosis sanatorium sponsored by the Workmen's Circle.

The sanitarium stay enabled him to return to Cooper Union in the fall. He also went back to working at the Weitzmann factory, but no longer full-time. In addition to trying to unionize the shop and participating in the organizing campaign for the 1913 mens' clothing strike, he picked up work as a waiter and as a tutor. This was much like how he made his living while traversing Lithuania as a professional revolutionary. The Liberty sanatorium saved his college career and his health, and contributed to his longstanding interest in cooperativism – he would maintain his Workmen's Circle membership even after he re-emigrated to the USSR. On the rare occasions that he wrote about America for the Soviet Jewish press, it was invariably on the subject of cooperativism. When he was arrested in 1937, there was a membership card in the Moscow cooperative society among his confiscated possessions.[31]

Noah's Bund was formally neutral between the Socialist Labor Party and the Socialist Party up to at least 1909. At first it tended to lean more to the SLP, even though the *Forward* was funding the Bund. As London would tell his Soviet readers, Jewish immigrants didn't join the SP during the 1905 Revolution because 'who would be interested in the politics of such a land with its yellow socialism?'[32] Daniel DeLeon's insistence on rigid socialist control over the labor movement would destroy his Socialist Labor Party, but this attitude was the cornerstone of Bundist labor policy in Russia, where it was a much more practical proposition.

Bundists in the New York garment industry had initially attempted to organize their fellow workers into the IWW. ILGWU Secretary-Treasurer John Dyche explained to his good friend Samuel Gompers that the ILGWU was weak because the Russian-Jewish immigrant 'keeps away because he is too radical, because his mind runs in the direction of revolution and revolutionary changes'. But the IWW was going through its own internal conflicts. The victory

31 Miril London, Avtobiografiia N.M. Londona, 1926, RGASPI, f. 17, op. 98, d. 8957; Arrest protocol, Oct. 29, 1937, London case file (sledstvennoe delo R-46033), TsaFSB (former KGB archive), Moscow, l. 4.

32 London, *Royte Velt* (Nov. 1928): 87; Orenstein, *Jewish Socialist Federation*, 55–6; Louis Levine, *The Women's Garment Workers* (New York: B.W. Huebsch, 1924), 122–6.

of Big Bill Haywood and his anarchist-minded followers over the De Leonists at the 1908 IWW convention repelled Bundist émigrés. Before Miril arrived in New York, the IWW locals in the women's garment industry were disbanded and liquidated into the ILGWU. This was a major factor in the revival of a union then on the brink of disintegration.[33] Bundists and anarchists had fought bitterly during the 1905 Revolution, in the leather industry and elsewhere. Vilna Bund leader Aron Devenishskii's companion died in an anarchist bombing. Conflict between Bundists and anarchists was due to the moderation of Bundist industrial policy, and also to the questionable attitude of some anarchists to pogroms. Even certain Jewish anarchists sometimes defended pogromists as popular rebels against Jewish capitalism.[34]

The American Bund activists who founded the JSF and built the Workmen's Circle were trying to shake off the dust of defeat in the old country. They were orienting themselves to the New World – *Di naye velt*, which was what the JSF called its weekly journal. Remarkably few articles about Russia appeared there. As for the Workmen's Circle or Arbeyter Ring, as London put it:

> Becoming Americanized on the one hand, and losing interest in Russia ... because of the defeat of the Revolution on the other hand, the active, conscious members of the A.R. began to seek their interest in the American movement here ... Beginning with the year 1910, great economic struggles of the Jewish workers began to develop ... The workers had taken up the living, concrete activity of real economic struggle ...[35]

Sometimes the JSF was critical of its parent organization. But it opposed the SP's anarchistic western radical wing led by Big Bill Haywood. Salutsky preferred Eugene Debs, the popular founder of the SP who led the great 1894 Pullman Strike and seemed to embody the true American radical spirit. By the time Noah and Miril arrived in America, Wobblies in the garment industry were mostly Italian. Jewish rank-and-file dissidence was firmly located within the Jewish unions, not outside. The JSF disapproved of Cahan's *Forward* dic-

33 Orenstein, *Jewish Socialist Federation*, 55–6; John H.M. Laslett, 'Jewish Socialism and the Ladies Garment Workers of New York', in *Labor and the Left: A Study of Socialist and Radical Influences in the American Labor Movement, 1881–1924* (New York: Basic Books, 1970), 104; Levine, *Women's Garment Workers*, 142.

34 Goldshmit, 'Khaver aron', 66–92; Frankel, *Prophecy and Politics*, 152–3. Ascher, *Revolution of 1905*, 146–54.

35 London, *Der Emes*, Sept. 23, 1921.

tating to the Jewish unions – partly because it believed Cahan's socialism was too moderate, but primarily because the Bundists leading the JSF believed that dictating to Jewish unions was their job.[36]

The Russian Bund in the aftermath of the defeat of the 1905 Revolution was moving closer to the more moderate Menshevik wing of Russian Social Democracy. In America, Jewish socialist veterans who became union officials, like former Menshevik Hillman and not so former Bundist David Dubinsky, were beginning to evolve from socialist revolutionism to socialist-flavored liberalism. They were realising that, as London put it, 'life is not play in revolution or romantics'. According to Louis Levine, the author of the ILGWU's 1924 official history, 'There was an influx into the locals of the International of the socialistic and radical workers in the industry who before 1909–10 had scorned the trade-union movement. Their influence was soon felt in various ways … Three years of practical experience with unionism made them think that their idealism must be tempered by a realism in method …'[37] The political trajectory of Jewish socialists in Russia always tremendously influenced American Jewish socialist exiles from Russia, who in turn powerfully influenced American garment unionism, connecting the American labor movement to its Russian counterpart.

But meanwhile, garment labor victories were inspiring shopfloor activists to militancy. Sharp internal conflict developed in the mens' clothing industry. UGW president Rickert and the 'old guard' Jewish Socialists tried to call off that mass tailors' strike in 1913 in which Noah London cut his teeth as an American labor activist. According to Hillman biographer Steve Fraser: 'The strikers were enraged. They marched *en masse* to the offices of the *Forward* in Union Square, where they proceeded to smash the windows of its newly erected building and threaten Cahan when he attempted to speak. The [Tailors] executive board naturally rejected the settlement, and the strike continued …' Noah remembered this long afterwards. Eleven years later, he would praise 'the revolt of the tailors against the bosses and against the Rickert-*Forward* dominion'; reminiscing how the *Forward* preferred strikebreaking to 'getting in trouble with … the Gompers machine'.[38] Cahan managed to smooth over the crisis by reversing field and coming out in support of the breakaway ACWA. But in the women's clothing industry where Miril was working, conflict escalated.

---

36 Epstein. *Jewish Labor in USA*, vol. 1, 56–63; Laslett, *Jewish Socialism and the Ladies Garment Workers*, 112.

37 Levine, *Women's Garment Workers*, 274–5.

38 Fraser, *Labor Will Rule*, 86; London, *Freiheit*, July 2, 1924; and 'Marshall, Pine un di "orime brider, nebakh"', *Freiheit*, May 14, 1924.

6 'Industrial Democracy' and the 'Slaves of the Protocol'

> For the first time since the Civil War, leaders of industry and finance spoke of the danger of an 'industrial and social revolution'. The 'New Freedom', 'Progressivism', 'Social Reform' became the slogans of the middle classes in a confused movement to create a 'New Democracy' which would dam the 'rising tide' of socialism. In the fear of Syndicalism, Industrialism and I.W.W.-ism, large sections of 'liberal America' accepted trade unionism and collective bargaining as lesser evils …
>
> LEVINE, *Women's Garment Workers*, 1924

Fraser called Hillman's reform policies in the mens' garment industry the 'dress rehearsal for the New Deal'. Miril's ILGWU was a central arena for experiments in something called industrial democracy, and this experience reveals the powerful impact of Russian-Jewish immigrants on the American labor movement.[39] It also had much to do with the birth of American Jewish Communism – and Noah London's role in it.

Industrial democracy was a pervasive catchword in those days, which meant all things to all men – and women too. Originally, socialists introduced the phrase into the labor movement as a translation of the concept of collective ownership of the means of production into language Americans could understand. Labor reformer Henry Demarest Lloyd, speaking for the SLP-backed socialist resolution at the 1893 AFL convention, proclaimed that the

> present aristocratic and monarchical government of industry stands a self-confessed failure … It is by the people who do the work that the hours of labor, the conditions of employment, the division of the produce is to be determined. It is by them that the captains of industry are to be chosen, and chosen to be servants, not masters. It is for the welfare of all that coordinated labor of all must be directed … This is democracy.[40]

---

39 Steve Fraser, 'Dress Rehearsal for the New Deal: Shop-Floor Insurgents, Political Elites, and Industrial Democracy in the Amalgamated Clothing Workers', in *Working-Class America: Essays on Labor, Community, and American Society*, ed. Michael Frisch and Daniel J. Walkowitz, (Urbana: University of Illinois Press, 1983), 212–55; Richard A. Greenwald, *The Triangle Fire: The Protocols of Peace, and Industrial Democracy in Progressive Era New York* (Philadelphia: Temple University Press, 2005).

40 David Montgomery, 'Industrial Democracy or Democracy in Industry?: The Theory and Practice of the Labor Movement, 1870–1925', in *Industrial Democracy in America: The Ambiguous Promise*, ed. Nelson Lichtenstein and Howell John Harris (Cambridge: Cambridge University Press, 1993), 24.

After beating off the socialist challenge, Sam Gompers made the slogan his own, redefining it as AFL craft unionism. Subsequently, progressive reformers like Louis Brandeis, one of President Woodrow Wilson's closest advisors, adopted it as well. By the end of World War I, it became identified as the industrial component of Woodrow Wilson's 'war for democracy',[41] but it still preserved a remarkable degree of ambiguity. Thus, London was to write in the JSF's *Naye Velt* as the war ended that Eastern European Jews were safe from pogroms only in 'industrially democratized Great Russia', the new Soviet republic.[42]

The Great Revolt of the cloakmakers in 1910 had been resolved through what was called a 'Protocol of Peace', brokered by America's premier industrial democrat, Louis Brandeis. He believed that this agreement would civilize American industry and bring business and labor in line with democracy, 'consistent with American spirit and traditions as well as with justice'.[43] Brandeis's vision of Progressivism, dubbed by Woodrow Wilson the 'New Freedom', was oriented to the needs of small businessmen, fearful of competition from monopolies and corporations and needing a cooperative relationship with unions more powerful perhaps than they were. It was thus well adapted to the women's garment industry, the domain of strong socialist-minded unions back then – and small sweatshops to this day. That Brandeis was also America's most prominent Zionist was useful in a Jewish-dominated industry. His Protocol was hailed as the model for permanent collaboration between capital and labor, a whole new economic order. Under it sweatshop conditions would be reformed, wages increased and strikes forbidden, with all disagreements settled through friendly conciliation.

But when the Cloak and Skirt Makers' Union appointed Isaac Hourwich as 'chief clerk' to administer the Protocol in 1913, this progressive pipe-dream began to go up in smoke. The New York Cloakmakers Joint Board sponsored their own newspaper, the *New Post*, and hired Jewish Socialist Federation leader B.Z. Hoffman ('Zivyon') to edit it. He used the *New Post* as a vehicle to denounce cloak manufacturers as thieves, attack top union officers and claim that cloakmakers had become 'slaves of the Protocol'. Zivyon would become an ally of London's a decade later in Communist factional strife.

Hourwich was a Russian-Jewish formerly socialist immigrant who had become a successful lawyer, a well-respected economist and a believer in mod-

41 Montgomery, 'Industrial Democracy'; Joseph A. McCartin, *Labor's Great War: The Struggle for Industrial Democracy and the Origins of Modern American Labor Relations, 1912–1921* (Chapel Hill: University of North Carolina Press, 1997).

42 London, 'An internatsionale idish-sotsialistishe konferents', *Naye Velt*, Nov. 1, 1918.

43 Greenwald, *Triangle Fire*, 77.

erate social reform. He was a model progressive, indeed he ran on Teddy Roosevelt's Progressive Party ticket for Congress in 1912. But he adhered to the version of Progressivism dubbed by Roosevelt the 'New Nationalism', oriented primarily to government regulation of business. The New Nationalism favored 'good' corporations who could afford concessions to their workforce, rather than Brandeis's small business progressivism. This was a version of progressivism more appropriate to the men's garment industry, already becoming the domain of large corporations, than to the women's garment industry. Sidney Hillman's New Deal-style socialism in the ACWA early on developed a cooperative relationship with wholesale garment manufacturers. When Hourwich tried to implement his progressive reforms in the cloakmaking industry, he fell into steadily escalating conflict with Brandeis, the employers and the union officials who hired him. The ILGWU was shaken by a massive cloakmakers' rebellion in Hourwich's name, led by Zivyon's *New Post*. Union officials struggled unsuccessfully to crush this democratic industrial rebellion against Louis Brandeis's version of industrial democracy.

Order was restored, temporarily. The *Forward* gave Hourwich a staff job, he rejoined the Socialist Party, the ILGWU's top officers got replaced by a new team linked explicitly to the Socialist Party, and the Protocol was allowed to lapse. Woodrow Wilson rescued Brandeis from garment industry turbulence, appointing him to the placidity of the Supreme Court in 1916. The imperturbable Cahan coined a clothing workers' aphorism, 'It will iron itself out', which became quite popular.[44] The 'Protocol of Peace' experience discredited moderate industrial reform in the eyes of thousands of rank-and-file cloakmakers. They would reinterpret the idea of industrial democracy as workers' control, responsive to Jewish Communists like London advocating a Leninist variant of the slogan, 'industrially democratized Russia'. Ongoing struggles within the Jewish unions would enable Jewish Communists to gain far more support in the labor movement than their gentile comrades. And radical Jewish unionism would become the first touchstone for Noah London's career in the American Communist Party.

According to the ILGWU's 1924 official history, because of the Protocol 'the largest and strongest locals of the International became divided into two warring groups which fought one another on the issues of industrial peace and industrial war, of leadership and democracy, of radicalism and compromise ...' This was not a conflict between socialists and nonsocialists, or even between

---

44 Epstein *Jewish Labor in USA*, vol. 2, 22. It even makes an appearance in London's 1934 secret manuscript.

pre-1905 old guard American Jewish Socialists and the post-1905 generation. Veterans of 1905 stood on both sides. In one camp were leaders of the new mass garment unions who had become more cautious, due to the responsibilities of union office and the impact of defeat in the old country. In the other stood rank-and-file activists whose militancy, first impelled by revolution in Russia, was reinforced by labor victories in America. This conflict foreshadowed the Socialist–Communist 'civil war' of the 1920s in which the Londons would participate.

Melech Epstein described the radicals as follows: 'The minority, mostly men and women under 20 on arriving here, carried with them the thrilling excitement of the underground movement in Russia ... These youngsters came, for the most part, from middle-class parents, had attended the *gymnasia*, and were driven to emigrate not by sheer poverty but by a pall of discrimination hanging over their heads. Here most of them went to work in the garment and allied trades'.[45] Miril Unterman and her sisters fit this description exactly.

The ILGWU opposition movement had two components: the feminist-influenced political radicalism of female waist and dressmakers like Miril; and the 'workers control' militancy of the overwhelmingly-male cloakmakers, on whom Noah would focus. Until 1917, these two movements had little to do with each other. Male Jewish cloakmakers had used sexual harassment to drive women out of the trade, previously mostly female. By contrast, revolt against sexual harassment by supervisors and employers was an important aspect of the 'Uprising of the 20,000' in the shirtwaist industry.[46]

Noah finally quit the factory in 1914, joined the Socialist Party and got a job running a readers' club. He moved uptown to 514 East 149th Street in Harlem, near the Untermans – a big step up the social ladder. He graduated from Cooper Union with a degree in civil engineering in May 1915, and was promptly hired as an engineer for a construction contractor. Now that he could support a family, Noah and Miril married in 1916. Noah received a civil service appointment with the New York State Highway Commission in Buffalo in June, Miril quit her job as a draper and they moved to Buffalo.[47] No longer was Noah London a mere *poluintelligent*. Degree in hand, he could now consider himself a full-fledged member of the socialist intelligentsia, and he would set about proving it.

---

45 Laslett, *Jewish Socialism and the Ladies Garment Workers*, 110–14; Epstein, *The Jew and Communism*, 54–5.

46 Bender, *Sweated Work, Weak Bodies: Anti-Sweatshop Campaigns and Languages of Labor* (New Brunswick, NJ: Rutgers University Press, 2004, 2004), 105–22.

47 London, *Biograficheskii ocherk*; Cooper Union transcript; Lichnyi listok po uchetu kadrov, RGASPI, f. 17, op. 100, l. 30b.

The Londons had left New York City for America's industrial heartland. But they had not left the domain of American Socialism. London would write a few years later that 'Buffalo once had a big socialist movement. There are a lot of workers there. The steel mills and the auto factories did not inculcate in the workers any love for capitalist paradise. Indeed the steelworkers in Lackawanna elected a socialist mayor' in the aftermath of the great 1919 steel strike.[48] But as the Londons arrived there America was moving to war.

7 Progress and Poverty in Jewish Buffalo

The Londons moved in to Buffalo's William Street, a miniature version of the Lower East Side, as Jews were starting to move out. Buffalo's Jewish ghetto was not as impoverished as New York's. There were few tenements, and most Jews owned their own homes, but overcrowding was turning it into a slum. During the war African-Americans emigrated to Buffalo from the South, attracted by wartime jobs in industry. William Street was transforming from a Jewish into a black ghetto.

The clothing industry was less important in Buffalo than in New York City, and Jews were less concentrated there. But the local women's garment trade, organized through a successful strike during the war years, likely with Miril's assistance, was overwhelmingly Jewish. William Street was the home of a small but fairly influential Jewish socialist movement which, as always, experienced strife between right and left. Its most effective branch was the Workmen's Circle. It organized a cooperative workers' bakery, maintained a Socialist Library and set up a Yiddish *folkshul* for the children. De Leonist radicals usually outvoted pro-Cahan moderates in internal battles, and truce was reached by shifting attention from political to cultural affairs.[49]

In Buffalo from 1916 to 1917, Noah built bridges and highways, and served as secretary for the Buffalo SP's Jewish branch. Meanwhile, Miril was a housewife not a garment worker.[50] She may well have had time to participate more actively in Jewish socialism and even garment unionism than in New York City, especially since the Londons were a childless couple for medical reasons. According to Susan Glenn:

48 'n.l.' (London), 'Iber shtedt un shtetlakh', *Der Emes*, Dec. 16, 1921.

49 Selig Adler and Thomas E. Connolly, *From Ararat to Suburbia: The History of the Jewish Community of Buffalo* (Philadelphia: Jewish Publication Society of America, 1960).

50 Miril London, Avtobiografiia N.M. Londona, l. 1–4; Avtobiog. Marii Efimovny Londona, RGASPI, f. 17, op. 98, d. 8956.

> For some women, marriage actually heightened political awareness and engagement, particularly when husbands were active in the labor and radical movements ... women who remained involved sometimes found they had more time for political activities than their husbands did. The men had to labor twelve or fourteen hours a day, said one former garment union activist, 'whereas we housewives ... could steal some of our time and devote it to political work.'[51]

Almost the only real light that can be shed on Noah's role as the secretary of the Jewish branch of the Socialist Party in Buffalo is in a letter from him published in the *Naye Velt*, March 3, 1917. This letter was his first contribution to the American socialist press. Its topic was the branch Sunday school, whose enrollment had dropped dramatically. Likely he was its director. He wrote that his branch had '89 members in good standing, with its own clubrooms with a piano and a library [presumably the WC Socialist Library], and maintains a Sunday school'. This branch was not distinguished by particular radicalism. In 1919, the overwhelming majority of the Buffalo Socialist Party would join the Communist Party – except for its Jewish branch.[52]

8 Jewish Socialism and the 'Great War' in Europe and America

World War I deeply demoralized the world socialist movement. The workers of the world had failed to unite. The great socialist parties of Europe decided that the workers did have something to lose besides their chains – their fatherlands. This marked the demise of international social democracy, a movement defined from then on by national boundaries. But Jewish social democracy reflected the Jewish labor movement, which had still not yet acquired a fatherland.

When World War I broke out, the Jewish Pale became a central theater of war on the Eastern front. As the Russian army suffered repeated defeats it took its revenge on a soft target – the Jews, who became scapegoats for its incompetence. Top commanding officers convinced themselves that Jews were collaborating with the enemy. Estimates of the number driven out of their homes

---

51 Susan A. Glenn, *Daughters of the Shtetl: Life and Labor in the Immigrant Generation* (Ithaca, NY: Cornell University Press, 1990), 241. A few years previously Miril's younger sister Anna drew up the founding constitution for the Young Socialist League, or so she told her daughter Beatrice years later. B. Holmes interview.

52 London, 'Vegen idishe sotsialistishe sondey-skuhls', letter to editor, *Naye Velt*, March 3, 1917.

range from half a million to a million. These mass deportations were ominously termed *polnoe ochishchenie*, 'full cleansing'. They rapidly evolved into full-blown pogroms, accompanied by looting, burning and mass rape. Terrified victims in response welcomed the German army as possible liberators.[53] In what was to become the independent state of Lithuania, 75 to 80 percent of the Jewish population was expelled.

In America as in Eastern Europe, Jewish public opinion sympathized with Germany's war against Nicholas the Bloody. Socialists followed suit. Cahan set the tone in the *Forward*, bluntly and short-sightedly stating that 'it would be fortunate for all of Europe and for the whole Jewish population if Germany would take all of Poland and also Lithuania from Russia'. Unfolding catastrophe in the Pale riveted the attention of Jewish immigrants. A widespread relief movement sprang up immediately and semi-spontaneously. It received universal support, even though relief was funneled through Berlin and Vienna. Woodrow Wilson proclaimed January 27, Samuel Gompers's birthday, as Jewish Relief Day.[54] The Polish Bund's neutralism acquired a pro-German tinge, as its main concern became organizing war relief. Noah London still considered himself a Bundist. However, he would claim in the Yiddish Communist paper he would edit in 1921 that he opposed this campaign. Instead he had advocated fundraising for revolution in Russia.[55]

The February 1917 Revolution in Russia completely transformed Jewish attitudes to the war. It abolished all Tsarist anti-Semitic legislation, immediately and permanently – one of the few major reforms successfully carried out by Alexander Kerensky's provisional government. In a country on the brink of civil war between red revolution and white reaction, Kerensky put forward socialist-flavored Wilsonian democracy as a pale pink alternative. The Mensheviks, the Bolsheviks' socialist competitors, were the backbone of the coalition behind Kerensky. In 1905 the Bund had allied with Lenin. But by 1917, Bundism was so indistinguishable from Menshevism that Bund leaders like Abramovitch

53 Eric Lohr, *Nationalizing the Russian Empire: The Campaign against Enemy Aliens during World War I* (Cambridge, MA: Harvard University Press, 2003); Peter Gatrell, *A Whole Empire Walking: Refugees in Russia during World War I* (Bloomington: Indiana University Press. 1999); Frankel, *Crisis, Revolution, and Russian Jews*, 133–6; Klier, 'Kazaki i pogromy'; Konrad Zielinski, 'The Changing Shtetl in the Kingdom of Poland during the First World War' in *The Shtetl: Myth and Reality*, vol. 17 of *Polin: Studies in Polish Jewry*, ed. A. Polonsky (Oxford: Littman Library, 2004), 123.

54 Marsha L. Rozenblit, 'The European Jewish World 1914–1919', 36–7; Daniel Rosenthal, 'Confronting the Bacterial Enemy', 135–6.

55 Epstein, *Jewish Labor in USA*, vol. 2; Orenstein, *Jewish Socialist Federation*, 138; London, 'A perzenlikhe erklerung', *Proletaryer*, June 20, 1921.

became central leaders of the Mensheviks as well. The 1905 Bund dream, a workers' insurrection to overthrow Bloody Nicholas, had been realized – but without Jewish participation. The dominating mood of a demoralized and fearful Russian Jewish population in 1917 was apathy and indifference.[56]

8.1 *Anti-war Socialism and European Immigrants to America*

Meanwhile, the American Jewish labor movement, empowered by garment industry victories, was galvanized by the Bolshevik Revolution – as were other European immigrants. The 'colossal industrial revolution which transformed America from an agricultural, smalltime country into what she is now', as London put it years later when donning the cap of a historian in the Communist *Freiheit*, 'demanded toilers in large numbers, the *chorny rabochy* [a Russian expression, literally "black workers"]. The element missing in America. The blacks were scattered around the cotton fields ... And it was not customary for white Americans to be 'laborers', exactly how once it was among us Jews ... So a great wave of immigration began from eastern and southern Europe ...'[57]

These new immigrants were 'strangers in the land'. When they first arrived in America escaping Tsarist pogroms, Jewish immigrants were 'welcomed with music', in Noah's words. But by World War I, hostility to European immigrants reached hysterical peaks. Traditional anti-Catholicism and fears of immigrant radicalism were envenomed by a witches' brew of 'Anglo-Saxonism', with ominous undertones of 'Aryan' racial anti-Semitism. '100 percent Americanism' became the wartime credo, and 'hyphenated Americans' were under suspicion as potential agents of the Kaiser. Many European immigrants had not yet learned to speak English. And whether they were from the German Empire, Russia, Austria-Hungary or even from England's Irish colony, few felt any natural pro-Allied inclinations.[58] This was particularly true for Russian-Jewish immigrants.

A case can be made that 1917, the year America declared war on Germany, was American Socialism's highpoint. If Jewish Socialist leader Morris Hillquit's New York mayoral campaign had won, as many thought it would, that would have been the greatest victory in a fundamentally electoral party's history. But

---

56 Zel'tser, *Evrei sovetskoi provintsii*, 18–28.

57 London, 'Der goy iz trif, zayn grobeyzn iz ober kshr', *Freiheit*, May 2, 1924. This is the third part of his series on immigration.

58 John Higham, *Strangers in the Land: Patterns of American Nativism 1860–1925*, 2d ed. (New York: Atheneum, 1975 [1955]). Slavic immigrants from the Hapsburg Empire sometimes supported the American war effort against their native land. And Italians, from a nation born out of rebellion against the Habsburgs, naturally were another matter.

it was in the Midwest that Socialist candidates received the highest ballot box percentages they ever achieved. Future Communist leader Charles Ruthenberg won more than a quarter of the votes when he ran for mayor of Cleveland. In America's industrial capital, Chicago, Socialist candidates in a judicial election racked up citywide vote totals of nearly 40 percent. Many Socialists were elected to various positions in other cities and towns all across America, especially in the Midwest.

In Buffalo, the Socialist Party received 32 percent of the vote in the September mayoral primary. The Socialist menace usually frightened Democrats and Republicans into uniting against it. Socialist John H. Gibbons was elected mayor of Buffalo's steel suburb Lackawanna two years later, because state law prevented Republicans from listing Lackawanna's Democratic mayor on the Republican ballot line. Similar rules elsewhere would have generated a remarkable string of Midwestern Socialist victories in 1917.[59]

The basis of Socialist success with the voters was opposition to the war. America was at first neutral in World War I, and so was its Socialist Party. When American Progressivism jumped to support Woodrow Wilson's war to 'make the world safe for democracy', American Socialism became the party of pacifist neutrality. The Socialist Party adopted its St. Louis Platform at its April 1917 Emergency Convention, as America was joining the war and Noah had just sent off his letter to the *Naye velt* describing life in his Buffalo Jewish local. It denounced Wilson's declaration of war as 'a crime against the people of the United States and the nations of the world'. As war fever mounted, most of the intellectuals and labor leaders who identified themselves with Socialism decamped – some out of patriotism, others out of fear. The 'grassroots socialism' flourishing in backwoods corners of America like Oklahoma and Texas, a heritage of Populism, was annihilated by a wave of brutal wartime repression whose main target was Big Bill Haywood's IWW. The Socialist Party was growing dramatically, but transforming from the left wing of American Progressivism and Populism into a radical party of European immigrant workers. This is why Socialist tickets did better in 1917 in places like Buffalo than in California or even New York City.[60]

59 James Weinstein, *Decline of Socialism in America, 1912–1915* (New York: Random House, 1969), 119–76.

60 Melvyn Dubofsky, *We Shall Be All: A History of the Industrial Workers of the World*, 2d ed. (Urbana: University of Illinois Press, 1988 [1969]); James R. Green, *Grass-Roots Socialism Roots Socialism: Radical Movements in the Southwest, 1895–1943* (Baton Rouge: Louisiana State University Press, 1978); Weinstein, *Decline*, 157. Socialist historian Weinstein made the claim that it was workers in general, rather than European immigrants in particular,

9 American Jewish Socialism and the Revolution of 1917

Five days after London published his Sunday school letter in the *Naye Velt*, hungry Russian women in Petrograd celebrated International Womens' Day by pouring into the streets and starting a revolution. The overthrow of the Romanov dynasty had a powerful but contradictory effect on American Jewish socialism. Throughout the twentieth century, Jewish immigrants were human transmission belts for political and social influences between Russia and America – in both directions. Thus in April 1917 Meyer London (no relation), the Socialist congressman from the Lower East Side, sent a telegram to the Menshevik president of the Petrograd Soviet of Workers Deputies, asking him to deny rumors that Russian socialists favored a separate peace with Germany.[61] Meanwhile, Jewish garment workers in New York City conveyed Russian influence in the opposite direction. Noah London wrote a few years later that 'the broad masses … boiled with delight, with excitement, with the most thrilled interest in everything coming from Bolshevik Russia. But this was partly from Russian patriotism and partly from traditional socialist sentiment, rather than from a positive, concrete desire to bring Bolshevism to America'.[62]

In Buffalo that summer, Jewish branch secretary London began publicly supporting the Bolsheviks. The workers' revolution in Russia was popular among European immigrants, and radical emigrés were jumping on the bandwagon. The Socialist Party's Russian Federation, mostly Jewish but tied to the Mensheviks rather than the Bund, abruptly went over to Bolshevism. Rapidly recruiting from the small ethnically Russian immigrant factory workforce, which the IWW-linked Union of Russian Workers was organizing, its membership ballooned dramatically. It became the backbone of a rapidly growing left wing movement in the Socialist Party. During the course of the revolutions in Russia, Germany and Austria-Hungary that ended World War I, these radicalized immigrant Socialists grouped themselves around the Bolshevik banner. They were the creators of American Communism.

who provided the large midwestern Socialist vote in 1917. But his own figures (173–6) do not back him up.

61 Epstein *Jewish Labor in USA*, vol. 2, 81.

62 London, 'Id. arb.-bavegung', *Freiheit*, Jan. 10, 1923.

CHAPTER 4

The Birth of American Jewish Communism

> Even those who later became leaders of the Left Wing … had not fully grasped in the deepest sense the October revolution … the only ones who … fully understood its real spirit, the only ones who had gone ahead and used the lessons of Bolshevism on American soil, were the conscious workers in the shops.
>
> NOAH LONDON, in *Freiheit*, November 1923

The Bolshevik Revolution in 1917 sparked the birth of American Communism in 1919. Revolutionary Jewish emigrants like the Londons carried that spark into garment sweatshops, and steadily sharpening conflict in Jewish garment unions provided tinder.

Those 'ten days that shook the world' were not the only reason this movement arose, an ocean away from Russia. Four other factors helped turn Jewish Socialists into Communists in the aftermath of the Great War. They were Jewish opposition to the war; the great American labor explosion of 1919; the revolutionary wave that swept over Europe simultaneously; and last but not least, the huge wave of anti-Jewish pogroms all over Eastern Europe that for several years accompanied revolutionary turmoil. Only Soviet Russia seemed immune. Noah London's transformation into a Communist would lead the way for other American Jewish socialists, radical or moderate.

Jewish garment unions initially followed the Socialist Party lead and opposed the war. But when American soldiers actually went 'over there' in 1918 Socialist union officers and moderate Socialists fell in line with the war effort – or decided that silence was golden. Initially, American attitudes to Soviet Russia were ambiguous. The New York subways hired Noah London in January 1918, and the Londons returned to New York City, moving to the Bronx. The engineering journals he was studying at the time were praising the Bolshevik industrial program. Many people had the misimpression that Woodrow Wilson was a friend of Red Russia. He had told Congress in January 1918 in his 'Fourteen Points' speech that America wanted to 'assure her of a sincere welcome into the society of free nations …' In March, Socialist leader Eugene Debs wrote

 | DOI:10.1163/9789004745384_006

that 'President Wilson, to his eternal credit, attempted to pave the way to the recognition of the Bolsheviki and back them up in their struggle to crown their revolution with victory'.[1] This belief gained traction among a number of radical immigrants and labor agitators. Events would soon puncture illusions in Wilsonian democracy. As Debs was penning these words of praise for Wilson, SP leaders were indicted for violating the Espionage Act.

American socialists, unlike Russians, were not used to the idea that police and agents of the federal government might bust up their headquarters, knock on their doors at night and haul them away to prison or even deport them. The Wobblies were, but their anarchist notions of how to deal with the repression they had so often encountered were failures – which contributed to the IWW's destruction as a mass movement.[2] More than half of American factory workers then were foreigners, overwhelmingly from Europe. They were always paid less and treated worse. When a newborn Communist movement of European immigrants from the Socialist Party's foreign language federations saw what was happening to the American IWW, they naturally looked to the successful European Bolsheviks as a model to imitate instead. Forced underground almost as soon as the movement was founded, it was wracked in its first years by a profound dispute over how deeply to go underground, and indeed whether permanently or temporarily. Was imitating Russian models in a very different country such a good idea anyway? And who should guide the movement? Theoretically knowledgeable Europeans, or Americans with more local experience? Life in the underground would be an unpleasant experience, aggravating all the movement's contradictions.

For Europeans, World War I was a bloodbath that discredited all responsible, even the theoretical victors. In the Russian, German and Austro-Hungarian Empires defeat led to revolution. Socialist opposition to the war thus had a powerful appeal to European immigrants – they did not want to be dragged into the meatgrinder. But by the time the US Communist parties were founded, the war was over and America had won. When the Yanks went 'over there', America experienced what Europe's rulers had promised and failed to deliver in 1914 – an exciting, successful adventure at a relatively low cost in blood and treasure. The immigrants would demand their fair share of the spoils instead of all becoming revolutionaries. Victory as a result diverted radicalization into patriotic channels. As London would put it decades later: 'Who better than the American workers can be rallied to fight for an ideal, though it be a false illusion as was

1 Eugene Debs, 'Views on the Double Attack on Russia', *The Eye Opener* (Chicago), March 16, 1918.

2 Melvyn Dubovsky's history of the IWW, *We Shall Be All*, tells the sad story.

the "fight for democracy" during the World War?' The marvelously ambiguous slogan of 'industrial democracy' dominated labor discourse as American troops helped drive the German army out of France.[3]

Like many other Jewish immigrants, Noah London had moved up in the world from the ranks of those conscious workers in the shops whom he saw as America's true Jewish Bolsheviks. He nonetheless became a central spokesman for this newborn movement. Its father was a mostly male *Linker Fligel* (Left Wing) he helped found in the Jewish Socialist Federation (JSF). Its mother was a labor rebellion in Miril's ILGWU local 25, born out of the famed women's 'uprising of the 10,000' in the shirtwaist trade. Its parents' marriage, like the marriage of Noah and Miril, was a happy one by all accounts. According to the ILGWU's first official history, produced as early as 1924:

> The beginning of this conflict may be traced back to the activities of a group of members in the New York Waist and Dressmakers Union, Local 25, who organized in 1917 the so-called 'Current Events Committee'. This 'Committee' voiced the general restlessness of a number of young women who were 'active' in Local 25 … It gave rise to an organized and persistent effort to 'rejuvenate' the local by getting rid of 'old' leaders and officers who were regarded as 'too practical' and 'too conservative' …[4]

Miril would certainly have been one of its founders were she not in Buffalo in 1917. The current event that occupied the committee was the Russian Revolution. According to Melech Epstein, 'The Current Events Committee mirrored the yearnings of a number of young people for a "soul" in the union … The girls went to work carrying [books by] Karl Marx and Kropotkin under their arms'. The reaction of the top officers of the ILGWU was perfectly captured by later ILGWU historian Benjamin Stolberg. He wrote that 'to all this transcendentalism of the girls the trade union bureaucrats reacted with bored indifference, and the heavy humorists among them offered cynical advice on how to get it out of their systems'.[5] The Jewish women in this committee joined forces with a mostly Italian New York Wobbly garment group to create the ILGWU Workers Council. Its first action was to organize a rally against American intervention

3 London manuscript, Appendix B; McCartin, *Labor's Great War*.

4 Levine, *Women's Garment Workers*, 352–3.

5 Stanley Nadel, 'Reds Versus Pinks: A Civil War in the International Ladies Garment Workers Union', *New York History* 66, no. 1 (Jan. 1985): 51; Epstein *Jewish Labor in USA*; Benjamin Stolberg, *Tailor's Progress: The Story of a Famous Union and the Men Who Made It* (New York: Doubleday, 1944), 109–10.

in Russia, at the peak frenzy of war-patriotism in 1918. Demonstrating garment workers were arrested in Harlem that summer.[6]

After the war ended in November, a militant mood took hold of the New York garment industry. The new movement grew rapidly. Under the influence of the Workers Council, which wanted to spread the Seattle general strike in the name of a 'workers, soldiers and sailors council' to the New York garment district, Local 25 called a general strike of all New York shirtwaist and dress shops in the spring of 1919. It touched off a nationwide strike wave in the industry. Noah London promptly became a public spokesman for the Workers Council. When the strikers returned to work, the council called an industry-wide conference at the Russian People's House on the Lower East Side. Some 320 delegates attended representing 14,000 workers, about half of Local 25's shops. The council's manifesto proclaimed: 'Soviets are being organized in almost every part of Europe, and the workers of America will NOT stand aside!' Workers needed to get ready to 'go on with production when the time comes for them to take over the industries ...' 'Industrial democracy' had definitely acquired a brand new meaning.

In Miril's shirtwaist and dress industry this was a women's movement. Male rebels in the trade Noah identified with, the cloak trade, were primarily non-Communist left Socialists, separated from Workers Council radicals by gender as well as politics (and by ethnicity with the Italian Wobblies). Cloak and dressmakers alike would join the Communist insurgency of the 1920s, but women did so more quickly. Noah, Miril's husband, would fight to build bridges between female Communist and male left-Socialist insurgents.

1 The Jewish Socialist Federation, the Russian Revolution and Noah London

As the Workers Council and the garment strike wave gathered steam, rebellion was brewing within the Jewish Socialist Federation. It broke out first in its oldest and largest chapter, the Downtown Manhattan Branch – the branch for the Lower East Side, the heart of the Jewish immigrant community. Here is where the labor revolts that lay the basis for the JSF's existence exploded. Dissidence spread rapidly, and Bronx branch member Noah joined in. He was already well known as a supporter of the Bolshevik cause.

6 Zimmerman interviews, Zimmerman coll., Labor-Management Documentation Center, Cornell, Box 1; London, *Freiheit*, Nov. 10, 1923.

The Jewish Socialist Federation was still basically an American offshoot of the Jewish Bund. Consequently, as Noah later put it, 'All those who had something to say in the Jewish workers' movement … either didn't understand the October Revolution or were against it'. The issue of the *Naye Velt*, the JSF weekly, that came out just before the storming of the Winter Palace barely mentioned historic events unfolding in Petrograd. The issue on the newsstands during the October Revolution featured the first pro-Bolshevik article ever to appear in its pages, 'Menshevism or Socialist Impotence'. Noah London, a teenage Bund Bolshevik from Lithuania who had grown up to become a respectable Socialist branch secretary in Buffalo, was a Bund Bolshevik once again.[7]

The ideas laid out in his first serious contribution to the Socialist press were those he would continue to believe in one form or another for the rest of his life. They offered a perch on a Bolshevik bandwagon for his fellow Mensheviks of the Jewish Socialist Federation. There was not a word about world revolution in it – the foundation stone of communism as Lenin or Trotsky or Marx understood it. Noah London's pragmatic arguments for Bolshevik tactics resemble instead Stalinist notions of 'socialism in one country'.

Bundists had dismissed Leninism as anti-Marxist. But as London put it: 'If we have to seek a rabbinical stamp of approval from Marx at every step, we should mention that the idea of a Communist Party is taken from the Communist Manifesto … When the workers of the whole country … are for the expropriation of land and capital, to search for a prohibition in the Jewish code of custom for a situation that nobody has ever seen before is, to put it mildly, impractical'.

Bundists and Mensheviks alike believed that Russian capitalism needed to develop further before Russian socialism was possible. Anticipating future sociologists, London answered, 'As a country becomes industrially developed, the revolutionary forces become weaker'. He had learned this from his American experiences. The main practical Bundist argument against Lenin was that Russia could not survive without foreign capital, especially from America. In London's opinion, after the war America 'would have its own ruins to rebuild and wounds to heal, rather than giving its capital or machinery or locomotives to a bourgeois Russian republic …' There was no reason why a socialist country could not trade with a capitalist country. If Germany had managed to survive blockade in wartime why could not Russia, with its immense natural resources, do the same in peacetime? He concluded that 'this can be a good warning to us

---

7 London, *Freiheit*, Nov. 10, 1923; London, *Naye Velt*, Oct. 30, 1917; London, 'Menshevizm oder sotsialistishe impotents', *Naye Velt*, Dec. 6, 1917.

Mensheviks of all lands: to avoid "impotence" we must strengthen and cultivate a sound, unsophisticated socialist spirit ...'

Noah London's initial reaction to the Bolshevik Revolution bears a definite resemblance to that of a better known Marxist thinker, Italy's Antonio Gramsci. A month after London's article appeared Gramsci published his own first piece that attracted much attention, 'The Revolution against "Capital"'. According to Gramsci, 'Events have blown out of the water all critical notions which stated Russia would have to develop according to the laws of historical materialism'. Gramsci went further than London, controversially proclaiming that the Bolsheviks 'renounce Karl Marx'.[8]

London's article prepared the way for a dramatic JSF ideological shift. Leader Salutsky's editorial note described the piece as 'very interesting and important', even though it 'idealized Leninism'. As soon as it became clear that the Bolshevik regime was not going to collapse right away, American Jewish Socialists joined a worldwide Socialist chorus of praise for the first successful workers' revolution in history. Abraham Cahan set the tone, as always. According to Bund leader Abramovitch, when he met Cahan in Berlin in 1920 the first thing Cahan had to say to him was 'you cannot write in the *Forward*'. When he tried to tell Cahan about the Red Terror and hunger in Russia, Cahan raised his hand to cover his eyes and shouted, 'Do not destroy my illusions!'[9]

Already, Cahan and his *Forward* had switched from a pro-German stance to American patriotism. The infamous Zimmerman Telegram from a German representative had been intercepted and publicized in January 1917. Germany had tried to inveigle the Mexican government to become a German ally and, if America declared war on Germany, to attack the US to regain Mexican territories lost in the Mexican War. *Forward* columnist and New York alderman Charney Vladeck wrote that if Mexico really was going to attack America, then it was the duty of every Socialist and citizen to rally 'round the flag. Vladeck's piece resulted in another *Forward* columnist, Russian visitor Leon Trotsky, storming out of the editorial office after a screaming match in Russian with Cahan shortly after the overthrow of the Tsar – and shortly before Wilson declared war.[10]

A year later, in May 1918, the JSF voted at a special conference to change its position on the war. Wilson had announced his famous Fourteen Points, advocating democracy and national self-determination as US war aims, after

8 Antonio Gramsci, 'The Revolution against "Capital"', *Gramsci: Pre-Prison Writings*, trans. Victoria Cox, ed. Richard Bellamy (Cambridge: Cambridge University Press, 1994).

9 Epstein, *Jewish Labor in USA*, vol. 2, 64.

10 Estraich, 'American Yiddish Socialists', 284–95.

Bolshevik Russia was forced to sign the oppressive Brest-Litovsk treaty. A huge revolution-wracked swatch of territory formerly part of the Tsarist Empire was surrendered to the German army and German quislings, some of them 'Socialist', including what is now the Baltic Republics, Moldova, most of Belarus and western and central Ukraine – but not the Donbass, not then seen as Ukrainian, or Crimea. The Brest-Litovsk treaty line was curiously similar to the line today dividing NATO influence and Russian influence.

The war according to the JSF had become a war for democracy against German imperialism, occupying ever larger swatches of Russian territory and threatening to crush the new Socialist idol, the Bolshevik Revolution. Sidney Hillman's ACWA, thriving on contracts for uniform production, wrote in its newspaper that the Bolshevik Revolution gave the 'struggle against German militarism new meaning'. JSF leader Salutsky edited this paper.[11]

London had written in the 1918 Fourth of July *Naye Velt* edition that whereas Britain and France were fighting for imperial interests, America was fighting for democracy, social progress and self-determination. 'Self-determination for all nations is the precept in Socialist Russia'. He would later apologize for this article, explaining that he thought at the time that as long as America was still at war with Germany, Wilson would be compelled to defend Red Russia in his own interests.[12] On July 6, the day after London's endorsement of Woodrow Wilson's war to make the world safe for democracy hit the newsstands, Wilson decided to send US troops into Russia.[13]

1.1 *From Pro-Soviet Socialism to Communism*

London now ventured beyond pragmatic support for Russian socialism in one country. The German Revolution that overthrew the Kaiser in November 1918 made Lenin and Trotsky's program for world revolution believable. By the spring of 1919, he had become a founding leader of American Jewish Communism.

Most Jewish Socialist activists and many of their leaders would follow his example, as did many Bundists in the former Tsarist Empire. According to

---

11 Orenstein, *Jewish Socialist Federation*, 201.

12 N. Paiezon [London], 'Vi Amerika hot oyfgenumen di Bolshevistishe revolutsie', London, 'Di parteyen in Amerike un di velt-mlkhmh', *Naye Velt*, July 5, 1918; and 'Perzenlikhe erklerung', *Proletaryer*, June 20, 1921.

13 David Montgomery, 'Nationalism, American Patriotism, and Class Consciousness', in *Struggle a Hard Battle: Essays on Working-Class Immigrants* (Dekalb: Northern Illinois University Press, 1986); *Der Emes*, Nov. 4, 1921; Betty Miller Unterberger, ed., *American Intervention in the Russian Civil War* (Lexington, MA: Heath, 1969).

Abramovich, the Bund's central leader: 'The Bund was until 1919 the strongest and surest fortress of Social Democracy in Russia ... But the German Revolution of 1918 and the German occupation ... raised strong Communist moods among the Jewish masses'.[14] The overthrow of the German Kaiser and the Hapsburg Emperor powerfully affected Bundists everywhere – indeed more than the Bolshevik Revolution itself.

One can pinpoint the exact moment when Noah London abandoned Bundism for Bolshevism. In November 1918 World War I ended, the German and Austro-Hungarian empires were overthrown—and Socialist congressman Meyer London lost his seat. All almost simultaneously. Civil engineer London later recounted how on Armistice Day,

> feeling the excitement in the streets that morning comrades go to the *Forward* building. Among the crowd are Meyer London, who had lost his Congressional election two days ago, and Jacob Panken ... Their audience pays close attention, waiting to hear what their leaders had to say. Meyer London is complaining about the 'comrades'. They hadn't worked hard enough ... It wasn't that he was defeated ... it was that the only Socialist congressman was defeated. Judge Panken, whose term still had some years to run ... tries to console the defeated congressman ... A member of the audience approaches them and tells them, 'look at the crowd collected together around the building. Historical events are taking place. The public is waiting on their leaders, speak to them'. The judge is delighted with the opportunity to distract his comrade from his sorrow. 'Look here, Meyer, he talks sense', he says. But Meyer London isn't comforted. What does he care about armistice, revolution, Bolshevism, he has greater concerns.[15]

One suspects Noah was the comrade who tried to draw attention to the bigger picture.

During the Russian Civil War that began in 1918 and reached its peak in 1919, the Jewish situation was even graver than in 1905. Hundreds of thousands of Jews were being murdered, raped, mutilated, orphaned or left homeless by Whites, Ukrainian nationalists and peasant bandits. Trotsky's Red Army was their only defense. Jews, the European ethnic group least interested in Bolshevism in Kerensky's Russia, streamed into the Red Army during the Civil War

14 Abramovitch, *In tsvey revolutsies*, vol. 2, 310.

15 London, Nov. 10, 1923.

to fight *pogromchiks* of every stripe, from monarchist Cossacks to anarchist Ukrainian peasants.[16] On November 1, 1918, Noah London published a piece in the *Naye Velt* on Jewish socialism and the European peace negotiations. He no longer believed, as he had a few months earlier, that American war aims could lead to 'a world free for the organized working class to prepare the coming of socialism'. Instead, Wilsonian self-determination was setting the stage for reaction in Eastern Europe, as newly independent Eastern European countries brought Wilsonian democracy and self-determination to their countries in the form of pogroms and jailing and murder of Jewish and other Communist 'enemies of democracy', the latter repression with Wilson's blessing. Jews were safe only in 'industrially democratized Great Russia'. But should Socialists 'wait until "industrial democracy" [that is, Bolshevik revolution] or better yet work for it and forget about the Jewish question? We would have to wait too long …' Meanwhile London was calling for a worldwide Jewish Socialist conference to put pressure on the Allies to protect Jewish rights.[17]

The *Naye Velt* published an open letter in the same issue calling for a Jewish National Workers Congress. A series of conferences ensued, marking the high point of the JSF's political influence in the American Jewish community. Its membership briefly ballooned to over 10,000. JSF founder-leader Morris Winchevsky, who later would follow Noah into the Communist movement, was chosen as one of American Jewry's official representatives at Versailles. And the delegates did get guarantees of Jewish rights in Eastern Europe inserted into treaties. The UK was given a League of Nations mandate to govern Palestine, giving the Balfour Declaration practical meaning. London commented in the *Naye Velt* that 'we have played *realpolitik*, and it seems that on paper at least, Jewish rights will be guaranteed'.[18]

But what did these words on paper mean in the real world? Noah wrote that the only real guarantee for Jewish safety in Eastern Europe was a workers' revolution after the Russian and German example. A world Jewish Socialist congress ought to mobilize workers for socialist revolution, not beg the Allies for protection or seek a refuge in Palestine. One-time Socialist-Zionist Noah London had now dropped the last remnants of past worldviews and fully become a Communist, the crisis of Eastern European Jewry providing the final

16 Gitelman, *Jewish Nationality*, 158–68.

17 London, July 5, 1918; and 'An internatsionale idish-sotsialistishe konferents', *Naye Velt*, Nov. 1, 1918.

18 Orenstein, *Jewish Socialist Federation*, 214–26; London, 'Di oyfgabe fun idishe arbayter kongres', *Naye Velt*, Jan. 17, 1919.

push. Six months later, he would write in his Yiddish Communist journal that 'it is true that there is a Jewish question but we say that it can only be solved when the international proletariat becomes the ruler of the world'.[19]

Nowadays Zionism has gotten a very bad press on the left, but before Israel became a leftist pariah, Jewish radicals for generations were torn between Socialist revolution and left-wing variants of Zionism. Noah London never shared the traditional anti-Zionist animus of the Bund. In the above-mentioned article, he would comment that 'Zionism is for some Jews a religion and therefore we regard Zionism as a private affair'. He opposed it only insofar as it could be used by British imperialism against the Arabs, something that seemed a lot less important to radicals in Europe and America then than it does now.

With notions of world revolution no longer seeming like pipe dreams, Noah London explored the theoretical implications of European revolutionary upheaval in a *Naye Velt* article series entitled 'Scholasticism or Action?'[20] He was an engineer, a trade unionist, a Bundist and therefore very much a pragmatist. These articles were his first and last venture into the realm of abstract Marxist theory – his proof that, degree in hand, he was no longer a 'half intellectual' but the real thing – ready, willing and able to guide the course of the movement. He applied proper theoretical polish to concepts which elsewhere he preferred to explain in popular terms. The resemblance to certain of Gramsci's writings is notable.

The questions he analyzed and the answers he derived parallel and sometimes prefigure the concerns and conclusions of other, better-known thinkers as well. Why did economically backward Russia have the most politically advanced working class in the world? Why did America, the most economically advanced country in the world, have the most backward? Did the Bolshevik revolution contradict Marxist theory, as the Mensheviks argued and Gramsci initially suggested?

All across Europe, Socialist parties were taking the reins of government into their hands that year. But in America the Socialist Party stagnated at the ballot box. And he pointed out, neither was America gradually moving to socialism through welfare measures, as its moderate wing maintained. America was far behind Europe in that respect. Before the Great War, American Socialists thought that they represented the inevitable wave of the future – just as did their European comrades, with more justification. What happened?

19 London, 'Di oyfgabe fun idishe arbayter kongres'; and 'Natsionale frage', *Kamf*, July 11, 1919.
20 London, 'Visenshaftlikhkeyt oder aktsion?', *Naye Velt*, Jan. 14, 1917 and Feb. 14, 1919.

Like Gramsci and countless other Marxist critics, he argued that Engels and Plekhanov, the Second International's classic expositors of positivist Marxism, had misused Hegelian dialectics. They had straightjacketed Marxism into a mechanical schema of economic determinism. What did they fail to understand? With a true Gramscian flourish, London argued that the rising cultural level of human society, stemming from economic progress and industrial revolution, meant that 'the impact of intelligence, the idea, on the ordering of our lives is increasing. The ideal is no longer the absolute slave of the material!'[21] This prefiguration of 'cultural Marxism' founded a simple, anti-positivist conclusion: 'We are therefore free from miscellaneous binding laws in our study of social science; we are free to select out the truly scientific in Marxism, and that is the economic doctrine, the doctrine of class struggle … and see to the realization of socialism when we are able'.[22]

His analyses of the contemporary world distinguished him as a creative thinker from the dogmatism that was usually the best American Communism could produce on the theoretical level, even in its early years before the straitjacket of Stalinist orthodoxy descended around it. Shortly after these words appeared in print he became a leader of the brand new Left Wing of the Jewish Socialist Federation.

2 Birth of the Left Wing

In the summer of 1918, while Noah London was still caught between Wilsonism and Bolshevism, an antiwar minority took control of the JSF's key Downtown Manhattan Branch, defeating moderate Socialist David Dubinsky. Later in life Dubinsky would become the leader of the ILGWU for over a quarter of a century, and one of America's central labor leaders. The new branch organizer was a young radical named Harry Hiltzik. He was closely allied with the Russian Socialist Federation, which exiles Trotsky and Bukharin took away from the Mensheviks shortly before their return to revolutionary Russia. Hiltzik and his friends had founded the Left Wing of the JSF in February 1919 and began issuing a newspaper called *Der Kamf*, or Struggle. The Downtown Branch was probably the first branch of the American Socialist Party to be expelled in what the Left would dub the 'Pink Terror'. Its leaders were hardly extremists, however. Their original program statement in the *Kamf* proclaimed that it was published 'with

21 London, 'Visenshaftlikhkeyt oder aktsion?', *Naye Velt*, Jan. 17.

22 London, 'Visenshaftlikhkeyt oder aktsion?', *Naye Velt*, Feb. 14.

the most peaceful of intentions ... to create a tribune for opinions that do not carry the O.K. of the official leaders'.[23]

Hiltzik died of tuberculosis early on, and the figures who replaced him came from a different group. Alexander Bittelman, secretary of the JSF Harlem branch, and Noah London from the East Bronx branch were its leaders. Several prominent national JSF functionaries were also involved. Like Noah, Bittelman had wavered in his opposition to the war in the spring of 1918.[24]

Bittelman and London, not satisfied with the Hiltzik group's vague program, decided to draft a manifesto and get it published in the *Naye Velt*. It attempted to adapt Bolshevik ideas to existing American reality, calling on Socialists to 'encourage the revolutionary elements in existing unions'. Most left-wing Socialists at the time were urging workers to abandon the AFL for the IWW. Their manifesto attracted broad attention and led to a merger of the two dissident groups, enabling the Left Wing to spread throughout the federation. London was elected as a Left representative to the Socialist Party's New York City Committee – but never seated, due to the 'Pink Terror' waged by the SP's leaders against the radicals, who were expelled wholesale.[25] According to Bittelman's memoirs,

> the left current in the Jewish branches was by far not as strong as in the Russian or Ukrainian ... What I found at the time by way of membership attitudes was a rather small grouping for the outspoken Right, which meant people who had supported the war, condemned the Bolshevik revolution and denounced the leftward trend in the world Socialist movement, especially in the United States. Support for the Left was much greater and very enthusiastic but a minority of the membership. The bulk ... preferred to go along with the official leadership ...[26]

The JSF moved rapidly towards a split. ILGWU organizer Bernard Chazanow described many years later how in his West Bronx branch,

23 Orenstein, *Jewish Socialist Federation*, 228–31; Epstein, *The Jew and Communism*, 68–9.

24 'Harry Hiltzik', *Funken*, Feb. 5, 1920; Bittelman, 'Outline for a History of the Communist Party in America', Exhibit 4, *Report of the Special Committee to Investigate Communist Activities*, 1930, 435–48; *Naye Velt*, Spring 1919 *passim*; Chazanow interview by J. Bloom, May 31, 1978, tape 1, side 2, Oral History of the American Left, Tamiment Library.

25 Bittelman, 'Things I Have Learned'; Bittelman, et al., 'Erklerung fun program fun a grupe fun zieben genosen', *Naye Velt*, May 9, 1919; London, *Biograficheskii Ocherk*, l. 6.

26 Bittelman, 'Things I Have Learned', 306.

> when we came to the elections the leaders of the branch … somehow managed that there was no lights in the local where we meet, a blackout, so everybody run out, but they went in a restaurant and they elected their delegates … We were waiting until we got lights, we continued our meeting, and we elected our delegates, I was one of the delegates. And we came to Boston to the convention. The convention was packed![27]

Ironically, those West Bronx branch leaders would later all join the Communist Party themselves. At the convention, the Left Wing called for the JSF to leave the Socialist Party. East Bronx delegate Noah London, the Left nominee for convention chairman, played the role of parliamentarian. According to a *Naye Velt* commentator, 'London exhausted himself so much with his points of order that, alas, he had no energy left to defend his position on the question of political action and contented himself with a couple of crackling phrases'. When the Left resolution was voted down, Bittelman somewhat reluctantly led a walkout from the convention. As he described it, 'Many left wing delegates … rose from their seats … and began tearing up their membership cards in the Socialist party. We had to ask them to take their seats again so we could make our final declaration and walk out in a body …'[28] The Left Wing was independent now. At first, Hiltzik was the main spokesman. Bittelman became editor of *Der Kamf*, with London as co-editor.

3 The Jewish Communist Federation and Alexander Bittelman

The Left Wing joined ranks with seven other foreign-language federations suspended from the Socialist Party a few days previously, primarily immigrant workers from the Tsarist or Austro-Hungarian Empires. They insisted on immediate formation of an American Communist Party, with or without any English-speaking members. Theodore Draper, the prime historian of American Communism, aptly commented, 'The Russian Federation's leaders began to develop unmistakable signs of delusions of grandeur – as if the genius of Lenin or Trotsky had rubbed off on all Russians'.[29]

---

27 Bernard Chazanow interview, OHAL. Chazanow was the organizer of ILGWU Local #38.

28 Bittelman, 'Things I Have Learned', 312–14; Liliput, 'Di 'fihrer' un dos 'folk' bay der konvenshon', *Naye Velt*, June 20, 1919; 'Protokolen fun'm bostoner tsuzamenfahr', *Naye Velt*, June 20 and 27, 1919.

29 Theodore Draper, *The Roots of American Communism* (New York: Viking Press, 1957), 159.

Naturally, this was not quite how Russian Federation leaders themselves saw things. Rather, they believed that they uniquely understood Marxist theory in the US, and that American radicals like John Reed, the author of *Ten Days That Shook the World*, were politically primitive and needed their guidance. Foreign-language federation leaders like Bittelman, Hiltzik and Russian Federation leader Nicholas Hourwich (son of Isaac Hourwich) would thoroughly dominate the Communist Party of America (CPA) when it was founded. Indeed, the CPA was essentially a federation of ethnic federations.[30]

London himself left the Jewish Communist Federation to join John Reed's Communist Labor Party (CLP). In a memorial article published on the anniversary of Reed's death he wrote that Reed, 'the most American of all American Communists ... did not believe in the communist competence of the federation leaders, he could not tolerate their narrow clique-sectarianism ... John Reed, closely connected with a general staff of giants in Russia, discerned a general staff of megalomaniac midgets in America'.[31]

Hiltzik's successor Alexander Bittelman soon realized that he, too, was not as politically close to the Russian Federation clique/sectarians as he had thought. The superficial similarities between the Slavic and Baltic Communist federations and their Jewish counterpart masked deeper differences. Jewish Communism, unlike that of the other foreign-language federations, was deeply rooted in the realities and traditions of American garment unionism.

Unlike London, Bittelman had no great interest in the Workers Councils in the garment trades, and even less in the IWW. He was the main author of the Left Wing manifesto, which mentioned neither and called for supporting revolutionary elements *within* the existing unions. Bittelman, a consistent opponent of 'dual unionism', the idea that revolutionaries should form revolutionary unions instead of 'burrowing within' the mainline unions, became someone who rivals would berate as a dogmatic 'Talmudist'. He would become William Z. Foster's closest political ally when the leader of the great 1919 steel strike, whose pre-World War I Syndicalist League had made opposition to Wobbly 'dual unionism' its platform, found his way into the Communist movement and quickly became one of its central leaders.

Bittelman's background helps explain the important role he would go on to play in American Communism. Whereas Pinsk, near London's birthplace, had the second-highest Jewish population by percentage of any city in the

30 Bittelman, 'Things I Have Learned', 319. The original 'federationist' Communist Party will hereinafter be referred to as the CPA, to differentiate it from the later united CPUSA or simply CP.

31 Paiezon [London], 'Dzhon rid – der revolutsionerer fihrer', *Der Emes*, Oct. 28, 1921.

world, Bittelman's hometown Berdichev had the highest. The Bund did not collapse as completely in all-Jewish Berdichev as elsewhere in the Pale in the aftermath of the defeat of the 1905 Revolution. Behind Bittelman's image as a Marxist Talmudist lay an adolescent background as a union activist in the Berdichev printing trade in the aftermath of a defeated revolution. It gave him a certain ability to translate everyday common sense into sonorous Marxist abstractions, which stood him in very good stead in the American Communist Party.

4 Noah London, the Workers Council Movement and the Spirit of 1919

London tried to ground Russian Bolshevism in American reality in a different fashion. As the Left Wingnik identified with the Workers Councils, he sought to bring the spirit of postwar labor revolt into Jewish socialism. All across America and Canada, labor radicals were thinking that the modern factory made craft unionism obsolete. They saw the British shop stewards' movement as the model of workplace organization that best corresponded to North American conditions.

Noah inherited his interest in British models from grandpa Joseph. Stewards' councils were arising as an ad hoc mechanism to get workers to cooperate across craft lines. In Seattle and Winnipeg, workers' councils coalesced on the basis of wartime shop committees and mass labor action.[32] In the summer of 1919, the New York garment Workers Council proposed a strike against US intervention in Russia to its left-wing backers who had just left the Jewish Socialist Federation.[33] Newfledged Communist Noah London was speaking at its rallies and analyzing workers council prospects in *Der Kamf*. In his opinion:

> The workers can accomplish more through popular councils than an unpopular trade-union administration ... Seattle and Winnipeg, not even speaking of Russia and England, demonstrate this. Who are the councils' foes? The government? ... Well, that is what the government is for, to fight the working class and that's why the workers have to organize themselves.

---

32 Montgomery, *Fall of the House of Labor*, 425–9.

33 Levine, *Women's Garment Workers*, 329-2; 'To the Workers of the Waist & Dress Industry', Box 84, U.S. Terr. Coll., YIVO; *Ohio Socialist*, June 11, 1919; Zimmerman interviews, 150–5; London, *Freiheit*, Nov. 10, 1923.

> The trade union leaders? ... If they commit the error of fighting the council movement, they will end up like [UGW leader] Rickert and company.[34]

By then, Sidney Hillman's ACWA had largely pushed Rickert's union right out of the men's garment industry. Analyzing the British experience, Noah London concluded that councils need not replace the unions. They did not in Russia, so why would they need to in America? He saw the main problem as an organic conflict between business agents, the backbone of the garment unions, and shop stewards' committees, the foundation stone of the council movement. When radicals briefly took control over Local 25 in the fall of 1919 and moved to implement a shop delegate system, the business agents, key to how that local operated, fought them tooth and nail. In most American unions, elected union officials appointed business agents, who carried out union business on a day-to-day basis. Electoral procedures were sometimes democratic and sometimes not democratic at all, the Jewish garment unions being a good example.

The shop delegate system in the garment industry, modeled after the British shop delegates movement, paralleled the way the Russian workers councils operated, or at least were supposed to operate. Workplace by workplace, on the shop floor, each shop would elect its delegates. If there was more than one union in a shop due to craft differences, all the workers in the shop would elect the delegates together. The shop committees were thus a step on the path of amalgamating craft unions into industrial unions – a central slogan of radical union oppositionists in the 1920s, and partially achieved by the CIO in the 1930s. The delegates, recallable on the shop floor at any time, would form a local-wide shop delegate council, which in turn would appoint all union officers and could recall them at any time. All elections would be 'stand up and be counted', without secret balloting, which would magnify the voices of the tongue-tied, the timid and the conservative. Instead the councils would be dominated by the loud, the aggressive, the militants, the radicals, once the weight of bureaucratic intimidation from the top down had been lifted.

This was also quite similar to the structure of the Soviet Communist Party of 'democratic centralism', again in theory, not necessarily practice. All unions by their nature have centralized decision-making. As a thoughtful union official said to me once, a union is like an army. Its purpose is to do battle with the employers. So the rank-and-file soldiers need to do what their officers tell them during battle. However, whereas all unions need to have centralized decision-making to win battles with centralized employers, unions unlike armies can be

34 London, 'Di bavegung far kounsils in di yunyons', *Kamf*, June 27, 1919.

democratic, although often they are not. So the 'democratic centralism' of the shop delegate system was tremendously popular in the garment unions.

In Great Britain, union leaders successfully co-opted the shop stewards' movement, incorporating stewards' committees into their structure. Such reforms gave British unions a reputation for militancy and democracy that lasted until Margaret Thatcher broke the National Union of Mineworkers in the 1980s. Likewise, in Noah's own old union the ACWA, Sidney Hillman gave radicals free rein for a while. Miril's ILGWU was less flexible.[35]

Labor activists then saw European immigrants like those in the foreign-language federations as the key radical factor. Noah London had personal experience in highway construction, where the overwhelming majority of the laborers were immigrants. He explained in *Der Kamf* that union organization was very difficult there. The workforce was migrant, seasonal and divided into many different language groups. Nonetheless, 'the New York subway workers are organized in a pretty strong union ...' Uniquely, unlike any other early white Communist, he believed that black workers could play a vanguard role in an American revolution: 'We have seen that they are worse paid and worse treated than any foreigners are treated anywhere, and at the same time the blacks occupy a very important place in the industry of the country ... a significant number [of foreign whites and native blacks] do not have the illusion that this is the best country in the world, the land of equal opportunity ... They can organize themselves very powerfully and fight for their rights'.[36]

The theoretical concept implicit here is that the working class has a vanguard and a rearguard. The revolutionary party should not be just the 'party of the whole class', in accordance with the classic formulation of the Second International of Karl Kautsky, Eugene Debs and the whole pre-World-War I Socialist movement. What may sound nowadays like an abstract political point was politically all important in the Socialist movement in the early twentieth century. The idea that the party of the working class should represent the vanguard of that class, not the whole class, was seen widely as a distinguishing feature of 'Leninism' and Communism. The notion that the party should instead represent the whole working class was seen as a distinguishing feature of Socialism *from* Communism.

This article reflected his abrupt political motion from the Jewish Bund and its American Jewish Socialist Federation into the new-fledged world Commun-

35 David Gurowsky, 'Factional Disputes within the ILGWU: 1919–1928'. Ph.D. diss., SUNY Binghamton, 1978, 52–62.

36 London, 'Der oyslendisher element in der produktsie un in der bavegung', *Kamf*, Aug. 1, 1919, and Aug. 8, 1919.

ist movement. But Noah London was still a Bund Bolshevik rather than a Lenin Bolshevik, and thus someone whose eyes were always turned to the masses and their welfare. For him, the distinction between vanguard and rearguard was economic and sociological, not ideological. The idea classically though not quite accurately associated with Lenin and Leninism that socialism was something to be brought into the working class from outside by originally bourgeois intellectuals was profoundly alien to Noah London.[37] London's admiration for Lenin was as a practical politician and revolutionary leader more than as a theorist. London was a pragmatist, never much concerned with the abstract theoretical musings of others. After all, he had some of his own.

London's unique concept of black workers as a potential vanguard for an American workers' revolution was expressed in *Der Kamf* as a wave of bloody 'race riots' inflamed cities all across America. During the 'Red Summer' of 1919, native Americans and less recent European immigrants engaged in assaults nationwide against the tidal wave of black emigrants from the South pulled north by wartime job opportunities. The Slavic and Baltic immigrants who were the prime constituency of the brand new communist movement usually tried to stay out of the way. In Chicago, Irish gangs donned blackface and set fire to the homes of Polish and Lithuanian immigrants in an unsuccessful attempt to get them to participate. The bloody conflict between often unionized white workers and black workers traditionally excluded from the AFL destroyed William Z. Foster's attempt to bring black stockyard workers into his union organizing efforts.

The use of black workers as strikebreakers in the nationwide wave of labor rebellion of 1919 cemented anti-black prejudices among these new arrivals to American shores. The new Communist Parties spoke out against anti-black violence, but they had no concept that racial oppression was a key problem American radicals needed to address. As late as 1925, Communist leader Charles Ruthenberg would berate black Communists for supporting the 'Great Migration' of black people to the north, still primarily seeing them as backward peasants and potential strikebreakers. It took the Communist International a decade of effort to pressure American Communists to take up the struggle for black liberation.[38]

American Socialism was largely indifferent to black oppression, treating it as a minor aspect of a broader class struggle. Some prominent Socialists were

---

37 Lars Lih, *Lenin Rediscovered*: What Is to Be Done? *in Context* (Chicago: Haymarket, 2008 [2005]).

38 Jacob Zumoff, *The Communist International and US Communism, 1919–1929* (Chicago: Haymarket, 2015), 291–2, 312.

explicit racists. Others were anti-racist, but their practical attitude was best expressed in Debs's infamous dictum that Socialists 'have nothing special to offer the Negro people'. According to Noah London, 'The Socialist Party never had any great urge to speak up for any idea or group discredited in the eyes of general public opinion and those who propagate it – the paid-off press, the paid-off colleges and churches. The Socialist Party never sought to organize the Negro in the South, because he had no right to vote'.[39]

As he mused a few years later, presaging 'whiteness studies' theorists, 'who are the white people in America? Jews, Italians, Poles, Syrians and all those who come from poor, backward corners of the continent are not reckoned as white people by the simple American public'.[40] While the Londons were living in Harlem, and on William Street in Buffalo, black people were moving in. Jews were less hostile to them than were other white Americans, facilitating the process. The similarities between the black situation in America and the Jewish situation in the Tsarist Jewish Pale were clear. Moreover, Jewish immigrants often understood America better than other Eastern European émigrés, who spoke less English and acquired citizenship less quickly.

Many young radical enthusiasts thought that an American revolution was around the corner in 1919. London knew better. In his opinion,

> as long as [the American worker] feels he is one rung higher than the foreign immigrant, as long as the immigrant is willing to pay the price of the native workers' privileges, no reconstruction of the capitalist system can take place … The path to Communism in America is to Bolshevize the millions of foreign workers, the millions of persecuted black workers, and through them to pull in the remaining workers in struggle for the dictatorship of the true proletariat …[41]

The concept that black workers might turn out to be the vanguard of an American workers revolution is common nowadays among the sparse ranks of would-be socialist revolutionaries in America. In 1919 it was unique to Noah London, at least among white radicals.

London, unlike Bittelman, did not believe that the foreign language federations needed to control the movement. He opposed their project to immediately form a new Communist party. He argued for tactical flexibility, writing

39 London, 'Der oyslendisher element'.

40 London, 'Der goy iz trif, zayn grobeyzn is ober kshr', *Freiheit*, May 2, 1924.

41 London, 'Der oyslendisher element'.

that 'we cannot always copy what other Communist parties do in different circumstances' in the last article he was allowed to publish in *Der Kamf*.[42]

American Communism was first organized at the height of the great 1919 strike wave, which gave newfledged American Communists the notion that America was on the brink of a revolution. The federationist Communist Party, the CPA, held its founding convention in Chicago just a few weeks before Chicago steelworkers hit the bricks – and just a few months after Chicago's 'Red Summer'. The Socialist Party managed to expel two-thirds of its membership in the 'Pink Terror'. Left-wing delegates who were denied admission, including entire delegations from thirteen states, staged a third convention and formed the Communist Labor Party. Noah London was ejected from the *Der Kamf* board for supporting this CLP, and he took few Left Wingniks with him. His new party did not bother to set up a Jewish section or issue a Yiddish journal. He instead participated in the general movement until the Palmer raids, serving on its New York City executive.[43]

Both new parties believed that the task of the hour was to turn the strikes sweeping the nation into revolutionary mass action. In his John Reed memorial article London wrote that:

> Right after the Chicago convention ... there was a conference of local Communist Labor Party activists in New York. The writer of this article defended the position that the party must attend to the daily economic struggles of the working class ... Then John Reed spoke out scornfully against half-baked Communists trying to make a revolution through a long-lasting historical process, going through their foolish struggles together with the workers, instead of ... pulling the great masses in behind the vanguard through immediate resolute action.[44]

5 The Red Scare, the Steel Strike and Wilson's War for Democracy

But Reed gravely misjudged the political situation. The ten days that shook the world touched off revolutions elsewhere, but a backlash as well. Counterrevolutionaries in Central Europe blamed Jewish conspiracy, and anti-Semitism took on malignant dimensions. When the backlash crossed the Atlantic it mingled

42 London, 'Vegen der grindung fun a nayer partey', *Kamf*, Aug. 1, 1919; and 'Printsip un taktik', Aug. 22, 1919.

43 London, *Biograficheskii ocherk*, l. 6.

44 London, *Der Emes*, Oct. 28, 1921.

with anti-immigrant hysteria to create the Great Red Scare of 1919–1921. In the words of Wilson's Attorney General A. Mitchell Palmer:

> Bolshevism has looted Russia not only of its material strength, but of its moral force. A small clique of outcasts from the East Side of New York has attempted this, with what success we all know. Because a disreputable alien – Leon Bronstein, the man who now calls himself Trotsky – can inaugurate a reign of terror ... because this lowest of all types known to New York can sleep in the Tsar's bed ... should Americans be swayed by such doctrines? ... My information showed that Communism in this country was an organization of thousands of aliens, who were direct allies of Trotsky. Aliens of the same misshapen cast of mind and indecencies of character ...[45]

Jewish domination of American Communism was music of the future at this point. Most Communists were gentile factory workers, craftsmen and miners, European immigrants but not Jews from the sweatshops of the Lower East Side. The steel strike graphically demonstrated that these immigrant Communists were isolated from their constituency. Their stance against racist pogroms in Chicago and elsewhere probably did not help, in the midst of widespread black scabbing.

The Bolshevik revolution coincided with election day across much of America, and Socialist candidates did quite well in Chicago. But by 1918, immigrant steelworkers were buying Liberty Bonds and crowding into union lodges with names like Democracy and Old Glory. The mantra of steel organizer William Z. Foster was that Wilson's war for democracy abroad required industrial democracy at home.[46] The foreign-language federationists could only play the role of Cassandras. The 1919 steel strike, the highpoint of the greatest strike wave America had ever seen, was the opposite of everything they stood for.

But steel was the beating heart of American industry. Buoyed by victory abroad, steel magnates were well prepared to crush the enemy at home, the immigrants who sweated inside their mills and now were picketing outside. In the euphoric atmosphere of 1919 they easily persuaded the general public that the strike was an outbreak of Bolshevism on American soil, regardless of patriotic protestations. Strikers were terrorized with the methods Palmer

---

45 A. Mitchell Palmer, 'The Case against the "Reds"', *The Forum* 63 (Feb. 1920): 175.

46 Weinstein, *Decline of Socialism*, 157; David Brody, *Steelworkers in America, Steelworkers in America: The Nonunion Era* (New York: Harper & Row, 1969), 220–3; McCartin, *Labor's Great War*, 156–7.

was applying to reds. The US army was mobilized, complete with field artillery and truck-mounted machine guns. In Cleveland, where future Communist leader Ruthenberg had run a remarkably successful 'red Socialist' mayoral campaign in 1917, two pickets were killed by what was reported to be machine gun fire from inside a struck plant. Sabotage by squabbling craft unions forcibly lassoed together in Foster's official strike committee applied the coup de grace. One of the greatest strikes in American history went down to defeat as the new American Communist parties were just getting off the ground.[47]

Now that the US army had made Europe safe for democracy, American business leaders made industrial democracy safe for America. They reinterpreted it once again as company welfare unionism. Immigrants turned away from unions, retreating into ethnic networks for protection against their employers and the outside world.[48] Radical immigrants retreated into their foreign-language federations in similar fashion, sinking into insular sectarianism. But the Communists gained one great victory. The strike experience convinced the most famous labor organizer in America of the errors of his ways. It pushed William Z. Foster into the arms of the Communist Party.

5.1 *Into the underground: America's 'Judeo-Bolshevik conspiracy'*

The Jewish Communist Federation represented most of what substance lay behind A. Mitchell Palmer's Judeo-Bolshevik nightmare. Its founding convention was a fairly impressive affair. An audience of more than 1,400 packed the opening session at the Continental Hotel in Philadelphia. National secretary Meyer Lunin reported that the circulation of *Der Kamf* had passed that of *Naye Velt* and defended Noah London's removal from its editorial board. A fund drive began for a Yiddish daily to compete with the *Forward*. Morris Holtman, another graduate of the Cooper Union engineering program, replaced London as Bittelman's co-editor. Because of London's departure *Der Kamf* was renamed *Funken* (Sparks) after Lenin's *Iskra*.[49]

The JCF's initial successes reflected the explosion of militancy in the garment industry. A few weeks later the Palmer Raids descended on the new organization. London later estimated that 'if it were not for the epoch of illegality, the persecutions and arrests, surely a daily newspaper would have been created

47 Brody, *Steelworkers in America*, 231–62; '1919 Steel Strike', in *Encyclopedia of Cleveland History*, ech.case.edu.

48 Lizabeth Cohen, *Making a New Deal: Industrial Workers in Chicago, 1919–1939* (Cambridge: Cambridge University Press, 1990), 53–97.

49 *Kamf*, Oct. 1919, *passim*.

then'.[50] Holtman, a capable organizer, became a central figure in the underground, though his primary contribution would be a sincere but misguided romanticism. A few years later he would tell the tale of how the JCF was driven underground:

> It was impossible to go on with the work like before. Everything was destroyed and broken in the office of the federation, and there was a real catastrophe in the editorial office ... It did not really occur to anybody that we would have to become an illegal organization ... But the second wave of raids, with a thousand arrests over the whole country, put us into a state of illegality before we had worked out any plans for an illegal organization.[51]

The Workers Council, headquartered in the Russian People's House near Union Square, was raided as well. According to its protest leaflet:

> Two rows of detectives stood by the door with blackjacks and revolvers in their hands and each of our comrades was forced to run the gauntlet. In the hall were the so-called guardians of 'law and order' ... Many of our comrades ... were thrown from the second and third floors. In the rear by the exit, they drew a hail of blows and blackjacks on their heads from the hired murder bands of capitalism.[52]

The finishing slogan of the flyer was 'Long Live the General Strike!' Unfortunately, calling a strike against the raids was not practical. Workers Council attempts to independently organize garment strikes had never succeeded before and did not do so now. The movement was forced to transform itself into an opposition movement within the Jewish garment unions – with Bittelman's full approval.

Workers Council advocate Noah London was of course now in danger. During the 1905 Revolution he had avoided Siberian exile or worse by hiding out with a cousin in the Pripet marshes, returning to underground work when the coast was clear. He repeated this experience in America. According to his Moscow industrial workbook, he managed to return to his old job as a highway engineer in Buffalo in April 1920. It seems that he fled to Buffalo during the Palmer raids, where his reputation was more respectable. But this worked out

50 London, 'Di anzager fun der freiheit', *Freiheit*, Dec. 28, 1924.
51 Holtman, 'Vi mir zeynen arunter in keler', *Freiheit*, April 1, 1923.
52 'A ruf tsu di arbeyter!', Box 84, U.S.T.C., YIVO.

only briefly. He soon took refuge with his older sister Chana and her husband Philip Weitzman – the same brother-in-law whose factory he unsuccessfully tried to unionize years before. According to Abraham Weitzman, five years old at the time: 'In 1920 there were the Palmer Raids, and by this time [Noah London] was a big shot in the Communist Party, and he was on the list to be shipped back to Europe … My family bought a big house in Linden, New Jersey, with a big attic, and the attic was fixed up, and he stayed in the attic for several months …'[53] These were not luxury accommodations. In a pamphlet written a decade later on the Siberian Birobidzhan project, infamous for insect infestation, London remarked that 'being one summer … in a little New Jersey town near New York, I had worse mosquito problems than in Birobidzhan'.[54]

Meanwhile Miril went back to work as a draper in a union dress shop. The June 1920 JCF convention protocols describe a protest by women from the Bronx JCF branch against lack of democracy in the organization. Miril surely was involved in this affair, and likely was its leader.[55]

5.2 *Underground Communism: Romance and Reality*

Underground existence was a terrible shock for the new Communist movement. It collapsed. Before the raids the two new parties claimed a combined membership of over 50,000. After the raids, probably no more than some 10,000 remained. Forced underground, both parties made a virtue out of necessity. Noah London avoided arrest unheroically but successfully. As soon as he returned to active duty, he would reclaim a prominent position in the Jewish Communist underground. However, his Russian and American experiences gave him an aversion to the romantic undergroundism expressed by fellow Cooper Union engineer Morris Holtman.

1920 was the darkest hour for American Communism. Under government persecution, English-speaking Socialist Party branches automatically pushed into the Communist Labor Party by the moderates' 'Pink Terror' melted away. The foreign-language federations held up somewhat better, if only because Hoover's agents rarely spoke their languages. Driven in on themselves, the new parties got caught up in destructive infighting. Well-founded fears of government infiltration and manipulation exacerbated a general atmosphere of distrust and paranoia.

---

53 Abraham Weitzman interview.

54 Noah London, *Mit der Amerikaner ekspeditsie keyn Biro-bidzhan* (Kharkov: Tsentralfarlag, alukrainishe opteylung, 1930).

55 'Lichnyy listok po uchetu kadrov', 1933, RGASPI, f. 17, op. 100, d. 126451, l. 3; 'Barikht fun der tsveyter konvenshon', RG 1400 (Bund Collection), Box 16, folder 62, 14–15, YIVO.

The federationist CPA went through an ugly split, marked by vicious personal recriminations. Ruthenberg, the most prominent former Socialist in the new party, branded the federation leaders as 'super-Bolshevik talk conspirators'. A certain individual named Belsky or Fisher, who apparently was a police agent, played the key role in this split.[56] The Ruthenberg wing of the CPA joined with Noah London and John Reed's Communist Labor Party to create a United Communist Party (UCP) at a convention in Michigan in May 1920. In the new UCP, federations were replaced by language sections, with very limited autonomy. Bittelman's Jewish Communist Federation vacillated between Ruthenberg and the other foreign-language federations and briefly attempted to go it alone as an independent organization. According to Bittelman: 'In the Jewish federation, most of us in the leadership ... were very much conscious of our Party's isolation ... We had ... a large number of trade unionists and these wanted Communist policies that would enable them to be active in their locals ... But we couldn't accept the destruction of the federation autonomy ...'[57]

The JCF collapsed at its second and last convention, where Miril perhaps led a Bronx women's rebellion. In Chicago, where Fisher-Belsky was the CPA leader, the JCF chapter issued a call to boycott the convention. The Chicago rebels branded Bittelman's idea of an independent JCF as 'a new form of Zionism ... in the Communist movement'. Most delegates who did attend wanted to stay with the CPA. Bittelman did not.[58]

5.3 *Undergroundism in Action in the Jewish Movement*

At this point Noah London was still in hiding in New Jersey. The leadership of the pro-UCP Jewish group fell into the hands of Fisher-Belsky's protégé Leon Hendin, a young Jewish dentist, who was possible as a Communist leader only in the hothouse atmosphere of the underground. His unrealism and irresponsibility exemplified the worst aspects of the undergroundism that London would fight against, and his story is worth examining as a cautionary tale. Hendin led the Baltimore Communist Party of America in the fall of 1919. When a Bureau of Intelligence agent was sent to interview him, he volunteered the identity of the party treasurer and the location of the party headquarters. When

56 Epstein, *The Jew and Communism*, 45–7. This work contains a number of errors. However, UCP CEC minutes in the Comintern archive and Department of Justice records confirm the key points of the Fisher-Belsky story recounted to Epstein by Leon Hendin.

57 Bittelman, 'Things I Have Learned', 335.

58 'Vegen a konvenshon fun der idisher K. P.'. and 'Idishe komunizm', *Der Komunist* 1, June 1, 1920; 'Barikht fun der tsvayter konvenshon ...'

his home was raided a treasure trove of membership lists and meeting minutes was seized. When the party went underground Hendin decided to restrict the Baltimore leadership to a small circle of trusted individuals – one of whom was a BI informant. The local party's situation improved remarkably when he left town for Chicago.[59]

At the UCP founding convention in the spring of 1920, Hendin was a vociferous advocate of 'armed insurrection'. It is easy to see why the agent Fisher-Belsky selected Hendin to run the party's Jewish affairs. The biggest controversy at the convention was over union policy. A young ex-Wobbly from Kansas, James P. Cannon, led a revolt by delegates with practical union experience. Cannon argued that 'the AF of L must be considered not from the side of the Gompers officialdom, that industrial unionism was having a development in many fields aside from the IWW'. This debate began the UCP's recovery from the worst vices of naïve ultra-leftism of which Louis Hendin was a human embodiment.[60]

In *Der Komunist*, the underground UCP Yiddish journal he edited, Hendin celebrated the extreme formulations his caucus managed to insert in the UCP program, such as a call to 'destroy the AFL'. His Jewish action program advocated boycotting all Jewish relief efforts in Eastern Europe, even if they benefitted Jews in the Soviet Union. It had not a word to say about what the UCP ought to do in the Jewish garment unions.[61]

At a summer 1920 Jewish conference the UCP took over Bittelman's *Funken* and transformed it. The new *Proletaryer* was intended to be a 'shop paper', an agitational Jewish labor journal, complementing the underground journal, the *Komunist*. The delegates refused to elect either Hendin or Bittelman as editor. For lack of another candidate Hendin became editor anyway, despite harsh criticism of his conduct. The *Proletaryer* letter files, seized and preserved for posterity by the Department of Justice, include a bitter protest from Bittelman's New York UCP Jewish group. It complained that his *Komunist* was 'simply rotten, both as regards matter and language'. When Hendin botched a Yiddish edition of Lenin's *State and Revolution* and the print run had to be destroyed, he was forced to resign from the UCP Central Executive Committee

59 Vernon L. Pedersen, *The Communist Party in Maryland, 1919–57* (Urbana: University of Illinois Press, 2001), 18–29.

60 'Y.F.' [Isaac Ferguson], 'The Convention of Revolutionists', *The Communist* (UCP) 1, June 12, 1920; Cannon, 'The Revival of the Socialist Party', in *The Left Opposition in the US, 1928–1931: Writings and Speeches*, ed. Fred Stanton (New York: Monad Press, 1981), 233.

61 'G. Delion' [Hendin], 'Problemen fun tsuzamenfahr', *Der Komunist*, July 15, 1920.

(CEC). Party leaders looked around for another Jewish editor,[62] and they found Noah London, who had escaped from his brother-in-law's mosquito-infested attic.

5.4 *Underground Communism and the Shop Delegate Leagues in the Garment Unions*

The Jewish Communist underground was far from isolated from the labor movement – unlike its gentile counterpart. London later commented that previous Jewish Left journals were hodge-podges of Marxist speculation and European revolutions. But the *Proletaryer* and even its federationist rival *Der Kamf* 'showed signs of being newspapers and not article collections, because the movement had gone ahead and come into relationship with the daily struggle here and now'.[63] The Workers Councils successfully transformed themselves into a shop delegate movement within the unions, with Bittelman's approval, and Noah London's as well.

The United Communist Party issued two labor journals. Cannon edited the other one, the English-language *Toiler*, predecessor of the *Daily Worker*. The UCP reported to the Comintern that 'the policy of the labor organs is to promulgate workers' control of production. Through the organization of shop committees we try to coordinate this work ... in the clothing workers unions in particular ... we have made our greatest inroads'. The *Proletaryer* industrial life column eagerly invited 'articles and correspondence from shop and factory workers'.[64] According to Hendin's editorial policy statement in the first issue:

> The *Proletaryer* will devote itself to the daily industrial struggle of the working class ... It will always propagandize the thought that the only way the workers can free themselves is to declare a great general political strike ... When the shop committees from a specific industry are united, they can all act together in a moment of crisis. United in community councils, they can transform themselves into workers' councils in a time of social revolution ...[65]

---

62 UCP CEC minutes 7–1, 31–1921, B. of I. case files, f. 202600-1775, r. 939, doc. 58; *Proletaryer* letterfile, r. 940, doc. 872; CEC minutes Nov. 10–13, 1921, doc. 500; UCP Bulletin #4, 8, 9–1920, CPUSA microfilms, op. 1, r. 2, d. 28, l. 15.

63 London, *Freiheit*, Dec. 28, 1924.

64 'To the Executive Committee of the Communist International', 'Paul Holt' [Nov. 1920 by internal evidence], CPUSA microfilms, Reel 1, d. 25, l. 4; 7; 'Fun industrielen leben', *Proletaryer*, Nov. 1, 1921.

65 'Di polisi fun *Proletaryer*', *Proletaryer*, Sept. 1, 1920.

Musings about revolutionary general strikes and 'community' workers councils were beside the point. Reality imposed a simple, workable union policy: to support the shop delegate movement. Every issue of the *Proletaryer* published statements, letters and manifestos from the shop delegate leagues that it and its rival *Der Kamf* were backing.[66] In practice, Communists found themselves working together in the Jewish garment unions, which already were becoming the bulwark of Communist strength and influence in the labor movement. CPA and UCP union policies were similar, except that CPA union groups collaborating with other union insurgents were enjoined to 'carry out their activities without revealing their identity'.[67]

The insurgency was rapidly gaining ground in 1920 and 1921, especially in Miril's ILGWU Local 25. When Local 25 voted to transform itself according to the shop delegate program, conflict came to a boil. The national officers decided to break up the local a few weeks after the *Proletaryer* started appearing. Their theory was that the radicalism of Local 25 was merely a heritage of the 1909–10 'Uprising of the 20,000' in the declining waistmakers' trade. Troublemakers could be stamped out in the rising dress trade, where Miril worked, if it were freed from waistmaker influence.[68] The *Proletaryer* printed a fiery shop delegates league proclamation in response:

> The workers in the industry have supported the shop delegate system in an overwhelming majority ... But the bosses of the International ... decided that this is 'undemocratic and unconstitutional' ... In the name of 'democracy' workers were packed off to the battlefield to fall in a capitalist war! In the name of 'democracy' Gompers and his clique declared war against Soviet Russia ... In the name of 'democracy' the best fighters for the American workers were murdered and caged in prison ... We must adopt the shop delegate system in the name of *proletarian democracy*.[69]

There was no longer much commonality between Wilsonist and Leninist conceptions of industrial (or proletarian) democracy.

66 *Proletaryer, passim.*

67 Communist union flyers collection, RG 117, U.S.T.C., Box 84, YIVO; 'Resolution on Communist Nuclei within the Unions', attached to CPA CEC minutes, Nov. 20–21, 1920, CPUSA microfilms, r. 2, del. 31, l. 48.

68 Gurowsky, 'Factional Disputes within the ILGWU', 64–5; Levine, *Women's Garment Workers*, 354.

69 'Tsu di veyst un dresmakher', *Proletaryer*, Dec. 1, 1920.

The breakup of Local 25 weakened the union in Miril's waist and dress industry. The shop delegate leagues, surely with her participation, nonetheless took over all the new splintered locals. The *Proletaryer* chronicled the spread of the movement to the cloakmakers' trade, which started falling into leftist hands as well. Jewish Socialist Federation supporters started joining forces with the far left. Cloakmaker leader Louis Hyman had been an enthusiast for Wilson's war for democracy, and had led the fight to expel Noah's Left Wing from the SP. He now wrote in the *Naye Velt* that 'the [shop committee] idea is also popular in the cloakmaker locals … True, the propagandists … are tactful and not as extreme as those among the waistmakers …' The shop delegate movement already had the majority of the membership behind it by the spring of 1921 in the New York dress, shirtwaist and cloakmaker locals, as the Jewish Communists were moving out from underground isolation. They included more than half of the national membership of the ILGWU.[70]

6 The *Proletaryer*, the Russian Civil War and the Jewish Socialist Federation

When Noah London took over the *Proletaryer*, he wrote that 'while there may possibly be some technical changes, the spirit of the time, the direction, the principles will stay as rock-solid as always'.[71] The first change he introduced was an aggressive orientation towards winning over JSF activists like Hyman. Bringing them into the Communist fold was a vital necessity, to unite the growing rank-and-file insurgency. London wrote an open letter to the JSF membership, appealing especially to union activists to

> take the so-called Jewish unions away from the American Federation of Labor … Perhaps, you would have already counseled [them] to free themselves … but for your illusion that the 'weak' Jewish unions needed the protection. You have long freed yourself from this illusion. You have found out how when a mass strike takes place under the protection of the AFL, like the steel strike, it is spoiled magnificently.[72]

70 Levine, *Women's Garment Workers*, 350–1; *Proletaryer*, *passim*; Hyman, 'Der kamf far "shap kamites" in unzere yunyons', *Naye Velt*, May 27, 1921.

71 'Iberblikn' (editorial notes), *Proletaryer*, Feb. 1, 1921, p. 8.

72 Paiezon [London], 'An ofener brif fun a gevezenes mitglid', *Proletaryer*, Feb. 1, 1921.

The JSF was essentially still an American subsidiary of the Jewish Bund. But Russian Jewish Socialists who supported Kerensky in 1917 were now mostly going over to Bolshevism, including the Russian Bund. The *Proletaryer* reported extensively on Bund affairs, hoping to encourage the Jewish Socialist Federation to follow suit. Meanwhile Moissaye Olgin, its most popular spokesman, returned from a six-month tour of revolutionary Russia on behalf of the *Forward*. The excitement of the revolution and the influence of old comrades was transforming his own political views. Olgin's old friend Max Goldfarb, formerly *Forward* labor editor, now was Red Army general David Petrovsky. In 1917, Olgin had accused Lenin of being a German spy. Now, Olgin became the most consistent supporter of reunification with the Communists within the Jewish Socialist Federation.[73]

American Socialists had enthusiastically supported the Bolshevik Revolution from the beginning, except for a few Menshevik and Bundist emigrés. The Socialist Party even applied unsuccessfully for membership in the Communist International. But as the political climate shifted rightwards, party leaders began to distance themselves from Bolshevism. The leftward-moving Jewish Socialist Federation, however, now wanted to accept Moscow's terms. When the SP finally rejected the Comintern once and for all, the JSF started looking for the exit door.[74]

But both SP and JSF were rapidly hemorrhaging members. The JSF in particular was suffering from guilt by association with discredited Socialist leaders of the garment unions. The final JSF convention voted in September 1921 to break with the party. Its leader Salutsky believed he had no choice. He proclaimed that 'if we didn't start talking about splitting from the SP, not only wouldn't we have 73 delegates here, we wouldn't have 73 members'. But unlike Olgin, he had no desire to unite with the Communists.[75] The convention issued a manifesto calling on Jewish workers to 'transfer the struggle into every union, every local, every Workmen's Circle branch ... Divide the sound elements from the sick, the viable elements from the rotten, the fighters from the petrified, the Socialists from the pseudo-Socialists'. Old Guard loyalists

---

73 Daniel Soyer, 'Soviet Travel and the Making of an American Jewish Communist: Moissaye Olgin's Trip to Russia in 1920–1921', *American Communist History* 4, no. 1 (June 2005): 1–20.

74 Michels, 'Socialism with a Jewish Face: The Origins of the Yiddish-Speaking Communist Movement in the United States, 1907–1923', in *Yiddish and the Left*, ed. Gennady Estraikh and Mikhail Krutikov (Oxford: Legenda, 2001), vol. 3, 36–7.

75 Paiezon [London], 'Revolt fun der idisher radikaler inteligents', *Der Emes*, Sept. 16, 1921; Michels 'Socialism with a Jewish Face', 37–8; J. Holmes and A. Lebowitz, 'Jewish Socialist Federation', *Encyclopedia of the American Left*, 2d ed. (New York: Oxford University Press, 1998), 404–5.

formed a feeble 'Jewish Socialist *farband*'. The reformed JSF had fewer dues-payers than the recently-reunited Jewish Communist Federation.[76] Its birth was significant only because a key component of the *apparatus* of the Jewish labor movement had gone left. What was to prevent the rest from following suit? Was a 'revolution on the Jewish street' on the agenda in America as well?

7 The Proletaryer and the ACWA

Communist and JSF union activists were working together in the shop delegate movement, laying the basis for unification. London's unity campaign helped lubricate the process. But the situation was complex in Noah's old union, the ACWA. J.B. Salutsky was also known as J.B.S. Hardman, Sidney Hillman's right-hand man. The first *Proletaryer* London edited printed a denunciation of ACWA officialdom side by side with his open letter to the JSF. He wrote that 'the sincere proletarians who want to infuse the spirit of devotion and self-sacrifice into the industrial struggle have the opportunity here to express their aspirations and just grievances'. A Chicago grievance was very serious: union leaders were accusing a union activist, an ex-rabbinical student named Albert Goldman, of being a police spy![77] More than a decade later Goldman would turn up as Leon Trotsky's lawyer before the 'Dewey Commission' in Mexico during the Moscow Trials. His personal experience as a frame-up victim was surely in the back of his mind as he represented Trotsky.

Socialist ILGWU leaders believed in fighting the Communist menace by any means necessary. Hillman preferred a subtler approach. He coated the bitter pill of wage cuts and speedup with red flags, revolutionary rhetoric and trips to the Soviet Union to consult with another advocate of industrial modernity, V.I. Lenin.[78] According to one writer in the *Proletaryer*: 'Has there ever been a more 'revolutionary' workers organization than the Amalgamated? ... Has any other workers' organization taken up the cause of the wretched of the earth, including the Indians, so many times? And what's the end of it? In the ranks of the very same organization we've surpassed the American Federation of Labor by a thousand percent'.[79]

76 Frank [Noah London], 'Ver shtelt di yunyons in gefar?', *Naye Velt*, Sept. 16, 1921.
77 'Fun industrielen feld', *Proletaryer*, Feb. 1, 1921.
78 Fraser, *Labor Will Rule*, 170–7.
79 'Maksim', 'Der algemeyne krizis un der shnaydersher', *Proletaryer*, Jan. 15, 1921.

7.1 *Noah London as Communist Realist*

As a brighter springtime for the Communist underground was unfolding, London was trying to lead its Jewish branch out of underground delusions. In a speech to ILGWU activists in Schenectady in May 1921, he insisted that 'the great masses are not ready to be heroes'.[80] All across Europe workers sympathized with the Russian Revolution. His audience knew that Jews in America felt similarly. But American Jewish garment workers were not ready for revolution. What they wanted right now was higher wages, shorter hours, job security and – fire escapes. No garment worker had forgotten the Triangle Shirtwaist tragedy, in which hundreds of young women died, burning to death or jumping out of fifth-floor windows.

Radicals might think such demands were naïve, but as London put it 'a child is naïve and foolish too, the elders speak the child's language and lead him by his little hand'. The job was to begin to speak the same language as the masses. Rank-and-file workers were ready to support left-wing slogans like the shop delegate system, uniting into one big garment union, and even joining the Red Trade Union International, which ILGWU Local 25 voted to endorse the previous fall. For more far-reaching slogans it was necessary to wait until 'the great masses begin to move'.

Der Komunist, no longer edited by Louis Hendin, published a union policy statement that month that laid out a scheme to organize the Communist underground by trade instead of territory, in order to forge a 'powerful machine' to win control over the unions. A nod was given to the Workers Councils in the garment industry, which London had advocated. They lay the basis for 'industrial councils' within the Jewish Communist underground, located near the peak of the organizational pyramid, beneath the industrial department head appointed by the UCP top leadership. But when the statement got down to the brass tacks of how to take over the unions, its answers were a bit schizophrenic.

Reflecting Noah London's realism, it stated that 'in peaceful times the masses cannot move too fast …' In general, it recommended that Communists should work together with 'radical and progressive elements' to oust the bureaucrats in 'bourgeois reactionary' unions. But then, still reflecting the influence of Hendin's ultimatism, it stated that after non-Communist reformers won office with Communist help, Communist-supported caucuses in the unions needed to confine their membership to advocates of proletarian dictatorship and 'abolition of trade unionism'. Referring specifically to allegedly Socialist unions like

80 'Organizirte arbeyt in di yunyons', *Proletaryer*, May 15, 1921. Speaker unidentified but clearly London.

the ILGWU, it advised that 'we will use every opportunity to expose to the workers their real character and their chicanery'.[81] This policy statement, despite its contradictions, was a possible basis for the new tactic of organizing rank-and-file opposition within the Jewish garment unions, rather than outside. It also left room for alliances with 'progressive' union leaders, notably Sidney Hillman of the ACWA.

In June 1921, as the party was emerging from underground isolation, Noah London believed that Communists needed a more realistic attitude to American politics, which differed from European politics, as well as a more practical approach to the labor movement. In his opinion, American Communists had failed to seriously address some fundamental questions. Just what is government in America? What do Americans think about politics? And what should that mean for Communist election policies?[82]

During the underground days Communists had boycotted elections altogether. According to London: 'Now comes the American agency of the Communist International, under the influence perhaps of Lenin's annihilating critique of infantile diseases of left wing communism, and demands that American Communist candidates carry out a campaign in the coming mayoral elections …' Zinoviev's emissary to the American Party that spring had forced down its throat the unpopular decision to run Benjamin Gitlow for mayor in the New York elections in the fall of 1921. Even after Gitlow had been ruled off the ballot by the courts as a Communist, this campaign was a miserable flop. Simply to garner the necessary number of signatures to put other candidates of the party's electoral front on the ballot, professionals had to be hired, as the membership voted no with their feet. As the official campaign committee dolorously reported, 'much criticism was offered by our members against the immediate planks of the platform and for this reason considerable trouble was encountered in its distribution, as many of our members refused to take them out'.[83] The movement, Noah London thought, had gone from left-wing to right-wing childhood sicknesses, because it was copying programs for other countries under external influence.

Both Communist Parties had argued in 1920 that running candidates for any executive office was against communist principles. This was also the position of the founding manifesto of the Jewish Left Wing, which London had signed in the spring of 1919. If elected, such candidates would be compelled to enforce

81 'Unzer arbayt in di yunyons', *Der Komunist* no. 6, May 1921.

82 'Der Amerikaner shtat un radikale parlamentarishe aktsion', *Proletaryer*, May 15, June 20, and June 27, 1921.

83 See marxists.org/history/usa/parties/cpusa/1921/12/1201-lindgren-wlcampaign.pdf.

capitalist law and order. That was certainly the experience with Socialist mayors, a number of whom were still in office. In 1921, election of Communist mayors in America was not, however, something to worry about.

London argued instead that Communists needed to base their electoral tactics on an understanding of how America was different from Europe. In Europe, the state was powerful. The people had illusions in government as their protector, and parliament as the voice of democracy. Lenin emphasized the importance of participating in elections and parliament in order to expose the truth to the people. In America, where government was relatively feeble and politicians were held in contempt, the problem was not the state, but the social power of the capitalist class.

> The numerous middle-sized capitalists, the control of business over the means of transportation, telegraph lines, weapon factories and arsenals, its complete control over food, its direct and complete control over the press, the churches and colleges – its, not that of the state. That is the power of the bourgeoisie ... In America everyone knows that the state is an employee of Wall Street, but the masses do not see this as a wrong, because they see Wall Street as a necessary evil. With Wall Street there is business, without Wall Street not.[84]

What conclusion did London draw from this somewhat Gramscian flourish? That the best and only reason for radicals to participate in elections in America was as a vehicle to spread socialist ideas. The central focus of Communist activity had to be fighting American capitalism where it was most vulnerable, on the economic front. Therefore trade unionism and shop delegate councils were not just a tactic for Communists to gain support from the masses, but the central strategy of struggle.

8 Uniting the Jewish Communists

The JCF trade union policy statement appeared in the last issue of the underground paper, as the two Communist parties were preparing to unite under pressure from the Comintern. London supported unification, but took the occasion to publish an article in the same issue arguing in sociological detail that the Russian Federation and most of the other Slavic federations, due to

84 Ibid., June 27, 1921.

their marginality in America and sometimes dubious social composition, were playing a negative role in the communist movement – whereas his Jewish Federation with its deep roots in the Jewish working class was playing a positive one.[85] This must have raised the hackles of the other Communist Party, dominated by Slavic and Baltic immigrants. For that matter, there were quite a lot of them in the UCP as well. London saw excellent prospects for a unified Jewish organization, both wings of which, whatever their mutual hostility, had considerable garment union influence. He then made an audacious proposal to the party leadership: 'The CEC ought to consider finances for *A Daily Jewish Paper*. There is a big field, a big demand, and enough talent'. But reunification of the Jewish Communist Federation did not go smoothly, and the subsequent wrangles paralleled those in the overall movement.[86]

During its first few months, the Central Executive Committee of the newly united Communist Party was paralyzed by caucus warfare. James P. Cannon, Alexander Bittelman and the 'City College boys', Jay Lovestone and William Weinstone, formed a new leadership team that gained a narrow majority and broke the deadlock. Lovestone and Weinstone were the first representatives of a new brand of American Jewish radicalism. They did not come out of the Bund or American garment unionism. Instead, they had been leaders of the Young Peoples' Socialist League chapter at the City College of New York. CCNY, like Cooper Union, did not discriminate against Jews and did not charge tuition. After World War I it became a central vehicle for Jewish upward social mobility in New York – and for middle-class Jewish radicalism. When Ruthenberg got out of jail and Foster joined the Communist Party, they joined this new collective leadership. These six figures, none of them from the Slavic or Baltic foreign-language federations, became the central leaders of American Communism for the rest of the decade.

When the new team started making tentative steps towards legal existence, the ex-CPA federationist caucus saw themselves as victims of intrigue and treachery. The Jewish Federation was caught up in the crossfire. Ex-CPA'ers did not want Noah London on the editorial board of the Yiddish paper. A writer in *Der Kamf* called him a former zealous patriot. A disgusted London walked out of a press meeting, published a partial *mea culpa* for past political sins, and suggested to the party executive that 'the comrade from Russia immediately

85 N. Kuznetsov, 'Di Rusishe federatsies un di kom. bavegung in Amerike', *Der Komunist* no. 6, May 1, 1921. 'Kuznetsov' is a transparent if somewhat ungrammatical Russianization of his English pseudonym, 'Smith'.

86 Smith, 'Proposals Relative to the Jewish … Conference', CPUSA microfilms, r. 3, d. 48, l. 3; also r. 4, d. 75 *passim*.

take complete charge of the Jewish press affairs'. Old Jewish Socialist Federation stalwart Shachno Epstein had just been sent back to America at the behest of ex-Bundists in the Soviet Jewish Section.[87] He indeed took complete charge of Jewish press affairs, and in response, the federationist executive secretary of the united party, Dirba ('Dow'), handed in his resignation in protest.[88]

Epstein was an experienced and well-known American Yiddish journalist who had been one of the JSF's most moderate leaders. He had returned to Russia in 1917, and like most Russian Bundists he initially opposed the October Revolution. After the Bund joined the Soviet Communist Party, he became the editor of *Der Emes* (Soviet-orthography Yiddish for *The Truth* or *Pravda*, there being no definite article in Russian), the Soviet Jewish Section daily. He merged the *Proletaryer* and *Der Kamf* and, naturally, named the result *Der Emes*. He selected London and Bittelman as his associate editors. It became the most successful of the Yiddish Communist weeklies. In London's opinion, *Der Emes* was a vast improvement over all its predecessors.[89]

After Dirba resigned, the new party leadership created an 'American Labor Alliance' (ALA) as a paper-thin legal front organization. Its ostensible purpose was to sponsor public speakers, distribute literature and handle legal defense. London was appointed secretary of an essentially fictitious 'ALA Jewish Federation'. The underground was receding into the background. Dirba's undergroundists walked out of the party when an agreement was negotiated with a new 'Workers Council', a loose left-wing fringe of the Socialist Party that seized on a popular name, to found a legal Workers Party. The backbone of this Workers Council was Salutsky and Olgin's Jewish Socialist Federation. London, who had been campaigning to win JSF activists over to the Communist cause, cautiously dubbed its newfound radicalism as 'the revolt of the Jewish radical intellectuals'.[90] When the JSF went independent, the Workers Council followed suit.

Its central political slogan was: 'For an Open Communist Party'. But an open Communist party was what Dirba's caucus feared. A sizeable section of the CPUSA rose in revolt against the risky experiment of attempting to create a legal party. The immigrant Eastern European factory workers who were the bulk of

87 RGASPI, Moscow, Russia, f. 445 (hereinafter '*Evsektsiia* papers'), op. 1, d. 58 *passim*.

88 Cannon, *The First Ten Years of American Communism: Report of a Participant* (New York: Pathfinder, 1973), 75; CPUSA microfilms, r. 4, d. 75, l. 25–40; and d. 51, l. 38–55 (CEC minutes, July 27, 1921); London, *Proletaryer*, 'Perzenlikhe erklerung', June 20, 1921; and politics series, June 20 and July 4, 1921.

89 Noah London, 'Heralds of the *Freiheit*', *Freiheit*, Dec. 28, 1924.

90 London, 'Revolt fun der idisher radikaler inteligents', *Der Emes*, Nov. 16, 1921.

the party were tired of risking arrest and deportation. But undergroundism had less appeal for Jewish garment unionists.

8.1 *Noah London as Jewish Communist Leader*

The Workers Party was born on Christmas Day 1921 at the New York Labor Temple. Cannon, the keynote speaker, became its national chairman. The move to a broader party pushed him to the fore – and London as well. London took his position as head of the ALA Jewish Federation seriously. As unity negotiations with the Jewish Socialist Federation proceeded, a daily *Der Emes* campaign gathered steam. It raised considerable enthusiasm among insurgent garment workers, and delegates from 51 Jewish labor groups attended a New York City campaign conference. London, the keynote speaker, told them: 'The present-day labor press of America serves the interest of the leadership, not of the workers'.[91]

Meanwhile the JSF's attempt to go it alone was stalling. Its break with the Socialist Party allowed it to get back some of the members it was losing. But its campaign to establish a daily paper was less successful than the *Emes* campaign. The opportunity to join forces with the Communists rescued it from imminent bankruptcy.[92] When agreement was hammered out to form a joint Jewish Workers Federation, London went on tour to promote it. His *Emes* travelogue illustrated his intimate familiarity with the state of the movement. His comments on Buffalo, where he had been JSF branch secretary, are of particular interest:

> There was very little sign of the Socialists in the last elections. Nowadays Buffalo socialism has collapsed ... With the *Farband* remained – not a single worker. One of [the farbandniks] said we already have socialism in America, we only need a few improvements. He thinks the 'Workers Party' is a party for *shlimazlnikes* (losers), because none of them are businessmen ... So, many went with the federation. They are against a centralised party ... our local comrades of the ALA say that it will take a lot of trouble to make the 'new' comrades into true revolutionary fighters ...[93]

Clearly, he did not have much luck in finding common language with his old branch membership. Elsewhere he painted a far more optimistic picture of the state of the movement.

91 'Di arbeyter konferents far'n teglikhen *"Emes"*', Nov. 25, 1921.
92 Michels, 'Socialism with a Jewish Face', 39.
93 'n.l.'. [London], 'Iber shtedt un shtetlakh', *Der Emes*, Nov. 16, 1921.

His national tour put him back on the radar screen of J. Edgar Hoover's Bureau of Investigation. Information that London's next stop would be Philadelphia reached the ears of Bureau of Investigation Director Burns. He sent a message to the Philadelphia office that 'I desire that the activities of this individual be covered very closely'. Special Agent in Charge Walter C. Foster informed Burns that the ALA had gotten a police permit for London to speak at a public meeting in Philadelphia, but that he would *not* inform the local police of the 'exact nature of the meeting ... because if I did, they would, without a doubt, refuse to allow the meeting to go very far'.

Bureau gumshoe Harold Nathan caught up to London in Baltimore on December 16 at the Brith Shalom Hall, where he spoke at a meeting 'ostensibly under the auspices of the Amalgamated Clothing Workers'. Nathan reported that 'subject's address was in support of the American Labor Alliance and the new Yiddish newspaper apparently to be published by this organization'. Agent Nathan's report, stamped 'Confidential', was not declassified until July 11, 1996, a few months before Noah London was finally 'rehabilitated' in Russia, with his conviction of treason and espionage in 1937 formally reversed.[94]

8.2 *Birth of the Jewish Workers Federation*

The Jewish Workers Federation (JWF) was formed at a shotgun wedding. The Workers Council was eager for unification. It had little non-Jewish following, and its leaders received representation on the National Committee of the new Workers Party far out of proportion to its numerical strength.[95] But the JSF and JCF had to be dragged to the altar. According to Bittelman, the JSF viewed the JCF

> as a group of immature romanticists playing in revolution without understanding much about the real business ... I was all in favor of having the Worker's Council group join with us in forming a legal party but I hadn't much confidence in their Communism ... I couldn't see why [they] should feel so superior in their wisdom. After all, if we, the Left Wing of 1918, were sick with some 'infantile' disorders of Communism, they, the Left Wing of 1920–1921, had been suffering with some 'old age' disorders of Socialism.[96]

London himself entertained public doubts about the sincerity of the JSF leadership's left turn. But in his opinion, 'We don't want to undertake to claim that the

94 NARA RG 65, FBI file 61-554, 'London, Noah', declassified per FOIA request NN94-991.

95 Cannon, *First Ten Years*, 44–5.

96 Bittelman, 'Things I Have Learned'.

new radicalism of the "Left" is only derived from chasing membership. Surely many of them mean a radical program seriously ...'[97] For London, uniting the union insurgency was more important than old rivalries.

Der Emes and the *Naye Velt* traded polemics back and forth until the merger agreement was adopted. Meanwhile in the garment district union activists were pressuring their leaders towards unity. As London later put it, 'A united front between *Der Emes* and the *Naye Velt* ... had existed in the union realm since the struggle began in general'. As the rival journals traded insults, the radicals who controlled the main New York cloakmaker locals were jointly organizing picket duty for the 1921–22 cloakmakers' strike. This was the first nationwide strike in ILGWU history, the largest the union had ever led – and a glorious success.[98]

William Z. Foster's Trade Union Educational League (TUEL) provided an umbrella for JSF activists to join forces with more radical elements. Shortly after returning from a trip to Soviet Russia, Foster joined the Communist movement. He brought along his TUEL, which became a vehicle for 'boring within' the AFL. Foster's own transit from Wilsonism to Communism closely paralleled the political trajectory of the JSF that London pioneered. Foster went on a national speaking tour for Sidney Hillman's ACWA in the fall of 1920. His excellent relations with Hillman and Salutsky certainly helped the cause of unity. When the Workers Party was founded, Hillman provided seed money to get the TUEL off the ground – as well as the JWF daily a few months later as well.[99]

Finally, organized Jewish socialism in America was reunited – under the banner of the Communist International. The garment union and Workmen's Circle staffers sponsoring the tiny Socialist *Farband* reacted with fear and hostility. The prospect that the left could take over was real, and they knew it. The stage was now set for the 'civil war' that wracked the American Jewish labor movement in the 1920s. The Jewish Workers Federation, whose first secretary would be Noah London, faced tremendous opportunities and tremendous challenges.

97 Paiezon [London], 'Der "vorkers kaunsil" – vos vil er?', *Der Emes*, Oct. 7, 1921.

98 London, *Freiheit*, Dec. 28, 1924; 'Der groyser zig fun der kloukmakher', *Naye Velt-Emes*, Jan. 21, 1922.

99 Johanningsmeier, *Forging American Communism*, 157–65; Fraser, *Labor Will Rule*, 178–97.

CHAPTER 5

Jewish Communism and Garment Unionism

Historians of the American Communist Party tend to focus on the 1930s and 1940s, when the party was largest and had the most influence in American society as a whole. But the peak of Communist influence in the American Jewish community was in the 1920s. Jewish immigrants still dominated the garment workforce in the 1920s and garment unions were central pillars of the Jewish community – and almost the only unions in America that thrived in the 'Roaring Twenties'. In the 1930s and '40s the success of the Communist Party was as union organizers and opponents of Hitler and fascism. In the 1920s the Communist Party had influence in the Jewish community on the basis of advocating militant unionism in the garment industry and the Soviet republic abroad, including its shop floor equivalent, the shop delegate system.

I once heard a ditty from an old friend and radical mentor, who told me that it was the only left-wing labor song in American history written by an actual rank-and-file worker. It went through changes down the years, as folk songs do. My mother told me many years later that she heard a different version when she was younger. Here is the song as I first heard it:

> Da cloakmakers' union,
> It's a no good union,
> It's a company union by da bosses,
> Oh dose right-ving cloakmakers
> An' da Socialist fakers
> Have been makin' by da voikers double crosses,
> De Hillkvits, Dubinskys an' da Thomases
> Have been makin' by da voikers false promises,
> Dey preach socialism,
> But dey pra-actice fascism,
> To prasoive cap'talism by da bosses,
> Hoo Hah!

A version similar to the one I heard is available on YouTube.[1] This bit of doggerel is a last vestige of the forgotten Communist garment insurgency of the 1920s.

1 See www.youtube.com/watch?v=N7gS25pfTDg.

 | DOI:10.1163/9789004745384_007

When the Jewish Workers Federation was born, it embodied a proud heritage of radical socialism rooted among garment workers. During the great labor upsurge of the 1930s and for a decade thereafter, a thoroughly Stalinized CPUSA would play a central role in the American labor movement – but as militant New Dealers, not revolutionists. The Jewish garment insurgency of the 1920s that Noah London helped to jumpstart was the only time in American history when Communism of a sort that a Lenin or a Trotsky might recognize as their own won mass support and serious success in a significant sector of the American labor movement.[2]

As such it deserves attention, especially from contemporary radicals, but from others as well. We live in an era when the performance of American capitalism has been faltering. Moreover, the story of American Communism in the 1920s is the missing link between the labor radicalism of the Progressive Era, recalled with nostalgia by radicals and labor historians, and the Communist-dominated New Deal radicalism of the Great Depression decade, whose reviews are more mixed.

Noah London, the first labor editor of the *Freiheit*, the daily newspaper of that Jewish Workers Federation, saw himself as the spokesman for the rank and file. He represented their spirit far better than fellow Cooper Union graduate Alexander Bittelman. Bittelman, the most prominent CP figure to emerge from the movement, was notoriously uninspiring as a writer, speaker or leader. Moreover, London represented the movement's radical heritage better than moderate Socialists such as Moissaye Olgin. It was no accident that London was its only early leader who became a dissident after Communism turned into Stalinism.

His experiences were emblematic of the story of the movement as a whole. It began with wide support. But the growing isolation of a radical enclave in an increasingly conservative America slowly pushed it into an insular bureaucratic mold. Upward Jewish social mobility accelerated the process. London's often heterodox articles and speeches foreshadowed future secretive dissidence in the Soviet Union. The gradual decline in his status in the movement paralleled its degeneration. The process was near completion by 1926, when he sailed from America to the promised land of socialism. At that point he no longer put his faith in rank-and-file initiative: a leader of rank and file rebellion *had* become a loyal Stalinist bureaucrat – for the moment.

2 For an overall history of the insurgency, see J. Holmes, 'American Jewish Communism and Garment Unionism in the 1920s', *American Communist History* 6, no. 2 (Fall 2007): 171–95.

1 Noah London's Moment as Jewish Workers Federation Leader

The JWF was the Jewish section of the Workers Party. In the first issue of the JWF weekly London expounded the official party labor strategy: 'boring from within' the AFL, through William Z. Foster's Trade Union Educational League. The party's 'highest attention would be applied to those points on which the whole capitalist structure is supported: railroad, coal, steel and transport ...' Subsequently he would explain that 'the League does not chase after easy successes in the more progressive unions, and concentrates its activity in the fundamental industries'.[3]

Personal experience molded his concept of the proper role of Jewish workers in the movement. He worked as a professional revolutionary in the Jewish Bund, where he sought to enlighten gentile leather workers in Lithuania during the 1905 Revolution. 1905 taught the Bund and London himself that no revolutionary movement could succeed unless it gained the support of non-Jewish workers in basic industry. In the summer of 1919 he had laid out and published his program for revolutionizing the American working class.[4] During his underground months he had plenty of time to refine it.

The formation of a legal Workers Party oriented to organized labor was well timed. It coincided with a moment when the AFL was probably more open to left-wing agitation than it would ever be again. Recession lingered. Labor was falling prey to a broad 'open shop' employer offensive. AFL unions were leading huge, grim, brutal defensive battles. Labor editor London would cover the 1922 coal and railroad shopmens' strikes in the *Freiheit*, two of the largest and most bitter conflicts in American labor history. They marked what labor historian David Montgomery called 'the fall of the house of labor' – the end of an era.[5]

Communist militants had a remarkable impact on these labor wars. Instead of denouncing the AFL root and branch, they campaigned for mass action to defend the very existence of unions. Agitation by Foster's TUEL for a national general strike got a powerful response. Gompers toyed with the idea himself during the 1922 rail strike. Party leader Charles Ruthenberg wrote that 'the fighting spirit shown by the rank and file of the labor movement in the miners strikes and the railway shopmen strikes ... shows a nearer approach to a revolutionary spirit than has existed in the recent history of the working class of

3 London, 'Di treyd-yunyon bavegung un di voyrkers parti', *Naye Velt-Emes*, Jan. 7, 1922; and 'Vos iz di treyd-yunyon edyukeyshonal lig?', June 11, 1922.

4 *Kamf*, Aug. 1 and Aug. 8, 1919.

5 London, *Freiheit*, July 7, July 17, Aug. 13, 1922, Jan. 3, 1923; Montgomery, *Fall of the House of Labor*, 407–10.

the United States'. The TUEL program called for amalgamation of craft unions into industrial unions, nationalization of industry, formation of a labor party, and 'the abolition of capitalism and the establishment of a workers' republic'. It provided an excellent umbrella for collaboration of moderate Socialist unionists like Louis Hyman with Communists. In the garment unions, the most radical section of the American labor movement, things looked good.[6]

The immediate concerns of the JWF were internal. Its unity was tenuous. Former JSF-ers wanted to get rid of the underground party altogether. London was one of six editors of its weekly *Naye Velt-Emes*, which immediately started printing polemics over the question of 'underground caucus control', which the Workers Party founding convention had avoided addressing. In the underground CP Central Executive Committee Bittelman raised a motion declaring that 'the advocacy of an open CP … is in effect advocating liquidation … and that the CEC considers persistency in preaching the above as sufficient cause for disciplinary action'. London's first and last act as national secretary of the JWF was to send out a public letter to all branches proclaiming: 'Only through unity and tireless effort can we fulfill our duty and our tasks … do your best to overcome petty trifles. Root out prejudices …'[7]

Petty trifles put an end to his brief career as the leader of organized radical Jewish socialism in America. Not only was the JWF divided, the underground caucus supposedly controlling it was divided as well. Noah London was the compromise candidate for the job, and the underground Communists were in no mood for compromise. The very fact that he was the most acceptable figure to the ex-JSF caucus meant that he had to go. The underground caucus narrowly voted to demand that he resign as JWF secretary. His replacement was Louis Hendin, the most dubious of the leading figures of American Jewish Communism.[8]

London's appeal to higher authorities is preserved in the Comintern archives in Moscow. It paints a sad portrait of the state of affairs. Internecine factional warfare had created deep-seated distrust and confusion. He commented that 'any argument to the effect that we must impose on our new allies such persons who are the most objectionable to them on the theory that what is bad

6 *Worker* (predecessor of *Daily Worker*) Aug. 12, Sept. 16 and Sept. 23, 1922; Ruthenberg, 'Where Do We Stand', WP Press Service, Oct. 24, 1922, CPUSA microfilms, r. 9, d. 149, l. 4–7; Foster, *Bankruptcy of the American Labor Movement*, 54–62; *Labor Herald, passim*; Edward P. Jonningsmeier, *Forging American Communism: The Life of William Z. Foster* (Princeton, NJ: Princeton University Press, 1994), 181–5.

7 CP CEC minutes 2-19-1921, CPUSA microfilms, r. 5, d. 94, l. 8; London, 'Tsu di brentshes fun der idisher federatsie "vorkers parti"', *Naye Velt-Emes*, Jan. 21, 1922.

8 CPUSA microfilms r. 7, f. 515, op. 1, d. 115, l. 39–54.

for "them" is good for "us", is not only foolish but shows an utterly harmful and most dangerous tendency ...' A profoundly annoyed Shachno Epstein chimed in that what was needed was to 'call to order not the accused ... but the accusers', and that 'I must give account to the comrades over the seas'.[9] But this was 1922, and appealing to Moscow authority at this point had no impact.

London's appeal was ignored because party leaders were as aware of his more conciliatory attitude to the 'centrists' as were 'centrists' Salutsky and Olgin – and recalled the patriotic black mark in his past. The party leadership was quite unhappy with the underground Jewish Federation. National Secretary Lovestone reported to the CEC that it was 'in very bad shape', but they could not agree on what to do about it.[10] Among the top party leaders, James P. Cannon was the nearest thing Noah London had to a defender. If London was the best representative of the original radical spirit of the Jewish movement, that was Cannon's role in the movement as a whole. Former Wobbly Cannon, the only top party leader other than Foster with experience in leading workers in struggle, would not just privately dissent against the degeneration of the movement. He would actively fight it and go on to become the founder of American Trotskyism.

Bryan Palmer's biography of Cannon describes him as the leading figure of an 'age of innocence for the Left'. He describes it as an era 'relatively uncorrupted by the cauterized complicities and worldly-wise knowledges that have calloused the politics of our time'.[11] What he means is that Cannon was uncorrupted by the Stalinist bureaucratism that would soon begin to cast its shadow over American Communism. London would react sharply to a few of its earliest manifestations. But there was also a certain quality of innocence about him in the usual sense – even of naivety. It would not serve him well in the factional warfare wracking the movement.

2 Birth Pangs of the *Freiheit* and the A Train

In its first few months the fragile JWF was virtually paralyzed, despite growing support in the unions. Fundraising for the daily *Freiheit* was not meeting its target. Recession lingered as New York men's clothing workers were recovering

9 'Smith' [London], 'The Steering Committee' p. 6, CPUSA microfilms, r. 7, d. 115, l. 45; 'Staley', l. 49–50.

10 CEC minutes, April 7, April 14, 1922, r. 5, d. 94, l. 22–7.

11 Palmer, *James P. Cannon*, 351–3.

from a lengthy lockout. A quaintly coded letter to Moscow warned that 'our Jewish customers are especially hard hit and unless immediate aid is received there they may have a falling out with their partners in their plans for the joint daily advertising'. But the Comintern refused to subsidize a Yiddish daily. The fund drive finally went over the top with a $3,000 donation from Sidney Hillman, whom the Communists were supporting against Socialist Party opponents in his union.[12]

The problems of the *Freiheit* were far from over. According to Paul Novick, an original staff writer who went on to become its editor for over half a century:

> [W]e had just a room in the print shop [of Ludwig Lore's *Volkszeitung*], 195 Canal Street, and that print shop, you know, they gave us one room about this size I would say, the editor was Olgin ... and there was Noah London, he was the labor editor. He was our first labor editor. He was an engineer, he was working for the subway, the New York subway, and of course making good money. But he gave up his job and he didn't get any money. You hardly got any wages once in five or six weeks, for at that time you know ... But somehow, he didn't fit in ...[13]

London had left his subway job during the Palmer raids. According to family tradition, he was one of the original draftsmen for what became the A train, the centerpiece of the municipally owned IND system. New York Mayor Hylan billed the IND as the 'people's subway'. In the spring of 1925, Hylan broke ground with a silver pickaxe for the first IND stop. He proclaimed 'the beginning of the emancipation of the people of the City of New York from the serfdom inflicted on them by the most powerful financial and traction dictatorship ever encountered'.[14]

Noah London wrote in the *Freiheit* that the Republicans and Democrats were just squabbling over graft, blocking desperately needed construction. Only when workers' parties were able to 'exert strong influence and introduce a really honorable management' could 'a little bit of order' be established.

12 Letter from 'Lewis' (national secretary Weinstein), Feb. 2, 1922, r. 6, d. 100, l. 12; ECCI protocol Nov. 15, 1921, RGASPI, f. 445 (*Evsektsiia* papers), d. 58, l. 53; Fraser, *Labor Will Rule*, 524. According to Melech Epstein, underground party secretary Lovestone also peeled off $1,500 from a bankroll in his pocket – without requesting a receipt, perhaps because the donation was unauthorized. Epstein, *The Jew and Communism*, 411n26.

13 Novick interview.

14 'Lichnyy listok po uchetu kadrov', Feb. 10, 1932, RGASPI, f. 17, op. 100, d. 126451, l. 3; Hood, *722 Miles*, 212.

He dismissed Hylan's municipal populism as a Tammany power grab versus the Republican state government. All the construction plans, Democratic or Republican, were designed to serve the richer neighborhoods. He advocated extending the subways through the Jewish Lower East Side, 'where there are absolutely no means of transportation eastwards from the Second Avenue Elevated to the East River'.[15]

Meanwhile, London proposed special measures to rescue the *Freiheit*. The underground CEC endorsed his proposition to 'send a messenger' to Moscow, to ask for money one more time. Messenger Bittelman reported to the CPUSSR Jewish Section that the party badly needed a Yiddish daily because of its successes in fighting for leadership of the Jewish garment unions. This could give the Workers Party a base to fight Gompers for control over the AFL.[16]

3 Jewish Communism and the Garment Unions

The JWF was scoring real victories in the unions, despite its problems. ILGWU leaders sought to use victory in the cloak strike to regain control over the cloakmaker locals. But the rank and file believed, as the JWF weekly put it, that it was their mass picketing that shut down the industry, not the legal maneuvers of union officers.[17] And now, gangster goon squads with knives and revolvers were trying to take over election meetings. London, keynote speaker at a *Freiheit* cloakmakers meeting attended by over a thousand workers, described a typical scene that fall:

> Men are stationed in different corners around the platform, they're afraid there will be trouble. 'Who are you expecting trouble from, the police?' 'No, we're afraid of hoodlums. Just today two pressmen were beaten up right next to the union office'. 'Who sends the hoodlums to fight, the bosses?' 'No, we have people who don't like us, the Left, the rank and file. We talk too much, we ask questions, they want to shut our mouths'.[18]

15 'Paiezon' [London], 'Politishens krign zikh un der oylm muz zikh dervayl shtiken in di sobveys', *Freiheit*, May 20, 1922.

16 May 23, 1922 CEC minutes, r. 5, d. 94, l. 33; *Evsektsiia* papers, d. 62, Cannon and Bittelman to ECCI, July 1, 1922, l. 164–5; Bittelman to *Evsektsiia*, July 10, 1922, l. 192–19.

17 Socialist leader Morris Hillquit had taken out a legally unprecedented injunction in court against the manufacturers. 'Der groyser zig fun der kloukmakher', *Naye Velt-Emes*, Jan. 21, 1922, 1; and *passim*, Feb./March 1922.

18 Paiezon [London], 'Oyf'n 'Freiheit' miting fun Nyu-Yorker kloukmakher', *Freiheit*, Sept. 19, 1922.

Strong-arm methods blew up in the face of ILGWU officialdom. Radicals consolidated their control over the key New York locals and gained seats and sometimes majorities on local executive boards all across America. At the underground Central Executive Committee meeting where Foster put in his first appearance, Cannon took charge of organizing 'left blocs' in the garment unions. A 'United Shop Delegates League' made a big showing at the 1922 ILGWU National Convention, despite an astonishingly undemocratic election system. Tiny rural locals in Tennessee or Texas received almost as many delegates as the giant New York locals. Top ILGWU officers could not even manage to be elected delegates by their own locals.[19]

But they managed to drive a wedge at the convention between the Workers Party and parts of the opposition. Until the Jewish Socialist Federation left the Socialist Party in the summer of 1921, Socialist office holders in the garment unions had supported the Soviet Union uncritically, regardless of struggles with radicals at home. Now they were on war footing. The convention took place on the eve of the 1922 Moscow trial of anti-Bolshevik Socialists for terrorism and assassinations. ILGWU leaders submitted a resolution demanding amnesty for all Socialist and anarchist Soviet prisoners. Communist delegates protested that this would aid counterrevolution. London commented that 'the *Freiheit* … has presented the proofs which the Soviet regime has that the arrested Socialist-revolutionaries are personally responsible for attempted assassinations of Soviet officials …'[20]

Socialist and anarchist supporters of the United Shop Delegates League peeled away. The Workers Party was able to muster only a quarter of the convention delegates to vote no on this resolution. In the aftermath, ILGWU dissidents hostile to the Soviet regime gradually fell back into line. After their departure the United Shop Delegates League was incorporated into a 'Needle Trades Section' of the Trade Union Education League. The *Freiheit* became the mouthpiece for a powerful rank-and-file movement explicitly identified with the Soviet Union.[21] Noah London saw himself as its spokesman:

> The labor editor of the *Freiheit* … knows the cloakmakers, they know him. They consult with him about their daily problems. They describe their

19 *Naye Velt-Emes, passim*; CP CEC minutes, April 7, 1922, r. 5, d. 94, l. 22; Gurowsky, 'Factional Disputes', 72–8; Levine, *Women's Garment Workers*, 354–6.

20 Noah London, 'Vos zeynen zey oysen', *Freiheit*, May 22, 1922.

21 *Labor Herald*, 1922 *passim*; Gurowsky, 'Factional Disputes', 89–90; M. Epstein, *Jewish Labor in USA*, 131–2.

> sufferings and joys to him. He doesn't talk with them about cloaks. He tells them that they are not alone. All across America a wave of workers has woken up … Against them stand not only the capitalists, but also the whole conservative labor bureaucracy.[22]

He believed that 'the human material of the cloakmakers is the best, the most intelligent and most conscious of all unions'.[23] He identified with the movement's male branch. But left-wing rebellion originated in the female branch, the shirtwaist and dressmaker locals to which his wife and her sisters belonged. Women workers were largely absent from his labor journalism. This blind spot was characteristic of this movement, in which women played a big role. Rose Wortis, the original leader, preferred to stay in the background during the 1920s. She pushed her ally Charles Zimmerman to the fore almost as soon as he entered the trade. He rapidly gained a leading position because he was a rare commodity – a male dressmaker.[24] She would take back leadership of the movement in its declining years, after he was purged from the party.

Noah's masculine focus surely had something to do with attitudes among the cloakmaker rank and file. They had driven women out of their craft more than a decade ago. Nor did it conflict as much as one might think with the values of radical women garment workers. Most of them, like the Unterman sisters, saw trade union militancy as an exciting adventure on the way to marriage and a family. Their model was Clara Lemlich, the original leader of the mass uprising of women workers that had rescued the ILGWU from oblivion. After a few years as a union activist she married, dropped out of politics, raised children – and then joined the American Communist Party and became its organizer of housewives. She became America's poster girl for the Stalinist slogan of 'building the family as a fighting unit for socialism'.[25] This concept was a natural extension of the 'New Womanhood' of Progressive Era America, at least in its Jewish garment variant.

Miril's influence on Noah is visible in an article he wrote for the *Freiheit* about three radical women in the Bronx, where the Londons lived.[26] They were arrested and sentenced to jail for distributing Communist literature. As he described them:

22 N. Paiezon [Noah London], *Freiheit*, Nov. 19, 1922.

23 Noah London, 'Der durchfall fun kloukmakher firershaft', *Freiheit*, Oct. 14, 1922.

24 Stanley Nadel, 'Reds Versus Pinks: A Civil War in the International Ladies Garment Workers Union', *New York History* 66, no. 1 (Jan. 1985): 55.

25 Bender, *Sweated Work, Weak Bodies*; Orleck, *Common Sense and a Little Fire*.

26 N. London, 'A nayer tip froyen in Amerika', *Freiheit*, May 12, 1922.

> An old woman in a poor neighborhood … what does she have to do with the public world, with the political world …? The second woman, a mother of children, a housewife from a worker family. Where does she have the time … when you have to go and wash and cook and sometimes, when there's a little money, take the kids out to a movie picture palace? And what does a 24 year old girl who needs to build her own little world … have to do with a movement … when it is so hard to dress well to attract men, when the family has so many worries, when you need to go out to have a little fun after a hard day's work in the shop …?

He saw them as a new type of women in America, reflecting Russian influence. Like the heroine of Maxim Gorky's *The Mother*, they were not publicity seekers. They 'worked for the revolution in the narrow circle of their friends and acquaintances'. Miril's role was much less public than Noah's. She did not publicly participate in her union. In the letter she wrote Beria from her *gulag* in 1939, she described herself as 'one of the organizers of the left wing of the [Socialist] party together with my husband'. When filling in her 1926 party transfer application, she stated that she had been a branch organizer and group captain. She was likely in charge of that literature distribution group arrested in the Bronx in the spring of 1922.

In Noah's own old union, the Amalgamated Clothing Workers of America, there was an alliance between the Communists and Sidney Hillman, America's premier progressive union leader. Labor officials associated with a loose reform movement were raising such issues as nationalizing the mines and the railroads. Cannon described this 'hazy sentiment' as 'general support of such proposals as the labor party, [union] amalgamation, recognition of Soviet Russia, etc., wherever it is not called upon to fight too hard for them'.[27]

The ACWA successfully withstood the 'open shop' business offensive of the early 1920s. It soundly defeated a lengthy New York lockout – but pent-up postwar consumer demand sputtered out. Hillman, like other progressive unionists, was turning to collaboration with progressive-minded manufacturers seeking higher productivity in unionized industries. The ACWA voluntarily adopted piecework 'production standards' in a fruitless attempt to establish order amid the chaos of the men's clothing industry.[28] He was more than willing to endorse everything the Workers Party advocated – as long as they did not interfere with

27 Cannon, 'The Workers Party Today—And Tomorrow', *Writings and Speeches, 1920–1928*, 139.

28 Fraser, *Labor Will Rule*, 160–70; Montgomery, *Fall of the House of Labor*, 420–4.

ACWA industrial policy. He defended his alliances with corporations such as Filene's as the American equivalent of Lenin's 'New Economic Policy'.

This line of argument was persuasive for some pro-Soviet radicals. ACWA garment cutter Benjamin Gitlow, a fairly prominent figure in the Communist Party, publicly expressed his admiration for Hillman even in the founding days of American Communism. He was far from the only leftist lured by Hillman's radical rhetoric. After all, Workers Party officer Salutsky edited the ACWA newspaper. In the *Freiheit* his partner Olgin was publishing encomiums to Hillman. Novelist Mike Gold wrote that ACWA production standards were compatible with revolutionary economics, adding that the union was 'bringing in the social revolution as fast as it can be brought'.[29] But Hillman's policy – labor-management collaboration to preserve the industry from non-union competition – pioneered the degeneration of American garment unionism. Once the most advanced section of the American labor movement, its current remnant is an outpost of Third World-style sweatshop exploitation.[30]

When the ACWA donated funds for the launching of the *Freiheit*, Cahan and the *Forward* launched a campaign against Hillman's production standards. This was a hypocritical maneuver, as Socialist officers were trying to introduce similar measures in the cloak industry.[31] Zivyon (B.Z. Hoffman), an ex-JSF leader whose ties to insurgent cloakmakers went back to the Hourwich affair, blasted the duplicity of ILGWU president Schlesinger in the *Naye Velt/Emes*: 'Sidney Hillman ... spoke to the tailors. He gave them the bitter pill nakedly, without any sugar coating, and they swallowed it with clenched teeth. They knew that their president told them the whole truth about the situation and they had no other alternative'.[32]

A sector of the party leadership seems to have suspected that rank-and-file resistance to the production standards was simply a Socialist provocation. Communist activists within the ACWA knew better. At the 1922 union convention, CP spokesman Robert Minor forbade them from waging a floor fight on the issue. A crisis broke out over Albert Goldman, whose frame-up as a labor spy had been pilloried in London's *Proletaryer*. According to Zimmerman, 'Hill-

29 Gitlow, 'Shop Committees in the Amalgamated', *Voice of Labor*, Aug. 30, 1919; Olgin, 'Hilman's linie in der arbeyter bavegung', *Freiheit*, May 14, 1922.

30 Liebman, *Jews and the Left*, 228–46; Philip Taft and Selig Perlman, *History of Labor in the United States, 1896–1932* (New York: Macmillan, 1936), vol. 4, 313–14; Myerson, 'ILGWU: Fighting for Lower Wages', *Ramparts*, Oct. 1969, 51–5; John Holmes, 'International Ladies Garment Workers Union', *Dictionary of American History*, 3rd. ed. encyclopedia.com.

31 Fraser, *Labor Will Rule*, 1991, 178–80; Levine, *Women's Garment Workers*, 344–45; Gurowsky, 'Factional Disputes', 70–71.

32 Zivyon [Hoffman], 'Tsu dem farendigten kloukmakher strayk', *Naye velt-Emes*, Jan. 28, 1922.

man wanted to get rid of Goldman ... Gitlow was at the convention ... He came to explain away this expulsion, why the Party wouldn't take any action against Hillman on this question. We almost threw him out of the hall.'[33]

After the convention a big conflict broke out in the New York ACWA between its Socialist Joint Board and the membership. At its height, the JWF and the Communist underground were both gripped by factional warfare. Minor and Gitlow's faction in the underground party, the so-called 'goose caucus', was momentarily in ascendancy over Cannon's caucus. It did not want to be dragged into a fight with Hillman. The official policy was that Hillman 'must be forced over to the left by means of energetic criticism'. The *Freiheit* chided top ACWA officers for their neutrality between the Rights and the Lefts, who stood for 'clean, democratic, fighting rank and file unionism'. Its narrow focus on democracy and corruption was due to a desire to avoid discussing Hillman's production standards, which the *Forward* was criticizing.[34]

Labor editor London avoided the issue as well, with personal experience shaping his attitude. He believed that 'the proof-stone for Hillman has not yet arrived' and regarded the 'enlightened absolutism' of the Hillman leadership as justified in the past by the social and economic backwardness of the industry, and its workforce as well. But the time had come for self-activity of the membership. The union should pass from the hands of officials to shop delegates, and enlightened absolutism should give way to 'democratic absolutism'.[35] A few years later he would become an official in another enlightened absolutism, the USSR. He would gradually acquire an attitude to the Soviet bureaucracy not dissimilar to his attitude to the Hillman bureaucracy in 1922 – or to the CPUSA's own budding bureaucracy.

Back in New York, Hillman stepped in to settle the crisis when anarchists started calling for a dues strike. The CP-backed TUEL caucus won new elections handily – with his support. During the ensuing period the TUEL caucus gained control over about half the union's locals, including all the big New York locals. But over the long run its alliance with Hillman 'killed the Left wing in the Amalgamated', as Goldman put it. When Hillman decided to purge it, the Left ACWA power base collapsed rapidly, despite sizeable mass meetings and even a work stoppage. In the end the ACWA, the most radical garment union, turned out to be the one where the Left was weakest.[36]

---

33 Epstein *Jewish Labor in USA*, vol. 2, 165; Zimmerman interviews, 173, 190.

34 *Freiheit*, Oct./Nov. 1922, *passim*; quote from 'Di shnayder hoben gezagt zeyer vort', lead editorial, Nov. 8, 1922.

35 London, *Freiheit*, July 10, Oct. 5 and Oct. 6, 1922.

36 Fraser, *Labor Will Rule*, 180–3; 'C.P. Expels Albert Goldman', *Militant*, July 8, 1933; Fraser 'Dress Rehearsal', 212–55; Epstein, *Jewish Labor in USA*, vol. 2, 166–8.

4 Noah London, United Fronts and Labor Parties

London committed his first public deviation from the Workers Party line in the *Naye Velt-Emes* – after it became clear that his appeal from removal as Jewish national secretary was futile. It concerned an issue far more important than the squabbles draining the energy of the Jewish Workers Federation: the long-standing debate among US radicals as to whether they should advocate forming a labor party.

In 1922, as London put it in a later Freiheit article, 'The creation of an independent labor party feels in the air'.[37] A new leading group had come to the fore in the Communist Party, made up of experienced unionists, new 'City College Boys' – and one veteran Socialist with serious political experience in American politics, Charles Ruthenberg. He had spent his political career leading Cleveland Socialism and scorning any notion of forming a labor party that would compete with his own party. This labor party idea that the Comintern seemed to favor was therefore outside their repertoire, and they were uncertain how to deal with it. Noah London had already given the issue of how and whether to participate in elections a lot of thought. Indeed, his view that they should only be used for propaganda purposes has resonated to this day among more radical American leftists.

In the decades preceding World War I, mass Socialist parties arose all over continental Europe, based in the working classes created by the Industrial Revolution. These parties usually claimed to adhere to Marxism. In England, and in England's white colonies such as Australia, labor parties came into existence instead, based on originally non-political trade union movements. Over time, these parties would all take on socialist colorations. In the English colony which gained its independence first, the United States, this did not happen.

After unpleasant early experiences, American Socialists of almost all stripes set their faces firmly against labor party experiments. The founders of the Socialist Party had witnessed the demise of Populism, following its fusion with William Jennings Bryan's Democrats in the 1896 election. Much of its original membership were former populists, including Debs himself. The SP opposed the idea of forming a labor party. As early as 1903, it went through a wrenching crisis over its relations with the notoriously anti-Asian racist Union Labor Party of San Francisco, the most successful labor party in American history. This res-

37 London, 'Iz a fareynigter politisher arbeyter front in Amerika noytig un meglikh?', *Freiheit*, July 3, 1922.

ulted in the replacement of its founding party secretary and the adoption of a resolution that was the official position for the next two decades, and which must have been axiomatic for Ruthenberg in his Socialist days:[38]

> Whereas, All 'radical' and 'reform' parties, including the so-called 'Union Labor parties', have, after a brief existence, uniformly succumbed to the influence of the old political parties and have proven disastrous to the ultimate end of the labor movement; and
>
> Whereas, Any alliance, direct or indirect, with such parties is dangerous for the political integrity and the very existence of the Socialist Party and the Socialist Movement;
>
> Resolved, That no state or local organization or member of the party shall hereafter under any circumstances fuse, combine or compromise with any political party or organization …[39]

But after World War I, the Socialist Party splintered and collapsed. The issue revived when William Z. Foster's friend, Chicago AFL leader John Fitzpatrick, formed a Farmer-Labor Party in Chicago, in the aftermath of the defeated 1919 steel strike.

Noah London's article called for an electoral united front between the Workers Party and parties like the Socialist Party and Fitzpatrick's party. For the JWF, this meant in practice that the Workers Party should support Socialist Congressman Meyer London in the 1922 elections. This was not a new idea for Noah. He originally wrote the piece as a conclusion for his series on American politics in the *Proletaryer* in the summer of 1921. When he submitted it to the *Emes*, Shachno Epstein and Bittelman rejected it as 'premature', as London put it.[40] Publishing such a proposal while the JSF was still debating whether or not to leave the Socialist Party would have been exquisitely poor timing.

He had argued in 1919 that the American working class was divided into a labor aristocracy and an underclass, and that the path to revolution was to 'Bolshevize the millions of foreign workers, the millions of persecuted black workers, and through them to pull in the remaining workers …'[41] Postwar labor

38 John Holmes, 'California in the Progressive Era: The Union Labor Party and the Socialist Party in the San Francisco Bay Area', Social Science History Association Conference presentation, Portland, OR, 2005.

39 'National Committee, Report of Proceedings', *New York Worker*, Feb. 8, 1903.

40 Noah London, 'A fareynigter front in Amerike', *Naye Velt-Emes*, March 11, 1922.

41 Noah London, *Kamf*, Aug. 8, 1919.

developments showed this could not be done directly. When American workers became class conscious, he anticipated that there would be a role for a reformist as well as a revolutionary workers party.

> The entire workforce can only be led by a united front of all labor parties, in which our party must occupy the left flank … Concretely our party … represents a certain layer of the immigrant elements … [and] can only pull out these elements to any kind of action. As far as the other layers go, because of their weak solidarity they will remain unmoved.[42]

He conceded that the SP and FLP were weak and getting weaker. This was because native white workers were not moving at the moment towards independent labor political action. When social crisis would push them in that direction, they would naturally join reform parties, because 'the worker masses will go with them and not with the Communist Party, until they have gone through all disillusionments and find out that the only way is revolution'. He still believed the main purpose of participating in elections was to make propaganda for socialism. He also proposed a united front labor-socialist radio program, a sort of pre-Pacifica. Radio was the internet of the 1920s, the exciting new technology which 'N. Paiezon' was eagerly explaining to the *Freiheit* readership.[43]

The resemblance between his conception and the brand new Comintern united front slogan was superficial. For the Communist International, a central objective of the 'united front' was to win workers away from the Socialists. As Lenin put it, Communists should support Socialist candidates in the same fashion a rope supports a hanged man. For Noah London the united front was a basic strategy, not a temporary tactic. A long-term alliance would require a conciliatory attitude. This 'centrist' orientation became the hallmark of his politics: he was already beginning to regret the division between Communists and Socialists in the aftermath of 1917.

His ideas were more timely by the spring of 1922 than they would have been the previous summer. The conservative railroad brotherhoods were facing a remarkably sweeping anti-strike injunction. They were seriously interested in political action, for the moment, and sponsored a Conference for Progressive Political Action in Chicago in February – to which the Workers Party was not invited.

---

42 London, 'A fareynigter front'.

43 Noah London, *Freiheit*, April 3, 4 and 27, 1922.

The Workers Party newspaper began a public discussion of how to apply the new united front slogan in America. Noah London weighed in with the only English-language newspaper article he ever wrote. He called for the party to 'immediately take steps to meet representatives of the Socialist Party, the Farmer-Labor Party, the Non-Partisan League and the radical labor unions with the object of forming a United Labor Party in America'. Its program should be 'adapted to the pressing needs for the moment', such as 'relief to the unemployed', 'legislation against open shop campaign', and 'recognition and trade with Soviet Russia'.[44] Calls for revolution and social transformation were distinctly absent. The issue was temporarily resolved at a public party meeting in New York, which over 500 members attended. Out of this discussion came the Workers Party Theses on the United Front, according to which: 'The Workers Party must not artificially force the development of a labor party … To enter into a political federation with existing political organizations, none of which have the support of the masses of workers, would be to negate the possibility of creating a real United Front of the workers politically'.[45]

Had American Communists stuck to that entirely sensible official policy, they would have saved themselves much trouble. London dissented, arguing in the *Freiheit* that 'the near future in parliament belongs not to the Communist party, but to the party of social reforms'.[46] He did not receive support from the ex-JSF 'centrists', who regarded the united front idea as a dubious Moscow scheme shoved down their throats by the 'underground caucus'. His idea of a United Labor Party was impractical, as he later acknowledged. After Meyer London was decisively defeated in the 1922 Congressional election, the SP attempted to sponsor a New York labor party. It was a purely bureaucratic affair. In the *Freiheit* London would describe how at its founding convention: 'Top secret invitations were sent out separately to each union office to send delegates to a conference … Even in the press it was only mentioned in passing … The SP basically invited itself. Whatever had an SP stamp in New York was represented there'.[47] The Farmer-Labor Party policy the Communist movement ended up adopting in 1923 would have a similar 'front group' flavor. He would question it as well.

44 Noah London, 'The Workers Party and the United Front', *Worker*, March 25, 1922.

45 Draper, *American Communism*; *Worker*, June 22, 1922.

46 Noah London, 'Fareynigter politisher arbeyter front', *Freiheit*, July 3, 1922.

47 London, 'An elekshon-mashin oder a mashin partey fun arbeyter?' *Freiheit*, Feb. 28, 1923.

5 Death Throes of the Underground

By the year 1922, the Communists badly needed to escape underground fantasy life and adapt themselves to reality, as London had advocated in his *Proletaryer*. The great Red Scare was winding down. America was not going Bolshevik. The steel strike had been crushed, labor was in retreat, Warren Harding was president and 'normalcy' was descending. The Workers Party and Foster's TUEL were functioning without molestation. Underground Communists were still being arrested, but more and more often were beating the rap. Increasingly, the underground merely duplicated the legal organization. As Paul Novick described it, 'They belonged to number one, to the underground, we were number two, the Workers Party'.[48] And nobody likes being number two.

But there was a final rebellion on behalf of undergroundism. Former UCP leaders sidelined after the UCP-CPA fusion by the new six-man leadership team argued that the underground party needed to stay in existence indefinitely, to control the legal Workers Party. Otherwise, they maintained, it would degenerate into reformism. The best-remembered figure among them was garment cutter Benjamin Gitlow. According to Gitlow, when one of the main leaders was accused of 'cackling like a goose', another jumped up and retorted that 'the geese saved Rome and we shall yet save the Party'. Whereupon Jay Lovestone dubbed them 'the goose caucus'.[49]

They in turn dubbed the new party leadership team as 'liquidators'. The 'liquidators' believed that it was possible to start moving in the direction of abolishing the underground. As Cannon put it, 'Our underground party ... is regarded by the masses as a good deal of a joke. They think it is illegal because we want to be illegal, and I must say that is true of a large majority of the illegal party'.[50]

In most branches of the movement the duplication of functions was just an annoying encumbrance. Parallel committees regularly changed hats and met on alternative weekends. But in the Jewish movement the legal and illegal organizations were definitely separate. Its two squabbling wings both saw the real issue as what kind of party the Workers Party should be. Would it be a Russian-style party of professional revolutionaries, or an American-style mass party of radical socialism? The former JSF caucus accused the underground

48 Novick interview.

49 Draper *American Communism*, 353–62; Cannon, *First Ten Years*, 43–57; Benjamin Gitlow, *I Confess: The Truth about American Communism* (New York: Dutton, 1940), 133.

50 James P. Cannon, Speech at American Commission of Fourth Comintern Congress, Moscow, Nov. 27, 1922.

caucus of acting 'as if the Russian Revolution had been bodily transplanted upon American soil'. They maintained that secret control by a secret organization was the only real issue dividing them from underground Communists. As historian Theodore Draper put it: 'There was a striking disparity ... between the broad principles and the narrow conclusion'. Their actual program was merely for an 'Open Communist Party'. Which was also what the 'liquidators' in the underground party really wanted, and indeed what Moscow wanted. This exacerbated distrust and poisoned the atmosphere.[51]

5.1 *The Crisis of the Jewish Workers Federation*

As the *Freiheit* financial crisis worsened, the JWF was slipping out of the hands of the underground caucus. At a June 'Number 1' bureau meeting, members concluded laconically: 'Financial situation bad. Editorial policy unsatisfactory. The tendency in the past of Number 2 to eliminate our comrades resolved to resist'. Then Hendin suddenly resigned his post as JWF national secretary.[52] Tensions exploded when he circulated a public manifesto advocating immediate liquidation of the underground party. He had gone over to the other side.

The JWF affair was a mirror image of simultaneous conflict in the underground party. It broke out on the eve of its 'Bridgman convention', which was supposed to settle whether 'liquidators' or 'geese' would run the party. On one key ballot the geese won by one vote, delivered by the police spy who tipped off the authorities. Had Hendin got elected as a delegate instead of resigning his secretary post, perhaps the vote would have gone the other way.[53]

When the police then busted the convention, undergroundism became an immediate question. Initially this was 'Sauce for the Geese', as Draper piquantly put it. Former Workers Council supporters in the WP tried to spin the affair in their direction as well. Salutsky ridiculed arrestees as 'children of a childish conspiracy'. But the raids backfired on the raiders. The government's *agent provocateur* tactics turned public opinion against them, and few Communists went to prison. 'Liquidator' Ruthenberg, who spent the rest of his life out on bail, believed that the raids actually facilitated escape from underground isolation. He publicly scolded Salutsky for maligning Communists 'at a time when they are meeting the hardest blows of the enemy' and asked: 'When before

51 'We Want An Open Communist Party', *Workers Council* no. 9, Nov. 15, 1921; Draper, *American Communism and Soviet Russia*, 334.

52 CPUSA microfilms, r. 7, d. 115, l. 18–19.

53 Draper, *American Communism*, 373–4.

… have central labor councils and state federations of labor concerned themselves with the defense of Communists?' Hendin, member and one-time leader of the underground party, was treated more harshly. An official 'Jewish Committee' demanded his expulsion on the grounds that he had 'openly published control of Number 2 by Number 1, thus endangering the very life of Number 2 and giving material [aid] to the enemy'.[54]

Bittelman regarded the ex-JSF caucus as pseudo-Communists masking their real political beliefs and launched a struggle against their control of the JWF when he returned to America, accusing Hendin of seeking to split the party.[55] London did not associate himself with Hendin. But he and Shachno Epstein both believed the time had come for an open Communist Party. They were tired of a pointless battle for control with the ex-Socialists and were willing to abandon it and get on with the work of building the federation. Epstein reluctantly went along with Bittelman, following underground party discipline. London did not. A 'Jewish Committee', headed by a brand new arrival from overseas named John Pepper, in response demanded his resignation from the JWF Executive Committee – the first political act in America of a man who would take over the party and send it on a wild ride. London refused to comply, and this disobedience pushed him willy-nilly into the ex-JSF caucus.

When the Workers Party came down on Bittelman's side, Hendin and Salutsky proposed an immediate split. London refused to follow them out of the movement. Jewish underground secretary Meyer Lunin, who had defended firing London from *Der Kamf* at the founding convention of the JCF, had regained his old post when Hendin resigned. He now labeled London as a 'coward'.[56] Public warfare broke out between a new majority in the JWF (including London) and the Bittelman caucus. Meanwhile, the Comintern was preparing to decide whether to overrule the razor-thin 'goose caucus' majority and order the underground party's dissolution. Most of the former JSF'ers wanted simply to get rid of a no-longer-necessary underground party. When word came back from Moscow that the 'goose caucus' had lost, Pepper, filling in as party leader

54 Salutsky, 'Labor Liquidates Revolution', *Liberator*, Oct. 1922; Lore, 'Wochen-Rundschau', *Volkszeitung*, Oct. 15, 1922; Ruthenberg, 'Where Do We Stand', Oct. 24, 1922; CP CEC minutes, Sept. 5, 1922, r. 5, d. 94, l. 71.

55 Bittelman, 'Ir shpalt di partey', *Freiheit*, Nov. 20, 1922. Hendin's answer, 'Ver shpalt di partey?', *Freiheit*, Nov. 22, 1922.

56 Letter from 'Max' to 'Miller', CEC minutes, Nov. 4, 1922, r. 7, d. 115, l. 29. This accusation seems to have registered deeply in his mind. In his 1934 secret manuscript he would write that 'the author prefers for the time being to be labelled as a coward … and to remain active within the movement, rather than to be driven into a position against it'.

while most of the others were abroad, found compromise solutions. The underground party was abolished, Bittelman became the new JWF secretary, and Hendin was expelled.[57]

With help from Moscow, Cannon and his liquidators had won out. But the undergroundists, led by Cannon's ally Bittelman, won out in the Jewish Federation – despite the lack of enthusiasm of Epstein, the putative Moscow representative. And then the underground party was abolished, just as the ex-JSF caucus demanded. Noah London fell victim to the multiple ironies of a complex, and rather odd, political dispute, one that poisoned the atmosphere and endangered his status in the movement.

5.2 *Noah London's Vision of Trade Union Communism*

London, unlike Bittelman, took the 'open Communist Party' slogan at face value.[58] Instead of calling for a more American brand of radicalism, as did his new allies, he raised the question: 'Is the American Communist Party really communist?' It was calling for votes for Fitzpatrick's Farmer-Labor Party, which was less socialist than the Socialist Party. Where was the guarantee that tomorrow it wouldn't tell the masses to 'give up their struggle … against their union leaders in order to make agreements with them in political elections?' A perceptive prophecy. What most bothered London was a brand new strategy. As he put it, 'You slip in a Communist disguisedly into … the central committee of a labor party, and it will become a tool in the hand of Communism'. This was pretty much Foster's scheme for 'boring from within' the AFL. Draper would call this the idea of 'the manipulated revolution',[59] and London's enemy Pepper became its theoretician.

Noah London had a different vision. The conclusion of his American politics series was that the central communist strategy needed to be trade unionism. In the fall, as the faction fight broke out, he wrote a series of 'letters from a worker about the movement'.[60] Allegedly a cloakmaker wrote those letters, in response to questions London sent out to 'some well-known workers'. He prefaced the series with a quote from Marx: 'The development of socialist sectarianism and of the real working-class movement always stands in inverse ratio to each other. Sects are justified historically so long as the working class is not yet ripe for an

57 Epstein, *The Jew and Communism*, 45–7, 109–10; Cannon, *First Ten Years*, 233.

58 London, 'Es fadert zikh an ofene komunistishe partey' and 'Der umzin fun an untererdisher komunistisher partey', *Freiheit*, Nov. 17, Nov. 28, 1922.

59 Draper, *American Communism*, 350 (note the quote from Foster).

60 Letter series, 'Brif fun arbeyter vegen der bavegung', Aug. 20, Aug. 21, Aug. 23, Aug. 25, Aug. 29 and Sept. 4, 1922.

independent (historical) movement. As soon as it has attained this maturity all sects are essentially reactionary'.[61] This was not just a polemical jab. It represented the essence of his political views. He would repeat the quote in 1934, as a centerpiece of his critique of Stalinism.

The cloakmaker was sympathetic to communism but skeptical of underground Communists. He wanted a movement rooted in the workaday reality of struggle against the bosses, not abstract theory. He was working with an underground Communist, a former Bundist, who didn't participate in the union, didn't socialize with other cloakmakers, and spoke a language they couldn't understand. They called him 'the philosopher'.

When the philosopher took the cloakmaker to a Communist meeting, he heard speakers discussing how to 'use the unemployed for our party'. The meeting decided to raise demands such as seizing the homes of the rich. When the government refused to grant them, the unemployed would learn that the government was their enemy. The cloakmaker asked, 'Who are "we" and who are the unemployed? Who should be using whom?' And he pointed out that the unemployed would hardly join a movement for demands that were unwinnable and provocative. Better would be to demand unoccupied apartments for the homeless.

In the last letter, the cloakmaker explains 'how a workers party should be organized'. Unlike the philosopher's movement, its whole structure would be based on union branches. Noah London still liked the idea of organizing a Communist Party on a trade instead of territorial basis, laid out in his old underground paper over a year ago. But the new scheme was different from the old one. When he described his plan to the philosopher,

> he called me a 'syndicalist'. I understand that is a bad thing. But since I don't care about names, I let him speak some more. I understand that he criticizes ... that I want to devote three times as much time to industrial questions as general political. He explained to me that the IWW also wanted to make the revolution through the industrial struggle and didn't want to know anything about politics ...[62]

The philosopher then lectured the cloakmaker about how this scheme would inevitably lead to trade union opportunism and reformism, to which the cloakmaker answered,

61 Letter, Marx to Bolte, Nov. 23, 1871, Marx and Engels, *Selected Works* (New York: International Publishers, 1968), 682.

62 London, 'Vi azoy darf zeyn organizirt an arbeyter-partey', *Freiheit*, Sept. 5, 1922.

> good brother, you are more learned than me, you have read books, you tell me about what has happened in other countries … But I know something about the IWW. I know two of them in the shop … The IWW doesn't believe in politics, they believe that when workers seize the factories then it's over with capitalism … as if the capitalists with their army and police would stay on the side and let us run things.

The cloakmaker's conclusion was that the Wobblies and the philosopher were both making the same mistake: seeking to pull the most class-conscious workers into a separate existence away from their brothers. (Sisters were not mentioned.) The workers party needed to arise out of the masses.

London's revised scheme for a union-based Communist party was an echo of his Bundist past as well as that old Jewish underground policy statement noted in the previous chapter. When he joined the Bund in 1905, it had already acquired an organizational structure not terribly different from that of Lenin's Bolsheviks – but it began originally as a trade union movement. This strategy had some plausibility in the strong and radically inclined American Jewish labor movement of the year 1922. It was hardly applicable elsewhere in America, where the great majority of workers were unorganized and averse to politics. As London himself had written, immigrant and black workers were often excluded from AFL unions. Moreover, employers all across America were firing radicals, and especially Communists. AFL unions were about to start expelling them.

The faction fight ended in a compromise at the December Jewish Workers Federation convention. London delivered a minority trade union report advocating restructuring the Workers Party on a trade union basis, as if it were a reborn Jewish Bund. Taking 'open Communism' to its logical conclusion, he proposed that WP union branches should act openly. Otherwise 'the machine, the true machine of the reactionary leaders will breathe out a crusade against us: "just think, an organization in an organization, a caucus, which wants to wreck" – and the masses would lend open ears …'[63] The concept of a tightly disciplined underground caucus machinery ultimately run from outside the unions could be vulnerable to exactly that sort of attack from union bureaucrats. Persecution was about to descend on Communists in the ranks of labor. The TUEL would shortly be booted out of the AFL. Would 'open Communism' have avoided this fate – or made radicals even more vulnerable to victimization? If London's plan had been implemented, the results could have been catastrophic.

63 London, 'Di Vorkers Parti un yunyon brentshes', *Freiheit*, Dec. 27, 1922.

A new figure in the Jewish Communist movement delivered the majority counter-report. He was Melech Epstein, future Jewish labor historian and former labor editor of a 'bourgeois' Yiddish daily *Der Tog* who would later refer to London as 'a man capable of being carried away by his imagination'.[64] One suspects Epstein saw the 'open trade union branch' scheme as the perfect example.

Meanwhile Noah was rehired as an engineer, working on the Holland Tunnel project. Once again he could contribute to the family budget, enabling Miril to quit her garment job. The project was no cushy office assignment. As he pseudonomously described it in the *Freiheit*, 'working in tunnels under heavy air pressure is the most dangerous work that you can understand. Not everyone can handle it. Before you send a worker or an engineer into the tunnels he is well examined by a doctor. You cannot be too healthy or have too strong a constitution to be suitable …'[65]

Miril followed her husband to Cooper Union. She studied chemistry while working part-time as a hospital lab assistant. By the time they moved to the Soviet Union she had learned enough to be hired at a Soviet chemistry lab.[66] Her youngest sibling Rose, the future transcriber of Noah's secret manuscript, was the only Unterman sister who never worked in garment. Instead she went to college. Family support made this possible – not the uncertain earnings of her father's garage, but the reliable income of her unionized sisters. She worked in small factories during Easter vacations. As she explained to her husband, that was more to learn working class 'discipline – the starching of my soul' than to afford her silk stockings.[67]

6 Labor's 'Lean Years' and American Jewish Communism

In the Roaring Twenties, militancy by and large evaporated from American unionism: labor had lost the labor wars. Defeat engendered demoralization and plunged Foster's TUEL into persecuted isolation. Collapse was the fate

---

64 Epstein, *Pages from a Colorful Life*, 70–1; Epstein, *The Jew and Communism*, 214.

65 N. Paiezon [Noah London], 'Vi azoy men grobt dem nayes tunel unter'n Hodson', *Freiheit*, Dec. 16, 192.

66 *Trudoviy Spysok* London, Noy Moiseevich, RGAE, f. 7297, op. 17, d. 2912; RGASPI, f. 17, op. 98, d. 8956, l. 2, 'Avtobiog. Mariia Efimovich Londona'; 'Registratsionnyi blank chlena VKP(b) Partbilet No. 1193080'.

67 Letter, Rose Unterman to Louis Discher, Kharkov, July 26, 1931. Collected correspondence in possession of Lucy Lewis, daughter of Louis Discher/Richard Lewis, Berkeley. Hereinafter 'Lewis Collection'.

of the labor-focused left-wing movements that flourished in America before World War I,[68] and Communism was nearly the sole survivor. In the Jewish community the story was different. Under the wave of anti-immigrant, anti-Bolshevik and anti-Semitic hysteria connected with the Red Scare, Communists became pariahs to the general public, but Jews remained sympathetic. The Jewish garment unions, uniquely successful in defending themselves from a nationwide 'open shop' offensive versus unionism, became the last bastion of left-wing power in the labor movement.

But this bastion was fragile. Greater Jewish access to higher education after World War I facilitated increasing upward social mobility – a path Noah and other Jewish radicals in the Cooper Union engineering program pioneered. The American Jewish community had begun a transition from the working class to the middle class. One of the factors making this possible was the greatly improved living standards of unionized garment workers. The higher wages, shorter hours and better working conditions they enjoyed made it much easier to take advantage of free tuition at CCNY and Cooper Union. Things were easier for Rose than they were for Noah. She could rely on family support, because Jewish immigrants were dirt poor no longer. But as they moved upwards on the social ladder, how would this affect their left-wing sympathies?

After his Holland Tunnel assignment ended, Noah became first a junior, then a senior designer for the New York subway system. As his career as an engineer progressed, his role in the movement receded. At the 1922 JWF convention Noah, who had lost his position on the underground bureau, lost his spot on the Federation Executive Committee as well. He would regain it, and again become a central figure in the movement, but no longer as a spokesman for Jewish labor radicalism. He lost his job as labor editor soon after the convention and wrote on garment affairs for the *Freiheit* far less frequently thereafter. His open trade union branch scheme surely had more to do with this than his subway job. He claimed in his convention report that it represented the opinions of 'the majority of those delegates who are active in the unions'. This may have been so, but it must have raised the hackles of experienced labor men like Foster and Cannon. His withdrawal from garment unionism after the convention was hardly by choice.

He had allied himself with Olgin's ex-JSF caucus and publicly criticized the underground party as sectarian and undemocratic. In so doing, he lost his lead-

68 Bernstein, *The Lean Years: A History of the American Worker, 1920–1933* (Boston: Houghton Mifflin, 1960); Montgomery, *Fall of the House of Labor*, 457–64.

ing status among Jewish Communists. To regain the full respect of his comrades, he would have to return to his land of birth and take up the task of building socialism in the USSR, where as a top-level industrial manager he would have the opportunity to view the rise of Stalinism from close up.

CHAPTER 6

From a Jewish Labor Movement to a Radical Subculture

The labor movement and socialism were central to the lives of Jewish immigrants laboring in garment sweatshops a century and more ago. Their descendants like to picture grimy, impoverished *shtetl* life in the old country in rosy colors. They prefer to remember American Jewish history as a celebration of winners, a narrative of immigrant achievement in America. Jewish Communism, to the extent it is remembered at all, is telescoped into a merely cultural movement, the radical subculture that evolved from Noah London's Jewish Workers Federation (JWF). It persisted for decades after the decline of the Jewish labor movement and served as a link between pre-1917 labor socialism and future middle-class Jewish radicalism.[1] The movement turned its focus away from unionism towards cultural pursuits, much as the Bund in Russia had done after the defeat of the 1905 Revolution, and for some of the same reasons. This turn was primarily due to social transformations in the American Jewish community, but also to the defeats the Jewish labor movement suffered in the late 1920s, beginning almost immediately after the Londons went home to a transformed Soviet motherland in the summer of 1926.

Shunted away from garment unionism in the party, Noah London would turn his attention to a Jewish Communist subculture he would play a significant role in creating. Its focuses were the *Freiheit*, the Londons' Camp Nitgedeiget, America's first 'red' summer camp, and especially the Bronx cooperative housing project celebrated in the PBS documentary film *At Home in Utopia*.[2] However, his shift of emphasis was not complete until the summer of 1924, when the Communist Party suffered a signal political defeat, one of whose consequences was renewed criticism of Noah for 'rightist deviationism'. The period from 1923 to that summer of 1924 marked the height of the influence of the Communist Party in American politics in the 1920s. London made his mark there as well, and for a brief moment regained his status as a party leader. But Stalinization began in the year 1924, in the aftermath of the defeat of the Ger-

1 Michels, *A Fire in Their Hearts* (Cambridge, MA: Harvard University Press, 2005), 16–21, 249; Paul Buhle, 'Jews and American Communism', *Radical History Review*, Dec. 1980; Liebman, *Jews and the Left*.

2 Michal Goldman, *At Home in Utopia*, PBS documentary, 2008.

 | DOI:10.1163/9789004745384_008

man near-revolution in 1923. That defeat shed cold water on dreams of world revolution, demoralizing the Communist movement and setting the stage for Stalinist degeneration, in the Soviet Union itself and everywhere else as well. Noah's party status would fall victim, and he and Miril would leave for the Soviet Union to regain his status in the movement.

1 Pepper Spray

> If to borrow the terminology of the economic cycle, the years 1920–21 can be called American communism's period of depression, and 1922 the beginning of the upturn, then the year 1923 can be described as the year of the boom. This boom was partly real and largely speculative, short-lived and fatally headed for a bust. It was the Pepper era.
>
> JAMES P. CANNON

The 1922 faction fights were molding experiences for American Communism in general and for Noah London in particular, with consequences positive and negative. On the one hand, the underground era of splintering and isolation was over. Communists had united and managed to learn how to bring their ideas to the American working class and gain a hearing. On the other hand, the way the internal battles were resolved set a bad precedent. The 'liquidators' did not defeat the 'geese' and the 'united toilers' through their own efforts. Moscow had the deciding voice.

The undergroundists surrendered because Moscow's support for their opponents placed them in an impossible position. Their whole line of argument was that the Bolshevik Revolution and the situation in Europe proved that a legal movement would inevitably either make peace with the powers that be or commit suicide. After the Bridgman convention, it was much less plausible to apply this logic to America. If the Bolsheviks themselves did not support the undergroundists, they had no leg to stand on.

It was John Pepper, the American Communist Party's new leader-by-accident who negotiated their surrender. In the fall of 1922, while the main faction leaders were still debating in Moscow, he utilized the confusion created by the discrediting of the goose caucus to seize control over the underground party. Cannon's biographer Bryan Palmer calls Pepper (real name József Pogány) 'a living articulation of the nascent degeneration of the Russian Revolution' and dubs his influence over the American Communist Party as 'Pepper Spray'. Pepper brokered an end to factional warfare by offering former 'geese' and former 'united toilers' leading positions in a new unified party leadership – on condition that they adopt a new, completely different program devised by Pepper himself, his version of the Comintern united front strategy as applied to America. Pepper's Labor Party pamphlet, published as he grabbed the helm, advocated campaigning for the creation of a labor party squarely based on Samuel Gompers's American Federation of Labor, something not to the taste of much of the party.[3]

The pamphlet set forth a potted version of American history, many features of which demonstrate that Hungarian immigrant Pepper did not understand America nearly as well as he thought he did, and certainly not as well as Noah London did. It did not mention the existence of black people in America, described Reconstruction as the reign of an 'open military dictatorship' and named Woodrow Wilson the leader of the 'radical wing' of the Democratic Party. Noah London based his Labor Party concept on the idea that there was a radical-minded wing of the American working class, the unskilled foreign immigrants and black workers, and a reformist-minded wing of skilled white natives – and that they should form a united front against capitalist exploitation. Pepper more crudely and less accurately claimed that a united workers party was now possible because friction within the working class allegedly was disappearing as European immigrants Americanized and the American working class homogenized. A solitary sentence, injected to ease radical consciences, suggests that this Labor Party really ought to adopt a socialist program. Perhaps because of its unusual moderation and timeliness, the pamphlet was, regrettably, the CPUSA's first bestseller.[4]

Worse was yet to come as Pepper tightened his grip over inexperienced American revolutionaries. American farming was in crisis in the 1920s, with crop prices plunging precipitously. The Non-Partisan League, a last gasp of farmer populism, was channeling unrest on the Great Plains into attempts to take over the major parties, especially the Republicans. In Minnesota, a Farmer-Labor Party based on a loose coalition of Scandinavian immigrant farmers and Minneapolis labor leaders became a major political factor.

Pepper had been the Commissar of War of the brief Hungarian Soviet Republic of 1919. Hungarian Communists had virtually ignored the peasantry, the majority of the population, during their regime. Within a year of his arrival on American shores, Pepper would assert that the USA was face to face with

3 Draper, *American Communism*, 56–71; Palmer, *Cannon*, 221; Thomas Sakmyster, *A Communist Odyssey: The Life of József Pogány* (Budapest and New York: Central European University Press, 2012), 82–6; John Pepper, *For a Labor Party: Recent Revolutionary Changes in American Politics* (New York: Workers Party of America, 1922).

4 Pepper, *Labor Party*, 9, 19, 29–32, 47; Sakmyster, *Communist Odyssey*, 85.

a 'farmer-labor revolution'. Its ideology would have, as he put it, 'elements of Jeffersonianism, Danish cooperatives, Ku Klux Klan and Bolshevism'. If the American Communist Party could seize the reins, it could lead the way – in the same fashion as he had seized the reins of the CPUSA, and as a small, just-born Communist Party had grabbed power in Hungary (indeed been handed power) as the government resigned.[5] This was precisely the kind of manipulative strategy that London criticized in the *Freiheit*, and which Theodore Draper would identify as the essence of the corruption of American Communism. 'Pepper Spray' cleared the decks for subsequent Stalinist degeneration and reinforced the early Communist Party's Debsian disregard of black aspirations as well.

Soon after the December JWF convention, Pepper forced through the removal of Olgin and Shachno Epstein as *Freiheit* editors, replacing them with former 'goose' Ben Gitlow. London was fired as labor editor, and Gitlow and his assistant Melech Epstein banned him from the *Freiheit* for a couple of months. As Paul Novick bitterly recounted more than sixty years later:

> Melech Epstein was his assistant, because that Ben didn't know Yiddish you know. He was the most, the most ... abominable, something which you couldn't understand. How you can remove Olgin as editor of the *Freiheit*, one of the main founders of the *Freiheit*, and *beloved by the masses*, Madison Square Garden was filled up when he was speaking there and put in Ben Gitlow there in his place ... but that's what happened with the Communist movement in those days, you know, there was Stalinism all over again.[6]

In late May, London managed to publish a piece in the *Freiheit* entitled 'Don't Strangle the Child with Too Much Love'. He asked: 'What happens when a leadership insists on nothing else but its right to dictate, to oversee every single step of its members? What happens is what happens with the foolish mother who continually presses and drags her child around until she squeezes the spirit out. You fan the party flag around so long that the flag remains, but the party is gone'. The military discipline Pepper was seeking to impose might be needed during war and revolution, but was highly inappropriate for peacetime.[7]

---

5 Draper 1960, 82–4; Sakmyster, *Communist Odyssey*, 36–50, 112–13.

6 Novick interview.

7 Noah London, 'Dershtikt nit dos kind fun tsufil libe', *Freiheit*, May 19, 1923.

London was now able to ridicule the new regime in the *Freiheit*, because he was far from alone in his opposition to 'Pepperism'. James P. Cannon was leading a revolt. When Cannon realized that Pepper's Farmer-Labor schemes were leading the party to the brink of disaster, he persuaded Foster and a number of leading union activists to join his rebellion. Both rival wings of the Jewish Federation immediately lined up behind him. Pepper's maneuvers accomplished a political miracle: they united the Bittelman and Olgin caucuses against him.

Cannon's revolt divided the central party leadership collective down the middle. Foster and Bittelman supported him. Lovestone, Weinstone and Ruthenberg supported Pepper. The history of the CPUSA for the rest of the decade would be one of warfare between these two camps. Foster gradually replaced Cannon as the leader of his wing of the party, made up primarily of Communists with a trade union background, Bittelman included. Pepper was the theoretician for the other camp, whose membership came by and large from the Socialist Party. Charles E. Ruthenberg, the most prominent former Socialist in the Communist movement, was its leader, publicly at any rate.

Ruthenberg did not confine his radicalism in the Socialist Party to articles in newspapers and speeches at party meetings. When he ran for mayor of Cleveland in 1917 and gained more than a quarter of the vote, his campaign was far from 'sewer socialism'. He ran against the war, illegally calling for defying the draft. London described in a biographical piece in the *Freiheit* how regular mass election rallies in Cleveland usually ended with fistfights with patriotic war veterans. The Mayday rally Ruthenberg led in the spring of 1919 in Cleveland drew 40,000 workers, closed down several large factories, and led to pitched battles on the streets of the city. Unlike the foreign federation caucus politicians who flocked to the Pepper-Ruthenberg banner, he was an attractive figure who knew how to speak the language of the American working class.[8]

2 John Pepper's Farmer-Labor Adventure

Government repression played a major role in labor's brutal defeats in the 1922 labor wars, focusing the attention of unionists on politics. There was broad interest in the creation of a political party to represent labor's interests, much

8 London, 'Tsharls E. Rutenberg, der nayer sekreter fun der "Vorkers Parti"', *Freiheit*, May 12, 1922.

along the lines Pepper was advocating. But the leaders of the conservative railroad brotherhoods sidetracked political discontent into support for the presidential aspirations of Wisconsin's Republican senator, Robert LaFollette. When their Conference for Progressive Political Action (CPPA) decided to stick to nonpartisanism, Chicago's AFL leader John Fitzpatrick walked out.

His Chicago Labor Party was a child of the 1919 steel strike, and, like the strike itself, it was a failure. Whereas Socialist candidates had won 34 percent of the vote in off-year Chicago judicial elections in 1917, running against the war, Fitzpatrick got only 8 percent two years later running for mayor on a platform of Wilsonian industrial democracy. After the steel strike was crushed, industrial democracy advocates were drawn into a national Farmer-Labor Party – and immediately started squabbling over what that phrase really meant. The FLP's 1920 presidential candidate received far fewer votes than went to Eugene Debs in his jail cell. Fitzpatrick's party declined, and the national FLP disintegrated.[9]

Fitzpatrick now saw an opportunity to revive the movement. He issued a call for a convention to re-form a national farmer-labor party, inviting the Workers Party to participate. When it opened in Chicago in June 1923, the West Virginia labor federation, several municipal labor councils and state farm organizations, and numerous union locals sent delegates. No national union leaders attended except for Fitzpatrick himself. Of the 500 or 600 delegates present, almost 200 were aligned with the Workers Party. Most of these were from Workmen's Circle branches, workingmens' choruses, Lithuanian literature societies, German sick-and-death benefit funds and so on. Not from unions. This was the boom that Cannon would describe as 'partly real and largely speculative'. An illusion floated in the air of much broader support than the movement really had. Most radicals attending, Communist or otherwise, wanted to found a new party on the spot, but Fitzpatrick believed this would be premature.[10]

The Communist delegates were particularly enthusiastic. Noah London represented Workmen's Circle Branch #561. His comments in the *Freiheit* capture the mood nicely:

> The traditional Socialist, the theoretical revolutionary ... had for years preached socialism, later Communism ... He split and he reunited, but always within the four cubits of these halls ... until he became acquainted

9 Weinstein, *Decline of Socialism*, 223–30, 272–4; McCartin, 197–8.

10 Draper, *American Communism*, 35–48.

> with the man of the earth, with the West Virginia miners, with machinists from Ohio, with farmers from Nebraska … Until now, we have talked about abstract workers and farmers, about their theoretical class struggle … At the convention in Chicago, we felt them with all five senses, how they live and breathe. And we have begun to breathe together with them.[11]

For London, the convention represented an authentic mass movement of real Americans, not a bureaucratic concoction like the SP's 'New York Labor Party'. He was slow to grasp the fictitious nature of the enterprise. He played a not insignificant role in the convention, whose airiest component was its 123 different 'fraternal bodies'. Of these 'broad mass labor organizations', 76 were branches of the Workmen's Circle – about two-fifths of the Communist bloc vote on the convention floor. When the Federated Farmer-Labor Party (FFLP) National Executive Committee was chosen, London sat on it as their representative.[12]

The Workmen's Circle had been the strongest branch of the Jewish labor movement until the mass strikes of the Progressive Era. In the mid-1920s, the organization was at its peak. It broadened its appeal into the middle classes, becoming a vehicle for Yiddish cultural expression and upward social mobility. However, its national leadership, closely aligned with the Socialist Party, boycotted the Chicago convention. The radical branches which sent delegates anyway were a poor basis on which to try to create a genuine American farmer-labor party.

As Foster told Cannon after the convention ended: 'You know, it's a funny thing. When people, who all want the same thing, get together in a closed room they tend to see what they want to see and they can talk themselves into almost anything … The trouble is, we've got the hangover, but the others in New York are still living in a fool's paradise'.[13]

Ironically, the Workers Party had originally cautioned Fitzpatrick against walking out of the CPPA, believing that Fitzpatrick had insufficient support to form a national labor party. But Fitzpatrick's cold feet at the Chicago convention let the Workers Party seize control. A precipitous break took place, and an ally of the Workers Party became a bitter enemy. Pepper's clever maneuver turned into a disaster. To the general public, the reason for the split seemed to

11 Noah London, 'Nit vi bay laytn, abi mmshus'dig', *Freiheit*, July 19, 1923.

12 NARA RG 65, FBI file 61-4203, Jacob Spolansky, 'Summary of the Proceedings of the National Convention of the Farmer-Labor Party of the United States … Held in Chicago, Illinois, July 3-4-5-6, 1923', declassified per FOIA request NND9470230, June 20, 2003.

13 Cannon, *First Ten Years*, 87.

be insistence of the Communists on running the show. The acceptance that the Workers Party had begun to receive on the left wing of the American political spectrum melted away.[14]

According to Leon Trotsky, the new-fledged Workers Party was a 'young and weak Communist Party, lacking in revolutionary temper'. It now was saddled with a fictitious farmer-labor party with a reform program devoid of revolutionary slogans. A smattering of Western populists and Noah's Workmen's Circle branches were the only other real participants. Minnesota Farmer-Labor Party leader William Mahoney, who boycotted the convention, saved the Workers Party from an immediate fiasco. He was interested in transforming his own party from a temporary coalition into a genuine political party based on individual membership, and he needed organizers. His FLP was really two separate political machines tenuously bound together under a single electoral umbrella, since farmer and labor economic interests were quite distinct and often counterposed. He was happy to enlist Communists as organizers – if they were willing to go along with a LaFollette presidential ticket in 1924. The Workers Party jumped at the opportunity.[15]

3 London, Lore, 'Loreism' and Traditional Left-Wing Socialism in America

Cannon and Foster's basic objection to Pepper's Farmer-Labor adventure was its break with Fitzpatrick. They were willing to go along with Pepper's theoretical flights of fancy, despite some skepticism. Aside from a handful of unreconstructed 'geese', the only opponents of Pepper's alliance with LaFollette supporters were a New York-based grouping. Its opponents labeled them as 'Loreites', since Ludwig Lore, the leader of the Workers Party German Federation, was the leader of Socialists like Olgin in the Jewish Federation from the old Workers Council who were not fully integrated into the Communist movement. Lore had a better understanding of basic American political realities than Pepper, or for that matter any of the other central party leaders at that time – and this attracted a disgruntled Noah London's attention.

14 Draper, *American Communism*, 49–51; Palmer, *Cannon*, 21–4; Weinstein, *Decline of Socialism in America*, 284–9.

15 Trotsky, *The First Five Years of the Communist Internationa*, ed. J.G. Wright (London: New Park, 1973 [1924]), 12–13; Weinstein, *Decline of Socialism in America*, 290–9; Draper, *American Communism*, 99–102; Hood, 'Hothouse Socialism: Minneapolis 1910–1925', in *Socialism in the Heartland*, ed. Donald Critchlow (Notre Dame, IN: Notre Dame University Press, 1986), 156–9.

A political maneuver by prowar SP dissidents was the initial basis of the postwar movement for a labor party that the Workers Party jumped into feet-first. Initially, it was scornfully rejected by Socialists and Communists alike. Only after the crushing defeat of the SP in the 1922 elections, including the loss of Meyer London's seat in Congress, did the party abandon its principles and endorse LaFollette in 1924. Lore had been a left wing Socialist before the Bolshevik Revolution, and a personal friend of Trotsky during his stay in America. He supported traditional left-wing Socialist principles, rather than Pepper's new-fangled maneuverism.

American Socialism had emerged from nineteenth-century German-American Socialism – but by 1919 the German Federation of the Socialist Party was a Socialist old age home. Revolution in Russia and Germany, anger at the persecution of German-Americans during World War I, and resentment of the refusal of the Socialist Party to oppose Prohibition pushed grizzled beer-drinking veterans into the Communist movement willy-nilly. Noah London had urged the foreign-language federations to at least wait for the Germans before founding a new party. Their leader, Ludwig Lore, joined John Reed's Communist Labor Party together with the Londons. He was a Jewish university graduate with decades of experience in the movement in Germany and America. His *Volkszeitung*, the oldest Socialist newspaper in America, acquired a reputation for literary brilliance under his editorship. It had opposed 'fusionism' ever since the Henry George New York labor party campaign in 1886.[16]

Lore, the spokesman for old-fashioned left Socialism in the Communist movement, in 1921 joined Salutsky and Olgin's Workers Council without bothering to resign from the underground party first, creating confusion and annoyance in its ranks. Criticism intensified after the French army occupied the Ruhr and touched off the great German inflation and social crisis of 1923. Lore expressed as much skepticism in his *Volkszeitung* about the possibility of a German revolution as he did about Pepper's American adventures. But Communists from Petrograd to New York briefly regained hope in immediate proletarian revolution. A tribute to the German worker Noah wrote for the *Freiheit* expressed this mood nicely:

> For him, there is no fatherland. Its flag is trampled, its statesmen and politicians turned out to be cowards, its scholars lackeys, its industrial

16 Noah London, 'Vegen der grindung fun a nayer partey', *Kamf*, Aug. 8,1919; Paul Buhle, *Ludwig Lore and the New Yorker Volkszeitung: The Twilight of the German-American Socialist Press*, in *The German-American Radical Press: The Shaping of a Left Political Culture*, ed. Elliott Shore et al., (Urbana: University of Illinois Press, 1992), 171–6.

> magnates clever speculators ... he marches with stick in hand, views how the guardsman points his rifle at him and is afraid, how the manufacturer is nervous, how the landlord is afraid ... and knows this is all because of him ... He knows when his time comes. He will take it. You have to believe in him. He is fit to make a revolution, he is fit to build a new world.[17]

All the 'Loreites' were enthusiastic about Pepper's Federated Farmer-Labor Party at the Chicago convention. But when Pepper came out with his theory of a 'LaFollette revolution', they sounded the alarm. Noah became Pepper's loudest critic, writing that 'the danger is now on the right'. He affirmed that: 'I am against, even decidedly against, the idea that the Workers Party in the next few years should enter into extra-parliamentary agreements and connections with petty-bourgeois parties'. The task of Communists was to win workers over to their program and lead them in struggle.

At the December 1923 National Convention of the Workers Party, Foster and Cannon defeated Pepper and Ruthenberg with the aid of the Lore caucus. Their objection was to the creation of a fictitious FFLP, not to the idea of voting for LaFollette. The issue of an alliance with pro-LaFollette populists was referred to the Comintern for final decision.[18] At the subsequent JWF convention, Cannon brokered a temporary end to the Jewish Federation's factional battles. The Bittelman and Olgin caucuses merged, and a united leadership took firm control. London returned to the Jewish Federation Executive Committee (JFEC) as Cannon's man, and even Bittelman's.

Olgin regained his editor's post at the *Freiheit*, and London again became one of its most prolific writers. His role as the leader of the 76-strong Workmen's Circle delegation at the 1923 Chicago Farmer-Labor convention restored his status in the movement. He was becoming a spokesman for a new Yiddish left-wing subculture.

4 From Garment Unionism to Cooperativism: The Birth of a Radical Subculture

London shifted from garment unionism to new Jewish projects, the first being the Workmen's Circle, seeking an arena where he would not be strictly bound

17 Noah London, 'Dem Kolner tsuefent, dos hitel on a zeyt', *Freiheit*, Oct. 28, 1923.

18 Draper, *American Communism*, 88; Cannon, *First Ten Years*, 188–9.

by party discipline. The Workmen's Circle was the obvious choice. Before the Chicago convention the Workers Party was barely aware of its existence. As he put it,

> The Arbeyter Ring with its hundreds of branches in hundreds of cities in the land, with its many-sided social activity (or inactivity) is thoroughly unreflected in our press … writers have written about everything in the world … But about the Arbeyter Ring, which is under their noses … about this they haven't written.[19]

He himself had suggested three years earlier in the *Proletaryer* that it was time for the Communist press to start talking about the Arbeyter Ring. But it was only after the Chicago Farmer-Labor convention that it 'captured the *Freiheit*', When the Jewish Socialist Federation split from the Socialist Party in the summer of 1921, its manifesto called for a struggle to drive 'pseudo-socialists' out of 'every union, every local, every Arbeyter Ring branch'.[20] At first glance the Workmen's Circle must have seemed the ideal field for a power struggle. The Jewish unions usually took their lead from Abe Cahan's *Forward* rather than from the JSF. The Workmen's Circle, however, was largely in the hands of former Bundists. Now that both the Russian Bund and its American branch the JSF had joined the Communist movement, why shouldn't the WC follow suit? London's future ally Reuben Saltzman was a member of its National Executive Committee, but other top officers all supported the Farband, the tiny SP-loyal splinter of the old JSF.[21]

A strong left-wing minority had developed in the Workmen's Circle but never posed as serious a threat as did the left-wing movement in the garment unions. This was primarily because of the transformation the WC was undergoing. In its early days it was the first institution Jewish immigrant workers could turn to for their material, social and cultural needs. In addition to cheap medical, dental and insurance benefits, it provided friendship, mutual aid and Yiddish cultural moorings in a strange land. It served as a vital support for the unionization of the garment industry. According to London, 'The social life of the masses in the branches bubbled, with socialism and revolution as their ideals. On top rot began to set in, just like with the Socialist Party'.[22]

---

19 Noah London, 'Vi azoy der Arbeyter Ring hot gekeptshurt di "Frayheyt"', *Freiheit*, Aug. 20, 1924.

20 London, 'Ver shtelt di yunyons in gefar?'

21 NEC minutes, Spring 1922, Workmen's Circle Coll., RG 575, YIVO.

22 London, *Royte Velt*, Nov. 1928, 88.

Once garment unions were solidly established, it was only natural that the Workmen's Circle, a support organization, would align itself closely with Socialist union leaders. As these unions became powerful institutions, they took over its practical functions. As radical immigrants began moving up the ladder from the working to the middle class, it assisted them in this transformation – as it had for Noah himself. At its peak, it was one of the most prosperous Jewish organizations in America, with over 80,000 members and a treasury of millions.

The cultural-educational orientation of the former Bundists who ran it facilitated a shift in its class composition, especially in non-metropolitan areas. Its old-country socialist values provided a haven for small town professionals and petty businessmen from widespread anti-Semitism in Middle America in the 1920s. The Workmen's Circle was becoming a socialist Yiddish subculture for middle-class immigrants who had climbed out of poverty. As London put it, 'Former well-paid workers became bosses, little peddlers became rich businessmen, former students and 'externs' [like Noah himself] became doctors and lawyers with rich practices. A class of *'alrightniks'* arose in the Workmen's Circle, who talked about socialism as a foolish youthful dream'.[23]

The sympathy of American Jews for Soviet Russia facilitated the support some of these *alrightniks* gave the left. Nonetheless, middle-class sympathy was no substitute for the solid backing disgruntled workers gave the left movement in the garment unions. Rank-and-file dissatisfaction with discredited Socialist union leaders gave Communists a ready-made battle cry, but the WC left wing had no fundamental grievance on which to base its struggle.

At the May 1922 Toronto Workmen's Circle convention, its leadership introduced a resolution demanding the release of Socialist political prisoners in the USSR. It was virtually identical to the parallel resolution passed at the 1922 ILGWU convention. Radical delegates walked out and formed a 'Left Action Committee' (LAC). It was a remarkable tribute to the degree of support that the Soviet Union had in the American Jewish community that a movement whose founding platform was to defend the right of the Soviet Union to put Socialists behind bars could find considerable support in the socialist Workmen's Circle. However, this was hardly an issue that spoke to the day-to-day needs of its working-class members, the primary support of the LAC.

London's 1923 campaign to get the Workmen's Circle to sponsor a national farmer-labor party was probably the most attractive campaign issue the Left

---

23 London, ibid.; Judith J. Shapiro, *The Friendly Society: A History of the Workmen's Circle* (New York: Media Judaica, 1970), 86–8; Liebman, *Jews and the Left*, 285–98.

Action Committee ever had. It gained particularly strong support in New York. The allure of an 'American' nationwide farmer-labor movement was powerful for Jewish radicals, since they were burningly conscious of their isolation from fellow Americans.[24] The FFLP fiasco deprived the LAC of a practical program. But Jewish garment workers were increasingly supporting the Communist-backed garment insurgency, steadily bringing working-class WC branches into the LAC.

The internal WC conflict reflected the struggle within the garment unions. Despite the absence of solid programmatic issues, it was equally brutal. Left Action Committee literature labeled it a class struggle between workers and bourgeois. Workmen's Circle officers denied this heatedly, pointing to the middle-class composition of many a radical branch. The LAC contention was not inaccurate, loosely speaking. Rank-and-file garment workers were flocking to the Left in the mid-1920s. The LAC got nearly a third of the delegates at a February 1924 WC conference, whose centerpiece was a provocative fund collection for arrested Socialists in Russia. Protesting radicals were chased off the platform.[25] London's convention article, 'The Class Struggle in the Arbeyter Ring', drips vitriol:

> *Forward* agents bustled around in automobiles over country paths and intercity roads into every hole ... to the pawn-brokers; to the bootleggers; to the ignoramuses who have squirrelled away money for years in their stockings to build themselves cottages and fill them up with furniture, linen and jewelry, and get dapper young men for their bepowdered and berouged little daughters ... they brought them all together on election day to rescue the Arbeyter Ring from the *arbeyter* danger ... But when the gang saw that the proletarian delegation was unimpressed by their howling, the majority measured out how to wound the workers ... how to make their hearts ache and hopes fail. The gang began to smear the worker government with blood and venom. Thus did brother take revenge for brother – NEPmen in America for NEPmen in Russia.[26]

The warfare within the Workmen's Circle would drag on for years. But raw class hatred was not a program for building a movement. When the inevitable split finally took place in 1929, at most 10 percent of the organization joined

24 NEC minutes summer 1923, WC Coll., YIVO; 'Der a. r. darf gehn mit Farmer Leybor Partey', *Freiheit*, July 10,.

25 Epstein, *The Jew and Communism*, 147.

26 Noah London, 'Der klasn-kamf in Arb. Ring', *Freiheit*, Feb. 28, 1924.

the Communist-backed International Workers Order, led by Reuben Saltzman. Noah London realized that if the Left wanted to create a radical Jewish cooperative movement in America, mere denunciation of the Workmen's Circle was worse than futile. The WC was providing an attractive Socialist subculture for Jewish immigrants. A Communist alternative was needed. So he set about creating one.

5 The United Workers Cooperative Colony: Camp 'What, Me Worry?'

The United Workers Cooperative Colony (UWCC) was a vegetarian 10-apartment communal housing cooperative of Jewish garment workers, in an apartment building in Harlem. It resembled a Sixties commune more than an underground Communist Party cell – perhaps not unlike the Socialist-Zionist Party commune in Vilna, London's first introduction to radical politics. Between the usual communal squabbles, its leaders organized cooperative summer holiday excursions into the countryside. A 1921 ad in *Der Emes* promised that 'you will sleep with mother earth, with your fist for a pillow. But you will be covered … by the lovely moon and the beautiful stars'. The excursions became popular. Soon, they opened a small weekend summer camp for adults in the rugged hills near Beacon, a midway stop on the Hudson River Day Line. They named it Kemp Nitgedeiget: 'Camp What, Me Worry?' would be a reasonable translation. About 50 campers participated the first summer, enjoying the sunshine, bathing in the Hudson, and performing all chores communally except cooking.[27]

In 1924, Noah London brought the Workers Party into the project – without bothering to go through party channels. The *Freiheit* would not write about Camp Nitgedeiget until 1925. Some 550 campers attended in the summer of 1924, with Noah London as camp director, who saw it as a field for constructive work without party interference. It rapidly became popular, growing from one year to the next by leaps and bounds. According to Mike Gold's 1926 account in the *Nation*:

> No one can come to this camp who is a boss or who owns a business of any kind. But any wage earner, and this includes intellectual workers, can come at the low rate of $15 a week. He is given clean linen and two wooly

27 *The Coops: The United Workers Cooperative Colony 50th Anniversary, 1927–1977* (New York: Semi-Centennial Coop Reunion, 1977), 7; Epstein *The Jew and Communism*, 214, 219–20; London, 'Unzere oyfgabe oyf'n kooperativn front', *Freiheit*, Nov. 1, 1925.

> blankets and can climb to his tent among the trees to rest … He can roam the hills. He can sing in the moonlight. He can swim, take sun-baths, listen to lectures, sing in the mass chorals, act in proletarian comedies, read in the library, talk, laugh, play games, go about all day in nothing but bathing trunks until his body is brown as a faun's.[28]

The *Freiheit* attracted a number of prominent Yiddish literary figures disgusted by the sensationalism and 'potato Yiddish' of Cahan's *Forward*. They saw it as a vehicle for high-toned Yiddish culture, and some started attending Camp Nitgedeiget, where they could link up with ordinary Jewish garment workers. It became a launching pad for left-wing projects, and it gave Noah London the opportunity to express his personal style of Jewish radicalism.

The camp newsletter called itself *Der Mamzer*, 'the bastard'.[29] The editors explained that *Der Mamzer* was 'an illegal child of a free-spirited mother'. The camp declaration proclaimed what the UWCC stood for: 'Ours is a *workers* cooperative, for workers. Those who have … any kind of interest in the current system of exploitation may not be members' As the newsletter's name implies, the family was *not* the fighting unit for socialism at this adult summer camp. Gender roles were more egalitarian, since communal living was the original UWCC idea. One of its three original leaders was a woman named Clara Farber.

Practically, the camp sought to provide a cheap, open air summer vacation for workers; to create a workers' cultural center; develop the cooperative spirit; and use the profits for future projects. *Der Mamzer* was devoted to humor and satire, to 'great biographies of little men' and 'little biographies of fat men', parodies of the *Forward* and the *Freiheit*, and a 'science for the people' column devoted to 'anatomy' for the benefit of 'fighters for freedom – for free love and free automobile trips'.

6 Noah London as Party Leader and Immigrant Advocate?

In the spring of 1924, as the Camp Nitgedeiget summer program was coming together, party chairman Cannon had attempted to send London as the American delegate to the Berlin 'Committee of Five' of the Workers International Relief (WIR), whose American branch was the Chicago-based Committee for International Workers' Aid. Out of this committee, later described by Cannon

28 Michael Gold, 'At a Workers' Vacation Camp', *Nation*, Sept. 29, 1926, 295.
29 *Der Mamzer* (June/July 1924) Bund collection, YIVO.

as a 'very quiet, inoffensive organization', would stem the more famous International Labor Defense, which under Cannon's leadership would conduct a worldwide campaign to defend Italian labor martyrs Sacco and Vanzetti. On the occasion of his departure from America two years later, London would tell Lovestone that one of Cannon's reasons for the appointment was 'to have me forget the traditional factional politics in which I was entangled … and to put me in closer contact with the leaders of our movement'.[30]

The purpose of the Committee of Five was to coordinate a 'Red Cross' for the revolutionary labor movement – the original function of the Workmen's Circle on a worldwide scale. One group of workers definitely needing help in America in the 1920s was immigrants. Anti-immigrant sentiment in America greatly intensified in the 1920s, following the outburst of anti-German paranoia during World War I. The Russian Revolution exacerbated this fear of radical foreigners from Europe, especially Jews. Anti-immigration laws were targeted first and foremost at preventing Slavs and Jews from emigrating to America, bringing over the virus of Bolshevism. Some sociological surveys seemed to indicate that the level of popular anti-Semitism in the USA in the 1920s was higher than in Germany.

Immigration was the topic of the most extensive article series of Noah London's journalistic career.[31] America, he wrote, had moved from open arms to open hatred for immigrants, not least Jewish immigrants. Immigration restrictions formerly blocked by business and public opposition were quietly passing into law with little resistance. America's prewar economic expansion was over, economic crisis was looming, industry no longer needed more workers, and Eastern European immigration raised the specter of Bolshevism. 'Open door' advocacy by Jews and liberals quieted to a murmur. Even Communist protest meetings attracted much less attendance than fundraising picnics and costume balls.

He set about examining the immigrant experience in the *Freiheit* a couple of years before his own decision to go back home. He based himself on American experience and history, not abstract Marxist theory, and his thoughts match the views of contemporary historians fairly well. His new realization was that unionism was not necessarily the path to radicalizing the working class. Steel trust magnates, he wrote, were in fact more liberal than Gompers with respect to immigration.

30 Zumoff, *Communist International*, 200–1; London to Lovestone, Feb. 22, 1926, CPUSA microfilms, r. 55, d. 770, l. 1–2.

31 *Freiheit*, April 24, April 27, May 2, May 4, May 11, May 14, May 24, 1924.

> A trade union is not a class organization, not a struggle organization, but an association, a trust for a limited number of people in a particular trade. The trade unions have taken the easy road, and that is not to let the foreigner … in the union, in the factory. And if he is in the factory, not to organize him and let the boss, better yet help the boss, to exploit the unorganized, so that they won't bother the organized.[32]

His conclusion was not a utopian call to return to the days of the open door. Rather, it was that 'communists cannot give a solution for the question in the realm of the existing order'. The immigration problem could only be solved 'in a world federation of Soviet republics'. Meanwhile, then as now, Communists needed to oppose both immigration restrictions and attempts by business to use immigrants to swamp the workforce and lower wage levels.

Contradicting himself slightly, he did come up with a positive program, one more plausible then than now. Mussolini had sponsored an international congress on immigration. A Swedish delegate proposed an international bureau to regulate immigration. Such a bureau under Mussolini's control would obviously be a disaster. But 'in the hands of the trade unions of all lands, let us say in the hands of the AFL and the Amsterdam International and the Red Trade Union International … it could bring order into chaos'.[33] Perhaps Noah London could facilitate such an arrangement in Berlin.

The Pepper-Ruthenberg faction objected to London's Berlin appointment. When it did not come through, Cannon counseled him that 'it should be of little concern to you. As matters are developing you may have the duty of playing an even more important role for the party – that of taking a leading post in bringing about the complete unification of groups in the party'. Cannon did manage to get Pepper sent back to the Soviet Union, and London's future in the movement looked good again. He was touring the country by rail on behalf of a farmer-labor convention in St. Paul in June 1924 that Minnesota FLP leader Mahoney was sponsoring. London enjoyed this vacation immensely, writing that 'it is good to get out and have a look at the workers movement … getting East Broadway politics out of your head'. In Schenectady, he helped negotiate an agreement to create a New York State Farmer-Labor Party.[34] But were his views on the matter the same as his sponsor Cannon's?

32 *Freiheit* series part 4, 'Ven geri iz liberaler fun Gompers'n', May 4, 1924.

33 London, final article in the series 'Imigratsie un internatsionale problem', May 27, 1924.

34 WP CEC minutes, April 2, 1924, CPUSA microfilms r. 20, d. 299, l. 45–46; and 4–24, d. 303, l. 34; Cannon to London, April 24 and April 29, 1924, Cannon Papers, Wisc. Hist. Soc., r. 3; London, 'Fun Nyu York keyn St. Paul', *Freiheit*, June 18, 1924; and 'Vos shtuft unzere yunyons rekhts', May 22, 1924.

7 Communism and American Politics in 1924

In 1923, Pepper had talked the Workers Party into an embarrassing fiasco. Now he was no longer in charge, but his ideas still lingered in the minds of American Communists. He justified the alliance with Mahoney's Minnesota populists by way of an elaborate theoretical edifice which dazzled even his opponents. There would be 'two splits'. LaFollette's Third Party movement would split the petty bourgeoisie from the big bourgeoisie. Then, the 'class Farmer-Labor party', whose convention was going to take place in St. Paul, would split the working class from the petty bourgeoisie. But as Trotsky put it, the Workers Party was simply building a movement 'around Senator LaFollette, or more correctly, around his name, for the Senator himself … has not yet found time to leave the ranks of the Republican Party'.[35]

In the *Freiheit*, Noah London avoided directly contradicting the party line, but he did challenge its theoretical underpinnings, introducing a badly needed note of realism. Practitioners of American politics viewed it as a form of business. Spectators saw political conventions as a sport, like the World Series. Campaigns did not hang on class issues, but on who voters saw as the 'better man'.[36] As London delicately put it, without mentioning Pepper's name:

> If you come from a European land and are a Marxist as well, you might try to guess that the Republican Party represents the big bourgeoisie, the Democratic Party the middle and smaller bourgeoisie. But those who are no longer quite greenhorns … think like SP stump speakers: both serve Wall Street … and seek out issues in order to fight over graft. The truth is that they both are right. Firstly both parties represent particular industrial interests. Secondly … both are loyal to the entire capitalist class in general and big capital in particular. Thirdly both parties are political firms that compete for the graft which comes with power.[37]

So what then did the LaFollette movement really represent? As London put it, 'We don't have a general revolt against big capital, as others of us are inclined to believe. If that were the case, LaFollette would not be playing cat and mouse with the other Republican politicians … This is not a Third Party movement, but

35 Draper, *American Communism*, 96–9; Trotsky, *First Five Years*, 12.

36 Noah London, 'Sdrh politishe konvenshons', *Freiheit*, June 4, 1924; and 'Di biznes fun politik in Amerike', June 9, 1924.

37 London, 'Di biznes fun politik'.

the political affair of certain sectors of the Republican Party'.[38] To be precise, the Wisconsin Republican machine of which LaFollette was a tool. Wisconsin, he wrote, was unique in the Midwest. Small- and medium-scale manufacturing and farming dominated the economy. Trusts and corporations were absent, and the railroads were run from Chicago and New York, so Wisconsin manufacturers were enthusiastic about Progressive campaigns against big business. LaFollette had opposed World War I because much of the population was German.

Did this mean that London opposed the St. Paul convention? No. Like the Foster-Cannon majority party leadership with whom he was allied, he accepted the concept of a 'class farmer-labor party' as good coin. During the runup to the St. Paul convention there was some convergence between London and Cannon's views on the farmer-labor movement. Whereas in April, Cannon cosigned a polemic in which he accused Loreites of 'dump[ing] all non-proletarian groups into one reactionary heap', by May, after Pepper and Lovestone vetoed Cannon's idea of appointing London to a key international post, Cannon shifted his stance a bit. Writing in the *Labor Herald*, Cannon denounced any support for 'a third party dominated by the petty bourgeoisie' and proclaimed that 'St. Paul Means Class Struggle'.[39] London for his part managed to broker a deal in Schenectady with liberal LaFollette supporters in which, in his opinion, the principle of working-class political independence was maintained. Elsewhere, Farmer-Labor conventions were usually made up entirely of Communist delegates. London was highly impressed with the Communist labor activists he met on his tour of America's industrial heartland. He was looking forward to a repeat of the WP's organizational victory in Chicago over Fitzpatrick and thought that the dubious LaFollette alliance would go by the wayside. As he put it in his final election piece, 'St. Paul will be all right'.[40]

A couple of weeks later, Foster brought the word back from Moscow that the party line had changed. The Comintern forced the Workers Party to break with Mahoney and LaFollette, under pressure from Trotsky's criticism. Another week later, LaFollette denounced Communists as 'the mortal enemies of the progressive movement and democratic ideals'. Mahoney followed suit. As Theodore Draper put it, the Third Party alliance 'came apart at both ends almost simultaneously'. Foster also brought back the message that the Comintern wanted a campaign against 'Loreism' as 'the American form of Trotskyism'.

38 Noah London, 'Klivland-Lafolet-St. Paul', *Freiheit*, June 12, 1924.

39 James P. Cannon, 'St. Paul-June 17th', *Labor Herald*, May 1924, 88–9; Palmer, *Cannon*, 228; Zumoff, *Communist International*, 133.

40 Draper, *American Communism*, 115; London, May 24 and June 18, 1924.

The CPUSA needed to be 'Bolshevized' – and troublemakers like Lore and Noah London needed to be brought to heel.[41]

8 Noah London's Marginalization: 'Bolshevization' and the Specter of Trotskyism

Lore's predilection for Trotsky was more personal than political – but his dislike for Comintern chairman Zinoviev was fundamental. Lore had proclaimed Pepper's defeat by Cannon and Foster to be a 'Trotskyist victory' in the *Volkszeitung*. The specter of Lore celebrating another Trotskyist victory over the LaFollette issue was potentially a grave embarrassment. 'Bolshevization' would thus dominate the life of American Communism in the coming period. Bryan Palmer aptly describes it as a 'two-edged sword'.[42] Cannon's embrace of Bolshevization would end his role as London's ally and protector. For Cannon, Bolshevization meant the transformation of the party into a hard-nosed working-class vanguard that could intervene more effectively in labor struggles. What he did not yet see was that it foreshadowed the bureaucratic corruption of the party into an American appendage of Soviet Stalinism. Initially, it would be a mixture of both processes at the same time.

Noah London attended the 1924 St. Paul convention as a Workmen's Circle delegate in June, but wrote not a word about this painful experience. St. Paul wasn't all right after all. Virtually every attendee who wasn't a party member wanted to endorse LaFollette for president. According to Foster, LaFollette 'could have controlled St. Paul for the mere asking'. All of the party's former Farmer-Labor allies clamored to climb onto the LaFollette bandwagon. A depressed London escaped north to Canada to cover a massive political strike for the *Freiheit*, and then fled to Camp Nitgedeiget for the rest of the summer.[43]

The Communist Party had suffered a dramatic defeat. Foster concluded that it was time to drop the labor party slogan and to run for president himself. The labor party movement was dead. According to Cannon, 'We all readily agreed with him. As I recall it, there were some objections from the Loreites such as Zimmerman'. And no doubt London as well. When he got back from summer camp, the Workers Party Central Executive Committee tried to fob him off with

41 Draper, *American Communism*, 104–14 (quote at 114).

42 Palmer, *Cannon*, 228.

43 Draper, *American Communism*, 115–16; Noah London, 'Der politisher strayk in kenede', *Freiheit*, July 2, 1924.

a job as *Freiheit* business manager in Philadelphia – not even New York. This would have been a tremendous step down from the role that Cannon had foreseen for him in the spring and would have required him to quit his job as a subway engineer. He refused. The CEC did not consider his reasons for refusal satisfactory, but accepted them 'in view of the many inconveniences which this appointment would cause Comrade London'.[44]

In the fall elections, Foster and the *Daily Worker* denounced LaFollette supporters in extreme language, even calling them future American fascists. London, who had always opposed LaFollette, had no difficulty following suit. In New York, the Socialist Party was the main force behind LaFollette – but LaFollette was playing political footsie with New York governor Al Smith. Smith had narrowly lost the Democratic Party nomination at its 1924 'Klanbake convention', where John W. Davis, an obscure conservative Southern Democrat, became the Democratic candidate for president, as a compromise between Smith and William Gibbs McAdoo, the Klan-backed candidate from California. Noah London condemned the SP-LaFollette-Smith alliance in the *Freiheit* as a corrupt political maneuver in the Tammany mold. But like other 'Loreites', he was unhappy with dropping the Labor Party slogan – and Ruthenberg and his Pepperite 'minority faction' were even more so. A year later, London would state at the final Jewish Federation convention that it was an illusion 'that the Foster group understands the American conditions better. Their tactics are not based on such a knowledge, for if this were the case, how could they jump from a LaFollette alliance to an extreme sectarian position, to negate a Labor party. Surely conditions in America have not changed so radically in a few months'.[45]

London was never in any sense a Trotskyist. His 1921 obituary article for John Reed in the *Emes* compared Reed to Trotsky but made clear that he admired Reed greatly while disagreeing with him politically. This was always London's attitude to Trotsky as well – including his private views as a Soviet official in later years. London's Communist role model was Lenin, not Trotsky, even before Trotsky was ousted from the leadership. Despite the anti-Trotsky campaign beginning to hit the Workers Party, London titled his 1924 October Revolution anniversary article in the *Freiheit* 'Seven Years of Permanent Revolution'. The

44 Draper, *American Communism*, 116–17; Cannon, *First Ten Years*, 129–30; CEC minutes, Aug. 1924, CPUSA microfilms, r. 20, d. 299, 61–2 and 70.

45 Draper, *American Communism*, 118; London, 'Tamani amol – di es pi haynt', *Freiheit*, Oct. 12, 1924; and 'Statement of N. London at the convention of the Jewish Federation of the Workers Party', CPUSA microfilms, r. 38, d. 561, l. 43–5.

article had no Trotskyist content other than its provocative 'Trotskyite' title.[46] Nonetheless, for an entire year after the publication of this piece he rarely appeared in the *Freiheit.*

Freiheit editor Olgin, having won his point on LaFollette, repudiated Lore and Trotsky and became a 'Fosterite'. London was more stubborn. A steady drumbeat of criticism of Lore, 'Loreism' and 'Loreites' started appearing in the *Daily Worker* – at first primarily from the Ruthenberg minority, but Olgin soon joined in as well. Jay Lovestone, who replaced Pepper as the mastermind of the minority, branded London as the leader of the Loreite group in the Jewish Workers Federation. Olgin went on to denounce London in both the *Daily Worker* and the *Freiheit* as the leader of the 'extreme right flank of the right wing opposition' in the JWF, blaming his own political errors of 1922 on London's influence,[47] though that was far from the truth. Noah London was hardly as 'rightist' as Moissaye Olgin had been in 1922, or beforehand.

London was not allowed to respond. A *Freiheit* piece on Camp Nitgedeiget expressed his feelings of frustration:

> The principle of the camp is *nit gedayget* ... Take a stick and climb up the hill. At the peak, where grass grows sparsely and the fragrance of the *mianter* makes your head spin and the sun pours over your head through the bluest heavens. You can roll on your back there, you can scream and sing freely. You can dance, make faces – you haven't done that in the shop, you haven't done that in the union local, you haven't done that in the party meeting. Do it there.[48]

He quit his New York subway job after all in November 1924 and went to work for the Amtorg Trading Corporation at its New York office. Amtorg originated as the US office of the All-Russian Cooperative Society and was the only legal representative of the USSR in America, serving Soviet import and export firms. His job title was senior engineer for construction and highway equipment. For a former garment workers' leader to play the role of a businessman had its difficult moments. He would tour middle America again in the spring of 1925 – but this time as an Amtorg representative, hobnobbing with capital-

46 Noah London, '7 yar permanente revolutsie', *Freiheit*, Nov. 9, 1924.

47 Lovestone, *Daily Worker*, Dec. 17, 1924; Olgin, 'Shoyn tsayt tsu vern gantse komunistn', *Freiheit*, July 30 and July 31, 1924; 'It Is Time to Become Communists', *Daily Worker*, Aug. 19, 1924.

48 Noah London, 'Kemp "Nitgedayget"', *Freiheit*, May 15, 1925. Presumably a 'mianter' is some sort of flower.

ists instead of socializing with radical workers. When he visited a huge steel mill near Pittsburgh, the company gave him red carpet treatment. Workers were forbidden to speak to him. As bosses escorted him through the plant, 'The workers looked at us, and in their glances I read hatred and contempt'. He assured his readership that this was a promising sign of incipient class consciousness.[49]

Noah London also joined the Presidium and Editorial Board of the Association of Russian Engineers. It began publishing *Amerikanskaia Tekhnika*, a purely technical journal little read in America but popular with Soviet engineers. According to the policy statement in its first issue, its goal was to study and analyze the latest American technology, 'from the standpoint of social, humanitarian engineering', in order to assist Soviet construction. London, who likely wrote the statement, was no great admirer at that time of American technology. He had criticized, in the *Freiheit*, its backwardness compared to Europe, and the way America wasted its immense national resources.[50] After participating in Soviet construction himself, he would change his attitude.

For Noah, Camp Nitgedeiget was not merely a refuge from factional persecution. It was also a place where he could help lay the basis for a cooperative movement – together with like-minded radicals and away from his critics.

> All agree on one thing, and that is that the cooperative ... must spread its activities to all areas: cooperative housing, cooperative stores, cooperative schools, theaters, banks. And who knows where fancy will take it ... There are class-conscious, goal-directed leaders there, who know that workers need to be taught to run their own affairs, so that they will be ready to handle the job when the time comes.[51]

It also was a good place for him to do some serious rethinking, during his second summer as camp director in 1925. The left-wing Jewish garment movement went off in new directions after his removal as *Freiheit* labor editor – directions he may not have been happy with. It was likely at this time that he began thinking about going to the Soviet Union.

49 Noah London, 'In mitl-Amerike', *Freiheit*, May 3, 1925.

50 London, *Biograficheskii ocherk*, l. 7; Bailes, 'The American Connection', *Comparative Studies in Society and History* 23, no. 3 (1981): 437; 'Ot prezidiuma assotsiatsii', *Amerikanskaia Tekhnika* 1, no. 1 (Nov. 1924); London, 'Vi Amerike farshvent ihre natirlikhe raykhtumer', *Freiheit*, April 20, 1992; and 'Di untershteligkeyt fun der Amerikaner tekhnik', April 27, 1922.

51 London, *Freiheit*, May 16, 1925.

8.1 *'Loreism', Noah London and Jewish Garment Unionism*

Was Noah London really a 'Loreite', as he was charged with being? Well, yes and no. Whereas Lore really was politically halfway between Communism and old-style left Socialism of the pre-World-War I era, Noah London was tempted by the idea of finding ways to bring the two warring halves of the workers movement into some sort of united front, if not outright unity. That often meant similar positions on practical questions, but not always. What it meant in garment unionism would lead London to take his distance from it.

The core of the Lore caucus was the ex-JSF caucus in the Jewish Federation. Most of the leading garment activists were 'Loreites', including Zimmerman, Wortis and Furriers leader Ben Gold. It had been not so long ago that Noah London had proclaimed that these people, the 'conscious workers in the shops', were the real Jewish Bolsheviks in America.[52] But were they?

In the 1920s, the AFL was expelling all Communists. In the ILGWU, the birth of the 'Lore group' coincided with a campaign by Sigman to remove officers affiliated with Foster's party-backed TUEL, which controlled many of the ILGWU's most important locals. Similar moves were afoot in other garment unions. London saw all this as a cynical conspiracy organized by Cahan's *Forward* to separate Communists from the masses through terror tactics. 'Let them hold onto their machine. Our work among the masses will go on … The masses are going over to our side', he assured his readers.[53]

How did these labor officials in Noah London's party caucus react? Foster's original TUEL had replaced the garment center Workers Council as their model. They were well aware that the labor movement was in retreat nationwide, and that the Jewish community was in the middle of a transition from the working class to the middle class. Unionists in New York's garment district, a short subway ride away from Wall Street, could not isolate themselves in a radical ghetto for long. If they did not want to bury themselves in a dissolving milieu as the world changed around them, they needed to adapt to the new situation. Foster's 1921 dictum that labor radicals should 'use their control to put across their radical philosophy, not use their radical philosophy to get control', suited them perfectly.[54]

Left-wing garment union officials were now taking their cues not from Noah London but from another Loreite, Juliet Stuart Poyntz. She was a former ILGWU Local 25 education director who became the first director of the New York

52 London, *Freiheit*, Nov. 10, 1923.

53 London, 'Zeyere zibn fete yorn', *Freiheit*, May 17, 1924.

54 Draper, *American Communism*, 350.

Workers Party's Workers School, where London taught as well. She was then the most prominent woman in the WP. Following her advice, they followed a policy the diametric opposite of the open communist trade unionism London had advocated in 1922. They simply signed *pro forma* resignation statements from the TUEL. This infuriated Sigman and led to escalating reprisals. By 1925 Zimmerman, now TUEL Needle Trades Secretary, was instructing left union officers to sign statements promising to discipline members distributing left-wing leaflets. In order to keep their jobs, they would agree to help Sigman against the rank-and-file members who had elected them to office, in line with Poyntz's recommendations.

This touched off a 'needle trades crisis' in the Workers Party, which fueled the campaign against Loreism. At a special Jewish Federation leadership meeting, 'Fosterite' Almazov stated that 'the great majority of the rank-and-file cloakmakers and even most of the executive board members ... are content with the *Freiheit* editorial' which had criticized the 'Loreite' union officials. London was conspicuously absent, touring the Midwest for Amtorg.[55]

Noah London of all people could hardly criticize the *Freiheit* for publicly chiding Left union officers for collaborating with ILGWU bureaucrats against the rank and file. The crisis must have seemed like a powerful argument against the emphasis on worker spontaneity that had been his hallmark as a Jewish Communist.

8.2 *The Stalinization of American Communism: Noah London's Capitulation*

By the fall of 1925 the Workers Party was fully 'Bolshevized'. Moscow, where Zinoviev was still head of the Comintern, ordered the party to expel Lore and install the Ruthenberg/Lovestone faction as its leaders, even though the Foster/Cannon faction had a clear majority at its August national convention. Marking the transformation symbolically, it adopted a new name: the Workers (Communist) Party of America. The Comintern's interference in American affairs in 1925 was the final step in the subordination of American Communism to Soviet needs and interests. After Lore's expulsion, London and other Loreites on the Jewish Executive Committee renounced Loreism at the final Jewish Workers Federation convention. According to the *Daily Worker*, 'All of

55 J. Holmes, 'Jewish Communism and Garment Unionism', 185–7; lead editorial, *Freiheit*, March 20, 1925; 'Statement on the Needle Trades Situation' and 'Statement ... submitted by Comrade Poyntz', Bell Collection, Box 10, folder 1, Tamiment; minutes, 'miting fun der ekzekutive un fun redaktsions kolegium', March 28, 1925 (in possession of author).

these comrades ... took the floor, acknowledged their errors and pledged themselves to follow the line of the party and the Comintern thereafter'.[56] None were re-elected.

Noah London's *mea culpa* did not have the groveling character such statements would take on in the future. It represented the conclusions he was forced to draw from the needle trades crisis. Ever since he helped found the Left Wing in 1919, he had upheld the revolutionary instincts of immigrant Jewish rank-and-file workers over abstract Marxist theory and party discipline. This 'syndicalist deviation' marked his earliest work as an agitator for the Workers Council movement, and it was indeed a red thread running through all his political activity. London's capitulation statement expresses the Stalinization of American Communism with crystalline clarity:

> The first, fundamental error was that at the first stages of our Communist movement I underestimated the role of the Comintern as a central guiding and ruling body ... If as it looked to me our movement locally would benefit by a more democratic form of organization, I was against the existence of the underground party ... Subsequently I realized that what counts at present, in the international situation, is a party molded along these lines of a military organization, that what really counts now is the defense of the Russian Revolution ...[57]

London ascribed his long-time adherence to the Lore caucus to 'the fact that I am less capable than others to change sudden front'. He inveighed at length against the maneuverings of his former allies, the prime persecutors of Loreism at that moment. He was particularly angry at Cannon, whom he felt had betrayed him personally. He announced that he had decided to 'surrender unconditionally' to the Ruthenberg minority, who were 'nearer to the Comintern'. They also had more or less the same position on the labor party question at that point as he did.

As early as 1917, London spoke out in *Naye Velt* as a pragmatic opponent of Menshevik impotence who saw Bolshevism as the practical alternative. Initially, he was more a supporter of a proto-Stalinist version of 'socialism in one country' in Russia than of the Leninist program of world revolution. By his own account, it was the radical activism of rank-and-file workers that pushed him into becoming a Communist. Radicalism was receding, however, even in the

56 Draper *American Communism*, 133–52; *Daily Worker*, Sept. 10, 1925.

57 London statement at JWF convention.

garment district. His fellow Loreites on the Executive Committee all joined the minority Ruthenberg faction.[58] Zimmerman, Wortis and Ben Gold would do so as well after Ruthenberg died in March 1927, when Lovestone granted them free reign in the garment unions. By then, their union policies were sometimes no longer terribly different from those of their Socialist rivals.

The American Communist Party was Stalinizing, and Noah London was pulled along by the current. And he was getting bored with the role of a privileged American engineer that the party was pushing him into, away from his original commitment to radical trade unionism. In the Soviet Union, where 'red' engineers seemed to have fewer social privileges than in America, could he take pride in the role of a red engineer, someone 'building socialism'? Was he hankering to return to the old country?

The campaign against Loreism was far from the sole impact of 'Bolshevization' on the party. The American working class was being 'Americanized' in the 1920s – not necessarily voluntarily. European immigrants were becoming assimilated into American culture and 'whiteness', a process facilitated in 1924 by the halting of European immigration for 40 years. Jewish garment workers resisted this process far less than Slavic or Italian steelworkers and coalminers. The cultural isolation of Eastern European Jewish immigrants faded rapidly.

'Bolshevization' was to some degree a reflection of this 'Americanization' within the CPUSA. In the interest of proletarian revolution, party leaders sought to put an end to the cultural and linguistic isolation of the European working-class immigrants, who formed the great majority of the membership, from the native working class. All the semi-independent foreign-language federations were reorganized into sections, with far less autonomy, on the Bolshevik model. Minutes in Comintern records of the bureau of the new Jewish Section are in English. According to Novick: 'We had a Jewish Federation … and we joined the party, and as we joined the party, English became the language, and we lost probably 90%. I remember Foster spoke to me, "What happened, what happened to the Jewish Federation, it was a big organization? Now there's just a thousand or two left?" I told him, you abolished the Yiddish language, many of them didn't know English …'[59] The *Freiheit* continued for many years to be an effective Communist voice in the needle trades unions. But garment industry agitation would henceforth be primarily conducted in English, which was rapidly becoming the lingua franca of garment unionism.

58 Saltzman, Siegal and Wiener statements, r. 38, d. 561, l. 46–53.

59 James R. Barrett, 'Americanization from the Bottom Up: Immigration and the Remaking of the Working Class in the United States, 1880–1930', *Journal of American History* 79, no. 3 (Dec. 1992): 996–1020; Draper, *American Communism*, 272–5; Novick interview.

After his 'Bolshevization' the pages of the *Freiheit* were open to him again. Soon after the last Jewish Workers Federation convention there was a convention of the American Federation of Labor, and London took the opportunity to demonstrate that he was no longer a syndicalist deviationist. He had begun his Communist career as a spokesman for the Workers Council movement, which expressed the radical spirit of the postwar labor upsurge in the garment industry. London sought to revive that spirit – but now under firm party leadership. His new ideas differed completely from his 1922 schema for an open Communist party based on union branches.

He pointed out that the vast majority of the American working class was non-union – and that the AFL was not about to organize it. In his opinion, 'Today there is no power ... which wants to and is able to organize the working class in America except for the power of Communism'. What America needed was a Communist-led 'American Federation of Workers' – in parallel with boring from within the AFL, but if necessary independently. He was seeking to prove that he was at least as good a Communist as his critics.[60]

His call for reorientation was timely. For a whole decade after the great defeats of 1922, virtually every major labor struggle in America was conducted outside the AFL – or in rebellion against it. It was not until the CIO was founded that the AFL took much interest in organizing the unorganized. London was not the only American Communist to see the need for a change. Cannon would advocate a shift away from Foster's AFL fetishism a few months later. The Passaic textile strike, which drew more public attention than any other labor struggle of the Coolidge Era, would be led by 'Ruthenbergite' Albert Weisbord.[61] It was not until the Great Depression that American Communists turned seriously towards organizing the unorganized majority of the working class.

The *Freiheit* was, however, the wrong venue for Noah London's new ideas. The Jewish labor movement was a radical island that had survived the fall of the house of labor. Organizing garment workers was not the question of the day. If London wanted to follow Weisbord's example, he would have to leave the world of Yiddish behind. And he would have to abandon his hard-earned career as an engineer. He had no intention of doing either.

60 London, 'Vohin mit der Amerikan fed. ov leybor', *Freiheit*, Oct. 15, 1925.

61 Palmer, *Cannon*, 257. Jacob Zumoff's recent book, *The Red Thread: The Passaic Textile Strike* (New Brunswick: Rutgers University Press, 2021), is a vital study of this underanalyzed but very important strike in the 1920s, and the role of the Communist Party in it.

9 Socialism in One Borough: 'From Vegetarianism to Communism'

On Christmas day in 1925, 400 people attended a holiday banquet to celebrate the commencement of construction of the Bronx 'coops', the United Workers Cooperative Colony Association's latest project. Noah London, its president, was the toastmaster. The UWCC had leased construction rights for a dozen city blocks of undeveloped land at the edge of Bronx Park, near the brand new Allerton Avenue subway station. When the complex was completed it was the tallest building in the Bronx, occupying two complete city blocks and including 720 multi-room apartments. It was the largest cooperative housing project in the US, and its low rents, high design standards, garden landscaping and architectural creativity rapidly filled the complex with some 2,000 tenants.[62]

London wrote its Yiddish manifesto, 'What Does Our Cooperative Movement Want?' It compellingly expresses the vaulting ambition of his vision. The purpose of the project was to 'raise a generation of managers, of business leaders, who can take charge of the economy of the land, without bosses or landlords or bankers or businessmen'. London wanted to combine the communal utopianism of contemporary Soviet experiments with American practicality and construction quality. Such dreams of fundamental social transformation flowered in the early Soviet Union, until smothered by Stalinism.[63]

His vision as *Freiheit* labor editor had been male-centered. The cloakmakers, not the female dress and waistmakers who galvanized the ILGWU in the first place, were his audience. But women's liberation was a significant focus of the coops project. As he put it,

> Had you belonged to a cooperative together with another hundred families like yours, only ten of the hundred would have to work to prepare and serve the supper. The other ninety would be free. That means that you would only have to spend one tenth of the time of your wife's work. That is money, if your wife is able to or wants to work in the shop. That is health and an easier life, if she has free time.

62 *Freiheit* clippings, 'Coops' collection, Tamiment; CPUSA microfilms, r. 62, d. 866, l. 2; *At Home in Utopia: Coops 50th Anniversary*, 7–9; Plunz, 'Reading Bronx Housing', *Building a Borough*, 51–3.

63 London, 'Vos vil unzer kooperative bavegung', U.S.T.C., YIVO, Box 6, folder 15. Melech Epstein erroneously attributes the authorship of the manifesto to Olgin. Epstein, *The Jew and Communism*, 215; Richard Stites, *Revolutionary Dreams, Utopian Vision and Experimental Life in the Russian Revolution* (Oxford: Oxford University Press, 1991).

Even in the cooperative, the family was still the fighting unit for socialism. Undoubtedly Miril's influence is seen here. But the manifesto was still addressed more to workingmen than to their wives.

The financial basis of the project would be the rising income levels of New York Jewish garment workers in the 1920s. London had argued that the key to creating an American revolutionary movement was to grasp that the working class was divided into two halves – a moderate-minded native aristocracy of labor and a radically inclined immigrant/black underclass. Now Jewish immigrants were moving up the social ladder, a handful becoming labor bureaucrats, Communist or otherwise, but far more were exiting the working class altogether. And the unusual strength of garment unionism in labor's 'lean years' of the 1920s was pulling immigrant Jewish garment workers out of any labor underclass. How then to keep them in the movement? The coops were his answer. As he put it: 'The more conscious wing stands at the front ... The less conscious also try to help their class – through cooperation'. He concluded that

> The possibilities of the cooperative movement among Jewish workers are now tremendous. All the necessary elements are present: (1) an active socially experienced mass of Jewish workers concentrated in great industrial cities; ... (3) whose income is relatively not bad ...; (4) with instincts for collective social creation; (5) and an ideological center and driving force in the form of the Communist Party ...[64]

He transferred his vision of a strategic united front between radical and moderate sections of the working class from politics to cooperativism. The Bronx coops would attempt to give Jewish garment workers a positive Socialist alternative to upward mobility. The manifesto proclaims:

> We want to show the worker that there is a life in well-lit clean houses, with music, with theater, with green fields, with healthy food, we want to show him a great world, which is his but doesn't belong to him, a world which the ruling class has completely taken away from him. The more he knows about the beautiful life the more he will seek to conquer the world.

How would this vegetarian utopia arise? By fusing the American 'can do spirit' with Bolshevik leadership. Before his own Bolshevization he had seen the UWCC as a manifestation of the spontaneous revolutionary instincts of Jew-

---

64 London, *Freiheit*, Nov. 1, 1925.

ish workers, which the party needed more to learn from than to guide. Now he warned *Freiheit* readers that there were still UWCC members 'who believe in cooperation for the sake of cooperation … And that the cooperative should be limited to a small number of the elect, who understand how to live a rational-idealistic life. The remnants of *pure and simple* [in English] cooperativism have hampered the growth of the organization …'[65] To avoid bureaucracy, it would be a cooperative 'of workers and for workers', with 'no place for bosses … and no cushy jobs', paying ordinary wages and choosing employees from the most experienced activists. It would be a movement of the masses, not a business institution.

The UWCC's membership had grown to 500, including 150 party members. It was now time to Bolshevize it, according to the party's new Jewish Bureau. 'Our work in the cooperatives used to be carried on in such a manner, that it was impossible to properly direct it … We therefore for the first time in the history of the Party worked out a policy …'[66] The new party policy was that:

> Party comrades shall combat any idea of the cooperative movement being self-sufficient and independent … 1. The UWCC shall extend aid to victims of class oppression … 2. That it will help and develop among its own members revolutionary educational and cultural work … 9. It shall extend the mass basis of the Cooperatives, increasing the proportion of non-Party membership to Party membership …[67]

This was all completely in line with Noah's ideas. Was he the leader the new movement needed, despite his deviationist past?

The New York party secretariat recommended bringing 'new blood' onto the Board of Directors.[68] Elias Watenberg, a leader of the American Left Poale-Zion recently recruited into the Communist Party, replaced London as the president of the UWCC after London departed for the Soviet Union. Lovestonites Gerson and Cohn would have free reign under Watenberg's loose supervision, and a number of the imaginative schemes outlined in Noah's manifesto were actually brought to life. But the cooperative movement, like the left-wing movement in the garment unions, turned out to be vulnerable to corrosion in the atmosphere of the times.

65 Ibid.
66 Report of Secretary to Jewish Bureau plenary, Jan. 23, 1926, CPUSA microfilms, r. 62, d. 868, l. 7, 9.
67 NY District 2 Political Bureau and Secretariat minutes, Jan. 5, 1926, CPUSA microfilms, r. 62, d. 866, l. 2–3.
68 Ibid., Jan. 5 and Jan. 29, 1926, l. 3 and 7; Epstein, *The Jew and Communism*, 216.

Risky financial propositions were extremely popular in America in the 'Roaring Twenties' – until the Crash. When money began to run short, Gerson and Cohn came up with a left-wing Ponzi scheme. They floated 'Gold Bonds' to finish construction on a second building, start building a third and even begin digging holes in the ground for a fourth. The party leadership backed the Gold Bonds enthusiastically. New York leftists took their savings out of capitalist banks and put them in the 'cooperative bank', the Consumers Finance Corporation, with a fancy office on Fifth Avenue. When the Crash hit in 1929, the Gold Bonds became worthless. During the Great Depression, the Consumers Finance Corporation failed its working-class customers as badly as any other bank.

10 'Our Cultural Front'

In the spring of 1925, London commented in the *Freiheit* that the most successful cultural programs at Camp Nitgedeiget dealt with literature. The coming task was to 'interest the camp visitors in proletarian culture'. The camp had some definite success in that direction. Vladimir Mayakovsky, the Soviet literary ikon of the 1920s, visited it on his American tour three times that summer, and even wrote a poem about it.[69]

London was very interested in Yiddish theater and reviewed Socialist plays in the *Freiheit*. In 1925, he addressed himself to satirist Moishe Nadir, one of the central cultural figures gracing the *Freiheit*. Nadir strongly sympathized with the Jewish Left, but believed that art was on a higher plane than 'a bread and butter idea' like communism. London attacked Nadir's conception of art for art's sake and satire without a program. 'The kings in their castles had court fools who ridiculed and laughed in the faces of the kings and their lords and ladies. That didn't make the court fool a revolutionary ... He was still the court fool ...' It was insufficient just to denounce the old order. The task was to create a new one. Artef, the Jewish Workers' Theater, arose simultaneously with the Bronx coops. At its founding convention, Noah London spoke on behalf of the UWCC and became a member of the Artef National Committee.[70]

69 London, *Freiheit*, May 16, 1925; Charles A. Moser, 'Mayakovsky's Unsentimental Journeys', *American Slavic and East European Review* 19, no. 1 (Feb. 1960): 93.

70 London, 'Broyt mit puter', *Freiheit*, Feb. 11, 1925; Kalmen Marmor, 'Di far-geshikhte fun Artef', in *Tsen yor Artef* (New York: Artef, 1937), 12; Edna Nahshon, *Yiddish Proletarian Theatre: The Art and Politics of the Artef, 1925–1940* (Westport, CT: Greenwood Press, 1998), 20; letter, Noah and Miril London to Secretariat, Feb. 22, 1926, CPUSA microfilms, r. 55, d. 770, l. 2.

As garment workers moved upwards into the middle class, the cultural front would gradually replace unionism as Jewish Communism's main arena of activity. The coops would become the bastion of this new subculture. In the mid-1930s, Alexander Pomerantz's history of American 'proletarian culture' would praise an article by Noah London on 'how are things on our cultural front'. Did London have a future as culture commissar?[71]

In the aftermath of the defeat of the Russian Revolution of 1905, the Bund sponsored radical Yiddishism, *Yiddishkeit*, as an alternative to broken revolutionary dreams. Ex-Bundists in America in the Workmen's Circle and the *Freiheit* sought to continue this tradition, each in their own fashion. The turn to *Yiddishkeit* preserved a Russian revolutionary heritage in America long after the Jewish labor movement itself died out. The Workmen's Circle, the last faint vestige of Jewish socialism in America, still exists, though it has moved with the times and now is called the 'Workers Circle'. Similarly, projects like Camp Nitgedeiget, the Bronx coops and Artef continued a radical Jewish tradition for decades after Jewish Communism had withered away.[72]

Communist-backed Jewish cultural projects were as successful as rival Socialist versions, if not more so. After World War II, the CP-backed Jewish Peoples' Fraternal Order rivalled the Workmen's Circle in membership, until its assets were seized by the government during the McCarthy era.[73] *Yiddishkeit* was the glue holding the movement together. Its summer camps, cooperative projects, choruses and theater groups would influence radicalism in America for decades to come. Its impact would not completely dissipate until the days of the New Left of the 1960s.

But Noah London was not satisfied with a role as leader of a New York-centered Jewish subculture. He had known virtually from the day he joined the movement that Jews could not be the decisive factors in a revolution. The first organization he joined, the Socialist-Zionist Party, characterized the situation of Jews in the Pale as hopeless. He was deeply aware of the upward social mobility lifting Jews like himself out of the working class in America. When opportunity came his way to move into a larger arena, he took it. His departure for the Soviet Union to build socialism must have seemed a brilliant solution

71 Liebman, *Jews and the Left*, 307–10; Alexander Pomerantz, *Proletpen: Etyuden un materialn tsu der geshikhte fun dem kamf far proletarisher literatur in Amerike* (Kiev: Farlag fun der alukrainisher visnshaftlekeher akademye, 1935), 43. London's article, in the Dec. 28, 1925, *Freiheit* is regrettably unavailable.

72 Liebman, *Jews and the Left*, 140–8, 283–325; Paul Buhle, 'Jews and American Communism: The Cultural Question', *Radical History Review* 23 (Dec. 1980), 8–33.

73 Shapiro, *Friendly Society*, 217; Liebman, *Jews and the Left*, 311–13.

to his difficulties in America, enabling him for the first time to fully apply his engineering skills to the revolutionary cause. It was the natural result of the ups and downs of his political career in the mid 1920's – and those of Jewish Communism and garment unionism in America as well.

11 'Building Socialism': From the Bronx to the Donbass

Donugol was the Soviet trust in charge of the coal industry of the Donbass, the Don River basin, the site of the former Donetsk and Lugansk Peoples Republics now annexed into Russia. In 1925, it sent a commission made up of five engineers and four worker-administrators to America. Their mission was to investigate the purchase of machinery in order to modernize production. Donugol was perhaps the single most important Soviet industrial trust, because Donbass coal was the Soviet Union's prime energy source. London took part in a nationwide mining tour that Amtorg arranged for the commission. The head of the commission, deputy Donugol director Semion Ivanov, was a former miner and an 'old Bolshevik'. London was highly impressed with him. When the delegation had to crawl through a mine tunnel on hands and knees, Ivanov, as London put it, 'turned out to be a better crawler by a mile than a typical American engineer, the writer of these lines included. [He] asked himself, looking at the blackened bent figures of the workers, well comrade, how do you solve the problem of hard labor in a communist society?'[74]

Ivanov was being paid about a third as much as the engineers he was traveling with. He described Donugol to London as a workers' trust. The workday was six hours, not eight like in America, and working conditions were civilized.

> With you, if a worker doesn't please the boss, he kicks him out. With us, we give the workers an account every month of every step we take. With you, the worker works for onions and garlic, with us he works for his own country. With you the worker drowns his sorrows with bootleg whiskey, with us the worker has hope and free spirit, lots of spirit.

After the commission returned to the Soviet Union, London sent Donugol a letter asking if they wanted to hire him. Red civil engineers with university degrees and years of experience were rare in the Soviet Union, and Ivanov promptly sent back a job offer. London applied for a party transfer, writing that 'only in

74 London, 'Mit der Rusisher komisie fun don'er koyln-rayon', *Freiheit*, Oct. 29, 1925.

USSR could be achieved the maximum usefulness of my work for Communism in … both my professional and my revolutionary party activities'.[75] Travelling to Russia was a golden opportunity to put his engineering skills to positive use for the cause – and to escape badgering by American critics. After all, he was just as vulnerable to persecution as a Loreite in the cooperative movement as in any other arena. And surely building a socialist utopia in the Soviet Union was more practical than in the Bronx. What he did not know yet was that, if the potential rewards for his efforts were higher in the Soviet Union, so were the dangers. Ironically, he would finally be placed on the Soviet purge lists in 1937 as a 'Loreite' deviationist in America.

An exchange between London and Lovestone hints that the clouds over his head were not yet fully lifted. London asked Lovestone to give him a statement to take along about his party activities in the USA. Lovestone coolly answered: 'You ask for an elaborate statement of your Party work. That is not necessary. When you get to Soviet Russia the Party authorities will ask you information, you will answer … In case you have any difficulties … please see Comrade Pepper'.[76] London might be leaving the country, but an old enemy was waiting to greet him there.

During his last few months in America, nostalgia and attempts at poetic flare marked his contributions to the *Freiheit*. How much influence he had over Artef is unclear, but it certainly had an effect on him. 'From Woolworth's to Leviathan', written on board the SS *Leviathan*, the ocean liner taking him back to Europe, borders on blank verse: 'The Moloch of American capitalism has built its workshops great and vast. From one ocean to the other, from the heaven-mount down into the great depths of the earth they spread out'. It is here where he described his personal experiences sewing sailor suits for little boys on Eldridge Street, as well as the black miners toiling in Tennessee tunnels.[77]

April 1926 was an appropriate moment for Noah and Miril London to leave America for the Soviet Union. His last article written on American soil celebrated the fourth anniversary of the *Freiheit* and looked forward to the future:

> I leave America with a certain nostalgia. I am leaving a corner of our world movement which … has spread out and developed with my participation

75 Ivanov to London, Jan. 11, 1926, CPUSA microfilms, r. 55, d. 770, l. 3; London to Lovestone Feb. 22, 1926.

76 CPUSA microfilms, r. 55, d. 770, l. 91 and 95.

77 London, 'Fun "Woolworth" tsum "lvisn"'.

> and before my eyes ... And now, when our comrades are leading a brilliant fur strike, lead the New York [ILGWU] Joint Board, when the *Freiheit* is the organ of the unions ... when workers burn copies of the *Forward* on the street ... when you watch the movement, the unions, the cooperatives, the progressive *arbayter ring* branches ... it warms your heart. And you feel sorry when it happens that you leave that corner, although you are already awaiting with pleasure and impatience the moment when you will arrive in a land where not only a corner is ours, but the world is ours.[78]

Jewish Communism had reached its historic apex in America, and decline was about to set in. The 1926 fur strike would lay the basis for a generation of left-wing control over the furriers' union. But in the men's clothing industry, Hillman had already used the 1924 LaFollette campaign as his excuse to break his bloc with the Communists. He reforged an alliance with the Socialist machine in the New York industry, and was busy driving the Communists out of Noah's own old union, the ACWA.

The great 1926 New York cloakmakers' strike broke out shortly after London arrived in the USSR. It led to a brutal, tragic Socialist–Communist civil war in the clothing industry that gravely weakened American garment unionism. The Socialist street general would be Abraham Beckerman, Sidney Hillman's new ally, who later served a prison term due to his involvement in the Lepke/Buchhalter gang, better known as 'Murder Incorporated'. In the aftermath of the struggle, sweatshop exploitation would re-emerge and left-wing strength would wither away. Defeat provided a perfect medium for the Stalinist degeneration of Jewish Communism in America.[79]

The Londons would never return to their adopted homeland. A few weeks before boarding the *Leviathan*, Noah expressed his hopes for America's future 'on a rainy Sunday in March':

> People say ... that the public can be kept in line with a full dinner pail, and if the pail isn't full they will put up with it if they believe in the cleverness of the system ... But the masses are disillusioned ... They look with contempt on the whole political edifice built by the ideologues of the ruling classes ... So now let's go talk to the Kremlin. The boot is coming soon,

78 London, 'A zay-gezunt un a skh-hkhl tsum 4tn yubileaum', *Freiheit*, April 4, 1926.

79 John Holmes, 'Jewish Communism and Garment Unionism', 191–5. It seems that Charles Zimmerman, the Communist leader, brought in other gangsters on the Communist side.

> that will shatter the whole thing with a kick. A rainy Sunday in March is not for dwelling on how long and boringly it drags out, and when it will end. Spring is coming.[80]

And the sun was rising in the east.

12 Postscript: What Happened to Other 'Loreites' after London Left?

Charles Zimmerman became Jay Lovestone's main labor lieutenant in the Communist Party. He would follow Lovestone into the arms of the ILGWU leadership in the 1930s, after they both were expelled from the party. After World War II, he would follow Lovestone yet further into collaboration with the CIA, in projects such as the infamous AIFLD in Latin America. The US Navy would name a ship after him. Rose Wortis and Ben Gold stuck with the party. She would be rewarded for her party loyalty with a remarkable plum, appointed head of the garment workers' union of her native Poland.[81] Ben Gold's furriers union became the most explicitly communist and most successful communist union in the American labor movement, despite failed attempts to organize a Socialist AFL loyal 'dual union'.[82] Its final demise, folded into a mainstream union in the 1950s, had as much to do with the decline of the American fur industry as anything else. After the Great Depression, Americans became much less interested in wearing dogfur coats, and mink coats and such were always a niche market for the rich.

Other Loreites would follow a kaleidoscope of different paths. Juliet Stuart Poyntz took her policy of behind-the-scenes maneuvering to its logical extreme, becoming, it seems, an American agent of the Soviet secret police in the 1930s. She would disappear mysteriously. According to famed Italian-American anarchist Carlo Tresca, her old personal friend, she like Noah London became disgusted with the Soviet Union and Stalinism. Her lover, London's old ally Shachno Epstein, had returned to the Soviet Union and become an ultra-loyal Stalinist. He was visiting America at the time of her disappearance, and was seen with her. Tresca believed that he was involved in it.[83] Tresca himself was murdered mysteriously a few years later. Paul Novick commented half a century later about the 'Poyntz affair' that this was

---

80 London, 'In a regndikn zuntik in martsh', *Freiheit*, March 12, 1926.

81 J. Holmes, 'Jewish Communism and Garment Unionism'.

82 Philip Foner, *The Fur and Leather Workers Union* (Newark, NJ: Nordan Press, 1950).

83 Tresca, 'Where Is Julia Stuart Poyntz?' *Modern Monthly*, March 1938, 12–13.

> one of the mysteries which I will not be able to add anything about … she disappeared, maybe she worked for the Soviets, maybe not, nobody knows what became of her … I knew her very well. I remember the last time we spent an evening together, we had a cup of tea and something, sang songs, of course she was quite a personality, and she disappeared, and what they said at that time, which we didn't believe, was probably true.[84]

Trotsky's ex-friend Lore was not given the opportunity to reconcile himself with the party. He would join an attempt to revive the Workers Party on an independent basis, at the height of the Great Depression. Reverend A.J. Muste's American Workers Party also included Salutsky-Hardman, then still editing the journal of Sidney Hillman's union. But after the 1934 Minneapolis Teamsters strike, the new party joined forces with its leaders, Cannon's expelled Trotskyists. In response, Hardman and Lore angrily departed left-wing politics forever. Lore became the European columnist for the *New York Post*. His patriotic columns advocated a broad 'popular front' anti-Hitler alliance – but were highly critical of the Soviet Union.[85]

Rumors spread that Lore was a Soviet agent in the 1930s. He died in unexplained circumstances during World War II, after he 'took over a special government assignment', as his *New York Times* obituary reported. In fact, by then Lore was a double agent, working for both the FBI and the Soviet NKVD. He reported to the FBI that his friend Whittaker Chambers headed a Soviet spy network of seventy or so government employees, including two private secretaries of assistant secretaries of state.[86] Retired Major General Julius Kobyakov, former head of the KGB American desk, stated a number of years ago that Lore 'was a con-man. He created fictitious sources and fabricated their reports. The KGB continued to use him for several years. In fact, after LEO's [Lore's] perfidy was confirmed, the Center for some time toyed with the idea of kidnapping him, either in Great Britain or in Spain, and shipping him off to Russia for interrogation, but that idea was abandoned and LEO terminated'.[87]

General Kobyakov did not clarify whether LEO was terminated with extreme prejudice.

---

84 Novick interview. The author encountered Ella Wolfe, the widow of Lovestone's longtime ally Bertram Wolfe, at the Hoover Institute in the 1990s. When asked what she knew about Noah London, she expressed the extremely improbable opinion that he was also an NKVD agent.

85 Cannon 1962, 176; Bell, *Marxian Socialism in the United States*, 134n220.

86 Obituary, *New York Times*, July 9, 1942; Tiger, ed., *In re Alger Hiss* v. 2, 208–9.

87 Kobyakov, 'Ales-HISS', March 23, 2004, H-DIPLO, http://www.h-net.org/h-diplo.

John Pepper, by the way, would die in the Soviet Union as a victim of Stalinist terror, like Noah London. The political fate of armed insurrectionist dentist Louis Hendin is also worth mentioning. He joined the Socialist Party a few years after his expulsion from the Communist Party, became a *Forward* staffer, and succeeded Abraham Cahan as editor when Cahan died, at a moment when the *Forward* had become the voice of the extreme right wing of American Socialism. It would walk out of Norman Thomas's Socialist Party in the 1930s as too left wing.

Lastly, when Noah London became a dissident once again in the Soviet Union, he would return to his semi 'Loreism' of the 1920s. In his 1934 manuscript he would advocate reuniting the world socialist movement, and criticize 'mechanical centralization' and 'so-called democratic centralism'. He had no objection to centralization within limits, but wanted some real democracy in the movement, whether in the Soviet Union or elsewhere, in parties or trade unions.

FIGURE 6 Family photo, photographer unknown, public domain. Young (Peoples?) Socialist League, 1912. Photo possibly taken by Anna Unterman, author's grandmother, whom according to family tradition authored the YPSL constitution. Her future husband Benjamin Hort in front row

FIGURE 7 London wedding photo, 1916, photographer unknown, public domain

FIGURE 8 Family photo, photographer unknown, public domain. Unsent postcard from Bronx studio, in the early 1920s

FIGURE 9
Family photo, photographer unknown. Crop from family photo, 1925–26. Noah and Miril, upper-left-corner. Rose, second from right. Bessie, Chaim and Anna Unterman, center

FIGURE 10 1926 design sketch for Bronx Coops. *Cooperation*, vol. 12, Dec. 1926

FIGURE 11 Photo taken by Andrew S. Dolkart of the first Bronx Coops project

FIGURE 12 Contemporary photo taken by author two decades ago of Coops door KJ, with hammer and sickle

PART 3

The Soviet Union

CHAPTER 7

The New Promised Land

What would things be like for the Londons in the land where the sun was rising in the East? As his old friend Paul Novick told me, when I interviewed him in the late 1980s, in America, 'somehow, he never quite fit in'. At first he seemed to fit in better over there. But his basic political attitude all his life, 'Londonism' if you will, was best expressed in the secret manuscript his sister-in-law smuggled out of Moscow in 1934. As he put it,

> Socialism means bettering the condition of the masses, enlightening them, not building cathedrals. Democracy built schools, hospitals, cottages – not citadels or monuments. It built roads and railways, filled up the dinner pail. Democracy built swimming pools, camps, organized gymnasiums and physical culture. Democracy spread ideas of equality, of communal spirit. We don't understand it here. So far very little is done for that.[1]

In theory, this was not incompatible with the Soviet party's line, that Soviet democracy was the only true democracy, and certainly with Soviet propaganda. He did not realize right away that it was not so compatible in practice, though it matched the official position well enough that it was some years before it led him into political trouble. That it really wasn't quite the political line of the Trotskyist 'Left Opposition' either confused matters. Not least for Noah himself. Indeed, not until the Great Purge in 1937 did it prevent him from being a well-respected and successful industrial manager.

Life in the Soviet Communist Party was different from life in the American CP. But not as different as many historians of American Communism believe, to say nothing of historians of Soviet Communism. There were many differences between the two parties, but the only fundamental difference was that the Soviet party was the ruler of a huge land, and the American only a small opposition party. It is usually only the most anti-communist historians of American Communism who emphasize this fact. The 'revisionist' historians of the party like to claim that it was an American party of American radicalism, whose bad features represented Soviet influence. This book maintains that the political degeneration of both parties was a parallel process with parallel causes.

1 Appendix B, page 396–397.

 | DOI:10.1163/9789004745384_009

The Soviet party strongly influenced the American because it was so much larger and more important. Its influence on the American party was not necessarily unfortunate, at first. Even after Stalinization, Soviet influence played a major role in cleansing the American party of the 'white blindspot' of American socialism.[2] Both parties went Stalinist, in the last analysis, because of the failure of the revolutionary movement in the aftermath of World War I to spread beyond the Soviet republic. It is true that power can corrupt – but so can lack of power.

Nor for that matter is the American labor movement as different from the more radical labor movement in Tsarist Russia, or from the Communist movement, as is generally thought. Emphasizing the negative, Noah wrote in his manuscript: 'There is absolutely no difference between the workings of the bureaucratic centralism of the AFL, which ruthlessly suppresses any expression of its rank and file, and the bureaucracy of the Communist Party towards its membership'. As an American trade unionist I can see what he meant, even though actually killing dissidents, American Londons, is unheard of, except in certain unions formerly under the influence of organized crime. Nowadays control by the US government has largely replaced other forms of criminal control in such unions. But there are positive comparisons as well.

Let us return to the London story, as they disembark in Britain and arrive in London, the city Noah was named after. May 1926 is a fine time for Communist tourism in Europe. Spring is in the air and revolution is on the march. They visit England on the eve of the 1926 General Strike, the high point of labor conflict in England in the twentieth century. Noah's travel writings gave him ample opportunity to express his faith in the Soviet banner as the beacon for mankind's future. His British correspondence, published in the middle of the General Strike, was the centerpiece of the *Freiheit*'s coverage of this vital chapter of European class struggle.[3]

Grandfather Joseph's choice of family name illustrates the ancestral roots of Noah London's interest in England. In the earliest days of American Communism, the postwar British shop stewards' movement was a major focus for his radical vision. His later scheme for an open communist party rooted in trade union branches would be realized in life by the British Communist Party. Its roots in the shop stewards' movement gave it broad influence despite its small size. As he put it in the *Freiheit*, 'As an American Communist I was simply envious of the English Communist Party ... [whose] work is more real, more

2 Zumoff, *Communist International*, 287–351.

3 London, 'England erv dem general strayk', *Freiheit*, May 9, 1926.

substantial, more fruitful, than ours'. But London was visiting the coalfields as a coal industry official, not a labor agitator.

London's tour of a Newcastle mine and his conversations with coal engineers persuaded him of the hopeless position of a declining, inefficient 'feudalistic' English coal industry run by 'real barons'. As for the miners themselves: 'I spent twelve hours, from six at night to six in the morning, in a coal mine a thousand feet under the earth. On emergence, I said a blessing that I was not an English coal miner. I was thinking that twelve hours was enough for people to crawl on their bellies and work like donkeys'.

His belief that England was going through a revolutionary crisis was good Comintern orthodoxy – but was not shared by the Communist Party of Great Britain (CPGB). Party union leader John T. Murphy was an engineer's apprentice who had been a leader of the shop stewards' movement that London had sought to emulate. In his opinion, 'To entertain any exaggerated views as to the revolutionary possibilities of this crisis … is fantastic'.[4] Nonetheless, the Comintern agreed with London that the CPGB was a praiseworthy model – obedient, well rooted in the masses, and best of all unriven by factional conflict.

London made a couple of favorable public references to Trotsky's views on England in the *Freiheit*, at the very last moment when doing so was politically safe. London arrived in the USSR as the Left Opposition was coming into existence, and the English General Strike would be part of its platform. It would take the CPGB to task for an insufficiently radical course of action. Stalin's roasting of the Opposition for their critical stance towards English Communism would alienate London from it. He himself was tired of being criticized for insufficient radicalism.[5]

1 The Polish Powderkeg

London's travels reinforced his faith in Communism and the Soviet leadership. He described his arrival in the Soviet Union as one of the happiest moments of

4 Gruber, *Soviet Russia Masters the Comintern: International Communism in the Era of Stalin's Ascendancy* (Garden City, NY: Anchor Press/Doubleday, 1974), 160.

5 E.H. Carr, *A History of Soviet Russia. Foundations of a Planned Economy, 1926–1929* (New York: Macmillan, 1978), vol. 3 pt. 2, 315–41; Gruber, *Soviet Russia Masters the Comintern*, 116–25, 151–71. The London manuscript makes clear that Noah's attitude to the 'Anglo-Russian Unity Committee', a formal alliance between the leaders of English and Soviet trade unions, which the Left Opposition saw as a betrayal, was rather like Stalin's and not at all like Trotsky's. By 1934 he was much less impressed with the British Communist Party than in 1926. As was Stalin for that matter.

his life. As soon as 'the rapture was over', he decided to follow the usual fashion, as he put it, and write up 'the truth about Russia' in a series for the *Freiheit*, before getting totally caught up in local affairs. He began with his impressions of Poland, a country 'standing on a powderkeg'.[6]

He had expected that the farther east he traveled, the greater would be the poverty. That is how things were before he emigrated to America. And the Great War was more destructive the farther east it raged. To his surprise, he discovered that Poland now was poorer than the Soviet Union. In Warsaw, even the fanciest tree-lined boulevards 'were simply weeping'. The Londons dined at one of Warsaw's finest restaurants for less than a dollar. It was almost empty. Why? 'A good worker, a carpenter for example in Brisk or in Pinsk [near London's birthplace], works for two zlotys [10 ¢] or one-and-a-half a day if there is work. Well, since a pound of flour, which a workers' family must have to live for a week to live, costs twelve zlotys …'

The Londons apparently had no contact with Communists while traveling through Pilsudski's Poland. That would have been dangerous. But Noah did talk with people from all walks of life, including a genuine landed noble, a Łódź manufacturer, a former Tsarist official, a bankrupt Jewish former merchant, Jewish workers and Polish peasants. All agreed that the economic situation was catastrophic, and blamed it on Poland's economic boycott of its Russian and German neighbors.

In the Polesian swamplands where he and Miril were born, the situation was even worse. Poorly coordinated Communist-led peasant insurgencies were sputtering out.[7] The forlorn corner of the Jewish Pale they grew up in was 'dripping today with blood from all its limbs, which they ripped out of White Russia [Belarus] and Ukraine'. On the train he overheard a conversation among soldiers on leave. One soldier recounted to his buddies how he had told his officer that, if ordered to fire to the East, he would fire to the West.

As for the Jews, 'There has never been in the history of the life of Jewish workers … such a bitter time, as it is now for them today in Poland'. For Noah London, it was 'good to dump Poland and come to Russia, to workers' and peasants' Russia'. Meanwhile he urged American Jewish workers to remember their sisters, brothers and kin in Poland, and organize 'constructive social assistance' to support their relatives and *landslayt* with food and clothing. He did not yet realize that the situation of *shtetl* Jewry under the NEP in the Soviet Union was not necessarily much better.

6 London, 'Poyln shteyt oyf a fas pulver', *Freiheit*, June 26, 1926.

7 E.H. Carr, *A History of Soviet Russia. Socialism in One Country, 1924–1926* (Baltimore: Penguin, 1972 [1964]), 205–6; Mendel, *Memoirs of a Jewish Revolutionary* (London: Pluto, 1989), 220–4.

His Polish experiences were not unusual. American Jewish travelers in Europe between the world wars unanimously preferred the Soviet Union. As London's New York colleague Moishe Nadir put it, 'Crossing the Polish border into Russia is like leaving a stuffy room full of medicinal odors for the bright outdoors. For the time being I am a bit blinded and can't see a thing'.[8]

2 The NEP in the New Promised Land

May 1926, the height of the NEP period, was about as pleasant a moment for the Londons to arrive in the Soviet Union as they could have found. Noah's first impressions were colorful and quite positive – not least because of the contrast with Poland. London was not one of those Communists who found the 'bourgeois' atmosphere of the New Economic Policy oppressive. In his opinion, 'compared to Poland, Russia materially speaking is heaven for all its inhabitants: workers; peasants; white-collar employees and NEPmen'.[9] He reported that in NEP Russia health care was free for workers, and they could easily afford the basic necessities of life. Because they had survived years of famine, they tended to overeat 'in Russian fashion'. He spent some time in Moscow before traveling on to Kharkov. Compared with New York City it was poor, because of Russian economic backwardness. The lack of gas, electricity, plumbing and garbage service was particularly difficult for housewives. Another thing he noticed that was missing was a 'Camp Nitgedeiget'. His impression was that the Russian worker was 'as content as a carpenter or cloakmaker in New York, or as discontent. But he feels that he is boss in the country and in his factory'.

What Russia needed was exactly what Noah London had come to help provide. Russians would be able to live as well as Americans 'when industry is more developed in general, when productivity grows'. He no longer believed that spontaneous revolutionary initiative of rank-and-file workers was the path to a brighter future. According to new coal executive London:

> There are workers nowadays who believe they are the boss of the factory, for example, not as a collective but that he is simply a boss of a little piece of the factory. And since he is a boss, he can be lazy, he can demand higher wages, he can goof off … One of the greatest evils in Russian industry has

8 Carr, *Socialism in One Country*, 394–400; Carr 1976, 586–8; Daniel Soyer, 'Back to the Future: American Jews Visit the Soviet Union in the 1920s and 1930s', *Jewish Social Studies* 6, no. 3 (Spring/Summer 2000): 132.

9 Noah London, 'Di ershte ayndrukn fun Sovetn-farband', *Freiheit*, July 15 and July 16, 1926.

> always been … the unproductivity of the workers … And I assure you, if the American worker produced as much as the Russian worker, the bosses would gather no great fortune.

As he had put it in his Bronx manifesto: 'Our Russian comrades, the Russian Communists, have to struggle against this "me-first" attitude among the backward workers and peasants'. But workers were making great strides in consciousness and collective responsibility because 'the different organizations, and first of all the Communist Party' were 'knocking it into their heads'. London now saw the role of the party as all-important, in industry and in the whole society.

> The administrator will want to pay the worker less. The union will want that the worker be paid more and work less. Therefore the Communist party must be iron, it must be a mercilessly precise mechanism, so that each one will feel himself simply to be a *shreifl* [*vintik*, little screw] in the great machine … Among the various currents and interests which exist in a great country with a heterogeneous population of nationalities, social and economic layers, the party must balance by means of its apparatus.

Many years later, at the height of the Great Terror, Stalin would praise the *vintiki*, the little screws in the machine, as the heart of the Soviet regime. London had proclaimed in his manifesto that he wanted the worker 'to learn to think of himself as a ruler, a master, fit for everything and able to do anything, who no longer feels degraded and depressed, that he is only a little screw, a worthless tiny thing …' Now London was getting into the party spirit. He was completely 'Bolshevized'. He had finally realised that the party apparatus was the key to everything.

3 Kharkov, the Capital of Soviet Ukraine

Noah and Miril London arrived at their new home in late May 1926 – minus all their luggage, lost in transit. The Donbass coal trust was headquartered in Kharkov, not in the Donbass. Kharkov, the Ukrainian Chicago, was the Red bastion during the Civil War. Even though it was just outside the old Jewish Pale, about a fifth of its population was Jewish by 1926 – a considerably higher proportion than in Moscow or Leningrad, and not far behind Kiev. Economic opportunity attracted growing numbers of *shtetl* Jewry to Ukraine before the revolution, despite pogroms. In the aftermath of war and revolution, Ukraine replaced Poland and the Tsarist 'northwest provinces' as the main center of Soviet Jewry. The young Ukrainian Soviet regime was seeking to turn its capital into a showpiece of avant-garde modernity in the 1920s. When the Londons arrived, the Gosprom building where Noah's office would be located was half finished. The building would be the centerpiece of Dzherzhinsky Square, planned to be the largest urban open space in Europe. This unique and striking complex, which foreshadows the brutalist style of American architecture of the 1960s, is Kharkov's prime tourist attraction to this day—that is, if Putin has not bombed it out of existence.[10]

London finished his series with a piece about his new homeland. He narrated Ukraine's history for the entertainment of his readers, from the day of the dinosaurs when Donbass coal deposits first began to form, through Tsarism, revolution and civil war, down to the contemporary scene. He described Ukrainians as a nation of dreamy, self-sufficient peasants uninterested in the modern world until war, revolution and foreign invaders were thrust upon them:

> They tread his fields, they take his horse and oxen – what do they want from him? ... He grabs his truncheon ... Beat the lords' soldiers? Sure. Beat Denikin's *moskali* [anti-Russian ethnic slur]? Sure. Drive out foreigners and build an independent Ukraine under a *hetman*? Under Petliura? Sure. Beat the rich, help the reds, who give land and freedom? Sure! Beat the Jews, even if they should be among the reds? Sure. Who are as cursed by God as the Jews! This accounts for the grand madness of the *Makhnovshchina*, of 'beat Jews, down with Bolshevism, long live Soviets' [in Russian]. The nightmare of Ukrainian banditism originates from this.[11]

According to Noah London, this peasant nation badly needed the industrialization and enlightenment that only the Soviet regime could provide. London employed a lengthy quote from Stalin – for the first and last time in his journalistic career – to explain the Soviet policy of 'Ukrainization', intended to help bring this peasant nation into the modern world. Ukrainian chauvinism, according to London, was no great danger, as Western Ukraine could only be liberated from Polish oppression 'in alliance with the other republics of the Soviet Union ...' He promised to tell his American readership about Jewish

10 Mordechai Altshuler, *Soviet Jewry on the Eve of the Holocaust: A Social and Demographic Profile* (Jerusalem: Yad Vashem, 1998), 36–40; Titus D. Henryk, 'Planning of the Capital in Kharkiv', *Harvard Ukrainian Studies* 16 (Dec. 1992): 325–59.

11 London, 'Ukraina', *Freiheit*, Sept. 8, 1926.

Ukraine later – a promise never fulfilled. The situation of *shtetl* Jewry under the NEP did not lend itself to the cheery optimism of his travel series. He had warned his *Freiheit* readership that he would soon be caught up in Soviet affairs, and his writings stopped appearing there. He had become an important official in the Soviet coal industry.

4 'Coal: A Driving Force of the Social Revolution'

> They say in Harlan County, there are no neutrals there.
> You either are a union man, or a thug for J.H. Blair.
>
> 'Which Side Are You On?', FLORENCE REECE, 1931

In its original version, 'Which Side Are You On?' was the anthem of the CPUSA-backed National Miners Union, whose brief but heroic lifespan was a realization in life of London's 1925 trade union perspective. One of its many versions went: 'I was born in Harlan County, Kaintucky born an' bred, but now that I've joined the NMU, they call me a Roosh'n red'. Coal miners have traditionally played a central role in the labor movement all over the world, in America, England, Poland, South Africa, the Donbass and elsewhere. Miners and former miners play a central role in the politics of the war-racked contemporary Donbass, despite the exhaustion of most of the mines.

They were the most powerful and militant unionists in America during Noah London's lifetime. Labor struggles in the coalfields in the early 1920s sometimes resembled scenes from the Russian Civil War more than conventional American labor battles. The Communist Party probably had more support in coal than in any other American industry in the 1920s – except garment.

London's interest in coal did not commence on the day Donugol hired him. This is how he described the West Virginia mine wars for the *Freiheit*:

> Within the borders of their counties and their state the miners are revolutionaries in the narrow sense of the word ... The miners union ... has grouped miners around the union who are ready to go through fire and water for the union. They believe that if they can drive out the corrupt dominion of the companies, all their troubles will be over ... This was a farmer's secession. They stood up with rifle in hand to protect their property and their rights.[12]

12 N. Paiezon [Noah London], 'Vi azoy di mayners in West Virdjinia leben', *Freiheit*, Aug. 13, 1922.

Coal, he had previously written in *Der Emes*, was 'a driving force of the social revolution', key to modern industry and the class struggle. Coal was fueling locomotives, powering factories and heating homes worldwide. Replacing it with oil or water power 'can only be realized in a future international Communist society'. (Solar and wind were not really much under consideration back then, to say nothing of nuclear power.) Meanwhile, experts believed that if coal was used more systematically to produce electricity, that would solve the industry's problems. But as he put it in the *Freiheit*, 'The greatest evil of the coal industry under capitalism is the bad conditions of labor'.[13]

The coal industry was in crisis everywhere in the 1920s. Even in America, John L. Lewis's mainline miners union, the UMW, was calling for nationalizing the mines. Engineers and experts were seeking to rationalize an extremely wasteful system in America. They wanted nationwide electrification – building coal power plants near the mines, as well as a system of electric cables to transmit energy wherever needed. Half a billion tons of coal were burnt annually to fuel locomotives to carry another billion tons all around the country. London argued that the world's fundamental industrial system could be transformed only when the workers took power, as in Russia.[14]

5 The Donbass

> 'One can't go to the Donbass without a gas mask'.
>
> LEON TROTSKY

The garment industry was widely seen as the 'European' sector of the American labor movement, with an unusually high level of cultural sophistication, socialist influence and class consciousness. By contrast the coal industry was quintessentially 'American', despite a large percentage of European immigrants in the workforce, and coal miners were renowned for their militancy. The center of the industry was in Appalachia, well known for its all-American social and cultural backwardness.

The (former?) Russian/Ukrainian border intersects the Donets River basin, universally abbreviated to Donbass in Russian or Donbas in Ukrainian (or Yid-

---

13 Paiezon [Noah London], 'Koyhlen: A treyb-kraft fun der sotsialer revolutsie', *Emes*, Sept. 30, 1921; London, 'Di mayners in West Virdjinia'; and 'Vi di koylen industrie vert fervaltet', *Freiheit*, April 28, 1922.

14 London, 'Vi di koylen industrie'; Paiezon, 'Mayners shlagen far natsionaliliziren di koyhlen industrie', *Freiheit*, Jan. 3, 1923.

dish).[15] It is surrounded on all sides by vast steppelands, fought over by many different peoples over the ages. When the Tsarist Empire expanded into the Donbass it was a borderland between the Don and Zaporozhian Cossack hosts. Cossacks were Slavic former peasants who fled serfdom from more settled lands for a free life in the wide open spaces. They usually preferred Russian to Polish rule. Cossacks like Stenka Razin and Pugachev would lead popular rebellions against the autocracy for centuries. By the time Noah London was born, they had become pillars of Tsarist authority on horseback. Contradictory Cossack traditions of anarchistic freedom and Tsarist subservience shaped the heritage of the 'wild steppe', the Russian counterpart of the American 'wild west'. Huge coal deposits in the Donbass began to be exploited after the abolition of serfdom, mostly by foreign investors. Shortly thereafter the Krivoi Rog iron mines were discovered across the Dnieper River, due west from the Donbass. Ekaterinoslav on the Dnieper rapidly transformed from a sleepy provincial capital into a major industrial center. Mines and factories sprang up in the arid, scantily populated region at an 'American tempo … never before seen in Russia', as Donbass labor historian Friedgutt puts it. The Donbass-Ekaterinoslav-Krivoi Rog complex became the Russian equivalent of the German Ruhr. In 1917, the Donbass alone produced 87 percent of Russian coal and 57 percent of Russian steel.[16]

Donbass coal miners could be called the 'American' sector of the Russian labor movement. They equalled and even exceeded Appalachian coal miners in militancy – and in social backwardness. Before 1917, the dominant characteristics of Donbass coal settlements were filth, disease, illiteracy, alcoholism and violence. There was also a considerable community of Jewish artisans and petty tradesmen spilling beyond the borders of the Pale. Anti-Semitism played a role in the Donbass almost as significant as that of white racism in Appalachia. A coal miner's life there was 'nasty, brutish and short'. According to a Donbass *chastushka* (rhymed folk verse, often sung):

> He rakes up money from the earth,
> On Sunday he drinks vodka,

15 As I had the opportunity to observe, nowadays the local population universally speaks Russian. And miners were by and large Russian speakers when the Londons were living in Ukraine. Therefore I use the Russian abbreviation.

16 Hiroaki Kuromiya, *Freedom and Terror in the Donbas: A Ukrainian–Russian Borderland, 1870s–1990s* (Cambridge: Cambridge University Press, 1998), 11–14; Theodore H. Friedgutt, *Life and Work in Russia's Donbass, 1869–1924*, vol. 1 of *Iuzovka and Revolution* (Princeton, NJ: Princeton University Press, 1989), 39–78.

He drinks vodka on Sunday,
On Monday he beats his wife.[17]

Coal miners' settlements in the Donbass were classic company towns. The foreign-owned companies that created them controlled everything and everyone. The largest, Yuzovka, was named after its founder, Welsh capitalist John Hughes. Later it became Stalino, and is now Donetsk. Managers and directors lived in palaces reminiscent of the estates of country nobles. Foremen occupied large, attractive flats with servants. Colliers huddled in *zemlianki*, filthy mud dugouts, or were stacked like cordwood in barracks, sleeping in alternating shifts. Flogging was the favorite method for disciplining the rebellious. The wild steppe was the land of wild exploitation.[18]

The first popular revolt in the Donbass took the form of the Yuzovka cholera riot of 1892. Miners assaulted and killed company doctors and attacked Jews as well. More blue-collar workers participated in anti-Jewish pogroms in 1905 in the Donbass than anywhere else in the Tsarist Empire. But the Donbass was also the site of the Gorlovka rebellion, the largest armed labor revolt in support of the Bolshevik uprising in Moscow. And the Menshevik-dominated Soviet of Workers' Deputies in Yuzovka took over much of civil authority for weeks. Yuzovka coal miner Nikita Khrushchev personally witnessed the October 1905 pogrom as an 11-year-old schoolboy. He wrote in his memoirs that 'workers realized that the Jews were not their enemies when they saw that many leaders of the factory strikes were Jews, and the main speakers whom the workers eagerly listened to at political meetings were Jews'.[19] Despite the Gorlovka uprising, radical Donbass workers mostly preferred the largely Jewish local Mensheviks to the Bolsheviks.

The 1917 revolution in the Donbass had a certain 'American' flavor. During World War I there was a peculiar mix of patriotism and pro-Bolshevism among many European immigrants when the Yanks went 'over there', which even influenced radicals like Noah London. In the Donbass there was an explo-

17 Friedgutt, *Life and Work in Russia's Donbass*, 112, 137–68; Kuromiya, *Freedom and Terror*, 30.

18 Friedgutt, *Life and Work*, 78–112; Loren Graham, *The Ghost of the Executed Engineer: Technology and the Fall of the Soviet Union* (Cambridge, MA: Harvard University Press, 1993), 9–10; Kuromiya *Freedom and Terror in the Donbas*, 50.

19 Friedgutt, 'Labor Violence and Regime Brutality in Tsarist Russia', *Slavic Review* 46 (Summer 1987): 245–65; and *Iuzovka and Revolution*, vol. 2, 1994, 135–72; Wynn, *Workers, Strikes and Pogroms: The Donbass-Dnepr Bend in Late Imperial Russia, 1870–1905* (Princeton, NJ: Princeton University Press, 1992); Nikita Khrushchev, *Khrushchev Remembers*, trans. and ed. Strobe Talbott (Boston: Little, Brown, 1970), 267.

sion of war patriotism and anti-Semitism when the war began. Popular patriotism lasted far into 1917, even as elsewhere in Russia the war was rejected. Crowds of miners lynched anti-war Bolsheviks as German agents. Meanwhile class conflict in the coal pits took on a unique, raw, apolitical intensity, reminiscent of American labor warfare in Harlan County – only more so.

The overthrow of the Tsarist regime gave miners the opportunity for revenge against their social superiors. Rather than unionizing as elsewhere in the Empire, they took direct action against hated foremen and engineers, arresting them and removing them from the mines. A coal miners' union was not formed until October 1917. Donbass miners wanted to kick out all the '*burzhui*' (bourgeois) and run the mines themselves. But whereas the desire to prevent economic collapse motivated the movement for workers control in Moscow and Petrograd, concerns were more basic in the Donbass. Miners seized horses from engineers in the summer, so that workers' families would be able to get away as soon as civil war broke out. At that moment, many Donbass miners still considered Bolsheviks to be 'enemies of the people'. They were slow to realize that the Bolsheviks were the only political force whose goals were congruent with their own. In February there were only 14 Bolsheviks in Yuzovka, one being a young Jew named Lazar Kaganovich from a dirt-poor family. But by fall there were 2,000, and the Bolsheviks gained more votes there than any other party in the Donbass Constituent Assembly elections.[20]

The Donbass became one of the Russian Civil War's bloodiest battlegrounds. Two-thirds of all coal miners fled the area with their families in 1918. Another 40,000 escaped with the Red Army when Denikin's White Guards seized the area in 1919. White Guard officers committed mass murder against miners, assuming all of them to be Bolsheviks. Mine owners and many of their engineers cooperated enthusiastically. Whenever a coal settlement was seized, workers by the hundreds were shot, hung and flogged to death. Survivors often would be starved and/or worked to death. According to Kuromiya, as many as 8,000 to 10,000 miners were killed in the Civil War in the town of Aleksandrovsk-Grushevski alone. Miners and Bolsheviks responded in kind, sometimes taking revenge even on engineers sympathetic with the Soviet government.[21] This heritage of ruthless class warfare was still poisoning the atmosphere when

20 Hiroaki Kuromiya *Stalin's Industrial Revolution: Politics and Workers, 1928–1932* (Cambridge: Cambridge University Press, 1988), 71–94; Theodore H. Friedgutt, *Politics and Revolution in Russia's Donbass, 1869–1924*, vol. 2 of *Iuzovka and Revolution*. (Princeton, NJ: Princeton University Press, 1994), 233–301.

21 Kuromiya, *Freedom and Terror*, 100–5.

the Londons arrived. Aleksandrovsk-Grushevski was renamed Shakhty under the Bolsheviks. It became the site of the infamous 'Shakhty Affair', for which the Londons would have a ringside seat.

Donbass conditions generated a peculiar brand of Bolshevism. There was not much of a revolution in Yuzovka. The Bolsheviks were essentially elected into office by coal miners and metalworkers, creating a separate Donets Soviet Republic which would be integrated into the Ukrainian Soviet Republic over considerable resistance. Party records from the immediate aftermath of the overthrow of the Kerensky regime are enlightening. The Constituent Assembly election results showed that the Bolsheviks had solid support in the population, but almost all of the membership consisted of freshly recruited miners and factory workers. They passively supported Bolshevism but rarely paid dues or attended meetings. Squabbles for control and pathetic campaigns against alcoholism and 'national prejudice' dominated party meetings. Political issues such as war and peace were rarely discussed. Yuzovka's daily problems were mostly ignored.[22]

The violence, social backwardness, political passivity and raw class hatred that had historically characterized the Donbass left a distinctive imprint on the local revolutionary regime, in which several of the figures in the top-level party clique that would form around Stalin participated. That regime collapsed quickly under White Guard attack, and Donbass Red Guards fled east to Tsaritsyn, where Joseph Stalin was in charge of the defense. They became the nucleus of Kliment Voroshilov's Tenth Russian Army, the primary nest of intrigue against overall Red Army commander Leon Trotsky.

Kaganovich and Voroshilov would become central members of Stalin's immediate entourage in the 1930s. During the revolution locksmith Voroshilov was the chairman of the Soviet in Lugansk, the capital of the former Lugansk Peoples Republic. Osip Stockman, the model Bolshevik locksmith of Mikhail Sholokhov's Nobel prize-winning *Quiet Flows the Don*, is a romanticized version of Voroshilov. Under Stalin, Lugansk would become Voroshilovgrad, Yuzhovka Stalino, and Tsaritsyn Stalingrad. The leaders of the refugees met first Ordzhonikidze, Stalin's original sponsor in the top ranks of the prewar Bolshevik party, and then Stalin himself in Tsaritsyn. This tiny coterie, which would become the sole top-level survivors of Stalin's Great Purge in the 1930s, was strongly connected to the Donbass. It first took shape in the summer of 1918, in the town to be rebaptised as Stalingrad. There Stalin won his Civil War laurels

22 Friedgutt, *Politics and Revolution*.

by successfully defending it from the Whites.[23] When the Reds retook the Donbass, Stalin's number one follower, Vyacheslav Molotov, was appointed party secretary.

Connections between the Donbass and Stalinism did not end with the Russian Civil War. Donbass coal remained the prime Soviet energy source as long as Stalin was alive. By 1937, at the height of the Great Terror, its share of Soviet coal production had declined to 60 percent. But the overall proportion of coal among fuel sources had risen to 75 percent. The Donbass would be a central focus for the Stalinist industrial revolution and its accompanying cultural revolution. And would be the birthplace of 'Stakhanovism', the Stalinist attempt to create a labor aristocracy on the shop floor loyal to the party. Donbass coal miner Alexei Stakhanov would become its most famous inhabitant.[24]

Recently in the Donbass, Stalin placards, banners and buttons have been reappearing. After the Soviet Union collapsed and Ukraine came apart, that original Donbass Soviet Republic was seen by some of the original leaders of the now-former Donbass Peoples Republics as their historic model, until the Russian nationalists took over.

---

23 Graziosi, *A New, Peculiar State: Explorations in Soviet History, 1917–1937* (Westport, CT: Praeger, 2000), 120–2; Oleg Khlevniuk, *Stalin: New Biography of a Dictator*, trans. Nora Seligman Favorov (New Haven, CT: Yale University Press, 2015), 54–9, 63.

24 Hiroaki Kuromiya, 'The Commander and the Rank and File: Managing the Soviet Coal-Mining Industry, 1928–1933', in *Social Dimensions of Soviet Industrialization*, ed. W.G. Rosenberg and L.H. Siegelbaum (Bloomington: Indiana University Press, 1993), 146, 160n2.

CHAPTER 8

The Stalinist Industrial Revolution

> Seldom, perhaps, in history has so monstrous a price been paid for so monumental an achievement.
>
> CARR AND DAVIES, *Foundations of a Planned Economy*, 1969

In the early days of American Communism, Noah London proclaimed that it was the conscious workers in the shops, not the leaders of the left wing, who represented the revolutionary spirit. But rank-and-file initiative was no longer his guiding star. In his application to transfer to the Soviet Communist Party, he placed his faith in party discipline and 'the leaders of our movement'.[1] This was a good position for a heterodox American Communist appointed an industrial administrator in a rapidly Stalinizing Soviet Union. His difficult experiences in American left-wing factional warfare were useful preparation for navigating the tricky shoals of Soviet political life.

Noah London went to the Soviet Union to use his engineering skills to help build a socialist utopia. And working in the heart of Soviet industry, he helped lead a genuine industrial revolution – a revolution from above stagemastered by Joseph Stalin that turned the Soviet Union from an agricultural into an industrial society. Stalin saw this agonizing metamorphosis as necessary for survival, as he asserted in 1931 in his famous speech 'The Tasks of Business Managers', the only Stalin speech worth reading. For once in his life, Stalin was speaking from the heart:

> One feature of the history of old Russia was the continual beatings she suffered ... All [her enemies] beat her – because of her backwardness, military backwardness, cultural backwardness, political backwardness, industrial backwardness, agricultural backwardness ... Do you remember the words of the prerevolutionary poet: 'You are poor and abundant, mighty and impotent, Mother Russia'. These gentlemen were quite famil-

1 Noah London, *Freiheit*, Nov. 10, 1923; transfer application letter, Feb. 22, 1926.

 | DOI:10.1163/9789004745384_010

> iar with the verses of the old poet ... Such is the law of the exploiters – to beat the backward and the weak ... We are fifty or a hundred years behind the advanced countries. We must make good the distance in ten years. Either we do it, or we shall be crushed.[2]

The USSR underwent one of the most remarkable transformations in history – fueled by Donbass coal. During World War I the Tsarist Empire was destroyed. By the early 1930s the entire world capitalist system seemed likewise to be disintegrating. The West was paralyzed by the Great Depression, and Hitler's Germany was a rising power. But in World War II the Soviet Union would defeat the Nazi *blitzkrieg*, and Hitler's Thousand-Year Reich would land in the dustbin of history. The USSR became a superpower.

For many Soviet enthusiasts this was what socialism meant. Soviet industry was the *spiritual heart* of the romance of Soviet Communism for them. Historian Stephen Kotkin describes the 'socialist city' of Magnitigorsk as its apotheosis, despite the 'idiocy of urban life' there, with its noise, smoke, and miserably inadequate housing, transport, sanitation and water supplies.[3] Noah London's concept of socialism was different – and as he made clear in his secret manuscript, he was no fan of Magnitigorsk. For him, socialism meant improving the lives of the people. As he put it, 'Was it an absolute necessity that Magnitogorsk could be built only at the expense of the bread, health, and life of the workers? The object of this writing is to prove that it was not so'.[4]

1 Cultural Revolution and Class War

The Stalinist 'proletarian cultural revolution' that accompanied this Great Transformation enabled huge numbers of workers to move up the social ladder into higher positions.[5] As London put it in his Bronx manifesto, echoing

---

2 Kuromiya, *Stalin's Industrial Revolution*, xi–xviii; Alec Nove, *An Economic History of the U.S.S.R.* rev. ed. (New York: Pelican, 1984 [1969]), 224; Stalin, 'Tasks of Business Executives', Feb. 1931, *A Documentary History of Communism*, vol. 2, ed. Robert V. Daniels (New York: Random House 1960), 21–9.

3 Kotkin, *Magnetic Mountain*.

4 Appendix B, 397.

5 Sheila Fitzpatrick, *Education and Social Mobility in the Soviet Union, 1921–1934* (New York: Cambridge University Press, 1979); and 'Cultural Revolution as Class War', in *Cultural Revolution in Russia, 1928–1931* (Bloomington: Indiana University Press, 1984), 8–40.

Stalin in advance, 'We want to make the workers into capable business-leaders, capable managers'. The upward mobility of hundreds of thousands of new working-class business managers in the Soviet Union paralleled American Jewish experience and seemed like practical realization of Noah's Bronx dreams. But it would further propel the Stalinist degeneration of the Soviet Union. As in America, upward social mobility reduced working-class interest in social transformation. In the course of the Great Purge, upwardly mobile former factory workers, the 'Brezhnev generation', would replace old, tired former revolutionaries in the Soviet bureaucracy. Including Noah.

During Lenin's New Economic Policy, old-regime engineers largely still ran Soviet industry. The vanguard of Stalin's 'cultural revolution' would turn out to be Noah London's Donbass coal industry. London's initial enthusiasm for Stalinist revolutions would not survive personal experience. By the time he left Ukraine in 1933, ugly realities of working-class impoverishment, bureaucratic privilege and peasant starvation reawakened dissidence.

1.1 *American Engineers in the Soviet Union in the 1930s*

When London was hired by Donugol in 1926, he was a doubly rare bird among Soviet engineers, as a Communist and a foreigner. The administrative structure of Soviet industry under the NEP was polarized into two camps: 'red directors', often former factory workers like Semion Ivanov, and old Tsarist 'bourgeois specialists', slightingly referred to as *spetsy*. A Russian diminutive for 'specialist'. There was a grand total of 80 foreign engineers in the Soviet Union in 1925. As late as 1928, the total number of university-trained engineers, foreign or domestic, at all levels of Soviet production who were party members was 139. Noah London and eleven others worked in mining.[6] This would change dramatically over the course of his career. By the time he was arrested in 1937, party membership and college training were commonplace among Soviet engineers – but foreigners were few and far between.

At the height of the Soviet industrial revolution, foreign engineers played a vital role. Over 1,000 American engineers were recruited to take part in the first Soviet *piatiletka* (Five-Year Plan). A handful were, like London, recruited through Amtorg. The overwhelming majority travelled to Russia under contract

6 Nicholas Lampert, *The Technical Intelligentsia and the Soviet State: A Study of Soviet Managers and Technicians 1928–1935* (London: Macmillan, 1979), 29–31; Kendall E. Bailes, *Technology and Society under Lenin and Stalin: Origins of the Soviet Technical Intelligentsia, 1917–1941* (Princeton, NJ: Princeton University Press, 1978), 63–6; E.H. Carr and W.W. Davies, *Foundations of a Planned Economy, 1926–1929*, vol. 1 of *A History of Soviet Russia* (New York: Macmillan, 1969), vol. 1, 599, 580n5.

with American engineering firms. The most important such firm was Freyn, and this is how H.J. Freyn described the life of an American engineer in the Soviet Union in 1931:

> Truly excellent meals are prepared by a capable Russian chef, assisted by a second cook and a scullery maid … entertainments are provided for the [Freyn] club as a whole … the initiation of new members is always the occasion for a gala frolic with special ritual and masquerade. The dinners served on these occasions will not easily be forgotten …[7]

These words were written as the Great Depression hit bottom and hunger stalked American streets. Shortly thereafter, outright starvation broke out in the Ukrainian countryside. Few of the American engineers were radicals. UPI correspondent Eugene Lyons described them as

> hard-headed, open-eyed men who knew their jobs inside out but neither knew nor cared two cents about economic theories and social ideals … The Kremlin leaders came to value the single-track minds of these strange apolitical Americans who were neither for nor against Bolshevism but merely doing a technical job well. In the various sabotage trials involving suspicion of foreign collusion, Americans were never even mentioned. The phlegmatic, cigar-smoking American, honest, efficient but politically illiterate, became a standardized type in the Soviet theater and screen plays of the Five-Year Plan era.[8]

Noah London was a different sort of an American engineer.

1.2 *From the Bronx to the Donbass 'through American Glasses': Cooperative Housing for Soviet Coal Miners?*

London became a coal industry official at a propitious moment. By 1926, the restoration process from the damages of war, revolution and civil war was essentially complete. Industrial production had returned to or exceeded the prewar level. Soviet Ukraine was playing a steadily increasing role in the eco-

7 Antony C. Sutton, *Western Technology and Soviet Economic Development, 1917 to 1930* (Stanford, CA: Hoover Institution Press, 1968), vol. 1, 347; Kotkin, *Magnetic Mountain*, 37–43; H.J. Freyn, 'The Life and Work of American Engineers in Soviet Russia', *Engineers and Engineering* 48, no. 6 (June 1931): 141.

8 Peter G. Filene, *Americans and the Soviet Experiment* (Cambridge, MA: Harvard University Press, 1967), 221; Eugene Lyons, *Assignment in Utopia* (New York: Harcourt, Brace, 1937), 234.

nomy. By 1926, some 23 percent of Soviet workers were employed in Ukrainian industry. Modernization had begun in the coal industry, completely non-mechanized in the Tsarist era. But the Soviet Union was still further behind the West in 1926 than Russia had been in 1913. Soviet industry needed to progress from the restoration of old mines and factories to the construction of new ones.[9]

Noah London was appointed *zamnachal'nik* (deputy director) of the Donugol Construction Bureau, or Stroibiuro, on May 14, 1926, immediately upon arrival. In Soviet industry, the pattern often was that the director was a political appointee, and his deputy really did the work. The Donugol Stroibiuro was in charge of almost all mine-related construction. Virtually every Donbass mine had an attached *stroikontor* (construction office), and almost a third of the Kharkov headquarters staff were working under London. The Stroibiuro had a particularly high percentage of old-regime engineers and a particularly low percentage of 'red specialists'. He was the sole foreigner in its Kharkov apparatus. His salary was 211 rubles a month, almost four times the average earnings of a rank-and-file miner. It would have been a lot more but for the 'party maximum', which still capped the salaries of party members. If he had not been a party member, it could have been eight times as much, not four.[10]

About 15 percent of all capital investment in Soviet industry in fiscal year 1926/27 went to coal. The Stroibiuro administered about a third of these funds. Opening new mineshafts was not necessarily the main focus. Almost half the budget went to building housing for miners.[11] In the Donbass, the coal barons had always been responsible for housing, medical, educational and indeed social facilities in general – such as they were. Noah's coal trust inherited these obligations. As it claimed to be a socialist trust run by a workers' government, it felt compelled at the time to take them more seriously. Its Stroibiuro handled all public construction needs in the coal settlements. Housing was a particularly sore point in the Donbass – much more than in the Bronx.

---

9 Carr and Davies, *Foundations*, 947, 951; R.W. Davies, *The Soviet Economy in Turmoil, 1929–1930*, vol. 3 of *The Industrialization of Soviet Russia* (New York: Macmillan, 1969), 26; Noah London, *Freiheit*, Oct. 29, 1925; and 'Ekonomik un teknik fun donbas', *Royte Velt*, Feb. 1927, 99–108; *The Soviet Union: Facts, Descriptions, Statistics* (Washington, DC: Soviet Union Information Bureau, 1929), 88.

10 *Trudoviy spysok* London, RGAE, f. 7297, op. 17, d. 2912; Itogi raboty i vyvody Tsentral'noi Komissii TsK KP(b)U po peresmotry administrativno-tekhnicheskogo personala 'Donuglia', (hereinafter *Itogi*), TsDAHO, f. 1, op. 20, d. 2952, l. 1–10; TsDAVO, f. 4181 (Donugol), op. 1, d. 62, l. 50; Carr and Davies, *Foundations*, 958.

11 *Soviet Union: Facts*, 77; Getsov, 'Khar'kov, 15 maia', *Vestnik Donuglia* 12 (May 15, 1927): 1–3; Lomov, 'K dokladu Donuglia na plenume VUK'a S.G.', *Vestnik Donuglia* 5 (Feb. 1, 1927): 3.

For the Soviet working class improved housing was one of the major gains of the Revolution. From 1913 to 1926, the average amount of living space per worker more than doubled – not from building new housing but through seizure and redistribution. The housing revolution in the cities, like the land revolution in the countryside, was a spontaneous affair that Soviet law merely regulated. But fuel shortages, snow and cold destroyed unheated residences. Water pipes froze and burst. Comfortable middle- and upper-class dwellings turned into squalid, overcrowded dumps. Only in 1924 did a party congress recognize that housing was becoming a serious problem. By 1926, as the Londons were arriving in the Soviet Union, the crisis was getting out of hand and the Left Opposition was making a major issue of it. At the December trade union congress, union leader Dogadov lamented: 'We live in huts, in cowsheds, in barns ... in the summer we live simply under the trees'.[12]

In the Donbass, there had been little to redistribute during the Revolution. Prosperous homeowners were a tiny minority in a vast sea of misery. Confiscating engineers' dwellings was dangerous. They were needed to keep the mines running. And a third of the miserable pre-war housing stock was destroyed in the Civil War. Only new construction could get miners out of the filthy, overcrowded barracks and mud huts they had endured under the old regime.[13]

As the former president of New York City's United Workers Cooperative Colony, the Bronx coops, Noah London saw building housing for workers as the most important task of Stroibiuro. He examined Donbass housing construction 'through American glasses' in the pages of the Kharkov Yiddish Communist daily newspaper, *Shtern*.[14] The ostensible purpose was to defend his Stroibiuro against unjust carping in the press. But a critical note was audible not far beneath the surface. Donbass construction reminded him of the feverish wartime construction boom in America. During World War I, 'people closed their eyes to the fact that waste and extravagance exceeded even American proportions'. The implications of this comparison were obvious, that Soviet waste was just as bad as in America.

---

12 Gregory D. Andrusz, *Housing and Urban Development in the USSR* (Albany: SUNY Press, 1984), 7–18; Alexander Block, 'Soviet Housing-I', *Soviet Studies* 3 (July 1951): 1–15; William J. Chase, *Workers, Society and the Soviet State: Labor and Life in Moscow, 1918–1929* (Urbana: University of Illinois Press, 1987), 27–31, 183–92; Trotsky, *Challenge of the Left Opposition (1926–27)*, *passim*; Carr, *Socialism in One Country* vol. 1, 1958, 432–7; Carr and Davies, *Foundations*, vol. 2, 612–16.

13 Friedgutt, *Politics and Revolution*, 450–3.

14 London, 'Vi azoy es boyt zikh der donbas', *Shtern*, July 17, 1926.

He assured his Jewish readership that the houses being built for miners were not only better than those Russian workers lived in before the Revolution, they were also 'bigger, cleaner, nicer and better than most of the houses of coal diggers which I happened to see in various parts of America'. (Given Appalachian conditions in the 1920s this was faint praise.) The biggest problem was the poor quality of the workforce. He blamed this primarily on the Russian winter. Because the construction season was so short, 'it wasn't profitable to anybody to proletarianize ... Now there is a great lack of qualified building workers'. He was equally unimpressed with the technical personnel, most of whom 'had gone through the school of the Tsarist "subcontractor", of bungling wherever possible ... We need to attract and raise a new generation of technicians and also retrain the current personnel, so as to have an element permeated with the spirit of socialist construction'.

He dismissed as an excuse the idea, popular among trade unionists, that the main problem was a lack of mechanization. In America, '75 percent of all railroads, highways and buildings are built with *simple hand labor*, with the same simple tools which are still used here'. The real problem was that workers thought that 'we have overthrown the old regime, we don't have to work hard'. For the next building season, more capable workers would be trained. They would 'apprentice, form model quality groups, and create standing cadres of workers who want to get down to their work and don't see it as torture'. Noah London had come a long way in a short time from his old trade union syndicalism, having been 'Bolshevized' in America. And he wanted to bring American quality into Donbass construction.

Some officials proposed simply giving miners money to build their own homes. Several advocated subsidizing cooperative housing.[15] One of the very first things London did on arrival in Kharkov was to write an article on the Bronx 'coops' for *Shtern*.[16] He saw them as an excellent model for Donbass miners. In America, they had to borrow money from capitalist banks at dangerously high interest rates, but he expected everything to work out better in the Soviet Union, where law favored worker cooperatives with low interest rates and almost a fifth of all housing construction was on a cooperative basis.[17]

15 'Zasedanie s uchastiem rudoupravlyayushchikh', Dec. 9, 1925, TsDAVO, f. 4181, op. 1, d. 52, l. 29; Maurice F. Parkins.

16 London, 'Vi azoy nyu-yorker arbeter boyen kooperative heyzer', June 6, 1926.

17 Alexander Block, 'Soviet Housing-II', *Soviet Studies* 3 (Jan. 1952): 229–57; Carr and Davies, *Foundations*, 617–18; Steven E. Harris, 'Moving to the Separate apartment: Building, Distributing, Furnishing, and Living in Urban Housing in Soviet Russia, 1950s–1960s', Ph.D. diss., University of Chicago, 2003, 264–72.

While London was running Donbass construction, cooperative housing received more funding than single-family dwellings. But nonetheless, cooperativism 'developed weakly' according to a union official.[18] Conditions for workers' building cooperatives were problematic. Soviet coal miners were paid less than many other workers during the NEP period. Their production was strictly for the state rather than the favored, semi-free market. Moreover, they could expect to receive free or low-rent housing (of sorts) from the coal trust. By contrast, Jewish garment workers in New York City were better paid than average in the 1920s, and could afford to buy into relatively inexpensive, high-quality cooperative projects.

Back in the Donbass, two and a half times as much housing was built in 1926 as in 1914, the previous peak year for construction. But London's hints about the dangers of waste were well founded. The mad rush to build the maximum possible number of units as quickly and cheaply as possible led to dangerous shortcuts. Low-grade wood as a construction material, which he had objected against, turned out to be a false economy. Moreover, wooden barracks and single-family homes, hurriedly cranked out and randomly scattered across the mine settlements, rarely had provisions for plumbing or electricity. Articles in the trust journal asserted that poor-quality construction was lowering the authority of the Soviet state in the eyes of the miners.[19]

Criticism of the Stroibiuro became intense. The coal miners' union accused the coal trust of 'hindering the development of housing cooperatives' and called for a reorganization of the Stroiburo. Trust protocols warned that the Stroibiuro had too many old-regime engineers and too few Reds. A party resolution proclaimed that 'last season there were abuses in a series of offices' and called on the GPU, the Soviet secret police, to investigate. But poor advance planning was just as much to blame as bad execution. Planning was supposed to be the responsibility of the Stroiotdel (Construction Department), rather than the Stroibiuro. On October 21, 1927, Noah London transferred to the Stroiotdel as its new head.[20] He was now responsible for choosing construction methods for the entire Donbass coal industry.

18 Litar', 'Zhilstroitel'stvo Donuglia', *Vestnik Donuglia* 12 (May 15, 1927): 15–17.

19 Getsov, 'Khar'kov, 15 maia'; Litar', 'Zhilstroitel'stvo'; Zorin, 'K Voprosam Zhilstroitel'stva i Blagoustroistva', *Vestnik Donuglia* 12 (May 15, 1927): 17–18.

20 'Zhilstroi' resolution, March 1927, all-Ukrainian committee protocols, DAKhO, f. R-1009 (Kharkov miners' union), op. 1, d. 200, l. 175–175ob; July 1927 Donugol board protocols, TsDAVO, f. 4181, op. 1, d. 321, l. 11; 'Rezolutsiia', May 16, 1927, DAKhO, f. P-4834, op. 36 (party Donugol fraction), d. 5, l. Aug. 13, 9; *Trudoviy spysok*.

In his article on Donbass housing construction, he promised to discuss industrial construction separately. He did so in an unlikely venue, *Royte Velt*, Kharkov's thick Yiddish literary journal. In his article on the American Donugol delegation for the *Freiheit*, he had reported that American machinery was being bought for the miners' benefit. Donbass coal shafts were so deep and narrow that miners had to crawl great distances. 'That means that you have to have some machines to spare and lighten work'.[21] He was more interested in benefitting the workers than in erecting a towering industrial edifice.

Now he laid out the workings of the Donbass coal industry for Yiddish literary readers. Its productivity was lower than in America or Germany. Production was falling behind other branches of Soviet industry. What was needed was rationalization and mechanization. What most needed mechanization was not the actual coal-digging, but 'bringing up the coal from under the earth'. Compared with American mines, Donbass coal mines were much deeper. Thus it would be more efficient to open new mines using the latest technology than to try to mechanize the old ones with their deep, narrow, winding tunnels. Coal power stations were needed to electrify the coal industry itself and the Donbass in general. It was important to remember 'construction work to satisfy the growing working population: schools; hospitals; clubs; bathhouses; and especially houses for living in'. The housing crisis was getting worse.

A tidal wave of mechanization hit the industry not long after this article appeared. But coal cutting was mechanized first, not hauling it to the surface as Noah London advocated. Miners' lives did not improve, nor did productivity increase. Indeed it dropped, as new machinery and untrained peasants flooded into the mines in the course of the Stalinist industrial revolution.[22]

It is unclear whether London's new post was really a promotion, or whether he was being kicked upstairs. His Stroiburo subordinates must have been glad to be rid of this critical, troublesome Jewish foreigner. At a March 1928 economic conference where reservations about the employment of foreign engineers were expressed, Donugol director Giorgy Lomov-Oppokov stated that employing them in planning had been highly successful, but not in production. Likely Lomov had London in mind, since foreigners were still few.

The Stroiotdel was a much smaller unit than the Stroibiuro, though arguably equally important. Its job was to decide proper methods. Meanwhile, most Stroibiuro headquarters staff were transferred to a new unit, the Upravlenie Novym Stroitel'stvom (UNS), and given the responsibility of overseeing the

21 London, *Freiheit*, Oct. 29, 1925.

22 London, *Royte Velt*, Feb. 1927; Kuromiya, 'Commander and the Rank and File', 147–54.

accelerating wave of new mine construction. The remaining under-administered Stroibiuro kept responsibility for everything else. The UNS director was Yuri Matov, a starry-eyed technocrat we shall hear more about shortly. He filled the pages of the thick trust journal with innumerable articles expressing his enthusiasm for building 'the new Donbass'.[23]

This reorganization was accompanied by a deep cut in the housing budget, despite protests from the miners' union. The 22 million rubles allocated for new housing in the 1926–27 season coincided with London's tenure as deputy director, but did not produce the desired results. As London complained, construction was not keeping pace with the expansion of the workforce. Nonetheless funds and personnel were diverted to industrial expansion, despite increasing dissatisfaction among the miners. This trend was far from unique to the coal industry. As industrialization gathered steam, housing funds everywhere were being squeezed.[24]

A major Stroibiuro corruption scandal broke out, in which a considerable number of its officials were arrested after Noah's departure.[25] There were no accusations of espionage or sabotage, in the fashion that would shortly become ubiquitous. Defendants were charged with bribery, forgery, embezzlement and poor-quality work. They were certainly guilty of the last charge. Worker witnesses complained that houses had cracks in the walls and were freezing cold in winter. Meanwhile local Stroikontor personnel were 'living large', throwing wild drinking parties. Funds for promised repairs had ended up in their pockets.

London's successor Ketkhudov was charged with ignoring all this while forging success reports to qualify for bonus awards. The trial did not follow the classic Stalinist pattern. None of the defendants confessed their sins and threw themselves on the dubious mercy of the court. They instead defended bribery as a necessary method for overcoming production bottlenecks. Ketkhudov himself sought to blame all construction problems on his superiors. The charges were certainly plausible, although it is unwise to put much faith in Stalinist jurisprudence. Stroibiuro staff apparently paid little attention to criticism from former boss Noah London, or anyone else.

Ironically, Ketkhudov himself would be rehired after he emerged from prison as head of a Stroiotdel for London's own Donbass water trust in the 1930s. London must have hoped that the trust could benefit from Ketkhudov's lessons

23 *Vestnik Donuglia*, 1926–7, *passim*.

24 Jan. 23, 1928, protocols, DAKhO, f. R-1009, op. 1, d. 200, l. 520b; Carr and Davies, *Foundations*, 612–21; Davies, *Soviet Economy in Turmoil*, 56–7.

25 *Pravda*, July 1, July 14, Aug. 4, 1928.

in the school of hard knocks. And in this post, his sticky fingers could be kept well away from actual construction. Surely it was not coincidental that this was the very same sort of post to which Noah had been shifted when Ketkhudov replaced him in 1927.[26]

London was simultanously appointed as head of a new Donugol water bureau. His interest was drifting away from Soviet housing construction. His general enthusiasm for work in the Soviet Union had already begun to ebb. CPUSA Secretary Lovestone had requested that London give him a written declaration that he was willing to return to America. London sent in a statement that 'if upon request from the CPA the AUCP will not object to my return back to the states, I, personally, will do it very willingly, inasmuch as I believe that my activity in the American party will be directly more useful for the movement, with the changed situation in the class struggle …'[27] Lovestone sent no such request.

2 Noah London's 'Struggle against Trotskyism'

> He never belonged to any opposition or anti-party grouping, on the contrary, he struggled with them … He was never linked in personal friendship with any former or current Trotskyists or rightists.
>
> Letter, Miril London to Lavrenti Beria, March 5, 1939

> At the time of the Trotsky opposition, the Trotskyites forced a discussion upon the party and its membership. Questions were openly raised at meetings, a spade was called a spade. But the oppositionists were driven out of the party by exile, abuse, and expulsion, and fired from their jobs.
>
> London manuscript, August 1934

Political life in the Soviet Union was dominated by internal party struggles similar to the American factional warfare that Noah London had fled. But in the USSR the stakes were larger. He arrived in Kharkov as the Left Opposition was forming. Its local leader was Yakov Abramovitch Livshits. Shortly before London's arrival Livshits became Donugol deputy director – replacing Ivanov, the veteran Bolshevik miner who impressed London so much in America. He was Noah London's new boss.

26 Protocol, Oct. 1, 1931, TsDAVO, f. 1279, op. 1 (1930), d. 21, l. 35–6 and *passim*.

27 Letter to Lovestone, Moscow, Aug. 21–8, transfer file, RGASPI. The date on the letter does not include a year. It was probably 1927.

Livshits was a youthful former Social Revolutionary who worked in the underground in Kiev under German occupation during the Civil War. When Trotsky's friend Christian Rakovsky became the head of the Ukrainian state, Livshits became chairman of the Kiev Cheka, and then deputy chairman of the all-Ukrainian Cheka. According to a 1922 'service reference' (*sluzhebnaia kharakteristika*), Livshits was a 'capable, energetic, original worker, skillful administrator, one of the better directors of government departments. [But] undisciplined, arrogant'. Noah London's first impressions of Livshits were definitely negative. At the Donugol housing construction conference that took place a few months before London arrived, Livshits was the prime advocate of spending as little as possible on housing for the miners. He even suggested giving Donugol 'the right to carry out cheap construction outside of labor norms'. A year later he changed his tune, signing a Left Opposition declaration protesting that 'housing conditions of the workers ... continue to deteriorate'. Understandably, Noah London might have questioned his sincerity.[28]

In Kharkov, Noah became a member of the Krasnozavodsk Party district organization, which included all the central political and economic institutions of Soviet Ukraine. He arrived around the time of its yearly conference, where critics sharply challenged the leadership. Likely he attended, and there had a good look at the Left Opposition in the process of formation. The minutes of this conference shed light on what 'Trotskyism' really meant in the Soviet Union in the late 1920s – in particular, what it meant to him.[29] Kharkov Party archivists were initially reluctant to grant me access to these documents, but became highly cooperative when I emphasized that I was primarily interested in records relating to Noah London's 'struggle against Trotskyism'.

Kharkov party leader Kirkizh emphasized NEP moderation at the conference. In the interests of good relations with the peasantry, it was necessary to hold down industrial costs – and in particular workers' wages. His treatment of Ukrainian national affairs, unsurprisingly, was similar to that of Noah London in his *Freiheit* piece published a few months later. Kirkizh even asserted that the 'Ukrainian bourgeoisie today sympathizes with and supports Soviet power' (Minutes, p. 10). The Trotskyist Livshits sardonically dismissed Kirkizh's ritualistic denunciations of the twin dangers of Russian and Ukrainian national chauvinism. He commented that Russian chauvinism was a real danger, but that Ukrainian chauvinism really only existed among

28 Yuri Shapoval and Valeri Zolotar'ov, *Vsevolod Balits'kyy, Osoba, chas, otochennya* (Kiev: Stylos, 2002), 63; 'Zasedanie', Dec. 9, 1925, TsDAVO, Donugol board protocols; Trotsky, *Challenge of the Left Opposition* (*1926–27*), 230, 238.

29 'x-aia Raionnaia Partiinaia Konferentsiia', May 29 to June 1, 1926, DAKhO, f. P-45 (Krasnozavodsk district party), op. 1, d. 31, l. 1–66.

> our responsible comrades. There are members of our party … who think that [they] represent a nationally oppressed mass … Comrade Grinko … a teacher in a Russian gymnasium for 20 years. He has nothing in general to do with the Ukrainian national movement. In 1920 he joined our party and now he is a nationally-backward element. Clearly … it is necessary to advance him into the Central Committee and the Presidium of TsIK and so forth. (pp. 23–4)

Livshits's ally, Ukrainian deputy finance commissar Grinshtein, cautiously noted that Kirkizh's remarks about holding down workers' wages were 'in my opinion the wrong way to pose the question' (p. 16). The critics' main emphasis was on advocacy of accelerated industrialization and party democracy. The call for more democracy and free discussion received broad support, including from speakers who explicitly differentiated themselves from Trotsky and Trotskyism.

Kirkizh was a relative 'softliner'. At points, he seemed in danger of losing control of the conference. He would be packed off to Uzbekistan in 1927 and replaced by a more famous Stalinist, Pavel Postyshev, who will reappear in this narrative. But Kirkizh managed to squelch the critics by labeling them as anti-worker.

Under 'war Communism', most industry was run by radical workers. But Red directors, such as Ivanov at Donugol, almost never had the necessary technical training to run a modern enterprise. Under NEP the 'bourgeois specialists' came back, and the polarization of Soviet industry between Red directors and *spetsy* became a constant source of conflict. Promotion of selected workers from the ranks, *vydvizhenie* in Soviet terminology, was the obvious solution. But would the criterion for promotion be ability – or political loyalty? Livshits was skeptical of the promotion of workers into management selected by the current party leadership:

> Without *vydvizhenie* for workers our party won't get very far. But I must say that it is necessary to promote definitely competent workers … This doesn't apply only to workers. We have a lot of absolutely incompetent intellectuals, who occupy themselves with toadying and they are promoted. (p. 23)

According to the conference minutes, Kirkizh responded demagogically but effectively that Livshits was 'against promoting new cadres of workers (applause)' (p. 42). By 1926, *vydvizhenie* was something everyone in the party agreed was a good thing. Earlier a subject of debate, seen by some as a route to creating an 'aristocracy of labor', it had become party orthodoxy by the time Noah London arrived in Kharkov.

The defeat of the 1923 German revolution had dashed the revived hopes of world revolution felt by hundreds of thousands of Communists worldwide, including Noah London, as well as considerable layers of the Soviet working class. When Stalin came up with his one semi-original idea, 'socialism in one country', it fit the political mood of the moment. Stalin's then-ally Zinoviev, filling in briefly as the party leader, thought that flooding the ranks of the Soviet Communist Party with 100,000 worker recruits in the so-called 'Lenin levy' would defeat what he was calling a 'petty bourgeois opposition' headed by Trotsky. While still alive, Vladimir Lenin, the author of *What Is to Be Done*, considered by some to be a charter for the rule of intellectuals over the workers, wanted to restrict party membership to revolutionaries. He feared the influx of social climbers into a party ruling the Soviet state, working class or otherwise. With Lenin gone, the floodgates opened. At first it did not work very well. Workers were being promoted directly from the shop floor, without receiving preliminary technical training.[30]

For Noah London in the audience at the party conference, Kirkizh's demagogic ploy around *vydvizhenie* was ideal for gaining his sympathy for the party majority. It is unlikely that he was pleased when he learned that Ivanov had been replaced by a youthful, arrogant factionalist who seemed to have little concern for the housing needs of coalminers. London did not need to come to the Soviet Union to appreciate the desirability of working-class upward social mobility. He proclaimed in his Bronx manifesto that a major purpose of his coops project was to 'prepare for the future generation great masses of educated, business-experienced, disciplined, proud and secure builders, creators, managers, helmsmen at the wheel of life'. *Vydvizhentsy*, to translate from Yiddish into CPSU Russian.

The conference must have helped seal his loyalty to the party leadership versus skeptical oppositionists. Ukraine had one of the largest Left Oppositions in the whole USSR. If the Donbass represented Stalin's original base in the party, much of the rest of Soviet Ukraine, most of which had been in the Jewish Pale, was a stronghold of Trotskyism. Trotsky himself was born in Nikolaev, not far from Jewish Odessa, that 'city of rogues and schnorrers'.[31] His friend Rakovsky was the leader of Soviet Ukraine until 1923. Trotsky's indus-

30 E.H. Carr, *A History of Soviet Russia: The Interregnum, 1923–1924* (Baltimore: Penguin, 1958 [1954]), 122–4.

31 Jerrod Tanny *City of Rogues and Schnorrers: Russia's Jews and the Myth of Old Odessa* (Bloomington: Indiana University Press, 2011).

trial lieutenant Piatakov led the first Ukrainian Soviet government, and his military lieutenant Antonov-Ovseenko had commanded the Ukrainian Red Army. Yurii Kotsiubynsky, the 'Red Cossack' son of popular Ukrainian novelist Mikhail Kotsiubynsky, organized the Bolshevik overturn in Kiev in 1918. He chaired opposition meetings in Kharkov in 1926. In 1923, Kiev Cheka party cells initially followed the lead of chairman Livshits and voted for the Trotskyist platform.[32]

Ukrainian party records report that Kharkov, the new capital, was 'colonized' by Kiev Trotskyists. In 1927, the party expelled 310 Kharkov oppositionists, including 57 in London's Kraznozavodsk district. Soviet secret police reports warned that Trotsky and Rakovsky were dangerously popular among Kharkov workers. The Trotskyist call for more democracy in the party and the Soviet Union, combined with a new willingness to raise economic demands for Soviet workers, distress at the increasing role of capitalist 'NEPmen' in the cities and 'kulaks' in the countryside, and the previous prominence of Trotsky and Rakovsky as Soviet leaders, attracted working-class support in Ukraine. The Trotskyist underground recruited many new supporters after the expulsions, almost exclusively from the factories. It waged power struggles for control over Ukrainian unions, and even led strikes in Kharkov.[33]

At Noah's coal trust, Livshits was packed off to Berlin as trust representative when the Left Opposition declared itself – and fired after it was expelled. Other top functionaries were 'closet' Trotskyists, in particular M.S. Dmitriev, head of the supply department. His deputy Doks, an 'open' Trotskyist, intervened into an official Kharkov Donugol 'self-criticism' session in 1928, attended by hundreds of headquarters staff, during the Shakhty affair. There were loud complaints about contract violations, layoffs and failure of a union representative to attend. One speaker proposed firing the head of the Kharkov regional miners' union. Doks commented that singling out one individual was inappropriate, as the entire regional union leadership was to blame for the situation.[34]

London was a member of the Kharkov Donugol party cell bureau – and had just been elected as a regional union official himself. As a former proponent of 'open Communism' in American unions, he would naturally have

32 TsDAHO, f. 39, op. 4, d. 103 (Kotsiubinskii); Shapoval, *Balits'kyy*, 63–5.

33 Isabelle Longuet, 'L'opposition de gauche en URSS (1928–1929)', *Cahier Léon Trotsky* 53 (April 1994): 38–9; TsDAHO, f. 1, op. 20, d. 2452, 2646, 2647, 2560, 2650, 2992 and 3058.

34 TsDAHO, f. 1, op. 20, d. 3058, l. 235; Donugol party purge commission, protocol #1, 7-4-1929, DAKhO, f. P-45, op. 2, d. 31, l. 91–91ob; Kharkov party cell secretary conference, May 28, 1927, DAKhO f. P-45, op. 1, d. 69, l. 15; 'Protokol obshchego soveshchaniia sotrudnikov Donuglia', July 13, 1928, DAKhO f. R-1009, op. 1, d. 325, l. 158–160ob.

opposed secretive boring from within by underground Trotskyists in the Soviet Union. When his record was reviewed in the 1929 party purge, he would be praised for fighting against 'Trotskyism and the right deviation'. However in 1927, at a Kharkov cell secretary conference, Donugol secretary Shishkin complained that one member of London's bureau did not vote for a resolution from Stalin's right-hand man Lazar Kaganovich because he wanted to 'read up about the question first'.[35] Quite likely this was Noah London. In his secret manuscript he would express nostalgia for the days of free discussion within the party before the expulsion of the Trotskyites, even though he had opposed them.

His only venture into public anti-Trotskyism was indirect and mild. In an article published in the spring of 1929 in *Royte Velt* he hailed the new Soviet five-year plan 'led by a conscious united party, which clearly and resolutely follows its path to the main goal … not falling into petty-bourgeois despair and intelligentsia waverings and doubts'. The plan would lead the way to socialism 'not with left phrasemaking, but with sound economics'.[36]

3 Shakhty: 'Cultural Revolution' in the Donbass

> In this country we find it pays to shoot an admiral from time to time to encourage the others.
>
> VOLTAIRE, *Candide*

Noah London had a ringside seat for the Shakhty Affair in the spring of 1928, the key moment of the Stalinist cultural revolution that accompanied Stalin's industrial revolution. It marked the breakup of the NEP-era alliance between *spetsy* and the Soviet regime – and between Stalin and 'right deviationist' Bukharin. Stalin took advantage of historic hatred between old regime engineers and coal miners in the Donbass going back to the civil war and before to advance his objectives and consolidate his authority. Noah London would take advantage of the Shakhty Affair for his own objectives.

A number of Donbass mining engineers working in Noah's trust were arrested and charged with sabotage. They confessed to deliberate wrecking on behalf of former owners living in exile and plotting the overthrow of the Soviet

35 Protocol no. 8, July 8 to July 15, 1929, DAKhO, f. P-45, op. 2, d. 31, l. 69–70; and Kharkov party cell secretary conference, May 28, 1927.

36 Noah London, 'Der finfyariker plan fun sotsialistisher boyung', *Royte Velt* 5–6 (May/June 1929): 89–90.

regime. The affair riveted the attention of the Soviet public, and the world public as well. At this first and most popular of the Stalinist show trials of the late 1920s and 1930s, more than 100,000 spectators and almost 100 reporters attended this months-long spectacle in the marble halls of the former Moscow Club of the Nobility. Jupiter lights glared and sputtered, movie cameras whirred and loudspeakers blared.[37]

The script concocted by the GPU asserted that coal trust representatives in contact with former coal barons abroad ordered sabotage. The only hard evidence produced was their confessions. Many if not all of them were stage-managed and rehearsed beforehand, as one GPU investigator cynically confessed in the 1950s. Convicted engineers insisted on their innocence in conversations with other prisoners.

It was, allegedly, organized from trust headquarters in Kharkov. The key player was Yuri Matov, head of the UNS, that new Donugol unit carved out of Noah London's Stroibiuro to oversee new mine construction. According to Soviet dissident Lev Kopelev, who fell in love with Matov's daughter, Matov briefly contemplated a declaration of innocence, causing another defendant to panic. So he resigned himself to performing as scripted. He told his lawyer that his testimony was false, but that cooperation with the prosecution was necessary. He told his wife and daughter that he was not a saboteur – but was indeed an opponent of the regime. His only crime, he said, was his reluctance to denounce the 'real wreckers' before he was arrested.[38]

The trial did not go as smoothly for the prosecutors as subsequent staged productions. Nonetheless, the charges were broadly accepted. German and Lithuanian diplomats thought that the Poles had financed the conspiracy, whereas Polish diplomats were sure that the Germans were responsible. Coal miners in the Donbass inscribed 'Long Live the GPU!' on their trolleys. (GPU was the new name of the Cheka, the Soviet secret police, later to be renamed

---

37 Robert Conquest, *The Great Terror: Stalin's Purge of the Thirties*, rev. ed. (New York: Macmillan, 1973 [1968]); Roy Medvedev, *Let History Judge: The Origins and Consequences of Stalinism*, rev. ed., trans. George Shriver (New York: Columbia University Press, 1989 [1971]); Kendall E. Bailes, *Technology and Society under Lenin and Stalin: Origins of the Soviet Technical Intelligentsia, 1917–1941* (Princeton, NJ: Princeton University Press, 1978), 69–73; Fitzpatrick, *Education and Social Mobility*, 113–16; Fitzpatrick, 'Cultural Revolution as Class War', 8–17; Julie A. Cassiday, 'Marble Columns and Jupiter Lights', *Slavic and East European Journal* 42, no. 4 (1998): 648–54.

38 Hiroaki Kuromiya 'The Shakhty Affair', *South East European Monitor* 4 (1997), 45–7. Kopelev identifies him as major Shakhty defendant 'M'. Matov is the only one who fits this description. Lev Kopelev, *The Education of a True Believer*, trans. G. Kern (New York: Harper & Row, 1980), 211.

NKVD, then KGB.) They bombarded Moscow with angry complaints about lenient treatment of the defendants, only a few of whom were shot. Some of these denunciations were flavored with anti-Semitism. It did not even occur to Trotsky in exile that Shakhty might be a frame-up. He wrote that the Shakhty affair was 'only the most flagrant expression of bureaucratic irresponsibility above, and material and cultural backwardness and passivity below'.[39]

Mining has been notorious since ancient times for its dangers and disasters. Under the Tsarist regime Russia had the world's second highest rate of mine fatalities, after the US. The state of the Donbass coal industry in the 1920s made wrecking accusations all too plausible. There were a remarkable number of frightening and suspicious incidents in the mines – fires, floods, dynamite found underneath rails, severed electrical cables, sand thrown into bearings. It remains unclear whether there was any fire behind the melodramatic, orchestrated smokescreen of a 'counter-revolutionary conspiracy'.[40]

Industrial sabotage was far from an unprecedented phenomenon in Soviet Russia. During the first few months of the Revolution, workers and Bolsheviks struggled with capitalists and engineers for control over production. At a January 1918 conference of the All-Russian Union of Engineers, members were forbidden to cooperate with workers' control or with Bolsheviks. Until June 1918, in half of all cases where workers nationalized enterprises, often without permission from above, the reason given was sabotage by management. As the original chaos of workers' control gave way to centralized authority, engineers began to reconcile themselves with the new regime.[41] But according to Rostov historian Kislitsyn, whose brief monograph is the most serious attempt at a post-Soviet study of the Shakhty affair, in the loose conditions of the NEP era:

> Certainly there was conscious sabotage from the side of formerly privileged layers of the population ... Analysis of archival sources that have recently become available lead the researcher to the conclusion that there were elements of resistance to the hardening politics of the regime ...

39 Kuromiya, 'Shakhty Affair', 45, 51–2; Trotsky, 'Crisis in the Right-Center Bloc', in *Challenge of the Left Opposition (1928–29)*, 330.

40 S.A. Kislitsyn, *'Shakhtinskoe delo'. Nachalo stalinskikh repressii protiv nauchno-tekhnicheskoi intelligentsii v SSSR* (Rostov: Izdatel'stvo NMTS 'Logos', 1993), 10–11; Friedgutt, *Life and Work in Russia's Donbass*, 277–88; Kuromiya, *Freedom and Terror*; Medvedev, *Let History Judge*, 257–60.

41 Bailes, *Technology and Society*, 19–23; Lampert, *Technical Intelligentsia*, 12–17, 161n7; E.H. Carr, *A History of Soviet Russia: The Bolshevik Revolution* (London: Macmillan, 1952), vol. 2, 64–80.

> Numerous leaflets were spreading among the specialists, calling on them to actively refuse to support Bolshevism, on the basis of worked-out platforms ...[42]

The Donbass coal industry was selected for a show trial for political reasons. In Kislitsyn's opinion, had Stalin been seeking a solid legal case against sabotage by *spetsy* he could easily have found one elsewhere. But its key role in Soviet industry, the profound hostility between miners and engineers in the Donbass, the historic dominance of foreign capital, and the sheer volume of disasters and accidents there made Shakhty ideal for Stalin's purposes. The actual degree of guilt of the *spetsy* in the dock was less important than their suitability 'to encourage the others'.

This stage-managed episode of class war between engineers and miners strengthened the authority of the Soviet state in the eyes of Soviet coal miners, and therefore in Noah London's eyes as well. The voluminous Shakhty trial testimony from miners mostly concerned engineers' behavior during the Civil War. Witnesses testified that engineers had ordered rebellious miners to be whipped or turned over to the Whites for execution. During the NEP years, the party and the miners' union campaigned against 'specialist eating', the demand for revenge of angry coaldiggers with long memories, and the suspicion that all of them were secret saboteurs. Now the floodgates were opened. Noah London saw Shakhty as a golden opportunity to shift Donbass construction priorities in a populist direction, with emphasis returned to housing – and, even more important, to clean, safe drinking water for the miners.

3.1 *Noah London and Shakhty*

The Londons responded to the Shakhty Affair on a personal level by giving up their US citizenship to prove their loyalty – a fateful decision.[43] Noah's attitude to the question of 'wrecking' itself was ambiguous. He shared the resentment of his fellow engineers against 'specialist eating'. But he also shared with Donbass miners their distrust of Russian *spetsy*. He had proclaimed in the Bronx manifesto that 'the *spetsy*, the well educated, they are the enemies of the working class'. In his *Freiheit* article on the Donbass coal commission's 1925 American tour, he wrote more measuredly: 'Immense labor has been performed by the workers ... disregarding sabotage or passivity of the *spetsy* ... The *spetsy* did what they could to keep the workers from learning [technology].

42 Kislitsyn, '*Shakhtinskoe delo*', 7–9.

43 Letter to Beria, Appendix D.

Naturally, since the workers can now hold their own technically, they get help from the *spetsy*'.[44]

After he became an industrial official himself his romantic enthusiasm for Soviet workers ebbed, his disdain for fellow engineers decreased. He became active in the Kharkov ITS, the engineers' section of the coal miners' union. He spoke at a Kharkov ITS conference on the eve of Shakhty, arguing that 'it is necessary to carry out a campaign so that engineers and technicians are not subject to repression for technical mistakes. This costs the government a lot of money, as it creates a tendency for unnecessary expenditures for safety'.[45] In his secret manuscript he would praise Lenin for 'his tolerance for Russian intelligentsia and specialists'.

London's naïve faith in Donbass mine safety may have surprised some of the engineers present. But his willingness to speak out against victimization made an impact. At this highly disputatious conference, other speakers carefully avoided the issue of 'repression for technical mistakes'. London was not on the party slate for union office, likely because cell secretary Shishkin distrusted him. He nonetheless received more votes than a number of the official candidates and narrowly missed election. When the Shakhty Affair exploded and most incumbents were discredited and even jailed, he was propelled almost automatically onto the union board.

The affair pushed London to the fore in other ways as well. The town of Shakhty is on the Russian side of the border dividing the Donbass, so Ukrainian Chekists had little direct involvement in the sabotage investigation.[46] What attracted their attention instead was cost overruns. The GPU reported to Ukrainian Party secretary Lazar Kaganovich that Donugol had exceeded its construction budget by nearly 35 million rubles. They blamed this on negligence and incompetence, not wrecking. On the eve of Shakhty, Donugol director Lomov sounded the alarm in the trust journal. Defendant Yuri Matov's UNS was the central culprit. Lomov assigned London the task of reviewing all design work for Matov's over-budget projects, and he reported his findings shortly before the trial began.[47] For the next few months, until the UNS was purged and reorganized, London played a central role in all Donbass coal industry construction decisions.

---

44 London, *Freiheit*, Oct. 29, 1925.

45 'Raionnaia konferentsiia ITS', Feb. 6–11, 1928, DAKhO f. R-1009, op. 1, d. 278, l. 106.

46 Kislitsyn, '*Shakhtinskoe delo*', 11.

47 Karlson (deputy director, Ukrainian GPU), 'O kapital'nom stroitel'stve', Oct. 1927, TsDAHO, f. 1, op. 20, d. 2504 (Donugol), l. 76–80; Lomov, *Vestnik Donuglia*, lead article, Jan. 15, 1928; London report 'o sostoianii proektirovaniia sverkhlimitnykh rabot', Donugol protocol, April 20, 1928, TsDAVO, f. 2602, op. 1, d. 2362, l. 39–40.

In the fall of 1928, the UNS and London's Stroiotdel (Construction Department) would be merged into Giproshakht (the Mine Design Institute). Definition of its tasks and duties was assigned to the productive-economic group of the Kharkov ITS, which London headed. Giproshakht was intended to be an independent planning agency modelled on Gipromez, a similar body for the metal industry. Most factories under construction were metal factories, so Gipromez effectively became the planning body for the Soviet Five-Year Plan. By 1929 it had considerably more staff than Gosplan, the official one. Capital project institutes like Gipromez and Giproshakht would become the heart of the entire economic planning system.[48] And Noah London was present at the creation.

3.2 *London and Lomov*

> I firmly stand on that position, that conscientious technical mistakes are not punished.
>
> GIORGY LOMOV-OPPOKOV, April 1928

Fedor Sokolov, London's protégé and successor as Donbass waterworks administrator, would tell NKVD inquisitors in 1937 that London was Lomov's protégé. Sokolov, Lomov's secretary during the Shakhty Affair, was in a particularly good position to know.[49] He typed all the trust circulars Lomov issued, including those marked 'secret'.

Giorgy Lomov in 1917 was the youngest member of the first Soviet government, its original Commissar of Justice. A well-liked, youthful 'old Bolshevik' with a reputation for honesty and integrity, he had been on the Party Central Committee since the summer of 1917. In 1918 he resigned his post as deputy chairman of Vesenkha, the administrative board for Soviet industry, complaining that 'the masses are being cut off from living creative power in all branches of our national economy'. He had been the prime defender of the idea of workers control among the top party leaders. But he was never seen as a political leader. By 1928 he was a member of the Ukrainian Politburo and a loyal supporter of Stalin – as at that moment was his protégé Noah London.[50]

---

48 Donugol board protocols, Spring–Summer 1928, TsDAVO, f. 2602, op. 1, d. 2362, *passim*; 'Plan Rabot Biuro ITS Kharraikom S.G.', DAKhO, f. R-1009, op. 1, d. 324, l. 432–3; London, *Biograficheskii ocherk*; Carr and Davies, *Foundations*, 358; Davies, *Soviet Economy in Turmoil*, 481–2.

49 *Registratsionnyi blank chlena VKP(b) No. 1639845*, F.G. Sokolov, 1936, RGASPI.

50 Simon Liberman, *Building Lenin's Russia* (Chicago: University of Illinois Press, 1945), 172–4; Carr, *History of Soviet Russia: The Bolshevik Revolution*, 91, 100–3.

Lomov seems to have been deeply surprised by the Shakhty Affair and ignorant of its fictitious character. In a top-secret circular sent out to all mine directors soon after the arrests were announced that spring, Lomov wondered how 'the participants in the conspiracy succeeded in leading us by the nose'. He expressed regret that 'many of the outstanding old specialists among the arrestees will be spoiled for us for a long time even if they come out of the trial vindicated', and asked the directors for their opinions of the situation. A party commission was set up after the arrests to review and purge the remaining trust staff. Lomov sent out another circular demanding that top-secret reports on all personnel be sent to Sokolov immediately. The commission recommended firing about a sixth of the Kharkov headquarters staff, including almost half of Stroibiuro personnel.[51] But meanwhile the main theme of Lomov's reports, circulars and public articles became a renewed fight against 'specialist eating'.

Lomov had been recruited into the Bolshevik Party by Alexei Rykov, the official head of the Soviet state during the Shakhty trial, who like Bukharin did not think it wise to accelerate. Lomov's line at Donugol seems to have been closer to Rykov's than Stalin's. When the Bukharin-Rykov 'right opposition' was defeated in 1929, Lomov was transferred to Moscow, where he became a central economic administrator. He would acquire a reputation for not quite knowing how to deal with 'wreckers'.[52] London would follow him there.

Bukharin's ally Rykov wrote the April 1928 Central Committee theses on Shakhty. Central Committee member Lomov must have been comfortable with their ambiguities. Stalin, however, used them as a platform for his cultural revolution from above. The theses emphasized 'bringing the working masses into the leadership of production'. There were some short-lived cultural-revolutionary experiments in democratizing industrial administration, but they were unsuccessful economically – though useful politically. In his secret manuscript, London would reminisce that 'Lenin's idea of the cooperative commonwealth was indeed cooperation, was that every man and woman should participate in running the affairs of the government'. Originally,

> the nucleus of the local party organization made the major decisions in running the business in every establishment, factory, store, and farm. The director or manager had to abide by these decisions ... Questions were dis-

---

51 Lomov, 'Vsem rudoupravliaiushchim', March 21, 1928, TsDAVO, f. 4181, op. 1, d. 316, l. 11–12ob; June 1, 1928 'top secret' circular, TsDAVO, f. 4181, op. 1, d. 316, l. 21; 'Itogi', TsDAHO.

52 Davies, *Soviet Economy in Turmoil*, 340.

> cussed by the entire body and the opinion of the masses was crystallized so that there was active help and understanding from everybody in carrying out decisions. This might seem like an absurdity under the capitalist system, but socialism also might seem like an absurdity.

In practice, the democratic rhetoric of Rykov's theses boiled down to 'self-criticism' sessions and *vydvizhenie*, the training of 'red specialists' from the working class to replace traitorous bourgeois engineers like the Shakhty defendants. Now large numbers of workers would be sent to engineering schools for technical training, the vital missing component from *vydvizhenie* before the Shakhty affair. The theses also demanded that 'industrial, union and party organizations consider every possible kind of concern for improving the daily conditions of the coal miners their nearest and invariable duty'.[53]

London's emphasis on the needs of rank-and-file coal miners fitted the political moment nicely. Since the theses placed 'particularly strict emphasis on the correctness of expenditures' on behalf of the miners, the Ukrainian Politburo appointed a commission to oversee revising the Donugol budget. London was one of the functionaries participating. It sent a resolution to Moscow calling for a special appropriation of 47 million rubles to improve miners' conditions. It stated:

> In the area of housing we [need] to talk about how to get workers' families out of the stables where they live now … out of stiflingly small rooms in which two-three families huddle together. Elementary improvements are necessary for barracks, where you still encounter workers sleeping on naked plank beds in the muddy work clothes which they arrive in from the mines.[54]

Over the next few months Kaganovich and other Ukrainian Politburo members bombarded Lomov with letters demanding immediate action. According to Medvedev, the chair of the Politburo Shakhty committee, the conditions the miners were living under – bad washing facilities, lousy work clothes, low

53 Bailes, *Technology and Society*, 84–9; Carr and Davies, *Foundations*, 586–7; Kuromiya, *Stalin's Industrial Revolution*, 15; Fitzpatrick, *Education and Social Mobility*, 117–19; Davies, *Soviet Economy in Turmoil*, 274–8; V.I. Bakulin and O.L. Leibovich, 'Rabochie, 'Spetsy', Partiitsy', *Rabochii klass i sovremennyi mir* 6 (1990), 105–8; N.V. Krylenko ed., *Ekonomicheskaia kontr-revoliutsiia v Donbasse*, 299–305.

54 'V Politbiuro TsK VKP(b)', TsDAHO, f. 1, op. 20, d. 2723 (Donbass workers' conditions), l. 38–49.

pay – were intolerable. 'LODGING AND WATER ISSUES ARE THE MOST HEATED AMONG THE WORKERS', he emphatically declared. The only good news he had to report was that deaths and injuries from industrial accidents were declining. Apparently management was being more careful. The turmoil was creating rapid turnover in the workforce, a 'division between "us" and "them"', and 'suspicion even towards good, dedicated administrators'.[55]

3.3 *Noah London as a Soviet Union Leader*

The coal miners' union played a powerful role at Donugol, especially during the Shakhty Affair. By the 1930s Soviet unions were largely subdivisions of management. But in the late 1920s in the Donbass it sometimes seemed to be the other way around, perhaps because Lomov ran the trust. Union and Donugol records paint a picture of continual conflicts with management, inside and outside of collective bargaining, in which the union usually seems to have the upper hand. Old Bolshevik Ivan Akulov was its leader.

Akulov had been promoted from head of the Donbass coal miner's union to become the chairman of the entire Ukrainian trade union federation as well as the miner's union in 1927. His role as official voice of the coal miners during the Shakhty Affair launched him into national prominence. He would become deputy director of the GPU in 1931. He held this exceedingly important post fairly briefly, soon becoming the Soviet procurator. Some historians identify him with the 'moderation' of repression in the mid-1930s. In 1935 he became secretary of the Supreme Soviet, turning over the procuracy to his deputy Andrei Vyshinsky, the prosecutor for the Moscow Trials.[56]

The Kharkov ITS was a branch of VMBIT, the Intersectional Bureau of Engineers and Technical Workers, which had some 150,000 members in 1928. Its leader, S.D. Shein, was a chemical engineer and former capitalist who joined the party after the Revolution. He was one of the 'peoples' prosecutors' during the Shakhty trial – and one of the main victims of the 1930 'Industrial Party' trial. Shein and his fellow defendants had participated in a small circle of believers in technocracy, a movement that attracted considerable support among engineers worldwide during the Great Depression.[57] London would express the fear in his manuscript that the Soviet Union was degenerating in a technocratic direction.

---

55 Medvedev, 'Vsem khlenam i kandidatam PB', TsDAHO, f. 1, op. 20, d. 2721 (Donugol), l. 154–5 (and *passim*).

56 Akulov file, TsDAHO, f. 39, op. 4, d. 3; Wheatcroft, *Challenging Traditional Views*, 122–8; 'Letter from Moscow', *Biulletin Oppozitsii* no. 31, Nov. 1932.

57 Bailes, *Technology and Society*, 58–9, 104–7.

Until the Shakhty affair, VMBIT primarily sought to defend engineers' material interests. The Kharkov ITS conference where London made his debut as union activist was mostly devoted to issues like vacation homes. But after the arrests, Rykov's Central Committee plenum theses criticized VMBIT for promoting caste isolation and a narrow corporate spirit among engineers. At the following VMBIT plenum Akulov delivered the report on Shakhty, on the very day that the trial opened. He attempted to soothe 'unfounded panic' about repression among engineers. In his opinion, *spetseeedstvo* or 'specialist eating' was due to bad treatment of workers and insufficient attention to their daily needs. The ITS sections needed more attention and support from the unions, and needed to pay more attention to 'productive-economic work' – which would become Noah's union assignment. If engineers demonstrated more social responsibility, their relations with the workers would improve, and it would 'free them from fear of calling repression down on themselves for possible, sometimes unavoidable mistakes …'[58]

Under Shein's leadership VMBIT tried to roll with the punches in the post-Shakhty era, while continuing to defend its members. Shortly before the Shakhty trial began the Ukrainian ITS Bureau ordered the dissolution of the Kharkov ITS *raibiuro* (regional bureau). Its head, Fridman, had been arrested. He was closely associated with Shakhty 'conspirator' Yuri Matov, a former leader of the Kharkov ITS. The conspirators, it was alleged, manipulated the voting at the conference where London was an unsuccessful candidate. Party cell secretary Shishkin, the scourge of Donugol Trotskyism, suffered a dangerous embarrassment. His name came up in trial testimony as someone with whom the saboteurs were on good terms.[59]

A general meeting to elect a new Kharkov Regional Bureau drew 150 engineers. Its presidium included several members of the all-Ukrainian ITS bureau, as well as D.F. Mel'nikov, the director of the Kharkov Coal Institute, who had hired Miril to work there. At the February conference, he had received the most votes of any candidate who missed election to office. The meeting resolution declared that 'it is necessary to renew the dissolved organization and draw into the newly elected organ socially well-recommended and suitable ITS members, and also young specialists'. Mel'nikov was elected head. London, second in the vote totals after Mel'nikov, became his deputy and the chief of the Donugol *mestbiuro* (local bureau) – which had just been purged of 'Shakhty conspirat-

58 Lampert, *Technical Intelligentsia*, 50–1; Akulov, 'Uroki shakhtinskogo dela', *Inzhenernyi Rabotnik* 6 (1928): 60–2.

59 Bailes, *Technology and Society*, 127–31; Prot. no. 10, May 12, 1928, TsDAVO, f. 2602, d. 2619 (Ukrainian ITS), l. 39–40; Krylenko, *Ekonomicheskaia*, 78.

ors'. Unlike other new officers, both were elected unanimously. None of the old bureau members kept their posts.[60]

London lamented at the conference that 'among us many serve but do not work'. The new Kharkov ITS *raibiuro* assigned him to direct productive-economic work to prove its newly discovered commitment to social responsibility. At the conference next year he would complain that rank-and-file engineers were insufficiently participating.[61]

During the period that London headed its coal branch, the Kharkov ITS took protecting its members' interests seriously and was immediately compelled to take up their defense against a wave of purges and layoffs that descended upon trust headquarters in the aftermath of Shakhty. Regional Bureau member Suktansky protested to the all-Ukrainian ITS bureau that management was trying to lay off Red Army veterans and ITS section workers, while keeping former mine owners on the payroll. And not even answering union letters! In August, Suktansky demanded that a reason be given for each layoff, and that jobs in the coalfields be offered to laid-off headquarters staff. The bureau threatened to file grievances against contract violations. Unfortunately, Kharkov coal trust union records for subsequent months are scanty.[62]

One ITS member on the layoff list was Miril London, then working in the chemistry laboratory at Mel'nikov's Coal Institute. She was elected as a representative of the Coal Institute on the Kharkov Regional Bureau plenum the following year, after her husband stepped down. By then he was being transferred out of the coal trust. Her main contributions would be in support of 'socialist competition', one of the campaigns begun during Stalin's cultural revolution to increase production. At one meeting, Mel'nikov complained that his chemistry lab seemed to be the only place in Kharkov where engineers were actually participating in socialist competition.[63]

Noah London was in the peculiar position of defending engineers' rights as a union leader while at the same time fighting for better conditions for rank-and-file coal miners as an industrial manager. A minor conflict over housing casts a spotlight on the contradictions Bronx housing activists Noah and Miril faced at Donugol. In the context of the housing crisis, cultural revolutionary control

60 Kharkov coal ITS general meeting protocol and resolution, May 24, 1928, DAKhO, f. R-1009, op. 1, d. 324, l. 535–536ob.; London, *Biograficheskii ocherk*.

61 Feb. 1928 Kharkov ITS conference, l. 106; Feb. 24, 1929 conference, DAKhO, f. R-1009, op. 1, d. 277, l. 224; Protocols 1–15, 2–19, 3–5, DAKhO, f. R-1009, op. 1, d. 277 (1929 *Raibiuro* protocols), l. 32, 64, 103.

62 Aug. 1928 ITS *Ukrbiuro* protocols, TsDAVO, f. 2602, d. 2619, l. 19–26; and DAKhO, f. R-1009, op. 2, d. 16, l. 61–3.

63 Layoff list, DAKhO, f. R-1009, d. 350, l. 188; 1929 *Raibiuro* protocols, *passim*, DAKhO.

commissions were here and there attempting to redistribute the fancy apartments of *spetsy*, in the spirit of 1917. A coal trust engineer named Trofimov was living in a housing cooperative together with members of the Kharkov party ZhK (the Womens' Committee). They asked him to give up a spare room for a worker's benefit. Miril, then a 'party and womens' organizer' serving on the Kharkov City Soviet, was surely involved in this affair.[64]

Trofimov agreed to give up the room but put a relative in it, explaining that 'workers are used to living in cellars'. According to Miril's ZhK, he was also making his maid sleep in the corridor. They demanded that Trofimov be excluded from the Kharkov ITS. Noah's local union committee naturally agreed with Miril's ZhK, but Trofimov appealed the decision to the regional bureau. Noah's comment there was that he 'considered Trofimov to be an ultra-formalist who knows how to make use of all nice points of law in his favor'. He wanted to bring up a motion for excluding Trofimov before a general membership meeting. Most of the regional bureau simply wanted to expel him on the spot.[65]

Noah and Miril London's 'United Workers' Cooperative Colony' was supposed to be as a cooperative 'of workers and for workers' with no 'careerists and jobseekers … trying to get in with us' – no Trofimovs. The Londons were attempting to marry Bronx communal utopianism to a Stalinist cultural revolution in this petty but revealing affair. The personal, as they say, is political.

At the February 1929 Kharkov ITS conference, Noah London and former party cell secretary Shishkin had a dispute over the conference resolution. London successfully insisted over Shishkin's objections that a clause criticizing the Regional Bureau for inadequately defending the interests of technicians be removed. From his point of view the Regional Bureau had done a fine job of defending its members' interests. But as the Trofimov case illustrates, it had not focused as much as previous bureaus on defending their material privileges.[66]

The long-term significance of Stalin's cultural revolution for Soviet engineers would be their transformation from 'bourgeois specialists' with autonomy and considerable material privileges into red specialists with even greater material privileges – but no autonomy. Ever-increasing numbers of them would come from working-class backgrounds, trained in engineering school for promotion – *vydvizhenie* – into leading roles in industry. Noah London supported

64 Bailes *Technology and Society*, 135; Letter, Miril London to Beria, 1939, Appendix D.

65 *Raibiuro* protocol Jan. 15, 1929, DAKhO op. cit., l. 102–3.

66 Feb. 24, 1929 Kharkov ITS conference, DAKhO, f. R-1009, l. 228.

vydvizhenie, what he would call in his secret manuscript the 'principle of boosting the worker into higher office'. But the results were already not quite what he had hoped for. Longtime *Freiheit* editor Paul Novick visited the Londons in Kharkov in 1929. According to Novick:

> We stayed, my wife and I ... in high state in their house, and of course they were as warm as they could be, particularly Miril ... and oh was he smiling ... even when he was angry he was smiling, you could never get me mad at him. That was in 1929, we spent there three or four days in their house, and of course, he already expressed certain dissatisfaction ... an American must be dissatisfied when he sees how they work, you know, how primitively they work, we are used to the technique here, so that was it, he was basically loyal ideologically, I don't think he was disappointed already by that time, but many people, particularly Americans, would find fault in their form of work, the slowness ...[67]

The 1929 Donugol party purge took place after London left the coal trust, while he was spending his summer in Siberia. He passed with fairly flying colors, characterized by his party organizer as a 'politically developed member of the party, an active participant in the struggle with Trotskyism and the right deviation, a keen comrade and good organizer of affairs assigned to him. Also his insufficient participation in daily party life should be noted'. London made crystal clear his distaste for the dreary internal life of the Soviet Communist Party by the late 1920s and '30s in his secret manuscript.[68]

But the purge commission also noted that he had been censured in America for 'participating in the Lore group'. When London returned he appealed the commission's findings, which described him as a white-collar 'employee' by social background. His appeal was granted, and it was duly noted that he had been a worker and a party organizer in America. His party censure in America, which he had accepted at the time and could hardly appeal now, remained on his record – with fateful consequences.[69]

By May 1929, new officers for the Kharkov ITS had been elected, Giproshakht, the mining design institute, was up and running, and construction was well under way for London's Donbass water projects as well. He left the coal trust to become Ukraine's new head highway engineer. He had previous experience for this post, in Buffalo during World War I. Nonetheless, this important-

67 Novick, interview 1988.

68 Donugol purge, July 8 to July 15, 1929, DAKhO, f. P-45, op. 2, d. 31, l. 69–70.

69 Donugol purge appeal *troika*, July 8, 1930, DAKhO, f. P-45, op. 2, d. 31, l. 1.

sounding job was the Soviet industrial assignment to which he devoted the least effort. During the year he occupied this position, his primary interest was in road-building in Birobidzhan in the Soviet Far East, a very long distance from Ukraine. Granted, the majority of Birobidzhan's Jewish pioneers were Ukrainian.

CHAPTER 9

'Soviet Zionism'

> The Jewish question can only be solved when the international proletariat becomes the ruler of the world.
>
> NOAH LONDON, *Der Kamf*, July 1919

The Broadway spectacular *Fiddler on the Roof* forms our contemporary image of Jewish *shtetl* life in the dying days of the Tsarist Empire. The play was loosely based on Sholem Aleichem's 1894 tales of *Tevye the Dairyman* and his daughters. In them, daughters Tsaytl and Shprintze represent the Jewish common people of Eastern Europe, who would be exterminated in the Holocaust. Shprintze kills herself. Tsaytl rejects a wealthy suitor to marry a poor tailor – who dies of tuberculosis. Other daughters leave the old world behind. Hodl becomes a revolutionary and Beilke flees to America. Daughter Chava represents what would become the Zionist alternative. She turns her back on Jewish tradition in the most practical fashion, by marrying a Christian. But in the end she repentantly returns to her father.

What happens to them? Tevye, Chava and Tsaytl get driven out of their homeland. Their Christian neighbors are kind enough to let Tevye do the job himself. "They're your windows, Tevel," said Ivan Paparilo, "and you might as well smash them yourself. As long as those damn officials can see there's been a pogrom." Tevye and his remaining daughters hope somehow to make it to Palestine or some other mythical refuge. Says Tevye:

> Anyone can be a *goy*, but a Jew must be born one. *Happy art thou, O Israel*—it's a lucky thing I was, then, because otherwise how would I ever know what it's like to be homeless and wander all over the world without resting my head on the same pillow two nights running? … Say hello to all our Jews and tell them wherever they are, not to worry: the old God of Israel still lives![1]

1 Aleichem, *Tevye the Dairyman and The Railroad Stories*, 130–31; Slezkine, *Jewish Century* 2004, 204–16.

 | DOI:10.1163/9789004745384_011

Noah followed daughter Beilke's example, and Hodl's as well. He abandoned his career as an American civil engineer to seek the revolutionary Holy Land, the Soviet Union. The Birobidzhan project represented Soviet Zionism, the Soviet variation of Chava's choice. Noah and Miril felt the need to do something for all the suffering Shprintzes, Tsaytls, Chavas and Tevyes in the Jewish Pale where they were born, whose fate would be bleak indeed if they did not manage to escape the Pale before Barbarossa.

Although recruited to work in the USSR as an engineer, his involvement in Soviet Jewish affairs was inevitable. Both Londons played prominent roles in UkrOZET, the Ukrainian branch of the *Obshchestvo po Zemel'nomu ustroistvu Trudiashchikhsia evreev*, the Society for Land Settlement of Jewish Toilers. OZET's mission was to help Soviet Jews become farmers, in Birobidzhan and elsewhere, something they had been legally banned from under Tsarism, with narrow exceptions. In the summer of 1929, Noah participated in an American experts' expedition to Birobidzhan. IKOR, OZET's American counterpart, was its sponsor. London had served on IKOR's National Executive Committee until he left America for the Soviet Union. The expedition was a key moment in the history of the experiment, and Birobidzhan's failure was a definite factor in his disaffection from the Soviet regime.

1 OZET and *Evsektsiia*

The *Evsektsiia*, or Jewish Section of the CPUSSR, created OZET in 1925, planning it to be a nonpartisan organization representing the general Soviet Jewish public. Its purpose was supposed to be solving the 'Jewish question' by turning *shtetl* Jewry into peasants. The leadership of this small activist society, staffed by unpaid volunteers, overlapped with that of KOMZET, the Soviet government department overseeing agrarian resettlement.

The *Evsektsiia's* official purpose was to be the voice of the party 'on the Jewish street', rather than to fight for Jewish rights. OZET's mission by contrast was to recruit, support and defend the settlers, acting as their advocates in conflicts with Soviet authority. OZET sponsored an attractive Russian-language magazine, *Tribuna*, the 'tribune of the Soviet Jewish public' according to its masthead. It exceeded all Evsektsiia journals combined in circulation and political influence as a vehicle for the Soviet campaign against anti-Semitism.[2] OZET essentially replaced the Evsektsiia as the official Jewish voice in the USSR. At its

2 Arkadii Zel'tser, 'OZET and the Soviet Self-Criticism Campaign of 1937', *Jews in Eastern Europe*

peak, while Miril London was serving on the presidium of its Ukrainian branch, it claimed a paper membership of some 400,000.

1.1 *Noah London, Evsektsiia and Soviet Yiddish Culture*

Noah London never participated in the Soviet Communist Party's Jewish section. In America, his Jewish Workers Federation was organically linked to garment unionism. However, the Soviet equivalent had little presence in trade unionism. It inherited the legacy, traditions and a good section of the leadership of the Jewish labor movement of Tsarist Russia, but that movement had been destroyed by war, pogroms, economic collapse, NEP social transformations and most of all, its crushing defeat during its hour of glory, the 1905 Revolution. The Evsektsiia fairly successfully realized the Bundist program of 'national cultural autonomy' in Soviet life. But Yiddish culture was not a primary Jewish concern in the Soviet Union of the 1920s. Jews wanted to learn Russian and escape *shtetl* poverty, not wallow nostalgically in tradition, socialist, secular or otherwise.[3]

About 61 percent of Soviet Jewry lived in Ukraine, and Kharkov was the center of the Soviet Yiddish newspaper industry. The daily Kharkov *Shtern* (Star) was the highest-circulation Jewish Communist publication. Nonetheless, its circulation was much less than that of the New York *Freiheit*, to which Noah had devoted so much of his talents. In Kharkov, he managed to squeeze in time to write for the *Shtern*, and for the Kharkov *Royte Velt* (Red World) as well, something unusual in Yiddish literature, a highbrow literary journal. Some of its content, and certainly everything Noah London wrote for it, was far from the world of Yiddish culture. It was sponsored by the official Ukrainian vehicle for secular Jewish culture, Gezkul't (Gezelshaft Kultur), the 'All-Ukrainian Society for Promoting the Development of Jewish Culture'. He served on its presidium as well.[4]

Gezkul't pursuits included art exhibitions, music, poetry readings and childrens' programs.[5] Its most popular efforts were in the field of Yiddish theater.

3, no. 40 (Winter 1999): 57–8; Yehuda Slutsky, 'Tribuna', *Soviet Jewish Affairs* 12, no. 1 (Feb. 1982): 45–53; Kostyrchenko, *Tainaia politika Stalina: vlast i antisemitizm* (Moscow: Mezhdunarodnaia otnosheniia, 2001), 107.

3 Vzi Y. Gitelman, *Jewish Nationality and Soviet Politics: The Jewish Sections of the CPSU, 1917–1930* (Princeton, NJ: Princeton University Press, 1972), 367–71; Estraikh, 'Yiddish Soviet Ukrainian trade unions', *Eastern European Jewish Affairs* 29, nos. 1–2 (1999): 51–60; Arkadii Zel'tser *Evrei sovetskoi provintsii: Vitebsk i mestechki 1917–1941* (Moscow: Rosspen, 2006), 143–7.

4 London, *Biograficheskii ocherk*, 1933; Estraikh, *In Harness: Yiddish Writers' Romance with Communism* (Syracuse, NY: Syracuse University Press, 2005), 121–2; Estraikh, 'The Kharkiv Yiddish Literary World, 1920s to Mid-1930s', *East European Jewish Affairs* 32, no. 2 (2002): 70–88.

5 *Gezkul't*, yivoencyclopedia.org.

Perets Markish wrote plays for the Kharkov Gezkul't theater. The foremost representative of expressionism in Soviet Yiddish literature, Markish had been the most popular Yiddish poet of Poland. Like the Londons, he came home to the Soviet Union in 1926. His widow, Esther Markish, was very young when she first met the Londons. She describes them as a 'remarkable, fine, noble pair of naïve, naïve people'. She remembers Noah from her first acquaintance as a 'big, strapping, really handsome man'. They were introduced by Khaike Vatenberg, the wife of Elias Watenberg, Noah's successor as head of the Bronx coops.[6] Perets Markish, like Noah London, had a reputation for heresy: the Soviet press had harshly criticized him for publishing a chapter of his epic poem *Nitgedeiget* in a Warsaw literary journal. It was no coincidence that the poem's name was the same as that of a certain summer camp.[7]

In America, Noah London's main work on the 'cultural front' was with Artef, the Jewish Workers' Theater. There he worked with Moishe Nadir, perhaps the most talented satirist of twentieth-century Yiddish literature. Like London and Markish, Nadir was a spokesman for Jewish Communism whose party orthodoxy was never quite 100 percent. He broke publicly with the party after the Hitler-Stalin pact – and London's execution. London's *Shtern* piece welcoming Nadir to Kharkov seems to have been his sole public contribution to Yiddish culture in the USSR. London portrayed this 'careless epicure' sympathetically and perhaps a bit enviously. 'And if you have a pen in hand, sharp and clever, then what else should you do but laugh. Ridicule bitingly and enjoy making a living from your clever pen'.[8] Stuck in his engineer's office, Noah London could not do the same.

1.2 *OZET and Jewish Agriculture, Jews and Ukrainians …*

The Londons got involved in OZET when it changed from a small activist society into a mass organization. The Kharkov province branch of OZET alone, which Noah was to head in the cruel spring of 1933, had 50,000 members – on paper. OZET began its work by supporting agricultural settlement where Jews were settling already. Impelled by hunger during famine in the aftermath of the Civil

6 Telephone interview with Esther Markish, Jan. 12, 2003.

7 Joshua Rubenstein and Vladimir P. Naumov, eds. *Stalin's Secret Pogrom: The Postwar Inquisition of the Jewish Anti-Fascist Committee*, trans. L.E. Wolfson (New Haven, CT: Yale University Press, 2001), 119–23; Podoprigora, 'Evreiskogo professional'nogo teatra', in *Materyaly konferentsii (Kyev 1994 g.) Evreis'ka istoriia ta kul'tura v Ukraini.* Proceedings in Ukrainian Judaica Conference, 1994; Estraikh, *In Harness*, 125–34.

8 Sol Liptzin, *A History of Yiddish Literature* (Middle Village, NY: Jonathan David, 1985), 107–9; London, Moishe Nadir, *Shtern*, Oct. 20, 1926.

War, impoverished Jews began farming unoccupied land in the vicinity of their *shtetls*. When this proved insufficient, a spontaneous search developed for new lands. The Soviet Jewish farm population grew by 45 percent in the early 1920s.[9] OZET was a response to this spontaneous movement.

The very first efforts at organized Jewish land settlement had been in southern Ukraine, in the nineteenth century. Post-revolutionary Jewish settlers travelled south to old settlements decimated by pogroms, war and famine. But Ukraine was overpopulated, so these settlements had little room to expand – and Ukrainian party leaders were suspicious of any projects on their soil that smelled of Zionism.[10]

Ever since the days of seventeenth-century Ukrainian hero/pogromist Bogdan Khmelnitsky, the interests of Ukrainian peasants and Jewish townsfolk seem always to have been counterposed. The Londons arrived in Ukraine at the peak of the Soviet policy of Ukrainization. OZET leader Yurii Larin was the leading opponent of this program, under which all public institutions were supposed to go over to the Ukrainian language – except for economic trusts run from Moscow such as London's coal trust. The Ukrainization program cost many Jewish officials their jobs and led to a big temporary plunge in Jewish enrollment in higher education in Ukraine.[11]

In Noah London's Ukraine article in the *Freiheit*, he expressed the opinion that certain Ukrainian Communists were going to extremes. Mykola Khvyl'ovyi, a leading Bolshevik literary figure, was urging writers to break away from Russian influence and look to Europe. As an adolescent activist in Lithuania, another peasant nation, London had dismissed local cultural pretensions contemptuously. Now he benignly characterized such 'shadows' as isolated excesses, remarking that

> [Khvyl'ovyi] … has become so excited that he has written that Ukraine should not learn from backward Russian culture. But there is a counter-reaction … from the 'Russian' intelligentsia, from the Jewish and even from a section of the non-party Russian industrial workers. But the

9 Jonathan Dekel-Chen, *Farming the Red Land: Jewish Agricultural Colonization and Local Soviet Power, 1924–1941* (New Haven, CT: Yale University Press, 2005), 20–2; Nora Levin, *The Jews in the Soviet Union since 1917: Paradox of Survival* (New York: New York University Press, 1988), 123–5; Allan L. Kagedan, *Soviet Zion: The Quest for a Russian Jewish Homeland* (New York: St. Martin's Press, 1994), 13–15.

10 Kagedan, *Soviet Zion*, 14, 76–9; Gennady Kostyrchenko, *Tainaia politika Stalina: vlast i antisemitizm* (Moscow: Mezhdunarodnaia otnosheniia, 2001), 93.

11 London, 'Di ershte ayndruk'; Robert S. Sullivant, *Bolshevik Politics and the Ukraine, 1917–1957* (New York: Columbia University Press, 1962), 125–46; Altshuler, *Soviet Jewry*, 119–20.

> party keeps an eye on all these moments. The rights of the national minorities are protected ...[12]

London saw himself as a voice for moderation and party orthodoxy.[13]

Former Menshevik underground organizer Yuri Larin, a prominent if eccentric Soviet figure, represented Jewish interests in the top party apparatus. He regularly took his holidays with Bukharin and Stalin himself on the Crimean Riviera, and he felt personally close to Stalin, calling him 'dear Koba'. His daughter Anna Larina married Bukharin. There was no Soviet leader more enthusiastic about collectivization and more hostile to kulaks than Larin. He proclaimed his eternal willingness to die for Stalin on his deathbed in 1932.[14] Jews, as Larin foresaw, would be among the greatest beneficiaries of the Stalinist industrial revolution. His Ukrainian counterpart in Stalin's entourage, Nikolai Skrypnik, committed suicide in 1933 during the collectivization famine.

2 Jewish Farmers and American Dollars

The first alternative to Ukraine that OZET found for Jewish agriculture was the sunny Crimea, where Larin, the son of a Zionist rabbi, was born. Larin wanted to create an autonomous Jewish area in northern Crimea and southern Ukraine. Due to its attractive reputation, low population density and proximity to the Pale, the Crimea, lately claimed by both Ukraine and Russia, seemed the ideal spot for Jewish settlement. But the northern Crimean steppes were not sparsely inhabited by accident. Northern Crimea is an arid steppeland which needed extensive, expensive reclamation work to become farmable. Larin was all too aware of how little the Soviet Union could afford such a program. The financial basis for the project was to be provided by American Jewish businessmen. The vehicle for collaboration would be 'Agro-Joint', a respectable philanthropic organization. Its prime financial backer was American Jewish community leader Louis Marshall.[15] This peculiar alliance was yet another example of the role of Jews in the twentieth century as human bridges between USA and USSR.

12 Sullivant, *Bolshevik Politics*, 118–32; London, 'Ukraina', *Freiheit*, Sept. 8, 1926.

13 London, 'Di ershte ayndruk'.

14 Kagedan, *Soviet Zion*, 25–33; Carr, *Socialism in One Country*, vol. 1, 259–335; Kostyrchenko, *Tainaia politika Stalina*, 92–3, 113–14.

15 Levin, *Jews in the Soviet Union*, 139; Yuri Larin, *Evrei i antisemitizm v SSSR* (Moscow: Gosudarstvennoe izdatel'stvo, 1929), 94, 171–84; Kagedan, *Soviet Zion*, 49–62; Kostyrchenko, *Tainaia politika Stalina*, 97–9.

In the US, London's IKOR, the American counterpart of OZET, and Marshall's Agro-Joint both came into existence in 1924, in direct competition. IKOR's first president was Socialist-Zionist Watenberg, whose wife would introduce the Londons to the Markishes.[16] Agro-Joint was putting the final touches on agreements with Soviet authorities while Noah London was lambasting Marshall in the *Freiheit* for his failure to oppose restrictions on Jewish immigration to America. Before World War I Marshall, the longtime head of the American Jewish Committee, was America's most effective publicist for an open door policy. According to London, Marshall fought restrictions then because industry needed immigrant workers, and liberal politicians needed Jewish voters. But 'today big capital does not need immigration. And moreover, today big capital sees in immigration the danger of a Bolshevik invasion, so our champions of the open door are silent'.[17]

The main purpose of the settlement projects was to help the Jewish poor. But organisers initially preferred 'bourgeois' *lishentsy*, Jews without citizenship as neither workers, peasants or officials, to *luftmentshn*, those 'living on air'. They were more likely to succeed, and of course to be able to pay back Agro-Joint loans.[18] Another objective was to soften popular anti-Semitism by proving that Jews were hard-working, self-reliant toilers. But the alliance with American capitalists choreographed by former Menshevik Larin could easily backfire. In 1927 the Ukrainian government discussed Jewish settlement in a closed meeting. Land had been given to small families and single individuals incapable of working it. Many settlers simply used the money to hire farm laborers. Not surprisingly, this led to 'condemnation' of Jewish settlers by local peasants of various nationalities. After Ukrainian authorities clamped down the problem shifted to the Crimea, where a pattern of hiring migrant Ukrainian farm labor developed.[19]

The theoretician of Noah London's old Socialist-Zionist Party, Jacob Lestchinsky, accurately and approvingly described these Soviet Jewish land resettlement programs in 1941 as 'Soviet Zionism'. The Crimea project ran into the same problem non-Soviet Zionism suffers from – what to do about previous Muslim inhabitants, the Crimean Tatars. An ugly squabble between Jewish and

---

16 Srebnik, 'Territorialism and the ICOR "American Commission of Scientists and Experts" to the Soviet Far East', in *1929: Mapping the Jewish World*, ed. Gennady Estraich and Hasia R. Diner (New York: New York University Press, 2013), 107–23, 109–10.

17 Dekel-Chen, *Farming the Red Land*, 35–7; Howe, *World of Our Fathers*, 54–5; London, 'Marshal, payn un di "orime brider, nebakh"', *Freiheit*, May 14, 1924.

18 Zel'tser, 'Soviet Self-Criticism Campaign', 59.

19 Zel'tser, *Evrei sovetskoi provintsii*, 59; V.I. Nikol'skii, 'Natsional'nye problemy 20-kh godov', *Novye stranitsy v istorii donbassa* 2 (1992): 689; Dekel-Chen, *Farming the Red Land*, 281n188.

Crimean Tatar Communists developed over Yuri Larin's Crimean scheme. It resulted in Larin's demotion, the discrediting of the Crimea project and the shooting of Crimean Soviet leader Ibraimov as, in Larin's words, a leader of a 'kulak-bandit gang'.[20]

According to Larin, the problem was anti-Semitic agitation by Soviet enemies. 'Everywhere, at the same time, talk began, "from who knows where": *russkikh otpravliaiut v Narym, a evreev – v Krym* [they're sending Russians to Siberia and Jews to the Crimea]'.[21] The Soviet leadership was not so sure about that. The government was offering millions of land-poor Ukrainian peasants farmland in the cold Ural mountains. Why wouldn't they resent Jewish farmers in the sunny Crimea, showered with foreign assistance? Semen Dimanshtein, a former rabbi won to Bolshevism in 1905, replaced Larin. Lenin had originally appointed him to run Bolshevik Jewish work, and he led the Jewish Section before its merger with the Bund. Under Dimanshtein, colonization was reoriented to the *shtetl* poor. OZET adopted a new goal – to become a mass organization. The *Tribuna* masthead changed to 'Workers of the World Unite'. OZET banned *lishentsy* and Zionists from its ranks and encouraged non-Jews to join. A network of OZET cells was established in factories and industrial enterprises.[22] The organization grew spectacularly, the Londons got involved, and OZET shifted resettlement to a new target unlikely to stir up resentment among the gentile peasantry, Birobidzhan.

3 OZET, Noah London and Birobidzhan

As Dimanshtein was replacing Larin, Noah London became the head of the Kharkov Coal trust OZET cell. This was only one of 150 such cells in Kharkov, and consisted of engineers and office workers, not coal miners. Nonetheless, the *Tribuna* wrote it up as a model. OZET Donugol sent a shipment of baseball equipment to an elementary school in a Jewish settlement in 1929, over and above its official commitments. Surely Noah provided this American touch.[23] After he left the coal trust in the spring, he spent his summer in Birobidzhan.

20 Yaakov Lestchinsky, *Dos Sovetishe Idntum: zayn Fargangnheyt un Kegnvart* (New York: Yidisher Kemfer, 1941), 187; Alan Fisher, *The Crimean Tatars* (Stanford, CA: Hoover Institution Press, 1978); Joseph Nedava, *Trotsky and the Jews* (Philadelphia: Jewish Publication Society, 1972), 213; Larin, *Evrei i antisemitizm*, 149–52.

21 Larin, *Evrei i antisemitizm*, 254; Kagedan, *Soviet Zion*, 75, 92.

22 National Minorities Dept., CC Ukrainian CP, 8-4-1931, TsDAVO, f. 1, op. 20, d. 4171, l. 27, 33–7.

23 'A.L.', 'Ozetiacheiki Khar'kova za rabotoi', *Tribuna*, Feb. 10, 1930.

Birobidzhan is a Belgium-sized chunk of the Soviet Far East on the Manchurian border. Centuries of Russo–Chinese conflict had greatly reduced the area's ancient nomadic population, and it was largely inaccessible for settlement until the completion of a spur of the trans-Siberian railroad in 1916. Revolution and civil war again cut it off from the outside world for years. As Larin's Crimean project was collapsing into controversy, the government decided to allocate Birobidzhan for Jewish colonization. Would-be Jewish farmers rushed there promptly – and most departed quickly, with loud complaints. As with so many other projects of the Soviet industrial revolution, there had been little or no advance preparation. A cloud now hovered over this Siberian experiment. Was it just a blunder, as Larin and his rich American friends maintained?

So IKOR stepped in. It organized an American expedition to investigate the Birobidzhan situation. This was not supposed to be a starry-eyed fellow traveling tourist jaunt. Its leader, Franklin Harris, was the president of Brigham Young University. He and fellow participant J.B. Davidson were among the world's leading agronomists.[24] Noah London, OZET's official representative on the expedition, instantly became a leading OZET spokesman.

His first letter from Birobidzhan in the *Tribuna* reported that 'it is clear to [expedition participants] that with respect to colonization Crimea's possibilities are not equal to Birobidzhan's'. His first article explained why OZET activists found Birobidzhan preferable. 'We need to organize the colonization system in such a way that ... settlers do not expect and do not need philanthropy'.[25] Solving the Soviet Jewish question with money from Jewish bankers was not Noah London's cup of tea.

3.1 *A Historic Test*

'Our Jewish Soviet public and we – its leaders – stand before a historic test',[26] was Noah London's pronouncement at the Moscow public meeting to celebrate the success of the Birobidzhan expedition. In the *Tribuna* he proposed a thorough reorganization of the Birobidzhan project. His article was a toned-down version of the scorchingly critical report delivered to Dimanshtein and the rest of the OZET leadership. In his public speech he emphasized the positive, dwelling on the Soviet patriotism of the Jewish youth. 'We got a telegram from the district that 120 Whiteguards had crossed the border ... that 40 volun-

24 Srebnik, Territorialism and the ICOR, 113.

25 London, letter to editor, *Tribuna*, Sept. 20, 1929; and 'Zadachi stroitel'stva Birobidzhana', Oct. 20, 1929.

26 Moscow speech, London, *Tribuna*, Oct. 20, 1929, 4.

teers were needed. … The march went by night, through impenetrable mud. And what do you think, instead of 40 there were 60. And they didn't know this was only a drill'. To emphasize their bravery, he later wrote that many of the young pioneers tramping heroically through Siberian mud were barefoot. Dimanshtein ended the meeting after London's speech, with his closing statements echoing London's challenge.[27]

The report pulled no punches. London judged that planners had chosen the wrong spots to colonize. The main locale, Birefeld, was far from the railroad or the Amur River or even the great Siberian woods, where lumber for housing was easy to obtain. It was unsuitable for rice culture, generally agreed to be the appropriate grain crop for a swampy area. He condemned the entire system of colonization, describing it as an attempt to transform *shtetl luftmentshn* into dirt-poor peasants with wooden ploughs, scattered here and there across the taiga. Given the difficult climatic conditions, with such methods

> only such elements as the Koreans and partially the forcibly-colonized Cossacks, hardy, stubborn and adapted to local conditions, could find their feet after many decades. Those lands which can be taken 'with bare hands' are already occupied … The old settlers in certain regions eagerly sold their 'farmsteads' to the Jewish settlers, which hardly speaks in favor of these 'comfortable' land allotments.[28]

London advocated abandoning scattered colonies acquired from previous settlers and starting all over again, because 'if in Crimea or Ukraine individual Jewish agriculture can limp along with the help of demoralizing philanthropy, in Birobidzhan *only concentrated, carefully-thought-out, scientifically enacted, planned, large-scale management* [emphasis in original] can exist and thrive without any philanthropy, creating a completely new type of farmer with a high level of life and culture'.

In his opinion not a single one of the settlements had a firm economic base. He sketched out an alternative colonization plan and elaborated it in a Yiddish-language pamphlet published a year later in Ukraine, 'With the American Expedition to Birobidzhan'.[29] The tone of the pamphlet is much more

---

27 London, 'Postroim sotsialisticheskuiu stranu', *Tribuna*, Oct. 25, 1929; Noah London, IKOR expedition report, 'Zamechaniia po voprosu o kolonizatsii Birobidzhana', GARF, f. 9498, op. 1, d. 47, l. 20–5; London, speech at Moscow public meeting, l. 14–18ob.; and Dimanshtein speech, l. 19, all Oct. 3, 1929.

28 London, expedition report, 'Zamechaniia po voprosu', 2.

29 London, *Mit der Amerikaner ekspeditsie keyn Biro-bidzhan* (Kharkov: Tsentralfarlag, alukrainishe opteylung, 1930).

upbeat than that of the private report, but its content is similar. It concluded that 'Birobidzhan can be mastered only ... with organization and system, with capital investment and with seriousness, otherwise it should be left completely alone' (p. 55).

According to Noah London's plan, pioneers would be sent to prepare the territory for colonization a year in advance, as wage-workers. They would build houses and roads, dig drainage ditches for the swamps and acclimatize themselves. Naturally, he wanted to build housing before anything else. When he was in Birobidzhan colonists were living in barracks as bad as anything inflicted on coal miners under the Tsarist regime. After the year was up colonists could choose: join *kolkhozes* (collective farms) and invite their wives and children to join them; or stay on as construction workers or tractor drivers or some other kind of proletarian; or take their wages and go home (pamphlet, p. 63). Instead of being tossed out into the *taiga* with loan money in their pockets and little idea of what to do with it, the colonists would get land ready for planting and live in homes they had built with their own hands.

OZET, a nonprofessional volunteer organization, was partially in charge in Birobidzhan – surely not the least of its problems. An attempt to give OZET a similar role in the Crimea had been disastrous.[30] London bluntly stated that it would be impossible for OZET to run the project. OZET was not an industrial trust. What was needed was a single government trust to run everything. Then colonization would not be a spontaneous affair, but planned and organized. And settlers would not have to run in circles among many different organizations to get their needs met. (pamphlet, pp. 60–2).

3.2 *A Model for Voluntary Collectivization?*

A few months before Noah traveled to Birobidzhan he published a piece in *Royte Velt* on the *piatiletka*, the Five-Year Plan for the Stalinist industrial revolution, calling it a step on the road to socialism. What did that mean in the countryside? It meant modern, scientific cultivation. Agriculture would be transformed 'in connection with the chemical industry and the widespread highway net'. London, Ukraine's new head highway engineer, and Miril at the Coal Institute could both do their part. By 1933 the percentage of grain produced in the socialist sector should shoot up from 2 percent to 38 percent, which would surely 'reduce the dependence on individual agriculture, on the *kulak*'.[31]

---

30 Dekel-Chen, *Farming the Red Land*, 53, 311n42; and 'Farmers, Philanthropists and Soviet Authority', *Kritika* 4 (Fall 2003): 872.

31 Noah London, 'Der finfyariker plan fun sotsialistisher boyung: a shtik veg tsum sotsializm', *Royte Velt* (May/June 1929): 86.

London's Birobidzhan pamphlet appeared in 1930, at the peak of Stalin's drive for the total collectivization of agriculture, which began while London was in Birobidzhan. Its concluding words concern the 'neutral and expectant' attitude of previous settlers. 'If Jewish colonization doesn't succeed in the next few years, the old settler population will start to complain that we should stop wasting good land. On the other hand, success in colonization would mean abundance for the old colonists. It would also mean rebuilding their affairs on a new foundation'. (pamphlet, p. 66)

London was suggesting collectivization of recalcitrant peasants through the power of Jewish example, rather than forcible 'dekulakization'. Collectivization began earlier with Jewish than with Ukrainian peasants. The spontaneous tendency of the original Jewish movement to the land seems to have been towards collectivism, under the influence of the Revolution. Until 1923, only peasants could get legal access to farmland – or be participants in agricultural cooperatives. And inexperienced Jewish townsfolk naturally found it easier to learn farming in a collective setting, where they could learn from others. This was as well a secret of the success of the Israeli *kibbutz*.[32]

Ukrainian peasants resisted collectivization because it destroyed their traditional way of life and placed city folk ignorant of agriculture in control of the land. Moreover, collectivization was forcibly inflicted on them before tractors were widely available, indeed before more than a handful of Soviet tractor plants were up and running. Without mechanization, the benefits of large-scale agriculture are questionable. As London put it in *Royte Velt*: 'Grain production is more profitable on great land masses with tractors and other machinery'. Both Agro-Joint and IKOR began sending tractors to Jewish farming colonies years before Stalin decided to collectivize the countryside. London had no direct involvement with collectivization, but was grimly aware of the famine that ensued. In his 1934 secret manuscript he commented that:

> Questions such as general collectivization, the exiling of the kulaks … questions vital to the existence of the country, which Lenin used to consider with the utmost care … have never been discussed. They were simply brought to membership meetings, reports would be given, specially assigned members would take the floor and praise the wisdom of

32 National Minorities Dept., CC Ukrainian CP, Aug. 4, 1931, TsDAVO f. 1, op. 20; Levin, *Jews in the Soviet Union*, 123–4; Gitelman, *Jewish Nationality*, 387; Gennady J. Estraikh, *In Harness: Yiddish Writers' Romance with Communism* (Syracuse: Syracuse University Press, 2004), 201; Dekel-Chen, *Farming the Red Land*, 108–10.

the proposer and the leadership that brought forth the proposal in their allotted ten minutes, and that would settle the whole discussion.

3.3 *Birobidzhan through American Eyes*

London modestly claimed that the colonization scheme laid out in his pamphlet was not his own, but merely what 'some of the expedition and the local activists' were calling for (pamphlet, p. 62). His plan deeply influenced the official commission report, which was highly favorable to the project. Its conclusions emphasized the need to form 'a single managing and planning body', warned against 'too hasty settlement' and urged that 'as far as practicable the prospective settlers who are in a stage of probation and training be used as workers'.[33]

When writing their report on the Trans-Siberian train back to Moscow, expedition participants discovered that finding common language was not hard, despite differing belief systems. They were Americans after all. Most urban Jewish spokesmen condemned the Birobidzhan project. But Professor Davidson, whom London called 'the father of modern agronomy' (p. 5), characterized Birobidzhan in his Moscow speech as the most suitable unoccupied spot on Earth still available for agrarian colonization. The commission reported that extensive ditchdigging to drain the swamps was vital. This would not be a trivial task, but would certainly be less difficult than the irrigation needed for Davidson's Utah, Larin's Northern Crimea or Noah's Donbass. Davidson asserted that the land then would 'drip with milk and honey' (p. 14).

Jewish Communist participants in the expedition got along quite well with its conservative Mormon leadership. American Jews had suffered discrimination in the nineteenth century, but Mormons had faced outright persecution. Mormon–Jewish relations were excellent in Utah, where a Jewish governor, Simon Bamberger, was elected during World War I. Land had been held in common in the early days of the 'State of Deseret'. As Mormon historian Juanita Brooks put it, the colonization of Utah was 'exactly opposite to the traditional idea of American "free enterprise", whose foundation stone is private property'. Indeed, early Mormonism had a close relationship with early nineteenth-century utopian socialism.[34] The Mormon expedition leaders were proud heirs of pioneer forefathers. Birobidzhan's climatic difficulties of course intimidated them less than they did New York Jewish businessmen. As for the IKOR

33 Srebnik, Territorialism and the ICOR, 114–15; *American Icor Commission for the Study of Biro-Bidjan and Its Colonization* (New York: ICOR, 1930), 86, 90.

34 Leon Talmy, *Oyf royer erd* (New York: 'Freiheit' farlag, 1931); Juanita Brooks, *History of the Jews in Utah and Idaho* (Salt Lake City: Western Epics, 1973), 10.

participants, as London put it: 'The difficulties of the first year of work in Birobidzhan did not shock the American comrades: conquering America was a long and hard process of colonization' (p. 4).

Donbass water expert London was highly impressed by the region's 'wonderfully healthy climate': not a single participant became sick from drinking or bathing in the local water, indeed nobody even caught a cold (pp. 25, 67). London viewed Birobidzhan with American eyes – but through spectacles of unusual prescription. He liked to compare the conditions Birobidzhan settlers faced with America's pioneer days. 'It's well known that in the United States we now have the most bloomingly healthy regions, where 50 years ago you had impoverished swamps with treestumps and fleas and mosquitoes' (p. 12).

London's attitude to settlers' complaints was complex. On the one hand, he did not like how they were being handled. He warned that leading personnel 'should be able to treat the colonists tactfully. In the difficult conditions of colonization, understanding and a good word plays a great role ...' (p. 38). But he sympathized with those officials who believed that all problems were due to the colonists being poor human material. He recounted colonist complaints about the dreadful housing situation, but counterposed the example of one settler with the American 'can-do' spirit. Instead of whining, he simply set about building his own house (pp. 36–8). Remembering his own immigrant experience, London recalled how

> also in America people would arrive and every day want to go back, but they couldn't go back, because there weren't any boat tickets. And as they saved up for a boat ticket, they slowly got used to things, began to earn a little money, so they could bring a little something home with them ... today, there's Birobidzhan, which is as far away as America, and where there's nothing but heaven, earth and mosquitoes. In America, you had no other choice, like that damn Columbus, but here you've got some kind of 'Soviet power', which gives you a ticket there and a ticket back, which gives you money for a house and so forth, you've got OZET, a social organization of *akheynu b'nei Isroel* [our Jewish brethren] to whom you can make certain complaints ... (pamphlet, p. 41)

3.4 *A Ukrainian Highway Engineer in Birobidzhan*

London's plan for Birobidzhan bore similarities to the recommendations of the first systematic Soviet effort to investigate the region. The report from KOMZET, a Soviet-wide agrarian settlement planning agency, called for settlement 'in accordance with a strict plan' instead of 'partial, spotty colonization'. Systematic preparation in advance was absolutely essential. It advocated using cheap Chinese labor, but also suggested forming labor brigades of unemployed Jewish youth who could become settlers.[35]

London's concept was different. He was not interested in using badly-paid Chinese workers for the dirty work. Moreover the KOMZET plan, unlike London's, recommended settling the Soviet bank of the Amur River first. Attempts to steer colonists there largely failed, due to the absence of any decent roads connecting the river valley with the Trans-Siberian railroad. KOMZET's solution was highway construction, and the task was assigned to OZET. Investigating the road situation was London's actual assignment on the IKOR expedition.

His conclusions were that spending millions on road construction in Birobidzhan would be premature. Immediate needs were far greater in Ukraine than in the underpopulated Soviet Far East. Birobidzhan settlement should have begun near the railroad, even if the Amur Valley was more fertile. After the first settlements were consolidated, settlers idle in the winter could be employed in roadbuilding. This conservative approach foreshadows industrial policies he would advocate in his secret manuscript.

London stated in his official reports that he spent the bulk of his time on roadbuilding questions. This is certainly how IKOR chairman Leon Talmy depicts him in his lengthy Birobidzhan travelogue, *Oyf royer erd* (On raw earth). London's first action was to protest the assignment of road construction planning to OZET, in a memo sent to Dimanshtein in Moscow. The tractors IKOR had given OZET were being used for roadbuilding in the off-seasons. The memo insisted that Birobidzhan roadbuilding needed to be integrated into general planning for the region as a whole. According to London, OZET had no particular expertise in road planning, no apparatus for it, nor even enough staff assigned to it.[36] His second action was to move to get the head of the local OZET road department fired. According to his report, 'The road department was given assignments of tremendous length, beyond its strength, insufficient money ... but the main fault was the criminal irresponsibility, incompetence and deception of the department manager Benkogenov'.

In *Oyf royer erd*, Talmy was more interested in beautiful scenery and adventures with Siberian tigers and bears than in settlers' complaints. Whereas London judiciously categorized them into 'justified and unjustified' (p. 27), Talmy took care to explain why complaints were always unfair when a Soviet official or institution was criticized. He made an exception for Benkogenov. When the

35 Schwartz, 'Birobidzhan: An Experiment in Jewish Colonization', in *Russian Jewry 1917–1967*, ed. G. Aronson (New York: Union of Russian Jews, 1969), 349–55.

36 London, Birobidzhan reports, GARF, fond 9498, op. 1, d. 47, l. 26–7.

tractor assigned to the expedition got stuck in the mud, Talmy described a self-satisfied 'Be-nov' sitting in his wagon, ignoring the tumult, and finally telling the crew to 'leave it there'. But when a film crew showed up, 'Be-nov' reacted immediately – by pulling out his pipe and lighting it for the camera, in best Stalin fashion.[37]

In his Moscow public speech, London put the best face he could on the fiasco, saying that 'although we have not had great successes in this connection, I must say that building roads in Birobidzhan does not represent a greater problem than around Moscow or Kharkov or anywhere else'.[38] This authoritative statement by Ukraine's head highway engineer throws light on the sad situation of Soviet highway construction in the year 1929.

3.5 *A 'Historic Test' Graded*

The panegyrics Talmy and other Jewish Communist spokesmen delivered for the Birobidzhan project did not reflect the view of the Soviet leadership. In the pages of *Sovetskoe Stroitel'stvo* (Soviet Construction), prominent Soviet journalist Victor Fink blasted the press for painting the situation in rosy colors.[39] Birobidzhan enthusiast Michael Rashkes, an old acquaintance of London's from the early days of American Communism, admitted at a 1928 Ukrainian OZET Conference that the colonists had been dispatched in a hurry. 'Were we not to begin colonization ... the area assigned to Jewish colonization would have been smaller because many non-Jewish settlers from Ukraine and Belorussia are rushing there'.[40]

The IKOR commission asked Alexei Rykov, the head of the Soviet government, whether such a single managing and planning body would be formed for Birobidzhan. Bukharin's ally Rykov, who would shortly be removed from his post, cautiously replied, 'I think that there will be no objections ...' According to Victor Fink such a trust – Birobidzhanstroi – was in the process of formation in the spring of 1930. One plausible candidate to head it – Noah London – was appointed in May 1930 to head Donbassvodtrest, a managing/planning body in charge of something more important, Donbass water supply. Birobidzhan was taken out of the hands of OZET, but simply turned over to the regional government.

The IKOR commission's proposals could hardly have come at a worse moment. Stalin's industrialization and collectivization programs were reaching

37 London report, GARF, l. 22 ob.; Talmy, *Oyf royer erd*, 54–5.
38 London, 'Postroim sotsialisticheskuiu stranu'.
39 Victor Fink, 'Birobidzhan', *Sovetskoe stroitel'stvo* 5, no. 46 (May 1930): 121.
40 Fink, 'Birobidzhan', 122; Gitelman, *Jewish Nationality*, 432.

new intensity, and the economy was suffering from extreme overstretch. The last thing the Soviet government wanted was another expensive project to suck up money, cadres, time and energy. When the commission asked Rykov whether more funds were available, he was forced to state that the government 'is at this time deprived of the opportunity to appropriate new additional means for this purpose'.[41] Birobidzhan became a propaganda showpiece instead of a practical project.

4 OZET and the Transformation of Soviet Jewry

In the initial period of Birobidzhan enthusiasm, OZET grew rapidly and became the spokesman for Soviet Jewry. It essentially replaced the Jewish Section, whose Yiddishism rendered it irrelevant to an increasingly Russian-speaking Soviet Jewish public. Like their American cousins, Soviet Jews were assimilating. OZET now received an additional function: to train Jewish youth to work in industry.[42] This became OZET's true historic significance. OZET's ostensible purpose, the transformation of Jews into peasants, became a Sorelian myth rather than a practical program. As the myth frayed over the course of the 1930s, and the Jewish poverty and popular anti-Semitism of the NEP era ebbed away, OZET declined.

Jewish proletarianization was transitory – a short stop on the path to white-collar bureaucratization. The private professionals, petty merchants and artisans, *luftmenshn* and starving unemployed who made up nearly half of the Jewish population in the former Pale when the Londons arrived in 1926 were almost completely eliminated as social categories by World War II. But the percentage of blue-collar workers went up only slightly. Affirmative action for workers and peasants was the central aspect of the Stalinist cultural revolution. Newly baptized Jewish 'industrial workers' and 'peasants' flocked to take advantage of preferential college admission.[43]

Class-based affirmative action was finally abolished during the Great Terror, from which Jews suffered less than Slavs in percentage terms. By 1939, 3.7 percent of the Jewish population in Ukraine and Belorussia had joined the top

41 Fink, 'Birobidzhan', 122; *Icor Commission*, 91–2.

42 Zel'tser, *Evrei sovetskoi provintsii*, 58–60; Mikhail Beizer, *Jews of St. Petersburg: Excursions through a Noble Past* (Melrose Park, PA: Jewish Publication Society, 1989), 240–50, 257–61; Levavi, 'OZET-GEZERD', *He'avar* (1969): 127.

43 Lestchinsky, *Dos Sovetishe Idntum*, 155–81; Sheila Fitzpatrick, *Education and Social Mobility*; Levin, *Jews in the Soviet Union*, 246–9.

Soviet elite, and an additional 42.2 percent had become white-collar government workers. In Moscow, more than 80 percent of the Jewish population were white-collar workers or higher. Soviet Jews were perhaps the greatest beneficiaries of the Stalinist industrial revolution and its accompanying cultural revolution.[44] The 1930s became a golden era for a Jewish Soviet elite. But not all Jews climbed the social ladder, even in Moscow. Mar'ina Roshcha acquired a reputation as a cross between a *shtetl* and an American-style black ghetto, famous for its high crime rate and its curious local custom of giving vodka and tobacco to children.[45]

5 UkrOZET and the Londons

When London's pamphlet appeared in 1930, OZET was reaching its peak. Over 600 delegates attended a Kharkov OZET city conference in December. Fewer than 100 were party members, more than half were factory workers, and 45 percent were non-Jewish. Following the standard ritual of the times, delegates denounced the leadership for its multiple failings. It was renovated in the usual fashion after the usual self-criticism sessions.[46] Local leader Viktorov's report mandated a transformation. The new agenda indicated what OZET was all about now. It consisted of: '(a) creation out of the Jewish poor, especially the youth, of a qualified labor force for industry and agriculture; (b) bringing the Jewish poor into the fundamental branches of industry and industrial cooperatives; (c) settling the poorest sections of the Jewish population in Crimea and Birobidzhan' (p. 55 of the report). But Birobidzhan came first.

The conference sent 16 delegates to the all-Ukrainian OZET conference. Fifteen of them are named in the protocol, but one is listed mysteriously as 'from Donugol' (p. 53). This it turned out was 'Maria' London. She was still working at the Coal Institute, where she had been promoted from lab assistant to 'scientific worker'. She represented it on the executive committee of the Kharkov engineers' section of the miners' union. At the all-Ukrainian conference 'comrade London, a working woman' was elected an alternate member of OZET's

---

44 Altshuler, *Soviet Jewry*, 27, 181–4; Gabriele Freitag, *Nächstes Jahr in Moskau!: Die Zuwanderung von Juden in die sowjetische Metropole 1917–1932* (Göttingen: Vandenhoeck & Ruprecht, 2004), 137–45.

45 Vetter, 134–35; Freitag, 312–15, 242.

46 'Protokol, 1-i Gorodskii konferentsii Khar'kovskogo otd. OZET', GAKHO, f. 1623, op. 2, d. 1, l. 45–57.

Ukrainian Presidium.[47] But unlike most members, she was living in Kharkov and was a regular and active meeting participant and so began to play a certain role there.

There was a public debate at the second all-Soviet OZET convention over Birobidzhan and Crimea. One-time Menshevik Larin advocated continuing to work with Agro-Joint in Crimea, and was covertly supported by former Bundists. Dimanshtein and former Socialist-Zionists like Mikhail Rashkes advocated Birobidzhan. In the middle of the controversy E.I. Veger, the Crimean party leader who succeeded Ibraimov, accused Larin and KOMZET of supporting kulak Jewish settlers and their American capitalist allies.[48] This touched off what was described as a 'lively discussion' in the UkrOZET Presidium in 1931. Miril and others repeatedly attacked the leadership for dragging its feet in reacting to the issue.[49]

That summer, *Freiheit* editor Moissaye Olgin visited Kharkov in the company of Miril's sister Rose, who had just finished her first year as a New York City schoolteacher. He gave a report to the Presidium, and a team including Miril was appointed to revive UkrOZET's laggard cultural sector. Miril was also assigned to handling communications with IKOR, the *Shtern*, and even the Ukrainian party's Jewish Section, which apparently hadn't been abolished quite yet in Ukraine. But when a proposal was made to send her out on an organizational tour, a resolution had to be passed to 'talk with the party secretary of the Coal Institute'. Authorization was not received, and her role in the organization subsequently diminished.[50]

Her work at the Coal Institute was not unimportant. She was working on scientific papers on coal chemistry and published two such papers in technical journals, presenting them at the Sixth Mendeleev Conference in Kharkov in 1932.[51] But the real reason she stepped back from a leading role in UkrOZET was different. Her maximum OZET activity coincided with the period when Olgin and Rose were houseguests. Miril and Rose spent summer weeks backpacking together across Ukraine and the Northern Caucasus. Miril thrived on this adventure, which severely affected her younger sister's health. During

47 UkrOZET Presidium Protocols, Dec. 8, 1930; GARF, f. 9498, op. 1, d. 218, l. 4.

48 Gitelman, *Jewish Nationality*, 435–6; Chimen Abramsky, 'The Biro-Bidzhan project', in *Jews in Soviet Russia since 1917*, ed. L. Kochan (London: Oxford University Press, 1970), 67; Hersh Smoliar, *Fun ineveynik: Zikhroynes vegn der yevsektsye* (Tel Aviv: Y.L. Perets, 1978), 401–6; Kostyrchenko, *Tainaia politika Stalina*, 112–13; Orgburo docs., 1931, RGASPI, f. 17, op. 114, d. 212, l. 146–87.

49 UkrOZET protocols, 1931 *passim*; GARF, f. 9498, op. 1, d. 229.

50 Oct. 12, 1931 protocol, l. 21; and *passim*.

51 Ibid.; Letter, Miril to Beria, Appendix D.

the month of September, when Presidium protocols seem to indicate she was beginning to take on a leading role in the organization, childless Miril was nursing her sick sister at home 'like a pet'.

Rose had accepted a well-paid job offer in childrens' education and was urging Louis Discher, her future husband, to join her in Kharkov. Discher's own ambition was to join the CPUSA and become a professional revolutionary. He lacked a high school diploma and was at the time working in a New York bookstore. Rose suggested:

> What prevents you from arriving here and applying for work in Traktorstroi ... Surely you will be accepted ... Then you will advance on a merit basis only, becoming an *udarnik* [shock brigader], participating in the work's numerous activities ... And if you are fit for it, you will be sent after a while to the work's own technical school ... You will share the extreme deprivation of the mass of the people who are being sweated for the rapid completion of the *piatiletka*. But ... you will become a worker ... [and] you will acquire an experience which will give you enough material for all the literary work you might wish to do during the rest of your life.[52]

When Rose finally decided to return home to New York and marry him instead, she wrote him that 'Mira is taking my change of heart very painfully. She cries when I mention going, and cannot bear once more to be isolated from everyone'. Her loneliness was not due to marital difficulties. According to her sister's description, 'evenings I lie on the couch and watch Mira and Noah. They are an unusually affectionate couple and bandy pet names and embraces as though they had been married yesterday'. Miril not long afterwards underwent a nervous breakdown, in connection with the great Ukrainian famine. A few years later, according to her niece Beatrice Holmes, mother of this book's author: 'Miril told Aunt Rose that there had been a famine in Ukraine and it had been hushed up whereas the famine after the Civil War was published and help was sought from the United States ... people were dying there, she told this story weeping ...'[53]

As Miril stepped away from UkrOZET, problems were developing. The *Tribuna* wrote extensively about UkrOZET's deficiencies, describing Kharkov as its worst branch. Jewish 'proletarianization' was already near completion. Jews

52 Letter, Rose to Louis, Sept. 7, 1931, Lewis collection.

53 Letters, Rose to Louis, Sept. 4, 1931; Sept. 13, 1931; Aug. 2, 1934; Rose to Sara, Aug. 2, 1934; Miril to Louis, July 21, 1934, Lewis collection; interview, John Holmes with Beatrice Holmes, Nov. 30, 1998.

were more assimilated there than anywhere else in Ukraine, and likely more blue collar as well.[54] UkrOZET's alleged task of Jewish peasantization was rapidly losing appeal. The Kharkov region was one of those worst hit by the famine.

A January 1933 Ukrainian Central Committee document described UkrOZET as highly unsatisfactory. Many branches existed only on paper, and the leadership did not know how many members or even branches it really had. The organization was getting ever more dependent on sales of lottery tickets and government subsidy. Cadre reinforcement was recommended. A very busy Noah London was saddled with the post of president of the Kharkov regional OZET (oblOZET).[55] He had his work cut out for him. According to an inspector's report to Dimanshtein, 'The oblOZET apparatus was picked in such a way that it cannot do any work … With the exception of the president of the *orgkom*, comrade London, none of the members of the *orgkom* is interested in the work. Presently, Kharkov oblOZET basically does not exist'.[56]

Not surprisingly, UkrOZET graded the work of the Kharkov oblOZET in June 1933 as 'clearly unsatisfactory'. The prime task KharoblOZET was assigned during Noah's presidency seems to have been selling lottery tickets. At one UkrOZET Presidium meeting, he remarked that due to the lottery campaign, little else was being done.[57] Surely selling lottery tickets to Kharkov factory workers to support Jewish agriculture in faraway Birobidzhan – in the middle of a famine killing millions of Ukrainian peasants, many near Kharkov – must have been a hard chore.

6 UkrOZET, Birobidzhan and Noah London

Despite the brave front presented in the *Tribuna* things were not going well in Birobidzhan either, as internal reports reveal. Noah's recommendations had been ignored. Few settlers were staying because, despite all warnings, no housing was prepared for them in advance. Meanwhile, Ukrainian settlement was not going well either. UkrOZET was publicly censured for 'hampering the build-

54 *Tribuna*, 1932–3 *passim*; Gennady Estraikh, 'From Shtetl to the City of the Sun Calling at the Schools of Communism: Yiddish Soviet Ukrainian Trade Unions of the 1920s', *Eastern European Jewish Affairs* 29, nos. 1–2 (Summer/Winter 1999): 51–60, 53; and Estraikh, *In Harness*, 119.

55 'Spravka o sostoianii i rabote "OZET" na Ukraine', TsDAHO, f. 1, op. 20, d. 6213, l. 18–21; Kharkov oblast secretariat protocols, Nov. 17, 1932, DAKhO, f. P-17-2, op. 1, d. 20, l. 119.

56 'Khar'kovskomu oblkomitetu I gorkomitetu KP(b)U, Ot Instruktorga Tsentral'nogo Soveta OZET chl. VKP(b) ROT', GARF, f. 9498, op. 1, d. 242, l. 107.

57 'Rezolutsiia', GARF, f. 9498, op. 1, d. 260, l. 25; UkrOZET Protokol #58, 12-18-1932, d. 241, l. 70b.

ing of Birobidzhan'.[58] In reaction to repeated agricultural failure the planners now changed emphasis to industrial development. The Birobidzhan experiment's original purpose, ending *shtetl* poverty, was tacitly abandoned.[59] The Soviet industrial revolution had rendered it irrelevant.

The final demise of OZET during the Great Terror had little or nothing to do with Stalinist anti-Semitism. The old Russian 'Jewish problem', in the terms traditionally posed, was solved. Soviet Jewry had been 'productivized', or rather bureaucratized. Shortly before her death in the 1980s, Rose Risikoff told the author's father that Noah regarded Birobidzhan as a failure.[60] Consequently, OZET no longer had any reason for existence. But the abolition of OZET meant that there no longer was any official Soviet body representing Jewish interests and tasked with fighting anti-Semitism.

For Noah London, this experiment in Soviet Zionism became a bad memory best forgotten. The historic test had been flunked. His 1934 manuscript evades any mention of OZET or Birobidzhan or indeed of the 'Jewish question' at all.

It is unclear whether or not Noah London's scheme to make a success of the Birobidzhan project was truly practical. In any case, what he recommended would certainly have worked out better than what was actually done. The question is whether the Soviet Union genuinely could have afforded to commit the human, material and monetary resources to Birobidzhan that would have been required for success. The Birobidzhan fiasco must have played a role in his disaffection. But the prime reason he lost faith in the party leadership was the profound social crisis that unfolded under his eyes in 1932 and 1933. After he returned to Ukraine he once again became a central participant in the Stalinist industrial revolution and a witness to the tragic famine that ensued. There were more important things to worry about than the fate of Birobidzhan or Soviet Yiddish culture.

---

58 'Soveshchanie pri kul'tprope TsK', Oct. 1, 1932, TsDAHO, f. 1, op. 20, d. 5288, l. 1–50; Eidel'man, 'Chto proizoshlo', *Tribuna* 13 (May 1932): 2–4; Pansenko, 'Dopovidna Zapyska', TsDAHO, f. 1, op. 20, d. 5252, l. 4–18; 'D.L.', 'UkrOZET i UkrKOMZET tormozit stroitel'stvo Birobidzhana', *Tribuna* 3–4 (Feb. 1933).

59 Barshchevsky, 'Zemel'noe ustroistvo trudiashchikh evreev', *Sovetskoe stroitel'stvo* 1 (Jan. 1934): 86–90; Robert Weinberg, 'Jews into Peasants? Solving the Jewish Question in Birobidzhan', in *Jews and Jewish Life in Russia and the Soviet Union*, ed. Y. Ro'i (London: Frank Cass, 1995), 87–102.

60 Interview, Jay Holmes with Rose Risikoff, Jan. 2, 1986.

CHAPTER 10

Donbass Water and Noah London

Noah London went to the Soviet Union to 'build socialism' – to build a better life for all the peoples of the former Russian Empire and provide a model for the rest of the world. His efforts to build socialism were focused on the Donbass, recently in the middle of a civil war between Ukrainian and Russian nationalists that has turned into a war between Russia and Ukraine. He was responsible for Donbass water supply under one job title or another for most of his Soviet career. He fought to provide clean, safe drinking water for the working population of the Donbass, whose coal was the prime energy source for the entire Soviet Union, and he was proud of the waterworks he built. They freed the Donbass from the Tsarist yoke of typhoid, dysentery and cholera. Water for the Donbass was a key Soviet priority – for industry, the uppermost consideration for the regime, and for the miners and the general population themselves, the fundamental concern for Noah London. The divergence between his priorities and Stalin's took a while to become truly problematic, due to the internal contradictions of the Stalinist system. But they did lead inevitably to the 'Stalinization' of the Donbass water trust he created, to the purge and replacement of its original staff by up and coming *vydvizhentsy*, with party blessing. And finally to his arrest and execution.

By the time he left Ukraine in the spring of 1933, 'kicked upstairs' to be deputy commissioner of Glavstroiprom, the trust in charge of industrial construction for the entire Soviet Union, Ukraine was in the grip of a famine that killed millions. And Noah London's expensive water projects helped put it there. In the zero-sum world of budget economics, any diversion of resources from agriculture was disastrous, even for projects as vital as the waterworks. Fundraising for Jewish agriculture in Birobidzhan among Kharkov factory workers only added insult to injury.

1 A 'Sewer Communist' Arrives in the Donbass

The official history of the water trust Noah London founded proclaims that 'V.I. Lenin repeatedly pointed out that in the development of industry it is necessary to pay heed to water resources, upon whose rational utilization everything depends'. According to environmental historian Simo Laakonen, 'Water is a global dictator which sets the limits for living nature', and the Don-

 | DOI:10.1163/9789004745384_012

bass has very poor natural water supplies.[1] In the Soviet Union's last years in the 1980s, rainfall per person in the Donbass was about 4 percent of the Soviet-era norm. The transformation of the Donbass into a thickly populated industrial center, like the simultaneous transformation of California deserts into suburbs, was ecologically questionable.

Prior to 1917, the Donbass had the highest death rate in the Tsarist Empire. The main cause was the drinking water, which caused frightening levels of disease. In the mines, water containers were few and far between, and usually empty. Toilets did not exist, and miners drank water trickling down tunnel walls, a particularly dangerous practice under the circumstances. They could bathe once a week, if lucky. Elementary public sanitation measures were lacking. In his official water pamphlet, London wrote that 'the task of water supply for the Donbass ... was not even within the range of vision of the mine owners'. In the only article he ever wrote for *Pravda*, he stated:

> In the old, prerevolutionary Donbass they 'solved' the water problem simply. They carted water in barrels out of filthy ponds and polluted wells to mine and factory settlements, they drank froggy water contaminated with wastes from outhouses and rubbish piles. Typhus and dysentery raged in the Donbass as nowhere else. But even this water was not enough in the hot summer months, when the rivers and wells dried up.[2]

During the NEP, the growth of industry and population in the Donbass aggravated the water problem. General health was improving remarkably as healthcare expanded. But when Noah London first visited the Donbass, water supply in its most important city was 'in a horrifying situation', according to a Soviet sanitation expert. He reported that:

> At the first water booth you see when you arrive in town there is a signboard with the inscription 'don't drink, you'll get sick' ... the Stalino district health service considers this water sufficiently satisfactory because

1 V.V. Solianik and Lutsenko, *Bol'shaia Voda Industrii: Ocherki iz istorii proizvodstvennogo ob'edineniia 'Ukrpromvodchermet'* (Donetsk: Izdatel'stvo 'Donbas', 1980), 5; Martin V. Melosi, *The Sanitary City: Urban Infrastructure in America from Colonial Times to the Present* (Baltimore: Johns Hopkins University Press, 2000), 1.

2 Friedgutt, *Life and Work in Russia's Donbass*, 152–60; Kuromiya 1998, 23; Solianik/Lutsenko, *Bol'shaia Voda Industrii*, 4–5; London, *Vodosnabzhenie Donbassa*, 1933; and 'Donbass trebuet vody', *Pravda*, Aug. 15, 1934, 4.

> it is safe bacteriologically, whereas the drinking water yearly causes outbreaks of typhoid fever.[3]

For London, building socialism in the largest country of the world seemed a more practical proposition than erecting a socialist Jewish utopia in the Bronx. Eliminating typhus and cholera in the Donbass became his personal project. Even housing was not as desperate an issue for the miners as clean water. In America, moderate American Socialists were dubbed 'sewer socialists'. In the Soviet Union, former American socialist Noah London became a sewer communist.

He attended a water conference a few months after arriving in Kharkov. There he advocated building a 120 kilometer water pipeline, from the Northern Donets river southwest across the Donbass to Stalino. He was appointed in March 1927 as director of a new water department for his coal trust, the Vodbiuro (Water Bureau). He began design work right away on his pipeline, the Almazno-Mar'evskii *vodoprovod*, and completed a first engineering schematic in May 1927. In the attached project description, he states that:

> At the same time as we have already achieved significant successes in our socialist construction in comparison with the pre-war situation … as we invest every year tens of millions for housing construction, hospitals, industrial education, Houses of Labor – we are completely lagging behind in water supply and are continuing the same amateurism that the capitalist entrepreneurs engaged in.[4]

Urban environmental reform was a major aspect of the Progressive Era in the United States. Its central feature was a 'bacteriological revolution' in urban water supply, and this was the model Noah London wanted to follow, pointing out that 'we see a lengthening of the average lifespan by ten years in North America … Sanitary authorities attribute these results to the great and wide development of water supply'.[5]

---

3 Friedgutt, *Politics and Revolution*, 437–9; Pervushin, 'G. Stalino (Donbass)', *Sanitarnaia Tekhnika* 1, no. 1 (March 1927): 83–4.

4 Noah London, *Poiasnitel'naia Zapiska k Proektu Donetskogo Vodoprovoda dlia Almazno-Mar'evskogo Raiona*, Vodbiuro Donuglia (1927), RGAE, f. 3429 (*Vesenkha*), op. 3, d. 2028, l. 37–49.

5 Melosi, *Sanitary City*, 103–16; N.M. Blake, *Water for the Cities: A History of the Urban Water Supply Problem* (Syracuse, NY: Syracuse University Press, 1956), 260–3; London, *Proekt Donetskogo Vodoprovoda*, 6.

The Donugol Vodbiuro was created in February 1927, after coal trust director Lomov called for action at a plenum of the coal miners' union. London became the official trust water advocate. *Vestnik Donuglia* (Don Coal Journal), the trust magazine, had ignored Donbass water issues for years. In its very first water article, Noah explained that until the Water Bureau was created, Donugol 'not only did not pay serious attention to the necessity of drinking water for the population, but did not even worry about water supply for steam-powered electric stations'.[6] Nevertheless, he faced considerable resistance in pushing his pipeline project, and it was not finally approved until after the Shakhty Affair. It was, after all, competing for funding with electric power projects, especially the Dneprostroi dam.[7]

2 Dneprostroi: A Peasant Buying a Gramophone?

> Communism is Soviet power and the electrification of the whole country.
> V.I. LENIN, November 1920

The Dneprostroi dam is downriver from Ekaterinoslav-Dnepropetrovsk, Soviet Ukraine's answer to Pittsburgh, then the center of the American steel industry. It was the most renowned single achievement of the Soviet industrial revolution. It physically embodied Lenin's electrification scheme, which London endorsed years before he arrived in the Soviet Union. Noah's first article in *Royte Velt* explained the project to his readers in ample detail. Its electricity 'according to the claims of the American experts would cost less than anywhere else in the world, except for the Niagara waterfall'. Stalin, however, was originally dubious about the project, which he compared to a peasant buying a gramophone.[8]

Leon Trotsky was originally the figure most closely associated with the Dneprostroi dam. His last official post had been as chair of the Board of Electrotechnical Development in 1926, the year the Londons arrived in Ukraine. The dam then became a central axis of Soviet industrial debates. Many planners believed that the dam would be too expensive or suspected that energy savings would be wiped out by transmission costs. Lomov opposed using Dneprostroi for Donbass power, because it was too far from the coalfields. But the Dnepros-

6 London, 'Vodosnabzhenie: itogi rabot', *Vestnik Donuglia* 48 (Nov. 15 1928): 14.

7 Lomov, 'K dokladu Donuglia', 4.

8 London, 'Der dnieprboy', *Royte Velt* 12, no. 27 (Dec. 1926): 71; Carr and Davies, *Foundations*, 898–912; Graham, *Ghost*, 50.

troi dam became a point of national pride for Ukrainian party leaders. They would throw their support to Stalin against Bukharin to some degree in return for Dneprostroi.[9]

London also opposed using Dneprostroi to supply electric power for the Donbass. His *Royte Velt* article discussed many possible uses for its electricity. But the idea of using it to power distant coal mines must have struck him as downright perverse. Years before his arrival in the Soviet Union, he had written about how American engineers were advocating a national electrification program. Power plants near the mines would save huge amounts of energy, transporting electricity by wire instead of coal by rail. The Dneprostroi dam had been approved before deciding exactly how to use its power and was completed two years before the factories assigned to consume its output were completed.[10] He expressed his final judgment in his 1934 secret manuscript:

> It is an open secret in the USSR that Dneprostroi has no economic base and was constructed purely for political reasons ... The country at large would have been much better off without it ... A new city [Zaporozhe] had to be erected ... in order to build the dam and the new plants. Otherwise all these plants could have been built nearer to the source of raw materials, in places already populated.

He would use Dneprostroi in 1934 in his secret dissident manuscript to analyze Soviet planning economics in general, coming to conclusions that foreshadow future concepts of 'market socialism'.

> The Russian economist generally does not figure any interest, because interest according to their interpretation of Marxism means parasitic capitalism. The fact is however that in order to raise capital for the purpose of construction, or any other purpose, interest is paid – either to foreign creditors ... or for postal savings and bonds ... To get capital from the people through taxes costs an overhead percentage ... of at least 15%.

The ultimate person to blame for the fiasco was Trotsky:

9 Graham, *Ghost*, 51–5; Anne D. Rassweiler, *The Generation of Power: The History of Dneprostroi* (Oxford: Oxford University Press, 1988), 30–55; TsDAVO, f. 2602 (miners' union), op. 1, d. 2362 (Donugol protocols), Dec. 30, 1927, l. 116–116ob.

10 London, *Der Emes*, Sept. 30, 1921, Carr and Davies, *Foundations*, 912; Davies, *Crisis and Progress*, 482–3.

> To Stalin's credit it must be said that, being a practical man with a more limited vision than his colleagues of the Lenin cabinet such as let us say the fiery Trotsky, he opposed the building of Dneprostroi as premature, according to reliable information ... Meanwhile many plants that are making shoes for example are not running at full capacity because of lack of materials while an army of 100 million peasants work the fields in *lapti* [bast shoes].

When Trotsky was in charge of planning the project he had actually advocated caution.[11] But Trotsky, unlike Noah, did think it was a good idea unless constructed Stalin style, before the factories that needed the power. The city of Zaporozhe arose from scratch around Dneprostroi, a new industrial metropolis in the historic heartland of the Zaporozhian (Ukrainian) Cossacks. But if the creation of Dneprostroi had something to do with Red Ukrainian nationalism, Noah London's opposition represented Donbass particularism. Dneprostroi was dubious as a power source for Donbass coal mines. But the dam is located smack in the middle of Tsarist Russia's answer to the German Ruhr, the Donbass-Ekaterinoslav-Krivoi Rog complex, which needed a power source.

3 Noah London versus 'Wrecking' in the Donbass Water Industry

> The grandiose project of the Donets pipeline ... provoked doubts among certain workers of the expediency of construction on such an enormous scale and of its realizability. Theoretical differences were used by wrecking elements (Prof. Osadchii and others) in creating every possible holdup in resolving the problems of the Donbass.
>
> NOAH LONDON, *Vodosnabzhenie Donbassa*, 1933

Noah London's function on the post-Shakhty budget commission was to deal with water supply. Its resolution dealt cursorily with water supplies ('drinking water is insufficient and so forth'), but 10 million of the 47 million rubles requested were for waterworks. The sums finally allocated were disappointing – 8.5 million rubles, 2 million of which went for water supply. But Shakhty did enable him to push through his pipeline project. A few weeks after the trial was announced, Stalin's favorite lackey Kaganovich sent out a Ukrainian Polit-

11 Rassweiler, *Dneprostroi*, 42–4; Trotsky, 'A Heart-to-Heart Talk with a Well-Meaning Party Member', Sept. 12, 1928, in *Challenge of the Left Opposition, 1928–1929*, 229.

buro circular stating that building the pipeline in the next construction season was 'absolutely necessary'.[12] The need of the miners for better water was only the immediate reason. After a brief flurry of attention to miners' complaints died down, a long-term factor working on the project's behalf kicked in. Accelerated Donbass industrial growth required a big increase in the water supply, especially for the coal mines. Further development was impossible based on local water resources alone – and without rapid expansion of coal production, the first Five-Year Plan would have collapsed.

On May 28, 1928, the Ukrainian Gosplan officially decided (1) that the Northern Donets would be the prime source for Donbass water; and (2) that construction of Noah London's pipeline should begin that year. Two days later, Lomov issued the order to create a construction administration for London's pipeline, to be headquartered at a nearby mine and headed by Lomov's secretary Sokolov.[13] One of the main criticisms of the Don coal trust in the purge commission report that Sokolov helped put together was that Kharkov headquarters was overstaffed. Many of its functionaries needed to be sent out into the coalfields. Was sending former coalminer Sokolov back to the coalfields a promotion – or a punishment? Perhaps it was a bit of both.[14]

London and his rival Shishkin got the pipeline approved by a Moscow technical council without much difficulty, despite certain ecological objections. The Water Bureau had already managed to obtain ten kilometers' worth of waterpipe for it – almost enough to reach a nearly finished steam-power plant that lacked any water supply. The council agreed to begin allocating preliminary funding right away, even though project design had not been completed yet. This was often the case during the Stalinist industrial revolution. As London explained in the trust journal, 'because nobody concerned themselves with researching [water supply] earlier ... it was necessary to design and build essential watermains in pressing order, without having enough materials worked up'.[15]

In August construction began, with Sokolov as its supervisor onsite. There was opposition to London's project from certain economic planners who believed that it was expensive and unnecessary. London was forced to cam-

12 TsDAHO, f. 1, op. 20, d. 2721, l. 117ob.; Kaganovich, March 30, 1928, TsDAHO, f. 1, op. 20, d. 2721, l. 24.

13 Protokol 300, *Tekhsovet Stroikom VSNKh* (hereinafter Prot. 300, *Tekhsovet*), June 11 and June 12, 1928, TsDAVO, f. 1279 (*Vodokanalstroi*), op. 1, *god.* 1930 d. 18, l. 218–25; and Lomov, *Prikaz* 96, May 30, 1928, l. 196.

14 Sokolov registration blank, RGASPI, *Uchëtnaia kartochka*, F.G. Sokolov, 1934, DADO-p.

15 London, 'Vodosnabzhenie', 14.

paign for it, visiting Stalino to speak before the regional Executive Committee in stumbling Ukrainian. The Gosplan Water Section, perhaps under the influence of Professor Osadchii, argued that the Donbass already had adequate underground water sources. But everyone knew there was a desperate shortage of clean drinking water. And the population was increasing rapidly – by 129 percent from 1926 to 1932. Extensive geological surveys seeking water hadn't found much.[16]

Perhaps some Gosplan planning experts thought that local water supplies would suffice if coal mine development came to a screeching halt? In that case, Stalin's industrial revolution would have run out of coal to fuel it. Were Osadchii or other 'bourgeois *spetsy*' seeking to use water, environmental historian Laakonen's 'global dictator', to bring the industrialization drive under control? At a Gosplan meeting in February 1928, Osadchii opposed the first Five-Year Plan as unrealistic, stating, 'If I were told: sign this variant as the basic one, I would refuse'. Osadchii, a former Kadet, was a top figure in Gosplan. He had chaired the committee that devised a quite conservative 'general plan' for Soviet industry in 1926, when Stalin and Bukharin were still allies. He was a key cooperating witness in the 1930 Industrial Party show trial, labelling himself a wrecker.[17]

It is understandable that London might have seen the resistance his project faced as wrecking. In his 1934 manuscript he would comment ambiguously that 'many believe that the trials against wreckers were played up to create the impression that most of the misfortunes that have befallen the working class of the USSR are due to those wreckers'. Whatever he really felt about the Shakhty Affair and the super-industrialization drive the Stalin regime undertook in its aftermath, they made approving his pipeline project possible. It was formally approved in December 1928, even though he had not yet finished all the design schematics. Sewer communist Noah London, seeking to supply miners with clean drinking water, was now a warrior against wreckers and Bukharinists.

Pipeline construction soon was well under way, and London was ready to leave Donugol and take up new projects. As he was packing for Birobidzhan, *Royte Velt* published his article on the Five-Year Plan. He believed it embodied working-class democracy:

---

16 London, Oct. 29, 1928, and Chubarov, director Glavgortop (Vesenkha coal directorate), Oct. 20, 1928, DADO-r, f. r-2 (Stalino *okrispolkom* protocols), op. 1, d. 159, l. 36–7 and 31–2; Likholobova and Kovalenko, 'Protsessy urbanizatsiia v Donbasse', *Novye Stranitsy v istorii Donbassa* 3 (1994): 59; 'Gidrologicheskie Issledovaniia', TsDAVO, f. 386 (Ukrvodkhoz), op. 1, d. 6, l. 14–18.

17 Bailes, *Technology and Society*, 111–12; Carr and Davies, *Foundations*, 837–9.

> Drop by drop, the plan crystallized at … cells and collectives of every plant and factory, of every cooperative, … from paper mills on the Volga and glassworks in White Russia, through the coal mines of the Donbass as far as the oil wells of the Caucasus and the cotton plantations of Turkestan, over a sixth of the globe of the earth, the drops streamed and flowed into the ramified and complicated system which is called the five-year plan of the peoples' economy. For the first time in the Soviet land, and thereby for the first time in history, a united methodical system has been worked out, based on the real forces of life …[18]

In Noah London's opinion, the plan was realistic, sound and sensible. Its tempo was not too slow and not too fast, but just right. Because if it were too fast, 'that could bring on a crisis'. And indeed, the original version of the Five-Year Plan seems in retrospect to be fairly sound – unlike later variants.[19]

London's account of the plan began with what he saw as most important. First and foremost, it would raise workers' standards of living significantly. It would improve housing, both in quantity and quality. He emphasized that it did not promise 'pie in the sky'. Workers would need to make sacrifices. He endorsed 'the tactic of the party which the rightists fight against. The party says, exert yourself today to be stronger tomorrow. Build heavy industry'. He particularly emphasized construction of power lines and stations to electrify the whole country. Dneprostroi, interestingly, is barely mentioned. Building a highway net was particularly important, to break down the barriers between town and country. 'Work and sacrifice', avoiding the 'opportunist path of the right deviation,' would mean 'a really significant improvement in the material condition of the masses'. 'Conscious organized proletarian will' would lead the way to socialism.

4 Bureaucratic Rationalism and Soviet Industry

> The decisive reason for the advance of bureaucratic organization has always been its purely technical superiority over any other form of organization. The fully developed bureaucratic mechanism compares with other organizations exactly as does the machine with the non-mechanical modes of production.
>
> MAX WEBER, *Bureaucracy*, 1921

18 London, 'Der finfyariker plan'.
19 Carr and Davies, *Foundations*, 894–7.

> Bureaucratic gridlock is caused by people with different priorities who practice good time management.
>
> SCOTT ADAMS, *Build a Better Life by Stealing Office Supplies*, 1991

When London returned from his summer in the Far East he took up new responsibilities as Ukraine's head highway engineer, after a few weeks of public speaking and writing on behalf of the Birobidzhan project.[20] This was the position he held in Soviet industry for which he had the most extensive previous experience. Perhaps it reminded him too much of his American career, because it did not hold his interest long.

According to his Five-Year Plan article, the Soviet Union was farther behind the capitalist countries in this respect than in any other. One of his lessons from the Birobidzhan experience was the necessity of proper organization. During the brief period he worked on highway construction, his prime role was as an advocate for system and order. Emotional distance perhaps gave him objectivity. A Ukrainian-language planning document he helped produce for the highway trust expresses an obsessive commitment to bureaucratic rationalism.[21]

A good dose of rationalism was what was needed in the spring of 1930. While London was in Birobidzhan, Stalin unleashed what was called a 'socialist offensive'. The 1929 party purge at Donugol was but a small chapter in a wide-ranging shake-up in the party and in industry that accompanied the turn to total collectivization in the countryside. The behind-the-scenes wrestling match in the party between Stalin's supporters and the so-called 'right opposition' finally went public – after the Bukharinists capitulated. As London would put it in his secret manuscript: 'There was almost no discussion on the question of the right opposition. The higher functionary would present his report and the membership would be asked, singly and as a whole, to approve it. Any dissenter, or anyone who did not understand, would find it more comfortable not to budge from his seat'.

In industry, the cultural revolutionary drive against '*spetsy*' went into high gear as the Five-Year Plan was repeatedly amended upwards. In December, a congress of shock brigades issued a call to fulfill it in four years instead of five. All across the Soviet Union, posters sprouted the interesting slogan 'two plus two equals five'. Crisis ensued, as London had suggested would happen: the

20 London, speeches and letters, *Shtern*, Oct. 8, 17, 18, 19, 20, and 22, 1929; London Moscow public speech, *Tribuna*, Oct. 25, 1929.

21 London, D'iakov, 'Shkhodo poriadku skladannia ta zatverzhdennia proektiv shliakhiv', Feb. 15, 1930, TsDAVO, f. 187 (Ukrdorstroitrest), op. 1, d. 169, l. 50–8.

economy headed deeply into turmoil.[22] He did get into the spirit of the socialist offensive at the highway trust, but in his own way. One of the major features of the breakneck industrial drive was an outright contempt for quality. London's attitude was different. The day after a national quality control conference had to be cancelled for lack of attendance, he sent out a trust circular threatening to turn over irresponsible construction administrators to the secret police.[23] Four years later, he would comment: 'The total mileage of hard surface, improved and even unimproved roads pales in comparison to American figures. Despite all the noise raised periodically in campaigns for road building, the improved roads are hardly being maintained'.

He had believed that what Birobidzhan needed was a single, authoritative trust for all aspects of the project. A week after his Moscow Birobidzhan speech, the Gosplan water committee determined that 'the grandiosity of forthcoming Donbass waterworks construction and the brief period allocated for its accomplishment advances the necessity of creating a special organ for carrying out the work of providing water for the Donbass'.[24] The Donbass Water Trust, Donbassvodtrest (DBVT), was founded in April 1930, and Noah London was chosen to lead it. But Donbassvodtrest was not in fact in charge of the whole process. It was responsible for planning, design, exploring for water and running the waterworks when built. They were actually built by other trusts such as Vodokanalstroi, the Water Canal Construction Trust. Donbassvodtrest was headquartered in Kharkov, Vodokanalstroi in Moscow, and the actual construction took place of course in the Donbass. Inevitably, London had to 'waste much time on interminable meetings and disputes, on a duplicate apparatus for supply, bookkeeping and technical oversight', as he complained to Ukrainian party leaders. He unsuccessfully advocated creating a supertrust to eliminate bureaucratic gridlock, after a couple of the subcontracting trusts went bankrupt.[25]

---

22 Davies, *Soviet Economy in Turmoil*, 75–80, 95–125, 187–95; Kuromiya, *Stalin's Industrial Revolution*, 139–57; Lyons, *Utopia*, 240.

23 Davies, *Soviet Economy*, 312–14; trust circular, London and Lisovik, April 12, 1930, TsDAVO, f. 187, op. 1, d. 169, l. 2.

24 Gosplan water committee, Nov. 1, 1929, TsDAVO, f. 1279 (Vodokanalstroi), op. 1 (1929), d. 2, l. 5–6.

25 TsDAVO, f. 1277 (Ukrvodstroi), f. 1278 (Yuzhvodstroi), f. 1279 (Vodokanalstroi), f. 386 (Ukrvodkhoz), *passim*. When I examined these materials I was told by archivists that in one case, I was the first person to consult them since 1932. London, 'V TsK KP(b)U, po voprosu raboty Donbassvodtresta', TsDAHO, f. 1, op. 20, d. 5338 (Donbassvodtrest 1932), l. 1–10b.

4.1 *The Story of Donbassvodtrest*

Immediate action was necessary because water and food shortages had sparked a strike wave in Donbass mines and factories in May and June. There was a great drought that summer, and virtually no water was available even for the miners' bathhouses. Disease was beginning to spread again, and 60 percent of Ukrainian anti-epidemic funds were spent in the Donbass that year. According to London's account in the spring of 1937, as the Great Terror was descending on Soviet industry, 'the situation was such that it was necessary to take all measures to get water'.[26]

Construction had not been going well in his absence. The centerpiece, his pipeline project, was being built almost exclusively by hand. There was little machinery on site, and only one old broken-down truck. Materials arrived on horseback from a railhead 10 roadless kilometers away. And Sokolov, its boss, had little or no technical training. His proletarian background was ideal to impress London favorably, but he had little management experience and none in construction. He was removed 'for health reasons' in 1929 and transferred to a less crucial job. London gave him a second chance. He brought him back to Donbassvodtrest and made him his deputy.[27]

In July, Donbass water was assigned 'shock' (*udarnyi*) priority, giving it first call on scarce resources. In 1937, Noah London would recount how Ukrainian Politburo members Kossior and Chubar repeatedly went personally to bat for Donbassvodtrest. Donbass revolutionary veteran Valerian Mezhlauk, a central Soviet economic planner and administrator who was the People's Commissar for Finance of the brief Donbass Soviet Republic during the Civil War, got assigned to oversee London's work. Mezhlauk was then deputy director of Vesenkha, the Supreme Council of People's Economy, which ran virtually the entire Soviet economy at that time. In 1937 London would describe the period of Mezhlauk's oversight as the 'golden age' of Donbassvodtrest.[28] Mezhlauk took over from Lomov the role of London's top-level patron.

---

26 Kuromiya, *Freedom and Terror*, 164–5; Komissii NKTP po vodosnabsheniiu Donbassa i Krivorozh'ia (hereinafter NKTP water comm.), April 16, 1937, RGAE, f. 7297 (NKTP), op. 38, d. 386, capital construction subcommission stenogram (hereinafter *kapstroi*), l. 8.

27 Solianik and Lutsenko, *Bol'shaia Voda Industrii*, 10; Donbass water conference, Dec. 15, 1929, TsDAVO, f. 1297, op. 1 (1929), d. 2, l. 18; Letter, Sokolov to Ul'mer, April 20, 1930, d. 18, l. 87; *Registratsionnyi blank chlena VKP(b) No. 1639845*, F.G. Sokolov, 1936, RGASPI; Sokolov case file, interrogation, Oct. 27, 1937, AUSBUDO, *delo* 18780, l. 15.

28 Rykov, Council of Labor and Defense (STO) order #85, July 16, 1930, TsDAVO, f. 386 (ukrvodkhoz), op. 1, d. 8, l. 83; Donbass water conference, Sept. 29, 1930, TsDAVO, f. 1279, op. 1 (1930), d. 22, l. 66–66ob.; NKTP water comm., kapstroi, April 17, 1937, l. 37ob.

On October 16, the Soviet government ordered that the primary segment of the water pipeline and a separate pipeline for Stalino be finished by January 1, 1931. Trust engineer Boris Kushin, who had the misfortune of being Donbassvodtrest chief engineer in 1937, would tell NKVD inquisitors that conditions were impossible back then: no equipment; no motor transport; no telephones; and hardly any technical staff. According to London, 'when the task stood before us of providing water for all regions of the Donbass as fast as possible, it was "super shock priority" [*sverkh udarnym*]. Only because ... comrade Molotov personally interested himself in this, we carried out the work in three months'. Molotov had just replaced Rykov as the head of the Soviet government.

Noah London acquired a reputation for taking good care of the workers under him. But that doesn't mean he wasn't a hard driver. In his Five-Year Plan article, he complained that the intensity of labor was less in the Soviet Union than in capitalist lands, and stated that 'the task of the party and the unions about this is to bring in stronger labor discipline'.[29] Even in his 1934 secret manuscript, he comments that 'capitalist-managed business squeezed out of the Russian miners about three or four times as much as does the Bolshevik commissar in the coal industry'.

The deadline was met. But the Stalino pipeline, which may have prevented an epidemic in a city that had doubled in population since 1926, had to use fragile wooden pipes instead of the originally planned ferroconcrete. This change led later to charges of wrecking. London would tell his interrogators in 1937 that the end of 1930 was when he began sympathizing with the views of 'the right'.[30] The pipelines were the first of many forced-draft water projects that the blitz-speed growth of the arid Donbass required. In 1926, only a third of its population was urban – already almost twice the Ukrainian norm. But by 1939, 73 percent would be urban. During its first two years Donbassvodtrest quadrupled the local water supply. But these were the peak years of industrial revolution and Donbass population explosion, and the breakneck pace of water construction was just barely fast enough to meet minimal necessities.

The whirlwind velocity of London's water projects was typical for the times. Shortages of everything were successfully resolved only because Donbassvodtrest had first call on materials and manpower during its 'golden era'. There were a series of dramatic successes. Donbassvodtrest constructed 500 kilomet-

29 London, 'Der finfyariker plan', 89.

30 STO order #311, Oct. 16, 1930, TsDAVO, f. 1279, op. 1 (1930), d. 22, l. 106; Kushin interrogation, Aug. 9, 1937, Rabukhin case file, AUSBUDO, *delo* 7606-2f, l. 49; NKTP water comm. plenary, April 25, 1937, RGAE, f. 7297, op. 38, d. 389, l. 21–21ob; 'Protokol doprosa Londona', Nov. 17, 1937, TsaFSB, *sledstvennoe delo* R-46033, 2.

ers of water pipeline, 11 reservoirs, and enough laboratories, filtration systems and chlorification stations that London could boast in his water pamphlet that by the fifteenth anniversary of the October Revolution, all Donbass drinking water was safe from disease.[31] But was it drinkable?

The wooden pipeline for Stalino was not the only decision with fateful consequences. There was a disagreement very early on over what to do when clean, unpolluted underground water was found where the pipeline pumping and filtration systems were planned to be built. London, still in charge of the Donugol Water Bureau, was called in. After consulting with Lomov it was decided to push construction forward anyway, dumping wagonloads of cement right on top of a just-discovered artesian well. The resulting controversy echoed into the future, reopening ecological questions raised about the project from the very beginning.[32]

The pipeline began downstream from Donsoda, a huge just-built coke plant that played a key role in the steel industry. Coke plants using the most up-to-date 1920s technology produced vast quantities of wastewater polluted with phenols and other unpleasant chemicals. The Northern Donets River was becoming severely polluted, unlike the underground water sources that project opponents preferred. Beginning the pipeline above Donsoda would have made it, in London's opinion, too long and too expensive. Moscow experts agreed. A 'sanitary protection zone' upstream from the pipeline was established, and Donsoda was supposed to treat its wastewater. The appropriate orders were duly issued by higher authorities – but never really carried out.

The standard technology then in use for treatment, quenching coke with the wastewater, was highly expensive, corroded equipment, and ruined coke for home heating because of the smell. The wastewater from Donsoda produced a remarkably foul taste and smell when chlorinated. As a result, the 'safe' drinking water from the pipeline created great discontent among the population. The trust was forced to resort to a variety of desperate measures to render it drinkable, even halting chlorination at one point.[33]

This problem was far from unique to the Donbass. The new profession of sanitary engineering was focused on protecting drinking water from disease

---

31 Likholobova and Kovalenko, 'Protsessy urbanizatsiia v Donbasse', *Novye Stranitsy v istorii Donbassa* 3 (1994): 56–73; London, *Vodosnabzhenie Donbassa*, 12–15.

32 Sokolov and Rabukhin case files, AUSBUDO, *delo* 7606-2 f., *passim*.

33 *Tekhsovet* Prot. 300 and 380, 6–11/12 and Aug. 21, 1928, TsDAVO, f. 1279 and f. 386, op. 1, d. 6, l. 79–82; and Vodokanalstroi technical report, f. 386, op. 1, d. 4, 75ob; A.I. Berzin, intro. to *Ugol'nye Filtry: Sbornik materialov o rabote ugol'nykh filtrov na Almazno-Mar'evskom (Donetskom) vodoprovode*, Donbassvodtrest, 1935, 3–7.

organisms. In America, sanitary engineers usually considered drinking water pollutants such as coalmine acid drainage a lesser evil, on the theory that they would at least kill bacteria. It was precisely phenol pollution from coke ovens that broke this consensus. Whether or not phenol was dangerous to humans, people simply refused to drink chlorophenolated water.

The solution found elsewhere was activated charcoal,[34] and one resource the Donbass certainly had plenty of was coal. London brought in a broadly respected Austrian expert, Alfred Taussig, to oversee construction of an activated charcoal filtration system for London's pipeline. Charcoal filtration had never before been attempted on such a large scale for a source as badly polluted as the Northern Donets. Nonetheless the system was highly successful. Contemporary Donbass water engineers say that it was so technically sophisticated that they never succeeded in rebuilding it after the Nazis destroyed it during World War II. According to London's water pamphlet:

> The colossal growth of technical water supply for the Donbass puts our enterprises already above the Europeans and Americans; and with respect to drinking water we have resolved the problem of first order importance of raising the everyday cultural conditions of the working population. We should surpass in the second Five-Year Plan the finest achievements abroad of industrial regions.[35]

But this filtration system was very expensive. The high cost would open London to charges of sabotage during the Great Terror.

5 Life at Donbassvodtrest

Noah met his sister-in-law Rose in Moscow in July 1931, on his way to England, where he was seeking to purchase metal pipes for his water projects. Whatever

34 Joel A. Tarr, *The Searth for the Ultimate Sink: Urban Pollution in Historical Perspective* (Akron: University of Akron Press, 1996), 360–4, 395–403; Melosi, *Sanitary City*, 135–48, 223–8; Moses Nelson Baker, *The Quest for Pure Water: The History of Water Purification from the Earliest Records to the Twentieth Century* (Denver: 1948), vol. 1, 452–5.

35 Berzin, *Ugol'nye Filtry* and 'Zakliuchenie po skheme vsedonetskogo vodoprovoda', Nov. 30, 1928, TsDAVO, f. 386, op. 1, d. 1, l. 13–14ob; interviews, Leonid Prishchepa, chief engineer, and Gennady Trikash, chief of technical department, Ukrpromvodchermet (current-day descendant of Donbassvodtrest), Donetsk, Ukraine, Oct. 9, 2003, and Sept. 21, 2004; London, *Vodosnabzhenie Donbassa*, 6.

political doubts he may have developed by that point, he did not share them. Rose wrote to her future husband Louis Discher that:

> Not till I came here did I realise what an important post Noah has. For private information only – he is president of the Don Basin trust which supplies hydro electric power to all factories and kolkhozes in that region ... Noah is both technical and party executive in his trust. Miril is assistant chemist in the laboratories.[36]

Apparently Noah was somewhat closed-mouthed with American friends and family about exactly what he was doing in the Soviet Union. Rose probably misunderstood what he did tell her because, like so many American and Soviet Communists, she was much more excited about the Dneprostroi dam than about something as prosaic as clean, safe water. Perhaps she felt differently by the end of the trip, much of it spent laid up with stomach problems.

Warfare between the party leader and the director dominated the life of many Soviet trusts. But at Donbassvodtrest Noah was both, according to Rose.[37] In choosing subordinates he adopted a highly unconventional policy by Soviet standards, or indeed many another. He deliberately appointed people who disagreed with him on vital issues. He wanted independent thinkers, not 'yes men'.

Shortly before he was fired as construction supervisor in 1929, future deputy Sokolov wrote a report criticizing London as a construction planner and expressing doubts about the wisdom of the decision to forge ahead with construction of the pipeline at its planned location, despite the discovery of clean underground water there. During the Great Terror, all the top trust staff under interrogation branded this decision as 'wrecking'. This is not, however, the opinion of contemporary trust engineers. According to contemporary technical director Gennady Trikash, underground water sources in the area are '*malodebitny*' (output too small).[38] London appointed Ivan Alekseevich Shakhov as the trust's chief engineer. Shakhov, the son of a prosperous peasant, began his career as an engineer working for the counterrevolutionary Whites in Turkestan. He was one of the planners of Dneprostroi – and one of the main critics of London's pipeline project on ecological grounds, challenging it at a water conference in Rostov. In 1931 Shakhov had a private discussion with Lon-

---

36 Letter, Rose to Louis, Moscow, July 23, 1931, Lewis collection.

37 I was unable to find Donbassvodtrest state or party records for the early 1930s, when London was in charge.

38 Sokolov to Donugol, 'Dokladnaia Zapiska', Spring 1929, f. 1279, op. 1 (1929), d. 4, l. 22–3; Prishchepa-Trikash interviews; Sokolov and Rabukhin case files.

don about the project. According to Shakhov's version under interrogation, London told him that 'perhaps the project is bad, but there is no reason to raise a fuss ... No need to hurry and worry. Soviet power has given you nothing good and is in no position to. Personally I am working to hold back the development of Donbass water supply, disrupting it, and a significant part of the engineers in our collective support me'.[39]

London's version of this conversation for the interrogators was quite different. What rings true is Shakhov's statement that London 'selected, according to his expression, people who were the most "independent thinkers"'. According to Sokolov's confessions it was in 1932 that London started to praise foreign technology and express discontent with party decisions, 'subjecting certain of its leaders to unhealthy criticism'.[40] His experiences as a Soviet industrial manager were turning him into a dissident.

Over the course of the 1930s Ordzhonikidze's Commissariat of Heavy Industry (NKTP) would become something of a haven for all sorts of ex-oppositionists and trouble makers, as long as they were capable and seemed loyal. In London's words in the secret manuscript, 'People are put in positions for their ability and willingness to serve ... There are many instances where excellent engineers were sentenced as saboteurs, and now are being put in the highest commanding offices'.[41] This was especially true at Donbassvodtrest. The trust staff was littered with alleged or real ex-Trotskyists, former White Guards and Black Hundreds, and several former 'wreckers'.

The Londons, believers in cooperative housing, shared their large and comfortable apartment with numerous friends, relatives and trust officials. Rose shared a couch with another American Jewish Communist visitor being hired as a specialist at another trust. According to Sokolov, there was a steady flow of foreigners staying there, especially in 1931 and 1932. He told the NKVD in 1937 that it 'provoked in me certain suspicions', but since everyone knew and London didn't hide it, it didn't really bother him at the time.[42]

Vasilii Il'enko, the trust drilling supervisor, lived nearby. He was an unusual figure in the trust, a last holdover from Donbass water supply under the Tsarist regime. He told the NKVD that the apartment was a social center where foreigners mingled with trust officials. Miril was often visited by 'alleged relatives, sisters and sisters of the husband and also a series of other foreigners

39 Shakhov testimony, Aug. 1, 1937, Rabukhin case file, l. 28.

40 Shakhov testimony, Aug. 1, 1937, Sokolov case file, l. 117; Sokolov testimony, Oct. 27, 1937, l. 16.

41 Khlevniuk, *1937-i*, 116; and *In Stalin's Shadow*, 48–61.

42 Sokolov case file, interrogation, Oct. 27, 1937, d. 18780, l. 16.

… bringing various foreign presents for the London family'. An unknown foreigner stayed there in 1931–2, never working and always typing. Il'enko's wife overheard a conversation there between him and an unknown woman from Moscow about the fate of her arrested husband. Il'enko's portrait of the London home differs from Rose's only in its xenophobia.

5.1 *The Donbass Needs Water: Noah London and the Iron Cage of Stalinist Industrial Politics*

Miril's husband reached the peak of his Soviet prestige in the mid-1930s. His name and photograph were placed on the All-Soviet Board of Honor for engineering-technical workers and published in the engineers' union journal, *Inzhenernyi Trud*. Usually only particularly famous experts received this honor. A recipient needed to be approved by blue-collar union members, and the union at the Donbass branch of Vodokanalstroi, the primary water construction contractor, sponsored this award. When I visited Donetsk, Gennady Trikash, the technical director of the current-day successor of Donbassvodtrest, had begun working there in the early 1950s. According to Trikash, veteran employees still remembered Noah London then, and respected him highly.[43]

Meanwhile, Noah was attempting with limited success to implement industrial policies a bit different from the official ones. During Rose's second visit in 1934, during which she took down his dissident thoughts, he published his *Pravda* article, 'The Donbass Needs Water'.[44] He reported that 'despite the great sweep and volume of work done, so far only the normal work of *active* industry is taken care of. The further growth of industrial enterprises and the working and city population requires a considerable increase in the water supply … There is still little additional water created through artificial structures, beyond natural resources. *It is necessary to supply this additional water'*. The printed version was toned down from a more scorching original, according to his later account during the Great Terror. It advocated a major program to build waterworks in the Donbass for agricultural irrigation, for which 'it is necessary to supply all materials, machinery and transport in sufficient volume and quantity, and not so meagerly as Donbassvodtrest has been supplied up to now'. This proposal was his bureaucratic response to the horrible Ukrainian famine that had just ended. He was seeking to increase food production in 'his' Donbass.

43 Trikash interview, Oct. 9, 2003. I am indebted to Moscow scholar Irina Garaevskaia, who informed me that documentation for the award can be found in GARF, f. 548, op. 13, and in *Inzhenernyi Trud*, 1935, no. 5.

44 Noah London, 'Donbass trebuet vody', *Pravda*, Aug. 15, 1934. Published while Rose was visiting.

5.2 *Donbassvodtrest from London to Sokolov*

The DBVT party secretary in the early days was one A.G. Biriukov,[45] but records indicate that at DBVT the party chairmanship was always the key post. Secretaries largely restricted themselves to taking minutes, in American rather than Soviet fashion, since Noah London had created the trust in the first place. That the name of the party chairman is not mentioned in the official history confirms Rose Risikoff's comment that her brother-in-law held the post in 1932. After London's departure for Moscow his critic, protégé and imitator Fedor Georgievich Sokolov led the trust. His statements under interrogation indicate that London shared with him some of his dissident notions. According to Sokolov's testimony,

> [London] said that the current leadership of party and government are unable to secure the elevation of prosperity for the masses, that there is a bad situation within the party, as the left and right deviations have not stopped their struggle, and strive to unite in order to come to power in the land, and that this would supposedly straighten out the situation, and that he also shared these views.[46]

The effective political leader of the trust after Noah London left was Rona Dolinskaia, until 1935. She headed both the cadre department and the engineers' union section (ITS) and edited the trust bulletin. In the early 1920s, she led the Cheka in the Ukrainian *shtetl* of Dubny. She was the secretary of the Donugol Construction Bureau when London was deputy director. According to Shakhov, she was a close friend of the Londons, often present at social gatherings at their Kharkov home, and Shakhov accused her of creating a 'cult of personality' around him. She and DBVT planning engineers Aleksandr Titov and Solomon Rabukhin had been co-workers and friends of Noah London since soon after he arrived in Ukraine. Titov and Rabukhin were London's co-designers for the Almazno water pipeline project, his trademark accomplishment as a Soviet civil engineer.

Noah benefitted from the patronage of superiors such as Lomov and Mezhlauk. At Donbassvodtrest, London himself was the patron, and Dolinskaia, Rabukhin and Titov were his clients. In 1935 they were caught up in a financial

---

45 V.V. Solianik, Lutsenko, *Bol'shaia Voda Industrii: Ocherki iz istorii proizvodstvennogo ob'edineniia 'Ukrpromvodchermet'*, Istoriia fabrik i zavodov (Donetsk: Izdatel'stvo 'Donbas', 1980), 10–11.

46 Sokolov case file, interrogation, Oct. 27, 1937, AUSBUDO (Donetsk SBU archive), d. 18780, l. 15–17.

scandal in the planning department. Dolinskaia was transferred elsewhere, and Rabukhin and Titov were 'sentenced to forced labor', which effectively meant merely a pay cut. Sokolov later told the NKVD that London used his influence on Lomov, then a member of the bureau of the Soviet Control Commission, to mitigate their punishment.[47] London found both of them jobs in Moscow, and Rabukhin later returned to a prominent post at Donbassvodtrest. But the affair must have weakened London's standing at his old trust. Moreover, it is a possible explanation for his mysterious departure in 1935 from the high Moscow post he had been kicked upstairs to, and the somber tone of his final letter from the Soviet Union to Rose Risikoff in late fall: 'What an interesting life we lived through … and alas how all of that is passing into the darkness it remains without a trace as the ripples on the surface of the sea'.[48]

Right in the middle of or just before this affair at Donbassvodtrest, there was an August 1935 planning conference for Western Donbass water needs, which Noah London essentially chaired.[49] The commission's purpose was to decide what to build to resolve growing water needs in the western part of the Donbass, centered on Stalino (today Donetsk). Eastern Donbass (Russian) water problems were believed to have been solved by then. Most experts advocated building a canal from the Northern Donets River. In his speech opening the conference, London sought to base discussion on fundamental principles, expressing his own ideas, which may or may not have been the official position:

> We judged up till now that the Donbass exists for industry, but it turns out that people live and labor in Donbass industry, and that we need to create decent living conditions for these laborers who work in the Donbass and we need to give them plenty of daily household water … Our judgments must be founded not only on economics, but also social and political knowledge and obligations.[50]

Later he stated that 'as culture and water needs rise, water for the population becomes more important than water for industry'. His speeches echoed themes emphasized in his secret manuscript of the previous summer, where he stated that Soviet canal projects do 'more harm to the cause of Communism than many other blunders that the All-Union Party could commit'. Threateningly,

47 Rabukhin case file, AUSBUDO, d. 7606-2f; Sokolov case file, Oct. 27, 1937, l. 52.

48 Noah to Rose, Oct. 29, 1935.

49 RGAE, f. 5679, op. 1, d. 124 (Donbass water conference). Officially chaired by his boss Ginzburg, whose name hardly ever appears in its minutes.

50 Opening speech, water conference, Aug. 25, 1935, f. 5679, op. 1, d. 124, l. 64–5.

he advocated 'all means' to put an end to them. At the conference, and in the manuscript, he argued that American experience proved that railroads were more efficient than canals for transportation. Moreover 'the climate has the bad habit of not allowing any navigation for 5–6 months each year'. Canals would freeze in the Russian winter. The manuscript blames projects to link up all Russian rivers on the heritage of Tsarism:

> Peter the Great deemed a canal system a necessary addition to the oxen used in those days, but there were no railroads at that time ... Russia has always been a land of dreamers, composed of a class of nobles who let the peasant masses toil while they indulged in art, philosophy, and sometimes politics; and an illiterate mass who could only indulge in instinctive primitive reveries. Nowhere did such a book as *The Tunnel* by Kellermann or Verne's *20,000 Leagues Under the Sea* or Wells' *The First Man in the Moon* have such popularity as in Russia.

Noah London presumably would have had a negative opinion of the Soviet space program. He also brought up irrigation, which other conference participants largely ignored, and pointed out that New York had rejected water supply canals on sanitary grounds.[51]

The discussion at the conference is 'of special interest ... from the standpoint of ice regime', as the collection guide in the Russian economic archive in Moscow puts it.[52] The professors argued that the canals would not freeze very often because Ukraine is not as cold as Russia. They finally managed to persuade him that building a canal from the North Donets River was unavoidable. Continuing pipe shortages made impractical London's scheme for a water pipeline instead. He finally gave the canal proposal his approval. But it would only be a water supply canal, not a grandiose transport project on the model of the Moscow–Volga canal then consuming so much of the budget and so many human lives. Ukrainian party leaders were sponsoring canal megaprojects to connect the Don and the North Donets with the Dnieper, Volga and even Moscow rivers. Their spokesman at the conference dominated its second day with a report of interminable length. London finally cut off his speaking time – his advocacy of 'all means' to halt such projects turned out to be the chairman's gavel.[53]

51 Water conference, Aug. 25, 1935, d. 124 l. 121–2.

52 Lebedev, water conference, ibid., 8.

53 Water conference, *passim*, esp. l. 4–62; TsDAHO, f. 11, op. 20, d. 6906, 1936.

The Stalino city soviet published a pamphlet after the conference arguing for linking up the entire southern Ukrainian industrial region, from the Donbass to the Krivoi Rog iron mines, with a grandiose canal. The editor was one Ian Semenovich Kanskii. This would have been the southern branch of the all-Soviet canal system London opposed.[54] But London had sabotaged Kanskii's canal project, something Kanskii would not forget. Unfortunately, budget cuts in any case prevented any work on the Northern Donets water supply canal. The contradiction between Noah London's industrial priorities and Stalin's were beginning to develop, against the background of insufficient economic resources in an isolated Soviet republic in a still socially and economically backward country. In 1937 they would explode.

---

54 *Glubokii Vvod Dnepra v Donbass*, ed. Kanskii, 1936.

CHAPTER 11

The Great Terror in Ukraine and the Donbass Water Crisis

Malenkov reported at a 1937 February–March CPUSSR Central Committee plenum that some 3,200 party members had been arrested thus far as 'enemies of the people'. Perhaps as many as half of these purges took place either in Ukraine or in the adjoining 'Azov-Black Sea territorial district', which shared the Donbass with Ukraine. As a 'Trotskyist wrecking trial' was unfolding, Ukrainian leader Pavel Postyshev and Azov-Black Sea leader Sheboldaev were transferred to lower-level posts, and a number of their underlings were arrested. Many had genuine if tenuous connections with Trotskyism.[1]

It was natural that the Great Purge began in Ukraine and the North Caucasus, the central fields of the Great Famine. The Ukrainian hierarchy had a remarkably high percentage of ex-Trotskyists at all levels, including in the NKVD. The Azov-Black Sea district included the town of Shakhty, as well as the main Cossack settlements. Cossack opposition to collectivization had been even more intense than Ukrainian, and the famine there was just as bad. And Alexander Beloborodov, the former head of the Russian NKVD, had recently been working in its capital, Rostov. He was the most prominent ex-Trotskyist still in high office.[2]

As discussed next chapter, Postyshev had been the theoretician of the transformation of the Soviet Communist Party from a largely blue-collar party at the height of the Stalinist 'industrial revolution' into an elite assemblage of bureaucrats allegedly well-versed in Marxism in the 'moderate' mid-1930s after the end of the Great Famine, despite, or because of, his own proletarian background. He implemented his ideas with great success in Ukraine. But after the assassination of Stalin's friend Kirov in 1934, Stalin became interested in purging former oppositionists, not the party's diminishing rank-and-file base. Stalin asserted in a party plenum speech that embittered ex-members outnumbered dues payers in some factories and blamed this situation on party leaders like Postyshev.

Despite all of Postyshev's purges, former oppositionists seem to have been commoner under his regime than any place else in the USSR. This was because

---

1 Feb.–March 1937 CC plenum, March 5, *Voprosy Istorii*, 1995 no. 10, pp. 4–8; RGASPI, f. 17, op. 21 (Donbass party 1937); Khlevniuk, *1937-i*, 93–108.

2 The Russian NKVD in the 1920s was in charge of police and prisons, but not the GPU.

 | DOI:10.1163/9789004745384_013

of the heritage of early Soviet Ukrainian leader Christian Rakovsky, and Ukrainian Trotskyism. As Postyshev's remarks at the February 1937 party plenum which unleashed the Great Terror indicate, he was not eager to purge former Trotskyists who had genuinely become loyal Stalinists – or at least 'Postyshevists'.[3] Khrushchev, in his famous 1956 'secret speech' against Stalin, selectively quoted those remarks to falsely paint Postyshev as someone who resisted the Great Purge – though they do have a somewhat different tone from those of other speakers. Truly enthusiastic supporters of the mid-1930s party line were hard to find in Ukraine, and Postyshev wanted to hang onto them.

By 1937, as the Great Terror unfolded, DBVT had undergone transformation. When its headquarters was transferred from Kharkov to Stalino in 1934, 54 of the staff made the move. In 1937, only a dozen of them remained. It employed about 1,600 people, about a tenth of whom were engineers. The small Stalino DBVT party unit seems to have been made up exclusively of engineers and other trust officials. There is no sign of a single rank-and-file worker in the extensive meeting protocols I found. This was far from a unique situation, but Donbassvodtrest was an extreme case.[4] Personnel and engineering issues dominate the protocols. Members occasionally accuse each other of treating the workers badly – but the workers' own voices are never heard. The union head, Maliarov, spoke rarely at meetings – and never on behalf of his rank and file.

Soviet industry impressed many foreign visitors with its formal democratism. The basic administrative structure was the *treugolnik* or 'triangle', whose three sides were management, union and party. Shop meetings at which union officials and sometimes even the rank and file criticized management shortcomings were common. Future American labor leader Victor Reuther, then working in the Soviet auto industry, sent a letter to an American friend in 1934, a few months before Miril's sister Rose visited the Londons in Moscow. Victor and his famous brother Walter felt that 'in all the countries that we have been in, we have never found such genuine proletarian democracy'.[5] The picture was less cheery to the native proletarians than to foreign semi-tourists.

The first labor hero praised in the official Donbassvodtrest history pamphlet is mechanic Ivan E. Ochichenko, who distinguished himself during the con-

3 Getty and Naumov, 359; Feb.–March 1937 CC plenum, March 5, *Voprosy Istorii*, 1995 no. 11–12, pp. 20–2; March 4, *Voprosy Istorii*, 1995, no. 6–7, 1–8.

4 Protocol, Feb. 15, 1937, DADO-p, f. 744, op. 1, d. 7 (Stalino dist. 1937), l. 21; Solianik, *Bol'shaia Voda Industrii*, 21.

5 Nelson Lichtenstein, *The Most Dangerous Man in Detroit* (New York: HarperCollins 1996), 40–1.

struction of the first leg of London's water pipeline. By 1937 he had been promoted to district manager. In his opinion, the 'triangle' was counterproductive. It would be better to have management in full charge, as workers would then be less afraid to criticize.[6]

1 The 1937 Donbass Water Crisis

A genuine crisis was at the root of the tensions that exploded in the Donbass water industry in the year 1937. The Western Donbass water problem was becoming critical. The Donets Canal plan approved at London's 1935 conference was stuck in bureaucratic limbo. Serious water shortages were starting to develop in the coalfields, while the Donbass was littered with unfinished waterworks. The main Stalino plant had no backup generator, and a breakdown could have led to disaster. And the critical Stalino water pipeline was still made of wood![7]

The immediate cause of the problems was no mystery and paralleled Soviet industrial difficulties elsewhere. When Noah London was transferred to Moscow, Donbassvodtrest (DBVT) lost its status as a 'shock' enterprise. In the mid-1930s, construction projects with second-tier status sometimes received less than a quarter of their budget requests.[8] Moreover, shortages of raw materials, especially pipes, meant that even inadequate budget allocations could not be spent.

2 The Great Purge at Donbassvodtrest

For years, Sokolov, who had served a term as party chairman, never even hinted at the gravity of the water situation in party meetings. The reports he sent to Noah at Glavstroiprom always maintained that everything was fine.[9] He finally broke the news at a meeting on December 23, 1936. The incorrectly drawn up

---

6 Solianik, *Bol'shaia Voda Industrii*, 10; March 7, 1937, DADO-p, f. 1646 (Krasnozavodsk dist. DBVT), op. 1, d. 5 (1937), l. 10.

7 Stakhanov, 'Dat' shakhteram pit'evuiu vodu', Za Industrii, letter, Aug. 16, 1937; Komissii NKTP po vodosnabsheniiu Donbassa i Krivorozh'ia (hereinafter Donbass water comm.), Stalino, April 1937, RGAE, f. 7297 (NKTP), op. 38, d. 385; 386; 387; 388; 389; 390; 391; 392; 393.

8 James R. Harris, *The Great Urals: Regionalism and the Evolution of the Soviet System* (Ithaca, NY: Cornell University Press, 1999), 146–90.

9 DBVT reports to *Glavstroiprom*, RGAE, f. 5679 (*Glavstroiprom*), op. 1, d. 33 (1933), 1–11; d. 63 (1934), 110–18.

and inadequately funded annual plan would not be fulfilled. The accident rate was too high. Nothing had been done about the Donets Canal project. The problem was a 'negligent attitude of certain workers, who only work to get money'. He put forward a resolution calling on the regional party committee to raise the question of additional funds for the Donets Canal project. In the course of the discussion, a new party chairman named Goloshchapov criticized the trust leadership and stated that 'the possibility that saboteurs are active is not excluded'. Pandora's box opened.

On February 1, 1937, while Sokolov was in Moscow, there was a special closed Stalino DBVT party meeting to report on the removal of Postyshev. Almost all the membership attended. The reason given was his 'lack of vigilance' against 'alien elements', especially Trotskyists. This touched off a full-blown rebellion against Sokolov, led by another former chairman named Mironov. According to Mironov, the reasons for removing Postyshev applied to Stalino DBVT as well, where '24 people from socially-alien spheres and former Communists' were working – slightly more than the number of full party members. One member after another bristled over Sokolov's suggestion at the last meeting that they were to blame for the crisis – and over his favoritism to non-party members for trust positions. They complained that ex-Trotskyists, ex-wreckers and ex-White Guards held higher positions and got better salaries than they did. They had heard chief engineer Kushin saying that the trust was run by 'Communists not specialists'.

Drillling supervisor Il'enko noted that foreigners frequently visited London when he was in charge. There was 'something disagreeable about him'.[10] But other officials did not yet feel comfortable with criticizing the founder of their trust. Another critic stated that unlike Sokolov, 'London dealt with living conditions well …'

The resolution passed confirmed the charge of 'the *zasorennost*' (contamination) of the apparatus of the trust with Trotskyists, former White Guards and kulaks', and called for a purge. The regional party committee drew up a purge list which included fully a quarter of all DBVT engineers. Many had checkered pasts. One prominent official had been tried as an alleged Black Hundred (Russian fascist). There was even a former Makhnovite.[11]

The greatest concern was the alleged Trotskyite menace. As to criticism for insufficient favor to party members: 'I have no special friendships with anyone, I require from everyone according to service'. He observed tartly that

10 Protocol, Feb. 1, 1937, DADO-p, f. 744, op. 1, d. 7, l. 10–19.

11 Chaplenko, 'O Zasorennost' Apparata DBVT', March 22, 1973, DADO-p, f. 326, op. 1, d. 1069, l. 91–4.

Mironov was discontent because Sokolov hadn't raised his salary. He insisted that wrecking was limited to a few situations where secret Trotskyite wreckers in high places had intervened. He pointed to the extensive staff turnover since the transfer from Kharkov to the Donbass as proof that he had already cleaned out plenty of 'foreign elements' from the trust. He promised to fire Kushin, ex-Trotskyist Toder and perhaps genuine underground Trotskyist Bezui within a month.[12] Critics complained that members felt intimidated in his presence.

The new meeting resolution 'upheld' Sokolov's December report, but criticized his failure to answer questions asked by members. But first and foremost it called on him to 'boldly promote young cadres to leading posts'. This slogan was a keynote of Stalinist discourse during the Great Purge, blaring from the pages of the press and expressing what was nearest and dearest to the heart of every *vydvizhenets* hoping to get the jobs of the revolutionary veterans being purged.[13]

The district committee began investigating Donbassvodtrest, and London's enemy Kanskii drew up its bill of indictment. On March 3, when Sokolov chaired the next meeting, he changed tone. He apologized for engaging in personal criticisms and agreed that a purge was needed. His turn to self-criticism restored harmony temporarily in the DBVT party unit. A few days later, a new style of 'party democracy', blessed from above, unfurled in a contested election for the party committee. Sokolov was returned with the second highest vote total, more than his sharpest critics like Mironov. Sokolov conceded in his campaign speech that there was wrecking at DBVT, but he blamed it all on Piatakov, Trotsky's former deputy, who had just been tried and condemned to death as a saboteur, and who had overseen Noah's Industrial Construction Trust (Glavstroiprom) in Moscow. Echoing London's later line of argument, he commented that the party committee was 'cut off from the masses'. It seems likely that Sokolov and London were coordinating their responses to the Donbass water crisis at this point.[14]

2.1 *The Decline and Fall of Comrade Sokolov*

At a special Donbassvodtrest '*aktiv*' conference of trust activists called to deal with the water crisis later in the ominous spring of '37, Sokolov gave his first full report on the sad state of affairs. He was subjected to a barrage of allegations

12 Their stories can be found in my Ph.D dissertation 'The Life and Times of Noah London', University of California, Berkeley, 2008, 458–9.

13 Fitzpatrick, 'New Elite', 171–2.

14 March protocols, DADO-p, f. 744, op. 1, d. 7, l. 29–56.

of bureaucratism. DBVT critics complained that he did not pay enough attention to his engineers. He had created an 'abnormal atmosphere', suppressing co-workers and paralyzing their initiative. Sokolov abjectly conceded that participants 'completely correctly criticized me personally in that my report was clearly unsatisfying'.[15] Unlike London, Sokolov limited criticism of local party leaders to gentle hints.

London told Sokolov at the *aktiv* that 'I know that you know your business, but you don't know your people. We cultivate our replacements. The former worker Sokolov learned the business ... now he needs to learn Bolshevism'.[16] 'We cultivate our replacements' was one of the most ominous of the catchwords Stalin circulated during the Great Purge. London's own formula from his Bronx manifesto, written shortly after his own 'Bolshevization' in America, was that 'the worker will be transformed from a messenger boy to a master, from an obedient slave to a seeker of power'.[17] London was not satisfied with his very own *vydvizhenets*, Lomov's former 'messenger boy' Sokolov. But would do his best to protect him and help him keep his job.

A Peoples' Commissariat of Heavy Industry (NKTP) commission was set to meet in April in Stalino to discuss the crisis – and look for culprits to blame it on. The initiative seems to have come from Donbass government officials who wanted to charge DBVT with wrecking. The NKTP named Noah London as the commission's president, and local leaders telegraphed Mezhlauk, NKTP's new head, to complain. They wanted instead to blame London as the wrecker-in-chief. After a telephone consultation with Mezhlauk's deputy Zavenyagin, Noah yielded to their protest. He stated that he had decided that it would be improper and un-Bolshevik for him to head the commission. But he still played a central role in choosing whom to invite and who should go on which committee.

Nikolai Gennad'evich Ivanov, the president of the Donbass regional state executive committee, replaced him as president. Ivanov poured scorn on London's 'gentlemanly' (*dzhentlmenskie*) statement declining the honor of chairing the commission, maintaining this was merely a consequence of his and his boss Sarkisov's telegram to Moscow. London replied: 'When I spoke to Zaveniagin he told me that ... he didn't consider it correct to remove me from the presidency. It was after I talked with Sarkisov and Ivanov here in this room that I made such a declaration'. The commission's records have a strange flavor: a technical conference with a curiously collegial atmosphere – whose purpose was to decide

15 Stenogram of Donbass water *aktiv.*, April 20, 1937, l. 29ob; 78.

16 Ibid., l. 33–33ob; 53.

17 See Appendix A.

which of its participants to arrest. The driving force and lead accuser was London's enemy Kanskii, now vice-chairman of the local planning department.[18]

2.2 *London's Duel with Kanskii*

The principal focus of the commission was its *kapstroi* (capital construction) subcommission. Kanskii chaired it, but London and Sokolov were also members. It spent a week exhaustively reviewing the history of Donbass water construction, arguing stormily over every last detail. Sokolov supported London and the local planners supported Kanskii. Industry representatives were neutral at first, but got irritated with Noah when he raised the issue of water pollution.[19] Kanskii seems to have sincerely believed that there was a conspiracy to wreck Donbass water supply, and that London, Sokolov and successive Donbassvodtrest chief engineers Shakhov and Kushin were at its heart. Kanskii's charges echoed the wrecking resolution at the recently-concluded Central Committee plenum. It identified one of the primary forms of Trotskyist wrecking as 'holding back construction of fundamental objectives, dispersion and spreading of resources on second-priority objectives by way of interminable repeated reworking of plans and estimates'. Kanskii identified this as DBVT's prime sin: deliberately starting innumerable minor projects and failing to finish the most important ones. And Noah London, the man in Moscow who handled all water questions, was the guilty party.[20]

Sokolov and London's defense was that Trotsky's old righthand man Piatakov, the deputy commissioner of NKTP until he was arrested, was the culprit. Sokolov stated that when Piatakov was appointed, 'the enemy applied his hand to Donbass water supply'. As London less dramatically put it, in 1934 'the planning sector gave DBVT not 40 but 20 million, and my job was to call Sokolov and tell him … everyone knew Piatakov related exclusively badly to Glavstroiprom …' It was at a session of this subcommission that London described the period of Mezhlauk's oversight as the 'golden age' of Donbassvodtrest. When London was in charge, and the trust and the Ukrainian government were both located in Kharkov: 'At that time Kossior and Chubar' would go to Moscow and raise those questions we raised in Kharkov before the Central Committee and Sovnarkom

18 Donbass water comm., d. 389 (plenary sessions), opening meeting April 14, 1937, l. 2–7; April 25 plenary, l. 20, 73, 82; secret report to Mezhlauk, May 20, 1937, f. 7297, op. 38, d. 393, l. 2.

19 Donbass water comm., d. 386 (*kapstroi* subcommission, April 16–24), *passim*; Davies and Wheatcroft, *The Years of Hunger*, 210–11.

20 CC plenum 'wrecking' resolution, March 2, 1937, *Voprosy Istorii*, 1994 no. 10, p. 3.; Kanskii, Jan.–Feb. 1937; Donbass water comm., plenary, April 25, 1937, d. 389, l. 9–14.

[government]. We had great support from Kossior. I would even visit comrade Kossior at his hotel, he would say I will give you pipes ...'[21] Kossior and Chubar' were on the short list of Politburo members to be executed during the Great Terror.

The subcommission was unable to reach unanimity. When the issue of whether DBVT committed wrecking came to a vote, Kanskii won – but the commission was supposed to be an NKTP commission after all. And London, the NKTP representative, refused to agree that he and Sokolov were wreckers. Despite the vote, the subcommission resolution was entrusted to editing by London and one of his critics.

At the final conference plenary session, London related that when he was in charge 'there was no talk of needing to cut back and concentrate work in one place ... The party and government told us to spread the work out all over'. But 'in 1933, when that scoundrel Piatakov began to smother us ... the situation was catastrophic'.[22] London then read from his 1934 *Pravda* article and letters to Ukrainian party officials, to prove that he was the only official campaigning for Donbass water while the crisis was developing.

This commission created to discuss a possible major catastrophe held its meetings behind closed doors. The nearest thing to a public session had been that two-day meeting of the Donbass water trust '*aktiv*'. At the February–March CC plenum that set off the Great Purge, Stalin and Zhdanov presented what they were unleashing as a restoration of 'party democracy'.[23] London tried to use this populist and 'democratic' rhetoric as his opportunity to criticize the bureaucratic machinery in which he was trapped.[24] This risky stratagem would prove no worse than any other for the difficult task of surviving the Great Purge.

In his lengthy and fiery speech at the NKTP Commission, printed in full in the official but secret commission report, London began by stating bluntly that he was going to focus first and foremost on drinking water for the workers, not industry. Industrial managers and 'even the local organizations' always put

---

21 *Kapstroi* subcommission, April 17 1937, l. 23ob.; 34ob–35; 28ob.

22 Plenary, April 25, 1937, l. 20–1.

23 'Revisionist' Soviet historian Arch Getty describes Zhdanov's 'party democracy' plenum speech as a culminating moment in a populist campaign against bureaucracy. Wendy Goldman presents a different view and explores the role of the 'democracy' campaign in Soviet trade unions and on the factory floor. Getty, *Origins of the Great Purges: The Soviet Communist Party Reconsidered, 1933–1938* (Cambridge: Cambridge University Press, 1985), 141–3; Goldman, *Terror and Democracy in the Age of Stalin: The Social Dynamics of Repression* (Cambridge: Cambridge University Press, 2007), *passim*.

24 NKTP water comm., d. 387, water *aktiv* session, April 19–20, 1937.

industrial water supply first. The wrecker Piatakov had tried to create a water crisis by cutting the budget. Doubtless he had planted agents ready to disrupt the water supply in wartime, 'to wreck in various directions, technically, chemically, bacteriologically and so forth'. But the heart of Piatakov's wrecking work was the planning atmosphere he created.

> They built factories without housing, they built factories without communal facilities, without those living conditions which the workers need. This is the rule through all industry as it is conducted. Here is where the hand of Piatakov was, all this to press the working class and call forth its discontent. Donbass water supply was the first victim of this wrecking hand. (p. 50)[25]

What allowed wreckers to do their work was '*samouspokoenie*' – self-satisfaction – at every level in the apparatus.

> I do not know ... if anyone raised a real shout, if anyone raised the simple question that the Donbass doesn't have water ... Workers don't have water for washing, for bathhouses ... I wrote a lot of documents and so did you, but the fact is what was needed was a living word ... I wrote an article for *Pravda*, but unfortunately *Pravda* did not publish it in the way I wrote it, they softened it ... (pp. 50, 51rev.)

And then Noah the deputy head of Glavstroiprom, the central industrial construction trust for the entire Soviet Union, turned to self-criticism: 'I must say that the head of Glavstroiprom [S.Z. Ginzburg] is a soulless *chinovnik* (Tsarist bureaucrat) and my guilt is that I became a squeezed-out Akakii Akakievich attached to him (commission final report, p. 51rev.)' London was comparing himself to the antihero of Gogol's short story *The Overcoat*, one of the most hopeless characters in all Russian literature. A clerk of limited competence at the lowest level of Tsarist bureaucracy whose life revolved around a quest for a warm fur coat, is frightened to death by a blustering superior after his coat was stolen by thieves. For his audience, this literary flourish was a standard trope of Stalinist discourse, of 'speaking Bolshevik'. But for Noah London himself, it expressed what he felt by then about his well-paid career as a Soviet industrial manager. He described the roots of his errors as bureaucratism:

25 Water *aktiv* session stenogram; inline citation of page numbers hereinafter.

> Bureaucratism is not a technical term, it is a political term that borders with wrecking. It is the spirit of contempt for the living person, contempt for the masses, for the people … We consider ourselves leading business managers, the water people, entrusted with water supply for Soviet industry, you can read about us in the newspapers … But it turned out that London occupied himself with paper, with planning, all kinds of problems, writes very beautiful documents, but London never stopped by to talk with the workers … (p. 53)

His conception of 'the tasks of business managers' was no longer the same as Stalin's. The day-to-day needs and interests of the working people came first. London next tried to turn the tables on his accusers. The local officials calling him a wrecker had done little or nothing to solve the water problem themselves. 'The speech of comrade Kanskii suffers from one small deficiency. Where is your self-criticism, comrade Kanskii? … I want to know, comrade Kanskii, what you did to mobilize consumers? … If you spoke with comrade Sergo [Ordzhonikidze] or comrade Molotov, they would have given you both people and pipes for Stalino' (p. 54). In the capital construction subcommission London was even blunter: 'If you comrade Ivanov … had gone to the late Sergo or Molotov or even higher, to comrade Stalin, and said that the workers of Stalino did not have enough drinking water … what do you think, would they have given us money or not?'[26]

Kanskii's protector Ivanov answered London's counterattack at the plenary session cynically, cleverly and effectively:

> You spent a lot of time telling how Piatakov did not love you and Glavstroiprom. That isn't serious. Nobody could prove whether he loved you or not. You produced many documents here … but the more documents, the more they speak against you … You had far more possibilities to raise the question in all its breadth [than] other comrades. You know how to describe this kind of attitude? I think it's *dvurushnichestvo* (double dealing). (p. 62)

Ivanov accurately branded London's pious repetitions of Stalin's plenum formulae as deceptive. He pointed out that according to London, 'Piatakov, Rataichak, Gvakhariia and so forth are guilty – those who already have been convicted by the high court and shot or those who have been arrested by order of

26 *Kapstroi* subcommission, l. 43ob.

the investigative powers as Trotskyist terrorists' (p. 76). Ivanov ridiculed London's *Pravda* article as 'wrong from beginning to end'. He charged that London's odd sounding irrigation proposals were deliberately designed to blind party leaders to the real problems, and were in themselves a form of wrecking (pp. 73–5).

London had called for a large-scale Donbass irrigation program because of the great Ukrainian famine – but as officially the famine had never happened, he could hardly bring this up to explain himself. Instead, he only weakly replied that perhaps he was wrong about irrigation, but at least he had warned of the danger of catastrophe (p. 82).

3 Soviet Industrial Politics and the Donbass Water Commission

The accusations against Noah London were carefully calibrated to the politics of the moment. But so were London's defenses. His praise of his patron Mezhlauk was hardly disinterested. And in the *kapstroi* subcommission London pointedly brought up a 1933 Donbass water supply conference, at which former Donbass leader Akulov 'became strongly interested in questions of Donbass water supply'. The message was that previous local leaders had taken water supply more seriously than the current team. Former Soviet secret police deputy director Akulov had a track record of opposition to excesses, and during the Shakhty affair was head of the coal miners' union in which London then was an officer. Kanskii vigorously defended the water record of the Sarkisov-Ivanov leadership team that replaced Akulov. (Sarkisov was a vulnerable former Zinovievite).[27]

London tiptoed delicately around his relations with his superior Ginzburg, defending him against accusations of wrecking but criticizing him for bureaucratism. This stance reflected his personal opinion of Ginzburg as well. Bureaucratic conflict between Glavstroiprom and Piatakov seems to have been genuine. According to London, Piatakov replied to his reports and letters on Donbass water problems by expressing agreement and – doing nothing. Former Trotskyist Piatakov believed that all Soviet problems stemmed from industrial backwardness, and that had to be dealt with first.

London blamed Piatakov for the low funding level for Glavstroiprom. But he conceded that Ginzburg had much influence over which of its projects would take the brunt of the budget cuts and 'Ginzburg underestimated funds

27 Ibid., April 14, 1937, London l. 23ob; Kanskii 38ob–39.

for DBVT'. London avoided the temptation to condemn him for this. 'It is necessary to recognize that out of these miserable resources Ginzburg tried to snatch something for defense needs. This did not help Donbass water supply'.[28] Final budget decisions reflected the differing priorities that London advocated in his secret manuscript, and that rare Great Purge survivor Ginzburg would advocate in his autobiography. Ginzburg always considered Soviet defense needs the number one industrial priority – an attitude that would serve him well under Stalin, Khrushchev and Brezhnev.[29]

Since NKTP had sponsored the commission, not the local government, NKTP official Noah London's refusal to accept blame for the water crisis could not be ignored. He asserted at the final plenary that most of the practical suggestions that the construction subcommission developed were his. No final resolution was adopted. Instead, Ivanov proposed that the heads of the subcommissions write one. Effectively, this meant that Kanskii would be the author. London insisted that Sokolov be added to the editorial committee.[30]

The Donbass party held a regional conference as the report was being written. Most of the top-secret conference resolution was devoted to 'wrecking'. The resolution states at the end on page 145 that 'there is wrecking in this area [water supply] also' in the form, naturally, of *raspylenie* (dispersion), the plague diagnosed at the February CC plenum. The very last sentence of this interminably lengthy resolution finally gets around to mentioning that there is an 'extremely difficult situation with Donbass water supply in 1937', and that a special NKTP commission is working on the problem. Thus spake the Donbass party leadership on the eve of destruction. The local party leaders were much more concerned with their personal fates than with the danger to the people's water supply.[31]

In the end, the commission report followed Kanskii's schema, labeling London, Sokolov and chief engineers Shakhov and Kushin as wreckers. Report editor Sokolov capitulated to Kanskii. All commission materials were sent to the 'investigative organs', in order to 'bring those guilty of wrecking Donbass water supply to criminal accountability'. In addition, 46 million additional rubles were demanded for DBVT. The report was sent to Mezhlauk ... and filed. It had no immediate impact on Noah London's status.[32]

28 Ibid., 34ob–35.

29 S.Z. Ginsburg, *O proshlom, dlya budushchego* (Moscow: Politizdat, 1970).

30 Plenary, April 27, 1937, l. 84.

31 'Rezolutsiia, III oblastnoi partkonferentsii Donetskoi organizatsii KP(b)U' (stamped *Sekretno*), Stalino, May 1937, RGASPI, f. 17, op. 21, d. 5162, l. 82ob-83 (144–5).

32 Water commission report, d. 393, l. 19–20; Siniichuk, 'O Vodosnabzheniem Donbassa', May 29, 1937, *Sotsialisticheskii Donbass*.

Mezhlauk's lack of response perturbed the Donbass party leadership. In early June the regional party committee decided to send Ivanov to Moscow to talk to Mezhlauk. But clouds were gathering over their own heads. Kanskii, like London, was a foreign Communist – but not, unfortunately, from the USA. Two days earlier the committee had been forced to 'ask comrade Kanskii to give [them] a detailed autobiography and documents confirming time and place of entry into the Communist Party and his work abroad in Poland and Czechoslovakia'. He was promptly arrested.[33] 1937 was not a good year for Polish Communists in the Soviet Union. Kanskii's arrest was quickly followed by those of Ivanov, Sarkisov and virtually the entire Donbass top party and state apparatus.[34] Noah London's argument that the local party leaders were the culprits in the water mess was the kind of charge that met broad resonance during the Great Purge.[35]

There were no DBVT party meetings for more than a month afterwards. But by June 8, Sokolov was no longer able to put off reporting to the membership. He was compelled to state that he, London, Shakhov and Kushin had all been branded as wreckers. Worse yet, he had to report that Moscow was offering not 46 million rubles in extra money, but only 12 million. Members pointed out that all they had was promises – no pipes. Like it or not, the Donets Canal was on the back burner. And worst of all, Kushin, the man who complained that Communists were in charge instead of specialists, was still chief engineer.

According to the censure resolution: 'Comrade Sokolov did not orient the party organization to the difficulties of Donbass water supply according to the general scheme in his December report ... For this it is necessary to censure comrade Sokolov for deceiving the party organization'.[36] In the next few weeks the local and Donbass party leadership who had sponsored the hounding of Sokolov were all arrested in succession. This did not help him in the least. Kan-

33 Donbass party committee protocols June 5 and June 7, 1937, RGASPI, f. 17, op. 21, d. 5490, l. 136, 151; report to Pramnek, DADO-p, f. 326, op. 1, d. 1016 (Feb.–Oct. 1937 corresp.), l. 47.

34 Sheila Fitzpatrick, *Everyday Stalinism: Ordinary Life in Extraordinary Times: Soviet Russia in the 1930s* (New York: Oxford University Press, 1999), 41; Z.G. Likholobova, '1936–1938 gody', *Pravda cherez gody* 5 (2001): 42–61; and *Stalins'kyi totalitarnyi rezhym ta politychni represii kintsia 30-x rokiv v Ukraini* (Donets'k: DonDU, 1996), 63–9; Burnosov, 'Nekotorye stranitsy 1937 goda', *Novye Stranitsy v Istorii Donbassa* 2 (1992): 102–10.

35 Polonskii, 'O vodosnabzhenii Donbassa', *Vodosnabzhenie i Sanitarnaia Tekhnika* 8 (Aug. 1937): 3–6.

36 DADO-p, f. 744, op. 1, d. 8 (1937 party committee protocols), l. 18–24; Protocol, June 8, 1937, d. 7, l. 63–4ob.

torovich, who had delivered the report back in December that set off the rebellion against Sokolov, returned at the July meeting to finish the job. Sokolov confessed that the reason the Western Donbass was facing a water crisis was that he had 'insufficiently strongly raised the question of water supply difficulties'. He admitted that he had allowed class enemies free reign. Goloshchapov answered that Sokolov had 'trailed out the wrecking idea of the Donets Canal [and then] went on the path of discrediting individual party members'. Mironov poured scorn on Sokolov's promises to clean out the 'alien elements' and bring in 'new young specialists':

> He doesn't even mention how to liquidate the consequences of wrecking, how to reconstruct the apparatus ... It seems to me that we should finally put the question today about Sokolov's remaining in the ranks of the party ... Sokolov has close ties with London, and London is a dark figure to us now. You have heard how London ... had close ties with foreigners, who they are we don't know, but the facts of the last days show that in this number there are a great number of wreckers and spies.[37]

This was the first time anyone other than xenophobe Il'enko ever attacked London at a DBVT party meeting. The meeting took a five-day break, while Sokolov tried desperately to save himself through abject self-criticism and denunciation of wreckers, including London. But when the meeting recommenced, Goloshchapov pointed out that:

> Sokolov here calls Rabukhin a wrecker, but a few days ago Rabukhin phones Sokolov ... and Sokolov tells him, I'm thinking of leaving Stalino in August and asks Rabukhin the wrecker to talk about him in Moscow. At the same time he warns Rabukhin that it is inconvenient to talk about everything on the city telephone. This is not simple.[38]

The meeting voted unanimously to remove Sokolov from the party committee and asked the district organization to expel him. But this did not happen right away. As 'alien elements' were purged, and members who had shown insufficient 'vigilance' were censured, Sokolov continued to attend meetings, speak, and even deliver a report on 'liquidating the consequences of wrecking'. But his fate was sealed. A week after Noah London was arrested, on November 7,

37 Protocol, July 23, 1937, DADO-p, f. 744, op. 1, d. 7, l. 66, 67, 73.

38 Protocol, July 28, 1937, ibid. l. 76. Rabukhin had resigned his post earlier and left for Moscow. Chaplenko, purge list, f. 326, op. 1, d. 1069, l. 91–94.

the twentieth anniversary of the Bolshevik Revolution, Goloshchapov reported that Sokolov had been arrested as an enemy of the people.[39]

New DBVT director Vorob'ev tried to extend the purge further, targeting party secretary Zemlianoi, the author of the protocols that are the basis of this 'micro-history' of the Great Purge in the Donbass water industry. Zemlianoi was an old drinking buddy of Sokolov's, who had nominated him for the party committee in March. But Vorob'ev met resistance from London's nemesis Il'enko and deputy director Nemchenko, whom the old party leadership had appointed as a watchdog over Sokolov back in May. It is worth emphasizing that this took place *before* the January 1938 Moscow Central Committee plenum at which purge 'excesses' of Postyshev and others were criticized. Zemlianoi fought back and was vindicated. The purge was over at DBVT, because its purpose was accomplished. The new generation was firmly in the saddle.[40]

The conflicts at Donbassvodtrest were highly similar to those that broke out elsewhere in Soviet industry on the eve of the Great Purge.[41] In the aftermath, *vydvizhentsy* from the factory floor trained in engineering school took the helm. Former steelworker Leonid Brezhnev is the most famous of this cohort. They became the core of the Soviet bureaucracy. Many Jewish *vydvizhentsy* became engineers, but few became top bureaucrats – the artificiality of their proletarian background was an obstacle to those who wished to climb the political ladder over the corpses of purge victims, as at Donbassvodtrest. They had more luck in becoming intellectuals and professionals – until the Cold War. The postwar explosion of anti-Semitism in the Soviet Union primarily resulted from the conflict between the Soviet Union and America, the true Jewish promised land. But the replacement during the Terror of often-Jewish former revolutionaries by overwhelmingly Slavic party and state functionaries from a working-class background had something to do with this as well.

At Donbassvodtrest the *vydvizhentsy*, whom Stalin (and London for that matter) favored enthusiastically, welcomed the Great Terror and indeed played an initiating role. All the old trust officials associated with London were purged. But the purge came to a screeching halt as soon as it began to touch the new generation, the people who would take charge of the Soviet Union for the next half century. Blue-collar workers at the trust played no role whatsoever in this ugly bureaucratic drama, the background for Noah and Miril London's arrest and trial in the fall of 1937.

39 Aug.–Nov. protocols, DADO-p, f. 744, op. 1, d. 7, l. 86–125 *passim*.

40 Jan. 1938 protocols, DADO-p, f. 744, op. 1, d. 10, l. 1–14.

41 Harris, *Great Urals*.

4 Why Was There a Water Crisis?

Was anyone actually guilty of 'wrecking'? There is no mystery as to why the waterworks budget was cut drastically after Noah London was kicked upstairs to Moscow. In 1934, Ordzhonikidze, the head of all Soviet industry, spoke before a coal industry conference in Stalino, now Donetsk. Many of its participants were complaining about the housing situation. He told them that 'the fact is that we are compelled to cut back capital investment'.[42] The budget cuts were not Piatakov's fault – they came from the top. And they were hardly Ordzhonikidze's wishes. Politburo minutes register sharp departmental conflicts pitting him against other Politburo members precisely over how much funding industry should receive. Stalin insisted on deep cutbacks due to the famine crisis, over Ordzhonikidze's objections. And on this issue, Stalin can hardly be faulted.

The Donbass water crises derived from systemic problems, not any one individual's incompetence or malice, even Stalin's. The USSR simply did not have adequate resources to avoid stumbling from one crisis to another. The problem was not false investment priorities, but the undemocratic, bureaucratic and indeed Stalinist way everything was done. Stalinism aggravated organic difficulties which the country would have had to face whoever was in charge and whatever the social system. Stalin's idea of 'socialism in one country' was not working. It managed – barely – to hold off the German invasion and delay the inevitable collapse of the deeply contradictory Soviet system by half a century. But the demoralization and resentment created by gulags, terror and bureaucratic privilege while workers tightened their belts and peasants starved nearly resulted in the collapse of the Soviet Union under the German *blitzkrieg*.

Lenin's vision for the Soviet Union was 'soviet power plus electrification'. Stalin delivered electrification, but the soviets, the organs of worker and peasant power during the Revolution, were abolished under the 1936 Constitution that Bukharin wrote for Stalin. Instead, the powerless shell that remained was structured like a traditional capitalist parliament, but had no input from workers and peasants whatsoever. It was simply the vehicle for untrammeled domination over society by a Stalinist bureaucracy. A project that in the long run turned out to be ... impractical.

In 1917, the Bolsheviks saw the October Revolution as something of a holding action. The notion that a Soviet republic in Russia could survive except briefly unless the revolution spread into Europe was something few thought was a real possibility – unlike Noah London, who argued in his Yiddish art-

42 Donetsk, April 18, 1934, f. 7297 (NKTP), op. 38, d. 108, l. 6.

icle that hit New York newsstands during the October Revolution that some sort of Russian socialism 'in one country' could be viable.[43] The Lenins and Trotskys thought correctly that a successful Bolshevik-led Russian Revolution would mean that the German and Habsburg empires would soon be overturned by popular revolutions. What they did not see was that the new regimes would turn out to be as hostile to the new Soviet republic as the old ones.

The prospect of a Communist-led German Revolution in 1923, stemming from the great German social crisis of that year, had led Communists around the world to briefly believe that the original Bolshevik prognosis of the spread of the Revolution was about to be realized. This consensus included Noah London, but not his factional ally Ludwig Lore. The only Soviet leader to express a bit of caution and skepticism was, naturally, Joseph Stalin.

In the aftermath, Stalin devised his theory of 'socialism in one country', which Noah London had prefigured in the *Naye Velt*. Depressed and disappointed Communists flocked to it, in the Soviet Union and around the world. For a while, the economic and social situation of the Soviet republic stabilized and popular standards of living recovered from the traumas of destruction and famine of the Russian Civil War. The Londons arrived in the Soviet Union at the peak of the NEP and enjoyed everything they saw. But the internal contradictions of the NEP broke down as the NEPmen and kulaks who had restored the Soviet economy gained strength and influence. The 1927 'kulak grain strike', with all peasants not just the richer ones refusing to sell their grain to the workers' state, was creating breadlines and threatened disaster. The slow, stumbling course of Soviet industrialization meant that the Soviet state could not produce enough goods to trade with the peasants at a price the Soviet Union could afford.

Stalin's solution was to cut the Gordian knot. He and his faction attempted to force through a massive industrial revolution and coercive agricultural collectivization, putting an end to Lenin's grand NEP compromise with the peasantry, by whatever means necessary and despite all attendant human suffering. The inevitable result was the Ukrainian famine the Londons witnessed, which destroyed their faith in the party leadership and placed a black mark on the socialist project worldwide. It turned out that world revolution, the original Bolshevik strategy that the Trotskyists still advocated, was the only really practical solution in the long run for Soviet economic problems.

43 London, 'Menshevism or socialist impotence?', *Naye Velt*, Nov. 6, 1917.

CHAPTER 12

Soviet Politics in the 1930s and Noah London

We've seen how things worked out in practice with Noah London's efforts to 'build socialism' in the Soviet Union – in housing for coal miners; in water supplies for Donbass miners and the general population; and for the benefit of the Jewish population of the old Jewish Pale where Noah and Miril were born. Now let us take a step backwards to take a look, against the background of the political turmoil in the Soviet Union in the 1930s, at what Noah London stood for and worked for in that tragic decade, as articulated in his secret manuscript, and cautiously in public as a Soviet official – and what relationship that would have with his arrest and execution in the 'Great Terror'.

When Miril's sister Rose visited the Londons in Kharkov in 1931, as far as she could tell they were still enthusiasts for the party line. In the egalitarian atmosphere of Stalin's 'cultural revolution', workers were favored and bourgeois engineers were under attack. This appealed to Noah, even though he was an engineer himself. By the next time she visited them, in the summer of 1934, things had changed. Noah revealed new thoughts in the quiet woods outside the London's dacha in the Moscow countryside. Rose took them down in Yiddish shorthand. 'The world at large probably does not know that in the year 1932–33, the famine in the USSR was in its scope no smaller or less horrible than the famine of 1921'. It stemmed directly from Stalin's decision to collectivize agriculture by force. London described this fateful step as 'second in importance only to the October Revolution itself'. Millions of victims died in Ukraine, where the Londons lived and worked. Ukrainians call this famine the *holodomor*, the hunger plague. Miril's reaction was a nervous breakdown. Noah's was to become a dissident again, but now in secret.

According to the manuscript Rose put together out of her shorthand notes back in New York City, Noah believed that 'socialism means bettering the condition of the masses, enlightening them, not building cathedrals'. The 'wonders of the Five-Year Plan' at which 'the whole world was gaping' were not his idea of socialism. In his words:

> Once there was walking along the shores of the Thames a young couple who were courting, a couple of moderate means. Now the young man was showing her the castles on the Thames and assuring her that he would soon become rich, buy her a castle, and install her as queen there. 'Ah', said the lassie, 'I wish we had a small apartment of our own with an oven.

 | DOI:10.1163/9789004745384_014

I would get me flour and bake me bread'. Now said the Englishman, 'What is the use of the castle? The bread is what counts'.

1 Present-Day Pipelines with Future Pipes?

Even before the famine, problems had begun to develop at Donbassvodtrest – especially the pipe shortage. No matter how many rubles the trust was allocated, it was impossible to construct today's pipelines with tomorrow's pipes, paraphrasing an article Bukharin wrote in his brief oppositional moment. Donbassvodtrest all too often found itself using rubber or even wooden pipes. This was not a problem particular to DBVT. It reflected a general Soviet steel crisis. In 1931, the Soviet economy suffered a half-million-ton deficit in rolled steel, and imports doubled. By 1932, Soviet steel pipe production had actually declined to 69 percent of its peak output two years earlier.[1]

Stephen Kotkin's tale of the construction of Magnitigorsk, the largest and putatively most modern steel complex in the world, shares features with the story of Donbassvodtrest. Kotkin portrays the 'magnetic mountain' as a cultural embodiment of the Stalinist vision of socialism – but dismisses the million tons of rolled steel per year it was cranking out by 1937 as 'production for production's sake', whose real function was to provide full employment.[2] At DBVT, those pipes were desperately needed.

When he was in charge at Donbassvodtrest, the man right above him in the hierarchy was one Semion Zakharovich Ginzburg. Ginzburg headed Glavstroiprom, the Moscow supertrust that oversaw all industrial construction. He was a ferro-concrete specialist who had studied at MVTU, Moscow's famed technical institute, and was promoted into a leading role in Soviet industrial construction immediately upon graduation.[3]

In the summer of 1931 Ginzburg sent London to England and Germany to buy pipes for Donbass water projects. He managed to knock down German pipe prices considerably, it being the height of the Great Depression. The deal he negotiated went all the way to the top. Stalin rejected Kaganovich's proposal to accept it, writing: 'You have evidently given into ... pressure ... since the municipal-economy people [e.g. London – JH] are ... demanding imports ... forcing the working class to pay with its own hard-currency resources for the

1 R.W. Davies, *Crisis and Progress in the Soviet Economy, 1931–1933*, vol. 4 of *The Industrialization of Soviet Russia* (New York: Macmillan, 1996), 6–7, 107, 230.

2 Kotkin, *Magnetic Mountain*, 37–71.

3 Ginzburg, *O Proshlom, dlia Budushchego*, 40–53, 134–8.

ineptitude, sluggishness, and bureaucratism of Vesenkha'.[4] A Soviet balance of payments crisis had arisen, and agricultural problems were aggravating it.

The Politburo had just previously resolved to cancel 'everything which is not absolutely necessary' from the fall import schedule. Stalin proposed cancelling steel pipe imports altogether, which proved impractical. Conflict broke out behind closed doors, against a background of previous disputes between Ordzhonikidze, the director of industry, and Molotov, the head of the government. On one of the very rare occasions that other Politburo members tried to overrule Stalin, or at least go behind his observant back, Kaganovich and Ordzhonikidze attempted to authorize additional steel imports a few days after a vacationing Stalin rejected London's German pipe deal. But Kaganovich (unlike Ordzhonikidze) crumbled immediately when Stalin laid down the law, expressing submission in groveling language.[5] The particularly low opinion London expresses of Kaganovich in the manuscript likely has something to do with this affair.

Years later, Noah London would tell NKVD interrogators that his disaffection stemmed from these industrial difficulties – and that Ginzburg shared it. Ginzburg was a Jewish radical from the Pale by family background. It was natural that he and London would get on well together.[6] Noah London would tell the inquisitors that it was his trip to England that convinced him that the capitalist system was not in its final crisis after all. He would carefully avoid mentioning his visit to crisis-ridden Berlin, where Trotsky's son Leon Sedov was putting his efforts into getting Trotsky's exile journal, the 'Bulletin of the Opposition' (*Biulletin Oppozitsii*), into the hands of visiting Soviet officials. The secret manuscript shows clear signs of familiarity with Trotsky's critique of Stalinist policies circa 1931.

According to his 1937 confession, this was when he began organizing a rightist wrecking conspiracy at Donbassvodtrest at Ginzburg's behest, to 'demonstrate the unreality of projected plans' and 'disrupt the tempo of industrial development projected by the party and government'.[7] This was obviously a fantasy cooked up for the NKVD's benefit. But it is worth noting how consistent its goals would be with thoughts expressed in the manuscript, whose existence he did not reveal to the interrogators. The summer of 1931 was a logical moment

4 Stalin to Kaganovich, Aug. 30, 1931. The Stalin–Kaganovich correspondence for the month of August refers to the issue repeatedly.

5 Davies, *Crisis and Progress*, 118–22; Khlevniuk, *Politbiuro* 1996, 83–8; Stalin–Kaganovich correspondence, Sept. 1931.

6 Ginzburg was, however, a Bolshevik not a Bundist. Ginzburg, *O Proshlom*, 19–22, 50.

7 'Protokol doprosa Londona', TsaFSB, 2–4.

for Noah's disaffection to unfold, with or without nervous perusal of dangerous documents to be burned after reading. The features of the Stalinist 'cultural revolution' that attracted him were disappearing. Populist anti-wrecking rhetoric was giving way to a campaign against 'petty-bourgeois egalitarianism'. And as he put it in the manuscript: 'If previously it was the custom to boost the workers into management and thus fulfill the slogan of Lenin, this process has now been stopped'. The status, security and social privileges of the 'bourgeois specialists' were restored, and their salaries increased sharply. Much less might he now be inclined to write off the worst features of the Stalinist industrial revolution as temporary unpleasantnesses.[8]

In the following year the regime was compelled to cut back grain exports drastically, as collectivization was going poorly and world food prices were declining. Unmistakable signs of famine began to appear in Ukrainian villages in the spring. Agricultural policies were moderated, and economic measures described by foreign critics and later historians as a slightly capitalist 'neo-NEP' were adopted. Foreign purchases like pipes were slashed dramatically. 'Shock' projects like Donbassvodtrest were still receiving lavish funding, but materials shortages made this meaningless. The investment cutbacks coincided with the first signs of the failure of the grain harvest. The barn door was closed, but the horse had already bolted.[9] And then the horse got eaten.

2 The 'Unbelievable Results' of the Stalinist 'Second Revolution'

The famine broke out right under the Londons' noses: the Kharkov region was one of its epicenters. The glorious successes of the water trust were losing relevance: miners were worrying about food, not water. Every ruble spent on the tremendous accomplishments of the Five-Year Plan, including Donbass waterworks, subtracted from resources available to feed the starving. While Noah London was building one of the most modern water filtration systems in the world, Ukrainian peasants were eating grass and dying with swollen bellies. He became a secret dissident first and foremost because of the Ukrainian 'hunger plague', a direct consequence of compulsory collectivization and the breakneck pace of Stalinist industrial revolution. As he put it in the manuscript, 'It is clear

8 Daniels, *Documentary History of Communism* vol. 2, 20–9; Sheila Fitzpatrick, *The Russian Revolution* (Oxford: Oxford University Press, 1982), 1, 42–3; Kuromiya, *Stalin's Industrial Revolution*, 263–86; Davies, *Crisis and Progress*, 65–88; Khlevniuk, *In Stalin's Shadow*, 44–8.

9 Davies, *Crisis and Progress*, 155–64, 201–41, 270–9; Davies and Wheatcroft, *The Years of Hunger*, 409–10.

that the bread situation in the seventeenth year of the victorious Revolution is unsatisfactory. Now wherein lies the reason for such unbelievable results?'

The story of Donbassvodtrest typifies the drama of the First Five-Year Plan as a whole. It illustrates in miniature how and why Stalin's policies led to enormous waste, grotesque human suffering and a crisis of the regime. As part of the drive against 'petty-bourgeois egalitarianism', coal miners and metal workers got substantial wage hikes while those in less vital industries like textile got paycuts, and strikes broke out. But even among workers in 'shock' industries, food was short – and peasants were starving. In 1932, peasant starvation and labor discontent seemed to be on the brink of breaking the Stalinist death-grip on Soviet political life. There was internal dissent at all levels of the party and state apparatus.[10] Stalinist agricultural policies faced resistance at the local level. As London told Rose:

> A rural Communist … cannot blind himself forever and carry out tax instructions from above which virtually strip the peasants of their bread and leave them with nothing for the rest of the year except hunger. [He] … cannot altogether be free of the influence of the ideas and desires and needs of the masses among whom he lives. That is why in most cases the local organizations have failed to carry out the wishes of the government – and in many cases were sabotaging their instructions.

Passive resistance and reluctance made their way through the apparatus all the way up to the Ukrainian members of the Soviet Politburo, who would be purged in 1937. 'Nationalist deviationist' Ukrainian party leader Skrypnik committed suicide.[11] And so did Stalin's wife.

The Trotskyist opposition revived. While Sedov in Berlin was cobbling together an 'opposition bloc' with disaffected capitulators in high places, in Moscow underground Trotskyists were agitating for a mass political general strike. In the spring of 1932 they attempted to spread the strikes in the Ivanovo textile region to Moscow. Workers at the huge Glukhova textile mill openly

---

10 Khlevniuk, *Stalin's Industrial Revolution*, 10–24; Davies, *Crisis and Progress*, 184–92; Jeffrey J. Rossman, *Worker Resistance under Stalin: Class and Revolution on the Shop Floor* (Cambridge, MA: Harvard University Press, 2005); Getty and Naumov, *The Road to Terror: Stalin and the Self-Destruction of the Bolsheviks, 1932–1939*, trans. B. Sher. (New Haven, CT: Yale University Press, 1999), 52–77.

11 Sullivant, *Bolshevik Politics*, 187–202; F.M. Rudich and R. Ya. Pyrih, ed., *Holod 1932–1933 rokiv na Ukraïni: Ochyma istorykiv, movoiu dokumentiv* (Kiev: Instytut istoriï partiï pry TSK Kompartiï Ukraïny, 1990); Shapoval and Vasil'ev, *Komandiri Velikoho Holodu*.

carried portraits of Trotsky at the 1932 May Day celebration.[12] But despite tremendous discontent and a high level of disaffection within the ruling party itself, no mass rebellion ensued. The regime survived.

Ukrainian peasants had already tried repeatedly to revolt against collectivization – and failed.[13] As for the workers, the Soviet regime at the time was a 'dictatorship of the ex-proletariat', in the words of Soviet historian Robert Davies. This is almost literally accurate. At the end of the Civil War, the total number of industrial proletarians on Soviet soil was about a million and a half. This is approximately the same as the number of blue-collar workers promoted to white-collar status or higher by the middle 1930s. At the height of the Stalinist 'cultural revolution' it was downright difficult for a worker to avoid such a promotion.[14] But even after wholescale *vydvizhenie* was curbed, key sectors of the Soviet working class possessed important privileges. Efforts to help starving peasants could only have been at their expense.

This was particularly visible in the Donbass. Its historic connection with Stalinism was graphically manifest at the peak of the famine crisis. Akulov, the former head of Ukrainian trade unions, was transferred from the secret police to the Donbass as party secretary. He pushed through a 20 percent wage increase for Donbass coal miners, on top of considerable previous increases. More importantly, food supplies improved remarkably. In February 1933 miners received meat three times a week. On May 10, at the peak of the famine, Akulov gave them increased butter rations and daily extra rations of groats for their children, as well as two-course meals to take home to their families. The Ukrainian government was explicitly forbidden to transfer any of this bounty to anyone else.

Coal miners were relatively well paid under the Tsarist regime, even if miserably treated. During the NEP era they were one of the worst-paid sectors of the labor force, since their mines were part of the state sector of the economy. But after Shakhty they became some of the best paid workers in the Soviet Union. They kept this status until 1991, when the Soviet Union finally collapsed. During the 1930s, miners who had previously been disgruntled now

---

12 Pierre Broué, 'Trotsky et le bloc des oppositions de 1932', *Cahiers Leon Trotsky* 5 (Jan.–March 1980): 5–37; *Protiv Techeniia* no. 1, Oct. 1931, RGASPI, f. 17, op. 120, d. 68, l. 2–3; Kevin Murphy, *Revolution and Counterrevolution: Class Struggle in a Moscow Metal Factory* (New York: Berghahn Books, 2005), 209–10.

13 Lynne Viola, *Peasant Rebels under Stalin: Collectivization and the Culture of Peasant Resistance* (New York: Oxford University Press, 1996).

14 Davies, *Crisis and Progress*, 448–51; Fitzpatrick, *Education and Social Mobility*, 187–8; Vladimir Andrle, *Workers in Stalin's Russia: Industrialization and Social Change in a Planned Economy* (New York: St. Martin's Press, 1988), 34.

had excellent practical reasons to defend Stalin against all opposition. It is far from accidental that Stakhanovism, that effort to create a 'western' style labor aristocracy, was born in the Donbass, with coal miner Stakhanov as its very first labor hero.[15]

How could an allegedly proletarian regime allow millions of peasants to die? Due to its economic blunders there was simply not enough food to go around. The Soviet government ultimately rested on the support or at least tolerance of the Soviet working class. Therefore famine struck the peasants, not the workers – not despite the ultimately working-class nature of the regime, but because of it. Such were the unbelievable results of the Stalinist industrial revolution.

3 'Moderation', a Congress of Victors and Secret Dissidents

The exact famine death toll has been thoroughly investigated, but is still subject to dispute.[16] Major investment cutbacks and concessions to the peasantry prevented total catastrophe. There was a good harvest in 1933, and the situation and the regime stabilized in the aftermath. Oppositional groupings that had revived at the height of the crisis collapsed. Former Trotskyists were appointed to prominent posts. Trotsky's one-time lieutenant Yuri Piatakov now essentially ran Soviet heavy industry. His protégé, London's former Donugol supervisor Livshits, became Kaganovich's deputy in the railroad industry. Ukrainian revolutionary hero Yurii Kotsiubynsky was promoted to become the head of the Ukrainian Gosplan. A former Trotskyist student leader named Giorgii Vissarionovich Gvakhariia became famous as the director of the Kirov Iron and Steel plant, one of the largest in the world. He became a personal friend and favorite of Ordzhonikidze, celebrated in the Soviet press as a model factory director.[17] The Donbass party leader who succeeded Akulov was former Zinovievite Sarkisov. Akulov, former head of the coal miners' union and former

15 Davies, *Crisis and Progress*, 384–7.

16 Davies and Wheatcroft, *The Years of Hunger*, 231–67. They estimate a total 'excess death' toll from all causes of 5.5 million for the entire Soviet Union in 1932–3, including at least 2 million in Ukraine (406–17). (And 1.5 million in Kazakhstan, but with no censuses and a nomadic population capable of fleeing across the border to China, that was mostly guesswork. In Kazakhstan unlike Ukraine the disaster was blamed on local officials who were purged. Even Stalin belatedly opposed forcibly turning nomads into steppe farmers, it turned out.).

17 Francesco Benvenuti, 'Industry and Purge in the Donbass', *Europe-Asia Studies* 45 (1993): 57–78.

second in command of the secret police, now became the Soviet Procurator General. As far as he was concerned, the job of the secret police was reforming the enemies of socialism, not extirpating them.

Noah was transferred to Moscow and promoted as the crisis was overcome, and as Miril was suffering her nervous breakdown from witnessing the 'hunger plague'. He became Ginzburg's deputy as Sokolov replaced him at Donbassvodtrest, and when the Ukrainian government moved next year from Kharkov to Kiev the water trust moved to the Donbass, lost its shock status and immediately began to suffer drastic budget cuts.

The Londons had left Ukraine, the Soviet Jewish heartland. Moscow was far outside the Tsarist Jewish Pale. Only 'wealthy Jews who lack for nothing' had been allowed to live there back then and search out bathhouses to sweat in. The new Jewish population of Moscow was made up of postrevolutionary newcomers, seeking to climb the Soviet ladder of Jewish upward mobility in the capital. Whether successful bureaucrats and intellectuals or the poverty-stricken failures of Mar'ina Roshcha, Yiddish language and culture was the last thing most of them were interested in. Once when Rose addressed him in Yiddish in Moscow, London told her never to speak to him in that language in public. Their involvement in Jewish culture took on a subterranean character. With their close friends the Markishes, at the peak of the Soviet Yiddish cultural world, they mostly spoke Yiddish. However, they did not speak Russian very well, according to Ester.[18] In its way, that must have been as much a detriment at the top of the social pyramid as it was for the urban *luftmenschen* in Mar'ina Roshcha at the bottom. And for the Birobidzhan fiasco Peretz Markish was heralding in public, we know from Rose that Noah by then considered it a failure. Miril, as she recovered, got a job as a chemist again at Moscow's Institute of Mineral Resources. But she was never again able to publish papers and present them at conferences.

London dictated his manuscript six months after the so-called 'Congress of Victors' in February 1934, at which old opponents of Stalin lined up at the podium to praise him to the skies. Stalin seemed to bask in the unanimous approval and support of all Soviet Communists now that the regime had survived intact. A more moderate party policy was accompanied by steps towards a relaxation of repression. Dissidence perhaps seemed slightly safer now, with a national public prosecutor with whom London had worked in the past.[19]

18 Interview, John Holmes with Beatrice Holmes, Jan. 30, 1998; Markish interview.

19 Stephen G. Wheatcroft, 'Towards Explaining the Changing Levels of Stalinist Repression in the 1930s: Mass Killings', in *Challenging Traditional Views of Russian History* (New York: Palgrave Macmillan, 2002), 122–4.

Perhaps the speaker who best reflected the mood of the moment was tolerant Leningrad party boss Sergei Kirov. He had replaced Zinoviev there in 1926, but allowed many former Zinovievites to occupy posts in his administration. The most famous industrial achievement of this brief 'era of moderation', Belomor, the White Sea–Baltic Canal, was under his purview. This was the first large-scale industrial project using gulag labor, and the model for all future such projects. Maxim Gorky and other 'engineers of the human soul' glorified Belomor. It allegedly rehabilitated and spiritually regenerated its workforce. Kirov's Congress speech praised the 'heroic labor' of 'our Chekists' who 'literally performed miracles' in building it so quickly. He neglected to mention the sufferings of over 100,000 gulag inmates who built the project, many of whom died. Soviet publicists would boast of how many prisoners were freed or had their sentences shortened, but even secret Soviet records maintain silence over the number of victims.[20] Nor did Noah London discuss their fate in the manuscript, many pages of which are devoted to his opposition to canal projects.

An explosion of bureaucratic privilege served as lubricant for the capitulation of Stalin's ex-critics. Former worker-Bolsheviks made up much of the Soviet apparatus. They had undergone untold hardship and stress during world war, revolution and civil war. As 'petty-bourgeois egalitarianism' came to an end, they received far greater privileges than did Donbass coal miners. But Stalin did not trust the authenticity of this support. He feared that, as Trotsky put it, 'there are those who ... demand the expulsion of Rykov and Bukharin, swear oaths of loyalty to the unique beloved leader, and at the same time have at the back of their minds: how to betray to their own best advantage'. Quite a few party cadre became *dvurushniki* – 'two faced' public supporters of the regime who were private critics among circles of friends. The paradigmatic example of this phenomenon was the Leningrad Zinovievite circle, whom Stalin blamed for Kirov's assassination in 1934. Nikolaev, the assassin, was acquainted with some of them. He mentions them favorably in his diary, which makes clear that his motivations for the assassination were political – ostensibly at any rate.[21]

---

20 Oleg Khlevniuk, *The History of the Gulag: From Collectivization to the Great Terror*, trans. Vadim A. Staklo (New Haven, CT: Yale University Press, 2004), 35–6; Dmitri Volkogonov, *Stalin: Triumph and Tragedy*, trans. and ed. H. Shukman (New York: Grove Weidenfeld, 1991), 195. Alla Kirilina, Kirov's biographer, maintains that he did intervene to improve the material condition of the prisoners, but concedes that this seems to have been solely in the interest of more production. *Neizvestnyi Kirov* (St. Petersburg: Neva, 2001), 127–30.

21 Trotsky quote in Anthony D'Agostino, *Soviet Succession Struggles: Kremlinology and the Russian Question from Lenin to Gorbachev* (Boston: Allen & Unwin, 1988), 124; Kirilina, *Neizvestnyi Kirov*, 257–9, and diary mention of the Zinovievites, 276.

But there were also *dvurushniki* who were former Stalinists, especially in famine-ridden Ukraine. Pavel Postyshev, the Kharkov party leader when London was at Donugol, was sent back from Moscow to purge the Ukrainian party of all troublemakers. He waged a bitter campaign against an alleged Trotskyist-Ukrainian nationalist alliance of secret followers of Rakovsky and Skrypnik. Kotsiubynsky was purged as just such a *dvurushnik* shortly after the Congress of Victors.

Another alleged *dvurushnik* was a Jewish protégé of Postyshev named Mikhailo Markovich Killerog. He played a fairly prominent role in Postyshev's entourage. Notably, he headed the Ukrainian party's National Minorities Department and oversaw UkrOZET. He must have had regular contact with Noah London, its regional director when Kharkov was the Ukrainian capital. It would seem possible that he cautiously shared his secretive dissidence with underling Noah. One-time Trotskyist Lev Kopelev depicted Killerog as a 'fop with a necktie' and a 'strutting pigeon' in his memoirs. Killerog fell into disfavor for 'rotten liberalism' in purging cultural institutions such as UkrOZET. He was arrested as a Trotskyist in 1936.[22]

There were many similar cases in Ukraine in the mid-1930s. What makes the Killerog case interesting is that the accusations were not baseless. In the 1920s, Killerog had been an active and thoroughly loyal Kiev Stalinist. But he was also a personal friend of several well-known Trotskyists (though not of Kopelev). In the aftermath of the famine he and a few of his old friends, all of whom had capitulated to Stalin, started criticizing forced collectivization and the absence of democracy in the party in private conversations – among whom a cautious Noah was presumably not included. According to one Ukrainian historian, 'Similar complaints were fairly widespread in party circles and reflected thoughts and moods of unprejudiced Communists of, one might say, prestalinist formation'.[23] Purges and arrests of such 'Trotskyists' ravaged the Ukrainian party in the mid-1930s, and in 1937 Killerog and his friends were executed as members of a 'parallel Ukrainian Trotskyist center' allegedly plotting to assassinate additional Soviet leaders besides Kirov.

22 TsDAHO, f. 1, op. 20, d. 6213 (circulars from Killerog); Kopelev, *Education of a True Believer*, 190–3; Arkadiy Naberukhin, 'Odyn z Psevdotrots'kistiv', *Z Arkhiviv VUChK, HPU, NKVD, KHB* 1/2 (1995): 341–5.

23 Naberukhin, 'Odyn z Psevdotrots'kistiv', 347.

4 Stalinist Party Purges and the Soviet Working Class

Stalinist purges of the CPSU were not a direct continuum leading up smoothly to the Great Purge of 1937–8. The first Stalinist purge in 1929 reflected to some degree the original conception of a party purge as a tool to rid it of 'petty-bourgeois elements'. The 1921 party purge, the first, was initially advocated by the Workers Opposition. The 1929–30 purge was directed primarily at administrative and rural party cells. London had passed that test with relatively flying colors. Workplace meetings were the vehicle of this purge at Donugol and elsewhere. They were a vital component of the 'cultural revolution' and cleared the way for the mass recruitment of workers into the party. In percentage terms, the CPSU was more blue-collar by 1932 than it had been since 1917, and certainly more than it ever would be thereafter.[24] Workers who supported the Bolshevik Revolution in 1917 were a solid majority but not the entire working class. And the working class itself was a fairly small percentage of the population of the Tsarist Empire. By the 1930s, the revolutionary-minded workers of 1917 overwhelmingly had been recruited into the Soviet bureaucracy or had fallen victim to the Civil War, or disease, or famine, or purges – if they were still politically active at all.

For that matter, hundreds of thousands of workers were perhaps not terribly enthusiastic about communism and world revolution but had, for whatever reason, stood behind the regime during the post-Civil War crisis whose peak was Kronstadt. Such workers joined the party on a massive scale during Zinoviev's 'Lenin Levy' of the mid-1920s. Simple arithmetic makes one suspect that many of the workers recruited to the party during the 'Stalin Levy' of the Stalinist cultural revolution, or at least remaining veterans of 1917 among them, were participants in the great strike wave of the terrible winter that preceded the adoption of the NEP in 1921. In the case files of Great Purge victims I am familiar with, references to that strike wave are noticeably absent. It was a rebellion against party-imposed sacrifices for the sake of the Revolution. Anti-Bolshevik worker moods in 1921 were sometimes colored with anti-Semitism, and often directed personally against Trotsky, militarizer of labor and impractical world revolutionary.

A decade later, Stalinist anti-Trotskyism was a natural evolution of such lower class moods in the context of rapid promotion of workers into a privileged Stalinist bureaucracy. Backward attitudes in backward sectors of the

24 Getty, *Origins of the Great Purges*, 38–48; T.H. Rigby, *Communist Party Membership in the USSR, 1917–1967* (Princeton, NJ: Princeton University Press, 1968), 176–90.

working class such as white racism are not a uniquely American phenomenon due to 'white skin privilege' or an ideological disorder.

The purge in the aftermath of the famine crisis differed from previous episodes, when party members were kicked out for various misdeeds, real or alleged, but which infrequently led to arrests or worse. The purge resolution targeted 'open and secret violators of the iron discipline of the party and state', as well as 'degenerates ... who do not struggle against kulak elements'. Its aim was to get rid of party members who were rebellious or at least disquieted. The target was the more than a million new members recruited from the factories during Stalin's 'cultural revolution'.

Ukrainian party leader Postyshev, London's old Kharkov party boss, provided the justification. He wrote that before 1929, mass factory recruitment brought people into the party who were firmly rooted in the industrial working class, even if they were uninterested in politics. Or outright opponents of the regime, for that matter. But since 1929, new members were often just recruited to factories from the countryside. This was a perceptive analysis, which recommended him to Stalin for the task of purging the Ukrainian party, where dissidence was rife. 'Old Bolshevik' Postyshev's insights did not derive from Marxist acumen. As a former blue-collar worker himself, he had a better feel for working-class life than former intellectuals – as well as a disdain for peasants. And for that matter, for new factory workers who hadn't participated in the Revolution. These were all useful attitudes for a ruthless party purger.[25]

At the height of the 'cultural revolution' almost half of all party members were manual workers, and nearly two-thirds were workers by social origin. Now the door swung shut. Party membership declined by about 1.2 million during the 1933–4 purge, and another half million during the lesser purges of 1935 and 1936 – in total about as many as joined during the 'cultural revolution'. The door did not reopen until after the Great Terror. In its aftermath, the blue-collar percentage among new recruits dropped to 24 percent. When *vydvizheniia* ended, hundreds of thousands of brand new working-class party members were discontent. They had endured the hardships of the Soviet industrial revolution and shut their eyes to the suffering of their peasant brothers and sisters, but had not received the rewards they expected. Not a few sought social advancement through illegitimate means, since the legitimate path was closing. They exited *en masse*, nearly as many voluntarily as through purges. In sheer numbers, as late as 1935 the majority of purge victims at the local level were expelled

25 Postyshev, 'On Purging the Party', April 28, 1933; Getty and Naumov, *Road to Terror*, 125–7; Rigby, *Communist Party Membership*, 190–6.

for embezzlement and other forms of moral turpitude. By 1937, a thoroughly working-class party in terms of raw numbers had become a party of the bureaucracy and the intelligentsia.[26] Noah London was dismayed by this transformation. As he put it: 'Intellectuals ... invariably serve the master class and act as one of its most effective tools ... we have ... not a dictatorship of the proletariat, but a technocracy'.

There was a 'verification' and then an 'exchange' of party documents, especially membership cards, in 1935 and 1936. That new rising star in the hierarchy, Nikolai Yezhov, supervised it all, removing hundreds of thousands of members from the rolls, Killerog among others. This was a transitional affair between earlier purges and the Great Purge of 1937 and 1938, of the leadership itself. Its motivation was not the social crisis of 1932–3, but a response to the assassination of Kirov in 1934. The justification was the claim that Leningrad ex-Zinovievists were responsible for the assassination of Kirov.[27] The objective was to kick dangerous two-faced *dvurushniki* out of the party. Stalin and Yezhov were targeting former oppositionists, not rank-and-file disgruntlement. But Postyshev and other local leaders seem to have treated the new purges as a continuation of 1933–4, still directed essentially against an unreliable rank and file. In a secret 1936 Central Committee transcript Yezhov stated that in the 1935 'verification' alone, 'we have expelled over 200,000 party members'. An annoyed Stalin commented that 'that's quite a lot' and that 'if we expel 30,000 [instead] ... and if we also expel 600 former Trotskyites and Zinovievists, then we would gain even more from that'.[28]

Internal dissent after the Famine was still Postyshev's main concern. His Ukrainian witch hunt against an alleged Trotskyist-Ukrainian nationalist alliance was directed against political dissidence, however secretively expressed. Such as that of his former protégé Killerog – or Noah London.

---

26 Rigby, *Communist Party Membership*, 185–90, 200–31; Goldman, *Terror and Democracy*, 67.

27 Alla Kirilina, *Neizvestnyi Kirov*, St. Petersburg: Neva: 2001, 281–303. This comprehensive and highly informative biography of Kirov argues convincingly that Stalin and the NKVD were not behind the assassination of Kirov, nor were the Zinovievites. Kirov, it seems, was one of Stalin's few personal friends. Kirov's assassin apparently had a mixture of personal and political motives for the assassination. Matthew Lenoe's *The Kirov Murder and Soviet History*, based on her work and expanded with additional research, gives English readers a more accessible version of her findings.

28 Rigby, *Communist Party Membership*, 205–9; Getty *Origins of the Great Purges*, 58–91; Getty and Naumov, *Road to Terror*, 236.

5 The Fate of Pavel Postyshev

Postyshev was certainly a loyal Stalinist. He would collaborate enthusiastically with the Great Terror – indeed, overenthusiastically. But he was doomed, because he failed to grasp that it was not just an arbitrary product of totalitarian whims. It would serve the social interests of the incoming masters of the Soviet world. Continuing friction began between Postyshev and other Politburo members, who understood after getting advance word from Stalin at that secret meeting in 1936 what was really going on. His transfer under a cloud in February 1937 from Kiev to Kuibyshev, a midsized city on the Volga, would launch the Great Terror in Ukraine. Then, a January 1938 Central Committee plenum would be summoned to rein in 'excesses' such as Postyshev's in his new post. In Kuibyshev, he had automatically changed all prison sentences to execution and disbanded more than half of all party committees, shooting their membership. At the plenum, Postyshev bizarrely stated that 'I am not so completely insane as to call everyone an enemy of the people. I never said that, I spoke only of the leadership …' As Kaganovich put it, 'What Postyshev has said here … is a repetition of conversations that were hostile to the party. He doesn't seem to see that in the last year we have promoted more than 100,000 new people. This is a great Stalinist victory'.[29]

The enthusiasm with which other plenum participants would jump on Postyshev reflected more than just fear and herd instinct. Unlimited blind purges after the Postyshev model would have destroyed the regime just as Trotsky was then predicting. Criticism of his actions at the plenum struck an unusual note of sincerity. And not always of hostility. As Khrushchev put it: 'So it turns out that you didn't have a single capable person on hand. It turns out that there is no one to promote. What you are saying is wrong'. In Stalin's eyes Khrushchev, the new head of the Ukrainian party, was striking exactly the right note. He replaced Postyshev on the Politburo by the end of the plenum, and Postyshev was purged and shot not long afterwards. As historian J. Arch Getty put it: 'Many of those speaking up forcefully against Postyshev were representatives of the new generation, the new *nomenklatura*'.[30]

---

29 Volkogonov, *Stalin*, 312.

30 Getty and Naumov, *Road to Terror*, 504, 512.

6 Bureaucratic Privilege, American Relatives and the London Manuscript

As purges drove out the rank and file, elite privilege crystallized. When Noah London was transferred from Postyshev's Kharkov to Stalin's Moscow in the summer of 1933, he got a big bump in salary. The 'party maximum' was abolished in a secret decree in 1932. For most Soviet bureaucrats the new privileges cemented loyalty to the regime. For London the death of egalitarianism was the last straw. He became exactly what Stalin worried about, a two-faced *dvurushnik*, a secret dissident.

When Rose Risikoff visited the Londons in 1934, Noah was a Stalin enthusiast no longer. According to her memory, half a century later, 'London ... lived in an elegant Moscow neighborhood, and had a car, a chauffeur, and a dacha in the neighboring countryside. During the 1934 visit, London drove Rose to an exclusive country club where food and fresh fruit were lavishly available during a period of widespread public starvation. He did this to illustrate his commentary about life in the USSR'.[31]

Several years after she died, I interviewed her then-husband Louis Discher. He had long ago changed his name to Richard Lewis. A former leader of the left-wing United Office and Professional Workers Union, he was retired and lived in a beautiful home in North Berkeley. According to Dick Lewis:

> Rose became more and more disturbed. And felt that she had to make another trip to see Miril and Noah ... When she returned, she was very uncommunicative ... whereas after the 1930 trip she told me and other members of the family all about Miril and Noah, and what she had done, and where she had been, and so on ... the second trip ... I don't remember any such thing ... I think primarily because she felt she had to protect Noah and Miril, I'm sure that she not only didn't tell me but didn't tell any other members of the family ... I feel that the reason for secrecy was primarily because she ... had been pledged to it ...[32]

He kept a collection of his correspondence with Rose in an old shoebox, which he found shortly before he died at the age of 96. His daughter Lucy kindly allowed me access to these letters, which describe in copious detail Rose's two vacation trips to the workers' promised land.

---

31 Risikoff interview, Jay Holmes, Jan. 2, 1986, Noah London Collection. Tamiment Library.

32 Interview, John Holmes-Richard Lewis, Berkeley, CA, Dec. 4, 1992.

In 1934, she was caught up in radical fervor in the revolutionary heartland of Leningrad, on her way to meet them. She wrote her husband that 'we must come here together ... as soon as possible. What can be done to hasten our own movement to bring about a new order ...?' But when she got to Moscow, Noah and Miril spirited her away to the London dacha in Kliazma, a country retreat 30 kilometers outside the city limits. She described it as a 'rough log house with 2 other families', where the vacationing Londons lived 'very primitively, somewhat reminiscent of Tel Aviv', where her father Chaim had moved after retirement. There 'the three of us ... talked ourselves hoarse'. Noah's 'Notes on the USSR' was dictated among the pine trees in the woods outside the dacha.

Rose wrote Louis from the dacha that she was 'a little grieved at the still-difficult food situation, the injustices caused by scarcity ... Don't take any decisive political step, please'. He was considering when to join the party, of which she was a member. As soon as she returned to Moscow, she dashed off a note on London's Glavstroiprom stationery that 'there are many heart-breaking moments in USSR – not yet, alas, a workers' paradise. Indeed we shall have many many things to talk about ...'[33]

Meanwhile, Louis was sending Rose enthusiastic correspondence and *Daily Worker* press clippings about the 1934 San Francisco general strike. On August 2, she wrote him that 'I founder in the stream of things to be said to you ... Shall I write you what I feel in the maelstrom of movement & change & conflict? The experience has been enormously complicated by an intellectual encounter which I cannot relay in a letter'. She hinted at feelings of revulsion for bureaucratic privilege by recounting her day:

> 3–5. Again in Moscow store, tempted to buy small Persian rug for 300 rubles.
>
> 5–7. Chauffeur knocks over woman, we go to police court for a grilling. I go home by car ...
>
> What do I feel? About Mira – worried over her mental health. About Noah – complete admiration for a strong & fine personality. About USSR – will tell you ...

On August 9, she wrote 'do you understand, my dear, the source of my discontents or would you disown me as a renegade? ... Or perhaps I should not blast

33 Rose to Louis Discher, July 12, 17, 21 and 31, 1934, Lewis Collection.

your illusory bubbles about the promised land with the steely point of reason and observation. Marxism, Leninism, are still beautiful truths – life in USSR – fighting in a revolutionary situation guided by inexpert & bureaucratic leaders. (May no censor open this or I will be expelled!)' It seems he did not reply as desired. Her last letter was devoted to praising a movie about 'the love of the Eastern peoples for Lenin'. In its last scene 'the White Sea Canal, Dneprostroi, the subway' realize Lenin's dreams. 'What would He say if he could see our land now?' Noah denounces the White Sea Canal, Dneprostroi and the subway in the notes which she smuggled out of the Soviet Union but never revealed to her husband, maintaining that Lenin would never have permitted the waste and suffering they created.[34]

The original plan was to publish the manuscript she would put together out of these 'Notes on USSR' anonymously. Noah preferred 'to be labelled as a coward who does not dare to wage an open fight', as during the 1922 conflict in the Jewish Workers Federation, 'and to remain active within the movement, rather than to be driven into a position against it'. The purpose was to provide the socialist public a comprehensive analysis of the sad state of the movement, in the USSR and worldwide. Its portrait of bureaucratic privilege reminds one of Trotsky's *Revolution Betrayed.* And both London and Trotsky saw capitalist encirclement of the Soviet Union as the ultimate root cause of what Trotsky called Stalinism. But Noah London was no Trotskyist.

Trotsky argued that the Bolshevik Revolution was betrayed by a Stalinist bureaucracy comparable to those dominating Western labor organizations – such as London's Jewish garment unions in America. Trotsky, and London as well, maintained that this bureaucracy arose because of the poverty, backwardness and isolation of the USSR and post-revolutionary demoralization of the Soviet working class. Soviet officialdom had abandoned Lenin's dream of world revolution for Stalin's slogan of socialism in one country.[35] Noah London himself was one such official. He now believed that Lenin's ambitious vision was premature, and wanted reunification of the movement. Like his old ally Ludwig Lore, he wished to return to the good old days of the socialist movement of his youth, before war and revolution chopped it into two mutually hostile pieces.

London thought that breaking with the socialists to focus on world revolution had been premature in the 1920s because the workers were not ready for

34 Rose to Louis, Aug. 2, 4, 9 and 19, 1934; Lewis interview.

35 Leon Trotsky, *The Revolution Betrayed: What Is the Soviet Union and Where Is It Going?*, trans. Max Eastman (New York: Pathfinder, 1970 [1937]).

that in the West, at that moment at least. He was writing his secret manuscript in the immediate aftermath of Hitler's triumph in Germany. His 'Loreism' was less distant from Communist Party orthodoxy than ever before – or since. Socialist parties were moving leftwards, and becoming friendlier to their Communist rivals. There was a united front against fascism that summer between the Communist and Socialist parties in France. The concept of 'organic unity' – i.e. fusion of the two parties – was in the air. Noah London saw France as the example to follow worldwide, though he had little interest in what he described as the 'bloodless, sapless' American Socialist Party.

But the Comintern was about to make a dramatic turn to the right, moving from united fronts to 'popular fronts'. By 1936 the CPUSA was supporting President Roosevelt, the Democratic Party and the New Deal. The Spanish Communist Party was engaged in bloody warfare against 'Trotzkyite fifth columnists' in the Republican camp, over some opposition from Spanish Socialists.

'Rightists' in the USSR such as Nikolai Bukharin strongly supported the new Comintern Popular Front strategy, which he may have played a role in formulating. Bukharin called for creating a broad popular anti-fascist movement in the pages of *Izvestiia*, which he edited, before this became the official party line. He enthusiastically supported the arrest and execution of real and alleged 'Trotzkyites' – even after he himself was arrested. The Politburo decision in the early fall of 1936 to intervene into the Spanish Civil War coincided with an initial decision to drop charges against Bukharin 'for lack of evidence'.[36]

Noah London's protégé Sokolov was to tell NKVD interrogators that London hoped for a Left-Right party bloc to displace Stalin.[37] This would have been a Soviet equivalent of the Spanish POUM, the radical movement whose story George Orwell told in *Homage to Catalonia*. Spanish workers seemed to Orwell and many others to be at least as ready for revolution in the 1930s as were Russian workers in 1917.

Rose divorced Louis and married Seymour Risikoff. According to Louis Discher/Dick Lewis,

> Rose never said anything about the Londons, the first word that I had of possible political differences were about Spain. I started to hear very vague rumors, your ex-wife is siding with the POUM, the Trotskyists … And the rumors started to circulate then that Rose and Si were Trotskyists …

36 D'Agostino, *Soviet Succession Struggles*, 142–8.

37 Sokolov testimony, Sokolov case file, l. 17.

> politics had nothing at all to do with [the divorce], we were both very active in the union. Rose was still active, very active, in the Teachers' Union, and I was very active in the Office Workers Union.[38]

Like the Office Workers Union, the New York Teachers Union was dominated by the Communist Party in this period. It enthusiastically supported the Communist 'Popular Front' policy in America and Soviet intervention into the Spanish Civil War and spoke out on behalf of the CP-backed Abraham Lincoln Brigade, Americans who took up guns and put their bodies on the line for the Spanish Republic in the struggle against Franco. But an opposition movement developed in the Teachers Union, the United Progressives, backed by Jay Lovestone's American 'Bukharinists'. It called for more union democracy and more militant union policies.[39] Did Rose stay with the Communist Party caucus to 'bore from within', or did she join the United Progressives? Either way, this would be consistent with the ideas Noah London expressed in the notes he dictated to her in 1934.

He would describe himself as a 'rightist' under interrogation in 1937, somebody who like Bukharin was dubious about the frantic pace of the Stalinist 'Industrial Revolution' and compulsory collectivization. But his political approach was at least as distant from the top-down moderatism of a Bukharin or a Gorbachev as from Trotsky, who, like the deceased Lenin, still saw the only possible solution for the problems of the Soviet Union in spreading workers' revolution worldwide. He disagrees respectfully in the manuscript with Trotsky, but barely mentions the Right Opposition. Its leader, Bukharin, was fervently loyal to Stalin in 1934.

6.1 *London and Soviet Industrial Policy*

Much of the manuscript is devoted to acid criticism of Soviet industrial policy. Metrostroi, the Moscow subway project, was his central target. London had recruited a couple of former New York subway co-workers to join him in the USSR. They were Ben Levine and Joe Mekhanik, a friend of Noah's brother Harry. Levine became a Moscow subway engineer.[40]

The subway was a major prestige project, overseen by Lazar Kaganovich with the involvement of his then-protégé Nikita Khrushchev as well. The huge construction budget was a major economic drain. In London's opinion, all Moscow

38 Lewis interview.

39 Clarence Taylor, *Reds at the Blackboard: Communism, Civil Rights and the New York Teachers Union* (New York, Columbia University Press, 2013), 34–56.

40 Risikoff interview; letter, Rose to Louis, July 7, 1934; Morris London interview, April 7, 2005.

really needed then was buses. As he himself was a New York subway engineer, his opinion of the project deserves quoting at length:

> There is a story about an old Polish noble, Radzivir, who spent most of his time in Paris. Once he reminded himself of his estate in dark Russia and old memories awoke in him a desire to go sleighing and bear hunting. He sent word to the management of his estate that he was coming and that he wanted to be met by his sleigh troika. This was sometime in June. One of the men, Mishka by name (every Polish noble has his Jew Mishka to serve him) spread salt all the way from the main road to the estate. Such methods are designated in Russian by the word *samodur* [petty tyranny]. The present Russian nobility, some of them recently themselves Mishkas, have inherited the same methods …
>
> The pyramids were apparently built by some Ramses who wanted posterity to know about his greatness. Medieval lords built fancy castles. Peter the Great had the building craze albeit with more practical results. Now our own Russian overlords who have ceased to be ordinary humans are building monuments to surpass the world. So Kaganovich beautifies Moscow, Petrovsky beautifies Kharkov, another viceroy introduces new ways of plowing fields and sowing from airplanes, but the harvests, alas, zero. All the viceroys of the USSR are making monuments for themselves.

London acidly criticized its costly deep tunnels. But they became a vital rallying ground during the siege of Moscow, safe from artillery fire and aerial bombardment – and the Battle of Moscow was the turning point of World War II. Moreover, the subway is highly valuable for the people of Moscow and a major focus of civic pride. When I was given the opportunity to report my research in stumbling Russian to a history working group of the Russian Academy of Sciences in Moscow, reactions to Noah London's opinion of the subway system ranged from astonishment to amusement.

One might argue that London was wrong about the subway system. But since the USSR lacked sufficient resources for all the many things that it needed in the 1930s, such questions are unanswerable. London accepted the Stalinist framework of 'socialism in one country'. Within its confines, a Metrostroi or a Magnitigorsk could only be built 'at the expense of the bread, life and health of the workers'.

During what historians have described as the 'three good years' of the Soviet economy, from 1934 to 1936, there was a definite shift in investment from heavy industry to consumer needs, and the popular standard of living recovered considerably. Noah London wanted to go much, much further. In Soviet political terminology, London's industrial priorities were 'Khrushchevist', with their prime focus on popular welfare. But if the Soviet regime had seriously tried to follow the ideas in London's manuscript in the 1930s, it would have immediately run up against the natural limitations that Khrushchev would butt his head against as Stalin's heir.[41]

Noah London's sharpest critique was directed at his own prime area of expertise, water construction – in particular, against canal projects. His remarkable statement in the manuscript that *all* means are justifiable to oppose them surely had something to do with their notorious abuse of gulag labor. The wasteful and deadly Stalinist mania for canal construction was finally exorcised by Stalin's last police chief, Lavrenti Beria, after Stalin's death in 1953.

6.2 *Noah London versus Technocracy*

London dictated his 'Notes' in the summer of 1934 while serving as Glavstroiprom director Ginzburg's deputy. Ginzburg was closely associated with NKTP head Ordzhonikidze, who committed suicide in 1937. Ginzburg survived and went on to become Minister of Construction under Stalin, Khrushchev and Brezhnev. During the collapse of the Soviet Union, pensioner Ginzburg publicly suggested that Ordzhonikidze was murdered by Stalin. The Khrushchevish minimalist industrial policy focused on popular welfare that London advocated was different from Ordzhonikidze's policies – as different as the Comintern policy London advocated was from Bukharin's popular frontism. Ordzhonikidze tried to defend his industrial managers against accusations of wrecking, and perhaps represented a certain technocratic trend in the Soviet leadership. But technocracy was the main menace London feared.[42]

Noah London viewed Stalin as a last guardian in the Politburo of communist egalitarianism. He preferred Stalin to his entourage, the 'new class which surrounds him', technocrats like Ordzhonikidze and 'viceroys' like Kaganovich, the most skillful flatterer, or Leningrad party boss Kirov. This attitude perhaps facilitated his survival in office somewhat longer than many other industrial managers. In London's opinion: 'The danger of the ruling class moving away from communism becomes greater as Stalin ages and gives over his functions to others'. Stalin's speech at the 1934 Congress of Victors was largely devoted to the struggle against 'bureaucrats and red-tapists'. Like many others, Noah was fooled by the image of asceticism Stalin projected. A life of bourgeois luxury

---

41 Davies, *Years of Progress*, 2014.

42 Khlevniuk, *In Stalin's Shadow*, 40–62; Bailes, *Technology and Society*, 141–56; Ginzburg, 'O gibeli Sergo Ordzhonikidze', *Vorprosy Istorii KPSS* 3 (1991); Khlevniuk, *In Stalin's Shadow*, 154–7.

lay behind an external proletarian facade. When Stalin's wife committed suicide in the fall of 1932, at the height of the Famine, she apparently took to her grave whatever personal commitment he still had to egalitarianism.[43]

The manuscript is unfinished. From the Caucasian resort town of Kislovodsk, Noah wrote to Rose in the fall that 'I was figuring to continue the work started in Kliazma. But ... it is not convenient to do it alone, there is no stimulus and inspiration ... You will have to come next year ... and then we shall find time somewhere in the hills to work'.[44]

That did not happen. He managed to smuggle a conclusion into a subsequent letter he wrote her from Siberia, on an industrial expedition. He packaged it in an elaborate Siberian fantasy, presumably to mislead censors. In it, he places the blame for Stalinism on the Soviet Union's encirclement by bourgeois enemies, and concludes ambiguously that 'the new class has become the victor ... The proletariat has *created the Siberian empire* because it is easier to conquer nature than to change the minds of peoples. Backed at the wall the Bolsheviks have created a superior civilization in technique than had hitherto been created in history by other classes'.[45]

It seems that Noah was vacillating about whether or not to publish the manuscript, even anonymously. According to another letter, 'I am sorry ... we had so little opportunity together to fix certain matters for an opportune time, though, one thing is to profess something, and quite the opposite is to say it under conditions and among people ... whom you consider your enemies ... Miril & I had our small quarrel on account of the books arrangement'.[46]

Likely he was hinting that Miril opposed publishing it, and Rose never did. Unlike Noah, Miril continued to participate in party life. According to her gulag letter to Beria, at the Mineral Institute she 'was party organizer of the chemical laboratory, discussion leader and propagandist. Always and at all enumerated jobs I strove to carry out the line of the party'. In the mid-1930s that was not the role expected of a wife of an industrial manager. Instead, they were encouraged to join the woman activist movement organized around a journal called *Obshchestvennitsa* (Lady Social Worker). This 'wives movement' originated in Noah London's Commissariat of Heavy Industry under the patronage of his top boss, Sergo Ordzhonikidze. Its job was to make society more cultured. Elite wives in industry were expected to ameliorate and prettify their husband's work

43 Stalin, 'Questions of Organizational Leadership', Jan. 28, 1934, Getty and Naumov, *Road to Terror*, 132–4; Radzinsky, *Stalin*, 300–1; Volkogonov, *Stalin*, 146.

44 Noah to 'little sis', Fall 1934.

45 Noah to Rose, Jan. 26, 1935.

46 Noah to Rose, May 30, 1935.

environments and the quality of life of the employees and their own selves through volunteer work and invitation only charity balls and give their husbands happy homes.[47] This was hardly Miril's conception of 'the family as a fighting unit for socialism'. She and her sisters could not be described as feminists, but they certainly believed in women's liberation. And this was definitely not that.

The world of Soviet industrial construction did not look good from Noah's vantage point at the top of the pyramid. In 1934,

> most of the work, even of the heavy industries in the vicinity of Moscow, had to be stopped because there was a shortage of construction materials and because the transport system could not deliver more materials than those absorbed by the subway and Volga Canal enterprises. Needless to say, almost all construction of homes, schools, hospitals, roads, and water works was curtailed because of scarcity of labor and even more importantly a lack of barracks for quartering workers ... The capital investment on the subway and canal for Moscow alone is larger than the capital investment for hospitals and public health all over the union.

Ordzhonikidze's regime in the NKTP was the classic example of the Soviet patron/client model. 'Sergo' protected 'his' people from the NKVD, but allowed them no space for creative thinking.[48] As London put it: 'The slogan now is to acquire technique. The slogan nowadays is less interference in business by politics and politicians. The rule is "all power to the manager". The rule is "shut up or we will shut you up."' The problem was not party domination but the strangling of the party by the bureaucratic machine: 'Rakovsky, the former staunch Trotskyite, used to call the party a category. Now even as such it is fading away. Should history proceed undisturbed, it will slowly do to the party what another dictatorship did brutally to its storm troops'. As things turned out, it was done quite rapidly.

7 London and Ginzburg

London's relations with Ginzburg at Glavstroiprom were not smooth. In his memoirs, Ginzburg conspicuously avoids mentioning Noah London's very

47 Fitzpatrick, *Everyday Stalinism*, 156–60.
48 Bailes, *Technology and Society*, 141–59.

existence. The memoirs do not indicate any sympathy whatsoever for a populist industrial policy. Instead, they emphasize the crucial role of Glavstroiprom construction programs in defeating the Nazis, especially what Noah called the 'Brest theory' of creating an alternate industrial base east of the Ural Mountains. London concedes in the manuscript that moving industry eastward did have 'this one absolutely positive feature, that unlike the Tsarist government, the USSR is now in case of an emergency, war, or blockade less dependent on the outside world than it ever was'. Ironically, even the 'purely civilian' Moscow subway system turned out to be a stellar example of the usefulness of Stalinist industrial priorities for military purposes.

While on vacation in Kislovodsk in the fall of 1934, Noah wrote Rose a letter about a new NKTP sanitarium being built there.[49] Rose herself visited Kislovodsk with Miril on her earlier visit in 1931. She described to her husband how at this beautiful resort, attractively perched on a hillside, 'narrow cobbled lanes wind about the incline. Throngs of well-dressed people (for USSR) parade in the gutter swinging Caucasian can bamboo sticks or carrying tiny silk parasols with long fringes. There is a huge park with orchestra, landscape gardens. And mineral springs bubbling out of the earth'.[50] But by 1935, this was no longer enough. 'Of course you might think', Noah wrote, 'that we have not solved yet our more urgent problems. For this one must have patience. We shall begin from those who *run* the industry, then when we get richer, we shall extend those benefits to those who *make* things'.[51]

8 'Londonism' versus 'Piatakovism'

London would blame People's Commissariat of Heavy Industry (NKTP) deputy director Yuri Piatakov for 'sabotage' of meeting Donbass water needs during the Great Terror. In the late 1920s, London had opposed alleged Trotskyist 'left phrasemaking' and 'superindustrialization'. Many Trotskyist 'capitulators', Piatakov especially, were won over by Stalin's authentic superindustrialization during the first Five-Year Plan. They believed that the problems of Soviet society were all due to industrial backwardness, and could only be solved through industrialization *at all cost*. 'Piatakovism' is an appropriate name for this concept.

49 Letter from Kislovodsk, Appendix C.
50 Rose to Louis Discher, Kislovodsk, Aug. 8, 1931, Lewis Collection.
51 Noah to 'little sis', Fall 1934; 'Protokol doprosa Londona', 11.

Piatakov, the son of an Ukrainian sugar magnate, was a true technocrat. His own conception of socialism was of 'building the first system of state industry in history'. His former mentor Trotsky described Piatakov after his capitulation to Stalin as a 'politically finished man', recounting how Piatakov had more than once told him that he wanted to leave politics and become a 'specialist'. Trotsky would reply 'half-jokingly and half-seriously, that if one fine morning, he awoke to find himself under a Bonaparte, he would still take his briefcase and head for the office'.[52] Not long afterwards, Trotsky started describing the Stalin regime as 'Bonapartist'. According to Piatakov's biographer he was the true architect of the NKTP:

> It was Piatakov who chose much of the higher echelons of the commissariat on the basis of merit, competence and devotion … It was he who made the NKTP into a 'reactionary' structure, as some American authors have written, grotesquely commenting on the prevalence of people with higher education and of 'dubious' social origin in its leadership. It was he who perfected the cultivated version of … methods to keep the bureaucratic machine under pressure …[53]

Ex-oppositionists like Piatakov were Noah London's polar opposites. Whereas 'Londonism' focused on workers' immediate needs and perhaps slighted longer-term necessities, 'Piatakovism' did the reverse. At Donugol London did not care for Piatakov's protégé Lifshits, who had little interest in housing for coal miners. London would claim during the 1937 water hearings that everybody knew that he and Ginzburg had continual problems with Piatakov:

> I can provide an example. We pushed through a Central Committee resolution, with great difficulty, about organizing the basis of construction. This Politburo resolution, Piatakov didn't carry it out. He didn't say that I won't … but from one quarter to the next he didn't give any money. A number of times Ginzburg had to write to Piatakov to ask him why a Central Committee resolution was not obligatory for him. It was impossible to talk to him in person, he was a big shot [*vel'mozh*].[54]

52 Andrea Graziosi, 'Piatakov's VSNKh and the Crisis of the NEP', *Cahiers du monde russe et sovietique* 36, no. 4 (1991): 539–80; Trotsky to Ishchenko, 'Pyatakov: A Politically Finished Man', March 17, 1928, in *Challenge of the Left Opposition (1928–1929)*, 64.

53 Graziosi, 'Piatakov's VSNKh', 54.

54 NKTP water comm., *kapstroi*, April 17, 1937, RGAE, f. 5679, l. 35.

Glavstroiprom records preserve an exchange London had with another ex-Trotskyist capitulator associated with Piatakov, Yakov Drobnis. According to Leon Trotsky, during the Civil War Drobnis was 'the chairman of the Poltava Soviet, whom the Whites placed before the firing squad but in their haste did not wound mortally. If Soviet power was able to maintain itself from 1918 to 1921, it was in large measure due to people of this type'. London first encountered a burnt-out Drobnis as editor of the Soviet technical journal on highway construction, when Noah was Ukraine's head highway engineer. Under Drobnis's editorship the journal distinguished itself by the supplicant tone of its hymns to Stalin and the party.[55] In 1935 Drobnis was the deputy director of Kemerokombinatstroi (KKS), the Kemerovo industrial construction trust in the Kuzbass, a new coal-mining region being developed in western Siberia. KKS employed some 30,000 of the 130,000 inhabitants of a brand-new city that, like Magnitigorsk, arose abruptly out of nothing during the Stalinist industrial revolution.

London complained to Drobnis about his budget for a major coal-distilling plant: 'On reviewing the list of estimates ... it turns out that ... estimates for communal-living and socialist-cultural equippage are completely absent'. Drobnis promptly sent off a new budget to London and the construction workers' union, appealing for their support for additional funds for cultural facilities. London backed this appeal with a letter to the head of the NKTP planning sector. He pointed out that 'satisfying the cultural needs of the workers and engineers at ... KKS stands on an extremely low level – in a city of 130,000 there isn't a single movie theater'. But he could hardly have had great enthusiasm for the new budget. The new plan included 2 million rubles for a club for 2,000 workers – and a million and a half for a rest home for 70 engineers![56] Kemerovo would play a fateful role in the Great Terror. Undoubtedly that is why this correspondence was preserved while other records relating to London were destroyed.

9 On the Eve of the Great Terror

Noah left Glavstroiprom in March 1936. His departure does not seem to have been voluntary. In the lists of industrial officials subject to purge compiled by

55 Trotsky, 'A New Moscow Amalgam', Jan. 21, 1937, *Writings of Leon Trotsky (1936–1937)* (New York: Pathfinder, 1978), 121; *Dorozhnoe Khoziaistvo i Avtotrans*, *passim*, 1929.

56 London to Kruglikov, Dec. 16, 1935, Drobnis to *TsK profsoiuza stroitel'stva tiazheloi promyshlennosti*, Dec. 12, 1935, London to Drobnis, Oct. 2, 1935, RGAE, f. 5679 (Glavstroiprom), op. 1, d. 52, l. 13–15ob. and 34.

Malenkov on the eve of the Great Terror, one states that he was fired. Another, and his job book, states that he was transferred to a new job. In fact, he became one of three deputy directors of Glavneft, the oil trust, in charge of capital construction. His monthly salary more than tripled, to the remarkable sum of 1,700 rubles a month. The fear he had hinted at in his last letter to Rose that he was about to be purged turned out to be premature. It is a good guess that his patrons in high places rescued him.

This was clearly an important job. Oil production was a problematic weak link of Soviet industry during the 1930s.[57] But Noah London had no particular interest in it. The plentiful but dull London materials in the Glavneft collection in the economic archives make this clear. He was always more interested in coal mines than oil wells. His American friends and co-workers Joe Mekhanik and Ben Levine returned to America. Levine put in a stint at Glavneft first, and taught engineering at London's old alma mater, Cooper Union, after his return to America.[58]

Noah London's name was never used in public at Glavneft. Ordzhonikidze's September 1936 Glavneft directive published in the oil industry journal assigns specific tasks to a whole series of trust officials by name. It refers to London only as 'the deputy director for capital construction'. Even a top-secret report on Glavneft to Molotov during the Great Terror would follow this peculiar xenophobic convention. Such a high status for a foreigner as late as 1937 must have been an embarrassment, and the obscure circumstances of his departure from Glavstroiprom surely played a role. London's name appears in the NKTP journal only once in this period, as one of a long list of co-signers of a Glavneft letter published when Ordzhonikidze died.[59]

Paul Novick visited the Londons again in Moscow in 1936. According to Novick:

> I used to spend a lot of time with them, and I remember he had the disposition of, a *droshky* in Russian, a horse and wagon, a little coach, you know ... he also had an auto. The driver's name was Kalinin [chuckles] ... so one day he gave us the disposition, and we went around Moscow ... and

57 Davies and Wheafcroft, *Years of Hunger*, 201, 310–11, 321.

58 RGASPI, f. 17, op. 71, d. 42, l. 105 and d. 43, l. 54; *Trudoviy spysok*, RGAE, f. 7297; Glavneft personnel list, Aug. 25, 1937, RGAE, Moscow, f. 7734, op. 7, d. 259, l. 31; 'Protokol doprosa Londona', *passim*; RGAE, *trudovii spiski*, d. 2835, 'Beniamin Solomovich Levin', Aug. 28, 1936; Cooper Union personnel records.

59 'Prikaz po Narodnomu Komissariatu Tiazheloi Promyshlennosti No. 1480', Moscow, Sept. 5, 1936, *Neftianoe Khoziaistvo*, Sept. 1936, 4–7; RGASPI, f. 82, op. 2. d. 565 (oil, 1936–1940), l. 4–55; 'Novye neftianye raiony – delo energii Sergo', *Za Industrii*, Feb. 22, 1937.

> the time we spent in Moscow we saw him many times, by that time he was thoroughly dissatisfied … 'An American, an American, what are you doing here' … maybe he wasn't careful enough in his dissatisfaction …[60]

Rose Risikoff told my father in 1986 that Noah 'had several opportunities for assignments in Germany, and was tempted to accept and defect. However, Miril objected because of her continued faith in Communism'. This story perhaps came by way of Noah's older sister Rochlea, who was visiting the Londons in 1937 when they were arrested. He had taken a business trip to Germany in 1931, and the Molotov papers confirm that Glavneft had secret dealings with German firms as late as the spring of 1937.[61] If Noah was seriously considering trying to escape the USSR by way of Nazi Germany, he was truly getting desperate.

In that last letter sent Rose Risikoff, dated October 29, 1935, he had hinted that he foresaw 'all what is coming'. He asked the question,

> when things are approaching the end one wonders – who will know of all the beautiful, marvelous although simple eternal things we knew and lived through? Where is our inheritance – to whom do we leave it in what form? Where are the books, the poems that were not written! Who is it that we will orally tell, impart there should be a continuance of our life – where & who? Such are the moods we are in these days …[62]

As his great nephew, I have taken up that task. That secret dissident Noah London managed to avoid being purged until the Great Terror was in full swing in the fall of 1937 is more surprising than if his earlier fears of being purged had proven accurate. I hope I have helped to explain why. Noah managed for years to jump through the political hoops of a Stalinized Soviet Union nimbly, while still attempting, under the nose of higher authorities, to carry out policies he wanted. His balancing act crashed in 1937.

---

60 Novick interview.

61 Interview, Jay Holmes-Rose Risikoff, Jan. 2, 1986, Noah London Collection, Tamiment Library; letter, Mezhlauk and Molotov to Stalin, stamped secret, March 14, 1937, Molotov papers, RGASPI, f. 82, op. 2, d. 565 (oil), l. 4–5.

62 Noah to Rose, Oct. 29, 1935.

CHAPTER 13

The Fate of Noah and Miril London

The Moscow Trial of the summer of 1936 signaled that massive repression was impending. Zinoviev, Kamenev and a number of their followers were convicted of mounting a terrorist conspiracy to murder Kirov and other party leaders and were executed. Georgii Maksimilianovich Malenkov replaced Nikolai Ivanovich Yezhov as the head of the Department of Leading Party Organs (ORPO), as Yezhov became head of the NKVD. ORPO, the party membership registration sector, supervised purges. As the trial proceeded, Malenkov ordered his deputies to study the files of responsible economic administrators – members of the *nomenklatura*, designated by the Central Committee as the ruling caste of the Soviet Union – for any signs of oppositional or suspicious activity in their past. They found compromising material on as many as a quarter of all top industrial managers. Ordzhonikidze's Commissariat turned out to be one of the biggest havens for troublemakers like Noah London.[1]

ORPO drew up an entire series of industrial purge lists in the fall and winter of 1936–7. They now reside in the ORPO collection of materials on oppositional activity in the Moscow Central Committee archives. Noah London's name appears on several. Thus, on the January list of '*nomenklatura* workers in industry, having participated in opposition in the past, and having wavered', the ninth name is that of Glavneft deputy director Noah London, 'censured in 1925 for factional activity'. Some of these purge lists clarify that this censure occurred in the *American* Communist Party.[2] He had seemingly passed the 1929 Donugol purge with flying colors. But the purge commission noted his censure in the US for 'participating in the Lore group'.[3] This now came back to haunt him.

He was fired from his job at Glavneft on October 16, 1937. On October 29 the Central Administration of State Security (GUGB) of the NKVD issued order No. A664, for the arrest and search of Noi Moiseevich London. He was taken that same day from his posh Moscow apartment on Ulitsa Koniukovskaia, building 28, apartment 8. Both Miril and his older sister Rochlea were present. Rochlea, visiting from America, returned home immediately. His property was confis-

1 Khlevniuk, *1937-i*, 116–17; Getty and Naumov, *Road to Terror*, 281–2.

2 RGASPI, f. 17, op. 71, d. 42, l. 40, 105, 120; d. 43, l. 54 and 105.

3 Donugol purge commission, July 8–15, 1929, DAKhO, f. P-45, op. 2, d. 31, l. 69–70.

 | DOI:10.1163/9789004745384_015

cated, including his typewriter, camera, binoculars, and his party, union and cooperative membership cards. The protocol compiled by the arresting officer was perfunctory.[4]

On November 16, he signed a confession that he had been recruited in 1931 into an anti-Soviet conspiracy at Donbassvodtrest, and later at Glavstroiprom (case file, 10). (He and his boss Ginzburg briefly 'conspired' with Kaganovich and Ordzhonikidze against Stalin in the summer of 1931 to approve German pipe purchases.) On November 20 his interrogator, NKVD lieutenant Alievskii of the 14th Department of the Third Division of the GUGB, wrote up the indictment (*obvinitel'noe zakliuchenie*) for case 14510. According to said indictment 'the Third Division ... received reports that London Noi Moiseevich is a member of an anti-Soviet organization of rightists and that by his order wrecking was carried out in Donbass water construction. According to the same reports London also carried out spy work for German intelligence' (p. 124).

Having confessed to his crimes he was 'subject to trial by the Supreme Soviet Military Collegium according to the law of December 1, 1934' (p. 127). This Kirov assassination 'anti-terrorist' law had a certain resemblance to post-9/11 American 'anti-terrorist' jurisprudence, though vastly more intensive. On December 7, 1937, Stalin, Molotov and Zhdanov signed a list of people 'subject to trial by the Supreme Soviet Military Collegium'. Noah London was the 143rd name on the list, in alphabetical order. His secretary, Irina Mukhina, was number 165.[5]

The trial took place two days later on December 9, before military jurists Matulevich, Goriachev and Zhdan. When asked how he pleaded, he admitted that he was partially guilty. But he stated that his earlier confession to participating in a counter-revolutionary organization was false (*lozhnyi*). The head of the tribunal read out former Donbassvodtrest chief engineer Ivan Shakhov's declaration that London had recruited him into such an organization. He answered that Shakhov's declaration was also false. He had neither participated in nor recruited anyone into a counter-revolutionary organization.

He explained that there was a lot wrong with his work. He had boasted of it as a model despite defects in its execution bordering on wrecking. But he never engaged in conscious wrecking or espionage. The head of the tribunal proclaimed the trial over and offered him a final word. He asked the court to give him the possibility of expiating his guilt through honest labor. The tribunal

4 London case file; Rose Risikoff interview 1986; interviews with London nephews; *Sledstvennoe delo N.M. Londona* (London case file) R-46033, TsaFSB (former NKVD central archive), Moscow, l. 1–9.

5 Memorial archive, Moscow, AP RF, op. 24, d. 413, l. 256.

retired to consult and issued its verdict, condemning him to execution. The entire trial lasted 15 minutes, from 9:45 p.m. to 10 p.m. He was shot that very night.[6]

Noah London was executed at the height of a countrywide bloodbath. Due to its crucial role in the Soviet economy, the Donbass, Noah's primary field of work, was a major target. Up to a third of all Ukrainian victims were from the Donbass. Shortly before London's arrest Stalin declared at a Kremlin reception for Donbass industrial managers and Stakhanovites that 'leaders may come and go, but the people will stay and live forever'.[7] But the party elite were very far from the sole victims. Soviet citizens named this bacchanalia of mass murder the *Yezhovshchina* (dirty Yezhov business), after Nikolai Yezhov, its direct perpetrator. Elsewhere it has come to be known as the 'Great Terror' – the most mysterious moment in the history of the Soviet Union. Historians have written many volumes to try to explain it. Some 800,000 Soviet citizens were executed in 1937, 1938 and the beginning of 1939, about half the grand total of people executed in the entire history of the Soviet Union.

Noah London's top boss, Sergo Ordzhonikidze, was the only Soviet leader who showed any sign of resistance to the mounting frenzy. He committed suicide on the eve of that February–March 1937 Central Committee plenum, the longest in the history of the Soviet Communist Party. It approved a massive purge of 'Trotskyist wreckers' in the economic apparatus. Stalin's concluding speech asserted that 'Trotskyism … has been transformed into a frenzied, unprincipled gang of wreckers, saboteurs, spies and assassins working under the orders of the intelligence services of foreign governments'.[8] *Pravda* published this speech, circulated throughout the country in pamphlet form. It was Stalin's explanation for the Great Terror – and its operating manual. It was not a call for mass terror. Instead, it motivated and explained how to root out *dvurushniki*, evil-minded secret opponents of the regime, masterminded by Trotsky. As Stalin put it:

> In order to spoil and wreck, you don't need a great number of people at all. To build Dneprostroi, you have to put tens of thousands of workers to work. But to destroy it, you need perhaps a few dozen, no more. To win a battle in wartime, you need several corps of Red Army soldiers. To ruin

6 London case file, l. 128–32.

7 Valerii Vasiliev, 'The Great Terror in the Ukraine, 1936–1938', in *Stalin's Terror Revisited*, ed. M. Iliç (New York: Palgrave Macmillan, 2006), 144–6; Kuromiya, *Freedom and Terror in the Donbas*, 225, quote on 245.

8 Stalin, 'Report on Trotskyist wrecking', Moscow, March 3, 1937, *Voprosy Istorii* 1995 no. 3.

> this victory at the front, for this several spies … capable of stealing the strategic plans and giving them to the enemy are enough … (pp. 13–14)

Was Stalin just being paranoid? Was this all a mask for another secret agenda? By 1937 the Trotskyist underground no longer existed outside the gulag. But as modern Soviet historian Oleg Khlevniuk puts it, 'The complex relationship between war and revolution, which had almost seen the Tsarist regime toppled in 1905 and which finally brought its demise in 1917, was a relationship of which Stalin was acutely aware'.[9]

1 War and Revolution

> While before the revolution Russia had 1.5 million proletarians, we now have in the neighborhood of 15–20 million. These workers will become settled, stationary; they will begin to lead an organized life. In some way or other their wishes and desires will find expression. It is difficult to foresee the way, but the way will arise. And maybe then the second revolution will be made – whether by force or by reform will depend on many conditions.
>
> NOAH LONDON, 1934

Did actual fear of collapse of the Stalinist regime during wartime lie beneath the rhetoric about wrecking and spying? At a safe distance of decades, even Molotov expressed skepticism in his memoirs about confessions of oppositionists to terrorism and sabotage. Nonetheless, the Great Terror was justified, as he bluntly put it, 'for the sake of the main objective – keeping state power!' As Lazar Kaganovich told his admirer Felix Chuev:

> You see, my friend, in our conditions of capitalist encirclement there were so many governments at large … There was a Trotskyist government, a Zinovievist, a Rykovist, this was very dangerous and impossible … Who could believe that old, experienced conspirators, using all the experience of Bolshevik conspiracy and Bolshevik cooperation in underground organization, that these people would not link up and organize? … Trotsky, who was a good organizer, could lead an uprising … We see nowadays various coups in all countries.[10]

---

9 Khlevniuk, *In Stalin's Shadow*, 174.

10 Felix Chuev, *Molotov Remembers: Inside Kremlin Politics. Conversations with Felix Chuevy*,

Was Noah London the only Soviet official who privately believed that the Soviet Union could use a different government? According to Volkogonov, Stalin's best-informed biographer: 'No one in fact opposed Stalin's personal rule, but he sensed that many, especially the Leninist old guard, secretly did not approve of his brand of socialism'. After Soviet intelligence agent Ignace Reiss defected to the Trotskyists in France and was murdered by the NKVD, Trotsky wrote: 'In Stalin's apparatus there are not a few who are wavering. The crimes of the Kremlin lord and master are prodding and will prod them to take the path of breaking with a doomed regime of falsehood and corruption'. This was far from the first time he engaged in such speculations. London commented in the manuscript: 'Any article or saying of Trotsky published abroad has more influence over the fate of the USSR today than Trotsky himself ever had as a party leader in the Soviet Union'. Volkogonov similarly maintained that Stalin studied all Trotsky's writings with care, often shaping his policies according to them. Yezhov was sent to hunt for those whom Trotsky thought were wavering ...[11]

The Stalin-Bukharin regime whipped up a war scare after Britain broke diplomatic relations in the 1920s, to smother opposition with Soviet patriotism. Trotsky responded with his 'Clemenceau thesis' that if war came, the Left Opposition would continue to oppose an incompetent Stalinist leadership, seeking to seize direction over the war from its hands. During World War I, Georges Clemenceau won the premiership by campaigning against the French government's military blunders. This 'Clemenceau thesis' was the foundation stone of Stalinist accusations of Trotskyist treason in the 1930s.[12] Beneath an alleged fear of Trotskyist sabotage, the official excuse for the Great Terror, lay a more rational fear. Stalin and his entourage could be undermined by wartime failures, as Trotsky suggested.

It is not hard to understand Stalin's desire for a blood purge to intimidate his own bureaucracy on the eve of World War II. Without one, would he have survived the embarrassment of the Hitler-Stalin pact, or the catastrophe that ensued? According to certain Politburo witnesses, he offered to resign shortly after the German invasion but was dissuaded by his colleagues. What about those Politburo members whom Stalin distrusted sufficiently to have killed dur-

---

trans. Albert Resis (Chicago: Dee, 1993), 264–5; F. Chuev, 'Tak govoril Kaganovich: ispoved' stalinskogo apostola'. In *Kaganovich. Shepilov* (Moscow: Olma-Press, 2001), 187–9.

11 Trotsky, 'A Tragic Lesson', Sept. 21, 1937, in *Writings (1936–1937)*, 451; Volkogonov, *Stalin*, xxiii, 228, 254–5, quote on 279–80.

12 Isaac Deutscher, *The Prophet Unarmed: Trotsky, 1921–1929* (Oxford: Oxford University Press, 1970), 349–51.

ing the Terror? Might they have been more inclined to accept a resignation, or even demand one? Certainly Stalin worried about such things, and wisely so from his perspective.

The Stalinist regime would narrowly survive Operation Barbarossa. Control over besieged Moscow would break down on October 16, 1941. Bureaucrats were burning their documents and attempting to flee. Some workers joined the exodus. Others seized control over their factories to prevent evacuation, assaulted factory directors deserting their posts and participated in mass street blockages of cars trying to escape the next target of the Blitzkrieg. Riots broke out all over Moscow. According to a journalist on the scene's diary:

> Everyone is boiling with indignation, talking out loud, shouting that they have been betrayed ... People are beginning to remember and to count up all the humiliations, the oppressions, the injustices, the clampdowns, the bureaucratic arrogance of the officials, the conceit and the self-confidence of the party bureaucrats, the draconian decrees, the shortages, the systematic deception of the masses ...[13]

Stalin considered fleeing Moscow himself. A special train was prepared. His decision to stay and fight saved the situation. The wastefully expensive deep subway tunnels whose construction London opposed played a vital role in organizing the defense. They made possible the mobilization of Marshal Zhukov's counterattack, which nearly shattered the German army. The Nazi war machine came close to losing World War II then and there. The siege of Moscow was the turning point of World War II – and thus of world history as well. But it was a very close thing.[14] Fascism found a temporary place in Trotsky's 'dustbin of history', and Stalin's regime stabilized. The no-longer-necessary Great Terror was never renewed.

But why did the Soviet bureaucracy allow itself to be decimated without resistance? To understand this, top-level state and party documents are insufficient. A look at what was happening 'from below' in the lower reaches of the apparatus was necessary. For the story of the 'Great Purge' at Noah London's water trust, I found rich informative records. But they can only be understood

13 John Barber, 'The Moscow Crisis of October 1941', in *Soviet History, 1917–53: Essays in Honour of R.W. Davies*, ed. E.A. Rees (London: Palgrave Macmillan, 1995), 201–18; Anne Applebaum, 'How Hitler Could Have Won', *New York Review of Books*, Oct. 25, 2007: 34–6.

14 David M. Glantz and Jonathan M. House, *When Titans Clashed: How the Red Army Stopped Hitler*. (Lawrence: University Press of Kansas, 1995); Heinz Guderian, *Panzer Leader* (New York: Ballantine, 1959).

against the background of developments in Soviet industry – in general, as well as in the Donbass water industry in particular.

2 The Industrial Context of the First Stage of the Great Terror

The 1936 Moscow Trial was directed against Zinoviev and his followers – former Left Oppositionists who were sometimes in significant posts, but who did not play central roles in the Soviet state. It was this trial which impelled Malenkov's ORPO to compile purge lists. Real and alleged former Zinovievists and Trotskyists in the apparatus were fired and arrested all over the Soviet Union. Victims at this stage 'merely' numbered in the thousands. The signal for a grand-scale purge was the January 1937 Moscow Trial of 'Trotskyists', most of whose defendants were industrial managers. The key defendant was Trotsky's former industrial lieutenant Yuri Piatakov of the NKTP.[15] Defendant Boris Lifshitz, London's old boss at Donugol, was the key administrator of the railway system. The purge gathered steam at the immediately subsequent February–March Central Committee plenum, where Bukharin was arrested, Postyshev was demoted and Ordzhonikidze was originally supposed to deliver the main report on 'wrecking'. His suicide removed all brakes.

Why was industry the focus? Soviet industrial performance under, essentially, Piatakov's leadership in the mid-1930s, the 'three good years' of economic progress, was highly successful. Stalin declared at the February–March plenum that success had caused the complacency that allowed 'Trotskyist wreckers' to operate. The main focus of investment shifted from basic heavy industry to the defense industry, the favorite priority of London's boss Ginzburg, and light industry. The general citizenry appreciated the increased production of consumer goods. But problems were not far below the surface. In heavy industry, sharp investment cutbacks coincided with growing pressure to increase output with existing equipment, compounded by disregard for physical limitations at the heart of 'Stakhanovism', artificially creating a labor aristocracy by staging dramatic production feats for which carefully selected workers received credit and social privileges.[16] Something had to give.

---

15 Fitzpatrick, 'Stalin and the Making of a New Elite', in *The Cultural Front: Power and Culture in Revolutionary Russia*, ed. Fitzpatrick (Ithaca, NY: Cornell University Press, 1992), 170. Piatakov's famous co-defendant, Karl Radek, was assigned the role of human link between the industrial managers and the Nazis.

16 Roberta T. Manning, 'The Soviet Economic Crisis of 1936–1940 and the Great Purges', in *Stalinist Terror: New Perspectives*, ed. J.A. Getty and R.T. Manning (Cambridge: Cam-

The flashpoint was not an economic downturn, but an industrial accident. On September 23, 1936, an explosion at the Tsentralnaia mine, which supplied coking coal for Magnitigorsk, killed 10 coal miners and gravely injured another 14. Tsentralnaia was one of the largest and most important mines in the 'Kuzbass' or Kuznetz Basin, a new mining center in Western Siberia developed to supplement the Donbass, accurately foreseen as vulnerable to German occupation in World War II. Two days afterwards, Yezhov replaced Yagoda as head of the NKVD. Four days later, the Commissariat of Justice sent out a circular demanding that procurators review all industrial explosions, accidents and fires over the last few years.[17]

The disaster was the central pretext for the January Moscow trial, after which Piatakov, Lifshits, Drobnis and 13 other industrial managers and ex-Trotskyists were shot. Yakov Drobnis, in charge of industrial construction there at the time of the explosion, was a key witness at the November 1936 Kemerovo wrecking trial, an out-of-town tryout for the Moscow spectacular. Confessions were the only evidence of sabotage produced. Indeed a visiting delegation of Soviet-sympathetic French coal miners' union officials labeled the accusations false and fraudulent. The Soviet press had repeatedly held up the Kemerovo mines as models for others to emulate.[18]

Both miners' testimony at the trial and records of interrogations of accused engineers describe unbearable working conditions and grossly insufficient attention to safety. Stakhanovites often worked standing in water, the ventilation system functioned very poorly, and of the miserably inadequate funding assigned for safety precautions, only a quarter was even spent. Moreover, there were serious water problems. Articles denouncing 'wrecking' in Kemerovo filled the pages of the main Soviet water supply journal during 1937. Drobnis's interest in spending money on workers' welfare was less than London's, as we have seen. As Trotsky's son Leon Sedov put it: 'It is well known that under the weight of insupportable plans, under pressure from above, industrial managers axe all kinds of secondary budget needs by hook or by crook, especially when they go for workers' expenses'.[19]

---

bridge University Press, 1993), 116–41; Davies, 'Soviet Economy and the Launching of the Great Terror', in *Stalin's Terror Revisited*, ed. Melanie Ilič (Basingstoke: Palgrave Macmillan, 2006), 11–37; Davies, *Years of Progress, passim.*

17 Goldman, *Terror and Democracy*, 95–100.

18 Goldman, *Terror and Democracy*, 100–2; Khlevniuk, *In Stalin's Shadow*, 111–12; Vadim Z. Rogovin, *1937: Stalin's Year of Terror* (Oak Park, MI: Mehring, 102–4); Leon Sedov, 'Novotsibirskii protsess', *Biulleten' Oppozitsii* (*Bolshevikov-lenintsev*) no. 54–55 (March 1937), available at https://iskra-research.org/FI/BO/BO-54.shtml.

19 Goldman, *Terror and Democracy*, 102–3; S.M. Polonskii, *Vodosnabzhenie i sanitarnaia tekhnika* no. 8 (Aug. 1937); Sedov, 'Novotsibirskii protsess'.

During the First Five-Year Plan many workers supported Stalin's 'Second Revolution' for the same reasons Noah did at first, and industrial disasters could be written off as necessary sacrifices for the cause. By 1936 this was no longer the case. Revolutions often stem from rising expectations. The USSR had allegedly achieved socialism, but the upward mobility of the 'cultural revolution' was now choked off. The explosion of bureaucratic privilege eased the pain of capitulation for tired, burnt-out former revolutionary heroes like Drobnis. It aggravated discontent among the rank and file toiling in the mines and mills. Should the party elite receive all the rewards for workers' sacrifices? The blatant disregard for workers' very lives that the Kemerovo mine explosion demonstrated could serve as a spark for political explosions, if not properly ventilated. As Ordzhonikidze put it in his final major speech, delivered right after receiving a dressing-down from Stalin: 'This is a very dangerous mildewing starting to inundate us ... when a dignitary or a functionary feels himself so detached from the masses'.[20]

Accident rates were skyrocketing – in the Urals, the Donbass and everywhere. More than half of all miners were injured at one Kuzbass coal mine in 1936. There were no less than 1,600 accidents. Workers were complaining loudly about safety, living conditions and factory organizations' lack of interest in doing anything about it. Trotsky, the alleged mastermind of the wrecking conspiracy, voiced the opinion that 'the numerous industrial catastrophes ... have aroused a burning indignation among the working masses. The ruling clique needs, therefore, expiatory victims'. And to make matters worse, the bad harvest of 1936 led to a famine panic in the countryside and urban breadlines.[21]

The wrecking accusations had a populist tone. They sometimes struck themes reminiscent of London's secret critique of Soviet industry. The CC plenum wrecking resolution denounces in its opening section the 'spoiling of everyday cultural construction' for workers in Kemerovo. This section of the resolution survived unchanged from Ordzhonikidze's original draft. Ordzhonikidze lifted the accusation word for word from London's 1935 correspondence with Drobnis, which he must have reviewed while working on the resolution.[22] Ex-Trotskyists in Soviet industry like Drobnis were fine scapegoats.

---

20 Ordzhonikidze collection, RGASPI, f. 85, op. 29, d. 156, l. 61–62; Khlevniuk, *In Stalin's Shadow*, 128–30.

21 Davies and Wheatcroft, *Years of Hunger*, 298, 325, 354–5; Harris, *Great Urals*, 183, 176; Kuromiya, *Freedom and Terror in the Donba*, 221; Rogovin, *1937*, 248–9; Fitzpatrick, *Everyday Stalinism*, 7, 41; Trotsky, 'Stalin in Partial Retreat', Jan. 30, 1937; and 'Industrial Sabotage', Jan. 26, 1937, in *Writings (1936–1937)*, 169 and 150.

22 Resolution on 'lessons of wrecking, sabotage and espionage of Japanese-German-

Ordzhonikidze's favorite factory director, Donbass steel boss Gvakhariia, was the perfect target. This former Trotskyist student leader seriously alienated his workforce through dictatorial behavior, market-oriented economic experiments that harmed worker interests, and even perhaps financial corruption. In the face of dreadful housing conditions for the workers at his plant, he diverted funds for his dacha, allegedly. His purge as a 'Trotskyist wrecker' was popular.[23] London would denounce him as a wrecker as well, for polluting the Northern Donets River. But official accusations reflected manipulation from above more than pressure from below. The Soviet people played little role in the ugly industrial purge drama. The lower levels of the bureaucracy itself, as we saw at Donbassvodtrest, played the central role.

2.1 *Sergo Ordzhonikidze Defends His People*

If the Soviet Union was in London's words 'not a dictatorship of the proletariat but a technocracy', then Sergo Ordzhonikidze was the head technocrat. His regime in the Peoples' Commissariat of Heavy Industry (Narkomtiazhprom, NKTP) was the classic example of the Soviet patron/client model. Piatakov, Trotsky's former right-hand man in industry, was Sergo's client. It seems that Sergo accepted the idea that Piatakov was a wrecker to protect other clients, after Piatakov was forced to confess in his presence. But Ordzhonikidze was skeptical of Shakhty-style populist wrecking accusations against his engineers.

The day after the January trial ended he gave a speech at a Moscow reception for staff of the oil refineries Noah was building, stating: 'Our engineer … is building his own home in his own Soviet Union … These are our own sons and brothers … the flesh of our flesh, our blood, our sons, our friends, our comrades'. The audience applauded wildly.[24] He sought to the last day of his life to defend his subordinates, trying to mobilize backing from regional party bosses with whom friction had developed with central authorities. He sent a number of NKTP officials out on the road as inspectors-general in the wake of the trial.

A professor named Galperin inspected Kemerovo. Another went off to the Donbass. London's old boss Ginzburg inspected Uralvagonstroi in Nizhnii Tagil in the Urals. This was one of the most ambitious projects of the second Five-Year Plan, slated to become the USSR's prime railcar plant. London wrote a

Trotskyist agents', Feb.–March CC plenum, March 2, 1937, *Voprosy Istorii*, 1994 no. 10, 3. Ordzhonikidze's first draft, RGASPI, f. 85, op. 29, d. 1569, l. 3.

23 Benvenuti, 'Industry and Purge in the Donbass', 57–8.

24 Khlevniuk, *In Stalin's Shadow*, 98–102, 119.

letter to Rose on a winter trip to the Kemerovo area to look at sites for locomotive plants. Likely he was the one who decided that the Urals would be a better place to build railroad cars than 'the cold, the dark, the terrible' Siberian *taiga*, as he put it.[25]

Both the head of construction and local party secretary had oppositionist connections. But according to Ginzburg, criticism of management was overblown. Uralvagonstroi was a model Soviet enterprise showing no signs of wrecking. Quality was higher than elsewhere. Molotov sharply criticized Ginzburg's report at the Central Committee plenum. According to the published version of his speech: 'Suffice it to say that this commission failed to cite a single instance of wrecking at the enterprise. It would appear that the notorious wrecker, Mar'iasin, and the other wrecker, Okudzhava, have only vilified themselves'. And Stalin criticized Ordzhonikidze himself for defending Okudzhava and other 'scoundrels'.

Shortly before the plenum, Ginzburg reported on his own Glavstroiprom in the NKTP journal, *Za Industrializatsiiu*, boasting of great improvements in its work. The editor, Valery Mezhlauk, cautioned Ginzburg that 'the trial of the anti-Soviet Trotskyist center showed that construction was one of the objects of the wrecking-sabotage activity of the Trotskyist bandits'.[26] Ordzhonikidze was aware of the fraudulence of wrecking accusations, and tried to fend them off. But there was a certain air of bureaucratic complacency around his defense of his commissariat. If all was for the best in the best of all possible industrial worlds, then why all the disasters? The Kemerovo explosion was far from an isolated incident. As Russian historian Khlevniuk puts it:

> Ordzhonikidze often signed off on impossible plans that he knew required the employment of projects yet to be completed. He himself strove for quantity, while closing his eyes to quality. He himself asked people to put off improving living conditions until better times and to build temporary barracks … Ordzhonikidze could every bit as much see himself and other leaders of the country as saboteurs.[27]

In his article on the Kemerovo trial, Trotsky's son commented: 'The industrial manager who doesn't squeeze the worker hard enough gets squeezed

25 Letter to Rose, Siberia, Jan. 26, 1935.

26 Ginzburg, 'O gibeli Sergo Ordzhonikidze', *Voprosy Istorii KPSS* 3 (1991); Khlevniuk, *In Stalin's Shadow*, 120–34; Rogovin, *1937*, 233; Ginzburg, 'Pervye Sdvigi', *Za Industrii* (Moscow), Feb. 11, 1937.

27 Khlevniuk, *In Stalin's Shadow*, 98.

from above, but the main squeezer – Ordzhonikidze – doesn't sit in the dock!' Ordzhonikidze's speech to the oil refinery staff reveals a guilty conscience. After his browbeating from Stalin he asked his assembled subordinates:

> Why did this happen? Were we really so blind to it all? You must ask yourself this question. That's because we didn't pay enough attention to what was going on around us … an accident happens in a mine, it does in 10–12 people, hey, they're dead, that's technical problems. But remember, many of you are old Bolsheviks, old revolutionaries … now when 20 people die, they pull them out of the shaft, put them in their graves, hide it and write that the mood of the workers has improved, everybody goes down into the mineshafts and works.[28]

His poor health and the urge to protest Stalin's witchhunt plans weren't his only motives for suicide. It seems that even the consummate technocrat, Sergo Ordzhonikidze himself, was troubled at the end by the memory that once upon a time he had been a revolutionary, not a bureaucrat. His death removed the last obstacle in the path of those like Stalin and his closest entourage who had forgotten this altogether – or, like the rising layer of *vydvizhentsy*, had never been revolutionaries in the first place.

2.2 *The New Regime: 'Every Industrial Accident Must Have Its Name and Patronymic'*

Valery Ivanovich Mezhlauk became the new head of the Commissariat of Heavy Industry after Ordzhonikidze's suicide. Mezhlauk was a veteran Ukrainian revolutionary who joined the Bolsheviks in 1917. In the spring of 1918 he was the commissar of finance of the short-lived Donbass Soviet Republic, out of which the Stalin clique originated. He became a central administrator, planner and theorist of Soviet industry and oversaw London's Donbass water projects in the early 1930s. Until Ordzhonikidze's death he was the deputy head of the Soviet government and the head of Gosplan, as well as the editor of the NKTP journal *Za Industrializatsiiu* (For Industry). An admirer of American technology, he was the first official representative of the Soviet government to visit the US, bringing home a Cadillac to bounce over Moscow's cobblestone streets. He was identified with the wrecker witch hunt in its original populist coloration and published its central slogan in *Za Industrializatsiiu* shortly before he became the commissar: 'every industrial accident must have its name and pat-

28 Ordzhonikidze collection, l. 61.

ronymic'. Under Mezhlauk, *Za Industrializatsiiu* harshly criticized Ginzburg for his 'paper-bureaucratic' style of leadership at Glavstroiprom. But he did not charge Ginzburg with wrecking.[29]

In the spring of 1937 much of the economy was still doing well, but lagging coal production was a problem. A directive from Mezhlauk blamed this on bad leadership and a failure to struggle against wrecking. His draft of a Central Committee coal resolution demanded a big increase in spending on construction for housing and other worker needs – as in the immediate aftermath of the Shakhty Affair. The secret report Mezhlauk sent Molotov and Stalin strongly criticized the Donbass coal trust, but cautiously stated that there had been 'some excesses' in unmasking wrecking. Too many engineers had been arrested. The Central Committee resolution adopted called for bringing the coal witch hunt to a halt.[30]

The other weak sector of Soviet industry was oil, where London was in charge of refinery construction. Whereas Ginzburg was closely identified with Ordzhonikidze, Mezhlauk seems to have been a patron of Noah London. In Mezhlauk's eyes, London may have represented American technology and know-how. Mezhlauk sent an inspector to the oil trust in April. According to his report, Glavneft, 'the most important trust in the NKTP', was grossly mismanaged. Director Barinov was incompetent, and his deputy Efuni was a wrecker. Efuni maintained that Soviet conditions made the production of lowgrade oil unavoidable. The inspector branded this idea as a form of wrecking. Fire disasters had killed 10 workers and seriously injured another 17. The party secretary unfairly blamed the dead workers themselves. According to the report, Efuni was the real culprit.

Efuni was probably right. Top trust officials had just returned from a widely publicized trip to America – on which Noah London was not included, for reasons that are not hard to guess. To bring Russian oil up to US standards might have required special measures along the lines of London's ultramodern, expensive Donbass water filtration system. The report criticized London's construction department less sharply than others. The inspector merely commented: 'The absence of immediate leadership and control over capital construction by the head of the trust is one of the reasons for the systematic failure

29 Mezhlauk file, RGAE, f. 71, op. 1, d. 133; hronos.km.ru-biograf-mezhlauk.html (accessed Nov. 12, 2007); Andrle, *Workers in Stalin's Russia*, 76; 'Glavstroiprom kak on est', *Za Industrializatsiiu*, April 1, 1937; 'Navesti bol'shevistiskii poriadok na stroikakh', April 4, 1937; 'Na aktive Glavstroiproma', June 23, 1937.

30 RGASPI, f. 82 (Molotov), op. 2. d. 580 (coal, May–July 1937), especially l. 82, 89 and 94; Benvenuti, 'Industry and Purge in the Donbass', 64.

to finish and put into production the most important factories'. In other words, London ran his department without interference. In the aftermath of the report he chaired several commission meetings and wrote numerous reports about refinery safety. He consistently refused to authorize completion of projects until fire dangers were eliminated.[31]

Glavneft financial reports indicate that while London was in charge of construction, expenditures for housing and other facilities for workers were considerably higher than elsewhere in Soviet industry. After he was arrested, the October Revolution anniversary piece published in the oil industry journal devoted much attention to how 'Trotskyist-Bukharinist wreckers' had damaged the industry, especially in construction. But even this article noted that: 'Much has been done in the area of elevating the daily cultural level of the workers and technicians of the oil industry. In the last five years alone more than 250 million rubles were invested in communal housing construction'. Noah London was still a communal housing man. And wages had doubled. In oil processing, London's arena, they increased more rapidly after he took over in 1936 than in any other sector of Soviet industry.[32]

While Mezhlauk was in charge, a populist policy stood Noah London in good stead. Mezhlauk's version of the witch hunt was relatively 'rational', at least compared to the grand madness of the Great Terror in full throttle, after Kaganovich replaced him. Noah London's downfall had little to do with his work in oil. What happened to him can only be understood in the context of what was going on simultaneously at the water trust he created. It sheds light on the mechanisms of the Great Purge in the Soviet Union as a whole. The records I found view them neither from the perspective of its victims nor from that of the totalitarian dictator supposedly masterminding everything. Instead, they show how it happened where it began, in Soviet industry – the social, economic, physical, emotional and moral heart of the Soviet system.

3 The Purge of Noah London and the Soviet Oil Industry

As the Stalino NKVD was interrogating water officials and collecting evidence against Noah London, parallel processes went on at the oil trust in Moscow.

31 RGASPI, f. 82, op. 2. d. 565 (oil, 1936–1940), l. 4–55; RGAE, f. 7734 (Glavneft), op. 5, d. 180 and 182 *passim*.

32 'Sovetskaia neftianaia promyshlennost', *Neftianoe khoziaistvo*, Nov. 1937, 13; Davies and Wheatcroft, *Years of Hunger*, 358.

During the summer of 1937, all of its leaders except London were arrested.[33] But then Kaganovich replaced Mezhlauk and appointed a new Glavneft director, A. Iskanderov. Machine-building was split off into a separate commissariat, which Mezhlauk continued to direct.

In his inaugural speech before a machine-builders' union conference, Mezhlauk did his best to demonstrate his enthusiasm for the purges then escalating to universal proportions. He even made an indiscreet public allusion to the mass terror against Soviet social outcasts just then beginning to accompany the Great Purge. According to Mezhlauk, 'Spies and saboteurs do not filter only into leading posts. They try to penetrate into the workers' milieu. Thus for example at one of the factories the former wrecker-director gathered about 600 former kulaks and anti-Soviet elements, former prisoners and camp escapees'.[34]

But he continued to try to dial down the 'wrecker' witch hunt. He reminded the audience of his coal resolution, which applied 'to all branches of industry without exception'. In Shakhty, he asserted, miners were *holding elections* to decide which engineers were wreckers! He also criticized unions for not fighting hard enough for 'daily cultural construction', especially housing, and blamed wreckers for insufficient attention to industrial safety.[35]

The speech appeared in the NKTP daily newspaper a week after a letter from Stakhanov himself complaining about drinking water for coal miners. A front-page article the next day branded the Donbass water situation a disgrace and blamed wreckers at Uralvagonstroi and other enterprises for 'deliberately creating a gap between production and consumer service'. Its author, probably Mezhlauk, maintained that 'the Stalin Constitution in great measure broadens the front of Bolshevik concern for the living person'.[36]

As the secret manuscript illustrates, London had a particularly low opinion of Kaganovich, and probably this view was reciprocated. In the departure of Mezhlauk from NKTP London lost a protector. Mezhlauk's relatively 'rational' witch hunt in industry exploded now into full, countrywide hysteria, as the NKVD temporarily displaced the Party as the dominant institution in Soviet society. Unleashed policeman Nikolai Yezhov began rounding up and shooting petty criminals, troublesome exiled kulaks, Orthodox priests, former landlords

33 G.G. Chakhmakhchev, 'Barinov', in *Veterany, Vospominaniia. Vypusk* 11, 42–3; RGAE, f. 7734, op. 5, d. 8 (apparatus circulars, 1937), *passim*.

34 Valerian Mezhlauk, 'Na s'ezde profsoiuza rabochikh tiazhelogo mashinostroeniia', *Za Industrializatsii*, Aug. 21, 1937.

35 Ibid.; Sheila Fitzpatrick, 'Workers against Bosses', in *Making Workers Soviet*, ed. David Siegelbaum and Robert Suny (Ithaca, NY: Cornell University Press, 1994), 319.

36 'Bol'she zaboty o rabochem byte', *Za Industrializatsiiu*, Aug. 17, 1937.

and capitalists, members of national minorities with fatherlands diplomatically aligned with Nazi Germany and other social pariahs *en masse*.[37]

London's 'Khrushchevite' industrial populism was no longer the flavor of the moment, as the Great Purge in the bureaucracy evolved into a true Great Terror against unruly categories of the general population. Kaganovich like Ginzburg was concerned first and foremost with military production. He took Ginzburg under his protection and made him one of his assistants.[38] Criticism of Ginzburg in the NKTP newspaper ceased abruptly. Articles had already begun to appear alleging wrecking in Glavneft capital construction. In June, Iskanderov accused Azerbaijani wreckers of deliberately delaying refinery construction to sabotage the flow of oil to Soviet industry.[39] Meanwhile London was holding up construction plans due to concern with fire dangers. A young Azerbaijani oil engineer named Nikolai Konstantinovich Baibakov wrote a letter from the Donbass to denounce the activities of a band of wreckers in capital construction at Glavenergo, the energy trust.[40] Kaganovich quickly brought him into Glavneft management. He became its deputy director for construction in 1939 – Noah London's former position.

Unsurprisingly, Glavneft records indicate that Iskanderov disliked London. He continually issued veiled threats in their correspondence. But London simply ignored Iskanderov's threats, not even responding except to pointedly sign all correspondence, no matter how trivial, as 'deputy director London'. The lead article in the October number of the oil industry journal proclaimed that many of the Trotskyist-Bukharinist bandits at Glavneft were 'already exposed, but not all yet have been eradicated. Even now their remnants are trying to carry out their wrecking activities'. The new trust leadership could only fulfill the vital tasks before the trust, such as 'quickening refinery construction', through boldly advancing Stakhanovites and young specialists to leading positions.[41] But this was not why London was arrested. His case file barely mentions

37 Khlevniuk, 'Party and NKVD: Power Relationships in the Years of the Great Terror', in *Stalin's Terror: High Politics and Mass Repression in the Soviet Union*, ed. B. McLoughlin and K. McDermott, 21–33 (New York: Palgrave Macmillan, 2003); Khlevniuk, *History of the Gulag*. (It is not only in the US that policemen do not think that the lives of social outcasts matter.)

38 Ginzburg, 'O gibeli Ordzhonikidze', 95; Kaganovich speech at construction conference, Jan. 11, 1938, RGASPI, f. 81, op. 3, d. 361, l. 145–176.

39 A. Iskanderov, 'Likvidirovat' posledstviia vreditel'stva v neftepererabotke', *Za Industrii*, June 23 1937.

40 Baibakov, letter, *Za Industrializatsiiu*, June 10, 1937.

41 RGAE, f. 7734, op. 5, d. 8, *passim*; 'Vydvigat' novye molodye kadry', *Neftianoe Khoziaistvo*, Oct. 1937.

Glavneft. London's difficulties there simply paralleled his problems in the water industry. The causes were identical. London was arrested in Moscow on October 27, 1937; Sokolov and several other Stalino water officials were arrested almost simultaneously. Mezhlauk was arrested the same month.

Industrial populism was now a thing of the past. Komsomol leader Kosarev wrote a letter to Stalin and Molotov a few weeks before London's arrest, sharply criticizing miners' living conditions.[42] Kosarev had been one of the most fervent and enthusiastic advocates of the 'cadre revolution' at the February/March CC plenum, boldly seeking to advance his fresh young cadres. He had voted for shooting Bukharin immediately, rather than having the NKVD investigate the case further, as Stalin recommended. He took the populist rhetoric of the wrecker witchhunt much too seriously, and he would be shot in 1938.

On October 28, the day after London's arrest, the NKTP newspaper published a glowing account of the just-opened luxury NKTP sanatorium in Kislovodsk. As Noah had written Rose in 1935, it was devoted to 'those who *run* the industry', not 'those who *make* things'. Beneath an attractive photograph, the piece explained that 'on the roof of the second building is a Chinese garden with dwarf plants, and on the roof of the main building a solarium'.[43]

3.1 *How the 'Donbassvodtrest Affair' Swallowed Noah London*

London's 136-page investigative case file is marked on the front cover '*khranit vechno, Osobyi Arkhiv*' (keep forever, Special Archive).[44] More than half of it consists of excerpts from interrogations of two witnesses, arrested DBVT engineers Shakhov and Kushin. The FSB in Moscow denied me access to this section of the file. For reasons Lavrenti Beria took to his grave, the case files of London protégé's Sokolov and Rabukhin were removed from the 'Special Archive' in January 1953 at the height of the anti-Semitic 'doctors' plot' affair, only a few months before Stalin died and Beria briefly replaced him. Jewish doctors were allegedly conspiring to medically murder various party leaders. Their files were transferred to the Stalino/Donetsk secret police archives, and these files also include much testimony from Shakhov and Kushin. They include as well excerpts from Il'enko's testimony, the most 'damning' in the atmosphere of the Cold War and the 'doctors' plot'.

Many years later, the Donetsk SBU, the Ukrainian successor to the KGB, graciously granted me access to the Sokolov and Rabukhin case files, during

42 Oct. 10, 1937, f. 82, op. 2, d. 581 (coal, 1937–1940), l. 2–9.

43 'Kislovodskii sanatorii Narkomtiazhproma', *Industriia*, Oct. 28, 1937.

44 London case file, TsaFSB, Moscow, *sledstvennoe delo* R-46033. The file had passed through a number of locations before landing in the Special Archive, file 952026.

the dramatic Ukrainian election campaign of the fall of 2004. A few weeks before I studied the files, one of the Ukrainian presidential candidates, Viktor Yushchenko, had a dinner rendezvous with the heads of the SBU elsewhere in the country. Candidate Yushchenko's encounter with the SBU went less well than mine. He apparently came down with dioxin poisoning afterwards.[45] On the other hand, he was elected president as a result.

Much has been written about the role of *donos* (denunciation, snitching) in the Great Purges.[46] One of the most famous practitioners of this black art was Nikolaenko, the 'little person' who snitched on Postyshev's wife, helping Stalin unleash the cadre revolution in Ukraine. Il'enko was DBVT's Nikolaenko: the 'little person' denouncing the 'big wheel' – in this case Noah London.

Although Il'enko played a central role in the *vydvizhentsy* rebellion against Sokolov, he was not himself a *vydvizhenets*. He was the only trust official involved in Donbass water supply under the Tsarist regime, as a geologic surveyor. Indeed, he appeared on the March DBVT purge list as a 'former kulak, previously censured, excluded from the party and fired'. Il'enko's own version of events was that Sokolov had briefly laid him off in 1933, after he wrote a letter about the Svetlichno well incident. Three years later, he proposed prosecution of his supervisor at the time, one Sychev. But Sokolov vetoed this.[47]

Sokolov himself may have opposed London's decision to build a pumping station right over an artesian well at Svetlichno. Noah London's personal friend Rabukhin, in charge of that project, resisted the interrogators more staunchly than anyone else. He denied that this decision represented wrecking, as Taussig's activated charcoal filters were being built for the phenol-polluted river water the pipeline was slated to use. The Svetlichno incident became the only direct evidence that Noah London was a 'wrecker'.

Under the Tsarist regime, water was obtained by drilling wells. This was Il'enko's field of expertise. His opposition to London's new methods is easy to understand. Il'enko's argument was that London's pipelines and foreign filter plants were wrecking because they were expensive and unnecessary. London himself had branded top-level opponents of his pipeline project as wreckers for making such arguments. Chief engineer Shakhov also opposed London's

45 Andrew Wilson, *Ukraine's Orange Revolution* (New Haven, CT: Yale University Press, 97–103).

46 Volkogonov, *Stalin*, 314–15; Sheila Fitzpatrick, *Tear Off the Masks!: Identity and Imposture in Twentieth-Century Russia* (Princeton, NJ: Princeton University Press, 2005), 205–39; Mark Junge and Rolf Binner, *Kak Terror stal 'Bol'shim'. Sekretnyi prikaz No. 00447 i tekhnologiia ego ispolneniia* (Moscow: AIRO-XX, 2003), 252n77.

47 Chaplenko, purge list, f. 326, op. 1, d. 1069, l. 91–94; Sokolov file, Il'enko testimony, l. 208–12.

pipeline, on ecological grounds. His NKVD testimony paralleled Il'enko's.[48] When Il'enko first raised the Svetlichno affair at the trust party meeting in February, Sokolov replied that Il'enko was not there at the time and did not know what he was talking about. But by the summer of 1937 he was echoing Il'enko's account.

Il'enko maintained that 'alleged foreigner' London was a suspicious character. His main proof was London's connections with foreigners – especially Jews, such as departed American engineers Mekhanik and Levine. Il'enko had socialized with the Londons in Kharkov, like other trust officials. According to Il'enko the Londons' home was a veritable transit center for innumerable American visitors, including 'alleged relatives' visiting his wife such as her sister (Rose, presumably). And for suspiciously acting Soviet citizens as well.

Il'enko was also accusing visiting Austrian filter expert Taussig of being a spy. By July, Sokolov was echoing Il'enko and denouncing Taussig as well. The malleable Kushin embroidered Il'enko's fairy tale for the NKVD, confessing that he himself was preparing to sabotage the water system under Taussig's direction in case of war.[49] Il'enko's insinuations that London was an American spy were not useful in 1937, unlike in 1953 when Beria decided it was wiser to pack certain records off to Stalino, out from under a dying Stalin's nose. But casting Taussig as German spy was perfect.

3.2 *Noah London's Duel with His Interrogators*

The records of his interrogation are highly revealing of his state of mind, unlike many other documents in former NKVD files. After about three weeks of questioning, he was willing to confess to being a 'member of an anti-Soviet organization of rightists'. But his initial confessions read like a carefully calculated ploy. They seem to have been composed by Noah London himself. The original hand-written version includes corrections in his own hand, most of which are for literary purposes. However, he did manage to persuade the interrogator to cross out the deadly accusation that he was a 'Trotskyist'. It does not appear in the official typed stenogram. His testimony gives the impression that he was trying to give the interrogators just enough of what they wanted to give himself a chance to survive, while trying to maintain as much personal integrity as possible. The task proved impossible.

He began by narrating how he became disaffected in 1930–1 because of the 'difficulties in the land at that time' and Donbassvodtrest's supply difficulties.

48 Rabukhin case file, Shakhov testimony, l. 36.

49 London case file, London *dopros* (interrogation), Nov. 17, 1937, p. 9, l. 33. The author was denied access to Kushin's Moscow *dopros*.

Ginzburg supposedly 'very carefully let me know that there was no reason to grieve about [them]'. After London's trip to England he was allegedly recruited into Ginzburg's rightwing wrecking conspiracy, whose purpose was to 'demonstrate the unreality of projected plans' through sabotaging water construction.[50]

By the time of London's arrest, Kaganovich had made it clear to all industrial officials that Ginzburg had his protection. London's testimony about Ginzburg closely reflects London's actual relation with Ginzburg. 'Wrecking activity' consisted of those policies Ginzburg followed but which London disapproved of. Naturally, this is equally true of the testimony about Noah London by Sokolov, Shakhov and Kushin. London's own biggest wrecking act at Glavstroiprom, he stated, was conspiring together with Ginzburg to build the Kislovodsk sanitarium.

> by means of consciously lowering the cost estimates, the government was pulled into additional expenditures to the sum of more than twelve million rubles. The fact is that if I and Ginzburg had made up proper estimates, they would not have given us permission to spend such a great sum of money, and it would be proposed to construct a less comfortable establishment.[51]

One gets the impression from London's testimony that he was deliberately claiming to have wrecked certain projects in the hope that this would persuade the authorities to fund them properly. By contrast, in the case of the sanatorium he was claiming that he and Ginzburg had *promoted* it as a form of wrecking. He admitted to committing a very peculiar species of wrecking on one occasion, namely stopping construction on 'the Bela river dam, which would leave the Alchevsky metallurgic factory without water. A catastrophe did not take place only because the factory was never reconstructed as was earlier planned …' And he had of course been trying to wreck the Donets Canal project. Aside from these crimes, his wrecking consisted of the budget cutbacks imposed on Donbassvodtrest by lack of funds, plus in Noah's words in the transcript, 'a series of wrecking acts, which I now simply can't remember'.[52] When I read that to the engineers at the current day successor trust in Donetsk, they laughed.

Like most of the Moscow trial defendants, he denied personally committing any acts of sabotage, or ordering anyone else to commit any. Initially, he was

50 Ibid., 2, l. 26; p. 3, l. 27.
51 Ibid., 11, l. 35.
52 Ibid., 10–12, l. 34–5.

only willing to name three carefully chosen co-conspirators at Donbassvodtrest (DBVT), all of whom had already left the trust. He was trying to preserve it from destruction. He claimed at this point that 'I recruited nobody else'. At the interrogator's insistence the word 'personally' was added here in the official transcript. The alleged co-conspirators were:

- Otto Martinovich Ul'mer, the DBVT planning department head when London was in charge. He was a major collaborator with London on his water pipeline and other projects. According to London, Ul'mer was his main co-conspirator. He had died in 1934.
- Shakhov, whose relationship to London was peculiar. It seems that the two of them indeed had a significant private conversation in 1931. London's version was quite different from Shakhov's. According to Noah London, 'I told Shakhov that I knew he conducted anti-Soviet conversation within the apparatus. Shakhov is honest by nature. He didn't deny it'. As Shakhov had been chief engineer, London's 'wrecking conspiracy' would hardly be plausible without him. Shakhov left the trust in 1935. Perhaps London thought that 'giving him up' was relatively safe for DBVT. And perhaps London knew or guessed that Shakhov had already testified against him. In any case, shortly after London made his statement about Shakhov, the interrogator read Shakhov's denunciation to him.
- Anatolii Nikolaevich Stekler, Shakhov's predecessor. Stekler also was working elsewhere by 1937, on the Moscow subway system, which London opposed. He had worked with London at the Stroibiuro when London first arrived in the USSR. Stekler seems to have been involved in the Stroibiuro corruption scandal in 1928. London describes him as a previously arrested engineer serving out his sentence at DBVT, and an 'embittered fellow with clearly expressed counter-revolutionary views'. Perhaps Noah thought Stekler really was a wrecker.

When the interrogator told London he had confessions 'proving' that London had recruited other engineers, such as Shakhov's, London added Titov and Rabukhin to the list. They were well known as London protégés, and had after all been convicted of financial malfeasance. And London may have suspected – correctly – that Titov and Rabukhin had already admitted to 'conspiring' with him. He also added various Glavstroiprom functionaries to the conspirators' list, including his successor Khaidukov, praised by Ginzburg in his memoirs as an innocent victim of Stalin.

But London refused initially to name anyone else at DBVT, insisting that 'Shakhov is in error'. He scornfully denied Shakhov's assertion that London had admitted to him that his pipeline project was a form of wrecking – even though he had conceded at the NKTP Commission that starting the pipeline at Svetlichno may have been a mistake. And he denied that he told Kushin or anyone else to sabotage the waterworks. He also confessed to wrecking at Glavneft by holding up refinery construction, but denied that he had any co-conspirators there.[53]

But shortly before the end of the transcript the inquisitor stated that 'the investigation turns to questioning you about espionage activity, about which accusations were presented to you … You must give exhaustive testimony about this'. This may be the point at which 'illegal methods' were applied. London now confessed that he was recruited as a German spy in February 1931 by the head of the NKTP foreign department, Mikhail Birentsveig. London first met him, naturally, at a Kislovodsk sanitarium.[54] I find it hard to believe he would have confessed to that without torture or threats against Miril. A few months previously, Stalin had formally authorized the use of torture in interrogations, a Soviet first, on paper at least.

Birentsveig's party autobiography depicts an individual who could hardly have fit very well at the top of the Soviet industrial hierarchy. The head of the NKTP International Department, he joined the revolutionary underground as early as 1900 and became a fairly prominent Bundist. He escaped from prison with the aid of his comrades and fled Russia after the 1905 Revolution. He then became a revolutionary 'rootless cosmopolitan'. He knocked around Europe, from Geneva to Warsaw to Brussels, where he received his engineering diploma, and then to Paris and back to Warsaw. At the end of World War I he joined the Polish Communist Party and became a party cadre in – Berlin. This peripatetic traveller went to work for the NKTP in 1931, after he was exiled from France.[55] Even from this sketchy account, one gets the impression that Birentsveig was a figure every bit as interesting as Noah London; and one who is even more forgotten. I found virtually no trace of him in the historic record. Stalin's extirpation of even the memory of so many of the best and brightest of the socialist movement is not the least reason why socialism lacks the appeal it once formerly had.

However, Birentsveig had a well-known relative. His sister Gina married the Bund's central leader, Vladimir Medem, but after his death joined the American Communist Party after a visit to the Soviet Union in 1926, the same year that the Londons arrived there. She became a pillar of American Jewish Communism and a Birobidzhan enthusiast until the day she died, as late as January

53 Ibid., 11, l. 35.
54 Ibid., 11–12, l. 35–6.
55 Birentsveig file, RGASPI, f. 17, op. 100, d. 51659.

1977.[56] Mikhail B. was in charge of recruiting foreign engineers for Soviet industry, but his exact relationship with his American sister, the Birobidzhan project and the Londons remains unknown. Likely he was also linked with Mezhlauk, well known for his foreign and especially American interests. Possibly the interrogators decided to 'use' London against Mezhlauk and against Birentsveig, who had been arrested on March 15.

Allegedly, Birentsveig offered London money for regular reports on Donbass industry that he accepted out of sheer greed. Why a top NKTP official like Birentsveig would have to pay him for such reports was unexplained. London also confessed to giving reports on the state of the oil industry in 1936 and 1937 to his American friends and co-workers, once to Mekhanik and quarterly to Levine. Both of them, conveniently, had already returned to America. In the handwritten version, he confesses to giving Birentsveig 'the following ready-made' intelligence reports, which then are listed in detail. In the official version, this becomes reports 'that interested him'. My best guess is that London was simply reading from a list the interrogator had handed him, and that the wording was corrected on editing to sound less like intelligence information.

In the 1990s, my family submitted several Freedom of Information Act requests to the US government for records pertaining to Noah and Miril London. Noah's FBI files are highly censored. They were much more difficult to access than his NKVD files. They include heavily blacked-out interview reports from the McCarthy period by FBI agents. In them there is discussion of an individual or individuals working with him in the Soviet Union in 1931–4 and 1937, and in particular, traveling there to work on a Crimean steel project in the early 1930s.

This fits Benjamin Levine's profile perfectly, according to his workbook in the Soviet economic archives. Levine, London's old coworker from the New York subway system, supervised the construction of a Crimean steel pipe plant for DBVT in the 1930s. He traveled back and forth between the USA and USSR more than once until his final return to America in the summer of 1937, just before the Londons were arrested. Cooper Union, Noah London's old *alma mater*, hired Levine for the fall semester to teach mathematics in its engineering school. He taught engineering there until he retired, dying in 1978. Rose described him in one of her letters to her husband from Kharkov as 'a dull naïve fellow ... awfully learned as an engineer and awfully simple as a human being'.[57]

---

56 Henry F. Srebnik, *Jerusalem on the Amur: Birobidzhan and the Canadian Jewish Communist Movement, 1924–1951* (Montreal: McGill-Queen's University Press, 2008).

57 Workbook, 'Beniamin Solomovich Levin', Aug. 28, 1936, RGAE, *trudovii spiski*, d. 2835; London *dopros*, p. 13. FBI materials on Noah London released per FOIA Request to Beatrice

In the course of document review, the FBI turned up material originating from the Central Intelligence Agency in the year 1965 and referred it to them. CIA official Lee Strickland wrote to my mother, Beatrice Holmes, that the CIA had made this determination: 'It must be withheld in its entirety on the basis of FOIA exemptions (b)(1) and (b)(3)'. The first exemption 'applies to material which is properly classified ... in the interest of national defense or foreign policy'. The second relates to 'obligations to protect from disclosure intelligence sources and methods, as well as the organization, functions, names, official titles, salaries or numbers of personnel employed by the Agency'.[58]

My parents appealed this decision and wrote several letters to top CIA officials. In one of them, my mother pointed out: 'The fact that the Russian government has disclosed some information about the trial and execution of Noah London, I hope, will reinforce my previous argument that disclosure of the information in your hands will not harm the United States'. Perhaps swayed by this argument, this four-page CIA memorandum was released. Unfortunately, all of it was redacted except for nine words.[59]

The decision to redact this memorandum might simply represent bureaucratic conservatism. But there was nothing in the Soviet Union in the 1930s of more interest to America than oil. The possibility that the US government obtained illicit oil information from Benjamin Levine cannot be dismissed, given the remarkable secretiveness of intelligence authorities about such an ancient matter.

However, the NKVD interrogator was peculiarly uninterested in Noah's 'confession' to spying for America. Germany not America was the subject of Soviet spy hysteria at the time. At the very end of the transcript, London finally 'confesses' that Kushin was telling the truth about his 'counter-revolutionary link with Taussig'. Allegedly, Taussig asked him in 1932 to recommend someone useful for espionage – before the Nazis came to power. He refused to the end to admit to working for the Nazis.

According to London, 'knowing Kushin as a fellow who loved money and had a petty nature', he recommended him to Taussig. At the NKTP Donbass water commission, Kushin had argued in his report to the plenary session

---

Holmes, Jan. 11, 1995, FOIPA No. 352.571 (Information on Benjamin Levine courtesy of independent researcher Linda Williams); Rose to Louis Discher, Oct. 1, 1934, Lewis Collection.

58 Letter, CIA Information and Privacy Coordinator Lee Strickland to Beatrice Holmes, Dec. 7, 1995.

59 Letter, Beatrice Holmes to CIA Director George Tenet, July 18, 1997; letter, Edmund Cohen, Chairman [CIA] Agency Release Panel to Beatrice Holmes, April 22, 1998. The nine words are '... in 1933 ... in Moscow ... Noah London, ... a construction engineer'.

that engineers' salaries at DBVT were insufficient – even though his own salary was a remarkable 1,500 rubles a month.[60]

Kushin agreed that in case of war he would wreck the pumping stations and infect the drinking water with typhus bacteria. Or was it the electric stations? That's how the handwritten version read originally, before it was corrected for consistency and plausibility in the typewritten version. London himself had suggested in his speech to the Donbass water *aktiv* that Trotskyist wreckers at DBVT might do such things. Moreover, in July the NKVD had been ordered to start 'a special purge of the water stations (especially the filtration systems)', in which all foreign nationals, naturalized foreigners and 'individuals related to foreign countries' were to be immediately arrested.[61] Oddly, the records do not indicate any connection between this order and Noah London's subsequent arrest. In any case, at this point the investigator had what he needed. The transcript ends abruptly.

Allegedly, the cynical Yagoda once commented that torture should not be used to extract confessions, because the 'client' is liable simply to repudiate such confessions at trial. Which is exactly what London did. But his trial was so secret that not even his district party committee was informed. He remained a party member for more than two years after his execution. In May 1940 his Moscow district party committee was finally told to expel him because he had been arrested by the NKVD. The district committee made a 'top secret' inquiry about his case. It received a 'completely secret' reply in October that London had been 'sentenced'.[62]

4 Donbass Water after the Great Terror

After the purges ended there was a different world at DBVT, well symbolized by a drunken brawl between union head Maliarov and party chairman Goloshchapov in 1938. Shortly thereafter former chairman Mironov was censured for corruption and fired. He somehow managed to get the chairman post back anyway, replacing Goloshchapov.[63] In short, while the 'cadre revolution' continued to rage elsewhere, Donbassvodtrest had made a 'great leap forward' into the Brezhnev era of corruption.

---

60 London *dopros*, 14–15, l. 38–9. Donbass water comm., plenary, April 25, 1937, d. 389, l. 50ob.

61 Khlevniuk, *History of the Gulag*, 144.

62 Personal file, N.M. London, TsAODM (Moscow party archive), f. 4, op. 30, d. 2485, korobka 110.

63 1938 protocols, *passim*.

Unlike other DBVT purge victims, Arkadii Kharchenko, the head of the Stalino DBVT unit under London and the last of London's 'Old Guard' to be purged, managed to survive. In 1955 he complained that his interrogators 'applied illegal methods of investigation' to him – i.e. torture. When all victims of the affair except London were posthumously rehabilitated in 1957, director Vorob'ev assured investigators that there had been no wrecking at DBVT. The waterworks built before 1937 were all still in operation and of high quality. Chief engineer Belanenko specifically stated that Il'enko's testimony about the Svetlichno incident, where an artesian well was buried by London's pipeline project, 'does not correspond to reality'. This is also the opinion of current trust engineers.[64]

The post-Terror history of Donbassvodtrest is a microcosm of the post-Terror history of the USSR. The waterworks were largely destroyed by the Nazis, so it is just as well that the Donets Canal project was delayed. They were rebuilt through intensive effort after the war. Like their role model Stalin, the 'victor' of World War II, the *vydvizhentsy* at DBVT burnished their reputation through their successful 'liquidation of the consequences of wrecking' – the real thing this time – by the Nazis. London and Taussig's high-tech activated charcoal filter system could not be rebuilt, to the regret of contemporary trust officials.[65] But wherever I went in the former Soviet Union in the first years of the new millenium, activated charcoal 'Brita filters' were ubiquitous for drinking water.

During the interregnum after Stalin died, one reform Beria introduced, as previously mentioned, was a halt to the wasteful and deadly canal megaprojects that Noah opposed. In the 1950s Donbassvodtrest became Ukrpromvodchermet, Stalino was renamed Donetsk and London's Donets water supply canal was finally built. It now supplies more than 80 percent of Donetsk water needs – or did before war broke out again. Russian media reports from the Donbass claimed that Ukrainian bombs and artillery shells destroyed much of the local waterworks during the ongoing Ukrainian civil war, as the Nazis did during World War II – bringing disease back to the Donbass.

By the 1970s, the economy and population of the Donbass had grown enormously, and the canal was seen as inadequate. Kanskii's old Don–Dnepr canal project was finally undertaken, but only as a water supply canal, not for transport purposes. It was abandoned unfinished after the collapse of the Soviet Union. Irrigation for agriculture became a central focus of Donbass water supply, just as Noah London had urged. While I was visiting a score of years ago,

64 Sokolov case file, l. 251–5; Trikash interview, Donetsk, Oct. 9, 2003.

65 Trikash interview.

the local press was issuing warnings of impending water catastrophe. But the trust officials I interviewed agreed with London that such a canal would be a boondoggle. They were probably right. Given the marked social, industrial, economic and population decline of Ukraine after the collapse of the Soviet Union, surely water needs were decreasing. And any new projects built would likely have been destroyed in the bloody warfare that would descend on the Donbass.[66]

5 Noah London's Successor: A Sketch of the New Generation

The tale of the Londons well represents the life stories of a whole layer of Jewish radicals in Russia, Eastern Europe, America and the Soviet Union. One Nikolai Baibakov replaced Noah London at Glavneft. Baibakov's life embodies the story arc of their replacements, the *vydvizhentsy*. His background was typical: he grew up in poverty, became an oil field worker and was sent to engineering school in the late 1920s. Not inclined to revolutionary dreams, he avoided the purges of possibly disgruntled former rank-and-file workers in the mid-1930s by serving in the army. After replacing London as deputy director in charge of construction, he went on to become oil minister under Stalin, and an important economic planner under Khrushchev. Under Brezhnev he became *the* central economic planner. How much economic wisdom did he gain from studying the files of his Glavneft construction department, from when Noah London was in charge? We shall never know.

Baibakov's autobiography was translated into English and published in the 1980s by the CPUSA. After the collapse of the USSR he wrote two more autobiographies. Their purpose was to defend Soviet planning, oppose Boris Yeltsin and advocate the so-called 'red-brown coalition' of Stalinists and anti-Semitic Russian nationalists, which Gennady Zyuganov's contemporary Russian Communist Party tries to organize. But he also supported the nationalist Aliyev regime of his native Azerbaijan, an American ally, whose post-Soviet travails are depicted in disguised form in Gary Shteyngart's well-received novel *Absurdistan*. He finally conceded in his last book that the turn to a market system was inevitable.[67]

---

66 Solianik; Tiutiunikov, 'Donbass mozhet ostat'sia bez vody', *Donetskie Novosti*, Nov. 7–13, 2002; Trikash interview.

67 Nikolai Baibakov, *The Cause of My Life* (Moscow: Progress, 1986); Baibakov, *Ot Stalina do Eltsina* (Moscow: GazOil Press, 1998); Baibakov, *Sorok let v pravitelstve* (Moscow: Respublika, 1993).

6 American Echoes

Back in America the arrest of the Londons received a certain amount of publicity in the socialist press. In 1938 Max Shachtman published an open letter to Noah's old ally, CPUSA leader Moissaye Olgin. Shachtman was an important behind-the-scenes figure in the largely Jewish 'New York intellectual' milieu, which played a central role in American intellectual life for much of the twentieth century.[68] It was centered on the *Partisan Review*, a journal that despite an always modest circulation exercised much influence on American literary life, and some political influence as well. Friendly to Trotsky and Trotskyism in 1938, it soured on Trotsky after Shachtman broke with him in 1940, and later went rightwards in the atmosphere of the Cold War. It was kept alive in the 1950s by covert CIA subsidies. Shachtman, his political followers, and most of that milieu followed the magazine rightwards, with Shachtman himself endorsing the Bay of Pigs invasion of Cuba and the Vietnam War in his old age. Many of his followers drifted into the camp of what came to be called 'neo-conservatism' after his death. Rose Risikoff told me, in my one and only conversation with her about the Londons, that she participated in 1938 in a *Partisan Review* summer camp, which likely bore a certain resemblance to Noah and Miril's old Camp Nitgedeiget.[69]

In that open letter to Olgin, Shachtman wrote that 'Noah London and his wife were tried a few years ago on a charge of 'sabotage' … He disappeared after that trial and recently the report reached here that he was shot by the Stalinist authorities'. A previous article in Shachtman's newspaper had written that:

> Some three years ago, London, his wife and two other engineers were tried in Russia on the customary charge of 'sabotage'. Old-time, devoted Communist that he was, this charge was as absurd as are most of the others. The two engineers were, however, shot; London and his wife sent to Siberia as exiles. London's sister was deported from the Soviet Union.[70]

---

68 Max Shachtman, 'An Open Letter to Moissaye Olgin', *Socialist Appeal*, July 9, 1938; Alan Wald, *The New York Intellectuals: The Rise and Decline of the Anti-Stalinist Left from the 1930s to the 1980s* (Chapel Hill: University of North Carolina Press, 1987).

69 I was not expecting this fairly short conversation with Aunt Rose at a family gathering to be the last I would ever have. I asked her about Noah London and Trotskyism, and she recalled her *Partisan Review* experiences.

70 'We Ask Once More: Is Noah London Alive or Dead?', *Socialist Appeal*, July 2, 1938.

The two engineers must have been Rabukhin and Titov, who indeed were tried some three years earlier. This version has enough similarities to the real story that it must have been based on what Rose heard second- or third-hand from other American visitors to the Londons. Noah's older sister Rochlea was visiting Noah and Miril when they were arrested in 1937. Possessing that final 1935 letter in which Noah expressed his fear of disappearing 'without a trace', did Rose put two and two together? It seems likely that she relayed the story to Trotskyists attending the *Partisan Review* summer camp, who printed it in Shachtman's paper with distortions and interpolations added along the way.

Moissaye Olgin did not answer Max Shachtman's open letter. Literary biographer Kalmen Marmor was an old friend and ally of Noah London, closer than Olgin. Marmor had been one of London's supporters in the CP underground caucus when London was national secretary of the Jewish Workers Federation in 1922. He was one of American Jewish Communism's most prominent Yiddish cultural figures. He worked at the Jewish Section of the Ukrainian Academy of Sciences in Kiev for several years, returning to America in 1936.

The Marmor archives preserve a copy of a coded letter to Noah London in Moscow in hard-to-read handwritten Yiddish. Presumably it was never sent.

> 4-1-37, to Nh. London: Too bad the Kiev people don't answer, I don't really blame them. Everybody has a relative, a little Goy in the hospital. Everybody's afraid to get sick. But with you in Moscow, and especially in your circle, there's no epidemic. I'm sure that you're all healthy and you are not in any hospitals. Even if in your dreams you must have written once a little letter …[71]

Marmor pointedly included praise of Noah London in an article on Artef, the Jewish Workers Theater, published in its tenth-anniversary pamphlet in 1937. Not long after this Yiddish pamphlet hit the 'Jewish street', reports appeared in the American socialist press of the Londons' arrest. Marmor seriously considered resigning from the American Communist Party when the Hitler–Stalin pact was signed a year later. Nonetheless, he remained a member until the day he died. Olgin too was deeply troubled by the pact. He couldn't summon the courage to quit, but died of a heart attack a few months later.[72]

Shortly after World War II broke out socialite Hester Huntington, the sister-in-law of a CPUSA leader, bailed party chairman Earl Browder out of jail. Jewish

71 Marmor papers, YIVO, reel 49, folder 604, items 21497-9.

72 Kalmen Marmor, 'Di far-geshikhte fun artef', in *Tsen yor Artef* (New York: Artef, 1937); Epstein, *The Jew and Communism*, 394–8.

NKVD defector Walter Krivitsky, seeking to keep Browder in prison, wrote her angry letters and gave copies of them to the House Un-American Activities Committee. He asked:

> Who murdered Noach London and Mirel London? ... Why does Noah London's body lay buried in the frozen earth of Siberia? Why does Earl Browder live on the fat of the land in these United States? Why? Is it because Noah London was a Jewish boy from the East side a son of a tailor. And Browder a Kansas accent man who can lie to heaven ... You and your boy friend Earl Browder will see and hear that it does not pay to be crooked. Justice and truth will triumph.

Krivitsky's testimony before HUAC, chaired by notorious anti-Semite Martin Dies, must have been an experience straight out of *Catch-22*. Krivitsky described Dies in his correspondence as a *Scheisskopf* – and his colleagues as 'ignorant cowboys'. Unsurprisingly, Dies failed to step forward to assist Krivitsky, born Samuel Ginsberg in a Galician *shtetl*, with his difficulties with American immigration authorities.[73]

7 The Fate of Miril London

Miril was arrested shortly after Noah. Yezhov's deputy Frinovsky signed the order himself. The arresting officer interrogated her quite briefly. He found letters to the Londons from Rose and other foreign relatives. Miril, a veteran of the American Communist underground, successfully concealed her husband's subversive link with her sister. When asked about her relatives, she chatted about several of them, including father Chaim in Palestine, her American Communist brother Morris and the author's grandmother Anna. But she left Rose out. When asked specifically about the letters, she suddenly remembered her youngest sister – but assured the officer that 'the correspondence is purely personal'. There is no further reference to Rose's letters in her file, or any others. Her passport was preserved, but all other memorabilia were destroyed – including all Rose's letters to Miril or Noah.[74]

According to Esther Markish, when Miril was arrested

73 'Schmelke Ginzburg' (Krivitsky) to Mrs. Hester G. Huntington, Nov. 11, 1939, and Dec. 27, 1939, Gary Kern, *A Death in Washington: Walter G. Krivitsky and the Stalin Terror* (New York: Enigma Books, 2003), 237–8, 246–7, 219 ('scheisskopf' reference).

74 *Sledstvennoe delo M.E. Londona* (Miril London case file), R-46598, TsaFSB, Moscow, Russia.

> those who were *very* good friends of theirs, they came tearing along to us, so that we would hide their things ... I said, we can hide them, but I don't see why you can't? Because the times then, as you know, were very difficult. Markish was – no, he wasn't yet a [Lenin] order holder, but he was a very famous poet ... Markish said leave it, don't touch it, that's all. I was very afraid that somebody was watching, but no, nobody came after us.[75]

Miril was sentenced to an eight-year term in a *gulag* in Kazakhstan – Alzhir, the Akhmolinsk *lager* for wives of traitors to the motherland. Over 5,000 wives of Soviet officials passed through its gates. She was inmate number 2420. According to Maria Moisseevich Goldberg, her camp companion and bunkmate, she was universally respected and loved there – even by the authorities. Goldberg described her as having 'the outward appearance of a kindly granny from an Andersen fairy tale'. She lifted everyone's spirits with endless stories about Noah. When the Markishes managed to find out where she was, Ester 'sprinkled her with parcels'. Miril used her old dressmaking skills to sew uniforms for Soviet soldiers, and was proud of contributing to the war effort. But she was working ten-hour days on bent knees, 'continually humming something reminiscent of familiar motifs from far away'. She lost the use of her legs due to tuberculosis, and suffered extreme insomnia as well.[76]

She described her disabilities in a 'declaration' to Lavrenti Beria, which is preserved in her case file and reproduced in Appendix D. She asked him to 'help her return to the useful and active life of a Soviet woman'. She narrated her career as an activist, and proclaimed that she and Noah had always been loyal to the party. She had

> never noticed any anti-party or anti-Soviet moods of my husband, much less activities. He never belonged to any opposition or anti-party grouping, on the contrary, struggled with them ... He was never linked in friendship with any former or current Trotskyists or rightists. His personal life was strict and modest, he never made use of those privileges which foreign specialists enjoy.[77]

---

75 Telephone interview, Esther Markish, Jan. 12, 2003.

76 *Alzhir* memorial book and Goldberg manuscript, l. 20–21ob., *Memorial* archive, Moscow; Markish interview.

77 'Zaiavlenie Narkomu N.K.V.D. t. Beria ot zakliuchennom London M.E.', March 5, 1939, Miril London case file. In Appendix D.

She pointed out that they had given up their American citizenship in the aftermath of the Shakhty Affair to prove their loyalty, and assured Beria that 'if I knew of any actions of my husband against Soviet Power, I would act as a Bolshevik should, to whom the party is dearer than life, and mercilessly expose him, regardless of our long life together'. She went on to say to him that 'you cde. Beria, closest counselor of cde. Stalin, understand the word of the Leader that to exclude an honest party member is the same thing for her as death …'

The initials 'L.B.' are scribbled on the front of the declaration, and the words 'concerning review of the case' appear in the upper left-hand corner. Beria had the reputation of a reformer, compared to Yezhov at least. The Londons' American connections could have proven very useful to the Soviet state, and to Beria in particular. If Noah had survived the Great Terror he would have been a logical figure to help oversee construction for the Soviet nuclear project, which Beria supervised. American Jewish Communist engineers like Julius Rosenberg surely must have seen Noah London as a role model.

When my grandmother, Anna Unterman Hort, went to the Soviet consulate in New York after World War II and asked permission to write to her sister Miril, she 'was told that Miril and Noah London did not exist'. But Miril was allowed to receive a letter from America from her younger brother Morris. He wrote that 'the main thing is that the USSR exists and calls us to struggle; woodchips fly when trees are cut down'. She managed to send him a reply, read at a family gathering which my mother, Beatrice Hort Holmes, attended. Unfortunately, that letter is lost.[78]

After Miril's release from Alzhir in 1945, she was forbidden to reside within 100 kilometers of any major Soviet city. Nonetheless, the Markishes invited her to stay with them in Moscow. They put her up for a few months, illegally. She was rightly afraid that they would be arrested on her account. One day the Markishes had guests over for dinner. They were curious about her. She was physically in poor shape, but very well dressed. She still had all her old American clothing, which the Markishes had kept for her. When they asked her where she was living, she broke out sobbing and sprang out of her chair. Ester ran after her and calmed her down, and told the guests that she was depressed because she had just lost her husband. She subsequently moved in with her friend Maria Goldberg in Kolchugino, an industrial town northeast of Moscow just outside the 100-kilometer perimeter.[79]

---

78 Letter, Beatrice Hort Holmes to Mikhail Gorbachev, Nov. 19, 1988; Goldberg, l. 210b.; Beatrice Holmes interview, Jan. 30, 1998.

79 Markish interview.

She and Maria lived on the second floor of a peasant's home. Soon they rented their own apartment, with one room and a terrace. Goldberg was working as a senior economist at a copper-smelting factory in Kolchugino. When another Alzhir veteran who was a friend of theirs showed up, she moved in as well. Maria Goldberg found Rakhil' Kaplan a job in her department. Because the apartment was small, Rakhil' soon had to move into the factory dormitory. Rakhil's daughter, Inna Shikheeva Gaister, remembers Miril as kind and hospitable.[80] Rakhil's and Maria's husbands, Aron Gaister and L.I. Genkin, had both been left-Zionists before they joined the party – as Noah London himself had been as a teenager. Aron Gaister was deputy people's commissar for agriculture when he was arrested. He was briefly a Trotskyist in the early 1920s, and apparently had shared disgruntlement over forced collectivization with a few old friends. Goldberg had a circle of friends in Moscow from her Komsomol days in Dnepropetrovsk, including Misha Svetlov, a famed Soviet poet. She introduced Miril to them.[81]

Freiheit editor Paul Novick visited Moscow in 1946 as a guest of the Jewish Anti-Fascist Committee. Two of its members, Leon Talmy and Elias Watenberg, London's Bronx coops successor, had worked with him in America and joined him on the 1929 American expedition to Birobidzhan. According to Novick:

> I made somehow some arrangements to get some money, you know, in the American embassy I could get a special rate … I sent over to [Miril] quite a sum of money … but what I remember is that when they came to arrest him, she cried out 'cursed be the day you ever came here, into the Soviet Union'. In Russian *'prochyat' bud' tot den' kogda my pridiom siuda* …[82]

He repeated this fairy tale, heard from his ultra-Stalinist Soviet brother, to Rose Risikoff and other Unterman relatives. They were the ones who gave him the money. Watenberg's wife, who had first introduced the Londons to the Markishes, made arrangements for Miril to get a high-quality sewing machine worth 1,200 rubles. Miril was able to make a decent living in Kolchugino with the help

80 Interview with Inna Shikheeva-Gaister, Moscow, April 27, 2002; Inna Shikheeva-Gaister, 'A Family Chronicle', in *In the Shadow of Revolution: Life Stories of Russian Women from 1917 to the Second World War*, ed. Sheila Fitzpatrick and Y. Slezkine (Princeton, NJ: Princeton University Press, 2000), 367–90; and Shikheeva-Gaister, *Semeinaia Khronika*, 79–81.

81 Gaister case file, *Semeinaia Khronika*, 189–96; Markish interview; Goldberg manuscript.

82 Paul Novick interview, May 26, 1988.

of that sewing machine, despite her problems with her legs. And the Markishes were still sending her money, always delivered by hand.[83]

Miril was finally informed by the authorities that Noah was dead. In December 1949, she hanged herself from the back of her iron bedstead. Ester found out about the suicide from the landlord, Shura Babilov. The Babilovs were a family of former kulaks, exiled in the aftermath of decollectivization. Ester met Shura at the Kolchugino train station, who told her all about it. She did not dare attend the funeral. As Maria Goldberg put it,

> As long as [Miril, Maria in Russian] hoped to meet her husband she was hardy, life-loving. The news of the death of Noah ate away at her. By the beginning of 1950 or the end of 1949, [Miril] was no more. She did not survive until the 20th Party Congress, until that time when all honest people, innocently ruined and blackened in the years of the cult [of personality] began to get their good names back.[84]

Miril London's official Soviet death certificate, which one of my relatives obtained a copy of from an émigré to Israel, is, oddly, in Belarusian, a language which possibly she did not know. This reflected Soviet nationality policy at the time of her suicide. Motele, where she was born, was then located in the Belorussian Soviet Republic, whose official language was still Belarusian. In the 1920s Yiddish was also an official language, but that was long ago.

Meanwhile, the secret police decided that Paul Novick was an American spy and a conduit to the Soviet Jewish Anti-Fascist Committee. His assistance to Miril surely was one of the reasons why. The secret trial of its leaders in 1952 resulted in the execution of a dozen Soviet Jewish community leaders, including Perets Markish and both Vatenbergs. Miril's sewing machine was one of the pieces of 'evidence' against Khaike Vatenberg.[85] The trial set the stage for the infamous anti-Semitic 'doctors' plot' affair, which poisoned the atmosphere in the Soviet Union during Stalin's last days. Denouncing the 'doctors' plot' as a fraud was one of Beria's actions during his brief reign in the aftermath of Stalin's death. The very names of Noah and Miril London disappeared without a trace, as Esther Markish commented in 2003 – and as Noah London had predicted in 1935.

83 Rose Risikoff interview with Jay Holmes, Jan. 2, 1986; Rubinstein and Naumov, *Stalin's Secret Pogrom*, 375; Gaister and Markish interviews.

84 Esther Markish interview; Goldberg, l. 21.

85 Rubinstein and Naumov, *Stalin's Secret Pogrom, passim.*

8 How the London Story Came to Light

Forty years later, as the Cold War was finally ending, Miril London was 'rehabilitated' through the Memorial society, presumably at the initiative of old friends or their children.[86] But Noah London's case was not re-examined during the tidal wave of rehabilitations of the Gorbachev era. On a spring day in the early 1980s, Rose Risikoff was a passenger in an automobile driven by my parents to a family event. 'I have a secret to tell you', Rose informed them. For the first time, she revealed the existence of the manuscript Noah London dictated to her in the summer of 1934.

Rose later said that she had chosen Beatrice and Jay Holmes to receive the manuscript because both of them were authors. Beatrice, employed by the US Department of Agriculture, had published official histories of water policy. Shortly before she died she told her son, the author of the book you are holding in your hands, that one reason she became interested in water policy was because she heard from her mother Anna that uncle Noah had been involved in building waterworks in the Soviet Union. Jay, a science writer and former journalist, author of *America on the Moon*, the first published account of the US space program, was then employed by the Department of Energy as a research director. Both were nearing retirement. Following repeated pleas, Rose produced the document on January 1, 1986. It had been hidden in a ceiling closet in her Manhattan apartment for half a century. I saw her climb a ladder to get it out. She gave my father permission to xerox a copy at a corner store the following day. Four months later, Rose became ill during a visit to a nephew in California and died in a hospital there at the age of 78.

During *perestroika*, as Miril was being rehabilitated, Beatrice Holmes wrote a letter to Mikhail Gorbachev. She expressed her 'hope that, in the spirit of *glasnost*, perhaps some records of my aunt and uncle could now be located in the archives of the Soviet government'. A year and a half later she received a letter from the American Red Cross, which reported that the 'Soviet Red Cross has contacted us ... They advised us that Noah London died on December 9, 1937, and as far as Miril London is concerned, the Soviet Red Cross was unsuccessful in locating her'.[87] It was no surprise in 1990 that Noah London was dead, as he was born in 1888. Forms were submitted to the Red Cross for a tracing inquiry. Finally, on November 25, 1996, the Red Cross relayed a report from the

86 I was unable to track down the woman who submitted the paperwork for the rehabilitation process.

87 Beatrice Holmes to Gorbachev, Nov. 18, 1988; letter, American Red Cross to Beatrice Holmes, March 1, 1990.

Russian Ministry of Internal Affairs that Noah had been arrested, convicted and executed by firing squad for 'participation in an anti-Soviet organization, carrying out espionage activities, [and] participation in preparation of diversionary activities'.[88]

My father, Jay Holmes, with the help of personal connections from his career in federal employment, got in touch with once-prominent Soviet dissident Pavel Litvinov, then living in New York. He is the grandson of Soviet diplomat Maxim Litvinov, and the son-in-law of dissident writer and former Trotskyist Lev Kopelev, whose name has popped up on the fringes of our tale. He was then the American representative of Memorial. He wrote to my father: 'What a sad and at the same time fascinating but not unusual story ...'[89] Noah London was rehabilitated through the offices of Memorial in the year 1997. This was exceedingly late but far from useless. If he had not been rehabilitated, I would not have obtained the broad access to his records that I received during my research in the former Soviet Union.

9 Final Epilogue: The Holocaust and Jewish Lithuania

The 'northwest provinces' of the Tsarist Empire, where Noah and Miril London grew up, became the very epicenter of the Holocaust. In what is now Lithuania and Belarus, a smaller percentage of Jews survived than anywhere else in Europe.

The Jewish population of Motele and Antopol, the old Unterman and London family *shtetls*, was virtually annihilated. The Motele Yizkor Book compiled by the few survivors mentions no Untermans and only one London, Shmuel London, as victims.[90] Apparently the numerous Untermans and less numerous Londons escaped to America – or Palestine. In Antopol however many Londons were murdered. The Antopol Yizkor Book narrates the story of Antopol under Soviet occupation:

> The Soviet army passed in a long line far out into the distance; motor vehicles, men, armaments and amiability ... Some of the officers in the

88 Beatrice Holmes, Red Cross tracing inquiry forms for Noah and Miril London, Dec. 15, 1995, and earlier (undated, probably 1990 or 1991); letter, Red Cross to Beatrice Holmes, Nov. 25, 1996.

89 Letter, Pavel Litvinov to Jay Holmes, Jan. 12, 1986.

90 'Destruction of Motele', Poliak 1956, http://www.jewishgen.org/yizkor/motol/motol.html, May 16, 2008.

> Soviet army were Jews. This was good news to us … Party Secretary Subatin occupied Bereh London's house on Pinsk street … Jews had to change their occupations. Instead of shopkeepers and middlemen they 'became' clerks, administrators, members of cooperatives or *artels* [collective independent labor unions]. On the side they did a little trading … The new regime took to purging the atmosphere of reaction, kulaks, ideological and economic opposition, etc. Among others, recent Polish settlers were carried off to the interior of Russia.[91]

But this relative Jewish paradise came to an abrupt end when the Nazis invaded. Noah London's relatives were exterminated with the rest of the population in an 'action' beginning on October 15, 1942. A few people fled to join the partisans. Of the 2,000 Jews living in Antopol before the Nazis came, only 8 survived. One of them, Itke Wolinetz, was probably a relative of Noah's mother, Pia Walensky or Wolinetz.

The partisans revenged this atrocity with a highly successful raid on the Nazi occupiers of Antopol the following year. Polesie, the Pripet Marshes where Noah and Miril London grew up, became the central base area for the partisan resistance movement against the Nazi invasion of the Soviet Union. In the crucible of Operation Barbarossa and the Holocaust, ethnic divisions in the swamplands broke down and serious blows were inflicted on the German occupiers. This facilitated the obliteration of Hitlerism but was too late to save the Jews of the Tsarist northwest provinces from the Holocaust.[92]

---

91 'Antepolie', Antopol Yizkor Book, 1972, http://www.stevemorse.org/yizkor/anteng/index.html May 16, 2008. The *shtetl* map on the website shows several homes owned by Londons.

92 See http://www.historylearningsite.co.uk/russian_resistance_movement.htm.

FIGURE 13 Contemporary (prewar) photo of *Gosprom* building in Kharkov where Noah London worked. Taken by author

FIGURE 14 Family photo, photographer unknown. Noah and Miril. Postcard apparently sent from the Soviet Union, September 1927

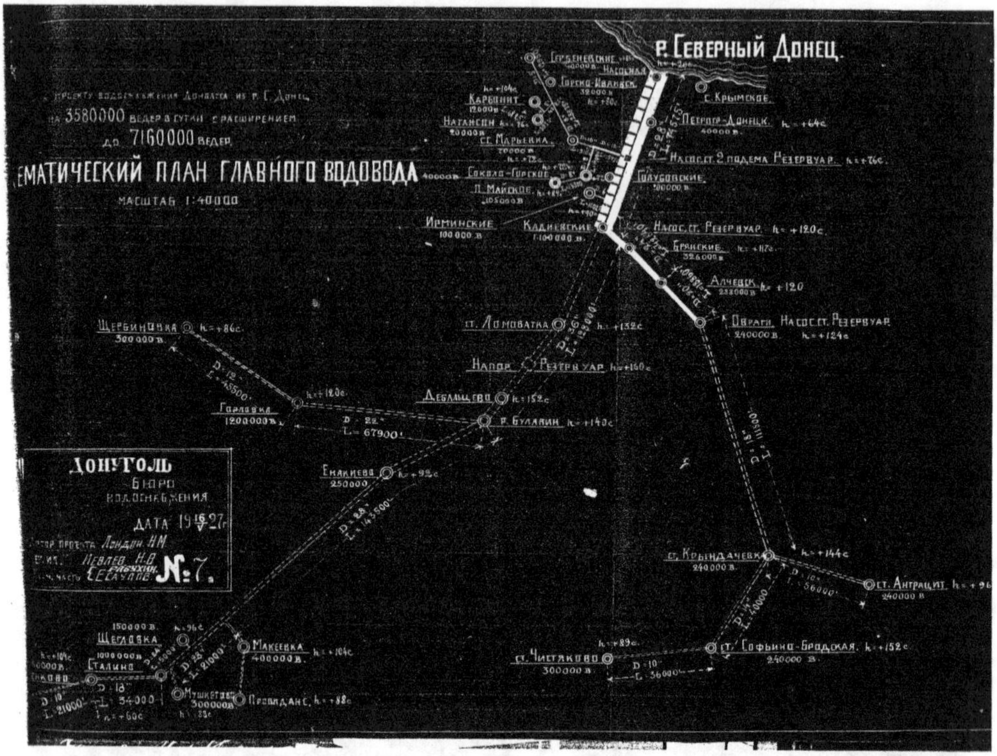

FIGURE 15 Soviet archives, files for Donugol Biuro Vodosnabzhenie. Noah London's design schematic for his first Donbass water pipeline, segment 7. May 16, 1927. The author has the right to his Soviet records as a relative of a victim of Stalinist repression under Russian and Ukrainian law

FIGURE 16
Dmitrii Debabov, 1930: Construction of Magnitogorsk. Found on website https://makinghistoryatmacquarie.wordpress.com/2012/11/17/the-great-leap-forward-the-rapid-industrialisation-of-the-soviet-union-between-1927-and-1940/

FIGURE 17
Wikipedia Commons file. Yakov Guminer. Arithmetic of a counter-plan poster (1931). https://en.wikipedia.org/wiki/File:Yakov_Guminer_-_Arithmetic_of_a_counter-plan_poster_%281931%29.jpg

FIGURE 18
Family photo, photographer unknown. Louis and Rose Discher-Unterman at grave in Palestine, early-mid 1930s

FIGURE 19 Family photo, photographer unknown. Clockwise from upper left. Party loyal Morris Unterman; Rose Discher-Unterman; Anna Hort-Unterman; her daughter Beatrice Hort, mother of the author. 1930s

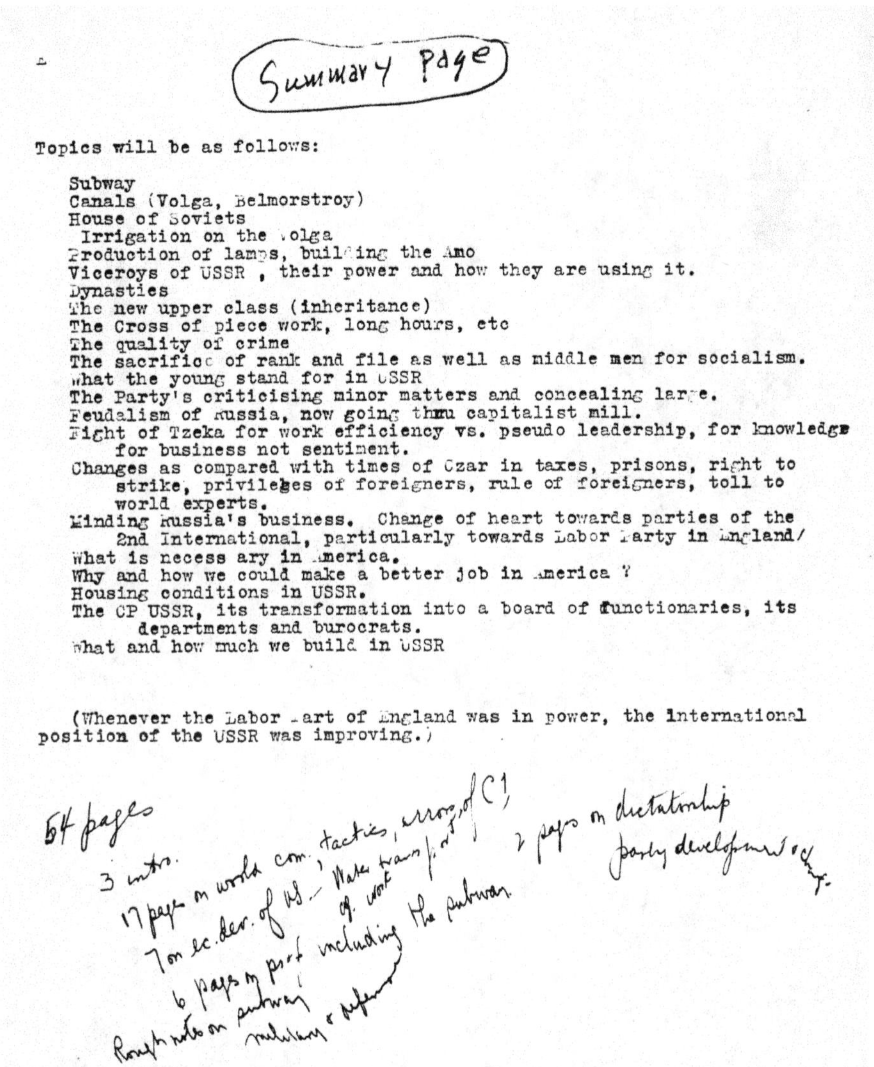

(Summary Page)

Topics will be as follows:

Subway
Canals (Volga, Belmorstroy)
House of Soviets
Irrigation on the Volga
Production of lamps, building the Amo
Viceroys of USSR , their power and how they are using it.
Dynasties
The new upper class (inheritance)
The Cross of piece work, long hours, etc
The quality of crime
The sacrifice of rank and file as well as middle men for socialism.
What the young stand for in USSR
The Party's criticising minor matters and concealing large.
Feudalism of Russia, now going thru capitalist mill.
Fight of Tzeka for work efficiency vs. pseudo leadership, for knowledge for business not sentiment.
Changes as compared with times of Czar in taxes, prisons, right to strike, privileges of foreigners, rule of foreigners, toll to world experts.
Minding Russia's business. Change of heart towards parties of the 2nd International, particularly towards Labor Party in England/
What is necess ary in America.
Why and how we could make a better job in America ?
Housing conditions in USSR.
The CP USSR, its transformation into a board of functionaries, its departments and burocrats.
What and how much we build in USSR

(Whenever the Labor Part of England was in power, the international position of the USSR was improving.)

64 pages
3 intro.
17 pages on world com. tactics, errors of CI,
7 on ec. dev. of US. – Water transport
6 pages on port including the subway
2 pages on dictatorship
party development
Rough notes on subway
military & defense

FIGURE 20 Photograph of copy of front cover of the London manuscript, in possession of author

FIGURE 21 Family photo, photographer unknown. Noah and Miril. Postcard sent from Soviet Union, probably mid 1930s

FIGURE 22
Family photo, photographer unknown. Benjamin Levine, 1934 or 5

FIGURE 23
Noah London's NKVD mugshot, 1937, courtesy of FSB

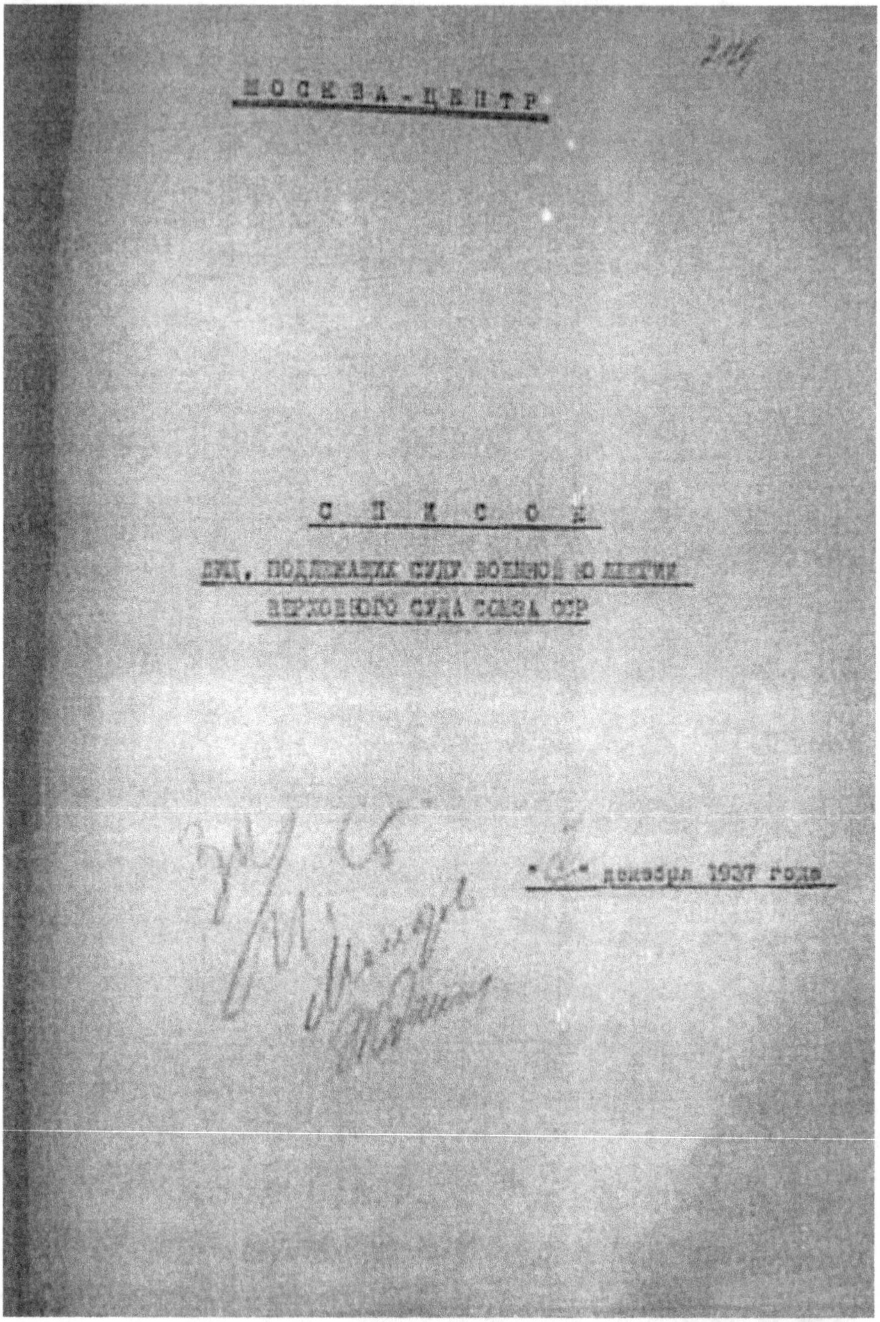

МОСКВА-ЦЕНТР

СПИСОК

ЛИЦ, ПОДЛЕЖАЩИХ СУДУ ВОЕННОЙ КОЛЛЕГИИ ВЕРХОВНОГО СУДА СОЮЗА ССР

"[illegible]" декабря 1937 года

FIGURE 24 Lengthy military trial (and execution) list initialed by Stalin and Molotov, after Noah London's execution, December 1937. Archive of the President of the Russian Federation, opis 24, delo 413, list 249

140. ЛИН-ДА-ШИН
141. ЛИПКИН Аркадий Маркович
142. ЛИФШИЦ Михаил Иосифович
143. ЛОНДОН Ной Моисеевич
144. ЛУКАШЕВСКИЙ Борис Петрович
145. ЛЮБИМОВ Владимир Виссарионович
146. ЛЮБИЧ Леонид Семенович
147. ЛЯПИС Яков Рудольфович
148. МАЛАМА Михаил Николаевич
149. МАНОВИЧ Арон Григорьевич
150. МАРКОВИЧ Андрей Филиппович
(он же Макаревич Игнат Григорьевич)
151. МАРЦИНСКИЙ Иосиф Владиславович
152. МЕЖЕНИНОВ Петр Сергеевич
153. МИЛЛЕР Генрих Иосифович
154. МИНСКИЙ Григорий Наумович
155. МИРОНОВ Иван Никитич
156. МИРОНОВ Сергей Алексеевич
157. МИХАЙЛОВА Зоя Ивановна
158. МИХЕЛЬ Карл Оскарович
159. МОЗЕ Альфред Оттович
160. МОЛДАВСКАЯ Элеонора Борисовна
161. МОЧАНОВ Михаил Николаевич
162. МОТОРИН Федор Александрович
163. МОУХАРАИН Булат Моухараинович
164. МУРАВКИН Герберт Ильич
165. МУХИНА Ирина Инокентьевна
(она же Худосовцева)
166. НЕЙМАН Алексей Федорович
167. НЕРОНОВ Иван Григорьевич
168. НЕСТЕРОВ Захар Антонович

АП РФ, оп.24, дело 413, лист 256

FIGURE 25 APRF, op. 24, d. 413, l. 256. Page with Noah London's name, number 143. His secretary, Irina Mukhina, is number 165

Беларуская Савецкая Сацыялістычная Рэспубліка
Белорусская Советская Социалистическая Республика

ПАСВЕДЧАННЕ АБ СМЕРЦІ
СВИДЕТЕЛЬСТВО О СМЕРТИ

ПЯ № 130923

Гр. ....
(прозвішча—фамилия)
....
(імя і імя па бацьку—имя и отчество)
памёр(ла)
умер(ла) ....
(прапісаю і цифрамі год, месяц і число—
прописью и цифрами год, месяц и число)
прычына смерці
причина смерти ....
аб чым у кнізе запісаў актаў грамадзянскага стану аб смерці
о чем в книге записей актов гражданского состояния о смерти
1949 года месяца 19 чысла
года месяца числа
утворан адпаведны запіс за
произведена соответствующая запись за № 509
Месца смерці: горад, сяло Минск раён
Место смерти: город, село район
вобласць, рэспубліка
область, республика
Месца рэгістрацыі
Место регистрации ....
(назва і месцазнаходжанне бюро ЗАГС—
наименование и местонахождение бюро ЗАГС)

Дата выдачи 19 . . . . 1949 г.

Загадчык бюро запісаў актаў грамадзянскага стану
Заведующий бюро записей актов гражданского состояния

М. П.

Белорусский яз. Гознак. 1947.

FIGURE 26 Graphic from family records. Official Soviet death certificate for Miril London in Belarusian-December 1949

FIGURE 27 City district channel dam picture, from Soviet Donbass water pamphlet, *Bol'shaia Voda Industrii*. 1980

FIGURE 28 Family photo, photographer unknown. Rose Risikoff-Unterman, teaching a class in 1940s or '50s

FIGURE 29 Front door of contemporary successor to Donbassvodtrest in Donetsk. Photo taken by author

Conclusion

The tragic odyssey of Noah and Miril London wanders through many dark corners of the blood-soaked twentieth century. What light does their story shed on the central axis of that calamitous century, the tale of the rise and fall of the Soviet Union? Among its ashes and diamonds, what do we learn about the nature of the Stalinist system? More narrowly, what does it have to tell us about the Great Terror – or at least about the Great Purge that set it off and to which they fell victim? So far as the light from the answers to these questions extends to our present condition, what does their story tell us about the twenty-first century? In America, where they were active participants in the socialist and labor movement, and worldwide?

According to Leon Trotsky's analysis in his most famous work, *The Revolution Betrayed*, the Soviet bureaucracy was a huge social layer, 12 to 15 percent of the Soviet population – a considerably larger percentage of the population than the working class represented in Tsarist Russia. This bureaucratic caste originated as a 'plenipotentiary of the working class' but acquired autonomy. It triumphed over the working class out of which it arose, betraying the revolution, in what he dubbed the 'Soviet Thermidor' of the mid-1920s. Analogies between the French and Russian Revolutions were ubiquitous in his day. Thermidor was the new revolutionary month in which Robespierre fell, more moderate Jacobins took power and the revolution went into reverse gear. To Trotsky, that's what happened in the Soviet Union after Lenin died. Much as, in the French Revolution, the Jacobins who overthrew Robespierre on the Ninth of Thermidor donned Imperial robes after Napoleon, the Stalin of the French Revolution, seized power.[1]

More recent historians have described how in the quicksand society of early Stalinism, rapid social transformation required the creation of a huge layer of administrators. They were largely recruited from the ranks of the relatively small Soviet working class, through the process of *vydvizhenie*, the Soviet version of upward social mobility. The upper ranks of the Soviet Communist Party became the *nomenklatura*, or as Trotsky put it a 'Bonapartist caste'. Noah London was a *nomenclaturchik*, denoted as such on Malenkov's purge lists.

By 1937, the year they shot Noah London, this bureaucratic caste was thoroughly homogenous – politically speaking. But behind the scenes a social divi-

1 Trotsky, *Revolution Betrayed*; Moshe Lewin, 'Society, State, and Ideology', in *Cultural Revolution in Russia*, 41–77; Isaac Deutscher, *Stalin: A Political Biography* (Oxford: Oxford University Press, 1967).

 DOI:10.1163/9789004745384_016

sion had unfolded. Inhabiting its upper levels were aging, burnt-out, disillusioned intellectuals and former workers, who had led a world-shaking revolution but eagerly embraced 'socialism in one country' after Lenin died: the Stalin loyalists, the Ordzhonikidzes, Postyshevs, Lomovs and Mezhlauks. Less enthusiastically, after intervals of varying length, the capitulators followed suit, the Zinovievs, Piatakovs, Lifshitzes and Drobnises. On the lower steps of the bureaucratic pyramid smothering Soviet society in the 1930s stood youthful and energetic *vydvizhentsy* – proletarian beneficiaries of the revolution, at Donbassvodtrest and everywhere else in the USSR. For the Baibakovs and Brezhnevs, the essence of that revolution was not social transformation, but upward social mobility – *their* upward social mobility. They saw Stalin as their leader, representative and role model. As Oleg Khlevniuk, Russia's best historian of the Stalin era puts it: 'In a matter of months, the purges destroyed the party's old guard and replaced it with fresh faces, unburdened by excessive knowledge of the past or ideas about how the country might be run differently'. After the Great Purge ended, most party secretaries were younger than 35.[2] And they became Stalin's heirs – the rulers of the Soviet Union – until they grew old and senile, and Mikhail Gorbachev organized their children to put them out to pasture.

Stalin was a central figure of the Bolshevik apparatus during the revolutionary days, but was largely unknown to the general public. He too, like the *vydvizhentsy*, entered the spotlight as dreams of world revolution faded away. He and his immediate entourage organized and supervised the Great Purge from the top. But it took shape at the bottom, in Soviet industry, the spiritual heart of the Soviet Union. And there, as we see from the Donbassvodtrest story, the *vydvizhentsy* were a driving force. Stalin was not an all-powerful totalitarian dictator, socially suspended in mid-air. A distinct layer in Soviet society, advanced into office during the Stalinist industrial and cultural revolutions, was the foundation on which the Great Purge rested. Without their support, Stalin's Great Terror could have turned out to be, as Trotsky prophesied, the last gasp of a regime on the edge of collapse.

Noah London's picture of Soviet reality in the mid-1930s in his manuscript was strikingly similar to the one painted by Trotsky. But their visions of where the Soviet Union was going were different. London saw it as moving 'from feudalism to industrialism', toward a technocratic state capitalism that could 'enslave labour as never before'. He thought it might serve a necessary historical purpose: the modernization of a 'backwards, Asiatic, filthy, lazy country'.

2 Khlevniuk, *Stalin*, 147.

Almost all American Jewish socialists, with Noah London a rare exception, supported the Mensheviks against the Bolsheviks before the October Revolution triumphed. They did not believe a socialist revolution was possible in a country as backward and uncultured as Tsarist Russia. Shortly before the seizure of the Winter Palace, London publicly ridiculed the Menshevik concept that history required Russia to go through a capitalist phase of development.[3] By 1934, the Menshevik argument that 'history does not skip stages' began to appeal to him. Subsequent developments could hardly have restored his faith in Bolshevik orthodoxy.

In his famous book, Trotsky treated Stalinism in the Soviet Union as a strictly temporary phenomenon doomed to collapse. He foresaw that:

> A collapse of the Soviet regime would lead inevitably to the collapse of the planned economy, and thus to the abolition of state property. The bond of compulsion between the trusts and the factories within them would fall away. The more successful enterprises would succeed in coming out on the road of independence ... The fall of the present bureaucratic dictatorship, if it were not replaced by a new socialist power, would thus mean a return to capitalist relations with a catastrophic decline of industry and culture.[4]

This is a startlingly accurate prediction of exactly what happened – more than half a century later. Trotsky's vision of the destiny of the Soviet Union was clearer than London's, but much water would pass under the bridge before that fall. I hope this book has helped to illuminate why.

So what happened to the former Soviet Union after the collapse of the Stalinist system? Since its inception, Stalinism depended on the support or at least tolerance of the Soviet working class in general and the coal miners in particular. Donbass miners were a relatively privileged layer of the Soviet working class. They produced the coal the whole country ran on, till it started to run out and the products of Noah London's and Nikolai Baibakov's oil refineries began to replace it. When the miners finally revolted in 1989, striking in mass and even seizing control of local government here and there, it was the death knell for the regime.[5] The return to free market capitalism did not come by popular demand. It was shoved down the throats of the Soviet people by the heirs of Stalin, Khrushchev and Gorbachev.

3 Noah London, 'Menshevizm oder sotsialistishe impotents', *Naye Velt*, Nov. 6, 1917.

4 Trotsky, *Revolution Betrayed*, 250–1.

5 Friedgut and Siegelbaum, *The Soviet Miners' Strike*.

Decollectivization had side effects all too similar to those of the forced collectivization of agriculture under Stalin. Much academic effort has been expended on trying to determine the exact number of people who died in the Ukrainian famine of nearly a century ago, but few seem interested in studying the more recent post-Soviet death toll. Those commentators who have addressed the matter often blame it on alcoholism – as if Soviet citizens first discovered vodka when Boris Yeltsin staggered to the helm. For that matter, if the response of the Soviet people to the restoration of capitalism was to drink themselves to death, that in itself would be a remarkable condemnation of the free market system.

The forced collectivization trauma at least *ended*. And perhaps, by transforming Soviet agriculture, it helped lay the basis for the Soviet Union's industrial triumphs, victory over Nazi Germany and rise to superpower status. By contrast, Russia and especially Ukraine descended ever deeper into misery and despair, as I saw with my own eyes on my research trips. During my first visit to Moscow in 2001, Alexander Zhelenin, a well-known journalist particularly interested in labor issues, told me that workers in Russia had never once gone on strike for higher wages since Yeltsin's seizure of power. Since then, Russian labor unionism has revived slightly, and the average Russian standard of living has headed back to some sort of impoverished normality. Meanwhile, Moscow now is tied with Hong Kong for more billionaires than any other city in the world after New York.

Gary Shteyngart's *Absurdistan* was a well-deserved literary success. It is the story of the post-Soviet odyssey of the son of a pious ex-Soviet New York Jewish gangster, forced to return to the homeland. After trials and tribulations, in St. Petersburg and 'Absurdistan', he finally happily gets to return to America by plane on – September 11, 2001. Not the least of its merits is its depiction of the bizarre situation of the remnants of the Soviet Jewish community. But how many of its readers thought it was merely a satire, and did not realize how accurate a portrait of life in the former Soviet Union in the 1990s it actually was? Until hostility between Russia and the US broke out, Western public opinion ignored the social horrors of contemporary Russia in pretty much the same fashion as Communists in the West used to turn their eyes away from the horrors of Stalinism in the Soviet Union – and for much the same reasons.

And Ukraine, where everything was just like Russia when I visited except worse, as it has no oil, descended into bloody civil war in the year 2014. The coal miners, whose aging rustbucket mines were the backbone of what is left of the Ukrainian economy, were prime victims of bloodshed and destruction. Even before Putin, frustrated by his inability to get NATO to promise not to admit

Ukraine, launched his brutal invasion, there were over 14,000 deaths in what began as an Ukrainian civil war.

And how about the rest of the world? The degeneration and collapse of the Soviet Union was one element of a broader late twentieth-century narrative. The world-historic defeat of fascism in World War II simplified a previous three-way death struggle into a geographical Cold War – between Communism in the East and "free market capitalism" in the West. The final collapse of the Soviet Union elevated the USA to be the world's single superpower, looming over everything like a colossus. Then 9/11 and American failures in Iraq and then Afghanistan pushed it off its perch, destabilizing a brief post-Soviet 'American Century'. It ended in the year 2008, when the demise of a US housing boom set off a grandiose worldwide financial crisis. In America, as Wall Street sucked the blood out of Main Street, the vampire motif began spreading in popular culture – often with the vampires as heroes, this being America. Worldwide, working class living standards have been declining almost everywhere except in China, which is now starting to develop troubles of its own. Upward social mobility in the USA is running into the brick wall of drastically rising college tuition levels. *Downward* social mobility led to the birth of Jewish socialism in Tsarist Russia. Will that have similar effects, here or elsewhere? It has not, thus far, in the former Soviet Union. Nor did it in Weimar Germany.

The worldwide revival of fascist movements seemingly swept into the dustbin of history during World War II imparts urgency to getting rid of capitalism. Margaret Thatcher used to defend the free market system on the basis that 'there is no alternative'. She had it backwards. If the coronavirus catastrophe doesn't make it clear that there is no alternative to getting rid of the capitalist economic system, what could? It lay bare the inability of the capitalist system to deal even with the horseman of the apocalypse that everyone thought modern medicine had bridled. And the other three horsemen, war, famine and that potentially lethal crisis in the background, global warming, are saddled up and riding as well.

So, what light *does* this book shed on the current situation of the world, and what to do about it? The Bolshevik-led Russian Revolution was a model for social transformation whose rise and fall shaped an entire century. Nobody has managed to come up with another that might actually work. What is the main lesson we can draw from the Soviet story, examined through the eyes of Noah London? That the fundamental reason for the Stalinist degeneration of the Soviet Union was its isolation, the failure of the revolution to spread worldwide as the Bolsheviks had expected.

Noah London fully understood, as he explained to Rose in one of his letters from Russia, the root causes of Stalinist degeneration. But he never broke from the core of Stalinist ideology. In the public statement in defense of Bolshevism he made in October 1917, he prefigured Stalin's theory before Stalin came up with it himself. Nowadays, in this era of globalism, socialism in one country is even less of a practical proposition than in Stalin's days. In his manuscript, Noah London turned back to his old 'Loreite' dream of reuniting a socialist movement irrevocably divided between reformists and revolutionaries by an actual revolution – another impractical proposition.

Has the original perspective of Marxism announced in the *Communist Manifesto*, worldwide proletarian revolution, become a survival necessity for the human race? As Rosa Luxemburg put it so long ago, the alternatives facing humanity are socialism or barbarism. Lenin's concept that what's needed for a socialist revolution is a vanguard party of the working class did get the job done, despite later Stalinist degeneration. Alternatives were possible, and what ensued was not automatic. In twenty-first-century struggles for the socialist alternative to barbarism, thorough study of the experiences of the Bolshevik Revolution, the Communist International and Soviet history is desperately necessary.

APPENDIX A

The Bronx 'Coops' Manifesto

The original Yiddish version of this manifesto, *vos vil unzer kooperative bavegung*, is a four-page flyer preserved in the YIVO American Collection, RG 1400, box 6, folder 15. This translation benefited from assistance from the producers of Michal Goldman's *At Home in Utopia* (Filmmakers Collaborative, Waltham, Mass. 2008).

What Does Our Cooperative Movement Want?
By Noah London

We want to strengthen the hands of the working class. We want to ease the life of the worker today. We want to raise a generation of managers, of business leaders, who themselves can take charge of the economy of the land – without bosses or landlords or bankers or businessmen – when the working class rules in the future.

We want to arouse the independence of the worker masses; to develop the dormant powers within them; to kindle their ambition for a social, independent, richly enjoyable life. We want to teach the worker masses to live in a collective, to live in solidarity, in cooperation with others. We want to accustom them to harmonious coexistence, to harmonious collective creativity. We want to prepare for the future generation great masses of educated, business-experienced, disciplined, proud and secure builders, creators, managers, helmsmen at the wheel of life. We want to create a fortress for the working class now against its enemies. Later – for power.

We want the working class to be able to keep as much as possible of its earnings, thanks to its cooperative enterprises. So that they are not wasted feeding a horde of parasites, middlemen and shopkeepers, a horde of enemies of the liberation of the workers. As much as possible let his earnings be used to make his life easier now, to strengthen the workers' cooperative in the future, to support unions in their strikes and their political party in its propaganda.

The Practice of Cooperation

You want to know how this can work? Let us accompany you from work to home, to see how you spend your wages, no matter how meager they may be.

 DOI:10.1163/9789004745384_017

You come home to eat your supper. Two people have worked for the supper. You in the shop, your wife at home. It costs you twice as much as you think it costs. Your time. Your wife's time. That is because you live for yourself, all alone, not with your brothers and comrades. Had you belonged to a cooperative together with another hundred families like yours, only ten out of the hundred would have to work to prepare and serve the supper. The other ninety would be free. That means that your wife would only have to spend a tenth of her work time. That is money, if she is able to work in the shop, or wants to. That is health and an easier life, if she has the time free.

Instead of using a hundred separate sets of dishes, instead of cooking on a hundred separate stoves, you save when the cooking is done in a single cooperative kitchen. But that is not all. Your wife bought groceries, milk, meat, vegetables for supper—from whom? From the middleman, from the storekeeper. They made a profit on that. But several hundred of you, or a thousand or more, could have your own cooperative stores. The profits could go into the cashbox of your cooperative. You could buy your shoes, clothes and linen in your own stores. Instead of the profits going to the middleman and the storekeeper, they go into the till of your workers' cooperative.

After supper, perhaps you go to the theater or to the movies. Several thousand of you could have your own theater, your own moving picture house. There is no need for you to enrich the theater magnates. You can give the profits to your cooperative. Instead of hearing and seeing cheap trash, foolishness or the rotten propaganda of clergy and bosses, you can get for your toil the theater and movies that you want. By your hundred thousand you can have your own studios, where you can make the movies you want. You don't have to make the movie trust rich, you can make your own cooperative fund rich. You don't have to subsidize capitalist propaganda, you can spread your own proletarian propaganda.

You get to your apartment. On the first you have to pay rent. You support your landlord. Your landlord takes rent from you not only for the interest on the money it cost him to build the house, but also for the money he paid real estate speculators and moneylenders. This means you support besides your landlord other speculators as well, percentage men and flesh skinners. You can have your own houses, better, airier, healthier than you have now. You can build with communal forces your own cooperative houses, with common kitchens, with day nurseries for your children, with gardens, to keep your wife free from housework.

You want to buy furniture for the apartment, you have to borrow money, or if there is a misfortune in the family, you go to the banks, to the percentage men, and they rob you blind. Several thousand of you could have your own loan-fund, your own cooperative bank. Instead of making the percentage men and parasites rich, you make your cooperative fund rich.

On Saturday or Sunday you go to the country in taxis or buses belonging to private businessmen. They get rich from your quarters. You could have your own cooperative buses. You could make your own cooperative fund rich. You go on vacation to private hotels, boarding houses, camps. You are supporting middlemen trying to make out like bandits for a whole year off of three-four months' work. You could have your own camps and country cottages. Only support your own cooperative enterprises.

What will the result of all these projects be? First of all, naturally all these things will cost you a little less. Secondly, the strength of your household will grow. Thirdly, you can support the whole working class pretty well in its struggle with your financial resources. But that is only one result. They have many more important uses.

Call Out the Will to Fight

Through cooperative work, workers' ambitions will be awoken, their eagerness for life, for enjoyment. Most workers are like 'Bontshe the Silent',[1] they know they won't be heros, they let themselves be content with whatever happens. They don't know what possibilities civilization has created for humanity. We want to show the worker that there is a life in well-lit clean houses, with music, with theater, with green fields, with healthy food, we want to show him a great world, which is his but doesn't belong to him, a world which the ruling class has completely taken away from him. The more he knows about the beautiful life the more he will seek to conquer the world. We want by this method to awaken the eagerness of the working-class for enjoyment of life, for power.

We want to reveal to the worker the workings of the current order. Today the worker knows about his own boss, and his neighbor or comrade's boss. If he has a little consciousness he knows that his boss is his enemy, he struggles against him. Through the cooperative, where the worker becomes the landlord, the banker, the simple property owner, and discerns the power of the trust, of finance-capital, of the great business combinations, how they have legislation, the state, and the lawyers along with the priests and rabbis and professors at their service against the worker-economy, against the working class. Then when

1 London refers here to *bontshe shvayg*, a famous Yiddish short story by I.L. Peretz. Its hero spends a quiet life in poverty and suffering. For his reward in heaven he requests that: "Every morning, I want to have a hot roll with fresh butter!"

he understands how his struggle is political, how the class struggle of the workers is political, then these members of the cooperative movement will become the most active defenders of the political party of the working class.

We have already seen an example: the farmers of the Northwest in America have through cooperation come to consciousness of their own farmer political party. Through worker cooperatives workers will come to their political workers' party.

We Want to Summon Workers to Self-Activity

We want him to learn to think of himself as a ruler, a master, fit for everything and able to do anything, who no longer feels degraded and depressed, that he is only a little screw, a worthless tiny thing, who only has his own little corner, and for the rest—the 'educated', the 'wise', the experienced specialist experts – the capitalists, they know the rest.

In reality, let's take a stroll together for a day and consider what happens with you, with every worker, in the course of the day. You go down into the subway, you pay your nickel, and it takes you to your shop. Someone is sitting somewhere high up in a big office, making decisions. Millions of dollars are collected and parceled out so the trains will run, in the banks and on the stock exchange. Somewhere they deliver coal to generate electricity for the motors, they forge steel and make subway cars. They dig tunnels, doors open and close, they take people in and spit them out, you among them. Of the whole operation you know one thing: you throw in the nickels; the doors suck you in and shove you out. In the great office on high the owners, the shareholders, come together; they talk, they hire people, they run the whole great machinery. They're the teamsters, we are the workhorses. You never think about this. This time you do. Do you have to play the role of the silent herring packed in the barrel? Are we not fit for anything else? Are those up there in that office on Broadway kneaded out of better dough than we are?

We go into a fully equipped shop. Somebody planned the building and invested capital to construct it. Someone gathered the machinery together and assembled it properly, someone sowed fields of flax, or raised sheep, sheared the wool, packed it, sent it to the spinning and weaving factories. Someone took orders for how many suits to make, somebody brought the material. They brought you a bundle, and out of the whole great operation, from the enormous organization sprawling over seas and fields, over the wide west prairie or the Australian mountains, to the banks and stock exchanges of Chicago and then New York—you just do one little thing. You sew the bundle on the sewing machine, you get your pay-envelope, and you know nothing else. If you have a good union your pay envelope is fatter, so you squirm a little less while you sew. You have no other say in the matter and you don't know any more about it.

You go into a restaurant to eat your lunch. Somebody has set out your herring from Scandinavia or Alaska, your meat from Nebraska, your bread from Kansas, your orange from California, your greens from Long Island, your napkins from Canada, your coffee from Brazil. You throw your nickels and dimes in the Automat and you get your meal readymade. Somebody sits in a big office and conducts the whole operation, produces whatever he wants for you, however much he wants, charges you what he wants to – you are only what they call in English the 'lemon' who gets squeezed. And so on endlessly.

If every worker goes into the cooperative organization, if he considers the cooperative enterprise his own affair, if he gets interested in the business, in every detail like buying the napkins, like digging the foundations for the cooperative buildings, in bosses and bankers, theater and music, the worker will be transformed from a messenger boy into a master, from an obedient slave – into a seeker for power. From somebody only out for himself, we will turn the worker into a community person. We will teach him through cooperative labor what concretely can be achieved together as a community, together in association with his brother fellow workers. We will pull him out of his own corner where he occupies himself with the boredom of passivity, with his own petty cares, into broad social activity where he will get momentum, where he and his fellow workers will care for the interests of the whole, his own interest included in the general interest.

We want to plant in the workers a respect for the interests and comforts of the community. We want to root out of him all tendencies toward private property, for his own household, for his own little corner. Through cooperation he will learn discipline, order, without which there can be no harmonious cooperation, without which there can be no economical life when the working class needs to run the collective economy in the future Communist order.

Our Russian comrades, the Russian Communists, have to struggle against this 'me-first' attitude among the backward workers and peasants. We want to do the preparatory work even before it will be our turn to take control over the country.

WE WANT TO MAKE THE WORKERS INTO CAPABLE BUSINESS-LEADERS, CAPABLE MANAGERS

On the morrow of the Revolution Lenin sent out a call to the Russian proletariat and peasantry. He called every worker, every housewife, every cook to the steering wheel of the state, to the management of industry, of banks and business.

The bosses, the *spetsy*, the well educated, they are enemies of the working class. When we take the economy away from them, we will confine them to giving assistance. We want the workers alone to take the places at the wheel, they can handle the normal course of work and business.

We want to create a giant branching network of cooperative enterprises, which will prepare workers for the great day to come when they will have to stop being the little screws that finish the ready bundles and sit down at the management desk, in the bank office, and steer their own lives.

After the devastation of war and counter-revolution the cooperatives in Russia were the first to get back on their feet and start rebuilding the ruins. They were the first cell around which an organized economic life began to develop. They were a powerful weapon of the proletarian government in struggling against catastrophe. We want to create for the working class and its dominion that kind of fortification and economic support.

But to make sure that the enterprises truly serve the interests of the working class in its current struggle as well as in the future, it is necessary for any class-conscious worker who has a bit of time left over from the union or the party to devote his work to the cooperative movement. To protect ourselves from bourgeois deviations, to protect ourselves from the danger of cooperative organizations trying to stay aloof and not get involved in helping the struggle of the working class, we will make cooperatives of workers and for workers. No place for bosses, full or half, for shopkeepers and business people, big or little. A pure proletarian organization, which must and will hold high the banner of proletarian ideals.

Our Cooperative a Purely Proletarian Organization

In order to avoid the danger of careerists and job-seekers wanting to turn the movement into a business trying to get in with us, as has happened in other cooperatives, we will create no cushy jobs. We will pay our employees ordinary working-class wages, and choose them from the most devoted, experienced activists of our movement.

In order to avoid the danger of a bureaucracy, which can naturally emerge where you have the management of great enterprises, and since we want our cooperative to be a movement of the masses not a business institution, we want the broadest possible masses to sign up with the organization. We want it to function continually, regularly, we want to have frequent membership meetings where all questions of the organization are considered and decided.

Our appeal is not only aimed at the workers of New York, where we began our activity. There are quite a few industrial centers in the country where great masses of workers are concentrated. There are thousands of conscious, active workers among them, who understand the meaning of collective action. The new revolutionary movement has awakened among them a striving for an active social existence, it has awakened great, unlimited ambitions. There is every possibility to create a great network of cooperative organizations throughout the land. Built by the workers of the new revolutionary movement and excited by the ideals of proletarian power, the cooperatives will be a success, will be an immense support for the working class.

Therefore it is the obligation of every honest worker, male and female, Communist or non-party, to join the cooperative workers' organization and help to forge the power of the working class, help to build its fortresses.

Published by the United Workers' Cooperative Society. Year 1926

APPENDIX B

'Notes on the USSR'

The London Manuscript

This is an edited but complete version of London's August 1934 manuscript, 'Notes on the U.S.S.R'. A shorter version was published with an introduction in *Labour/Le Travail* in 2007.[1] The original, available in the 'Noah London Collection' at the Tamiment Institute at New York University, represents the efforts of his sister-in-law Rose Risikoff to organize her old notes from dictation sessions in the woods outside London's dacha in Kliazmo, a vacation settlement in the Moscow suburbs. These now-lost notes were likely in shorthand. They may have been in Yiddish, judging by the syntax and sentence structure of the typed manuscript. The manuscript is undated, unfinished, disorganised, and does not follow its table of contents, probably dictated in Kliazmo and photographically reproduced in this book. Rose's handwritten notations on it sketch out more or less accurately the structure of the final typed version – except that they indicate a length somewhat longer than that of the final product. A few handwritten pages in the manuscript must be holdovers from a lost previous draft, which may have included additional material. Parenthetical notes by Noah London or Rose Risikoff are in parentheses. Parenthetical notes in brackets are by the author of this book, as are footnotes.

Foreword

The author is a Communist, a member of the Communist International (CI). The object of this writing is to present to Communist and revolutionary workers ideas of reorganization of the revolutionary movement, of changing tactics in order to serve more effectively the only goal of the true Communist, to serve the only end of the true Communist, that is, the daily struggle for betterment of the material and cultural conditions of the working masses through the creation of a socialist state, where exploitation, suppression, arbitrary rule are impossible. While the author considers the present tactics and organizational forms of the CI and its sections to be fundamentally wrong in that they fail to best serve the ends described above, he knows that the revolutionary impetus is concentrated within the bounds of the organizations within and around the Communist

1 'Noah London's "Notes on the USSR"', *Labour/Le Travail* 60 (Fall 2007): 181–215.

 | DOI:10.1163/9789004745384_017

Party of the World, with its symbol of working-class revolt and victory embodied in the USSR, a beacon pointing the way towards world revolution.

To divorce oneself from this organization means finally to divorce oneself from the revolutionary movement, and therefore the author writes under an assumed name in the hope that soon the Communist movement as a whole or in part will realize the justice of these criticisms, which will undoubtedly be received at present as a hostile action against Communism. The history of the last decade has shown that all the oppositionists who waged an open fight against the movement finally, by the logic of the offense, found themselves among the ranks of the enemies of the revolution and of the working class. The author prefers for the time being to be labelled as a coward who does not dare to wage an open fight, and to remain active within the movement, rather than to be driven into a position against it.

Many will surely consider it an outrage to expose to the enemy the weak spots of the revolutionary movement at a time when bloody fascism and world imperialism are conspiring to destroy the Communist movement and the land holding the flag of revolution and representing the hope and ambition of the downtrodden world masses. Is this betrayal of the revolution? The author holds that hiding one's sores, wrapping them in rags so that nobody may see them, is not as healthy as painful surgery, cleansing, and exposure to sun and light. Sores will heal away when treated.

1. The World Communist Movement

It is 17 years since the revolutionary party of the working class of Russia seized power and became the standard bearer for all the revolutionary organizations of the world. It is 15 years since this party obtained organizational hold over all the revolutionary parties all over the world, exerting a control even the Catholic Church never exerted over the minds and bodies of its faithful in the worst times of the dark ages and the inquisition. But with what results? The object of this essay is to speak plainly and to find the reasons and remedies for such discouraging results.

The Crisis of the World Working Class

At no time in history, since the French Revolution, was the working class so disunited, so disorganized, its organizations so physically and morally crushed as now. At no time in the existence of the so-called Second International were the socialist parties, then the only fighting labor organizations, as weak, as ineffective as the Communist parties, the revolutionary organizations of the present, are now.

The Communist Party of Germany was simply brushed aside by fascism, driven underground without having the working class put up any struggle for its existence. The glorious and vain struggle of the Austrian proletariat against fascism started with the Communist Party of Austria deeply absorbed in organizational and dogmatic casuistries and acrobatics. The barricades in Amsterdam woke the Communist Party from its deep study of the latest circular of the staff of the world revolution, the CI, in which the grandeur and wisdom of the leader of the world revolution was extolled. The French workers without the leadership of the super-organized 'revolutionary movement' step forth to battle with their breasts bare against fascist cohorts, rousing the leadership to resume meaningless talk about united action. In spite of huge unemployment, in Great Britain, the classical land of the labor movement, a land where world politics and world imperialism are being shaped, where various schemes are made for arming and disarming, for pacts and anti-pacts, the land of classical parliamentarism, the Communist Party has some 3,000 members. Fluctuating plus or minus that figure for a decade, mustering under its banner a few hundred marchers in the various marches, drives and campaigns so carefully contemplated, organized, and super-organized according to all the slogans on how to attract the masses expounded in the latest CI circular. In Eastern Europe and the Balkan states, the Communist parties are making no headway at all. Some give no signs of life. There remains the All-Union Communist Party, the CPUSSR, which we will deal with later.

American Communism

At a time of the greatest crisis that America has ever known, when government and politics are dominating (no longer is government confined to policing; *laissez faire* is past and forgotten), the Communist and Socialist vote together amount to a half or so of what the united revolutionary movement mustered under the leadership of Debs in 1912, with the number of voters doubled since then! The party which continuously, almost thrice weekly, annoys the police by gathering again and again the same crowd of people at various squares of the street without the masses knowing what all the noise is for; the party which every year changes its tactics from dual unionism to boring from within and vice-versa; the party which cannot reap the harvest of the great upheaval in America while even the defunct American Federation of Labor (AFL) almost doubles its membership, while the bloodless, sapless Socialist Party still has a hold on several big unions and wrests the needle trades away from the influence of the Communists. Such is the American Communist Party!

Marx said in one of his letters to (Bolte): 'Sects are multiplying among the workers in inverse ratio to the growth of the movement … They continue to squabble and quarrel among themselves, in part artificially, until the real struggle begins, when sects disappear and a real movement begins'.[2]

The present period cannot be characterized as one which has no real issues for the working class. The menace of a new world fascism is spreading, the rights of workers are being suppressed. The tasks before the labor movement are gigantic. Who maintains that artificial division, the artificial issues on which the working class of the world is divided against itself? Sects do not want to disappear by themselves, there must come some power which derives its authority from the wide masses of the working class to wipe away the sects. The working class must be united not over a 'front', but for life!

We Communists are prone to throw the blame for our failures on the working masses. This is not true. The American workers, for instance, are not more 'dumb' than were their brethren who destroyed the Bastille in 1789, than were the Russian peasants and soldiers who made the October Revolution, than were the English peasants who revolted in 1381. The Executive Committee of the Communist International (ECCI) tries to explain the failures by blaming the leadership for not knowing how to approach the masses. With them the question is purely geometrical, the angle of approach, certainly an incorrect viewpoint.

Who better than the American worker, used to the dirty politics of the ruling parties, distrusts the bureaucrats who make a business out of the movement? Who more willing than the American worker, used as he is to a high standard of living and ready to fight for it at a time when it is being mercilessly depressed? Who better than the American workers can be rallied to fight for an ideal, though it be a false illusion as was the 'fight for democracy' during the World War? Today the workers of the world do not see before them a leadership whom they can trust, in whose hands they can boldly place their faith, a leadership ready to sacrifice itself for the masses instead of a group that plays politics at the expense of the masses. Furthermore, a leadership whom the masses can trust must not be a holy body like an academy of immortals. It must consist of living persons, living fighters who have shown by their individual acts their energy and wisdom. The Communist movement of the world has not produced such individuals – just the reverse is the case. Whatever was genuine, whatever was singled out in a potential leader, whoever displayed bold reasoning and

2 This quote, misidentified in the manuscript as a letter to 'Bracke', is a very loose paraphrase from Marx's Nov. 23, 1871, letter to German-American socialist Friedrich Bolte. It does convey the gist of Marx's argument. More than a decade earlier London quoted this letter to Bolte accurately, to the same effect, in his article 'Brif fun arbayter vegen der bavegung', *Freiheit*, Aug. 20, 1922.

had the guts to fight for his opinion was ousted from the Communist Party and finally from the revolutionary movement. Those Liebknechts and Luxemburgs who were not killed by the Whites were disabled or maimed or removed by the Communist International itself. Every country, every section of the CI has its Trotsky in exile – be it Thalheimer, be it Tranmael, be it Doriot, be it Bordiga.

Take the case of the American, Foster. Once upon a time he was the leader of the national steel strike against the greatest odds. Then he became a national figure. Now the machine has distorted and twisted him; he is just a spoke in the wheel. The new leader of the Communist movement is a man who does not inflame the masses with his rhetoric, logic, or powers of persuasion, as did Lenin, but who laboriously studies and transmits to his machine the latest encyclicals of the general staff of the revolution.

The Errors of the Communist International and Their Sources

Since world revolution was proclaimed in 1917 by the greatest revolutionary there ever was, Lenin – and he was the greatest strategist of revolution as well – the Communist parties in most of the countries have not made much headway so far as actual leadership of the masses goes. Indeed, some of them have been rolling down an inclined plane. What has caused such a state of affairs? What specifically is wrong with the theory and practice of the CI? How should it be amended?

As to theory: the first wrong assumption is that the way of the revolution in other countries must be almost identical to the way of the Russian Revolution. Lenin tried to drive this point home in his booklet *'Left-Wing' Communism: An Infantile Disorder*. There he points out a whole set of coincidences and conditions which ensured the success of the Russian Revolution. Yet the leaders of the CI do not grasp that truth, most probably because none of them is capable of understanding anything outside of previously worked-out theory.

Specifically, let us consider 1905, the time of the so-called first revolution, when there was a movement of national scope against Tsarism. Lenin did not advance for the vanguard of the workers the slogan 'Overthrow Tsarism, Establish a Dictatorship of the Proletariat!' He was against the leftist slogan of Trotsky and other prominent revolutionists, 'Down with Tsarism – For a Workers' Government!' Why is it that the greatest revolutionary, Lenin, at the time of the greatest upheaval history has ever witnessed, only 12 years before the actual overthrow of the Tsar and the establishment of the dictatorship of the proletariat, opposed the slogan of dictatorship? Did the German Communists have the right in 1921, 13 years before the landslide of fascism and the almost complete erasure of any revolutionary activity, to call the workers to the final social revolution, for the establishment of a workers' government? Was it not silly, historically speaking?

Lenin did not call for the immediate establishment of a workers' government because faith in capitalism was not yet shattered in 1905, even though Tsarism had failed miserably, in war as well as in its internal policies, leaving the country in a belligerent, semi-civil state. The German masses had not entirely lost their faith in capitalism, which sold the country to the conquerors under the Versailles Treaty, which together with the whole array of peace treaties constituted a stabilization scheme for the whole capitalist sector. The slogan to overthrow Germany, one part of the capitalist sector, was therefore equivalent to the slogan to overthrow the entire capitalist world, including victorious France, Great Britain, Italy and America – a manifest absurdity. Yet the Russian Communists, who were able so well to seize the right moment and lead a successful revolution in their own country, who could size up so well the internal situation and the international factors which enabled the Russian Revolution to succeed, were and are completely ignorant of the internal situation in the Western countries, believing the situation there to be similar to the Russian.

If we can believe the account of a Russian *New York Times* correspondent, Lenin warned him that he might return and find a revolution in America. Karl Radek, one of the first leaders of the revolutionary CI, wrote that the splitting of the Socialist parties of the world and creating the Communist International was done because of the expectation of an immediate social revolution. Otherwise, he said, there would have been no sense in creating a separate CI ('Three Years of the CI', *Communist International*, 1922). If the slogan of immediate establishment of a workers' government, the battle cry of millions of German workers, was a failure because of its prematureness, because the theory of universality of laws of revolution as promulgated after the Russian Revolution does not hold true, was it not all the more silly to put forth the slogan of a workers' government in the victorious nations, such as Italy, France, Great Britain and the US? Who does not recollect the way in which the Communist Party called the masses for an armed insurrection in Rutgers Square in 1920? But that insurrection was postponed because some of the leaders got word that the chief of police was preparing special squads to handle it. Can the working masses of these countries take seriously such parties with such untimely slogans? It is no wonder that such large parties as the German and French, heirs to a membership of millions, have dwindled from year to year, almost to the vanishing point.

It is easy enough to explain why the Russian leaders, men with vision and experience, did not size up the situation in the Western countries correctly. The first reason was the isolation of Russia from the West during three years of war followed by two years of revolution, which made it simply impossible for them to know what was going on in the other countries. Certainly the wish was father to the theory. The desperate conditions in which the Russian Revolution found itself during the intervention period raised the hope of a revolution of international dimensions, so that even the most cool-headed of the leaders based his tactics on the assumption of an impending world revolution.

The greatest mistake, however, was the question of organization, the question of tactics. The leaders of the CI applied the theory of government control to the theory of control of parties. In his famous book *The State and Revolution*, Lenin theorized that a revolutionary government must not leave the apparatus of the former government intact, since this could only serve as an instrument for furthering the aims of that former government. Instead, the old apparatus must be destroyed and a new one, completely controlled by the newcomers, must be created. Proceeding from this premise, the Russian Communists decided that in order to win the support of the working class of other countries, the respective working-class parties must be smashed as a part of the apparatus of former governments, and a new apparatus must be created, capable of being completely controlled by the Russian working-class party. This assumption was entirely wrong, because mechanical control of a governmental apparatus gives one control of the functions of the citizenry served by these governmental departments, because the relationship between government and citizenry is compulsory rather than voluntary. In the case of political parties, however, the best mechanical control of the party apparatus does not guarantee control of the membership of that party, since the membership has the privilege of leaving and the masses have the privilege of not listening, of ignoring the party and its apparatus. The best rigid control of a party may be like steering a device in a vacuum, and this is just exactly what has happened in almost every country, as we will see later. On the other hand, the theory that the former Socialist parties could not help to serve the aims of the new revolutionary government was totally wrong. When the sentiment of outside countries did not support the revolution, no party or party apparatus could by mass action or political pressure raise any effective aid. (Lobbying and diplomatic exertions not based upon actual mass strength are worthless, as Marxists know.) When there is sentiment among a goodly portion of the masses upon which any party builds its strength, even a reactionary Socialist party, then the leadership of that party, which is seemingly altogether a free agent with respect to the Russian government, cannot ignore the sentiment of the masses in that party for the revolutionary government of the USSR and must give expression to their friendly feeling for the Russian government.

During the time of the Polish war, British and German workers gave effective aid to Soviet Russia by refusing to load ammunition for Poland. That the Labour Party leadership was inherently hostile to the USSR did not prevent the existence of the Anglo-Russian Committee. This was due to the sentiment of the laboring masses for the USSR, a warmth not raised by the propaganda of the lilliputian CI-controlled British section. No matter how effective were the techniques of propaganda practiced by that section, that party failed to reach the masses because its numbers were too small to have broad contacts, and because its writings, periodicals, and pamphlets had a negligible circulation. This example is cited to prove that it is not the propaganda of the CI which creates favorable sentiment, nor is it the party apparatus that gives effective expression to that sentiment. Rather there exists an innate and real feeling of fellowship for the first and only government where the workers drove out their hated exploiters. The problem then for the Russian Communist Party was to establish such relations between itself and the existing socialist parties of the Second International that these might not thwart the friendship of the masses. Instead of vainly trying to destroy the Socialist parties and to create a new apparatus totally controlled by the Russian Communist Party – an effort that met with little or no results – it must be pointed out with all historical truthfulness that the splitting of the old parties, in the main instances if not in all, immediately and directly harmed Soviet Russia. In splitting away from the Socialist parties their most revolutionary part, the most ardent fighters for the cause of the Russian Revolution, the other portion, the reactionary element, was placed on the other side of the barricades. The leadership of a united party could never have permitted itself the outrages that were committed after the split.

For example, let us take the leadership of the German Independent Social Democratic Party before and after the split. Or to take a nearer case, let us look at the American Socialist Party. Before the split, this party, with all the unions and organizations under its influence, had at least given 'lip service', as the *Communist* called it, to the revolutionary government of Russia. But 'lip service' is still service, and it is better than actual counterrevolution. Now instead of that service, there arose clear expression of hostility. The truths that Lenin was trying to hammer in about 'boring from within' the mass organizations – why it is wrong for revolutionaries to leave those mass organizations thereby giving the reactionaries a free hand – the same policies were applicable to the parties of the Second International, in a sense mass organizations, each with a membership of hundreds of thousands with widespread affiliations, auxiliaries and publications.

The Fundamental Task Was Internal Affairs

In the light of history, it must now be stated that the split of the Second International and the creation of the Communist International was a blunder, insofar as the direct, immediate needs of the Russian Revolution were concerned. This policy resulted in crystallizing hostile action against the revolution in influential circles throughout the world, rather than in establishing effective counteraction to the hostility of the world, giving time for the building of a socialist stronghold in Russia which might be secure against external intervention. Since the revolutionary wave outside of Russia failed, it was the business of the revolutionary government to concentrate on internal policy without trying to become a center for world revolutionary propaganda, which because of the mechanical methods chosen could not be effective. More plainly, the Russian government should have at the very beginning stated clearly, specifically and in good faith that it permits the workers of each and every country to fight their battles alone, by their own ways and methods. That the Russian revolutionary government by snatching power from its capitalist class has undertaken responsibility for the life of the western Russian empire. That its herculean task is to organize, feed, clothe and clean its own land and build there a true socialist state. Would then the laboring masses, the revolutionary workers of the world have accused the Russian government of nationalism? Would they have demanded that the Russian revolutionary army should march into the world bringing socialism on the tip of its sword? Perhaps some hotheads would have wished the Russian army to relieve them of the difficult task of organizing and conducting their national revolutionary struggles. Nevertheless the Russian army could not and did not attempt such a gigantic task, despite the sentiment in some circles which favored such an extremist policy.

Hence the creation of the CI has cost the Russian workers and peasants tremendous additional suffering, since it served as a bugaboo for all the reactionary forces of the world to increase their attacks on the Soviet Union by economic and political pressure, as well as armed intervention. It should be said that Lenin made attempts to correct this mistake. As a matter of fact, Lenin understood better than anyone else that the fundamental task of the Russian Communist Party was internal affairs. Immediately after seizing power, he recognized the tremendous responsibility of the Communist Party to Russia; he realized that socialism must be introduced with the maximum care and consideration; that the classes of Russia will have to be appeased; their hostility neutralized by all means at the cost of any principle except the holding of power. This he thought would guarantee that the Revolution would not deviate from its general course and would finally reach its goal.

When Lenin introduced the slogan of the 'United Front', he meant it. He meant a united front, such as (and perhaps more unconditional than) the united front being carried on in France at present, where the common enemies are being fought by full strength, common issues and common slogans, rather than the Jesuitic maneuvering carried on during the past 12 years to discredit and break down the leadership of the socialist parties, a policy which did not succeed. Was not the German Socialist Party, the most treacherous of all to the cause of the working class, destroyed not by the maneuvers of the Communist Party but by Hitler?

Lenin, whom the author does not wish to present as an infallible God, undoubtedly made a mistake in sizing up the international situation in the period of 1917–19. Simply because he was not acquainted with the technique and economics of Western countries, he made mistakes in the economic policies of Soviet Russia. Lenin with his 'United Front' slogan, with his New Economic Policy, with his emphasis on caution and care in handling the peasant question, with his tolerance towards Russian intelligentsia and specialists, with his close contact and responsiveness to the masses, who was insistent but not stubborn, who though a leader took advice from his comrades, Lenin would have led the Russian Communist Party and with it the Communist International along different policies which would have born entirely different and better fruit than what we have now without Lenin. Due to his sickness, Lenin could not overcome the inertia of Military Communism and develop the policy of the United Front and the New Economic Policy, which were later amended or misrepresented. There is ample evidence in his writings of the latter years as well as in his actions and decrees. About the Leninist cult in general, later.

The Communist-Socialist Split Was Avoidable

The mechanical transplanting of Russian tactics and organizational forms to Western Communist Parties was wrong. On what issues of burning interest to the working masses, on what practical quarrels did the splits occur? The only country where a split was justified at the time was Germany, where the official leaders of Social Democracy pandered to the machinations of the imperialist clique in dividing the spoils of the World War and intervening in Soviet Russia. Although the primary policy concerned a foreign country, no worker could remain indifferent to the action against the first and only workers' government. The second burning issue of the day was the question 'Shall the workers of Germany make an attempt to seize power?' It is true, as shown by history, that the workers of Germany could not successfully seize and hold power there, but in making a revolution one cannot calculate to the last decimal point, and without making the revolutionary attempt there can never be a successful revolution.

Some of these attempts must surely fail. The question, then, was actually one of creating a party which could organize the revolution in Germany. Was it necessary to create a Communist International for this? What issue was of interest, let us say, to the American workers in the clash between Communist and Socialist parties? The relationship to Soviet Russia? There was no real issue between the two parties in this respect. As for the national interests of the working masses, there was actually no issue which could not have been ironed out inside and not outside party walls.

Let us take the current postwar period. What are the workers interested in? Employment, living wages, insurance, safety, more power. Could there have actually been any question on these issues between the Socialist and Communist parties, as if the socialists could mete these benefits out to the workers but did not want to and the Communists had to fight the Socialists for them? Obviously there could have been a difference in opinion as to how to present these demands and how to organize. But such questions were not of vital interest to the workers of America. Therefore, the squabbles of the parties, the very existence of the Communist Party, was not justified from the point of view of the daily interests of the masses. The fundamental error was that the Communists applied the organizational tactics of an actual revolutionary situation to the tedious task of acquiring mass support via long-drawn-out struggles. In an actual revolutionary situation, the widest masses are drawn into the struggle, are looking for leadership and organization, and seek a determined group of organizers and leaders who by close coordination and direct organizational activity can occupy a strategic position. At such a time a group of conspirators, by proper maneuvering, can accomplish the task and direct the revolutionary stream into channels prepared by them. Acting under this assumption, the Communist parties of the world and particularly of America try to occupy all strategic positions or gateways through which the wave of the mass movement must pass.

Let us enumerate some of these gateways. Unemployment groups – since there are over 10 million unemployed, there must be a mass movement of the unemployed. To get a hold of this group and direct it, it is necessary to create an organization to serve as a net to get the catch. Now there is surely a mass resentment against fascism, and there must be a movement to organize the unorganized. Certainly there must be a mass movement to help political prisoners. There must be a mass movement of poor farmers and of Negroes. How about the groups of foreign-born workers? What about the protection of the rights of women, youth, and children, a mass movement of students, sports organizations, self-education and so on? At every strategic point the Communist Party organizes its special groups.

But somehow or other the masses do not move and the party remains very small. What is the positive strength of the party? Wherein lies the enormous amount of energy necessary for all these organizations, transformations and continual charges into vacuum and space? The revolutionary charge which releases such tremendous energy comes not from the heart of what some may call the nation, but from an order, a group of individuals who have consecrated themselves to Communism as in earlier times did the Christians in their struggle for survival and then power in the Roman Empire. Whatever may be said of a leadership inspired by a lust for power, of the 'professional revolutionaries' who have been drained by machine politics of every revolutionary sentiment and turned into mere strategists, the only thing that can be said of the rank and file is that they are literally martyrs, be it from the persecution of police and bosses or from overwork in their organizations.

The Negative Effect of So-called 'Democratic Centralism'

In passing it must be said that although the Russian Revolution had a great stimulative effect on class-conscious workers and revolutionaries, opening new horizons and showing the masses a better future before them instead of generations and generations of seemingly hopeless struggle, nevertheless the leadership of the Russian movement had in many ways a negative effect. First, an unbecoming lust for power appeared among the 'strategists'. Second, the aping of Russian tactics, sacrificing contact with the masses and fights on live critical issues for maneuvers and organizational stunts. The worst thing was the adoption of the principle of so-called 'democratic centralism'. Democratic centralism, in principle, means that the leadership derives its power from the will and choice of the masses. The principles and tactics are then mapped out by wide and free discussion and choice of the masses. This is the democratic part. Whatever policy is then chosen, the masses must unconditionally and uncritically obey until discussion and election again take place. Without going into questions of principle, it must be said that it worked to the preservation of genuine democracy in the first years of the October Revolution under the centralism of a Lenin, who more than anyone else trusted the free will of the masses when organized in the proper fashion. However, under the centralism of the ordinary functionary of the CI and its sections, there has been no taint left of democracy in the Communist movement. Centralism, military discipline, law and order infringing upon the elementary rights and wishes of the masses, are necessary and effective only in time of great upheavals, the war of one nation with another, or of one class with another; that is, when the general cause absorbs and sweeps away every individual whim. Such a centralism is possible in peacetime only in an army whose incumbents serve a brief term. Then periodic drilling of discipline and centralism is bearable for soldiers and helps make them ready to endure the greater discipline of wartime. However, centralism in an army of long-time service has brought very sad results because, instead of thinking persons ready to adjust to conditions and exigencies, soldiers become automatons. More than one army was beaten because it consisted of automatons. Just that centralism, originating in the Comintern, caused the greatest detriment to the revolutionary movement in America.

There is absolutely no difference between the workings of the bureaucratic centralism of the AFL, which ruthlessly suppresses any expression of its rank and file, and the bureaucracy of the Communist Party towards its membership. The bureaucracy of the AFL suppresses its membership and perpetuates its hold of power because it pays and in the name of the policies of pure Americanism. The functionaries of the Communist Party perpetuate their power because it pays (strange as that may seem) and in the name of service to internationalism. (The material advantages of Communist functionaries are poor as compared with the salaries and bonuses of AFL officials, but a good many 'professional revolutionaries' would otherwise have to look hard about making a living.) By the way, both AFL officials and Communist bureaucrats sincerely believe in their service; the difference is in the tactics employed. The AFL bureaucrat combines skillful application of Robert's Rules of Order with cajoling, bribery and terror when necessary, keeping live persons out of the organization, while the Communist functionary applies the holy cross, not allowing any discussion or any real live issues before the party membership. This is sufficient for a membership which has consecrated itself to the cause; heretics are of course expelled.

What Is to Be Done?

In conclusion, it seems that the Russian revolution, the Russian masses, and Russian socialism would benefit more by a policy of strict Soviet nationalism. Plainly speaking, minding exclusively the business of the nation; abandoning hold of the Communist International; and letting slip our control over the other Communist parties of the world.

Trotsky criticizes Stalinism because of its nationalistic limits. He is absolutely right in stating the cause and absolutely wrong in drawing conclusions. What is worse, the old man is aware of Trotsky and his criticisms and therefore clings to internationalism.

If we adopt a Soviet nationalist policy, the capitalist nations of the world would cease looking upon the Soviet Union as a force undermining their existence. They would consider the USSR a nation with which they would have normal controversies or agreements. Secondly, the wholesome effect upon the

Communist parties of the world would be tremendous. They would start to act and think by themselves, according to the needs of the working class and the requirements of their movement. They would become real leaders of struggle of the working class instead of agents of propaganda. Medvedev said it long ago, but he was repudiated by a leftist wave.[3] The organized masses in revolutionary parties around the world would be much more effective help to the only working-class republic than any number of hired agents.

II. Building Socialism in the USSR

The Five-Year Plan: The Price of Defense

Now what of the Piatiletka, the Five-Year Plan? What of the great accomplishments of the USSR in heavy industry – Dneprostroi, Magnitogorsk, Traktorstroi, gigantic auto factories, plants producing agricultural machinery, new factories, mines, newly reconstructed metallurgical plants, machines, ships, airplanes, new chemical plants, the production of pig iron at the rate of 11 million tons per year instead of 4–5 million as in prewar times, etc.? Since so much is said in glorification of these achievements, I will not stop here to point out the real positive sides of these projects, which have this one absolutely positive feature, that unlike the Tsarist government, the USSR is now in case of an emergency, war or blockade less dependent on the outside world than it ever was. While few countries outside of the USA could withstand a defense of their borderline relying on their own resources, even efficient Germany collapsed because all its resources were drained. It does not become us to maintain that the USSR, because it has built so many plants and made such progress, will be able to rely on its own resources in defending the socialist fatherland.

Almost everything is built in the name of defense. The construction of a new base for heavy industry is a second-line trench in case the southwestern base should be taken. The theory is that it is important for the revolution to retain some corner in the event of invasion, be it in the far north, be it a small territory, in the expectation of a new wave of revolution – the theory of the Brest peace.

But what is the price of moving north? Take, for instance, the much advertised Magnitogorsk-Kuznetsk combination. The idea is to haul ore from Magni-

3 Medvedev, a principal Ukrainian party leader and Politburo member according to Ukrainian historian Robert Sullivant, was 'repudiated' so thoroughly that his full name is uncertain. Likely he was purged as a Bukharinist. Sullivant, *Bolshevik Politics and the Ukraine*, 167, 430; Bakulin and Leibovich, 'Rabochie, 'Spetsy', Partiitsy', *Rabochii klass i sovremennyi mir* 6 (1990): 107.

togorsk to Kuznetsk and on the way back to haul coal from Kuznetsk. Ordinarily the return trip would be entirely empty. But the fact remains that one has to haul coal and iron 750 miles, which of course would not be economical anywhere in the world. In South Russia the distance between the ore basin and the coal basin is 300 to 350 miles, half as far. But even this is not the main thing. It was necessary to build new cities, hauling food and materials great distances to build in a place where things cost double. And further: it will be necessary to continually compensate people for the inconvenience of living in the north in severe climates. How much quicker and more effective it would be to build in the south. Of course, things were built there as well, because people do not lay all their eggs in one basket. This is the price of defense – people should know it. Maybe the price is too high. Maybe if it becomes necessary to withdraw east, the whole thing will prove worthwhile.

What does moving north mean? Take the example of Canada, a country as free and democratic as the United States, larger in territory, a people under liberal rule and of the same origin and capability as the people of the USA. However, the USA has a greatly larger population. What is the reason? The main reason is that Canada lies in the north. The climate is harsher on the people, it takes more energy to fight nature. In the USA the climate is moderate, it helps people. Alaska is part of the US. It is manned by the most robust, physically capable people. But now that the Klondike rush is over, Alaska is a barren country. Gold, coal and metal are less important than whether people can work and enjoy living somewhere.

'The Bread Is What Counts'

If however we talk from the point of view of everyday economics, if we seek what constitutes the strength and happiness of a nation, we should say about the wonders of the Five-Year Plan what one Englishman said about the German successes during the late imperialist war. At the time when the German army made its terrific onslaughts on both Eastern and Western fronts, and the whole world was gaping in wonder at the great tactical achievements of the German army, one of the chief Allied propagandists told the following anecdote. Once there was walking along the shores of the Thames a young couple who were courting, a couple of moderate means. Now the young man was showing her the castles on the Thames and assuring her that he would soon become rich, buy her a castle, and install her as queen there. 'Ah', said the lassie, 'I wish we had a small apartment of our own with an oven. I would get me flour and bake me bread'. Now, said the Englishman, 'What is the use of the castle? The bread is what counts'.

Socialism means bettering the condition of the masses, enlightening them, not building cathedrals. Democracy built schools, hospitals, cottages – not citadels or monuments. It built roads and railways, filled up the dinner pail. Democracy built swimming pools, camps, organized gymnasiums and physical culture. Democracy spread ideas of equality, of communal spirit. We don't understand it here. So far very little is done for that. Everything is done at the expense of living conditions. They believe that socialism means greater monuments than capitalism.

Surely there must be something fundamentally wrong with things in the USSR if 17 years after the revolution the country produces less bread than it did before the war, sells less than it did in 1913, and keeps the population on a ration which only in the case of heavy industry workers, engineers, army men, GPU higher officials and responsible Communists is sufficient for an adult. This privileged group may comprise about 3 to 5 million people. So far as the rest are concerned, the peasants have what is left after the government has taken away its due for the government and all its agencies. What is left is enough to feed the peasant family all year around only in such sections or even farms where the harvest is exceptionally good. Otherwise, the great majority of the peasants have not enough bread to last them the whole year round. The world at large probably does not know that in the year 1932–3, the famine in the USSR was in its scope no smaller or less horrible than the famine of 1921, with the difference that the excuse for the former famine was an exceptional drought and prolonged civil war, while no such excuse existed in 1932–3. So far as the great masses of the country people are concerned, the rations vary from a kilo of bread down to 100 grams or nothing for the members of the family. To Americans it may seem that a kilo of bread is quite a big ration. Of course it is when in addition one has cereals, potatoes, meat, milk, eggs and the rest of the items that make up the American diet. However, when in addition to the bread one is getting a few pounds of meat per year, maybe 10 or less, it may be more in heavy industry, then it is clear that the bread situation in the 17th year of the victorious Revolution is unsatisfactory.

Now wherein lies the reason for such unbelievable results? Was it an absolute necessity that Magnitogorsk could be built only at the expense of the bread, health and life of the workers? The object of this writing is to prove that it was not so. While it is true in principle that the country had to build itself up in the first place along lines which strengthened the defense resources of the country, and that it was incompatible for the revolutionary USSR to remain the same backward feudal agricultural country that it was, the methods of construction, the very objects of construction, the time and place were correct neither in time nor place.

The Folly of Dneprostroi

Let us take the example of Dneprostroi. Who does not know about Dneprostroi? It is an open secret in the USSR that Dneprostroi has no economic base and was constructed purely for political reasons, for display purposes. The country at large would have been much better off without it. Dneprostroi was supposed to be a combination of plants, whereby the potential energy of the Dnieper would be converted into electricity, and on the basis of that electrical energy industries which consume large amounts of power would be built nearby, such as aluminum plants and high-grade steel mills. It should be remembered that the raw materials have to be transported from other districts. A new city had to be erected, with all that goes with it, in order to build the dam and the new plants. Otherwise all these plants could have been built nearer to the source of raw materials, in places already populated. Already-existing plants might have been converted, with a power cost not much greater than the Dneprostroi power cost in the case of high-grade steel production. (Metallurgists all over the world know that the best way to completely utilize all the heat generated in pig iron or steel plants by the combustion of coal or coke is to utilize part of the heat, which would otherwise be lost, in generating electrical energy.) Even in the USSR where there are no such things as private property and separate interests such as metal, power and coal interests, the metallurgical, coke and chemical plants are building their own power stations, even though there may be big power stations in the vicinity, which due to their demands should furnish cheaper power.

A few words about the Dneprostroi cost figures. According to the original figures of Professor Alexandrov, the cost of power should have been very low. He figured an interest on capital of only 4 percent, taking this not as a practical figure designating the actual cost of capital, but as a figure accepted in the USA, for example. The Russian economist generally does not figure any interest, because interest according to their interpretation of Marxism means parasitic capitalism. The fact is, however, that in order to raise capital for the purpose of construction, or any other purpose, interest is paid – either to foreign creditors, amounting to at least 12 percent with various commissions and deductions; or for postal savings and bonds for which the government actually pays 10 percent or more, not to mention all the overhead expenses involved in the campaigns to raise the capital. To get capital from the people through taxes costs an overhead percentage surely greater than the above figures. So it is obvious that during the time of the exceedingly heavy capital outlays of the *Piatiletka*, the cost of obtaining capital, or interest on amortization and capitalization, should be figured to be at least 15 percent.

Now if we take the cost of Dneprostroi at about 200 million rubles (note that the figure is approximate but near enough for the sake of comparison. This figure denotes gold rubles because a great part of the cost is expended in foreign countries for equipment, machinery, consultants and travel. The balance is spent on bread, lumber, cement, and steel, which in the USSR has virtually gold value. The resulting yearly cost could be figured in gold values.) Now if we take the actual yearly output of Dneprostroi, 3 billion kilowatt hours, and distribute on these kilowatt hours the cost of interest on capital and amortization of these 200 million gold rubles at 15%, that would mean 1 kopek in gold per kilowatt hour produced – an interest amount not figured by the original designers of the project. This extra outlay above the building cost could have been used to pay the cost of coal consumed in generating that electrical energy. Now it is two years since the completion of Dneprostroi was hailed all over the world as the greatest victory, and only a negligible part of the electrical power of the Dneprostroi is being actually used at present. It is not yet known when those 3 billion kilowatt hours per year will be used.

Besides electricity, Dneprostroi had to provide facilities for extended navigation along the Dnieper. The fact is that changes in navigation along the river from what existed before are so negligible that this cannot be considered at all as a factor in transportation in that sector of the country. About the water transportation craze of the USSR we shall speak further.

To Stalin's credit it must be said that, being a practical man with a more limited vision than his colleagues of the Lenin cabinet, such as, let us say, the fiery Trotsky, he opposed the building of Dneprostroi as premature, according to reliable information. And premature it was. In a country like the USA, which is much more industrialized than the USSR and which has vast amounts of free capital and huge capacity for utilizing all kinds of new plants, Muscle Shoals or St. Lawrence Seaway projects are practical and feasible. Now, because of the 200 million rubles invested in Dneprostroi, the country is making manifold addition capital outlays in that region in order to make use of those millions. Meanwhile many plants that are making shoes for example are not running at full capacity because of lack of materials while an army of 100 million peasants work the fields in *lapti* [bast shoes].

Samodur and Monument Building

There is a story about an old Polish noble, Radzivir, who spent most of his time in Paris. Once he reminded himself of his estate in dark Russia and old memories awoke in him a desire to go sleighing and bear hunting. He sent word to the management of his estate that he was coming and that he wanted to be met by his sleigh troika. This was sometime in June. One of the men, Mishka by name (every Polish noble has his Jew Mishka to serve him) spread salt all the way from the main road to the estate. Such methods are designated in Russian by the word *samodur* (petty tyranny). The present Russian nobility, some of them recently themselves Mishkas, have inherited the same methods.

An example of this is the most extravagant, the most wasteful manner of planning and building the municipal program of Moscow. Russian Communists, internationalists though they may be, are patriots of their particular territory and residences. The practical American bourgeoisie understood that Washington need not necessarily be the largest city in the world, leaving it to New York and Chicago to compete for the honor. But the Russian Communists believe that the capital of the world revolution, Moscow (and why not Leningrad, and why not eventually Berlin or New York?), must exceed all other cities of the world. Not only must Moscow have a subway, but it must be the best in the world. A stadium or a peoples' theater must have the largest seating capacity in the world, towering over the Eiffel Tower and the Empire State Building. The city's river must not be the present Moscow stream, but something bigger. If London has its Thames and New York its Hudson, Moscow must have the largest river that Europe can afford, with the Volga turned toward the city (unfortunately the Amazon and Mississippi are too far away for even the Moscow leaders to dream of turning into streams around the Kremlin.)

Now there is another feature which can be noted in feudal or oriental countries. That is the ambition for exterior decoration or monuments. The pyramids were apparently built by some Ramses who wanted posterity to know about his greatness. Medieval lords built fancy castles. Peter the Great had the building craze albeit with more practical results. Now our own Russian overlords who have ceased to be ordinary humans are building monuments to surpass the world. So Kaganovich beautifies Moscow, Petrovsky beautifies Kharkov, another viceroy introduces new ways of plowing fields and sowing from airplanes, but the harvests, alas, zero. All the viceroys of the USSR are making monuments for themselves.

Some Notes on the Subway

The case of the Moscow Subway project, Metrostroi, is very characteristic of the methods of planning and realizing building projects. Metrostroi is headed by one of the chief engineers who built Dneprostroi, Roberts, a non-party man whom the party trusts along with a few other non-party men at the head of very important institutions. But the head of our city administration is the mayor, and on top of all is the secretary of the Moscow party, L.M. Kaganovich. This individual will be discussed separately and at length. In the USA, the ordinary practice is that the city administration decides the routes, to whom to give the contracts – all questions of politics, quite often of graft – but the question of design and methods of work is handled by the engineers. Not so in Moscow. There is no distribution of graft in high quarters (though plenty among the small fry). But the activities of the orators, journalists and propagandists who are fathers of the city included decisions on special technical questions, decisions against the explicit advice of higher technicians and even Roberts himself, so rumor has it.

The questions were: Shall Moscow have a subway or not? What shall be its routes? What method of construction shall be used, open cut or deep tunnel? A large body of experts were invited, Russian, French, English and German. However, the question of whether or not to build a subway was not placed before the experts. Some volunteered, with good reason, that Moscow could get along for the time being without a subway. There is no great problem of distance, as is the case in New York or Chicago. If you draw two concentric circles from the middle of Moscow, one with a radius of two kilometers and the other with a radius of five kilometers, you would find that about 60 percent of the population of the city lies within the first circle, and the second would practically reach the city limits and would in many places coincide with the railroads which serve to connect all railroad lines and terminals around Moscow. The maximum distance is five kilometers, a little over three miles.

Would New York City consider building a subway to travel a distance of about 60 city blocks? Traffic on streetcars in Moscow is less congested than that in most big American cities, particularly Chicago. What the experts advised was to improve street pavements, covering rough stone paving with asphalt for example, and running an additional hundred busses. This would solve the problem of transportation in Moscow for a good many years.

Russia Has Always Been a Land of Dreamers

Two hundred years ago, when Russia was still riding on oxen and Sweden, Germany and England were sailing the seas, Peter the Great decided that he must bring the sea nearer to Russia. A system of canals was planned which the Bolshevik government began setting out to accomplish in the year 1930. Briefly, the system is as follows: connecting the White Sea with the Baltic; connecting the Baltic with the Black Sea by canals and dams; and connecting the Baltic with the Caspian Sea. The main features of the system are the following projects: the partially completed White Sea Canals, with a system of dams over the River Svir; deepening and widening the Maria Canal system which connects the Baltic with the Volga River; a canal turning the Volga into the Moscow River; and a system of dams to enlarge the carrying capacity of the Volga. In addition, a canal connecting the Volga and the Don rivers; another canal connecting the

Don through the Manich system to the Caspian Sea; and finally a system of canals and dams joining the Dnieper to the Don. At the dams, power stations are to be built, part of the power generated to be utilized in operating the canal system; part for irrigation purposes; and whatever is left for building new industries. Certain 'strategists' believe a fleet can be built up that can maneuver freely through the Arctic, the Baltic and Black Seas into the Atlantic Ocean, outmaneuvering the Empress of the Seas. These planners forget one thing it seems – that if the enemy chooses to fight in January, the whole continental armada is as icebound as the Cheluskin in the Baring Straits. The climate has the bad habit of not allowing any navigation for 5 to 6 months each year.

As for the value of canals in general for transport, it is true that the greatest problem in Russia today is transportation. A good system of water transportation would be of great help. However, the conditions of transport are such in Russia that the greatest difficulties are met in the fall and winter, when the transport of grain and coal is heaviest. In the summer times, the only difficulty is the transport of construction materials. Certainly a nicely organized transport of construction materials along river lines would be of great help. But for that it is necessary to make such a tremendous investment in joining one river system to the other, building dams, and deepening and widening canals, especially since building materials require local and not transcontinental transportation. Peter the Great deemed a canal system a necessary addition to the oxen used in those days, but there were no railroads at that time.

A very striking example proving the absurdity of these projects from the point of view of navigation is the Barge Canal connecting the Great Lakes with the Atlantic Ocean. There one sees a ready system passing through the most populated and cultivated section of a continent, joining two of the largest deep water systems, with a tremendous amount of transport going from the East to the upper Midwest and vice-versa. Still the Barge Canal is almost covered with grass. A good deal of the difficulty is attributed to the interest of railroad owners who will not let water transport develop. If such artificial hindrances could be removed, the value of transport would increase somewhat. Still, common sense would say that it could not be a paying proposition, because time lost in shipping costs money nowadays. A good system of railroads, roadbeds, rolling cars, self-dumping cars with good loading and reloading equipment makes rail transport very economical. In the Russian canal system, sometimes over 100 kilometers one passes through ten sluices, each with an enormous loss of time and energy and maintenance costs. The cost of water transport becomes prohibitive from any economical point of view.

There is, however, another feature to these projects. Russia has always been a land of dreamers, composed of a class of nobles who let the peasant masses toil while they indulged in art, philosophy, and sometimes politics; and an illiterate mass who could only indulge in instinctive primitive reveries. Nowhere did such a book as *The Tunnel* by Kellermann or Verne's *20,000 Leagues Under the Sea* or Wells' *The First Man in the Moon* have such popularity as in Russia. Russian journalists burst aflame at the idea of some daring project – at the idea, not its materialization. Russia believes in heroes.

The Revolution, which accomplished the almost unbelievable, the overthrow of the Tsarist regime, also freed medieval and primitive dreams and ideas. Any idea of overpowering nature, changing the face of the earth by organization, is near to the heart of intellectual dreamers as well as Bolshevik theoreticians, who also claim that proper organization and willpower can change the world. Engineers have emerged, who present the idea of stopping the Volga River from flowing into the Caspian Sea by drying it out and turning the land to a useful purpose. They propose to let the Volga inundate the deserts and turn millions of acres into fertile lands. To accomplish this it is necessary only to build a huge water system, which will block the river and turn it into other channels. Strangely enough, this proposal, which seemed wild to ordinary citizens, was in substance accepted by the TseKa [Central Executive Committee], which decreed that a huge dam be built according to the plans of these engineers. To give a section of the country which suffers from periodic droughts an additional 10 miles of irrigated land, or about 3 to 4 million tons of additional grain, is the aim of the project. But the problem in the USSR now is not to reclaim additional land either by drainage or irrigation. The problem is to secure a larger yield from the land under cultivation. Yield per acre is far higher in the USA than in the USSR, due of course to fertilization, proper selection of seed and proper cultivation. If the USSR were to improve its yield only 10 percent, the result would be better than the reclamation of 10 to 15 million hectares [25 to 40 million acres] of land. Furthermore, the last decision by the Central Executive Committee of the All-Union Communist Party brings out the idea that by proper organization of the harvest alone, that is the gathering of the crop and proper disposal of it, 1934's yield, despite the drought, will not be less than last year's harvest. The facts show better organization of agriculture this spring than last year. In spite of the drought, in the main sections of the country the harvest will be saved. Now all friends of the USSR, all friends of the working class, must exert all the influence of their advice and criticism to stop the government of the USSR from the tremendous waste of building this system. All means are justifiable in fighting that harmful tendency. It does more harm to the cause of Communism than many other blunders that the All-Union Party could commit along political or organizational lines.

In Absolute Controversy with Common Sense and Sound Economics

Dneprostroi, the Moscow subway, the various water system projects, are all in absolute controversy with common sense and sound economics. What is the local and political effect of such waste? A few examples will illustrate. During the year 1934, most of the work, even of the heavy industries in the vicinity of Moscow, had to be stopped because there was a shortage of construction materials and because the transport system could not deliver more materials than those absorbed by the subway and Volga Canal enterprises. Needless to say, almost all construction of homes, schools, hospitals, roads and water works was curtailed because of scarcity of labor and even more importantly a lack of barracks for quartering workers. The figures paint a picture of the waste. The capital investment on the subway and canal for Moscow alone is larger than the capital investment for hospitals and public health all over the union. In terms of materials, labor, and food values, these projects receive more than the construction of dwellings and municipal works all over the country.

Many things, if not most, are being done for the sake of propaganda. Take for instance the decision of the Central Executive Committee against cheating and misrepresentation of weights and measures. High-level officials were reprimanded for cheating on weights and measures, to give the impression that cheating had assumed proportions calling for strenuous measures and causing shortages. People in the USSR claim that the shooting of several scores of men for producing bad canned goods was the same type of propaganda. Many believe that the trials against wreckers were played up to create the impression that most of the misfortunes that have befallen the working class of the USSR are due to those wreckers.

Condition of the Soviet People

What is the condition of living quarters in the USSR? What is the condition of municipal works generally? What is the condition of the life of the people as compared to the life of American workers? If one were to draw a line from West to East, passing from the USA through England, France, Germany, Poland and Russia, one could say that the further East one goes, the poorer are the working masses. The same principle holds true going from Russia into Turkey, India and China. One can therefore say that housing and living conditions in Russia are a little bit better than those in Turkey and China.

How do the peasants live in Russia? Practically speaking, nothing has been done to improve the housing or living conditions of the peasantry. For 17 years, absolutely nothing for the housing of the peasants, while a good deal has been accomplished in the cities. Rural families live in one room; the room usually has an earthen floor; windows are small and near to the ground; ceilings are low and covered with smoke. On particularly cold winter nights, newborn calves are brought in to share the warmth with the family, which may consist of as many as 10 or 15 persons. Right in the yard, among heaps of dung, is the water well. Streets are impassable in spring after the thaw. In the fall the rains render the roads impassable again. During the rest of the season when the roads are not frozen, they are full of mudholes where pigs are bathing and sunning themselves. One or two houses in each village may be found in better condition. These belonged formerly to kulaks and are now occupied by village councils or functionaries.

The Russian peasant may know what plates are but he does not have them. Families eat out of a common pot with wooden spoons. Forks are found only in the more cultured homes. Tin plates, forks and spoons in factories are fastened to the table in factory restaurants so that they will not be stolen. If not fastened, another system of control is used to check up on the cutlery. In a Russian village, there may be a bathhouse which functions on the occasions when there is fuel. The great mass of the peasantry consider lice their ordinary bed and clothesmates, as are flies, mosquitoes and bedbugs. These lice carry typhus germs, disease and death.

How about roads? The total mileage of hard surface, improved and even unimproved roads pales in comparison to American figures. Despite all the noise raised periodically in campaigns for road building, the improved roads are hardly being maintained. Some are deteriorating. Some roadbuilding is being done for strategic purposes, and improvements are also being made around a few centers like Moscow.

III. Party and Class

The Dialectic of Dictatorship

Any dictatorship, even of the proletariat, results in a dictatorship of the few. In Russia it started with the dictatorship of a class, the whole proletariat participated in expropriating the exploiters – the land, the factories, houses, dwellings and works. Workers were put in charge of factories and estates, were quartered in houses of the bourgeoisie. Laws were issued in the name of the free proletariat. That was at the beginning.

Then there crystallized a distinct layer within the class and that was the party. Distinctions began between the party and non-party man in respect to jobs, quarters and rations; in representation; in government; in all walks of life. Civil law was for the rest of the country, but party law was their law. A party member could not be arrested nor prosecuted nor fired from his job without a specific decision of the party.

Within that party, members had the right to criticize the government and its policies, to put up demands, express opinions, take initiative – rights which nobody else enjoyed. It became the dictatorship not of the class but of the party, the upper layer of the class. Then the logic of dictatorship abolished such privileges for the mass of party members. All these rights came to be reserved only to the groups which led the party, the various committees. The privilege of the rest was to obey, to approve by vote as they were asked by the higher officials.

So far as the ordinary worker was concerned, the very principle of boosting the worker into higher office was abolished. Little by little power and privilege were concentrated exclusively with the higher party committees under the leadership of the official party plenipotentiaries of the government – section, district or state.

Now rank-and-file party members are equalized to ordinary citizens with respect to rations, jobs and quarters. They were lowered, the rest were not raised to a higher level. In every district there are about 30 families that enjoy the privilege of an increased ration in all the benefits of life. They get their food and products from the special exclusive stores called *Tridtsika* or *Dvadtsika* – meaning for 30 or 20, or whatever is the number of beneficiaries.

In the Politburo, only a few count beside the leader in shaping policies. The first of them is the Vice-Secretary Kaganovich. Another is probably Molotov, nominal head of the government. He has not forgotten that he was vice-secretary and still dares to express an opinion. Then there is probably Ordzhonikidze, chief of industry, and possibly Voroshilov of the War Department, who dare to say something. The rest of the Politburo are just honorary members permitted to express sentiment rather than opinion, and in many cases to be mouthpieces for the leader. One of these is Kalinin, the president of the country. Then there are the other two members, who are viceroys of the most important centers outside of Moscow.

Outside of meetings of the Politburo, each of the ten is completely his own boss and the unrestrained ruler of his political domain. Moreover, anyone who does not use a strong hand in ruling his domain is deposed. There is no criticism, no questioning the doings of these viceroys. They in their turn have their plenipotentiaries, the satraps of the various districts who are in turn unimpeachable except by the will of the superior. Under such conditions skill in flattery of superiors rather than real ability has the day. Kaganovich derives his power because he is the most skillful flatterer. To him belong the various epithets glorifying Stalin.

First it began as the 'best disciple of Lenin'. At that time this seemed to be the highest conceivable praise. Then the term 'co-fighter of Lenin, the best co-fighter'. Then equality was reached – 'leaders of the working class, Lenin and Stalin'. Then equality was introduced between Marx, Lenin and Stalin. Next the term 'Great' was introduced. But there were already various 'Greats', such as Alexander, Peter and so on – hence the form 'Beloved' was evolved. Now 'Great and Beloved' and even 'Greatest and Most Beloved' is not sufficient. It is necessary to have the masses feel with their heart and soul their blood relation to the greatest of leaders and men. What the next thing will be is unknown, maybe 'Superman', 'Giant of Ages', or 'Brain of the Cosmos' will come into use.

Meanwhile factories, city after city, mountain peaks are named after the leader. Pretty soon the study of geography will be the most difficult subject in the USSR as it will be impossible to know whether a place is situated in Siberia or the Pamir or the Donbass, and which is the machine-building and which the metallurgical plant. There is no editorial, no leading article, which does not quote the leader. There is no book of fiction or magazine issued without glorifying him in one way or another. Histories which do not pay proper tribute to the leader are being rewritten.

The shame of it is that foreign statesmen who want to carry out their politics and USSR-friendly journalists who are seeking popularity and recognition at home and abroad have joined the host in praising the greatest statesman, the great etc. With not one at the top, including Stalin himself, noting the shame and impropriety of it. Never in the history of Soviet Russia under Lenin was such an outrage possible.

The Party Is Fading Out

How does the party function? It does not function as a party. Originally the nucleus of the local party organization made the major decisions in running the business in every establishment, factory, store and farm. The director or manager had to abide by these decisions as a member of the nucleus. Questions were discussed by the entire body and the opinion of the masses was crystallized so that there was active help and understanding from everybody in carrying out decisions. This might seem like an absurdity under the capitalist system, but socialism also might seem like an absurdity. But socialism can be established, built and maintained only with the active help, support and understanding of the widest masses. Lenin's idea of the cooperative commonwealth was indeed cooperation, was that every man and woman should participate in running the affairs of the government. Every member of the total socialist community should be as active and conscious of the end as are the cells of a growing active living body, each cell fighting its own as well as the common battle. You can drive ideas upon machines, you can force labor upon slaves, you can hire mercenaries whose loyalty will not last – or you can call an army to battle. When we come to the workings of the various cooperatives and talk about labor, we will dwell longer upon this subject.

Now what has become of the party nucleus and its power? It was replaced by a committee called the *biuro*, chosen at a general meeting. That *biuro* would draw in a few more comrades, called the *aktiv*, who were arbitrarily chosen either by the *biuro* or the secretary of the *biuro*. Later the principle of one-man management was introduced and proclaimed as the greatest principle of Socialism, that is, that the director is the complete boss of the establishment. The committee of the nucleus and the nucleus as a whole remained responsible for any major changes in policy. However, one-man management alongside an active board of party members asking questions does not jibe very well. Discussion is becoming more troublesome, and means are sought to avoid it at all.

At the time of the Trotsky opposition, the Trotskyites forced a discussion upon the party and its membership. Questions were openly raised at meetings, a spade was called a spade. But the oppositionists were driven out of the party by exile, abuse and expulsion, and fired from their jobs. There was almost no discussion on the question of the right opposition. The higher functionary would present his report and the membership would be asked, singly and as a whole, to approve it. Any dissenter, or anyone who did not understand, would find it more comfortable not to budge from his seat. The vote would be taken without opposition – just like at company union meetings in the free United States, except that no heavy gavel would fall on the table when calling the question. With one exception – dissention at company union meetings might mean firing from the job and a beating at the end of the meeting, while at the meeting described above dissention might even mean imprisonment or exile.

Questions such as general collectivization, the exiling of the kulaks, the amount of taxes, the price of bread and produce – questions vital to the existence of the country, which Lenin used to consider with the utmost care, which he warned time and again that the utmost care should be taken over – have never been discussed. They were simply brought to membership meetings, reports would be given, specially assigned members would take the floor and praise the wisdom of the proposer and the leadership that brought forth the proposal in their allotted 10 minutes, and that would settle the whole discussion.

The last party congress removed all possibility of discussion, all possibility of asking questions, all 'interference' in the affairs of the state and the government, by giving a final blow to the party nucleus. It was done in this way: A slogan was presented against excessive meetings, which is in itself a good slogan when it means business, but not when it refers to a party. Party committees are now chosen only in establishments or factories where there is a large party membership. The local nuclei of the various departments or branches have no committees and no meetings except when the party organizer calls a meeting. These party organizers are actually designated from above, but voted upon by the membership as if nominated by them. Note that it is easier for a manager to explain matters to a single party organizer than to several members of a party committee. All committees are named from above and mechanically elected from below, including the Central Executive Committee of the party.

The Party Convention has abolished RKI, the Workers' and Peasants' Inspectorate, which existed side by side and parallel to the party organization. Lenin planned to introduce a checking mechanism into party affairs, like the two-chamber system of the American Congress. Although the RKI was never as effective as the two-chamber system, due to tradition and the personal influence of this parallel control commission, much abuse of power and many minor irregularities were exposed or checked. Now this organization has been abolished and a board of 'chosen' men put in charge of control work. This new board, like the party apparatus, has become a weapon in the hands of the leadership to control the country, like the extra system of special guards beside the regular army and the police. This special board reports on the various provinces to the Control Committee, not to the local party committees as previously. This makes it an instrument for doubly controlling the party committees below.

How does the party look now? It consists of several departments conducting various branches of activity – governmental, social work, business. The departments hand down their decisions to the corresponding governmental, social, and business *aktiv*, while an army of party cardholders pay dues and have the duty of carrying out the instructions of the party. Whenever it is necessary to call the masses to public demonstrations, meetings or volunteer service, these members are summoned. In return for such duties, party members have certain privileges, corresponding to their position in the party. The very lowest strata have negligible privileges, higher and higher layers get increasingly more. Rakovsky, the former staunch Trotskyite, used to call the party a category. Now even as such it is fading away. Should history proceed undisturbed, it will slowly do to the party what another dictatorship did brutally to its storm troops.

Technocracy, and the New Apparatus Supplanting the Party

The apparatus that is running the country is supplanting the rule of the party; it fulfills the wishes of the upper ten or five. Those who are carrying out these wishes are not necessarily party men. No party affiliation determines their capability, but simply ability to serve. There are a few cases here and there where people are placed in high positions because of personal connections and nothing else. In the majority of cases, people are put in positions for their ability and willingness to serve a set purpose to carry out a particular function. While in the beginning they were necessarily the revolutionists, the party men, the trusted old guard, now this alone without knowledge of the business does not suffice. There are many instances where excellent engineers were sentenced as saboteurs, and now are being put in the highest commanding offices.

What qualities are necessary to run the country? To begin with, literacy; second, specialty; third, endurance; fourth, willingness to serve the cause or the master who pays. These qualities lie in whole or in large measure with the intelligentsia (bearing in mind that those who belonged to the bourgeois class and opposed the present system were exiled, crushed, demolished). Only the remnants of this class are serving the master as the intelligentsia of every epoch and system does. Intellectuals as a whole invariably serve the master class and act as one of its most effective tools. Intellectuals are literate, they are specialists – engineers, mechanics, agronomists, chemists, teachers, physicians, jurists, economists, accountants, experts in government and propaganda. If previously it was the custom to boost the workers into management and thus fulfill the slogan of Lenin, this process has now been stopped. The pretext was that the workers are needed for the machine. Actually, this process was stopped because men are being selected who possess the qualities above enumerated, instead of workers who do not have these qualities. Paradoxically, we have in the USSR not a dictatorship of the proletariat, but a technocracy. But it differs from what American technocrats aspire to. They believe that under technocracy machines will perform all the work and mankind will be busy only four hours a day, and will play the rest of the time. The Russian technocracy carries not only power but material privileges, with hard manual labor performing the work very inefficiently in lieu of machines to come, and the technocrats taking the cream of production. Very little is left over for the workers to maintain themselves by.

Political Departments: The New Parallel Structure

In the rural sections of the country the local party organization became an obstacle rather than a conveyor of the *ukases* (decrees) of the government. Take for instance the question of the tax, that is how much bread each *kolkhoz* (collective farm) has to give from its fields. A rural Communist, no matter how high his consciousness and discipline, cannot blind himself forever and carry out tax instructions from above which virtually strip the peasants of their bread and leave them nothing for the rest of the year except the prospect of hunger. The local Communist, who is himself part and parcel of the peasantry, cannot altogether be free of the influence of the ideas and desires and needs of the masses among whom he lives. That is why in most cases the local organizations have failed to carry out the wishes of the government – and in many cases were sabotaging their instructions. The party leadership had to resort to the establishment of *politotdely*, political departments, which virtually abolished the party in rural districts, and in any case made it an auxiliary to the political departments.

Political departments work like this. The apparatus of the Central Executive Committee of the section appoints the district political commissar for agriculture. These appointees can be removed only by the CEC of the section and constitute a parallel organization to the district party committee with respect to agricultural policies. The districts are further subdivided into sections and subsections, in each of which political commissars are appointed. The lower down the chain of command, the more power is given to the political commissar and the less to the local party organization, in proportion to the mistrust that the top has for the bottom.

A tendency towards creating such *politotdely* in all other branches of activity prevails. In the coal industry, the question was to squeeze out more work from the miners. Certainly capitalist-managed business squeezed out of the Russian miners about three or four times as much as does the Bolshevik commissar in the coal industry. The local party organization proved itself in many instances actually to be a hindrance to the leadership, because it could not continually take on additional quotas without proper real compensation in means of subsistence. There too the political department was introduced in the form of a party organization expressly appointed from above and independent of the local organization. The political department has also been introduced in transport, although with much less effect.

It must be stated that this method is in general more effective at present than the party method. But what is the political significance of these political departments versus the party? First, the party method means drawing the masses into socialist activity, social sacrifice, into real cooperation by persuasion, by appeals to their conscience, their enthusiasm. The method of real socialism, the only one proposed by Lenin, means the voluntary expression of the conscious desires of all the active elements of society. The political department method means forcing upon the masses higher taxes, longer hours, more intensive labor, etc. by decrees and by crushing resistance. Secondly, it signifies that even one single party, considered to be Communist and supposedly the leader of the masses, without freedom of speech and press becomes an expression of antagonism to the leadership – or as the apparatus labels it, becomes the expression of the class enemy. Therefore the leadership begins to see in the existence of the party itself a danger to the sacred drive for power and systematically and persistently reduces the party as a whole to a rubber stamp.

At the time of the bitterest Civil War, at the time of the greatest danger to the revolution, at the time of Military Communism, Lenin had a party congress every year, and in between a conference, featuring wide-open discussion of the problems before them. Even when the German armies were at the gates of Leningrad, a discussion was going on as to the terms of the peace. It is true Lenin said on a similar occasion that discussion was too much of a luxury. Now we have a party congress once in three years, with no discussion either before or at the congress. No questions of importance are ever discussed. Everything is decreed from above. There was no discussion on the question of collectivization, which was second in importance only to the October Revolution itself. Why is all this being done? Because the party has become a menace to the revolution. Because it seems that the leadership is doing what is against the wishes of the majority of the working class as well as the peasantry.

IV. Whither the USSR?

Wherein lies the guarantee that the leadership will not by the logic of events depart onto the path of a new capitalism? The guarantee is in the growth of the proletariat, both in quantity and quality. The creation of many factories and plants draws in millions of new workers. While before the revolution Russia had 1.5 million proletarians, we now have in the neighborhood of 15 to 20 million. These workers will become settled, stationary; they will begin to lead an organized life. In some way or other their wishes and desires will find expression. It is difficult to foresee the way, but the way will arise. And maybe then the second revolution will be made – whether by force or by reform will depend on many conditions.

The danger of the ruling class moving away from Communism becomes greater as Stalin ages and gives over his functions to others. The point is that the old man has one ambition in his life: to get the crown of Marx and Lenin. This is his greatest weakness. Those who want to curry favor, from the second man Kaganovich to the opposition leaders Zinoviev and Kamenev, found that the best way was to compare Stalin with Lenin. Surely he does not care for riches and worldly comforts as do his contemporaries (and colleagues)[4] Hitler and

4 This parenthetical phrase, which does not jibe politically or analytically with the rest of the manuscript, is an interlinear insertion, presumably by Rose Risikoff.

Mussolini. Until now the weakest spot in his life was the mention of Trotsky, the placing of Trotsky's name next to that of Lenin, the very hint that Trotsky was a bigger man. That is why, strange as it may seem, Stalin has carried out almost every policy that Trotsky ever proposed. Stalin has exceeded all the super-industrialization than Trotsky ever dreamt of. Stalin established greater militarization of the country as a whole than Trotsky ever suggested. Any article or saying of Trotsky published abroad has more influence over the fate of the USSR today than Trotsky himself ever had as a party leader in the Soviet Union. For the moment, this keeps the Old Man sticking to his Communism and respecting old Bolshevisk traditions such as idealism, sacrifice and discipline. The weakening of his spirit due to age and/or the pressure of the new class which surrounds him could create the danger of moving away from Communism.

The Wheels of History

The slogan now is to acquire technique. The slogan nowadays is less interference in business by politics and politicians. The rule is 'all power to the manager'. The rule is 'shut up or we will shut you up'. Should history continue this way, no one can tell where the process will stop, whether a new class of technocrats will in the name of the building of socialism enslave labor as never before, substituting heartless functionaries for the former nobility, a decadent class of dreamers. A new class hardened by revolution and famine, men and women cynical to emotion and all ideals, brutal in their methods, having one idea before them – to have the wheels of history grind and grind the nation into what it should be: a civilized, industrialized nation instead of the backwards, Asiatic, filthy, lazy country it was before.

History it seems does not skip stages. In spite of everything said and written about Communism; Socialism; abolition of crises; world revolution; the rule of the downtrodden and the proletariat, Bolshevism in Russia may be the unconscious rule of history driving the country forward, maybe inefficiently and surely wastefully, from feudalism; primitive economic production; a state where the great majority of people are small peasants living in simple big undeveloped villages, into some new form of capitalism different from what exists now in the rest of world. Military Communism, wars, the greatest upheavals and transformations that history ever witnessed, have arranged the economic lineup where it should be according to this phase of history: from feudalism to industrialism. Where the driving force is not private property but the whip of the government and economic necessity, the whip which harnesses the underprivileged uncultured population in the hard task of building up a new continent.

To understand these social phenomena one must dwell further upon the economic situation of Russia, of the inheritance that fell into the hands of the Bolsheviks. [The manuscript ends here, except for the 'rough note for future elaboration' below. Its conclusion, elaborately packaged in a 'Siberian fantasy' to fool Soviet censors, can be found in Noah London's January 26, 1935, letter from Siberia to New York in Appendix C.]

Rough Note for Further Elaboration

The raw organization of distribution is like the story of the quartet, the Goy, bear, ass and goat. There is an army of two million which leaves the village, the land for construction jobs. One has 500 workdays but gets nothing except one kilo of oats a day. At the construction job he is a guard and gets 70 rubles a month. His wife carries brick and earns 26 rubles every fortnight. But here he gets 800 grams of bread a day and this is what counts.

Dictated by Noah London to Rose Unterman-Discher-Risikoff, his visiting American sister-in-law, in the woods outside his dacha in Kliazmo, August 1934. Translated and edited by her. – JH

APPENDIX C

Noah London's Letters to America

These letters were found among Rose Risikoff's personal effects when she died. They continue the themes of the London manuscript, and the second letter represents its conclusion. They frequently use Aesopian language 'in a Martian way' as Noah puts it, to elude the eyes of censorship. The final letter nostalgically recounts Noah and Miril's lives together. Its somber tone indicates that he suspected it would be his last communication with the outside world. To maintain as much as possible of the original flavor I have transcribed them fully and literally, without correcting grammar or punctuation. Ellipses in parenthesis indicate illegible words. Explanatory interpolations are bracketed or placed in footnotes, with words difficult to read indicated by question marks.

Undated Letter, Fall 1934

Dear Little Sis:

In Kislovodsk I was figuring to continue the work started in Kliazmo. But alas: First, it is not convenient to do it alone, there is no stimulus and inspiration. Second we are so busy idling and getting the most of Kislovodsk that no time is left for any mental or other kind of work.

You will have to come next year, and we shall manage to spend the time in Kislovodsk or Cora, and then we shall find time somewhere in the hills to work. Of course I do expect to find time here & there before that. What do you think about the proposal of next year? Take Kliazmo & raise it to the nth degree and you have Kislovodsk. It is worth while.

By the way. We are building here a Sanitarium for the *Narkomtiazhprom* à la Tomilino to accommodate 350 people at one time. Of course you might think, that we have not solved yet our more urgent problems. For this one must have patience. First we shall begin from those who run the industry, then when we get richer, we shall extend those benefits to those who *make* things.

This simply to confirm a certain theory in our society of inequality (but equal opportunity) that brains, knowledge, culture what counts & what will count foremost in the near future the more complicated the social machinery become due to planning & systematizing things. Remark: in your Country: not brains or culture but title to money what counts.

 | DOI:10.1163/9789004745384_017

Of course you can say that title to power is the same as title to money. About this next time.

Regards & love to sister & brothers, Noah.

Siberia, January 26, 1935

Dear little sis:-

Son (Ben) [Benjamin Levine] & I are on the fifth day, the last day of our journey to Kuznetsk (Siberia). My mission is at the head of a group of engineers to pick out sites for 3 Locomotive & R.R. Car plants in this district.

Ben I borrowed from *Metrostroi* to help me & keep me company. He with his inquisitive mind and insight into engineering economics fits in very well into the job.

As we pass in this midwinter the endless stretches of Siberian snowfields, with the frosty sky showing only small specks of light, Son & I have a midwinter vision of the Siberia of the future. And this is what we see.

Sparkling cities extending deep into the arctic. Young folks on skis (*lyzhen*) floating on snow waves dressed in light silk (Rayon) padded with electric [mat?]. The Rayon comes from the forests, the electric energy radiated through the ether from the most powerful hydroelectric stations on the Ob, Yenisei, Augava, Lena, Amur and thermo-electric stations utilizing the coal resources of the Kuzbass & Bureia. These same stations will supply heat enough to grow lettuce & oranges in the polar regions & run aeroplanes & dirigibles through the Siberian *Purga* (snow storm) carrying the elderly people to the Siberian Central Opera House.

Folks will be sturdy with long legs & long arms, fair complexion, will not know what a draft, a sneeze or a cold is. They will read that somewhere, when you cross the arctic, on the Western hemisphere going south through what was Canada & U.S. you get to a hot place called Florida. That Florida is populated by a nation which was formerly a class (the capitalist class) in America. After many years of NIRA [Roosevelt's National Industrial Recovery Administration – JH] (so history tells) the people got sick of Capitalists running the country under the protection and limitation of NIRA, and one of the descendents of F.D.R. passed a bill by which the title to all the property was turned over to the nation and those who owned the property (through money, stocks, bonds) were given an eternal & handsome annuity with the condition that they give up their claim to run the country. In order to isolate them & the same time to let them have it as easy as possible the peninsula of Florida was reserved for them. The story further tells that the inhabitants of Florida do nothing except bathing, dressing

& undressing, making love & gossiping and dreaming of a still warmer planet, and dying out little by little from the grippe.

The story further says, that some of the new rulers of former America come sometimes to Florida to learn good manners or get an aristocratic wife. This is what our arctic folly will hear and wonder about the funny doings on the side over the Arctic.

Now the folks on the Siberian side of the Arctic will consider themselves and will really be a superior nation commanding from the top of the world (the North pole) the rest of the earth. And, the textbooks of geography & history will in a Martian way explain the creation of the Siberian empire thus [the rest of this letter represents a conclusion for the secret manuscript – JH]:

The Russian people chased out their landlords & capitalists. This was done while the rest of the world was busy and simply failed to take notice in time. As soon as the other capitalists & landlord and their households got wise they started in everyway and used all the tricks to do harm to the Bolshevik Country. First they refused to sell anything on credit as is done in the family of nations. Then for their internal game they have taken them into their political circle still ostracizing them socially and economically.[1]

America flirted with Russia to frighten and bring to terms Japan. France let herself be kissed & hugged to make jealous Germany & Poland. Meanwhile the nations all around Russia formed an iron ring of fire, of epidemic bacillae, which did not for a minute release the energy of the Russian nation for purposes of raising standard of living, for creature comfort. The nation had to entrench itself against invasion, against subjugation by superior forces of the [s/o?] of the rest.

Seeing an insurmountable barrier on the west in the face of an armed Europe with their fleets, same thing with Japan & England on the Pacific, with U.S.A. always ready to get in the game on the side of the stronger to get a share of the spoils—the only way for entrenching and expansion remained the north. The cold, the dark, the terrible.[2]

Without being safe in the beautiful sunny Caucasus the rich, fat Ukraine, that section of Russia, which can create enough wealth and give a life of comfort to all Russia's population if properly industrialized, the nation had therefore to make the most strenuous efforts to move over part of its population into the uninhabitable lands of Siberia and make them habitable. If the British

1 This letter was written soon after the USSR was admitted to the League of Nations, the USA granted it diplomatic recognition, and the Franco–Soviet Pact was signed.

2 i.e. "cold, dark, terrible" Stalinism, "the Siberian empire," is the consequence of Russia's encirclement by enemies.

& Japanese & German fleets rule the warm waves, there is left the Arctic Ocean for Russia. Therefore the exploration of the Northern Route, the *Cheliuskina*, the Siberian *Libke*.

Russia went conquering the Arctic, conquering the *Purga*, the uncontrollable world elements of Siberia not because of lack of land or work, or in search of gold, but because **the rising (proletarian)**[3] **class wants to perpetuate his power**, to retain the independence of the nation. That social stimulus has caused the Russian nation to plunge itself into **War & Conquest of Nature.** In this warfare the new class has become the victor, the same way as the rising Bourgeoisie the tradesmen have in their time conquered the Atlantic, conquered America, **created the American empire.** The **Proletariat has created the Siberian empire** because it is easier to conquer nature than to change minds of peoples.[4] Backed at the wall the Bolsheviks have created a superior civilization in Technique than had hitherto been created in history by other classes. This is how history will explain the creation of the Siberian Empire.

Moscow, May 30, 1935 (Decoration Day)

Dear Rose:

We are so disappointed this summer remaining alone that I am almost ready to propose you should repeat the trip to us instead of staying away. Only I understand how impractical it is.

We are going back to Kliazma to the same house, except that we have there two rooms, and no kids. We are just through remodelling our new rooms, and this morning Miril & I had our small quarrel on account of the books arrangement.

Today, the layout, we were not going out but attended to the house (the first time for many months). Miril is going to have her vacation the month (July) in Kliazma, and then in October with me in the Caucasus. Health and mood O.K. I am sorry though, we had so little opportunity together to fix certain matters for an opportune time, though, one thing is to profess something, and quite the opposite is to say it under conditions and among people who have altogether different motives than you, and whom you would not like to identify with, whom you consider your enemies.[5]

3 The word "proletarian" is inserted above the line in the original, again presumably by Risikoff.

4 i.e. the original Bolshevik program of world socialist revolution or "changing minds of peoples," is off the historical agenda and needs to be replaced with something else.

5 He is expressing qualms about publishing the manuscript. Perhaps he and Miril had "a small quarrel" about it.

I hope though my little comrade to have the opportunity to talk to you about serious matters.

Yours, Noah

Cora, Sanatorii ul. Frunze, October 29, 1935

Dear Rose:

We are half a month at our vacation, and so metamorphosed (changed) that Kap'y would not recognize us. Kap'y undoubtedly told you that Miril is again cranky, sick, depressed, quitting work; Noah worn out, gray, sick looking, old. Now during these 14 days, both of us became younger 14 years (7 each). We are bathing, rowing, walking lots, having all the fun in the evenings, movies, talkies, concerts, forgetting there is work or worry in the world.

I am writing this to you to show that you have in USSR not old worn out sister & brother but a robust couple in the middies (for middle age) alive and kicking. Tell it to the rest of the family who undoubtedly were troubled by hearing from Kap'y what she saw and knew about us.

As we walk along in leisure and have time to look over the 25 years we are pulling together we see what an interesting life we lived through, what an interesting world we went through, and alas how all of that is passing into the darkness it remains without a trace as the ripples on the surface of the sea.

Nobody has yet told the story of our East side of 1910–1914, our immigrant years, the years of struggle and adaptation to a new life, of a multitude of Miril's & Noah's which taken together made up a social group, with its social thriving giving to its individual doings a social color & meaning.

That period I would define like this: Realization that life is not play in Revolution or romantics. That life is individual steady work & struggle for ends that have a collective significance.

The immigration of the preceding five years was of people who traveled with the drum of the 1905 Revolution in Russia still ringing, with the Romanticism and inexperience in life inherent to the Russian intelligentsia of that period.

And so we, your sisters & myself among the cohorts of others like us, have thrown ourselves into the fight to become a good draper, a sleevemaker, to overcome the 3rd and the 10th reader (do you know what a 1st & 5th reader, is it made only for grown up immigrants – personally I never studied a reader), and then to live a love in the parks, go to theater, have a good time in a E.B-way [East Broadway – JH] restaurant and enjoy all of that, without suspecting that for Central Park there are villas on the Hudson, for Coney Island there is Newport, that for our Sullivan County boarding houses there is Corn or Crab Long Beach, that there are the wide spaces.

I call these our childhood years in America.

Then came the years when the start in life was made. All the initial difficulties were overcome. We acquired a trade or a profession, the language, acquired **citizenship**, in its direct and implied meaning. We started as full-fledged members of the Community to fight for a Better America.

When I think of these two periods, I don't know which raises more tender memories, whether those initial years of childhood when we learned how to make our first steps in life, or the 2nd Period when we started to walk on our own feet. Whether I love the old-fashioned Madison St. where I used to come only for supper with pumpernickle and lots of soup and boiled meat and pickled tomatoes, with the Sunday morning spending in the barber shop waiting for the next to be shorn, and hear all the neighborhood gossip for the week, including the gossip in and about the Forward and *Warheit*, or the City Island swimmings with the Unterman family, baking ourselves in the hot mud in bundles of bodies and legs and young laughing faces, or whether I have better memories of the struggles at the meetings for leadership, fight for ideas the struggle for a Better America.

And then we have memories of trips across the Continent, of trips across the ocean, of trips to Siberia, Caucasus, Crimea – and when things are approaching the end one wonders – who will know of all the beautiful, marvelous although simple eternal things we knew and lived through?

Where is our inheritance – to whom do we leave it in what form. Where are the books, the poems that were not written! Who is it that we will orally tell, impart there should be a continuance of our life – where & who?

Such are the moods we are in these days, while we are not earnest in the business of recuperation.

Now enough of ourselves. For less than a month from now we shall be back to our interesting work in Moscow, with all what is coming with it. An outing to a country place on a "Sunday," to a theater once in a while etc. etc. until next summer when you will come to see us and we shall not let you go away back.

Now **Sarahle!** [Yiddish script] remember Sarahle what a good little ribber you were! And how we liked each other. Now you are so serious caring for Bobbette and worrying for Gelfie. Do you smile & jump as in the older days? Well sister, I shall have space for a few lines for Miril. Some other day I shall write to the older side of the family. My best regards for Louis and for Gelfie.

Noah

Dear sisters!

I have very little to add, it's a wonderful place very much like California, we receive everything we are about to eat and drink, and if you do not want to obey you eat what people eat when they are not afraid to gain weight. The main thing is that we are getting old and will hardly be able to enjoy our new prosperous country. 20 years ago we couldn't even dream of such a beautiful days to come, but your health and days bygone have left their mark.

In order you should get some idea of this sanatorium of ours I will write to Anna a detailed letter. My love and kisses to all.

APPENDIX D

Miril London's Letter to Beria

I found this letter to the head of the NKVD in Miril London's investigative case file at the former KGB archive in Moscow.[1] She sent it to him on March 5, 1939. She was then beginning her second year in the *gulag* – at Alzhir, the 'Akhmolinsk *lager* for wives of traitors to the motherland', in Kazakhstan. As the initials 'L.B.' are scribbled on the front page in pencil, it is reasonable to think that he actually read it. He may have been the one who underlined certain phrases in the letter. Someone, not necessarily Beria, scribbled in the upper left-hand corner 'concerning review of the case'. Many *gulag* prisoners sent such letters to Beria, but he read few of them. Even fewer were carefully preserved in the files for half a century. Ellipses in parenthesis indicate words missing due to physical damage – JH

To NKVD Peoples' Commissar cde. Beria
from prisoner London, M.E.
DECLARATION

I am turning to you because I hope that you can help me to return to the useful and active life of a Soviet woman. It is already about a year and a half that I have lost freedom. Arrested on 11-23-1937, as a member of the family of homeland-betrayer Noi Moisseevich London, former deputy director of *Glavneft*. Condemned Spec. Conf. 12-25-37 for 8 years to corrective labor camps.

I am 47 years old, and have worked for 31 years, for 16 years as a dressmaker, and 15 years as a chemical analyst. I have been in the revolutionary movement since 1912, first as a member of the Socialist Party of the USA, after that in 1918 as one of the organizers of the left wing of the party together with my husband, him being a founding leader of the American CP, a member of which I and my husband have been since 1919, since the day it was organized.

I and my husband ardently strove after the USSR from the very beginning of the revolution, as my husband, as a construction engineer, believed that his knowledge and experience would be especially useful for the young republic with its colossal construction tasks. We only succeeded in realizing his dream in 1926. We received sanction for departure from the CPUSA. I and my husband were registered as members of the AUCP(b) in July 1926.

1 *Sledstvennoe delo* R-40598, Maria Efimovna London, TsaFSB, Moscow, Russia.

 | DOI:10.1163/9789004745384_017

For 11 years worked as an analytic chemist. 7 years in the Kharkov Coal Institute and 4 years in Moscow at the Institute of Mineral Resources (*Ryzhavsky rep. d. N7*). I never received any reprimands. Despite my unfinished higher education, I succeeded in producing 2 scientific works on coal, which were published in 2 scientific-technical journals, and which I presented at the Sixth Mendeleev Conference in 1932 in Kharkov.

Besides my principal work, I convictedly and conscientiously participated in party life in the capacity of agitator, propagandist, and party and womens' organizer. I was a member of the bureau of the Coal Institute cell for 4 years, party organizer in the chemical laboratory where I directly worked for 5 years. Along the line of volunteer work I was a member of the leadership of the 'Third International' Seamstress Club (…) member of the presidium of UkrOZET 4 years (…) Kharkov City Soviet 2 years, member of city committee of Coal Miners Union 1 year. In Moscow at the Institute was party organizer of the chemical laboratory, discussion leader and propagandist. Always and at all enumerated jobs I strove to carry out the line of the party. I never received any party censures. My party card was taken away by the NKVD organs on the night of my arrest.

I was with the interrogator for 30 minutes, filling out the questionnaire with 4 questions, he personally presented no charges against me, also he did not say concretely what my husband was charged with. And for my part I declare with full responsibility that I never noticed any anti-party or anti-Soviet moods of my husband, much less activities. He never belonged to any opposition or anti-party grouping, on the contrary, struggled with them (*Donugol* cell, Livshits and Dimitrov). He was never linked in personal friendship with any former or current Trotskyists or rightists. His personal life was strict and modest, he never made use of those privileges which foreign specialists enjoy (*Spetsstavki, Insnab, Torgsin*). He had no party or Soviet censures, his party card was also taken on the night of arrest. With respect to how solidly my husband and I linked our fate with the fate of the USSR, it is visible perhaps, in that we took Soviet citizenship right away after the Shakhty affair, since it more solidly convinced us that it will be possible to build the first Socialist Homeland only with its own specialists.

I have not comprehended the arrest of my husband up to this day, but as an honest Communist, I can assure you that if I knew of any actions of husband against Soviet Power, I would act as a Bolshevik should, to whom the party is dearer than life, and mercilessly expose him, regardless of our long life together.

31 years of productive labor, 25 years of intense revolutionary activity, have turned me into a complete invalid. I suffer from insomnia, I often cannot sleep for whole months in a row. In connection with this I have various illnesses, dur-

ing the time of my residence in the camp my ailments have aggravated more and more, the only thing which supports me is this deep belief that the Soviet Union, my Socialist Homeland will return me to freedom in the end.

You cde. Beria, closest counselor of cde. Stalin, understand the word of the Leader that to exclude an honest party member is the same thing for her as death, so much the more to convict, to disgrace, to throw into prison an honest person!

I turn to you and ask you to investigate my case, help me to become such a person as I was, perhaps I can show again through my work and devotion, that I am not lost for the party with which I was linked for about 20 years and without which life is completely no use.

For a year now I am working in the camp as a seamstress at the sewing factory, the head of the camp will give a description of my work attitude and a general reference, I can only say that in the camp too I work with the same enthusiasm that I work all year in freedom.

London, Maria Efimovna
3-5-39

Annotated Bibliography of the Writings of Noah London

Noah London was a prolific writer, but almost exclusively in Yiddish. He is listed in several lexicons of Yiddish writers. The most comprehensive listing is in the multi-volume *Leksikon fun der nayer yidisher literatur*, published by the Congress for Jewish Culture in 1961. As Yiddish is essentially a dead language, all Yiddish titles are translated here into English. Russian titles appear in the original. As the Yiddish-language journals and newspapers he wrote for are now difficult to find, I have indicated where they are available. They are mostly on microfilm by now—in the case of the *Proletarier* or *Proletaryer* at my initiative. I have provided brief explanations of the significance of certain titles. An earlier, less complete and accurate version of this bibliography, compiled in 1992, is available in the Noah London collection at the Tamiment Institute at New York University.

During the early 1920s in America, he wrote for the legal Yiddish Communist press under the pseudonym N. Paiezon.[1] Articles by "the engineer Paiezon" sometimes but not always concern industrial subjects. The pseudonym is no longer used after January 1923. Articles written under the pseudonym will be indicated by an asterisk.

In addition London wrote for *Der komunist*, an underground party organ he edited, under the name "N. Smith." (His father was a blacksmith.) Holdings of *Der komunist* are true bibliographic rarities. In documents in the Comintern archives from the Communist underground his pseudonym is also "Smith." However, others used the same pseudonym as well.

Bibliography of Noah London

Di naye velt, 1917–1919. Organ of the American Jewish Socialist Federation. Tamiment Institute, New York University.

1917

"About Yiddish socialist sunday schools," letter, March 3, 1917.

"Menshevism or socialist impotence?" November 6, 1917. Went to press just prior to the

1 His nephew Jonas Weitzman, who had also attempted to research his uncle's career and fate, informed me of this pseudonym in the late 1980s. Telephone interview, California-New Jersey, late 1980s. Unfortunately his memory was lost by the time I commenced serious research.

Bolshevik revolution, and was apparently the first pro-Bolshevik article ever appearing there. An editorial footnote accuses London of "idealizing Leninism."

1918

"The parties in America and the world war," July 5, 1918.

"A chapter in history," August 30. About Mexican Revolution. Ironic praise for Woodrow Wilson

"An international Jewish socialist conference," November 1.

1919

"Scholasticism or Action?," article series: Part 1, January 10; Part 2, January 17; Part 3, February 14.

"The tasks of the Jewish workers congress," January 17.

"Declaration and Program by a group of seven comrades." Subhead: "discussion of party questions for the coming convention of the A.S.P." May 9. Manifesto of Jewish Left Wing. Written primarily by Alexander Bittelman and Noah London.

Kamf, 1919, organ of Left Wing of Jewish Socialist Federation, and subsequently of the Jewish Communist Federation. NYPL Jewish Division. London on masthead as one of three co-editors, from no. 9, June 17, 1919, through no. 18, August 27, 1919. Articles:

"The movement for councils in the unions," no. 9, June 27.

"National questions," no. 11, July 11. On Zionism (opposes). Note at end: "comrade London expresses his personal opinion. – ed."

"The foreign element in production and in the movement". Series, only first two parts of which were printed. Part 1, no. 14, August 1; Part 2, no. 16, August 15. Notable for treating black workers jointly with immigrants as the most militant layer of the American working class.

"About the founding of a new party," August 1. Short statement at the end of Part 1 succinctly expressing his support for the Communist Labor Party.

"Principles and tactics," no. 17, August 22. Polemic against ultraleftism.

1921

Der komunist. Yiddish-language underground journal of illegal United Communist Party. Part of the file was lost during the Bund Archive's merger with YIVO in the 1990s. Not microfilmed.

"N. Smith," "Unity discussions," no. 5, February 1921. Half of this issue and this article is in the possession of author. Xeroxed during a visit to the Bund archive in the late 1980s. Some unsigned articles were probably also by Noah London.

"N. Kuznetsov," presumably London, "The Russian Federation and the Communist Movement in America," no. 6, May 1921. Copy in Harvard University Library Judaica collection, recently digitized. 16-page convention issue, most articles official statements or unsigned. Several other pieces possibly by Noah London.

Proletaryer. Biweekly Yiddish legal newspaper sponsored by UCP, September 1920 to July 1921. Full collection on microfilm at New York Public Library, partial collection at YIVO. London became its editor in issue no. 9. All editorial notes thereafter likely also by London.

"An open letter from a former member to the members of the Jewish Socialist Federation of the Socialist Party of America,"* no. 9, February 1, 1921. Focuses on trade union questions.

Change in editorship announced in editorial notes (*Iberblikn*).

"From the industrial field," a series initiated by the previous editor. Letters or statements from union activists, sometimes with editorial introductions. In no. 9: editor's introduction for appeal on behalf of Albert Goldman re: his persecution as an alleged "labor spy" in ACWA.

"Economic surveys,"* no. 10, February 15.

"Once again about the Jewish Federation of the A.S.P.,"* no. 11, March 1.

"The crisis and American great finance,"* no. 12, March 16.

"Dictatorship of the proletariat, a speech by Noah London" (in Syracuse), no. 14, April 15.

"Organized work in the unions," speech to ILGWU members, unidentified but almost certainly by London, no. 16, May 15.

"A personal declaration," no. 17, June 20. London partially apologizes for old political mistakes, in particular pro-Wilson articles in *Di naye velt* in the summer of 1918.

Also, "The American state and parliamentary action,"* Part 1, no. 17, June 20; Part 2, no. 18, July 4. Last issue. The third part was submitted to *Emes*, but was rejected for publication.

Emes, weekly Yiddish legal organ of CPUSA, fall 1921. Editor: Shachno Epstein; co-editors London and Bittelman. New York Public Library and Hebrew Union College. Final few issues on Reel 323 of the CPUSA Comintern collection. Unavailable elsewhere.

no. 5–6, September 2. "Amsterdam and the American Federation of Labor."*

no. 8, September 16, "The revolt of the Jewish radical intellectuals (about convention of Jewish Socialist Federation)."*

no. 9, September 23. "The Workmens' Circle—what it is and what it should be." London by now publicly identified as head of Jewish section of legal Jewish CPUSA front organization, the "American Labor Alliance."

no. 10, September 30. "Coal—a driving force of the social revolution."*

no. 11, October 7. "The 'Workers Council'—what does it want?"* (WC united with CPUSA later.)

no. 12, October 14, "The railroads, the current crisis and the worker."

no. 13, October 21. "The unemployed under Hoover's guardianship."*
no. 15, October 4. "How America reacted to the Bolshevik Revolution."*
no. 16, October 16. "Three years after the armistice."
no. 19, December 2. "About the program of the 'Workers Party.'"
no. 21, December 16. "Over towns and townlets (shtetls)." Report from a national tour about Jewish workers' reactions to unification of Jewish communists with Jewish Socialist Federation.

1922

Naye velt-emes, January–March 1922. New York Public Library. London one of six editors.
First issue, January 7. "The trade union movement and the Workers Party." On the TUEL.
no. 2, January 14. "Capitalism in a proletarian state." On NEP.
no. 3, January 21. "To the branches of the Workers Party Jewish Federation," signed "Noah London, Secretary."
Also in no. 3: "The Genoa Conference (in the light of numbers and facts)."
no. 10, March 11. "A united front in America." Third part of the old *Proletarier* series. Discussion article.

Worker, Communist Party's English-language newspaper. March 25, "The Workers Party and the United Front." The only article London published there.

Freiheit, highest-circulation American Communist daily paper during the 1920s. London was labor editor until late winter 1923.
April 2. First issue, "Do you know what?: A series by the engineer N. Paiezon."* Part 1. Scientific explanation of radio and radio waves.
April 3. "How information moves from a thousand miles in a moment."* Part 2 of the explanation of radio and radio waves.
April 4. Repeat of Part 1.
April 5. "Workers' parties in Germany." On the question of the united front.
April 6. "The American proletariat grows."* On a New England textile strike.
April 11. "French workers parties."
April 17. "The Italian workers parties."
April 20. "How America squanders her natural resources" (unlike Europe).
April 27. "The backwardness of American technique," also "Workers propaganda through radiophone, a practical proposal to all workers' organizations."* United front radio station proposal.
April 28. "How the coal industry is run."
April 30. "The month of May should be tools month for Russia," appeal for material aid.
May 4. "A new way to fight unions," critique of progressive reformer Untermayer.

May 7. "The tailor shop that makes clothes for Russia."*
May 12. "Charles E. Ruthenberg, the new secretary of the W.P.," also "A new type of woman in America,"* on Bronx housewives arrested for leafleting.
May 18. "A communist colony of Americans in Siberia,"* on the Kuzbass colony.
May 19. "How the highest American courts openly prostitute themselves for capitalism," about child labor.
May 20. "Politicians fight and the public suffocates in the subways."*
May 22. "What are they after? Once again about the famous 'resolution' of the Workmen's Circle convention." Resolution called for freeing Soviet political prisoners.
May 26. "Larceny, robbery, graft,"* about the Teapot dome scandal.
June 11. "Medem the leftist, Lenin the rightist," about Bund leader Vladimir Medem.
June 5. "The convention of the Furriers' union."
June 11. "What is the T.U.E.L.?" (Trade Union Education League).
June 19. "When a union suffers from too much politics," on the Furriers union.
June 18. "The shop delegates and the last Supreme Court decision."
June 25. "Images from the cutters' (shneiders) strike"* (ILGWU Local no. 10).
July 3. "Is a united political front in America possible and necessary?"
July 7. "The railroad workers must have one big union."*
July 10. "Our Jewish union leaders."
July 12. "The agreement in the cloak industry."
July 17. "How an American railway magnate tricked two states."*
July 22. "The strike wave in the Jewish unions."
July 25. "The stoppage in the cloak industry."
July 26. "Should the Workers Party become an open communist party?"
August 13. "How the miners live in West Virginia."*
August 17. "We need one Amalgamated union in New York." For local mergers.
August 20. "Letter from a worker about the movement, introduction by Noah London." Part 1.
August 21. "Letter from a worker," Part 2.
August 23. "Unemployment insurance in the needle industry."
August 25. "Letter from a worker," Part 3.
August 29. "Letter from a worker," Part 4.
September 4. "Letter from a worker," Part 5: "How a workers party can be organized."
September 6. "A doctor finds a remedy for the worst sicknesses."*
September 7. "Again about the doctor who heals all sicknesses."*
September 8. "About Dr. Abrams' theory of healing disease."* Unconventional practitioner shunned by medical profession but advocated by Upton Sinclair. Argues that his theories should be tested.
September 19. "At the New York cloakmakers' Freiheit meeting."*
October 5. "The leaders and masses in the Amalgamated."

October 6. "Self-activity by the membership is needed in the Amalgamated."
October 11. "The aches and pains in the cloakmakers' union."
October 14. "The failure of the cloakmakers' leadership."
October 26. "In the capmakers' union."
November 7. "Bolshevism in the unions."
November 17. "An open communist party is needed in America." Factional polemic.
December 10. "The nonsense of an underground communist party in America." Factional polemic.
December 16. "How they are building the new tunnel under the Hudson."* Has the tone of personal experience. Confirms the family story that he worked on the Holland Tunnel project.
December 25. "The brand of shame on the cloakmakers' leaders."
December 27. "The Workers Party and Union Branches, report at Federation Convention about the necessity of party trade branches." Minority report, proposed industrial reorganization of the federation into "trade branches." Majority counterreport by Melech Epstein.

1923

January 3. "Miners fight for nationalizing the coal industry."* Last time the pseudonym was employed.
January 6. "Where arbitrariness in a union comes from." About the needle trades.
January 11. "Our defeats—our victories." About the needle trades.
January 19. "Notices from the workers' movement." About the needle trades.
January 30. "Timely questions from our union life." About the needle trades.
February 15. "A union needs a president, but a president must have a union." About the ILGWU.
February 28. "An election machine or a machine party of workers?" Critique of the Socialist-run "American Labor Party" in New York.
March 14. "Socialist authors with old heretical thoughts." Review of "Rich Paupers," a Yiddish play by Chone Gottesfeld, editor of *Forward* humor page and later president of Yiddish Writers Union.

Two-month gap. London was replaced as labor editor by Melech Epstein.

May 29. "Don't smother the child with too much love (about the discussion on party discipline)." Polemic against new American Communist Party leader John Pepper.
June 10. "The donkey knows his bosses' trough." On poet David Einhorn's correspondence from Berlin in the Forward. Article stirred up public controversy.
June 25. "The culture bearers and the party doers." Reply to response to Einhorn article in Tog, a non-socialist Yiddish daily.

July 19. "Not like among the upper crust, but it's important anyway." About the 1923 farmer-labor convention.

September 29. "Parlor communism or living communism." Reply to Zivyon (B. Hoffman), a Freiheit editor who had just left the Workers Party and published a critical pamphlet. States that London had agreed with Zivyon on many issues when he was still a party member.

October 20. Series Part 1, "notes from a reader." "The twilight of civilization." About an article in the Nation on the rise of barbarism all over the world, from fascism in Italy to the KKK in America.

October 28. Part 2. "The collar open, the cap on the side." About the German near-revolution in 1923. Title from European correspondent's description of German communist attire.

November 10. "The October Revolution and the Jewish workers movement in America." Historical article which gives London's viewpoint on the birth of American Jewish Communism.

December 28. "The danger is now on the right (on the discussion about a third party)," vs. supporting LaFollette in 1924 presidential elections.

1924

February 24. "The class struggle in the Workmen's Circle."

March 26. "Homo Sapiens for $125 a week." Scathing critique of modernist Polish novelist Stanislav Pshibishevsky.

April 20. "How the Workmen's Circle has captured the *Freiheit*."

April 24. Series about immigration politics, Part 1, "From open arms to open hatred"

April 27. Part 2, "Soft idealism for hard cash."

May 2. Part 3, "The goy is *treyf*, but his digging tool is kosher."

May 4. Part 4, "Where Gerry [steel magnate] is more liberal than Gompers."

May 7. Part 5, "The crisis becomes an American citizen."

May 11. Part 6, "The specter of Bolshevism in America."

May 14. Part 7, "Marshall, Pine and the poor, unfortunate brothers." Max Pine was the head of the United Hebrew Trades; Louis Marshall a prominent Jewish businessman and public spokesman.

May 17. "Their seven fat years." About the *Forward*.

May 22. "What pushes our unions to the right."

May 24. "Immigration and international problems." Last article in the immigration series; expounds Workers Party program on immigration.

May 29. "Tomorrow's liberalism and *Forward* socialism."

June 4. Series on political conventions, Part 1, "The theme of political conventions." Implied theme of the series: opposition to CPUSA line of support to Lafollette, which would be overruled by the Comintern.

June 9. Part 2, "The business of politics in America."

June 12. Part 3, "Cleveland, LaFollette, St. Paul."

June 18. Part 4, "From New York to St. Paul."

July 22. "The political strike in Canada."

July 16. "Isaac the Patriarch and Abe Cahan" About Cahan and the late Isaac Hourwich.

October 24. "Once Tammany, now S.P."

November 9. "Seven years of permanent revolution." October revolution anniversary article. Presumably the "Trotskyist" title of this piece did not help London's status in the party.

November 16. "Is there a difference between Marxism and Leninism?" (Answer: no.)

December 28. "The heralds of the *Freiheit*." Historical piece about the predecessors of the *Freiheit*.

Amerikanskaia Tekhnika, journal of the Russian Association of Engineers, began appearing on November 1, 1924. London was a member of the five-man editorial board of this journal, which later became the Amtorg journal. Purely technical. Available at the Library of Congress and elsewhere. London was probably the author of the unsigned manifesto in the first issue.

1925

Freiheit.

February 11. "Bread with butter." About playwright Moishe Nadir.

March 9. "From Archangelsk to Turkestan." About Amtorg, where London was employed.

May 3. "In middle America." Travel impressions.

May 15. "Camp Nitgedeiget," Part 1. London directed Camp Nitgedeiget that summer.

May 16. "Camp Nitgedeiget," Part 2.

No articles by London appeared from May 15, 1925, to October 29, 1925. During this period he was being pilloried in the *Daily Worker* and the *Freiheit* as a rightwing deviationist.

"Statement of N. London at the Convention of the Jewish Federation of the Workers Party," September 1925. In this statement he renounces the Lore caucus, criticizes the pro-Foster Jewish Federation majority, and announces his adherence to the Ruthenberg minority. Available in both the Comintern CPUSA microfilms and in the Lovestone papers at the Hoover Institute.

Gap in New York Public Library *Freiheit* microfilm series for the last three months of 1925. The period from October 7 to November 7, 1925, is available on YIVO microfilm.

October 29. "With the Russian Commission for the Don coal region."
November 1. "Our tasks on the cooperative front."
November 7. "America and Russia."

According to A. Pomerantz, *Proletpen* (Kiev: 1935), there was an "an interesting article by Noah London" in the Novermber 28, 1925, *Freiheit*: "How are things on our cultural front."

1926

"What Does Our Cooperative Movement Want"? United Workers Cooperative Colony manifesto. Apparently published winter or spring 1926.

Freiheit.
February 26. "Political activity about the rent question." Discusses bills before the New York state legislature.
March 12. "On a rainy Sunday in March." About reading Sunday papers—and leaving for Russia.
March 14. "In cheder." About the Communist Party New York Workers' School, in which London taught.
April 4. "A goodbye and a summary for the Fourth Jubilee." On the fourth anniversary of the *Freiheit.*
April 28. "From Woolworth's to the Leviathan." Travel impressions. Written on the SS *Leviathan* as he crossed the Atlantic.
May 9. "England on the eve of the General Strike." Front-page article, written en route to the USSR, after his visit to England.
June 26. "Poland stands on a powderkeg." Travel impressions. Written in the Soviet Union after his arrival there from Poland.
July 15. "First Impressions of the Soviet Union," Part 1.
July 16. "First Impressions of the Soviet Union," Part 2.
September 8. "Ukraine"

No further articles with London's byline appear in the *Freiheit* for at least six months thereafter. Perhaps more appeared subsequently.

Shtern, Kharkov. Daily Yiddish newspaper of the Ukrainian *Evsektsiia*, the Jewish section of the Ukrainian Communist Party. On microfilm at YIVO.
June 5. "How New York workers are building cooperative housing."
July 3. "To the history of the cooperative movement in America."
July 17. "How the Donbass is being built (seen through American eyeglasses)." Housing construction in the Donbass.

October 20. "Moishe Nadir" (then visiting Kharkov).

Di royte velt, Kharkov. Yiddish literary journal. On microfilm at University of Texas, Austin, Judaica library.

December no. 12, "The *Dneprostroi* [*dnieprboy*]: how to make electricity from water," pp. 70–5.

1927

Di royte velt, February no. 2, "The economics and technique of the Donbass," pp. 99–108.

Poiasnitel'naia Zapiska k Proektu Donetskogo Vodoprovoda dlia Almazno-Mar'evskogo Raiona. Vodbiuro Donuglia. Engineering schematic and exposition of London's water pipeline project. RGAE, Moscow, f. 3429 (*Vesenkha*), op. 3, d. 2028, l. 37–49. Map dated May 1927.

1928

Di royte velt, November no. 11, "The Workmen's Circle of the United States and Canada (on the occasion of the arrival of the delegation in the Soviet Union)," pp. 84–90.

1929

Di royte velt, May/June, no. 5–6, "The five year plan of socialist construction (a piece of the path to socialism)," pp. 75–90.

Shtern.

August 4. "With the American Expedition to Birobidzhan," letter.

October 8. "We will master Birobidzhan," London's and other speeches at Kharkov OZET *aktiv*.

October 17. "A land with a rich future," Part 1. Series on Birobidzhan.

October 18. "A land with a rich future," Part 2.

October 19. "A land with a rich future," Part 3.

October 20. "A land with a rich future," Part 4.

October 21. "A land with a rich future," Part 5.

Tribuna, Russian-language journal of OZET. Widely available, at Library of Congress and elsewhere.

no. 18, September 20. Excerpted letter from Birobidzhan, "Birobidzhan nuzhdaetsia v khoroshikh rabotnikakh!"

no. 20, October 25, "Postroim sotsialisticheskuiu stranu;" and "Zadachi stroitel'stva Birobidzhana (Rezul'taty raboty ekspeditsii 'IKOR')."

1930

Tribuna no. 6, February 20. In bibliography section, review in Russian of "Report of the IKOR American Experts' Commission," signed "N.L."

"With the American Expedition to Biro-Bidjan," Kharkov, 1930. Yiddish pamphlet published by OZET. London was the official representative of OZET on this expedition. His official reports are to be found in the OZET papers at GARF in Moscow, f. 9498, op. 1, d. 47. Much of this pamphlet comes from his articles on Birobidzhan in the *Shtern* and *Tribuna*.

1933

"Vodosnabzhenie Donbassa," Kharkov, 1933. Pamphlet on London's Donbass water projects.

1934

Pravda, Moscow, "Donbass Trebuet Vody," August 15, 1934.

"Notes on USSR," 47-page mostly double-spaced typewritten manucript. Original dictated to visiting American sister-in-law, Rose Unterman-Discher-Risikoff, in August 1934 and smuggled out of the Soviet Union. In Noah London Collection at Tamiment, and in Appendix B.

1934 and 1935

Four letters to Rose Risikoff from the Soviet Union: Appendix C.

General Bibliography

A Documentary History of Communism. Robert V. Daniels, ed. Vintage Russian Library, vol. 2. New York: Vintage Books, 1960.

Abramovitch, Raphael. *In tsvey revolutsies: di geshikhte fun a dor*, vol. 2. New York: Farlag "arbeter-ring," 1944.

Abramsky, Chimen. "The Biro-Bidzhan project, 1927–1959." In *Jews in Soviet Russia since 1917*, edited by L. Kochan, 62–75. London: Oxford University Press, 1970.

Adler, Selig, and Thomas E. Connolly. *From Ararat to Suburbia: The History of the Jewish Community of Buffalo*. Philadelphia: Jewish Publication Society of America, 1960.

Aleichem, Sholem. *Tevye the Dairyman and The Railroad Stories*. Edited and translated by H. Halkin. Library of Yiddish Classics. New York: Schocken, 1996.

Altshuler, Mordechai. *Soviet Jewry on the Eve of the Holocaust: A Social and Demographic Profile*. Jerusalem: Yad Vashem, 1998.

American Icor Commission for the Study of Biro-Bidjan and Its Colonization. New York: ICOR, 1930.

Andrle, Vladimir. *Workers in Stalin's Russia: Industrialization and Social Change in a Planned Economy*. New York: St. Martin's Press, 1988.

Andrusz, Gregory D. *Housing and Urban Development in the USSR*. SUNY Series in Urban Public Policy. Edited by Mark and Richard Schneider. Albany: SUNY Press, 1984.

Ascher, Abraham. *The Revolution of 1905*. Stanford, CA: Stanford University Press, 1992.

Bailes, Kendall E. *Technology and Society under Lenin and Stalin: Origins of the Soviet Technical Intelligentsia, 1917–1941*. Princeton, NJ: Princeton University Press, 1978.

Bailes, Kendall E. "The American Connection: Ideology and the Transfer of American Technology to the Soviet Union, 1917–1941." *Comparative Studies in Society and History* 23, no. 3 (1981): 421–48.

Bakulin, V.I., and O.L. Leibovich. "Rabochie, 'Spetsy,' Partiitsy." *Rabochii klass i sovremennyi mir* 6 (1990): 98–110.

Ball, Alan M. *Russia's Last Capitalists: The Nepmen, 1921–1929*. Berkeley: University of California Press, 1987.

Barrett, James R. "Americanization from the Bottom Up: Immigration and the Remaking of the Working Class in the United States, 1880–1930." *Journal of American History* 79, no. 3 (December 1992): 996–1020.

Barshchevsky, D. "Zemel'noe ustroistvo trudiashchikh evreev." *Sovetskoe stroitel'stvo* 1 (January 1934): 86–90.

Beizer, Mikhael. *Evrei Leningrada, 1917–1939*. Jerusalem: Gesharim, 1999.

Bender, Daniel E. *Sweated Work, Weak Bodies: Anti-Sweatshop Campaigns and Languages of Labor*. New Brunswick, NJ: Rutgers University Press, 2004.

Benvenuti, Francesco. "Industry and Purge in the Donbass, 1936–37." *Europe–Asia Studies* 45 (1993): 57–78.

Bernstein, Irving. *The Lean Years: A History of the American Worker, 1920–1933*. Boston: Houghton Mifflin, 1960.

Bittelman, Alexander. Tamiment Institute, Collection 62. 1962. *Things I Have Learned.* New York.

Blake, N.M. *Water for the Cities: A History of the Urban Water Supply Problem*. Maxwell School Series, vol. 3. Syracuse, NY: Syracuse University Press, 1956.

Block, Alexander. "Soviet Housing: The Historical Aspect: Some Notes on Problems of Policy-I." *Soviet Studies* 3, no. 1 (July 1951): 1–15.

Block, Alexander. "Soviet Housing—The Historical Aspect: Some Notes on Problems of Policy-II." *Soviet Studies* 3, no. 3 (January 1952): 229–57.

Brody, David. *Steelworkers in America: The Nonunion Era*. New York: Harper & Row, 1969.

Brooks, Juanita. *History of the Jews in Utah and Idaho*. Salt Lake City: Western Epics, 1973.

Budnitskii, Oleg. "Jews, Pogroms and the White Movement: A Historiographic Critique." *Kritika* 2, no. 4 (Fall 1991): 751–72.

Budnitskii, Oleg. "The Causes of Pogroms, or Gunshots from Behind." Unpublished paper presented at Institute of Slavic, East European and Eurasian Studies, University of California, Berkeley, November 9, 2005.

Buhle, Paul. "Jews and American Communism: The Cultural Question." *Radical History Review* 23 (December 1980): 8–33.

Buhle, Paul. "Ludwig Lore and the New Yorker *Volkszeitung*: The Twilight of the German-American Socialist Press." In *The German-American Radical Press: The Shaping of a Left Political Culture*, edited by E. Shore, K. Fones-Wolf, and J. Danky, 168–81. Urbana: University of Illinois Press, 1992.

Cahan, Abraham. *The Rise of David Levinsky*. New York: Penguin Books, 1993.

Cannon, James P. *The First Ten Years of American Communism: Report of a Participant.* New York: Pathfinder Press, [1963] 1973.

Cannon, James P. "The Revival of the Socialist Party." In *The Left Opposition in the U.S., 1928–1931: Writings and Speeches*, edited by Fred Stanton, 231–9. New York: Monad Press, 1981.

Cannon, James P. "The Workers Party Today—And Tomorrow." August/September 1923. In *James P. Cannon and the Early Years of American Communism: Selected Writings and Speeches, 1920–1928*, 127–49. New York: Prometheus Research Library, 1992.

Cannon, James P. "We Want the Comintern to Give Us Assistance," November 27, 1922, In *Spartacist*, No. 60, Autumn 2007.

Carr, E.H. *A History of Soviet Russia. The Bolshevik Revolution, 1917–1923*, vol. 2. Baltimore: Penguin Books, [1952] 1966.

Carr, E.H. *A History of Soviet Russia. The Interregnum, 1923–1924*. Baltimore: Penguin Books, [1954] 1958.

Carr, E.H. *A History of Soviet Russia. Socialism in One Country, 1924–1926*, vol. 1. Baltimore: Penguin Books, [1958] 1970.

Carr, E.H. *A History of Soviet Russia. Socialism in One Country, 1924–1926*, vol. 3. Baltimore: Penguin Books, [1964] 1972.

Carr, E.H. *A History of Soviet Russia. Foundations of a Planned Economy, 1926–1929*, vol. 3, part 2. New York: Macmillan, 1978.

Carr, E.H., and R.W. Davies. *Foundations of a Planned Economy, 1926–1929*. A History of Soviet Russia, vol. 1. New York: MacMillan Co., 1969.

Cassedy, Steven. *To the Other Shore: The Russian Jewish Intellectuals Who Came to America*. Princeton, NJ: Princeton University Press, 1997.

Cassiday, Julie A. "Marble Columns and Jupiter Lights: Theatrical and Cinematic Modeling of Soviet Show Trials in the 1920s." *Slavic and East European Journal* 42, no. 4 (1998): 640–60.

Charney, Daniel. *Vilne* (*memuarn*). Buenos Aires: Industria Argentina, 1951.

Chase, William J. *Workers, Society and the Soviet State: Labor and Life in Moscow, 1918–1929*. The Working Class in European History. S. Meacham, J. Scott, and R. Zelnik, gen. eds. Urbana: University of Illinois Press, 1987.

Chazanow, Bernard. Interview by Jonathan Bloom, 31 May 1978, New York. Tape 1, side 2. Oral History of the American Left, Tamiment Institute: Series I.

Cohen, Lizabeth. *Making a New Deal: Industrial Workers in Chicago, 1919–1939*. Cambridge: Cambridge University Press, 1990.

Conquest, Robert. *The Great Terror: Stalin's Purge of the Thirties*. Revised ed. New York: Macmillan, 1973 [1968].

Conquest, Robert. *The Great Terror: A Reassessment*. New York: Oxford University Press, 1990.

Critchlow, Donald T., ed. *Socialist in the Heartland: The Midwestern Experience, 1900–1925*. Notre Dame, IN: University of Notre Dame Press, 1986.

D'Agostino, Anthony. *Soviet Succession Struggles: Kremlinology and the Russian question from Lenin to Gorbachev*. Boston: Allen & Unwin, 1988.

Davies, R.W. *The Soviet Economy in Turmoil, 1929–1930*. Vol. 3 of *The Industrialization of Soviet Russia*. New York: Macmillan, 1969.

Davies, R.W. *Crisis and Progress in the Soviet Economy, 1931–1933*. Vol. 4 of *The Industrialization of Soviet Russia*. New York: Macmillan Co., 1996.

Davies, R.W., and Stephen G. Wheatcroft. *The Years of Hunger: Soviet Agriculture, 1931–1933*. Vol. 5 of *The Industrialization of Soviet Russia*. New York: Palgrave Macmillan, 2014.

Davies, R.W., and Stephen G. Wheatcroft, Oleg Khlevnyuk, and Stephen G. Wheatcroft. *The Years of Progress: The Soviet Economy, 1934–1936*. Vol. 6 of *The Industrialization of Soviet Russia*. New York: Palgrave Macmillan, 2004.

Dekel-Chen, Jonathan. "Soviet–Jewish agricultural colonists, 1937–1945." *Jews in Eastern Europe* 3, no. 46 (Winter 2001): 34–56.

Dekel-Chen, Jonathan. "Farmers, Philanthropists and Soviet Authority: Rural Crimea and Southern Ukraine, 1923–41." *Kritika: Explorations in Russian and Eurasian History* 4, no. 4 (Fall 2003): 849–85.

Dekel-Chen, Jonathan. *Farming the Red Land: Jewish Agricultural Colonization and Local Soviet Power, 1924–1941*. New Haven, CT: Yale University Press, 2005.

Deutscher, Isaac. "The Non-Jewish Jew." In *The Non-Jewish Jew and Other Essays*, edited by Tamara Deutscher, 25–41. London: Merlin Press, 1981.

Draper, Theodore. *American Communism and Soviet Russia*. New York: Random House, [1957] 1986.

Draper, Theodore. *The Roots of American Communism*. Communism in American Life Series, edited by Clinton Rossiter. New York: Viking Press, 1957.

Dubofsky, Melvyn. *We Shall Be All: A History of the Industrial Workers of the World*, 2d ed. Urbana and Chicago: University of Illinois Press, [1969] 1988.

Epstein, Melech. *Jewish Labor in U.S.A., 1914–1952: An Industrial, Political and Cultural History of the Jewish Labor Movement*. New York: H. Wolff, 1953.

Epstein, Melech. *The Jew and Communism: The Story of Early Communist Victories and Ultimate Defeats in the Jewish Community, U.S.A., 1919–1941*. New York: H. Wolff, 1959.

Estraikh, Gennady, and Diner, Hasia R., eds. *1929: Mapping the Jewish World*. New York: New York University Press, 2013.

Estraikh, Gennady, and Diner, Hasia R., eds. "The Kharkiv Yiddish Literary World, 1920s to Mid-1930s." *East European Jewish Affairs* 32, no. 2 (2002): 70–88.

Estraikh, Gennady, and Diner, Hasia R., eds. "The Soviet Shtetl in the 1920s." In *The Shtetl: Myth and Reality*, edited by A. Polonsky, 197–212. Polin: Studies in Polish Jewry, vol. 17. Oxford: The Littman Library of Jewish Civilization, 2004.

Estraikh, Gennady, and Diner, Hasia R., eds. "From Shtetl to the City of the Sun Calling at the Schools of Communism: Yiddish Soviet Ukrainian Trade Unions of the 1920s." *Eastern European Jewish Affairs* 29, no. 1–2 (Summer–Winter 1999): 51–60.

Estraikh, Gennady, and Diner, Hasia R., eds. *In Harness: Yiddish Writers' Romance with Communism*. Judaic Traditions in Literature, Music and Art, edited by K. Frieden and H. Bloom. Syracuse, NY: Syracuse University Press, 2005.

Feuer, Lewis S. "American Travellers to the Soviet Union." *American Quarterly* 14, no. 2, part 1 (Summer 1962): 136–44.

Filene, Peter G. *Americans and the Soviet Experiment*. Cambridge, MA: Harvard University Press, 1967.

Filtzer, Donald. *Soviet Workers and Stalinist Industrialization: The Formation of Modern Soviet Production Relations, 1928–1941*. Armonk, NY: M.E. Sharpe, 1986.

Fink, Victor. "Birobidzhan." *Sovetskoe stroitel'stvo* 5, no. 46 (May 1930): 117–23.

Fisher, Alan. *The Crimean Tatars*. Stanford, CA: Hoover Institution Press, 1978.

Fitzpatrick, Sheila. *Education and Social Mobility in the Soviet Union, 1921–1934*. New York: Cambridge University Press, 1979.

Fitzpatrick, Sheila. *The Russian Revolution*. Oxford: Oxford University Press, 1982.

Fitzpatrick, Sheila. "Cultural Revolution as Class War." In *Cultural Revolution in Russia, 1928–1931*, 8–40. Bloomington: Indiana University Press, 1984.

Fitzpatrick, Sheila. *Stalin's Peasants: resistance and survival in the Russian village after collectivization*. New York: Oxford University Press, 1994.

Fitzpatrick, Sheila. *Everyday Stalinism. Ordinary Life in Extraordinary Times: Soviet Russia in the 1930s*. New York: Oxford University Press, 1999.

Flores, Marcello. "The American Attitude Toward the First Soviet Five-Year Plan." *Storia nordamericana* 1, no. 1 (1984).

Foster, Willliam Z. *The Bankruptcy of the American Labor Movement*. 2nd ed. Chicago: Trade Union Education League, 1922.

Frankel, Jonathan. *Crisis, Revolution, and Russian Jews*. Cambridge: Cambridge University Press, 2009.

Frankel, Jonathan. *Prophecy and Politics: Socialism, Nationalism, and the Russian Jews, 1862–1917*. Cambridge: Cambridge University Press, 1981.

Fraser, Steve. *Labor Will Rule: Sidney Hillman and the Rise of American Labor*. New York: Macmillan, 1991.

Fraser, Steve. "Dress Rehearsal for the New Deal: Shop-Floor Insurgents, Political Elites, and Industrial Democracy in the Amalgamated Clothing Workers." In *Working-Class America: Essays on Labor, Community, and American Society*, edited by Michael Frisch and Daniel J. Walkowitz, 212–55. The Working Class in American History. Urbana: University of Illinois Press, 1983.

Freitag, Gabriele. *Nächstes Jahr in Moskau!: Die Zuwanderung von Juden in die sowjetische Metropole 1917–1932*. Schriften des Simon-Dubnow-Instituts. D. Diner, gen. ed. Göttingen: Vandenhoeck & Ruprecht, 2004.

Freyn, H.J. "The Life and Work of American Engineers in Soviet Russia." *Engineers and Engineering* 48, no. 6 (June 1931).

Friedgutt, Theodore H. "Labor Violence and Regime Brutality in Tsarist Russia: The Iuzovka Cholera Riots." *Slavic Review* 46, no. 2 (Summer 1987): 245–65.

Friedgutt, Theodore H. *Life and Work in Russia's Donbass, 1869–1924*. Vol. 1 of *Iuzovka and Revolution*. Studies of the Harriman Institute. Princeton, NJ: Princeton University Press, 1989.

Friedgutt, Theodore H. *Politics and Revolution in Russia's Donbass, 1869–1924*. Vol. 2 of *Iuzovka and Revolution*. Studies of the Harriman Institute. Princeton, NJ: Princeton University Press, 1994.

Gatrell, Peter. *A Whole Empire Walking: Refugees in Russia during World War I*. 1999. Indiana-Michigan Series in Russian and East European Studies. A. Rabinowitch and G. Rosenberg, gen. ed. Bloomington: Indiana University Press.

Getsov, S. "Khar'kov, 15 maia." *Vestnik Donuglia* 12 (May 15, 1927): 1–3.

Getty, J. Arch. *Origins of the Great Purges: The Soviet Communist Party Reconsidered, 1933–1938*. Soviet and East European Studies. Cambridge: Cambridge University Press, 1985.

Getty, J. Arch. "The Politics of Repression Revisited." In *Stalinist Terror: New Perspectives*, edited by J. Arch Getty and R. Manning, 40–62. Cambridge: Cambridge University Press, 1993.

Getty, J. Arch, and Oleg V. Naumov. *The Road to Terror: Stalin and the Self-Destruction of the Bolsheviks, 1932–1939*. Translated by B. Sher. Annals of Communism. J. Brent, gen. ed. New Haven, CT: Yale University Press, 1999.

Ginzburg, S.Z. "O gibeli Sergo Ordzhonikidze." *Voprosy Istorii* KPSS 3 (1991).

Ginzburg, S.Z. *O Proshlom, dlia Budushchego*. 2d ed. Moscow: Politizdat, 1986.

Gitelman, Zvi Y. *Jewish Nationality and Soviet Politics: The Jewish Sections of the* CPSU*, 1917–1930*. Princeton, NJ: Princeton University Press, 1972.

Gitlow, Benjamin. *I Confess: The Truth about American Communism*. New York: E.P. Dutton, 1940.

Glenn, Susan A. *Daughters of the Shtetl: Life and Labor in the Immigrant Generation*. Ithaca, NY: Cornell University Press, 1990.

Gold, Michael. "At a Workers' Vacation Camp." *Nation* 123, no. 8195 (September 29, 1926): 294–95.

Gold, Michael. *Jews Without Money*. 2d ed. New York: Carroll & Graf, 1930.

Goldberg, Robert A. *Back to the Soil: The Jewish Farmers of Clarion, Utah, and Their World*. Salt Lake City: University of Utah Press, 1986.

Goldman, Wendy. *Terror and Democracy in the Age of Stalin: The Social Dynamics of Repression*. Cambridge, Cambridge University Press, 2007.

Goldshmit, A.I. "Khaver aron." In *vayter-bukh: tsum andenk fun a. vayter*, edited by Sh. Niger and Z. Rayzen, 66–92. Vilna: Br. Rozental, 1920.

Graham, Loren. *The Ghost of the Executed Engineer: Technology and the Fall of the Soviet Union*. Cambridge, MA: Harvard University Press, 1993.

Gramsci, Antonio. "The Revolution against 'Capital,'" translated by Victoria Cox. In *Pre-Prison Writings*, edited by Richard Bellamy. Cambridge: Cambridge University Press, 1994, pp. 41–42. Original, "La Rivoluzione contro il Capitale," *Avanti*, December 24, 1917.

Graziosi, Andrea. "'Building the First System of State Industry in History,' Piatakov's VSNKh and the Crisis of the NEP, 1923–1926." *Cahiers du monde russe et sovietique* 36, no. 4 (1991): 539–80.

Graziosi, Andrea. *A New, Peculiar State: Explorations in Soviet History, 1917–1937*. Westport, CT: Praeger Publishers, 2000.

Green, James R. *Grass-Roots Socialism: Radical Movements in the Southwest, 1895–1943*. Baton Rouge: Louisiana State University Press, 1978.

Greenwald, Richard A. *The Triangle Fire, The Protocols of Peace, and Industrial Democracy in Progressive Era New York*. Philadelphia: Temple University Press, 2005.

Gruber, Helmut, ed. *Soviet Russia Masters the Comintern: International Communism in the Era of Stalin's Ascendancy*. Garden City, NY: Anchor Press/Doubleday, 1974.

Gurowsky, David. "Factional Disputes within the ILGWU: 1919–1928." Ph.D. diss., SUNY Binghamton, 1978.

Harris, Steven E. "Moving to the Separate apartment: Building, Distributing, Furnishing, and Living in Urban Housing in Soviet Russia, 1950s–1960s." Ph.D. diss., University of Chicago, 2003.

Hellbeck, Jochen. "Fashioning the Stalinist Soul: The Diary of Stepan Polubnyi, 1931–39." In *Stalinism: New Directions*, edited by Sheila Fitzpatrick, 77–116. London: Routledge, 2000.

Hellbeck, Jochen. *Revolution on My Mind: Writing a Diary under Stalin*. Cambridge, MA: Harvard University Press, 2006.

Henryk, Titus D. "Planning of the Capital in Kharkiv." *Harvard Ukrainian Studies* 16, no. 3/4 (December 1992): 325–59.

Higham, John. *Strangers in the Land: Patterns of American Nativism 1860–1925*. 2d ed. New York: Atheneum, 1975 [1955].

Hobsbawn, Eric. *The Age of Extremes: The Short Twentieth Century, 1914–1991*. London: Little Brown & Co. 1994.

Holmes, Beatrice. "The Young Girl as Heroine: the Aspirations and Self Image of the Eastern European Jewish Woman Immigrant Trade Unionist." Term paper. George Washington University, January 1992.

Holmes, John. "California in the Progressive Era: The Union Labor Party and the Socialist Party in the San Francisco Bay Area." Presented at the Social Science History Association. Portland, Or., Nov. 5, 2005.

Holmes, John. "International Ladies Garment Workers Union," *Dictionary of American History*, 3rd. ed. (Gale Group, 2003).

Holmes, John. "American Jewish Communism and Garment Unionism in the 1920s." *American Communist History* 6, no. 2 (Fall 2007): 171–95.

Holmes, John, and Arieh Lebowitz. "Jewish Socialist Federation." In *Encyclopedia of the American Left*, edited by M.J. Buhle, P. Buhle, and D. Georgakas. 2d ed., 404–5. New York: Oxford University Press, 1998.

Hood, Clifton. *722 Miles: The Building of the Subways and How They Transformed New York*. Baltimore: Johns Hopkins University Press, 2004.

Howe, Irving. *World of Our Fathers*. New York: Simon & Schuster, 1976.

Instytut istorii partii pry TSK Kompartii Ukraïny. Documentary collection. In *Holod 1932–1933 rokiv na Ukraïni: ochyma istorykiv, movoiu dokumentiv*. Edited by F.M. Rudich and R. Ya. Pyrih. Kiev, 1990.

Ivanov, Alexander. "From Charity to Productive Labour: The World ORT Union and Jewish Agricultural Colonization in the Soviet Union, 1923–38." *East European Jewish Affairs* 37, no. 1 (2007): 1–28.

Johanningsmeier, Edward P. *Forging American Communism: The Life of William Z. Foster*. Princeton, NJ: Princeton University Press, 1994.

Kagedan, Allan L. "Agro-Joint Project, 1924–1937." *Jewish Social Studies* 43 (1981).

Kagedan, Allan L. *Soviet Zion: The Quest for a Russian Jewish Homeland*. New York: St. Martin's Press, 1994.

Katzenelenbogen, Uriah. "Der pionir fun der leder-industrie in lite—chaim frenkl." In *Lite*, edited by Mendel Sudarski, Uriah Katzenelenbogen, and J. Kissin, 941–70. New York: Futuro Press, 1951.

Kazovsky, Hillel. *The Artists of the Kultur-Lige* (Khudozhniki Kul'tur-Ligi). Translated by J. Klein. "Sovremennye issledovaniia." Jerusalem; Moscow: Gesharim; Mosty kul'tury, 2003.

Kenez, Peter. "Pogroms and White Ideology in the Russian Civil War." In *Pogroms: Anti-Jewish Violence in Modern Russian History*, edited by John D. Klier and Shlomo Lombroza, 293–313. Cambridge: Cambridge University Press, 1992.

Kessler-Harris, Alice. Foreword to *Bread Givers*. 3d ed., vii–xvii. New York: Persea Books, 2003.

Khlevniuk, Oleg. *1937–i: Stalin, NKVD i sovetskoe obshchestvo*. Moscow: "Respublika," 1992.

Khlevniuk, Oleg. *In Stalin's Shadow: The Career of "Sergo" Ordzhonikidze*. Translated by D.J. Nordlander. The New Russian History. London: M.E. Sharpe, 1995.

Khlevniuk, Oleg. *Politbiuro: Mekhanizmy Politicheskoi Vlasti v 1930–e gody*. Moscow: Rosspen, 1996.

Khlevniuk, Oleg. *The History of the Gulag: From Collectivization to the Great Terror*. Translated by Vadim A. Staklo. Annals of Communism Series. New Haven, CT: Yale University Press, 2004.

Khlevniuk, Oleg. *Stalin: New Biography of a Dictator*. Translated by Nora Seligman Favorov. New Haven, CT: Yale University Press, 2015.

Khrushchev, Nikita. *Khrushchev Remembers*. Edited and translated by Strobe Talbott. Boston: Little, Brown and Company, 1970.

Kirilina, Alla. *Neizvestnyi Kirov*. St. Petersburg: "Neva," 2001.

Kislitsyn, S.A. *"Shakhtinskoe delo." Nachalo stalinskikh repressii protiv nauchno-tekhnicheskoi intelligentsii v SSSR*. Rostov: Izdatel'stvo NMTS "Logos," 1993.

Klier, John. "Kazaki i pogromy. Chem otlichalis' 'voennye' pogromy?" In *Mirovoi krizis 1914–1920 godov i sud'ba vostochnoevropeickogo evreistrva*, edited by O. Budnitskii, 47–70. Moscow: Rosspen, 2005.

Kopelev, Lev. *The Education of a True Believer*. Translated by G. Kern. New York: Harper & Row, 1980.

Kostyrchenko, Gennady. *Tainaia politika Stalina: vlast i antisemitizm*. Moscow: Mezhdunarodnaia otnosheniia, 2001.

Kotkin, Stephen. *Magnetic Mountain: Stalinism as a Civilization*. Berkeley: University of California Press, 1995.

Kozerod, Oleg. *Perelomnye Gody: Evreiskaia obshchina Ukrainy v pervoe poslevoennoe desiatiletie (1919–1929 gg.)*. Biblioteka Narodnogo universiteta evreiskoi kul'tury v Vostochnoi Ukraine, no. 2/98. A.M. Nekrasov, gen. ed. Kharkov: "Evreiskii mir," 1998.

Krylenko, N.V., ed. *Ekonomicheskaia kontr-revoliutsiia v Donbasse. Itogi Shakhtinskogo dela: Stat'i i dokumenty*. Moscow: Iuridicheskoe izdatel'stvo NKIU RSFSR, 1928.

Kuromiya, Hiroaki. "The Commander and the Rank and File: Managing the Soviet Coal-Mining Industry, 1928–1933." In *Social Dimensions of Soviet Industrialization*, edited by W.G. Rosenberg and L.H. Siegelbaum, 146–65. Indiana-Michigan Series in Russian and Eastern European Studies. Bloomington: Indiana University Press, 1993.

Kuromiya, Hiroaki. "The Shakhty Affair." *South East European Monitor* 4, no. 2 (1997): 41–64.

Kuromiya, Hiroaki. *Freedom and Terror in the Donbas: A Ukrainian–Russian Borderland, 1870s–1990s*. Cambridge Russian, Soviet and Post-Soviet Studies, vol. 104. Stephen White, gen. ed. Cambridge: Cambridge University Press, 1998.

Kuromiya, Hiroaki. *Stalin's Industrial Revolution: Politics and Workers, 1928–1932*. Soviet and East European Studies, vol. 60. Cambridge: Cambridge University Press, 1988.

Lampert, Nicholas. *The Technical Intelligentsia and the Soviet State: A Study of Soviet Managers and Technicians 1928–1935*. Studies in Soviet History and Society. R.W. Davies, gen. ed. London: Macmillan, 1979.

Larin, Yuri. *Evrei i antisemitizm v SSSR*. Moscow: Gosudarstvennoe izdatel'stvo, 1929.

Laslett, John H.M. "Jewish Socialism and the Ladies Garment Workers of New York." In *Labor and the Left: A Study of Socialist and Radical Influences in the American Labor Movement, 1881–1924*, 98–143. New York: Basic Books, 1970.

Lenoe, Matthew. *The Kirov Murder and Soviet History*. New Haven: Yale University Press, 2010.

Leon, Abram. *The Jewish question: A Marxist interpretation*. New York: Pathfinder Press, 1970.

Lestchinsky, Jacob. "Di ekonomishe lage fun di yidn in lite (1919–1939)." In *Lite*, edited by M. Sudarski, U. Katzelenbogen, and J. Kissin, 827–940. New York: Futuro Press, 1951.

Lestchinsky, Yaakov. *Dos sovetishe idntum: zayn fargangnheyt un kegnvart*. New York: Yidisher Kemfer, 1941.

Levavi, Y. "OZET-GEZERD: Khevrah lesidur khakla'i shel yehudim a'melim b'vrit hamo'atsot." *He'avar* (1969): 118–30.

Levin, John F. and Earl Silbar, eds. *You Say You Want a Revolution: SDS, PL, and Adventures in Building a Worker-Student Alliance*. San Francisco: 1741 Press, 2019.

Levin, Nora. *The Jews in the Soviet Union since 1917: Paradox of Survival*. New York: New York University Press, 1988.

Levine, Louis. *The Women's Garment Workers*. New York: B.W. Huebsch, Inc., 1924.

Lewin, Moshe. *Russian Peasants and Soviet Power: A Study of Collectivization*. Translated by I. Nove. New York: W.W. Norton, 1975 [1966].

Liberman, Simon. *Building Lenin's Russia*. Chicago: University of Illinois Press, 1945.

Liebman, Arthur. *Jews and the Left*. New York: John Wiley & sons, 1979.

Likholobova, Zoia G., and V. Kovalenko. "Protsessy urbanizatsiia v Donbasse (1926–1939 gg.)." *Novye Stranitsy v istorii Donbassa* 3 (1994): 56–73.

Liptzin, Sol. *A History of Yiddish Literature*. Middle Village, NY: Jonathan David Publishers, 1985.

Litar'. "Zhilstroitel'stvo Donuglia." *Vestnik Donuglia* 12 (May 15, 1927): 15–17.

Lohr, Eric. *Nationalizing the Russian Empire: The Campaign against Enemy Aliens during World War I*. Russian Research Center Studies, vol. 94. Cambridge, MA: Harvard University Press, 2003.

Lomov, G. "K dokladu Donuglia na plenume VUK'a S.G. 1 fevralia 1927 g." *Vestnik Donuglia* 5 (February 1, 1927): 1–5.

London, Noah. "Mayners shlagen far natsionaliliziren di koyhlen industrie," *Freiheit*, January 3, 1923.

London, Noah. "Ukraina," *Freiheit*, September 8, 1926.

London, Noah. "Vi azoy di mayners in vest virdjinia leben," *Freiheit*, August 13, 1922.

London, Noah. "Der finfyariker plan fun sotsialistisher boyung," *Royte Velt* 5–6 (May/June 1929): 89–90.

London, Noah. "Di ekonomik un teknik fun donbas." *Royte Velt* 4:2 (February 1927): 99.

London, Noah. "Di ershte ayndrukn fun sovetn-farband," *Freiheit*, July 15 and 16, 1926.

London, Noah. "Poyln shteyt oyf a fas pulver," *Freiheit*, May 26, 1926.

London, Noah. "Vi azoy es boyt zikh der donbas," *Shtern*, July 17, 1926.

London, Noah. "Vi di koylen industrie vert fervaltet," *Freiheit*, April 28, 1922.

London, Noah. *Mit der amerikaner ekspeditsie keyn biro-bidzhan*. Pamphlet. Kharkov: Tsentralfarlag, alukrainishe opteylung, 1930.

London, Noah. "Birobidzhan nuzhdaetsia v khoroshikh rabotnikakh!" Letter to the editor. *Tribuna*, September 20, 1929: 13.

London, Noah. "Donbass trebuet vody." *Pravda* (Moscow), August 15, 1934, 4.

London, Noah. "England erv dem general strayk," *Freiheit*, May 9, 1926.

London, Noah. "Postroim sotsialisticheskuiu stranu." *Tribuna*, October 25, 1929, 13.

London, Noah. "Vi azoy nyu-yorker arbeter boyen kooperative heyzer," June 6, 1926.

London, Noah. "Vodosnabzhenie: itogi rabot po vodosnabzhenie Donbassa za 1927–28 god." *Vestnik Donuglia* 48 (November 15, 1928): 14–18.

London, Noah. "Zadachi stroitel'stva Birobidzhana (Rezul'taty raboty ekspeditsii 'IKOR')." *Tribuna*, October 20, 1929, 3–4.

London, Noah. ["N. Paiezon"] "Koyhlen—a treyb-kraft fun der sotsialer revolutsie." *Emes*, September 30, 1921.

London, Noah. *Poiasnitel'naia Zapiska k Proektu Donetskogo Vodoprovoda dlia Almazno-Mar'evskogo Raiona*. Vodbiuro Donuglia. 1927.

London, Noah. *Poiasnitel'naia Zapiska k Proektu Donetskogo Vodoprovoda dlia Almazno-Mar'evskogo Raiona. Vodosnabzhenie Donbassa*. Pamphlet. Kharkov: Vugillia i Ruda, 1933. Korolenko Library.

Longuet, Isabelle. "L'opposition de gauche en URSS (1928–1929)." *Cahier Léon Trotsky* 53 (April 1994): 33–61.

Lyons, Eugene. *Assignment in Utopia*. New York: Harcourt, Brace & Co., 1937.

Margulies, Sylvia R. *The Pilgrimage to Russia: The Soviet Union and the Treatment of Foreigners, 1924–1937*. Madison: University of Wisconsin Press, 1968.

Mariagin, Georgii A. *Postyshev*. Zhizn' zamechatel'nykh liudei. Moscow: "Molodaia gvardiia," 1975.

Marmor, Kalmen. "Di far-geshikhte fun artef." In *Tsen yor artef*. New York: Artef, 1937.

Mayer, Arno. *Why Did the Heavens Not Darken? The "Final Solution" in History*. New York: Pantheon, 1988.

McCartin, Joseph A. *Labor's Great War: The Struggle for Industrial Democracy and the Origins of Modern American Labor Relations, 1912–1921*. Chapel Hill: University of North Carolina Press, 1997.

McKay, Claude. *A Long Way from Home*. New York: Furman, 1937.

Medem, Vladimir. *The Life and Soul of a Legendary Jewish Socialist: the memoirs of Vladimir Medem*. Translated by Samuel A. Portnoy. New York: Ktav, 1979.

Medvedev, Roy. *Let History Judge: The Origins and Consequences of Stalinism*. Translated by George Shriver. Revised edition. New York: Columbia University Press, [1971] 1989.

Melosi, Martin V. *The Sanitary City: Urban Infrastructure in America from Colonial Times to the Present*. Baltimore: Johns Hopkins University Press, 2000.

Michels, Tony. "Socialism with a Jewish Face: The Origins of the Yiddish-Speaking Communist Movement in the United States, 1907–1923." In *Yiddish and the Left*, edited by Gennady Estraikh and Mikhail Krutikov, 24–55. Studies in Yiddish, vol. 3. Oxford: Legenda, 2001.

Michels, Tony. *A Fire in Their Hearts*. Cambridge, MA: Harvard University Press, 2005.

Montgomery, David. "Industrial Democracy or Democracy in Industry?: The Theory and Practice of the Labor Movement, 1870–1925." In *Industrial Democracy in America: The Ambiguous Promise*, edited by Nelson Lichtenstein and Howell John Harris, 20–42. Woodrow Wilson Center Series. Cambridge: Cambridge University Press, 1993.

Montgomery, David. *The Fall of the House of Labor: The Workplace, the State, and American Labor Activism, 1865–1925*. Cambridge: Cambridge University Press, 1987.

Moser, Charles A. "Mayakovsky's Unsentimental Journeys." *American Slavic and East European Review* 19, no. 1 (February 1960): 85–100.

Mother Jones. *The Autobiography of Mother Jones*. Chicago: Charles Kerr, 1925.

Murphy, Kevin. *Revolution and Counterrevolution: Class Struggle in a Moscow Metal Factory*. International Studies in Social History. M. van der Linden, gen. ed. New York: Berghahn Books, 2005.

Myerson, Michael. "ILGWU: Fighting for Lower Wages," *Ramparts* 8, no. 4 (Octobrt 1969).

Naberukhin, Arkadiy. "Odyn z Psevdotrots'kistiv." *Z Arkhiviv VUChK, HPU, NKVD, KHB* 1/2 (1995): 341–55.

Nadel, Stanley. "Reds Versus Pinks, A Civil War in the International Ladies Garment Workers Union," *New York History* 66, no. 1 (January 1985).

Nahshon, Edna. *Yiddish Proletarian Theatre: the Art and Politics of the Artef, 1925–1940*. Westport, CT: Greenwood Press, 1998.

Naumov, Vladimir P., A.A. Kraiushkin, and N.V. Teptsov, eds. *Stalin's Secret Pogrom: The Postwar Inquisition of the Jewish Anti-Fascist Committee*. Translated by L.E. Wolfson. Annals of Communism. New Haven, CT: Yale University Press, 2001.

Nedava, Joseph. *Trotsky and the Jews*. Philadelphia: Jewish Publication Society of America, 1972.

Nikol'skii, V.I. "Natsional'nye problemy 20–kh godov i ikh reshenie." *Novye stranitsy v istorii donbassa* 2 (1992): 51–70.

Nord, David Paul. "Hothouse Socialism: Minneapolis, 1910–1925." In *Socialism in the Heartland: The Midwestern Experience, 1900–1925*, ed. Donald T. Critchlow. Notre Dame: University of Notre Dame Press, 1986: 133–66.

Nove, Alec. *An Economic History of the U.S.S.R.* Revised ed. New York: Pelican Books, [1969] 1984.

Novick, Paul. Interview by John Holmes, May 26 1988, New York. Noah London Collection, Tamiment Institute, NYU.

Orenstein, Eugene. "The Jewish Socialist Federation of the U.S. (1912–1921)." Ph.D. diss., New York, Columbia University, 1978.

Orleck, Annelise. *Common Sense and a Little Fire: Women and Working-Class Politics in the United States, 1900–1965* Chapel Hill: University of North Carolina Press, 1995.

Palmer, A. Mitchell. "The Case Against the 'Reds.'" *Forum* 63 (February 1920): 173–85.

Palmer, Bryan D. *James P. Cannon and the Origins of the American Revolutionary Left, 1890–1928*. Urbana: University of Illinois Press, 2007.

Palmer, David. "Organizing the Shipyards: Unionization at New York Ship, Federal Ship, and Fore River, 1898–1945." Ph.D. diss., History of American Civilization, Brandeis University, 1989.

Parkins, Maurice F. *City Planning in Soviet Russia*. Chicago: University of Chicago Press, 1953.

Patenaude, Bertrand M. *The Big Show in Bololand: The American Relief Expedition to Soviet Russia in the Famine of 1921*. Stanford, CA: Stanford University Press, 2002.

Pedersen, Vernon L. *The Communist Party in Maryland, 1919–57*. Urbana: University of Illinois Press, 2001.

Pepper, John. *For a Labor Party: Recent Revolutionary Changes in American Politics. A Statement by the Workers Party*. New York, Workers Party of America, 1922.

Pervushin, A. "G. Stalino (Donbass)." *Sanitarnaia Tekhnika* 1, no. 1 (March 1927): 83–84.

Pinkus, Benjamin. *The Jews of the Soviet Union: The History of a National Minority*. New York: Cambridge University Press, 1988.

Plunz, Richard. "Reading Bronx Housing, 1890–1940." In *Building a Borough: Architecture & Planning in the Bronx, 1890–1940*, 30–77. Bronx, NY: Bronx Museum of the Arts, 1986.

Podoprigora, A. "Puti stanovleniia evreiskogo professional'nogo teatra v Ukraine v 20–e gody XX stoletiiia." In *Materyaly konferentsii (Kyev, 8–9 dekabria 1994 g.) Evreis'ka istoriia ta kul'tura v Ukraini*. 2005. Conference materials. Proceedings in Ukrainian Judaica: 1994, article 42.

Pomerantz, Alexander. *Proletpen. Etyuden un materialn tsu der geshikhte fun dem kamf far proletarisher literatur in Amerike*. Kiev: Farlag fun der alukrainisher visnshaftlekeher akademye, 1935.

Prometheus Research Library. Introduction to *James P. Cannon and the Early Years of American Communism: Selected Writings and Speeches, 1920–1928*, by James P. Cannon, 1–70. New York: Spartacist Publishing, 1992.

Radzinsky, Edvard. *Stalin*. New York: Doubleday, 1996.

Rafes, M. *Ocherki po istorii "Bunda."* Moscow: Moskovskii Rabochii, 1923.

Rassweiler, Anne D. *The Generation of Power: The History of Dneprostroi*. Oxford: Oxford University Press, 1988.

Reunion Committee. Souvenir collection. In *The Coops: The United Workers Cooperative Colony 50th Anniversary, 1927–1977*. New York: Semi-Centennial Coop Reunion, 1977.

Rigby, T.H. *Communist Party Membership in the U.S.S.R., 1917–1967*. Princeton, NJ: Princeton University Press, 1968.

Rittersport, Gabor T. "The Omnipresent Conspiracy: On Soviet Imagery of Politics and Social Relations in the 1930s." In *Stalinist Terror: New Perspectives*, edited by J. Getty and R. Manning, 40–62. Cambridge: Cambridge University Press, 1993.

Rosenberg, William G. "The Social Background to Tsektran," in *Party, State, Society and the Russian Civil War*, ed. Diane P. Koenker, William G. Rosenberg and Ronald Grigor Suny, 349–73. Bloomington, Indiana University Press, 1989.

Rosenthal, Jerome C. "Dealing with the Devil: Louis Marshall and the Partnership between the Joint Distribution Committee and Soviet Russia." *American Jewish Archives* 39, no. 1 (April 1987): 1–22.

Rossman, Jeffrey J. *Worker Resistance under Stalin: Class and Revolution on the Shop Floor*. Russian Research Center Studies, vol. 96. Cambridge, MA: Harvard University Press, 2005.

Rozenblit, Marsha, and Jonathan Karp, eds. *World War I and the Jews: Conflict and Transformations in Europe, the Middle East, and America*. New York, Berghahn Books, 2017.

Sakmyster, Thoma. *A Communist Odyssey: The Life of József Pogány*. Budapest and New York: Central European University Press, 2012.

Schwartz, Solomon. *The Jews in the Soviet Union*. Syracuse, NY: Syracuse University Press, 1951.

Schwartz, Solomon. "Birobidzhan: an experiment in Jewish colonization." In *Russian Jewry 1917–1967*, edited by G. Aronson, 342–66. New York: Union of Russian Jews, 1969.

Schwarz, Solomon M. *Labor in the Soviet Union*. New York: Praeger, 1952.

Shapiro, Judah J. *The Friendly Society: A History of the Workmen's Circle*. New York: Media Judaica, 1970.

Shapoval, Yuri, and Valeri Vasil'ev, eds. *Komandiri Velikoho Holodu: Poïzdki V. Molotova i L. Kaganovicha v Ukraïnu ta na Pivchnichnyj Kavkaz. 1932–1933 rr.* Kiev: "Geneza," 2001.

Shapoval, Yuri, and Valeri Vasil'ev, eds. *Vsevolod Balits'kyy, Osoba, chas, otochennya.* Kiev: "Stylos," 2002.

Shofat, Azriel. "History of the Jews of Pinsk, 1881–1941." In *Pinsk Historical Volume*. Chapter 1. Translation from Pinsk Sefer Edut ve-Zikaron le-Kehilat Pinsk-Karlin. 26 Dec. 2002. Yizkor Book Project. July 19, 2007 http://www.jewishgen.org/yizkor/Pinsk1/Pinsk1.html.

Slezkine, Yuri. *The Jewish Century*. Princeton: Princeton University Press, 2004.

Slutsky, Yehuda. "'Tribuna'—a Soviet Jewish Russian journal, 1927–1937." *Soviet Jewish Affairs* 12, no. 1 (Feb. 1982): 45–53.

Smoliar, Hersh. *fun ineveynik: zikhroynes vegn der yevsektsye*. Tel Aviv: Y.L. Perets, 1978.

Solianik, V.V., Lutsenko. *Bol'shaia Voda Industrii: Ocherki iz istorii proizvodstvennogo ob'edineniia "Ukrpromvodchermet."* Istoriia fabrik i zavodov. Donetsk: Izdatel'stvo "Donbas," 1980.

Soyer, Daniel. "Back to the Future: American Jews Visit the Soviet Union in the 1920s and 1930s." *Jewish Social Studies* 6, no. 3 (Spring/Summer 2000): 124–59.

Soyer, Daniel. "Soviet Travel and the Making of an American Jewish Communist: Moissaye Olgin's Trip to Russia in 1920–1921." *American Communist History* 4, no. 1 (June 2005): 1–20.

Srebnik, Henry. "Territorialism and the ICOR 'American Commission of Scientists and Experts' to the Soviet Far East." In *1929: Mapping the Jewish World*, edited by Gennady Estraich and Hasia R. Diner. New York: New York University Press, 2013, 107–23.

Stalin i Kaganovich. Perepiska. 1931–1936 gg. Moscow: ROSSPEN, 2001.

Stalin, Joseph. "Tasks of Business Executives." Speech, February 1931. In *A Documentary History of Communism*, edited by Robert V. Daniels. Vintage Russian Library, vol. 2. New York: Vintage Books, 1960.

Stave, Bruce M., ed. *Socialism and the Cities*. National University Publications, Interdisciplinary Urban Series, gen. ed. R.A. Mohl. London: Kenikat Press, 1975.

Stites, Richard. *Revolutionary Dreams: Utopian Vision and Experimental Life in the Russian Revolution.* New York: Oxford University Press, 1989.

Sullivant, Robert S. *Bolshevik Politics and the Ukraine, 1917–1957*. New York: Columbia University Press, 1962.

Suny, Ronald Grigor. *The Soviet Experiment: Russia, the USSR, and the Successor States.* New York: Oxford University Press, 1998.

Sutton, Antony C. *Western Technology and Soviet Economic Development, 1917 to 1930.* Hoover Institution Publications, vol. 1. Stanford, CA: Hoover Institution Press, 1968.

Taft, Philip, and Selig Perlman. *History of Labor in the United States, 1896–1932*. History of Labor in the United States, vol. 4. John R. Commons, gen. ed. New York: Macmillan, 1936.

Tainy natsional'noi politiki TsK RKP. Stenograficheskii otchet sekretnogo soveshchaniia Ts RKP, 1923 g. Edited by Bulat Sultanbekov. Moscow: Rossiiskii mezhdunarodnyi fond kul'tury, 1992.

Talmy, Leon. *Oyf royer erd.* New York: "Freiheit" farlag, 1931.

Tanny, Jarrod. *City of Rogues and Schnorrers: Russia's Jews and the Myth of Old Odessa.* Bloomington: Indiana University Press, 2011.

Taylor, Clarence. *Reds at the Blackboard: Communism, Civil Rights and the New York Teachers Union.* New York, Columbia University Press, 2013.

Teptsova, N. "Monarkhiia pogibla, a antisemitizm ostalsia. Dokumenty Informatsionnogo otdela OGPU 1920–x gg," edited by V.A. Kozlov and S.M. Zav'ialov, 324–58. Neizvestnaia Rossiia, XX vek, vol. 3. Moscow: Istoricheskoe Nasledie, 1993.

"The Soviet Union: Facts, Descriptions, Statistics." Pamphlet. Washington, D.C.: Soviet Union Information Bureau, 1929.

The Stalin–Kaganovich Correspondence, 1931–36., ed. R.W. Davies, Oleg V. Khlevniuk, E.A. Rees, Liudmila P. Kosheleva and Larisa A. Rogovaya, trans. Steven Shabad. New Haven, CT: Yale University Press, 2003.

Trotsky, Leon. "A Heart-to-Heart Talk with a Well-Meaning Party Member," translated by David Keil, September 12, 1928. In *The Challenge of the Left Opposition, 1928–1929*, edited by Naomi Allen and George Saunders, 225–49. New York: Pathfinder Press, 1981.

Trotsky, Leon. "A New Moscow Amalgam." In *Writings of Leon Trotsky* (*1936–1937*), ed. N. Allen and G. Breitman. 2d ed., 115–27. New York: Pathfinder Press, [1937] 1978.

Trotsky, Leon. "Crisis in the Right-Center Bloc," 301–35, November 1928.

Trotsky, Leon. "Pyatakov: A Politically Finished Man." Letter to Ishchenko, March 17, 1928. In *The Challenge of the Left Opposition* (*1928–1929*), edited by N. Allen and G. Saunders, vol. 3, 64–6. New York: Pathfinder Press, 1981.

Trotsky, Leon. "Thermidor and Anti-Semitism." *The New International*, May 1941.

Trotsky, Leon. *The First Five Years of the Communist International.* Edited by J.G. Wright. London: New Park, [1924] 1973.

Trotsky, Leon. *The Revolution Betrayed: What Is the Soviet Union and Where Is It Going?* Translated by Max Eastman. New York: Pathfinder Press, [1937] 1970.

Trunk, Isaiah. "The Cultural Dimension of the American Jewish Labor Movement." *YIVO Annual of Jewish Social Science* XVI (1976): 342–93.

Unterberger, Betty Miller, ed. *American Intervention in the Russian Civil War*. Problems in American Civilization. Edwin C. Rozweno, gen. ed. Lexington, MA: D.C. Heath and Company, 1969.

Verbeeten, David R. *The Politics of Nonassimilation: The American Jewish Left in the Twentieth Century*. De Kalb: Northern Illinois University Press, 2017.

Vetter, Matthias. *Antisemiten und Bolschewiki: Zum Verhältnis von Sowjetsystem und Judenfeindshchaft 1917–1919*. Reihe: Dokumente, Texte, Materialien/Zentrum für Antisemitismusforschung der Technischen Universität Berlin, vol. 17. Berlin : Metropol-Vel., 1995.

Vilkova, Valentina. *The Struggle for Power: Russia in 1923*. New York: Prometheus Books, 1996.

Viola, Lynne. *The Best Sons of the Fatherland: Workers in the Vanguard of Soviet Collectivization*. New York: Oxford University Press, 1987.

Viola, Lynne. *Peasant Rebels under Stalin: Collectivization and the Culture of Peasant Resistance*. New York: Oxford University Press, 1996.

Volgin, A.S., and S.N. Orlovskii. *Glubokii Vvod Dnepra v Donbass: gipotesa vodnoi magistrali "Donbass-Dnepr-Krivorozh'e."* Donoblispolkom Obplankomm no. 640, edited by Ya. S. Kanskii. Stalino: Oblit, 1936.

Volkogonov, Dmitri. *Stalin: Triumph and Tragedy*. 1988. Edited and translated by H. Shukman. New York: Grove Weidenfeld, 1991.

Weinberg, Robert. "Jews into Peasants? Solving the Jewish Question in Birobidzhan." In *Jews and Jewish life in Russia and the Soviet Union*, edited by Y. Ro'i, 87–102. London: Frank Cass, 1995.

Weinstein, James. *The Decline of Socialism in America, 1912–1915*. New York: Random House, 1969.

Wheatcroft, Stephen G. "Towards Explaining the Changing Levels of Stalinist Repression in the 1930s: Mass Killings." In *Challenging Traditional Views of Russian History*, edited by S. Wheatcroft, 112–46. Studies in Russian and East European History and Society. New York: Palgrave Macmillan, 2002.

Wisse, Ruth. *A Little Love in Big Manhattan: Two Yiddish Poets*. Cambridge: Cambridge University Press, 1988.

Wohl, Robert. *French Communism in the Making, 1914–1924*. Stanford, CA: Stanford University Press.

Woroby, Maria. "Russian Americans." In *Encyclopedia of the American Left*, edited by M.J. Buhle, P. Buhle, and D. Georgakas. 1st ed., 661–3. Urbana: University of Illinois Press, 1992.

Wortis, Rose. "Shop Delegate League in Needle Trades." *The Worker* (New York), May 13, 1922.

Wynn, Charters. *Workers, Strikes and Pogroms: The Donbass-Dnepr Bend in Late Imperial Russia, 1870–1905*. Princeton, NJ: Princeton University Press, 1992.

Zel'tser, Arkadii. *Evrei sovetskoi provintsii: Vitebsk i mestechki 1917–1941*. Moscow: Rosspen, 2006.

Zel'tser, Arkadii. "OZET and the Soviet Self-Criticism Campaign of 1937." *Jews in Eastern Europe* 3, no. 40 (Winter 1999): 57–67.

Zielinski, Konrad. "The Changing Shtetl in the Kingdom of Poland during the First World War." In *The Shtetl: Myth and Reality*. Vol. 17 of *Polin: Studies in Polish Jewry*, edited by A. Polonsky, 119–31. Oxford: Littman Library, 2004.

Zimmerman, Charles. Interview by Henoch Mendelsund 1975–1977. Zimmerman collection, Labor-Management Documentation Center, Cornell University: Box 1.

Zorin, Z. "K Voprosam Zhilstroitel'stva i Blagoustroistva." *Vestnik Donuglia* 12 (May 15, 1927): 17–18.

Zumoff, Jacob. *The Communist International and U.S. Communism, 1919–1929*. Chicago: Haymarket Books, 2015.

Index

www.ingramcontent.com/pod-product-compliance
Lightning Source LLC
LaVergne TN
LVHW010658300926
849161LV00005B/1160
* 9 7 8 9 0 0 4 7 3 0 6 2 5 *